ONE WORD SHAPES A NATION

Integration Politics in Germany

One Word Shapes a Nation demonstrates that integration politics limit how immigrants, refugees, and their descendants can participate in German society and how Germans imagine their national future. By reconstructing recent polemic media scandals, re-interpreting historical narratives about migration after the Second World War, and conducting extensive fieldwork with social work organizations that implement "integrative" programs, Johanna Schuster-Craig explores the intersection between media, capital, nation-building, and human lives in contemporary German society.

The book reveals that while anti-immigrant tropes are long-standing in German post-war history, integration is not the only potential model. Schuster-Craig argues that "integration politics" in Germany is defined by a selective approach to who qualifies as a citizen, as well as beliefs about German national identity that require assimilation to cultural values beyond mere naturalization.

Drawing on media analysis of key public speeches and debates, historical analysis, and ethnographic observation and interviews, Schuster-Craig examines the nature and impact of an integrative apparatus. *One Word Shapes a Nation* ultimately asks what it would take to reimagine immigrant incorporation as a form of citizenship that applies to everyone.

(German and European Studies)

JOHANNA SCHUSTER-CRAIG is a former associate professor of German and global studies at Michigan State University.

GERMAN AND EUROPEAN STUDIES

General Editor: James Retallack

One Word Shapes a Nation

Integration Politics in Germany

JOHANNA SCHUSTER-CRAIG

UNIVERSITY OF TORONTO PRESS
Toronto Buffalo London

ISBN 978-1-4875-5116-2 (cloth)   ISBN 978-1-4875-5119-3 (EPUB)
ISBN 978-1-4875-5117-9 (paper)   ISBN 978-1-4875-5118-6 (PDF)

(German and European Studies)

Library and Archives Canada Cataloguing in Publication

Title: One word shapes a nation : integration politics in Germany /
   Johanna Schuster-Craig.
Names: Schuster-Craig, Johanna, author.
Series: German and European studies ; 53.
Description: Series statement: German and European studies ; 53 | Includes
   bibliographical references and index.
Identifiers: Canadiana (print) 20240315960 | Canadiana (ebook) 2024031607X |
   ISBN 9781487551162 (cloth) | ISBN 9781487551179 (paper) |
   ISBN 9781487551193 (EPUB) | ISBN 9781487551186 (PDF)
Subjects: LCSH: Immigrants – Cultural assimilation – Germany. | LCSH: Social
   integration – Political aspects – Germany. | LCSH: Immigrants – Government
   policy – Germany. | LCSH: Minorities – Government policy – Germany. |
   LCSH: Germany – Ethnic relations. | LCSH: Germany – Emigration and
   immigration – Government policy.
Classification: LCC JV6342.S38 2024 | DDC 305.9/069120943–dc23

Cover design: Will Brown

The German and European Studies series is funded by the DAAD with funds from the
German Federal Foreign Office

DAAD   Deutscher Akademischer Austauschdienst
         German Academic Exchange Service

We wish to acknowledge the land on which the University of Toronto Press operates. This
land is the traditional territory of the Wendat, the Anishnaabeg, the Haudenosaunee, the
Métis, and the Mississaugas of the Credit First Nation.

University of Toronto Press acknowledges the financial support of the Government of
Canada, the Canada Council for the Arts, and the Ontario Arts Council, an agency of
the Government of Ontario, for its publishing activities.

Canada Council   Conseil des Arts   ONTARIO ARTS COUNCIL
for the Arts   du Canada   CONSEIL DES ARTS DE L'ONTARIO
                                         an Ontario government agency
                                         un organisme du gouvernement de l'Ontario

Funded by the   Financé par le
Government   gouvernement   Canadä
of Canada   du Canada

Contents

Acknowledgments

There are many people who have contributed to this book – no scholar writes a book in isolation. I developed this research in conversation with colleagues at German Studies Association conferences, the Transnational German Studies Workshop, the Transdisciplinary Colloquium at ZIFG at the TU-Berlin, and in conversation with colleagues at Michigan State University and Cornell College. During my Humboldt German Chancellor Fellowship in Berlin, which funded some of the preliminary ethnographic and research work for this project during the 2010–11 fellowship year, my host at the Technical University of Berlin's Centre for Interdisciplinary Research on Women and Gender (ZIFG), Prof. Dr. Sabine Hark, and the members of the Transdisciplinary Gender Studies Colloquium, were influential in shaping the arc of this project. I was introduced to Sabine's work by the Gender and Women's Studies program at Duke University, which I consider the home of my theoretical training, and – they may not know this – but I owe a lot of my ability to think conceptually to Robyn Wiegman and Ara Wilson and what I learned in their courses on Feminist Theory and Transnational Feminism. The junior faculty writing group at Cornell College was an excellent place to get my footing: Hans Hassell, Rebecca Wines, Ari Hagler, and Ellen Hoobler provided helpful commentary on many of the ideas in these chapters. Some of this research was also funded by Humanities and Arts Research Program development and production grants, as well as a College of Arts and Letters Summer Fellowship, all from Michigan State University. I received a Humboldt re-invitation grant in 2015 to continue my fieldwork. Dan Nemeth and Temilade Adegoke, as my research assistants at various times in the writing process, helped with various tasks. I appreciate their assistance.

Beverly Weber was one of the first people to show excitement for a book like this back in 2015, when I emailed her cold, and Kristin

Dickinson has truly been a lifesaver in terms of providing feedback when drafting seemed an insurmountable task. I can always count on Ela Gezen for suggesting interesting new impulses and providing excellent structural commentary on chapters.

Audra Wolfe was an insightful developmental editor to work with and provided space for writing-as-process-and-experimentation that created the foundation for turning ideas into chapters and chapters into a book. Her line edits on early drafts were transformative. Stephen Shapiro has been a wonderful editor with whom to go through the publishing process for the first time, and he provided such a high level of engagement with drafts and review that I was, am, and continue to be astounded by my luck. This book would have been far less than what it became if I had lacked both Audra and Stephen's commentary. Many thanks as well to the three peer reviewers who spent time with the manuscript when it was admittedly far too long. Finally, in the era of social media, several citations that became useful were forwarded to me by scholars I barely know. The people thanked in those footnotes are being given the credit for those offhand suggestions that often turned out to be very fruitful places to look. Given how competitive and vitriolic academic debates can become, I find it important to mark those scholars who are generous with their time and suggestions, especially with junior scholars they have never met.

While it seems like a million years ago, I must also credit the faculty at Duke for being quite willing to let me go off in new directions, even when I rarely did so well or diligently as a student. Their willingness to let me try new things indirectly led to this project and is atypical in graduate education. Many thanks to my committee chair, Erdağ Göknar, as well as Tina Campt, Ann Marie Rasmussen, and Jochen Vogt.

The people I spoke with at the social work organizations represented here have been incredibly generous with their time and support. I cannot name them individually, but this book would not exist without their input and their reframing of interactions I may have initially misunderstood. For those in whom I did not necessarily inspire confidence at first, but who were willing to talk with me anyway: thank you. I also want to thank the people who completed an online survey for me during the start of the pandemic, as everything suddenly changed and all of us were scrambling to figure out how to do things in new ways. Any misrepresentations or mistakes I have made in quoting their statements, explaining their work, or interpreting their aims are my own. And last but not least, a brief note on representation and cover design: both I and my editor wanted to include Arabic on the cover. However, there was no way to do so with the font software available to us during the design process. The result – no representation for Arabic-speaking Germans – was not intentional, but instead an obstacle encountered through the printing process.

To the policymakers whose work I often critique here: activists, scholars, and cultural figures uttered critiques similar to this book's arguments long before I had ever stepped foot in Germany for the first time as an exchange student in 1999, and the arguments I make in this book – there are mountains of evidence that this is the case – had already been made by citizen-activists, social workers, immigrants and permanent residents in local communities for decades before this book had even been conceived. Continued participation in a society that does not always accept one's engagement is, for me, the essence of democratic participation. This is true in many countries, and the lack of participatory opportunities is hardly a singularly German affliction. Journalists, publishers, and tech moguls also hold a great deal of responsibility in choosing which stories to cover and where to direct their resources in ways that can negatively affect civic participation and amplify extremist ideas. It is a democratic duty to ensure that citizens and permanent residents are respected and honoured for their honest engagement to improve access to social, political, and economic systems and networks of social care. Engaged citizens do not need scandalizing rhetoric or media scandals to participate democratically or socially. In stark contrast, the celebrity critics analysed here demand polemic attention at high volume – and often generate high profit by doing so – all the while escalating the problems to which they offer no real solutions. Learning to distinguish between engagement and polemic is what civic education requires in the face of extremist politics and disinformation. This discernment is the primary task I set for myself by writing this book.

Abbreviations

AfD	Alternative für Deutschland	Alternative for Germany
AmkA	Amt für multikulturelle Angelegenheiten	Office of Multicultural Affairs (NGO in Frankfurt am Main)
ARD	Arbeitsgemeinschaft der öffentlich-rechtlichen Rundfunkanstalten der Bundesrepublik Deutschland	Consortium of Public German Broadcasters, also known as Channel One (Das Erste)
AVPO	Ausländerpolizeiverordnung	Foreigner Police Ordinance
AWO	Arbeiterwohlfahrt	Worker Welfare Office
BAMF	Bundesamt für Migration und Flüchtlinge	Federal Office for Migration and Refugees
BKA	Bundeskriminalamt	Federal Criminal Police Office
BMI	Bundesministerium des Inneren	Federal Ministry of the Interior
BPK	Bundespressekonferenz	Federal Press Conference
CDU	Christlich Demokratische Union Deutschlands	Christian Democratic Union of Germany
CSU	Christlich-Soziale Union in Bayern	Christian Social Union of Bavaria
DGB	Deutsche Gesellschaftsbund	German Trade Federation
DİTİB	Diyanet İşleri Türk İslam Birliği (Türkisch-Islamische Union der Anstalt für Religion e. V)	Turkish-Islamic Union for Religious Affairs

DM	Deutsche Mark	German currency, 1948–2002
DP	Deutsche Partei	German Party
DRP	Deutsche Reichspartei	German Imperial Party
DVU	Deutsche Volksunion	German People's Union
GB/BHE	Gesamtdeutsche Block/Bund der Heimatvertriebenen und Entrechteten	All-German Bloc/League of Expellees and Those Deprived of Rights
LSVD	Lesben- und Schwulenverband Deutschlands	Lesbian and Gay Association of Germany
NPD	Nationaldemokratische Partei Deutschlands	National Democratic Party of Germany
NRR	Neue radikale Rechte	New Radical Right
NVA	Nationale Volksarmee	National People's Army
PEGIDA	Patriotische Europäer gegen die Islamisierung des Abendlandes	Patriotic Europeans against the Islamicization of the Occident
RM	Reichsmark	German currency, 1924–1948
SPD	Sozialdemokratische Partei Deutschlands	Social Democratic Party of Germany
SRP	Sozialistische Reichspartei Deutschlands	Socialist Imperial Party
SVR	Sachverständigenrat für Integration und Migration	Council of Experts on Integration and Migration
ZDF	Zweites Deutsches Fernsehen	German Channel 2 (Public Broadcasting)

ONE WORD SHAPES A NATION

Introduction: Integration Politics

On 14 July 2006, 86 participants met with Chancellor Angela Merkel and some members of Parliament at the *Bundeskanzleramt*, the Office of the Federal Chancellor, for the first *Integrationsgipfel*, the integration summit.[1] Maria Böhmer (CDU), the Federal Commissioner for Integration in 2006, made sure to emphasize before the event that nearly 30 of the 80 or so participants were "migrants," thus declaring that the choice of the participants was representative.[2] Critics argued that this representation was selective, and that Muslim leaders had not been invited, but representatives of churches and synagogues had. Noting that multiple Muslim organizations had been invited to the Federal Ministry of the Interior's upcoming *Islamkonferenz*, a consultation structure focusing on both the recognition of Islam as a national religion and the integration of Muslim Germans, politicians declared that several Muslim organizations were currently on a watch list for possible illegal activities and thus would not be welcome nor would their presence be fitting at the Office of the Federal Chancellor (BKA), the site of the *Integrationsgipfel*. Instead, these organizations could be properly surveilled at the Federal Ministry of the Interior (BMI), where the *Islamkonferenz* would take place.[3] Despite politicians from both the SPD and the opposition parties who speculated that the summit would become a *Showveranstaltung*, a performative act, the press coverage that followed was fairly positive.[4] And the images of Merkel walking past the "migrants" during a photo op at the Office of the Federal Chancellor – with the most visibly different Black and Asian participants standing in the front row – showed a friendly, confident, and smiling Chancellor who was similarly greeted with smiles by the participants Böhmer had invited to the summit.[5]

After the four-hour event, Chancellor Merkel declared herself to be "exceptionally pleased" with the outcome of the summit.[6] Participants and the government would work together to produce a National

Integration Plan over the course of the coming year, with six working groups meeting either four or five times before March 2007 to prepare their reports.[7] Merkel called the summit an "almost historical event,"[8] and both the chancellor and participants, like Bekir Alboğa, the Dialogue Commissioner of the Turkish-Muslim organization DİTİB, spoke positively about it, with Alboğa noting that he was "positively surprised by the chancellor," and that "integration will shape our future."[9]

The summit did produce a 400-point plan by July 2007.[10] Working groups on the topics of integration courses, German language acquisition, education and vocational training, gender equality, local integration, and civic participation were organized.[11] Participants were invited back to the BKA to take part in what would be known as the Second Integration Summit in July 2007; however, this time, multiple Turkish-German organizations threatened to boycott due to the revisions to integration policy included in the 2007 amendments to the *Zuwanderungsgesetz* (Immigration Act), which made it more difficult for Turkish citizens to immigrate to Germany by limiting residency through marriage and family reunification laws.[12] The amendments demanded Turkish women speak German before they emigrated and made it more difficult for parents to bring their children to Germany.[13] In the end, all but three of the 20 Turkish-German organizations Böhmer had invited continued to participate in the Integration Summit, and the German government assured participants that in spite of the boycott, all 20 participants would continue to be invited to future summits as a gesture of goodwill.[14] Merkel declared the First National Integration Plan (presented at the second summit) to be a "milestone in the history of integration politics."[15]

By 2021, 13 integration summits had taken place.[16] I call this nexus of highly specialized philosophies, rhetoric, policy programs, and citizen responses – of which the integration summits are a part – the integrative apparatus. The integrative apparatus exists in the networks that lie between the different cultural, social, and economic facets of German society that engage with both social and systemic integration as well as how politics and policies direct German attitudes towards foreigners, immigrants, refugees, and their descendants. This apparatus has been starkly influenced, especially during the 16 years of Merkel's chancellorship, by conservative ideas about nation-building that struggle to adjust ethnonationalist integrative rhetoric to the realities of contemporary German life. These summits organized by the German government represent a late-stage development in the integrative apparatus. In contemporary Germany, the positions people take towards German national identity range from adjusting that identity to better reflect and represent a diverse populace to preserving the historical construction of German national identity as an ethno-national one. Whether in politics, the media, or the program design of social work interventions, debates about Germanness and belonging are implicated in all the discussions German citizens and residents have about encouraging and demanding "the integration" of newcomers (*fördern und fordern*). In Germany, as is also common elsewhere, ethnic animus walks in lockstep with migration and is inseparable from the governmental apparatus that manages social arrival, systemic integration, naturalization, and ultimately the incorporation of newcomers into the body politic.

How Germans mediate and engage with this process of incorporation is the focus of this book. The demand that newcomers integrate themselves has become so culturally powerful that this discourse structures nearly every avenue of German social, political, and cultural life, and the word "integration" shapes not only national identity but also national debates about what Germany is, what it means to be German, who can claim belonging in the nation, and what kinds of values will structure a German future.

But what does it mean to integrate, exactly, and who should integrate? What is included under the broad heading of "integration politics" or an "integrative apparatus"? *Integration* in everyday usage has many synonyms. Assimilation, inclusion, incorporation, unification, and consolidation are just some of the words that all describe the basic process of incorporating a part into a greater whole. Scholars also use integration in a variety of disciplinary contexts: sociologists distinguish between systemic and social integration; economists talk of European integration as the process by which politicians and policy-makers consolidated markets and introduced a single currency across the European Union; educators talk about integrating students with special needs into mainstream classrooms.

Although "integration" has become politically charged in the contemporary moment, we can mark the entry of the word in the context of political conversations in the 1960s and 1970s when other potential synonyms (like assimilation) were considered to be far more offensive. Karin Hunn, a German historian of Turkish migration to Germany, clearly articulates the difficulty in explaining what integration means in the context of migration and German politics. Politically, in Germany, the concept of *Integration* came into vogue in the 1970s as the government commissioned scholars to address the "integration problems of foreign worker families."[17] The scholarly studies that the German government commissioned at that time became inseparable from government politics. For scholars, integration had long been an analytic category that Hunn deems "indispensable" for examining the various processes associated with immigration and the differences between integration, assimilation, and segregation.[18] The sociological concept of "integration" serves as a heuristic through which to examine the relationship of parts to a whole; these relationships may then be taken together to constitute a structured whole, such as a society.[19] When this scholarly terminology entered a politicized discursive space, integration in Germany took on additional meanings. Journalists, politicians and citizens began using "integration" to their own ends. Historian Rita Chin argues that "by the mid-1980s, both ends of the political spectrum framed integration according to a strict set of parameters and defined it as a one-way process."[20] This new political inflection of integration was only partially related to how scholars had previously applied the term as an analytic. Integration, when used in a political context, also started to resemble various forms of compulsory assimilation. Integration politics thus operates at the nexus of historical, political, and cultural concerns about a deceptively simple question: Who and what is German? In the context of immigration to Germany, this question reflects broader concerns about the process of integration: Is it possible *to become* German?

Politicized in this way, "integration" no longer functions primarily as a scholarly analytic. Instead, "integration" can serve as a potentially harmful signifier for an apparatus that works to limit the role immigrants, refugees, and their descendants can play in German society. Of course, bringing newcomers into national cultural, political, and social life is crucial – segregation is not only socially unjust; it limits the life chances of individuals and poses a constant threat to the stability of democratic societies. But "integration" as a term strongly politicized in Germany needs to be kept separate from "incorporation" or "inclusion." The political instrumentalization of "integration" has largely invalidated its use in examining how immigrants and refugees become part of the nation. Furthermore, the conditions under which "integration" moved from scholarly discourse into political discourse did not end in the 1970s: over the past decades, integration politics has strengthened its hold on virtually all areas of German social life. I argue that "integration" has now become an apparatus of governmentality of great scale and scope that exists in between the networks between discourses, institutions, legal philosophies, politicking, and German cultural life.[21]

Because integration in Germany has taken on so many competing definitions, in what follows I will use the term "incorporation" to denote the practices, policies, and processes that are critical for bringing immigrants and refugees into social, cultural, and political life. I use "integration" whenever I discuss the politicized version of these practices, policies, and processes included under the banner of "integration politics." I hope that this distinction will provide clarity and also distinguish between the sociological term and its political instrumentalization. Because of the terminological overlap in German discourses, however, some slippage may be unavoidable.

Contemporary integration politics and discourses are deeply incoherent and intentionally contradictory. This incoherence can be mobilized by journalists and politicians to underscore the political urgency of integration as a social good and a social goal precisely because such debates are unable to articulate the theoretical contradictions between various approaches to integration. In the absence of definition and context, political affiliation, affect, ideological beliefs, and cultural identity dominate the approaches people take towards questions of integration.[22] The political right, for instance, often engages with a value-oriented approach to cultural integration (i.e., immigrants must value a secular public sphere and traditional Christian holidays). Politicians across the spectrum also often emphasize the role of the individual in processes of assimilation and portray changing national values as a crisis of social (dis)integration. Those who emphasize assimilation to "German values" are often unable to see the institutional structures that prevent immigrants, refugees, and their descendants from having equal chances to thrive.[23] At the same time, Germans of colour and other marginalized groups often critique integration politics as a systemic form of oppression that neither acknowledges the differences among and between marginalized groups and the majority, nor does it provide an avenue through which marginalized German citizens and residents can claim their legal right to participate fully in German civic, social, and political life.[24] More importantly, the heavy weight "integration" carries limits the ability of all Germans to imagine a different future.

Contemporary integration policy builds on three specific strains of cultural logic that inform public policy, journalistic discourse, and even everyday interactions. The first logical assumption of integration politics justifies the need for integration policies through a narrative of past mistakes. Many Germans subscribe to the idea that politicians failed to integrate postwar immigrants because they did not expect them to stay.[25] Immigrants arriving between 1955 and 1973 mostly came as foreign workers, and rhetoric about policy-making suggests that politicians and German citizens assumed their stay would be temporary.[26] Many contemporary commentators argue that the lack of formal integration policy for foreign workers who came to (West)

Germany on short-term contracts to provide labour for the "Economic Miracle" led to the widespread segregation of marginalized communities in contemporary German society.[27] Right-wing nationalists (and many German citizens) also see segregation as a threat to national cohesion.[28] According to critics, segregating "unintegrated" immigrants into so-called parallel societies produced a space in which harmful traditional practices could persist and in which second- and third-generation immigrants radicalized.[29]

A narrative of historically failed integration, however, obscures the fact that East and West Germany incorporated over 12 million newcomers from the now Polish "eastern areas" after the Second World War, as well as ethnic Germans from Czechoslovakia, Hungary, Romania, Austria, and the Soviet Union, and that in the 1950s, the (two) German governments congratulated themselves for doing so quickly and efficiently.[30] The primary long-term successes or failures of incorporating Eastern expellees and foreign workers, respectively, can be partially traced to their ethnic identity and rapid access to citizenship. Expellees were granted the participatory rights of citizenship when the postwar German states were founded.[31] Foreign workers, in contrast, waited decades for citizenship reforms to speed up the process of naturalization.[32] Some refugees and asylum seekers still do not have a path to citizenship, and ethnic and racial difference can still serve as a barrier in Germany for those who attempt to claim the full rights and benefits of citizenship.[33]

The second assumption embedded in integration politics posits that newcomers need not only to learn the German language, but also how to perform German civic responsibilities. Embedded within this demand is a second, subtextual concern: that newcomers need to learn German values to take up a German national identity.[34] These values – which, depending on whom you ask, might include accepting democracy as the best form of government, prioritizing gender equality over traditional gender roles, maintaining a secular public sphere, agreeing to pay taxes, and voting – can be taught, but immigrants must also willingly internalize them. In the logic of integration, groups who refuse to do so can be categorized as "unwilling to integrate" or "in need of integration." They can be compelled to take "integration" and "orientation" courses offered by the German government to teach them these skills.[35] While it would be absurd to deny the usefulness of having residents learn the majority language, compelling German immigrants to ascribe to values that German citizens may themselves reject raises a wide variety of cultural, ethical, and philosophical questions about the nature of national belonging.

Finally, the way that these first two cultural assumptions are negatively defined – guest workers were not integrated; immigrants will not easily internalize the German language or democratic values – shape a discursive environment in which integration policies must take the form of "integrative demands" (*Integrationsaufforderungen*).[36] In this context, integrating immigrants requires legal measures that both "encourage" and "demand" their participation in the process of integration. Such demands also serve as the legal means to inculcate values and language skills in immigrant populations.[37] Legal measures introduced in 2005, 2007, and especially in 2015, after Chancellor Angela Merkel opened the borders to allow more than 1.1 million asylum seekers to enter or pass through the country, laid the groundwork for politicians to pass Germany's first Integration Act in 2016. This law links social welfare benefits and potential residency status to integration "achievements." In effect, this law creates a system in which immigrants and refugees can be punished for not integrating successfully. Critics point out that this system of sanctions implies that immigrants do not want to integrate willingly; government policy treats them with a certain level of distrust.[38] And yet the data show that immigrants are far more willing to take advantage of integration courses than is generally believed.[39] The demand for such courses has always exceeded the supply.[40] Bureaucratic structures – like this law, or the rhetoric of "encourage and demand" (*fördern und fordern*) – can set up obstacles that prevent immigrants from accessing services and, in the process, actually hinder incorporation.

As the German sociologist of education Paul Mecheril argues, integration deserves our attention because there's a great deal at stake: integration not only pokes at the emotional discomfort migration produces as a matter of course, but is also intricately interwoven not only with how people construct society at large, but also with the way that privileges and resources are distributed within it.[41] In contemporary Germany, "integration" is not simply a descriptive term to analyse social organization or the interplay of social systems in a complex society. Integration politics in Germany has woven ideas of social access, national identity, and culture together in such a way that integration has become inextricably linked to both the future of the German nation and the establishment of hierarchies based on class, religious, ethnic, and racial identities. Despite continued migration to Germany, the demands of integration have become more rigid with time, which limits chances for upward mobility and for access to representation in the media and government. While gains continue to be made with each successive generation, I ask in this book what it would require to envision a political landscape where ideas of inclusion, access, and participation in the public sphere circulate without recourse to the rhetoric of integration and its subtext of compulsory assimilation. Such a project would admittedly require a radical shift in the terms of debate: it would require abandoning certain national myths as well as investing in a progressive political vision. Incorporation and participation would thus become the national values of importance, rather than cultural preservation and the assimilative subtext of integration. This vision would reimagine a German national identity that *starts* from a place of diversity rather than attempting to recuperate the myth of a homogenous past.

Imagining a new future, however, clearly requires some understanding of the past. *One Word Shapes a Nation* combines close readings of contemporary media-driven polemics about immigration with historical perspectives on the development of integration policies in Germany. Many contemporary political debates about migration begin with polemic scandals and crises, which include concerns about gender-based violence and human rights; the relationship between terrorism, religion, and ethnic identity; the contemporary acceleration of right-wing extremist rhetoric and white German nationalism; the role of the state in both accepting and incorporating refugees; and historical legal changes that finally opened up German citizenship to immigrants.

In Germany, as in every other immigrant-receiving nation, it is absolutely necessary to provide newcomers with explicit explanations of legal and social codes, offer opportunities for them to learn and practise the German language, and limit the obstacles that might prevent entry into a complex economy or the public sphere. What is up for debate is *how* best to structure these interventions – as well as whether assimilation should be their ultimate goal. While politicians view integration as an issue worthy of new policies and legal measures, the grammatical demands of the German verb *integrieren* (to integrate) also place a heavy demand on individuals. Since the verb is often reflexive in German (*sich integrieren*), the burden to integrate – despite laws and policy changes – falls squarely on the shoulders of immigrants. In a common formulation, immigrants must integrate *themselves* into German society (*sie müssen* sich *in die Gesellschaft integrieren*). Common rhetoric thus renders the role of government and the effects of discrimination invisible. While activists have formulated these critiques for decades, without language to describe how these institutions and practices work, the obstacles that prevent some immigrants from being able to participate fully in German public life remain unarticulated in mainstream political rhetoric.

Theories of Integration

The greatest challenge in writing about integration politics is to identify not only *what* integration is, but also *how to frame* any discussion
of integration. Any framework must offer the benefit of precision and
protect against a descent into the depths of abstraction. There are two
ways in which public debates about the integration of immigrants have
devolved over time: first, there are so many social factors referenced in
integration debates that too many things "count" as signs of integration (or disintegration) in the public sphere.[42] Second, in sociological
discourse, terms such as integration, assimilation, and adaptation are
riddled with conflict. Neither public opinion nor scholarly discourse
can agree on how best to define the terms of integration and whether
or not integration (if we can define it) should be a cultural, social,
and political goal. Such contradictory and confusing debates reflect a
deeply rooted ambivalence to immigration. The ambivalence towards
newcomers becomes evident in the tension between media polemics,
political rhetoric, social work interventions, and German reactions to
integration policies in everyday life.

Given that sociology is a discipline that studies how humans develop
and sustain societies, sociologists have developed a particularly rich
body of knowledge about "integration" as a theoretical term. The more
complex the society, the more sociologists expect that society to create
avenues for integration, whether this means ensuring that the economy, law, politics, education, and civic life function together to stabilize
a society, or whether it means insisting that marginalized groups have
access to and can participate in any of these arenas.[43] Sociologists interested in how societies created these processes developed terminology
to describe two types of integration: systemic and social integration.
Systemic integration describes how various institutions and systems
come together to create the conditions out of which a complex society
emerges. These foundational institutions include the economy (trade
and currency), jurisprudence (the legal duties and rights of citizens),
education (institutions such as public schools), and cultural institutions
(including the arts and journalism). Systemic integration also describes
how people integrate into societies through participation in broad,
interrelated systems like financial and trade markets, or come to share
interests, rhetoric, and values.[44] One of the best modern examples of
systemic integration can be seen in the example of the European Union.
The European Economic Community (EEC), which arose after the Second World War to facilitate economic partnerships across European
countries, eventually incorporated multiple European economies into

a shared system of trade and exchange. When this economic community transformed into a political and economic union with a common currency and freedom of movement between states, officials spoke of "European integration" as a form of systemic integration that permitted citizens of member states to participate in broad, interrelated systems of trade, governance, and even migration to other member states.

Systemic integration may succeed and yet still separate groups from either each other or from different areas of social and cultural life. Social integration describes how citizens and residents access and participate in the interrelated systems of a society. When scholars focus on how immigrants access the job market, what kind of social relationships they develop with local populations, and whether or not they participate in the political sphere, they are looking at social integration.[45] In the context of immigration, analyses of social integration ask whether, and how, ethnic minorities and immigrants can create connections with other groups in a diverse society as well as to society at large.[46] While systemic integration and social integration focus on different arenas of societal integration, they are interrelated and interdependent concepts. When systemic integration works well, one of its byproducts is social cohesion. Conversely, if social integration functions erratically or not at all, the lack of social cohesion could threaten systemic integration.[47] Disintegration, however, should not be seen as synonymous with collapse: one outcome of disintegration might be segmentation (for instance, downward mobility).[48] Segregation can also play a role in keeping society stable by reproducing racial, ethnic, or class hierarchies that control the distribution of labour and wealth.

Framing the integration of immigrants through the lenses of systemic and social integration is a structuralist approach to the integration of immigrants and their descendants into society. But this approach has its limits. Systems theory – an interdisciplinary approach for understanding how systems are bounded and structured and influence behaviour – built upon structuralist sociological theories and was quite en vogue among German sociologists analysing migration beginning in the 1970s.[49] Chin argues that early studies about guest workers in Germany were rooted in systems theory, and that this research primarily focused on cultural conflicts which seemed to emerge from confrontation and conflict between the "traditional systems" of the Global South and the "modern system" of West Germany.[50] Within this framework of cultural clashes, the goal of immigrant integration became indispensable and served as "a crucial antidote for the instability created by the clash of the so-called modern and traditional systems."[51] As Chin notes, the main geographical focus of systems theorists in Germany was Turkey, which they saw "as the most traditional nation of all the labour-sending countries."[52] Chin's research specifically charts how the application of systems theory in migration studies led to the development of a political discourse of integration that she argues was adopted by every major West German political party by the mid-1970s.[53]

This political agreement across parties obscures the depth of scholarly conflicts about the process of incorporating immigrants. Scholars, for instance, disagree about whether or not integration is the same as assimilation, whether or not integration is the product of individual efforts, and whether or not immigrants and their descendants should move towards integration. Researchers even disagree about the order of individual stages immigrants might move through as they experience the process of integration or assimilation. While the melting pot theory would propose a straight line that eventually and always leads to assimilation, more recent data has taken into account how some groups might move towards assimilation and then change course to strengthen an ethnic identity – or, due to racial or ethnic discrimination, some groups might assimilate into an underclass (rather than become upwardly mobile).[54] Integration is often considered the necessary precursor to full assimilation, since differences between groups rarely disappear if groups remain starkly differentiated.[55] But integration and assimilation are neither synonymous nor unidirectional. Take, for instance, this example offered by German sociologist Silke Hans: mothers who come from countries where women usually work outside the home move to Germany, where many mothers stay at home. The more immigrant mothers assimilate to German norms, the lower the rate of female integration into the job market will be.[56]

Integration Politics as an Apparatus

In addition to the conflicts of definition and analysis in scholarly debates, politicians and journalists often sensationalize urgent integration "problems," but ignore the cultural and historical contexts that likely led to the specific social developments they mark as problematic. This active forgetting, for instance, is pervasive in media discourse about ghettos and criminality among immigrant youth.[57] Without looking critically at how integration for adolescents is quite complicated and involves a number of interrelated factors, including family structure, traumatic experiences, racism, school policies, and urban planning, journalists and politicians are quick to criticize and blame immigrants for situations over which they may have little control. In this way, theoretical disagreement in scholarly discourse can combine with media sensationalism to produce an incoherent understanding of integration that later provides fertile ground for polarized rhetoric to gain enough traction to inform public policy.

Structuralist approaches to systems offer some foundational ideas that can be very useful to understanding integration as a conceptual term: societies arise from foundational systems and knowledges, and it is crucial for immigrants and citizens alike to be able to access these systems if societies are to be even moderately democratic. But because structuralist approaches emphasize the bounded nature of institutions and systems, they miss how porous boundaries between institutions (and people and nation-states) are. The networks created between these various structures are perhaps more important for understanding integration politics than the structure of the systems themselves.

Poststructuralist thinkers – theorists who were interested in examining semiotics, who engaged in the practice of deconstructing rhetoric, and who charted the relationships between the historical generation of knowledge and its relationship with power – took up the task of understanding how rich the networks *between* people, places, systems, institutions, and experiences can be. Whether they focused on actual territorial borders, linguistic exchange, or personal identity, poststructuralists often argued that analysing a system without including the historical and cultural contexts of such a system – as well as the power relationships embedded within them – is insufficient. The question of historical urgency – why certain social formations are seen as problems at a specific place in a specific time – is also crucial to understanding how systems are both constructed, and how people interact with, in and across these systems.

One of the most productive veins in twentieth-century research into the history of ideas – especially in the work of Michel Foucault – was to discern to what degree the relationships between power and knowledge were intertwined. Knowledge about groups can be used in the service of power, both through the creation of policies designed to know, manage, and discipline groups, and through the terms, discourses, and categories humans create in order to label, define, and subsume unique individual biographies into groups that social institutions can later mobilize. And yet, one central authority, acting in isolation, hardly wields the power to determine who belongs. Humans generate and disseminate knowledge through diverse networks of relationships in which they hold varying levels of power. The essence of much of Foucault's work is the assertion that power *and* resistance to power exist simultaneously and are also always in flux. Foucault developed the term "governmentality" to describe how government in modern states relies on complex and wide-ranging techniques to manage large, diverse, and complex populations.[58]

The integrative apparatus connects the institutions that implement integration policy, the rhetoric that compels people to integrate, the language used to describe a process of integration, the cultural identities integration policy shapes, the feelings people have about integration, and the activities of people's daily lives that mark them as integrated or (un)integrable. It would be impossible to chart each intersection between discourse, practice, knowledge, and power, just as it would be incredibly difficult to trace causality from a particular policy to the details of a specific life. A precise sketch, similar to an architectural blueprint, of every network embedded in an apparatus of governmentality is impossible to create. But it *is* possible to conceive of an abstract space in which networks of practices, discourses, and processes of cause and effect connect. That integration politics is primarily an apparatus (although it also has disciplinary features, including some limited forms of punishment) is evident in the laissez-faire quality inherent to an apparatus that permits a broad spectrum of integrative behaviours (including dissent, or "counter-conduct").[59]

Within an apparatus, discursive and non-discursive practices are the two primary mechanisms through which subjects can actively participate in producing or reproducing a discourse. The distinction between discursive practices and non-discursive practices lies in the role linguistic and symbolic practices play in how subjects participate in constructing both meaning and their own subjectivities. People can participate in discursive practices by using language or other symbolic practices to both speak and be heard. Within a discourse, however, there are also non-discursive practices built on various forms of action or gesture that attempt to reproduce, support, or even change a discourse.[60] Discursive practices must be related a social occasion during which subjects take part in verbal and non-verbal practices that have social consequences for the relationship to the self and that serve as processes of exchange.[61] Although an apparatus serves as the infrastructure for a discursive formation, it would be a mistake to see a clear and causal connection that marks an apparatus as always emerging before discourse or to see discourse as always responding to an apparatus. These concepts work in a polyvalent manner both with and upon each other, and discursive and non-discursive practices can be mobilized by a variety of apparatuses. These apparatuses, then, have different effects depending on the constellations of power embedded within the institutional and philosophical structures required by systems of knowledge.

In complex modern states, institutions play a formidable role in generating knowledge about groups, especially governmental institutions and the press. Technologies of power define when, where, and how any particular social formation becomes a problem.[62] In other words: we problematize social issues through discourses that are historically situated and produced through social exchanges of knowledge. These discourses, in turn, produce various subjectivities. Guest workers exist as a demographic category that can be recognized because journalists, politicians, and foreign workers participated in a variety of practices through which they could be known.[63]

Systems of governmentality are inherently political because they – according to urban scholar Kim McKee – "[translate] political ambitions into something inevitably more practical."[64] As I have argued elsewhere, thinking of integration politics as an apparatus of governmentality is a helpful way to understand the implicit goals of integration politics: "integration translates political ambition (full assimilation) into practical measures (sufficient "integration" to participate in society)."[65] The intricate interplay of whether, when, or how the government decides to label immigrants, refugees, or their descendants as a political problem also shapes the kinds of policies politicians and policymakers design to intervene in the lives of various groups.

Politicians do not develop policies in a vacuum. Instead, each step builds on the historically and culturally situated legislative changes that came before, thereby strengthening the networks between institutions, philosophies, discourses, practices, and legal measures. The 2005 Immigration Act, for instance, first categorized some groups of immigrants as being bearing a duty to integrate.[66] The 2016 Integration Act went a step further, regulating not only who could take integration courses funded by state subsidies, but also where asylum seekers would be permitted to live upon arrival.[67] These legal regulations – when combined with journalistic tropes – strengthen the subtext of integration laws and policies, which often imply that immigrants and refugees are unwilling to integrate and congregate in ghettos. When we look at a collection of cultural objects, discourses, and practices – here, the language of a "duty" to integrate; the legal changes in 2005 and 2016; residency regulations; and journalistic reporting – we can see how the trope of unintegrated immigrants performs multiple functions. First, it frames immigrant neighbourhoods as a social problem – both for cultural life and for the self-interests of a nation-state invested in democratic practices and equality. Second, and somewhat counterintuitively, this trope itself acts as a barrier to social integration. The remedies proposed to solve the problem of immigrant isolation combine to form a network through which politicians, journalists, and academics generate knowledge about a group. The government then acts upon this knowledge to maintain the prevailing (and normative) social order.

Because integration politics reaches into so many spaces, analysing "integration" requires a framework that can accommodate multiple disciplinary perspectives. I find it helpful to think of integration politics not just as a field of public policy, or a collection of journalistic tropes, or even as the proposed pathway into the systems of German social and political life. Instead, integration politics is a broad network of practices that society has developed to control and manage the participatory roles available to immigrants, refugees, and their descendants in German society. Due to the combination of policy changes since 2000 and the heightened urgency of media attention to immigration since September 11, 2001, integration has moved beyond discourse and now constitutes a highly complex and intricate apparatus of governmentality. Moreover, I argue that the construction of this apparatus began earlier than many contemporary critics of immigrant incorporation remember. It is not an artefact of unification or the War on Terror. By the 1960s, politicians in West Germany were already laying the foundation for the integrative apparatus. This book uses the framework of the integrative apparatus to analyse how contemporary German cultural and political ideas about integration politics invoke, categorize, maintain, and manipulate gendered, racial, class, ethnic, and national identities. The consequences of these demands are far-reaching, affecting not just immigrants, but all German citizens and residents. In this context, the most urgent question becomes: What kind of society will emerge from contemporary German debates and conflicts?

Legal Changes and the Development of the Apparatus

An apparatus is not merely a legal philosophy and is certainly not synonymous with legal or policy changes writ large. But a number of legal changes have affected how integration politics developed and how the apparatus expanded. These legal changes shape the interactions of citizens and residents with the state as well as how the state funds policies and programs. Attention to legal documents is different based on each discipline, and I want to be very clear that this book is firmly rooted in the methods of discourse and apparatus analysis after the ethnographic and transdisciplinary turns in cultural studies. I am neither attempting nor would I be capable of applied legal critique. What the inclusion, however, of legal policies offers me are ways to chart the pre-emergence of, impetus for, and the consolidation of an apparatus between multiple networks of subjects, discourses, and institutions.

There are roughly three different periods of legal changes. The first addressed the residency and incorporation of expellees and refugees after the Second World War and extended into the guest worker period (which includes the post-recruitment period after 1973). The Federal Law on Expellees and Refugees (1953) as well as the Aliens Act (1965) and the Recruitment Stop (1973) managed the postwar movement of human beings into West Germany. The end of this period came in 1980, when the Asylum Procedure Act and the amended Aliens Act changed how newcomers could be granted visas and residency permits. Both the 1973 Recruitment Stop and the 1980 Asylum Procedure Act were legal measures that sought to slow, if not stop, the flow of newcomers into West Germany.

The second period mixed limits to immigration with nationalist rhetoric. The social backlash that emerged in the 1980s and that persisted past the unification of the East and West German states in 1990 included Helmut Kohl's Act to Aid Return (*Rückkehrhilfegesetz*, 1983), which attempted to reward former guest workers remuneratively if they left West Germany, and the Asylum Compromise (1993), which reinterpreted the right to asylum embedded within the German Basic Law in order to limit asylum claims following the collapse of the Soviet Union and decolonization across the Global South in the early 1990s.

By the early 2000s, a third collection of legal changes accelerated the expansion of the integrative apparatus. These changes are the focus of the chapters in this book that examine the interplay of media scandals, politics, and historical developments. They exhibit some interesting characteristics that are ripe for future scholarship about the relationship between media profits, cost-saving policies promoting the ideologies of neoliberal efficiency, and population management policies that alternately embrace both the rhetoric of inclusion/participation *and* nationalist exclusion. The labour market reforms known as the Hartz Reforms were a package of legal measures that were passed between 2003 and 2005 that had significant impact on unemployment services as well as job re-training and career counselling programs like those I examine in chapter 9. The Hartz reforms also instituted a new class of citizens with permanent welfare status, known as Hartz IV. The Hartz IV reform took effect in 2005 – the same year that Necla Kelek, the author I examine in chapter 1, published her bestseller *Die fremde Braut* (The Foreign Bride), and the same year that Hatun Sürücü was murdered by her brother, a case study of the media racialization of domestic violence that I examine in chapter 2. These two events captured the national media landscape at the same time that various consultative structures were developed at the federal level: the first Integration Summit and the first German Islam Conference both took place in 2006. Nationalistic polices were also instituted at the regional level in some places that same year – see, for example, my discussion of the so-called Muslim Test in Baden-Württemberg in chapter 1. By the start of the next decade, these types of media spectacles had intensified: Thilo Sarrazin's polemic *Deutschland schafft sich ab* (Germany Is Doing Away with Itself) made millions of dollars in 2010 and prompted a nation-wide conversation about integration politics and race. At the same time, regional states began to publish their own integration policies: Berlin's Integration Act took effect in 2010; North-Rhine Westphalia followed in 2012; and Baden-Württemberg in 2015. These integration policies were correlated with an ascendant right-wing presence on the national stage: in 2013, the right-wing extremist party Alternative for Germany (AfD) was founded; in 2014, the so-called right-wing citizens movement known as PEGIDA organized several very large protests that attracted global attention. German integration policy polarized alongside politics writ large: as many of the regional integration acts created policies to facilitate the inclusion of newcomers and assure opportunities for their participation in the democratic process, nationalist groups and parties worked hard to denigrate immigrant and refugee agency through their nationalistic and racist statements. These extremist groups predominantly garnered social interest through posting and agitating on social media. This third group of legal changes culminated in the Federal Integration Act of 2016, which was followed by an explicitly nationalist Bavarian Integration Act later that year.

Integration politics emerged and was shaped by the conditions of both the postwar and post-unification periods. If the postwar policy changes revolved primarily around population management, with a clear turn in the 1980s and 1990s to attempts to "re-sort" the demographics of West Germany through return "aid," nationalist paroles, or constitutional limits on asylum, the post-unification policy changes welded together an ideology of economic efficiency in late capitalism with more detailed forms of population management. Politicians viewed these changes as necessary against the backdrop of a populist political landscape on which the right wing garnered more power, more visibility, and more formal representation at the federal level of government. I describe this particular intersection of vectors as the "late-stage integrative apparatus" – both to reflect the constant presence of late capitalist economic ideologies (like neo- and ordoliberalism), and to mark how the integrative apparatus continually expands its influence into the cultures and practices of daily life.

Integration and Racialization

Understanding integration as a term originating in scholarly sociological literature sheds more detail on the differences between integration and assimilation. In its politicized context, however, integration rhetoric is often hardly distinguishable from assimilative demands. Demands to assimilate are, in turn, often linked with nationalist ideology. Across the world, politicians, journalists, and other elites mobilize nativist ideas because of their political expediency. But this expediency comes at a cost: nativism and nationalism lead to violence. The effects of the Trump presidency and Putin's brutal war against Ukraine have made this reality glaringly obvious. But even before the extremes of war and persecution, nativist and nationalist ideas can prompt individuals to pursue violent, isolated assaults on people perceived to be different, or provide justifications for excluding these groups from higher education or political representation. By exploring one national context in depth, this book offers a way to understand which elements of integration politics are culturally specific and which elements are relevant to understanding migration as a transnational or global phenomenon. Nationalism in Germany is heavily racialized: assimilative demands are consequently built upon racialized hierarchies and reinforce both ethnic Germanness and white supremacy.

It is impossible to think about social organization without understanding the hierarchies of power that structure German society and how these hierarchies are unique and particular to every national or regional context. I grew up primarily in Louisville, Kentucky, with brief stints in the far west, middle-class suburbs of St. Louis County, Missouri, and the semi-rural, small-town of Fayetteville, Georgia. Both Louisville and St. Louis County are communities with a long history of school busing to desegregate school districts. As a white student, I was bused into downtown Louisville public schools that were predominantly Black and Vietnamese. Primarily Black students from downtown St. Louis were bused out into my predominantly white and South Asian suburban middle and high schools. While racial and ethnic groups were still segregated through academic tracking programs in all the schools with a busing program, I grew up expecting a certain level of Black and Asian diversity in a school environment – even if my classes were predominantly white. When I became an exchange student in northern Germany in 1999, I was shocked to walk into my first classroom and be greeted with what looked like a sea of white faces. It made me feel uneasy because of my own national history of segregation, but it also seemed to confirm the worst of National Socialist racial ideologies that I had grown up learning about. It wasn't until several years later that I realized that my 12th grade German classroom had been much more diverse than I first assumed: I had German classmates of Polish, Turkish, Kurdish, and Filipino descent. The small neighbourhood school I attended also had younger students of Indian, Chinese, and Russian descent. There were likely other students who passed for me as white who were *not* passing as white to their classmates, and the complexity of class divisions as well as rural–urban disparities in the state of Schleswig-Holstein, where there is high unemployment and low economic output, were lost on me during my exchange year.

Racialized hierarchies are shaped by culture. As Nell Irvin Painter declares: "What we can see depends heavily on what our culture has trained us to look for."[68] It is not surprising that the language of race in Germany is most often substituted by the language of culture (*kulturalisieren*). In a national context where the German word for race is forever associated with memories of the Holocaust, the use of the German word for race is taboo. The English word "race" as well as the verb racialization (*rassifizieren*), the German word for racism (*Rassismus*), or the term *migrantisieren* (to turn someone into a migrant, coined by Fatima El-Tayeb) are all workarounds in contemporary German speech to avoid reproducing the racial language of National Socialism.[69] Avoiding the language of race, as many scholars have pointed out, does nothing to render racial ideology and unequal material conditions obsolete. Racialized hierarchies are embedded in cultural discourses and reinforced by culturally sanctioned mechanisms of power and exclusion, while simultaneously being shaped and informed by historical precedent.

The Black-white-Asian trifecta that I encountered as a child in the United States was prevalent across the suburbs of the Midwest and the Southeast in the 1980s and 1990s. These US discourses about race were no longer just reproducing a Black-white binary – at the same time, discourses of racial solidarity and terms like BIPoC had not yet entered everyday speech. When I walked into that German classroom in 1999, I was confronted with a radically new expression of cultural dominance that was absolutely invisible to me because it lacked both the cultural vocabularies and demographics with which I was most familiar.

The longer I spent living in Germany and studying German culture, the clearer the distinctions between German and American social hierarchies became. However, I continued to make some severe interpretive mistakes that were facilitated by both my own socialization as well as how certain groups are treated in Germany. When I started looking for research topics for applications to graduate school, I consistently misread Turkish-German authors as white. Necla Kelek and Seyran Ateş were white to me, not the least because my own mother looks a little bit like Kelek. I also share the greying dark hair and skin tone I saw on Seyran Ateş' cover photograph, which I inherited from my father. The visual identification primed by media coverage and cover photographs combined with my own identification with a narrative "I" that is inherent to reading autobiographical texts.[70] Based on other experiences I had while in Germany on a student exchange, I mistakenly assumed that the problems both authors sought to illuminate were German problems that were typical in (white) German families. I completely overlooked – in a rather stunning early misreading informed by personal experiences – how they were writing explicitly from a marginalized perspective that demanded Turkish-German integration into German social norms. Eventually, I became curious about the construction of race and ethnic belonging in a German context. As a graduate student, the first visit I spent abroad was in Essen, where I lived for a month and visited university courses. The level of diversity and physical crowding in a large city in Germany's most densely populated state shocked me and made it clear that my perception of German society presented a very urgent *Nachholbedarf* (need for an update).

Historian and theorist Fatima El-Tayeb's 2011 book *European Others: Queering Ethnicity in Postnational Europe* argues in cogent theoretical detail just how clearly race and racism continue to be important for understanding how Europe constructs its own identity as both white and colourblind. El-Tayeb rejects the idea that Europe – as the site of origin for the ideologies of colonialism and imperialism that found their way to the farthest corners of the globe – could ever be seen as a "colorblind continent."[71] Many white European scholars view critical race theories as American imports, preferring instead to see class as the fundamental category of difference for European societies.[72] El-Tayeb acknowledges that "the continent's racial paradigms differ from the US context [...] in a number of ways that still need to be fully explored."[73] However, those differences do not preclude being subjected to racializing logics:

> Race, at times, seems to exist anywhere but in Europe, where racialized minorities have traditionally been placed outside of the national and by extension continental community. Europe can thus be situated within the larger context of ideologies of colourblindness that prohibit discourses

around racialized oppression. [(...)] In its European version, this ideology is characterized by the convergence of race and religion as well as the externalization of racialized populations (rather than their relegation to second-class citizen status).[74]

The racialization of Muslims and the widespread notion that Germans of colour must come from "somewhere else," when situated within an ahistorical, colourblind framework, make it difficult to name and negotiate the power afforded to whiteness. German journalists and political commentators often assert that bullying against Germans exists and that Germans of colour promote "anti-white racism" in their critiques of racist German practices, which is a false equivalency that upholds hegemonic German whiteness.[75] In early 2021, the most publicized debate of this kind centred around the work of one of the only Black professors in Germany, Maisha Auma, who is also one of the foremost authorities on race and racialization in education.[76] Racializing discourses are themselves immaterial, but they still have material consequences – and while racialized hierarchies can shift and morph, that changeability rarely unsettles white subjectivity. Political ideology is the clearest indicator as to whether or not whiteness is seen as an acceptable descriptor of "German" cultural hegemony and whether other European groups who are not German can be considered white. Those with a vested interest in hegemonic German whiteness use white invisibility and reject naming whiteness to reproduce their dominant status.

The efficacy of whiteness as an analytic continues to be debated despite the obvious fact that whiteness and white supremacy exist. There are very real concerns that the study of whiteness reproduces and re-centres the white subject and is potentially irredeemable as a theoretical approach. Scholars are also grappling with how the focus on scholarship about identity, as well as research about whiteness that is insufficiently antiracist and critical, provides white supremacists – or even white "allies" – with scholarly evidence they can invert and appropriate to support their political goals. However, ignoring whiteness or rejecting it as a US theoretical import allows whiteness to continue to be rendered irrelevant and invisible in spite of the fact that white supremacist politics are on display every day in German public spaces. Integration policy is built on long-standing tropes of hegemonic German whiteness and rewards those groups who slowly are able to garner proximity to whiteness. The structures that permit what Matthew Hughey terms "hegemonic whiteness" determine the role immigrants and Europeans of colour can play at all levels of German society as well

as the demands white Germans can make of newcomers.[77] There is no
way to study integration policy without taking into account the obstacles created by whiteness and how whiteness serves as the foundation
for claiming German belonging.

Nell Irvin Painter argues in *The History of White People* that medieval
Europe was home to multiple white races with complex histories and
shows – primarily through the history of European migration to the
United States – how the boundaries of whiteness are constantly in flux.
Indeed, the malleability of whiteness affirms its dominance – it allows
white people to determine who counts as white. In Germany, race and
ethnicity represent the two features required to claim a dominant white
identity. German ethnicity combined with visually passing as a white
German are *both* required to be considered "fully" German. Members
of the Afro-German community, many of whom are *also* ethnically German, are frequently lumped together with immigrants to Germany and
targeted with an integrative discourse. This constant misreading of
both how racism works and of the mere existence of Black Germanness
prompted *ADEFRA e. V. – Schwarze Frauen in Deutschland* (ADEFRA –
Black Women in Germany) to release a 2020 statement against the parliamentary decision to grant €9 million in research funds for the study
of racism to the Center for Integration and Migration research. Not only
have German scholars of anti-Black racism consistently been ignored
for their achievements, they argue, but racism is also not the same as
migration or integration and is unlikely to be sufficiently understood
under an integrative paradigm: "research about racism as integration
research is not an appropriate, future-oriented approach for a hyperdi-
verse, post-migrant society oriented towards a critique of racism and
discrimination."[78]

As a person with a German name living in a white body, I am frequently granted white privilege in Germany despite the fact that I am
not German, I did not grow up speaking German, and German society
continues to be a foreign environment to me, no matter how much time
I spend trying to master the language and engage with German culture.
Sometimes this misrecognition provides me with benefits – the more
people think that you are like them, the more likely they are to connect
with you. Sometimes this serves as a hindrance. If you have had a negative experience with a white German, reading my name and appearance
as evidence of German whiteness can hardly be comforting, especially
if I am interviewing you about your life or silently observing you work
during a period of ethnographic fieldwork. Recently, even the possibility that this mistake could occur has become intensely uncomforta-
ble for me. More and more often, I find myself often preempting any

misunderstandings by identifying as an American and a German language-learner earlier than seems necessary in the general flow of conversation. This is especially true in interactions that require politeness in a foreign language: sometimes I recognize the social and cultural codes, and sometimes I don't. Misunderstandings become clear either by visible incomprehension or the stunned silence that follows offence.

The political and politicized forms of German whiteness associated with social and cultural dominance do not foreclose the existence of other white identities. When German critics and commentators insist that whiteness has nothing to do with skin colour, what they are arguing for is often a differentiated understanding of whiteness and power. Different forms of whiteness and different expressions of whiteness are present in the German social context and may or may not be bound to political and social privilege. Immigrants from multiple countries pass as white in a German context, especially if no one knows their name, which can obscure ethnic identity. Thus, it is possible to be a member of an ethnic minority, have a personal history of migration to Germany, be an immigrant, or be marginalized, and *still pass* in general, anonymous situations as white.[79] It is also equally possible for immigrants from any of these origins to be *excluded* from hegemonic whiteness based on physical features such as hair texture or skin tone that do not match colourist assumptions about the construction of Germanness. Colourism plays a strong role in German society: the visual perception of someone's identity determines how they are treated, whether or not the person who is looking looks accurately. Tiffany Florvil addresses how colourism affected Afro-German communities in her book *Mobilizing Black Germany*, when she addresses reports of tensions within ADEFRA due to differences in skin tone and the privileges that the proximity to whiteness afforded some members.[80] Anecdotal evidence in literature and social commentary also reveals how a North American Black-white binary can be disrupted in a German context: the playwright and novelist Sasha Marianna Salzman, who confirms anecdotes I have also heard from Jewish Americans doing research in Germany, writes about the fascination Germans express with Salzmann's curls in a mode that bears striking similarities to the discourses and tropes about Black hair in the United States.

Adding to this complexity is the reality that immigrants of European descent who may pass as white live alongside other Germans – to invoke Tina Campt's study of Black Germans during the Holocaust – who cannot and will never pass as white.[81] Black Germans and Germans of colour face different and complex forms of discrimination, especially compared to those who experience intermittent privileges of passing. Proximity to whiteness absolutely affects who is marked as a subject in need of integration and who is not. The complex diversity of contemporary German and European society thus requires that we attend to difference in all of its registers. Non-hegemonic whiteness, political Blackness, and visibly Black, Brown and genderqueer bodies are all subject to power and discipline in different ways. The demands of integration thus affect all subjects differently, bringing with them a variety of consequences and multiple forms of oppression. Racialization and integration politics – as ADEFRA states – are not synonymous. But it would be impossible to deny that racist structures inform the contours of the policies and discourses of integration.

There will be many people who contest this approach to understanding racial hierarchies in Germany, insisting that Eastern European immigrants and Eastern Europeans of Jewish descent (as well as Jewish people) cannot ever be considered white in a German context, especially after the Holocaust. I fully agree that none of these groups are groups I would include in what I am calling hegemonic whiteness. But it would be specious to argue that hierarchies of whiteness do not exist or that they do not elevate even Eastern and Southern Europeans above Black, Roma, or Asian Europeans. That does not mean, however, that Eastern Europeans always pass as white. There are also forms of precarious whiteness that exist alongside hegemonic whiteness. When compared with the profound global presence of anti-Blackness, anti-Asian sentiment after the pandemic, or the centuries-old suspicion of Roma communities, members of marginalized groups who can pass as white in anonymous settings are having a fundamentally different experience than those who cannot pass as white. This book is partially an attempt to explain to North American scholars working from different theoretical models of race and ethnicity as well as to North American students how these racialized dynamics play out in German society. Both the visual and political assumptions of how race and ethnicity structure public space in the United States or Canada neither consistently nor fully translate to a German context.

The ideology of divide and conquer that structures a colonial imaginary also readily explains how non-hegemonic whiteness can produce a targeted identity but still simultaneously profit from anti-Black ideologies. This tension between white-passing Germans with a history of immigration and those who cannot pass as white comes up frequently in events and other social settings that I have observed during various periods of fieldwork in Germany. Comments audience members made during Q&As at panels or talkbacks after theatrical performances made it clear that not all immigrant subjects or subjects of colour share the same concerns or the same obstacles. While this statement reads as a truism, it cannot be repeated enough given our tendencies as humans to read affinity groups as monoliths. The difference in media attention to refugee protests in 2014 led by refugees from the Middle East versus those led by refugees from African nations offers an additional case study in the clear presence of anti-Black racism in Germany. Understanding the complexities of whiteness in both hegemonic and non-hegemonic forms in order to render the mechanisms of cultural and racial dominance visible can be useful if we are attentive to situational specificity and are careful not to re-centre white subjects. I believe that any attempt to remedy an unjust distribution of power and dominance must attend to whiteness and name it. Whether I successfully do so here is an open question to the reader.

Participation in the Integration Nation

Questions of migration and integration intersect with two topics of critical importance for democratic societies: citizenship and political participation. Where one stands on integration often provides insight into where one stands on the political spectrum. Any one-way definition that defines integration as a process that only applies to outsiders requires an ethnonationalist subtext. It is this subtext that makes integration politics an arena ripe for appropriation by the far right.

Anti-immigrant sentiment appears in contemporary far-right European politics as nativism and ethnonationalism; political scientist Cas Mudde even maintains that nativism is *the* core feature of radical right ideologies.[82] Political scientist Hans-Georg Betz traced the origins of the term "nativism" to nineteenth century American populist movements and, along the way, showed how nativism and populism exhibit some core, shared traits. Among these shared traits are the desire to look backward and reclaim a nostalgic version of the past, as well as to conflate the people with the nation.[83] Populism thus often mobilizes a vision of "the people" as a homogenous entity. Citing Benjamin McLean, Betz argues that "populism's 'insistence on homogeneity' means that within the 'populist logic, difference can never appear as a potential basis for unity'."[84] This ideology clearly poses a theoretical problem for super-diverse, democratic, and pluralistic societies that can only succeed by expanding the opportunities for participation by all citizens. Expanding and ensuring access requires either granting citizenship more easily to permanent residents or finding ways for noncitizens to access both the public sphere and the political process.

The integrative apparatus that demands assimilation to German culture and values – rejecting difference as a matter of course – has an implicitly nativist logic built-in. This does not mean that integration policy is *only* a political tool of the far right, despite the simultaneous reality that its rhetoric is most often deployed in this way. That social and systemic incorporation into national life requires some explicit introduction can simply be pragmatic. But within the integrative apparatus, the ethnonationalist subtext of integration politics opens up connections between centrist and far-right tropes, illustrating how integration politics can so easily be pulled to the right. The ethnonationalist subtext of integration politics, and its appropriation in multiple instances by the far-right political actors driven by notions of nostalgic nativism, make it impossible to reject whiteness, race, and ethnicity as categories of importance. Marking certain populations as "unwilling to integrate," "unintegrable," or as the causes of societal disintegration performs the externalization of racialized populations theorized by El-Tayeb.

Although minority segregation, segmentation, or "dis-integration" might seem to be a problem only for those who remain excluded, one of the great misunderstandings of integration is the idea that integration politics only affects immigrants. Indeed, the degree to which any group is socially incorporated reflects how the broader social system functions. Integration politics and rhetoric have a number of negative effects on marginalized groups who feel compelled to integrate or challenged by the terms of "integration," and for white Germans, the rhetoric of integration ultimately reflects a conservative approach to national identity. But integration also demands conflicting behaviour from white Germans by painting ethnic German citizens either as "benevolent gatekeepers who offer opportunities for immigrants to integrate, [or] as stern sentinels tasked with guarding a national cultural threatened by ethnic, racial, and religious diversity," as I have argued elsewhere.[85] The integrative apparatus ultimately serves to define both the social and cultural identities of "us" (Germans) and "them" (foreigners or immigrants), as well as the national identity of the Federal Republic itself. Studying integration politics reveals a much broader – and potentially more critical – concern than just charting the contours of German national identity. Imaginative work here is critical: What kind of German society would be possible if the cultural and rhetorical demands to integrate were to disappear?

PART ONE

Polemic and Scandal: How Integration Became a Household Word

Chapter One

Demanding Integration

When Jörg Lewin picked up the phone in the middle of the night, he was confused. It was 12 September 2001. A former co-worker had called him up after seeing the identities of the terrorists who had attacked the World Trade Center broadcast on TV. "I just saw a picture of the attacker," Lewin's colleague reportedly said. "It's our Mohammad." Lewin recounted this story for the German newspaper *Der Tagesspiegel*, adding: "We're actually the only ones who called him that."[1]

Mohammad Atta was an Egyptian citizen who had studied in Germany and later attended flight school in the United States. In 1995, he began to work for the Hamburg-based city planning firm Plankontor, which Lewin had founded. Back then, Lewin had hired Atta as a student worker. Atta's primary task for the urban planning firm was drawing up maps, a small contribution to the larger project of revitalizing East German cities after unification. As a model immigrant, whom Lewin described as "reliable and skilful," Atta worked for Plankontor for several years until computer programmers automated many hand-drawn tasks.[2]

How could such a nice man have committed such a heinous crime? News media identified Atta, along with several other Muslim men, as part of the "Hamburg Cell."[3] The Hamburg Cell was a group of terrorists radicalized by Al-Qaeda who were responsible for the attacks on the World Trade Center in New York on September 11, 2001. Lewin and his colleagues were hardly the only Germans shocked that this terrorist attack had been planned right under the noses of the German police. If Mohammad Atta – "our Mohammad" – could fly a plane into a Manhattan skyscraper, how many other terrorists were lurking on German soil? What else were Muslim immigrants hiding – and what was the German government going to do about it?

In Germany, reductive commentary from both journalists and politicians has allowed many elements of a neocolonial, Orientalist discourse to converge in a public arena called "*Islamkritik*," or "criticism of Islam." *Islamkritik* overlaps strategically with integration debates: the two most foundational questions for German politicians trying to design integration policies centre on whether Muslims can be democratic and whether Muslim women are oppressed by their religion. Other areas of debate include whether public servants should be able to wear headscarves, whether handshaking should be required in professional settings, and the relationships between Islam, terrorism, and national security. An additional flashpoint has focused on whether Islam can be recognized as a state religion with the corresponding political rights currently afforded to Christianity and Judaism.[4] A quick Google NGrams search – a digital tool that tracks the discursive emergence of certain terms – suggests that *Islamkritik* is indeed a post-9/11 phenomenon.[5]

The September 11th attacks heightened stereotypes of Muslims as violent, and the subsequent discovery of a German sleeper cell placed Muslims in Germany under a broad, general suspicion of criminality and radicalism.[6] The discovery of the Hamburg Cell also expanded the German security apparatus: in December 2004, the *Gemeinsames Terrorismusabwehrzentrum* (Joint Anti-Terrorism Centre) began operating with a focus on Islamic extremism and jihadist terrorism.[7] No matter how kind they appeared to be, any Muslim could be harbouring terrorist, anti-democratic ideas. The basic elements of contemporary Islamophobic discourses in Germany are part of a global trend that builds on long-standing tropes and images deeply rooted in the intellectual traditions of the West. The same security discourses that stereotyped Muslim men as violent also portrayed Muslim women as the victims of religiously sanctioned gender oppression. The powder-blue burqas of Afghanistan – the Taliban's clothing requirement for women – appeared in striking press photographs throughout Europe and the United States after the NATO invasion of Afghanistan in 2001.[8] The Bush Administration used these images as yet another justification for its military project: not only did the masterminds of the attack on the World Trade Centers need to be brought to justice, but Afghans also needed to learn internalize democratic ideals, like gender equality.[9]

In the early 2000s, *Islamkritik* was less likely to perform critiques of terrorism and more likely to enter the public sphere through discussions of gender and women's rights. On 27 January 2005, the highbrow political newspaper *Die Zeit* published an excerpt of Necla Kelek's first book for general audiences, *Die fremde Braut*.[10] Having an excerpt printed in *Die Zeit* is an achievement for any German public intellectual – the paper has high journalistic standards and is known for its weekly intellectual commentary on politics, economics, and the arts. Each edition is also massive: according to urban legend, one weekly issue contains as much text as a copy of Thomas Mann's *Buddenbrooks*, a modernist novel of many hundred pages. The excerpt from Kelek's book, entitled "The Bride as a Bargain," appeared under a photograph of opulent wedding dresses on page ten of the politics section. By placing the title and image in this configuration, editors linked the consumer behaviour associated with weddings to the traffic in women as brides.[11]

The anecdotes in *Die fremde Braut* – based on interviews Kelek conducted with "import brides" – are tragic and heart-wrenching. Emine, 32, suffered miscarriages, an abusive mother-in-law, and a brain tumour after moving to Germany. She turned to religion as a way to survive the brutal stressors of her daily life. It worked: Emine tells Kelek that she now beats her son less – although she can feel her brain tumour growing back. Kelek's second story focuses on a beautiful Turkish girl, just turned 18, who was purchased for 10,000 German marks by her mother-in-law, a Turk who has lived in Germany for 20 years. When Kelek tries to speak with the young bride directly, her mother-in-law quickly banishes the bride to the kitchen. "We don't need any more tea," the older woman says. Kelek implies in this excerpt that this young bride is nothing more than a domestic servant; in the full book, she argues that import brides are purchased through dowries and essentially become household slaves who serve their husbands at the mercy of their mothers-in-law. That terrorism and gender oppression are both stereotyped as practices handled with the utmost secrecy links the discourse of Muslim communities as suspicious with the discourse of Muslim communities as antidemocratic.

Kelek is an important figure in German integration politics because of her rapid consolidation of political power over a brief period from 2005 to 2007. This otherwise unknown academic, who completed her PhD in 2002, transitioned in merely three years from holding an obscure teaching post to becoming a media and political juggernaut. Very few of Kelek's ideas are original – her arguments mix Islamophobic rhetoric with defences of democracy. But she was nevertheless highly influential in changing the tenor of integration politics in the early years of the twenty-first century. While integration had been part of the vocabulary used to describe how immigrants adjusted to German everyday life since the 1970s, Kelek welded demands to integrate with the cultural criticism of *Islamkritik*, imbuing long-standing discourses about the integration of foreign workers and their descendants with a distinctly discriminatory slant. In the short term, this move allowed

Kelek to pursue political influence. In the long term, the widespread attention paid to Kelek in the media and in politics primed the pump for future commentators to invoke rhetoric that became more racist and nationalistic over time. Kelek's arguments may have even provided convenient cover for the mistakes and oversights in the development of state-sponsored integration policies.

Kelek was not the only public figure in the early 2000s who argued that the German state should demand that immigrants integrate. But she was one of the loudest voices and one of the most successful personalities to garner media attention. Kelek's celebrity and her ability to consolidate political power left an indelibly conservative mark on integration politics: national debates about German identity and immigration – which were already moving farther to the right – were presented by a Turkish-German celebrity who confirmed they were moving in the right direction.

Die fremde Braut (The Foreign Bride)

Necla Kelek's first book, Die fremde Braut, was published on 9 January 2005 – just a few weeks before Die Zeit published her excerpt.[12] In Die fremde Braut, Kelek combined her own autobiography with interviews with traumatized "import brides." Both parts of Kelek's work strengthened a long-running narrative that Muslim women were oppressed by their families and by the patriarchal expectations that governed and shaped their lives. In her exposé, Kelek reveals a subculture in which young women are reportedly "imported" to Germany to serve as wives for second-generation Turkish-German men, where they suffer a variety of abuses at the hands of their in-laws and husbands. Kelek argues that the state must do more to crack down on abuses of power sanctioned by tradition, which requires tougher policies that demand integration as a form of cultural assimilation.[13] Kelek's own identity as a Turkish-German woman – even though she offers no autobiographical evidence that she has suffered in analogous ways to import brides – validates her demand for stronger integration policies because she supposedly has insider knowledge about a community to which few white Germans have access.

In the months that followed her book's publication, Kelek garnered a great deal of media attention: she was one of several authors smeared by the Turkish-language daily newspaper Hürriyet for demonizing Turkish men as "violent brutes."[14] The Federal Interior Minister Otto Schily – a centre-left Social Democrat – positively reviewed her book for the weekly magazine Der Spiegel.[15] She won literary prizes, worked as a consultant for the Hamburg Office of Justice, and volunteered her services as a consultant to the state of Baden-Württemberg.[16] Kelek's second book, *Die verlorenen Söhne* (The Lost Sons), published a year later, incorporated interviews with Turkish-Muslim men in German prisons and functioned as a gendered companion text to *Die fremde Braut*.[17] The Orientalist dichotomy of savage men and beautiful, oppressed women was predictable. Kelek made the rounds of German radio and TV talk shows and even garnered attention in the American press: the *New York Times* profiled her in December 2005.[18] In September 2006, she was appointed to the first German Islam Conference – a new government advisory body created to solve various problems attributed to a growing Muslim population in Germany.[19] The University of Duisburg-Essen also awarded her a prestigious professorship in 2006, the Mercator Professorship, a position for which she gave two well-attended public talks in 2006 and 2007.[20]

The women Kelek interviews – whom she depicts as trafficked goods who immigrate to Germany through forced or arranged marriages – may be victims, but Kelek also portrays them as cultural threats: "Import brides generally don't want anything to do with Germans. They don't speak their language or understand their culture, and their lifestyles are generally despised by religious Muslims. They [import brides] turn away [from Germany] and turn towards their traditions. Islam is and remains their homeland."[21] Kelek correlates the level of a bride's animosity towards German culture with both increased religiosity and an increased risk of abuse. Despite the abuses these women have suffered, Kelek distrusts their turn towards religion as a form of survival. Assimilated Turkish immigrants know of this "problem," Kelek says, but fear being associated with such an "embarrassing" cohort.[22] Kelek argues that both Germans and open-minded Turkish immigrants are therefore losing contact with this (unintegrated) group. And she demands the government fix the problem.

Lest I give Kelek too much credit for being politically savvy, it is important to acknowledge – as journalist Patrick Bahners also argues – how her career profited from (or was even the product of) good timing.[23] Her first book was published after the attacks on September 11, 2001, in New York and the invasions of Afghanistan (2001) and Iraq (2003), all of which were global events that brought Islamophobic ideas to the centre of most Western political discourse. Part of Kelek's success in Europe was related to broader trends: her first book was published shortly after the highly publicized murder of the Dutch provocateur Theo van Gogh in 2004, and just a couple of months before both the French riots in the *banlieues* and the Danish cartoon controversy in

2005. All of these events raised questions about whether Europeans accepted Muslims as participants in European society. Van Gogh, for instance, was known for off-colour remarks about Muslims and was murdered by a Dutch-Moroccan man, rumoured to have terrorist ties, who reportedly had been upset by van Gogh's most recent film.[24] The riots in France were a response to police brutality against marginalized groups, including Muslims, and the Danish newspaper *Jyllands-Posten* deliberately tried to provoke Muslim communities that honoured a strong tradition against creating graven images by printing a collection of cartoons of the Prophet Mohammed.

Kelek describes her political project at the beginning of *Die fremde Braut* as if she were a meddling aunt: "I meddle *because I want integration* [italics in the original]," Kelek writes. "Mind you, integration has a price. 'You can't have the cake and eat it' [sic] applies here, too. Integration is not a declaration of mutual love, but rather a kind of contract. Certain conditions hold for both sides, and they must be adhered to. This is what's lacking. On both sides."[25] Kelek then argues that immigrants retreat into ethnic communities and isolate themselves from the German mainstream because of a lack of coherent integration policy. Once isolated, communities are ripe for radicalization. Despite this brief attempt at even-handed critique from the second page of *Die fremde Braut*, much of Kelek's subsequent writing and rhetoric asks Germans to stand up for what they believe in by demanding immigrants assimilate to German norms. The demands of integration in Kelek's rhetoric are *not* equally shared by "both sides." For Kelek, the "price" of integration – the effort required to change – squarely falls on the shoulders of those who are different.

Native Testimonials

The cover design for *Die fremde Braut* makes it difficult to ignore the relationship between the genre of the exposé and the colonial and Orientalist stereotypes amplified by journalistic commentary about the Taliban's treatment of women and the post-9/11 justifications for the wars in Afghanistan and Iraq. Against the backdrop of a black patterned fabric, a single, white, female hand reaches out between the folds, conjuring images of burqas, abayas, and chadors, and overtly referencing the visual and sexual unavailability of the veiled Muslim woman. This image is nearly iconic in the historical context of the territorial land grabs and civilizing missions of European imperial conquest in the Middle East and North Africa. As male imperialists exercised their political and economic dominion over the colonies, imperialists' wives took a special interest in Indigenous women supposedly oppressed by traditional cultures, conveniently ignoring white women's experiences of patriarchal domination at the hands of their husbands or their respective national cultures.[26] As colonial feminists tried to "save" Indigenous women, their particular style of feminist engagement was built upon racist portrayals of Indigenous men as violent savages and Indigenous women as victims in need of rescue. As feminist theorist Gayatri Spivak put it in her famous and neatly packaged description, colonial feminism was a system in which "white women save brown women from brown men."[27] Kelek's project – similar to those of many Critics of Islam (*Islamkritiker_innen*) – seems strikingly similar to the projects of colonial feminists, as German feminist theorist Birgit Rommelspacher later argued.[28]

In Germany, *Islamkritik* commandeered national debates about immigrants through books like Kelek's. The late anthropologist Saba Mahmood named this mass market literary genre "native testimonials."[29] "Native testimonials" are memoirs by Muslim women with a distinctly political bent. According to Mahmood, "native testimonials" blend long-standing Orientalist tropes with fervent rhetoric about the value of liberal democracy. It's important to note that Germans are a reading public: they boast a variety of high-quality newspapers, translate fiction from across the world into German, and have a nonfiction genre – the *Sachbuch* – which is highly popular and includes a great deal of political commentary. German authors of "native testimonials" thus benefitted from a ready and accessible audience receptive to political argument.

The "native testimonial" – which Mahmood argues is a transnational phenomenon – bears a few shared, salient markers. First, the authors of these texts almost always identify as Muslim women, whether or not they practise their faith publicly. By claiming an identity as a Muslim woman, the author of a native testimonial certifies her claim to authentic expertise and simultaneously protects herself from the criticism that she discriminates against Muslims. Second, these narratives often garner conservative or neoconservative political power for their authors, who may or may not share the typical political or theological credentials associated with elite positions. Finally, many of these narratives critique patriarchal power in ways that reproduce elements of colonial discourse, from colonial feminism to the portrayal of Islam or non-Western cultures as savage.[30] This combination of author identity, colonial rhetoric, and the pursuit of conservative political power is highly expedient in domestic politics – and it sells a lot of books. Finally, according to Mahmood, the authors' "shrill polemic against

Islam" often reproduces Western assumptions about Islam and Muslims, such as the purported prevalence of Muslim misogyny.[31] In addition to Kelek, the works of Seyran Ateş (Germany), Serap Çileli (Germany), Fadela Amara (France), Irshad Manji (Canada), and Ayaan Hirsi Ali (The Netherlands) fit into this genre of "native testimonials."[32] Such polemic texts do not require that neoconservative politicians adjust their ideology to welcome the authors of "native testimonials" into their political ranks – after all, why would you criticize someone who shares your views?

Kelek's celebrity thus rests on a simple formula: since she published *Die fremde Braut* as a partially autobiographical text, German media and politicians see her as an "authentic" victim of the patriarchal practices within Islam against which she struggles. Kelek's identities as both a woman and a Circassian-Turk with a German passport thus protect her from charges of misogyny and racism.[33] Kelek additionally purports to argue from a centre-left, feminist position and maintains that her demand that immigrants assimilate is based on a sense of moral justice rather than on nationalist politics. Secular European countries should not tolerate human rights abuses, she argues, much less the systematic abuse of women. In order to protect individual freedoms, to see women's rights *as* human rights, and to honour the rights guaranteed by Germany's Basic Law, Kelek rejects Islam. (The Basic Law functions as Germany's constitution.) At the same time, her rhetoric about Turkish immigrants to Germany confirms German stereotypes about Muslims as backward, violent, and sexist. Her rhetoric both legitimizes political discourses that demand Muslim assimilation to German national identity and attempts to advocate for freedom from religion and for women's rights.

Kelek's celebrity was not merely the result of a coordinated PR campaign and her willingness to appear on television to defend her position. At the start of 2005, high-ranking German politicians in the Social Democratic Party had just spent three years of political capital debating the role of immigrants in society. These negotiations had been relatively successful. Parliament passed a new Immigration Act that took effect in January 2005, right before *Die fremde Braut* was published. Five years earlier, German Parliament had also revised the laws that governed citizenship, introducing the possibility of limited birthright citizenship for the first time.[34] In this context, German politicians saw the publication of *Die fremde Braut* as worthy of comment.

In April 2005, then-Federal Interior Minister Otto Schily wrote a review of Kelek's book published in the national magazine *Der Spiegel*, which had been founded after the Second World War, purportedly as an imitation of the US magazines *Time* and *Newsweek*, as well as similar British publications.[35] Schily was a Social Democrat who in 1999 had been influential in drafting citizenship reforms that made it easier for children born in Germany to foreign parents to naturalize. That Kelek secured an early review from a high-ranking political official with a position in the chancellor's cabinet reflected a tacit endorsement by the German federal government of Kelek's political rhetoric. The Schily review is thus one of the first markers of Kelek's growing political power.

In the review, Schily praised the overall contours of *Die fremde Braut*, noting that both sides of the political spectrum had suppressed debates about the integration of immigrants – those on the right insisted that Germany was not an immigration country (*Einwanderungsland*), while those on the left insisted that everyone could live together in "multi-culti-bliss" without specific policy.[36] Kelek's book, Schily noted, would make it possible to "lead the integration debate more intensely than before."[37] Schily also used his forum in *Der Spiegel* to note that two recent legislative changes improved conditions for "import brides": first, in 2004, Parliament passed a law that made it a crime to force someone to marry. The offence carried a sentence of up to five years in prison.[38] Second, the Immigration Act, which Schily called "the first step towards a systematic policy of integration," had gone into effect in January 2005.[39] Parliamentary measures had thus already started to fortify integration policy at the same time that Kelek mobilized public opinion in favour of policies that compelled assimilation.

Schily's review criticizes the historical implausibility of Kelek's claims about Islam, pointing out that women's inequality in Islam can hardly be "the root of all patriarchal evil."[40] But overall, his review is positive and his critiques are limited. By absolving Kelek of her more egregious counterfactual statements, Schily's review promoted the idea that integrating Muslims is an important and valid area for state policy-making. As a centre-left politician, Schily's endorsement of Kelek also represented a broader rightward shift in German politics.

The Immigration Act not only replaced legislation written during the foreign worker era, but also substantially revised integration policy, laying out a national policy of "Encouraging Integration" as well as a federal *Integrationsprogramm* (program of integration). This 2005 Act instituted the integration course system and identified who would be required by the government to take such a course. If immigrants could not make themselves understood verbally, were receiving social welfare payments, or were "in need of integration in a specific way," federal officials at the Foreigner Registration Office (*Ausländerbehörde*) could determine that these individuals were mandated to complete an integration course.[41] People could also be sanctioned for not participating in or not completing the course by reducing their social welfare payments by ten per cent.[42] The law also determined who would be eligible for permanent residency based on (among other incorporative demands, such as adequate housing and income), whether or not someone could speak German and understood the basic requirements for law and social order as well as the living conditions in Germany. Both of these requirements could be fulfilled by the successful completion of an integration course.[43] Finally, the Act expanded the Federal Office for Refugees into what is now known as the Federal Office for Migration and Refugees (BAMF).[44] In some ways, these changes offered federal support for immigrant incorporation by consolidating and laying out funding policies for integration courses and explaining who would be entitled to federal course fee subsidies or be required to participate in the program. However, the first paragraph of the law also appeared to articulate a limited ability of the state to both accept and incorporate immigrants and declared that the purpose of the law was to shape "immigration under the considerations of the capacity to absorb and capacity to integrate as well as [under] the economic and political labour market interests of the Federal Republic of Germany. The law also simultaneously serves to fulfill the humanitarian duties of the Federal Republic of Germany."[45]

Over the course of 2005, Kelek promoted her work in any venue to which she gained access. The Federal Ministry for Migration and Refugees invited her to participate in a conference about Islam and integration that June.[46] She was awarded the prestigious Scholl Siblings' Prize in November, which is named for Hans and Sophie Scholl, a brother and sister who bravely resisted the Nazi dictatorship and were murdered for their activities. The Scholl Prize comes with a €10,000 award and is given to authors who demonstrate "intellectual independence" and who demand "civic freedom, as well as moral, intellectual, and aesthetic courage."[47]

If the press and politicians found that Kelek's stories made compelling headlines, scholars were alarmed by Kelek's celebrity. Not only did they take issue with her reductive ideas, but they were also frustrated that an author who had a PhD in sociology and had worked as an academic lecturer could utter such reductive statements about the dangers of Islam with a straight face. Furthermore, scholars overwhelmingly rejected Kelek's conclusions in *Die fremde Braut*, especially since the book contradicted the findings of the author's own dissertation, which had been published in 2002.[48] In her dissertation, *Islam im Alltag* (Islam in Everyday Life), Kelek found that the adolescents she interviewed adapted Islam to the conditions of German daily life, and stated that Islam could thus facilitate (rather than hinder) integration.[49] The arguments Kelek made in *Die fremde Braut* foreclosed this option.

The debates between journalists, politicians, and scholars about the veracity of Kelek's claims in her books for general audiences reflect a critical struggle for power. To many Germans, it was not only unclear who was authorized to speak about minority communities, but also who – in this now agitated public discussion – could be considered truthful and an expert. Kelek's media engagements were highly effective at casting her as a blunt personality willing to talk sense. The convergence of years-long political debates with the publication and media attention to *Die fremde Braut* created something of a crisis for more moderate (and more rigorous) migration scholars. As most scholars know, common sense often stands in conflict with verifiable research results – and human beings cling tightly to their cognitive errors. The willingness of the German government to subscribe to Kelek's arguments – many of which do not hold up under the rigours of scholarship – was a signal to migration researchers that policy-making would continue to be driven by discourse rather than data. In hindsight, one of the most remarkable effects of Kelek's work is how eerily her books and their reception seem to presage a broader shift to the right in societies where policy-making is driven by ideology and facts are considered debatable.

Critiques by Researchers and Kelek's Influence on Policy

Critiques of integration politics, whether they appear in journalism or scholarship, often bemoan policy-makers' lack of interest in research: commentators, scholars, and journalists chide politicians for promoting policies about how immigrants adapt that are ideological rather than rooted in evidence.[50] The refusal to incorporate evidence-based research into integration politics makes it difficult for integration policy to succeed. As Kelek's work continued to generate public interest and publicity, a wider community of scholars began to raise the alarm about the potential consequences of building integration policy on the foundation of Kelek's exaggerated polemic.

In February 2006, a group of migration researchers published an essay in *Die Zeit* that criticized Kelek's work. The essay was printed alongside a petition signed by 60 people, including Kelek's dissertation adviser. Years later, Kelek complained in an interview that her adviser had organized the petition.[51] Yasemin Karakaşoğlu, a professor of education, and Mark Terkessidis, a psychologist, teacher, and independent scholar, co-wrote the petition, entitled "Justice for Muslims!" Although the petition was nominally directed against Islamophobic rhetoric and "native testimonial" literature by Kelek as well as her contemporaries Seyran Ateş and Ayaan Hirsi Ali, Kelek stands out as the main target. By focusing on Kelek, the authors portray her as a symbolic figurehead for a larger group of critics who were demanding that the government take more forceful steps to integrate Muslims into German society.

What alarms Karakaşoğlu and Terkessidis is the alliance between Kelek and city administrations. The district of Berlin-Neukölln, they report, started an internet campaign against forced marriage in response to Kelek's exposé, citing Kelek's book as proof that Islam was the source of such atrocious behaviour. The authors sarcastically paraphrased the rhetoric of the Neukölln campaign in the following terms: "It is the incorrigible, backwards Islam that is responsible for forced marriages and other cruelties. The only antidote is the 'integration' into German (read: Western) society."[52] Although the sarcastic tone of this statement matches the tone of Kelek's polemic by suggesting that Islamic radicalism will make German democracy obsolete, the researchers' basic criticism holds. *Die fremde Braut* uses individual tragic stories of abuse to demonize Islam as the source of abusive and antidemocratic behaviour in Muslim families.

The researchers were deeply concerned that state and municipal institutions were using narratives like Kelek's to hide their own political mistakes in the context of integration and immigration policy. By distracting viewers and readers from a more complex discussion of why integration policy might have stagnated or been ineffective, the media attention to *Die fremde Braut* facilitated the state's desire to redirect blame. Karakaşoğlu and Terkessidis argued that the consequences of this false rhetoric about integration were dire. Various federal institutions, in their view, were pursuing a hopelessly misguided form of integration politics:

> That the former Interior Minister reviews Necla Kelek's book; that she receives the Scholl Siblings' Prize for her deeply unserious work, and that she is warmly welcomed as a consultant in the Federal Office for Migration and Refugees; that large swaths of the administration, federal ministries, and the media would rather refer to unserious pamphlets while rigorous scientific research is hardly noticed – this development is indeed cause for concern.[53]

Kelek's rhetoric did not need to be rigorous to generate political interest in integration policy, nor did she need to temper her Islamophobic rhetoric to generate political power. In fact, it was exactly her intemperance that resonated in politics, because her ideological demands about integration overlapped with long-standing conservative ideas about nation-building.

Die Zeit allowed Kelek to publish a rebuttal to the petition in the very same issue, which she composed in a highly defensive tone. Kelek accuses the researchers of being upset that she stole their thunder; they are upset, she says, that "my book received the attention that they actually deserved." She accuses scholars of wasting decades of work in their "well-financed" research projects, blinded by the ideology of multiculturalism:

> In the past decades they could have had the time, means, and opportunity to examine the question[s] of forced marriage, arranged marriages, honour murders, segregation, and Islam. They could have asked the questions I did. They didn't do it because these questions don't fit into their ideology of multiculturalism. In this way, they accepted the taboo, however, and permitted others to suffer.[54]

In addition to blaming researchers for the persistence of segregation and family violence, Kelek tries to gain the upper hand by encouraging her colleagues to read one of the foundational works of Turkish-German migration studies, Werner Schiffauer's *Die Migranten aus Subay* (The Migrants of Subay, 1991), which she argues confirms her theses.[55] She ends her rebuttal by holding scholars responsible for the failures of integration politics. In a highly illogical turn that cements Kelek's reputation as a polemicist, she demands that scholars "put [their evidence] on the table!" Scholars have, of course, "put their evidence on the table" through decades of publication.

What is deeply unsettling about the petition and its rebuttal is that Kelek used her scholarly credentials both as a way to lay claim to irrefutable expertise *and* to bring journalistic polemic into the academy. Her refusal to stand by her previous scholarly work (her dissertation) at the same time that she insists her work for general audiences is both scholarly and an improvement on three decades of migration research is an attempt to discredit evidence-based research. This effect of Kelek's celebrity on public discourse is far more troubling than sensationalist journalistic attention to her exposé alone. Discriminatory rhetoric against marginalized groups can certainly mobilize public opinion in ways that create hardship both for members of that group and for civil society as a whole, but Kelek's refusal to play by the rules of both scholarship and measured civic discourse created a space in which the very foundations of the democracy Kelek purportedly loved underwent a transformative shift. Having successfully discredited migration research as the product of a leftist multicultural ideology, Kelek used her celebrity to promote an ideological brand of policymaking that invokes nationalist integration politics as a way to protect democratic values.[56]

From 2005–6, German politics underwent some profound federal shifts. Angela Merkel had been elected chancellor for the first time in late 2005 and took office that November. Merkel's election returned the control of Parliament to the centre-right Christian Democratic Union (CDU) after a seven-year period during which the country had been governed by a left-wing coalition of Social Democrats and Greens. Nationwide, Merkel's election signalled the entry of polarizing conflicts between conservatives and progressives that have since become intractable in German politics. The election results between the SPD and the CDU were so close in 2005 that both the incumbent Gerhard Schröder and challenger Angela Merkel claimed electoral victory. Merkel assumed the chancellorship after three weeks of negotiations, which eventually produced a so-called Grand Coalition between the SPD and CDU. Against this backdrop, Necla Kelek's influence in 2006 extended beyond her position as a media darling and political commentator. That year, both the state government of Baden-Württemberg and the federal German government took up measures designed to "solve" some of the problems that Kelek had purportedly identified and made public.

Nation-states built on federalist systems often have regional governments that pass more conservative or radical measures than would be possible at the federal level. In 2006, the state government of Baden-Württemberg approved a naturalization test designed to interrogate individual attitudes about questions they imagined would represent social taboos for Muslims. Some examples of questions from the attitude test include items like, "What do you think about critiques of religion? Are these critiques permissible?" And "What do you think about the statement that women must obey their husbands, and that he is permitted to hit her if she doesn't?"[57]

This survey, which was designed with Kelek's help, was known colloquially as the "Muslim Test." The test earned this name partially because it was only supposed to be administered to citizens of the 57 member states represented by the Organization of Islamic Cooperation and partially because the questions are clearly animated by tropes common to *Islamkritik*. The test supposedly proved whether applicants for naturalization would be considered fit for democracy. This survey immediately generated a great deal of controversy – so much so that merely a couple of weeks after the test went into effect, the interior minister of Baden-Württemberg had to partially recant. He asserted that this test was not just for Muslims, but could be implemented in any case "whenever sufficient doubt [about democratic attitudes] was present."[58] His statement came after a debate in the Federal Parliament about whether or not states could legally require candidates for naturalization to answer opinion questions and whether such a test could be restricted to Muslim immigrants.[59] Despite the controversy, this attitudinal test was administered from 2006 until 2011, when Baden-Württemberg's state politics swung left and the newly elected SPD/Green Party coalition jettisoned the requirement.[60]

Kelek's influence on the development of the "Muslim Test" is evident in the questionnaire itself, which features many of the points she made in *Die fremde Braut*. Although not hired formally by the state, Kelek developed an informal relationship with Rainer Grell, the civil servant who developed the survey. In response to the controversy about the test, Grell electronically published a 230-page manuscript about the process on a right-wing website. In his acknowledgments, he explicitly and profusely thanks Kelek for her support:

> Dr. Necla Kelek supported me time and again in the development of the discussion guide, and also supported me afterwards [by assuring me] that I was on the right path. Her courage to tell the truth and her love for her new German homeland and its liberal democratic order touched me to a great degree. Without *Die fremde Braut* and *Die verlorenen Söhne*, I never would have thought some thoughts, let alone dared to have uttered them.[61]

As Grell's comments attest, Kelek stood ready to advise him in developing the test between 26 April 2005 and 31 May 2006, a period that overlaps with Kelek's political ascent.[62] Grell argues that it was obvious to him from the beginning that various groups would criticize the ministry's protocol as discriminatory.[63] However, it was still important to proceed because of the stakes for German democracy:

> We should hold ourselves here to the emphatic admonition of Necla Kelek: "Germany has created a constitution and a country since the war that is unique in the world. We live in a very rich country – rich in democracy and rich in social security. Please don't give all that away to people who will exploit it for themselves and who are unable or unwilling to treasure it. We must protect our achievements against abuse."[64]

The willingness of a state government to develop and enact such a discriminatory measure shows how a variety of events converged to make it possible for Kelek to wield political influence. The intense early marketing campaigns of Kelek's book (excerpts in *Die Zeit*, reviews in *Der Spiegel*) combined with the success of the book as a bestseller and introduced a broad audience to Kelek's ideas. Conservative, white, German middle-aged peers, who may have had little contact with Muslim immigrants, proved more than willing to accept Kelek's narrative of unintegrated Muslims because it confirmed either their stereotypes or their fears. Kelek understood how to move through spaces (like the media and universities) generally reserved for the German elite and was also willing to *reveal* the purportedly hidden social realities of a marginalized group. Kelek was thus able to influence many elite stakeholders. In the case of the "Muslim Test," Grell was not only a sympathetic ear, but also a bureaucratic functionary who held substantial regional political power. His "Muslim Test" certainly had consequences for the fates of immigrants attempting to naturalize in a populous, diverse state between 2006 and 2011 – and he acknowledged that Kelek had strongly influenced how he thought about Muslims and their role as citizens in German democracy.

Kelek exercised similar influence at the national level via a new advisory body known as the German Islam Conference, which met for the first time in September 2006. After Merkel's election, Wolfgang Schäuble replaced Otto Schily as Federal Interior Minister. Schäuble created the German Islam Conference to bring together representatives of the federal and regional governments, community leaders, and commentators, including representatives of Muslim organizations and Kelek, to further the dialogue between the German state and Muslim residents and citizens.

On 28 September 2006 – one day after the Islam Conference's first meeting – Schäuble opened a parliamentary debate with a speech that declared why such a conference was necessary:

> Ms. Parliamentary President! Ladies and Gentlemen! Somewhere between 3.2 and 3.5 million Muslims live in Germany today. The majority came to this country decades ago with their traditions and customs, with their religion, and with their culture. Many of them, like film director Fatih Akin described, "forgot to go back."[65]

Schäuble declared Islam to be part of Germany's present and future and said that Muslims are "welcome" in Germany and should be allowed to develop their talents and "bring the country forward."[66] Nevertheless, he continued, the presence of so many Muslims in Germany had caused certain problems that the government must address. He continued, "In order to develop a vision for a common future, we need to try to solve the problems that strain living together with Muslims in our country: Religious instruction in Quran schools and in public schools, headscarves, training imams, the role of women and girls, ritual slaughter – to just name a few keywords."[67] These keywords are practically a list of the most pressing concerns for *Islamkritiker*. In a speech that framed the coexistence of Germans and Muslims as a problem, Schäuble laid the groundwork for his government to regulate the integration of Muslims in the future.

In the transcript of this plenary session in Parliament about the Islam Conference, Kelek's rhetoric bleeds through a lively debate. Politicians yelled out disparaging commentary from the floor, and a newly elected freshman MP from the Green Party engaged in a bit of performative politics by handing Interior Minister Schäuble a German copy of the Koran, asking him to read the actual text, not just read "about it."[68] CDU/CSU politicians frequently incorporated rhetoric from *Die fremde Braut* into their statements. One MP for the CDU even thanked Kelek by name for accepting an appointment as one of the fifteen representatives to the Islam Conference, saying that including members like Kelek and formal leaders of Muslim organizations finally "reflected social reality."[69] This rhetorical gesture is a technique common to both *Islamkritik* and right-wing politics more generally, where commentators frequently insist that politicians, journalists, or citizens who defend Islam or take up culturally relative positions are refusing to acknowledge "reality." While religious radicalism *is* a global concern, there is little evidence to suggest that radical Muslim communities pose a serious enough danger to German society that they could succeed in toppling the democratic order. That power is generally only attributed to the far right. Although the trend would not be apparent to most observers in the first years of the twenty-first century, deeply divisive arguments about "truth" were already becoming a transnational element of far-right politics. Kelek intuitively understood how to mobilize a post-factual framework a decade before the far right made stark electoral gains in German politics.

One of the contradictions of Necla Kelek's celebrity is that she uses her Turkish-Muslim identity to claim expertise about Islam – but it is primarily Christian-German politicians who mobilize her rhetoric. The majority of MPs with a Turkish migration history (Lale Akgün, Hakkı Keskin, and Sevim Dağdelen) spoke as members of the Left and the Social Democratic Parties and positioned themselves against compulsory assimilation. That Kelek's rhetoric is attractive to conservatives confirms that the aims of integration are inherently conservative, irrespective of the identities of either critics or supporters. In this parliamentary debate, members of the Christian Democratic Union were most likely to revert to stereotypes of Muslims as violent or to portray German democracy as an institution in need of defence.

The similarities between Kelek's book and statements by members of the CDU show a number of variations on a theme. In *Die fremde Braut*, Kelek criticizes the mayor of Hamburg, a Social Democrat, who believes schoolteachers should be able wear headscarves in the classroom. She asks the reader rhetorically, "Where is this politician's understanding that we live in a constitutional democracy founded on the separation between religion and the state?"[70] (The logical fallacy of this argument is obvious, since many schools in Catholic areas of Germany still permit crucifixes in the classroom and in post-Holocaust Germany no one would dare to criticize a kippa or tefillin worn in public.) MP Hartfrid Wolff (FDP) took up a similar argument in the parliamentary debates about the Islam Conference: "Freedom from violence in no uncertain terms and recognizing the separation of religion and state are essential prerequisites [for accepting the basic values of our society]."[71] Wolff and Kelek both implied that public displays of faith are incompatible with the basic tenets of either constitutional law or "the basic values" of German society. Kelek's entire book, in fact, rests on a vision of the state that sees the state as responsible for enforcing compliance not only with the Basic Law, but also to cultural norms such as marriage practices.

Elsewhere in *Die fremde Braut*, Kelek declares, "When people come to us, to Germany, then they have to accept the requirements that exist in this country. And a basic requirement for the ability of our democracy to survive is freedom and the protection of the individual. This is not up for negotiation."[72] This quotation sounds similar to comments made by other members of the CDU in the debate about the Islam Conference, including MP Köhler, Interior Minister Schäuble, and MP Hans-Peter Uhl. MP Uhl argued in debate that many Muslims isolate themselves from Germans – and that this shows disrespect towards the state and German culture: "We demand respect for our system of values and respect for our Basic Law. Whoever isn't ready to do so must ask themselves exactly why they want to live in our country."[73] All of these statements presume that (Muslim) immigrants are unwilling to assimilate to German values and are antagonistic towards either democratic order or the German State.

Necla Kelek is, of course, not solely responsible for the emergence of nativist or Islamophobic ideas in German politics. These ideas were in circulation long before Kelek even contemplated embarking on a political career. Her media celebrity, however, facilitated a public embrace of conservative interpretations of the compulsory power of the state in integration politics. These parliamentary statements are but a small sample of the convergence between Kelek's rhetoric and the politicians of the CDU. There are many, many more to be found in the parliamentary record. The result of this convergence in 2006 was that Chancellor Merkel's newly elected conservative government in 2006 now had the charge to develop an integration policy that would, in the face of a purportedly growing Islamic threat, attempt to compel Muslims to assimilate to protect German values and a democratic social order.

The primary assumption that informs Kelek's work is that Muslims must be compelled to integrate: they should speak German, adhere to German cultural norms, and practice their religion privately. They should also internalize a vaguely articulated program of democratic values. Kelek's pro-integration and Islamophobic arguments are evidence of an emerging (or re-emerging) right-wing nationalism in Germany that would slowly and steadily begin to sanction white supremacy through integration politics and integration discourse. The effects of this discourse were not obvious to a broad section of society in 2006 – despite the fact that scholars immediately sounded the alarm. Today, it is much more obvious that these sorts of arguments can make ideas considered taboo since the Holocaust part of the political mainstream, and that they work against the liberal democratic project of the European Union in favour of nationalist politics.

What Kelek's polemics and the subsequent mobilization of her ideas into the spaces of government render visible is also the inherent intersectionality of an integrative apparatus. Gender may be the identity that seemingly carries the most weight in Kelek's demands, but Kelek's analysis mobilizes racializing tropes through her reduction of Islam's influence on family violence. Her class bias – visible in her invocation of her Circassian identity, her devotion to notions of a secular Turkish identity, and her postdoctoral positions as a member of the educated elite – surface at various points in *Die fremde Braut*. While Kelek is most interesting to me due to her early mobilization of discursive techniques now common across the global right wing, the intersectional bubbling up of her multiple identities also influences how I conceptualize an integrative apparatus.

What happens – practically speaking – when rhetoric like Kelek's begins to enter and occupy all those interstitial cultural spaces that serve as the infrastructure of the integrative apparatus? Rather than rendering the pain and suffering of domestic violence and sexual assault more visible and spurring effective interventions, this rhetoric negatively affects the ability of many white Germans to empathize and notice the all-too-human and common indicators of family and intimate partner violence and abuse. Discourses about a culture of honour in Muslim communities are one – and only one – example of how this foreclosure of empathy appears in German culture.

Chapter Two

Failed Integration

He murdered his sister on a February evening in 2005.[1] While standing at a bus stop, Ay. S. shot his sister multiple times, and her injuries were severe enough that she died at the scene.[2] Court documents only identified the young man by his initials, although the names of the family members are by now common knowledge. The son of former guest workers of Kurdish descent who had immigrated to Germany from Turkey, Ayhan Sürücü had seven siblings and was born and raised in Berlin.[3] The family practised a fundamentalist form of Islam that required veiling and the strict separation of genders when visitors entered the apartment, at which point female family members would retreat behind closed doors.[4] According to the 2007 verdict on appeal from the 5th Criminal Division, Ayhan Sürücü declared in no uncertain terms to investigators that he murdered his sister because he deemed her behaviour to be dishonorable.[5] As a male family member, Ayhan Sürücü also considered it his duty to restore the family's honour by murdering his sister.[6]

In August 2007, the 5th Criminal Division of the Federal Court reversed the verdict that the Berlin District Court had issued in 2006: Ayhan Sürücü was found guilty of murder and sentenced to nine years and three months in prison.[7] The sentence was relatively short due to his status as a minor when the crime was committed: the legal maximum was 10 years. His two older brothers, who investigators assumed had also collaborated in planning and executing the murder, were found not guilty due to lack of evidence.[8] While the Federal Court declared the need for a new trial for the two older brothers, by 2007 Mutlu and Alparslan Sürücü had already fled to Turkey.[9] Because the Turkish police refused to extradite them, the Berlin prosecutor's office closed the case in 2009.[10] Multiple trials in Germany and Turkey have followed, including one as late as 2018, always leading to verdicts of not guilty due to lack of evidence for Mutlu and Alparslan Sürücü.[11]

Ayhan Sürücü was promptly deported to Turkey upon his release from prison in 2014. When he was born, Germany did not have a system of birthright citizenship (*jus soli*). It was legal to deport Ayhan because he was not a citizen, despite the fact that he had been born and raised in Germany. According to the deportation order, Ayhan Sürücü was deported because the state held concerns about his ability and willingness to integrate: "Your behaviour leads us to believe that even in the future you will not be willing and ready to integrate yourself into the current social and constitutional order."[12] The deportation order also states that Ayhan Sürücü has not shown remorse for his crime.[13]

Despite the incredible diversity of immigrant communities in Germany, many elements of integration politics reflect – both explicitly and implicitly – a debate about Muslim difference, especially gendered Muslim difference. In integration debates, Muslim men are routinely demonized as aggressive and violent, while "emancipated" Muslim women are permitted to assimilate – as German Studies scholar Beverly Weber points out – primarily through a process that requires their sexualization.[14] While many people perceive Western or European communities as societies made up of individuals whose behaviour is psychologically motivated, Western and European discourses on cultural difference portray immigrants who commit crimes as motivated or even brainwashed by traditional thinking or cultural logic.[15] This insistence on cultural or traditional motivations denies immigrant perpetrators agency by blaming their behaviour on cultural norms, and overlooks the universal complexity of individual subjectivity.[16] Political actors can thus invoke "culture" in ways that substitute cultural belonging for "race" or "ethnicity." As Fatima El-Tayeb and Yasemin Yıldız have shown, political commentators frequently use gender and sexuality as a proxy for debates about "Muslim difference," which shows how religion can be racialized and thus appropriated as an essentializing category.[17] The controversies about honour-related violence in Germany are also long-standing debates in which gender and sexuality are the mode through which Europeans stake a claim to universal human rights. According to El-Tayeb, such debates perpetuate racializing logics that portray Muslims as inferior:

> the claim to the "incompatibility" of Islam and Europe is not framed as a conflict between a Christian majority and a Muslim minority, both of whom are European, but between European humanism, committed to the protection of rights, namely those of gender equality and sexual freedom, and a hostile, intolerant, foreign culture. Within this unequal dichotomy, Europe invariably stands for the universal, while Muslims represent the

particular and thus inferior. As a result, while the European Muslim community as a whole is judged to present the "wrong," (i.e., misogynist and homophobic) type of heterosexuality, feminist and queer Muslims too appear as limited by their culture, deviating from the dominant norm of liberal and progressive cosmopolitanism.[18]

Media coverage of Hatun Sürücü's murder coalesced around several specific topics deemed critical for integration politics: immigrant masculinity, culturalizing racial logic and the idea that the integration of "inferior" cultures was doomed to failure from the start.[19] Several events converged to render this murder exemplary and of broad interest to a national audience. First, a criminal act marked as an honour killing and the cultural narrative about the motives of the perpetrators confirmed stereotypes about Muslims and, as Weber points out, "could easily be appropriated for a particular script of violence" through which domestic violence is attributed to immigrant communities.[20] Second, a principal at a school near the crime scene made the disparaging comments from some of his students public, prompting broad protest against violent adolescent masculinity and the conservative religiosity embodied by both the teenaged perpetrator and the students who shared his views. Third, the notion of ethnic neighbourhoods in German society as so-called parallel societies – interest in which had grown exponentially after the release of Necla Kelek's *Die fremde Braut* and debates about German *Leitkultur* – prompted widespread political agreement among commentators who instrumentalized the murder as proof that integration had failed, often blaming culture and religion. This high-profile murder case combined both public interest *and* public outrage and had specific consequences for how German integration politics focused a good deal of energy on demanding assimilative behaviour from Muslims. At the same time, the tragedy of Sürücü's murder led commentators to assert that integration was destined to – or had already – failed. Through the trope of the "parallel society," integration rhetoric mobilized gender and sexuality to shape the very definition of cultural and social integration as the successful pursuit of progressive gender roles, private religiosity, and a rejection of criminality and violence.

Culturalization (Racialization through Culture)

The murder of Hatun Sürücü is the most infamous case of honour killing in Germany. It is also still the most visible case of a so-called failure of integration. Her murder is so infamous that she became a martyr in German integration debates: yearly vigils are held at the bus station at the edge of an apartment complex on Oberlandgarten where Sürücü was killed, and the District of Neukölln declared in 2018 that a bridge would be named after her.[21] The mayor of Tempelhof-Schöneberg placed a large memorial stone at the site of her murder in 2008, which bears a plaque written in German and Turkish that commemorates Sürücü's life: "Hatun Sürücü (b. 1982) was murdered here on February 7th, 2005, because she would not submit to the pressure (*Zwang*) and oppression of her family – but rather wanted to lead a self-determined life. In memory of her and the other victims of violence against women in this city."[22] The memorials held near the stone on the yearly anniversaries of Sürücü's death are still often televised by local news, further attenuating Hatun Sürücü's martyr-like status.[23] As a paradigmatic example of a crime of honour, the media's sensationalist coverage of Sürücü's murder exaggerated and expanded the intensity of integration debates, especially those focused on the role of cultural practices in sanctioning such violence.[24] I attended one of these vigils in February 2011, and overheard another attendee comment with frustration on the political speech given by one of the local politicians: "*Din, din, din … und nicht Gewalt*," she said in a mix of Turkish and German – religion, religion, religion … and not violence. The focus of this politician's speech posited that Islam, rather than the dynamics of domestic violence, offered a paradigm for understanding what had happened to Sürücü, and the attendee's commentary confirmed that at least one community member understood the repeated mistake of seeing religion, rather than the dynamics of violence, as the source of such behaviour.[25]

As chapter 1 illustrated, the terms of these debates were hardly new. Discussions about honour killings and the inherent violence in Muslim families pervaded the opinion pages after Sürücü's death and reflected tropes about the Muslim family as violent that appeared in books like Necla Kelek's *Die fremde Braut* and *Die verlorenen Söhne*. The gendered dichotomies between female victims and male criminals were certainly reinforced by Kelek's pair of books due to her meteoric rise and commercial success, but Kelek's narratives were hardly anomalous. Books by the journalist Güner Balcı (*Arabboy* and *Arabqueen*) or the 2010 pair of books by Kirsten Heisig (*Das Ende der Geduld*) and Sineb el-Masrar (*Muslim Girls*) reflected similar narrative structures.[26] Journalists and commentators frequently described the brutality of Sürücü's murder on an open street as an "execution," and the traumatic details of Hatun Sürücü's biography – even years after her death – seemed to confirm the worst stereotypes about Muslim family life.[27]

But who or what, exactly, was responsible for this failure of integration? Mutlu Sürücü had completed his *Abitur* and, according to journalists Matthias Deiß and Jo Goll, radicalized during his compulsory military service with the *German* army. In the ARD documentary Deiß and Goll directed, all of the Sürücü siblings speak German.[28] The key witness in the murder trial was Ayhan's ex-girlfriend, a Turkish-German woman from a secular family who reported comments made after the murder to the police, testified against the brothers during their trial, and then entered the witness protection program fearing her own murder in retaliation.[29] Hatun Sürücü had emancipated herself from an unhappy marriage and had attended the most academically challenging school form, the *Gymnasium*, as a child – despite her parents' delinquency in registering her at school for two years (she was first enrolled in school at the age of 8!). One brother has cut all ties with the family and at the time of Hatun's murder was studying law in Cologne, which is no small feat in the German educational system.[30] If we start from the premise that incorporation requires some form of *systemic* integration and access to systems of education, economics, politics, and culture, it would appear that the Sürücü family had managed to find access to employment and education in Germany; it was another Turkish-German woman who was willing to report the case to police.[31] The systemic integration of Turkish-German immigrants – their incorporation into German systems and institutions broadly conceived – does not appear to have failed when compared to this list of facts. Instead, it is a diffuse and nebulous internalization of German values and practices – *social* integration – that purportedly failed, at least in terms of the familial violence of the Sürücüs. And even then: the lack of social integration does not neatly overlap with familial or ethnic identity. The question of what constitutes the successful internalization of values (values that violent German perpetrators have also not internalized) is therefore debatable. The ambivalence of such questions makes integration debates ripe for sensational reporting and prompts opinion journalism to dominate news coverage.[32] These debates about social integration also obscure the dynamics of violence, the causes of violence, and the overlap between the dynamics of violence in both immigrant families and violence in white German families.

Hatun Sürücü had certainly *not* failed to integrate, despite the obstacles that had come her way. Multiple newspapers assert that Sürücü's father had removed her from school as early as the 8th grade, when she was formally withdrawn from a Kreuzberg *Gymnasium*.[33] Subjected to an arranged (and likely forced) marriage to an older cousin in Turkey as a 16-year-old, Sürücü returned to Berlin in 1999, pregnant with her son and divorced from her husband.[34] Back in the city where she had grown up, she stopped wearing a headscarf, found her own apartment, naturalized as a German citizen, and was completing a vocational training program as an electrician at the time of her death.[35] Numerous newspaper reports and the summary of the Berlin investigation in the 2007 appeal are also sure to mention in the context of her biography that Hatun Sürücü dated German men.[36] Sürücü thus serves as an exemplary case of successful systemic and social integration under the terms often required by German integration discourses. She wanted to lead a "self-determined life," as the memorial plaque states; had chosen a technical career as a trained electrician (progressive gender roles); she was no longer visible as an observant Muslim without her headscarf (private religiosity); and her desire to train and find a job meant she could not be seen as a financial burden to the state (rejection of criminality – in this case, welfare dependence or "fraud").[37] The mention of dating also serves to prove – as Weber has argued – that her integration was truly complete. Sexualization serves an important role in the integration of immigrant women because "becoming German" links freedom to sexuality: "The Muslim woman's emergence into European subjecthood appears to come only to the degree to which she 'frees' herself from Muslim control by exposing herself [through clothing and sexuality – jsc] to the German gaze."[38] In spite of Sürücü's integrative success, Weber points out that the subtext of a great deal of the media coverage of her death implied that Sürücü's integration was bound to fail: "[Sürücü's] integration is often imagined as both necessary and impossible, and [her] murder inevitable – she 'had to die.' The inevitable fact of her death is considered a consequence of her being 'too modern' or 'too German.'"[39]

Within this rhetoric of failure, all of Sürücü's achievements constituted insufficient protection against the cultural traditions of her Kurdish, fundamentalist, Muslim family. When culture and religion purportedly hold this much sway, even the state cannot possess sufficient power to compel a family to abandon violence. In Sürücü's case, various authorities were aware of the family violence she had experienced, but that knowledge did not prevent her murder.

Was Sürücü's death a more general failure of authorities to act, or did stereotypes about Muslims as violent prompt authorities to miss obvious signs of domestic violence due to "culturalizing" logics that framed certain types of violence as traditional behaviour? In Deiß and Goll's ARD documentary about the murder as well as in their book-length account, Sürücü's social worker reported that she *knew* Hatun Sürücü was subjected to verbal and low-level physical abuse, as well as stalking-like behaviours, at the hands of her brothers.[40] She may have been sexually molested by one brother, which the district attorney in Berlin interpreted as a possible motive for her murder.[41] The 2007 decision from Federal Court also describes an anecdote where several years before her death, Sürücü's older brother Mutlu had slapped her for refusing to sit next to their father.[42] Several journalistic accounts assert that Sürücü had even filed complaints with the police about her brothers' violent behaviour, but was told that the police could not act preemptively.[43] In their book, journalists Deiß and Goll even recount an anecdote that Sürücü had asked her social worker to adopt her son if something were to happen to her and struggled with depression due to the psychological pressures of her family members.[44] Despite the fact that all of these behaviours (verbal and physical abuse, as well as psychological terror) are well known to scholars and social workers as characteristics of domestic violence, this particular social worker told the ARD journalists that she never suspected Hatun would be murdered by her own family.[45]

Purna Sen, former Executive Coordinator and Spokesperson on Addressing Sexual Harassment and Other Forms of Discrimination at UN Women, argues that honour-related violence *is* different from domestic violence because a community, rather than one individual perpetrator, often plans the act together – both men and women.[46] While all forms of violence are certainly shaped by the cultural discourses in which they are enacted, it is difficult to separate honour-related violence completely from the mechanisms of power and control intrinsic to patterns of domestic and relationship violence since both are forms of violence more common in societies with stark gender roles. Legal scholars like Lama Abu-Odeh have pointed out that crimes of honour and crimes of passion hold similar status and similar justifications in Western and Middle Eastern legal systems.[47] Understanding cultural interpretations of behaviour may require a form of translation; however, the mechanisms and red flags that signal a need for intervention in cases of domestic violence, sexual assault, and femicide are often similar across cultures. Shame, abusive behaviour that escalates in intensity over time, and the psychological dehumanization that undermines individual confidence exist in both individually perpetrated and collectively organized forms of abuse. Witnessing abuse raises the likelihood of perpetrating or being subject to abuse; women's isolation is also linked to higher rates of violence. Finally, as three researchers argue in a review of domestic violence research: "violence against women is most common where gender roles are rigidly defined and enforced and where the concept of masculinity is linked to toughness, male honour, or dominance."[48] In anticipation of potential critiques that I am reinforcing a stereotypical view of Muslim men as aggressive and "traditionally masculine," I want to point out that it would be a mistake to assume that German culture does not also link masculinity to toughness or dominance.[49] Methods of power and control inherent to domestic violence can be seen through stalking, generating rumours, and other forms of social control, including low-level violence like slaps that can escalate into more extreme violence over time. These methods *are not particular to immigrant communities* – they are well known and well documented across the world.[50] That these red flags did not prompt stronger protections in Sürücü's case may be attributable to caseworker or police stereotypes about Muslims as inherently more violent and violent in a different way than Germans, which obscures the ability of white Germans serving marginalized populations to assess threat and pain along a human continuum.[51]

The tendency to attribute behaviour to ethnic and cultural traditions has a long history in German research about immigrant populations (as well as in German politics). German scholars call this particular mode "culturalization" (*Kulturalisierung*): the practice of marking (individual) behaviour as the product of traditional practices and foreign cultural logics.[52] North American scholarship frequently portrays this scholarly mode as research that is predicated upon a modern–traditional divide or as a product of the colonial gaze.[53] Within the integrative apparatus, culturalization is more likely to be invoked than racism to describe a process of essentializing differences. Following Kathrin Osterloh and Nele Westerholt, I interpret culturalization as a German mode of cultural essentialism that invokes culture as a substitute for race and in this way uses cultural or religious justifications to racialize groups based on their heritage, traditions or culture.[54] Seeing Sürücü's murder as culturally specific and separate from the interdisciplinary understanding of domestic violence as a form of power and control reflects how behaviours that appear in multiple cultures can serve, through their essentialization as a cultural practice, to racialize and pathologize both perpetrators and victims.

Sürücü's murder was neither immediately interesting to the public nor was it – in and of itself – immediately subject to culturalizing interpretations. As Anna Caroline Cöster points out in her dissertation about honour killings in Germany, the media interest in Sürücü's death was not immediate.[55] The murder itself was not even mentioned in the press until Volker Steffens, the principal of the Thomas Morus Upper School in Neukölln, released a public letter about ten days later. The Morus School stands a couple of blocks away from the crime scene. Principal Steffens was outraged by comments several students had made during a bereavement counselling session.[56] According to his open letter, three male students defended the murder during the 2005 counselling session because Sürücü had "behaved like a German."[57]

When *Der Tagesspiegel* covered a demonstration to honour Sürücü several days later, journalists interviewed girls from the same class who identified the boys in question as having "Turkish, Arab, and Polish backgrounds."[58] An article in the *Berliner Zeitung* asserted that the boys were of Arab, Polish, and German backgrounds.[59] Six months later, in an article from *Spiegel Online*, the ethnic identities of the boys changed again: this author asserts that three students of "Turkish descent" had made those comments, as do most subsequent press reports.[60] The consolidation of ethnic identities in press coverage is important. Early reporting – before the game of "telephone" so common in high-intensity scandals obscures or twists facts – likely had no reason to instrumentalize the students' ethnic identities. But later reporting, such as the *Spiegel* article, which appeared after the subtext of the cultural debates at the national level became clear, might reflect the subtle twisting of material in multiple retellings due to individual bias and journalistic error. Later coverage thus appears to confirm stereotypes of violent, Muslim boys who condoned the murder (and, if fears came true, might later perpetrate one).[61] According to cultural anthropologist Katherine Pratt Ewing: "These schoolboys came to stand in for Turkish men and their unassimilable masculinity."[62]

Steffen's public letter quickly created a media frenzy. Outraged by the callousness of the student comments, Steffens asserted in his letter that the school would neither tolerate attacks against "freedom" nor student behaviours that reveal a "lack of respect for fellow human beings."[63] He did not include any mention of the ethnic backgrounds of the students. Press attention to the murder proliferated after Steffens' letter became public.[64] German politicians and commentators rushed to comment on the danger of "parallel societies," the need to promote German values, and vented outright hostility towards Muslim Germans who quite literally seemed to be getting away with murder.[65] Newspapers claimed that the number of honour killings in early 2005 were an epidemic, citing five or six murders in half a year (these numbers are difficult to verify).[66] The details of the Sürücü case and the public outcry about the students' comments seemed to pose the question to many Germans as to whether or not it would ever be capable to integrate long-standing immigrant communities into German society due to misogyny, perceived hatred towards German culture, and perceived animosity towards German civil society. At the Morus School, young men who embodied the kind of machismo and ethnic animus seen as characteristic of Muslims were viewed through the lens of the adults they would become: men who enforced problematic norms of shame and honour that led to sexual and domestic violence in parallel societies.

And yet, it is important to note that the consolidation of stereotypes was not an inevitable outcome of media attention. Sürücü's murder could have prompted political solidarities between groups, which appears to have taken place on a smaller scale. The Gay and Lesbian Alliance of Germany (LSVD) and the Gay Crisis Line were the first groups to hold a vigil at the bus stop where the murder had taken place. The vigil on 22 February 2005 took place more than two weeks after the murder, but only about five days after school director Steffens published his letter.[67] They invited the *Islamkritikerin* Seyran Ateş, who is publicly out as bisexual and identifies as Turkish-Kurdish-German, to give a speech. Ateş had been shot by a Turkish nationalist while working at a domestic violence prevention project in Kreuzberg in 1984, and was thus personally affected by both ethnic nationalist and misogynist violence.[68] Multiple other Germans of many ethnicities signed the LSVD call to protest.[69] Ateş is also well known for defending domestic violence victims through her legal practice, and Sürücü's murder could be seen to represent a crime well known to the queer and feminist communities: violence designed to limit the free expression of sexual orientation and gender identity, no matter one's gender, orientation, or nationality. Enlisting a lawyer specializing in domestic violence cases to speak also provides an entry point for approaching the murder not primarily through a culturally essentialist lens, but rather as a clear case of femicide. About 100–150 people attended the rally, including politicians from the SPD and Green parties and, as one newspaper report notes, "Turkish, African and German women."[70] But just as El-Tayeb argues, a coalition of queer, immigrant, Muslim, feminist, and leftist groups against domestic violence was too illegible to the mainstream to ever permit the LSVD or the Turkish-Kurdish-German community to truly take ownership of the media spectacle. And despite multiple Turkish-German women entering the debate, as Weber shows, ethnic expertise was unlikely to flip the script about violence.[71]

The debate about parallel societies arose at the intersection of multiple debates about culture, religion, and gender-based violence. The debate became so heated because its themes overlapped with other legal and media events already in motion within the integrative apparatus. The popularity of native testimonials that framed narratives of problematic Muslim masculinity was at its peak in 2005; the new Immigration Act establishing and regulating access to the integration course system took effect on 1 January 2005; and a broader debate about schools and equal educational opportunities for immigrant children (an area in which Germany was sorely behind in terms of equity) had faded in and out of national conversation for decades.[72] Debates about parallel societies also stoked fears of both segregation (a taboo topic in Germany) and the loss of German culture to a hostile minority (a long-standing fear of so-called *Überfremdung*).[73] The trope of a parallel society is uniquely German, although debates about segregation, integration, and Muslim communities are common across Europe. Other European nations have different words for neighbourhoods in which immigrant cultures and violence are said to create dangerous spaces: in France, journalists talk about the *banlieues*; polemicist Oriana Fallaci in Italy talks about the *second city*; Necla Kelek appropriates a Turkish word and calls it *kaza*.[74] What is shared between terms are the purported isolation and separation of Muslim neighbourhoods that are dangerous spaces of disintegration segregated from the mainstream, in which a code of honour sanctions those who try to leave.[75]

A Parallel Society

The origins of the term "parallel society" are often attributed to sociologist Wilhelm Heitmeyer and his research team in Bielefeld.[76] In 1997, a team of German researchers conducted an extensive study of adolescent Turkish-Germans in the state of North-Rhine-Westphalia titled *Verlockender Fundamentalismus*.[77] This team was led by Heitmeyer, who then directed the Institute for Interdisciplinary Research on Conflict and Violence at the University of Bielefeld, and the goal of the study was to identify the risk factors and processes by which young people found themselves drawn to Islamic fundamentalism. The Heitmeyer study provides some insight into how or why the media trope of a parallel society portrays Muslim inhabitants as hostile to German values and culture.

A critical argument of the study is that fundamentalist violence arises out of complex patterns of socialization that implicate the majority society and their discriminatory behaviour towards marginalized groups. The researchers emphasize that experiences of discrimination are strong predictors of whether or not Turkish-German teens choose to socialize in spaces that are predominantly Turkish. Teenagers who were subject to higher rates of discrimination in the public sphere were much more likely to spend their time only with other Turkish teenagers and were less likely to express a desire for more contact to German teenagers.[78] (The majority of Turkish-German teenagers – 65.6 per cent – said they would like to have *more* contact with German teenagers).[79]

Hostility does not emerge in a vacuum – negative responses to contact with Germans can be viewed as a reaction against contact itself. Of prime importance for understanding what draws young people to Islamic fundamentalism were social temperament, experiences of discrimination, and the presence of identity-based superiority complexes (*Überlegenheitsansprüche*).[80] Those drawn to extremism tended to spend more time socially isolated or prefer being alone; these youth experienced higher rates of discrimination for their ethnicity or religion than other Turkish-German youth; and they were more likely to interpret experiences of discrimination as a reason to retreat into an ethnic identity (which they then inflated in importance to produce feelings of superiority).[81] Boys were also much more likely than girls to experience public discrimination, violence, or negative encounters with the police.[82]

While the number of those actively drawn to fundamentalism and willing to act on those beliefs in a violent manner was quantitatively small, it was still significant.[83] Right-wing German extremist youth in the same age cohort show similar attitudinal patterns, and did so especially during the period of post-unification violence.[84] The overall conclusions of the study hardly imply that a predisposition to violence is something for which immigrants can be blamed, nor that this type of identity formation is the predominant mode activated by Turkish-German youth. Instead, these behaviours are worrisome for the small minority predisposed to violence and more critically, the study emphasizes the role German discrimination plays in activating that predisposition.

How did a research study published by an academic press generate a metaphor so vivid that the phrase "parallel society" is now a common trope used frequently in both media debates and private conversations? Like many scholarly works from Suhrkamp Press, my dark blue paperback copy of the study is completely devoid of any cover imagery or marketing design. Yet, the brief blurb on the back suggests that a cursory interpretation of the study could be phrased in such a way that it could be easily appropriated by the media:

> When they can't feel at home in Germany, a substantial proportion of Turkish teenagers find comfort in the Koran and security in Islam. How susceptible are they then to fundamentalism and radical political ideologies? The social scientists Wilhelm Heitmeyer, Joachim Müller, and Helmut Schröder have analyzed this for the first time: they point to the consequences of increasing disintegration and the problems of the development of a Muslim parallel society.[85]

This blurb suggests that the development of a parallel society is both a problem for Turkish immigrants as well as a description of a developing social reality. Treating a parallel society as a fact of contemporary life, however, stands in contrast to how the term is used in the study. "Parallel society" appears only once in the study's conclusion, and is dropped into the text in quotation marks and articulated in the subjunctive case, illustrating its metaphorical and theoretical – rather than factual – character:

> On the whole it would be a dangerous development for the integration of the *entire society* if a broadly de-traditionalized, secularized, and functionally differentiated majority society were to come into confrontation with re-traditionalized, religio-politically oriented subgroups of a developing "parallel society" of minorities. Then, a revival of religio-cultural resources for mobilizing in majority society would be conceivable, because disputes about "cultural capital" (Esser 1996) are always intensely inflammatory. This is even more often the case because attitudes do not automatically turn into actions, nor do processes of formation and their intensification into violence develop in causal and linear ways. [86]

The conclusion continues as if the study authors had presaged the media's later appropriation of the term:

> Violent conflicts are often instigated through "coincidental" singular events, develop their own dynamics, or are inflamed particularly by elites; thus, they are not inevitable. One should remember that inflammatory attitudinal patterns frequently develop long before political or violent sequences [of events]. Even the contemporary example of German teenagers should serve as a warning. Already by the mid-1980s, the proliferation of right-wing extremist attitudes was identified through empirical studies (Heitmeyer 1987, 1995). During the xenophobic wave of violence at the beginning of the 1990s this age cohort participated in this violence to an especially high degree.[87]

Media attention that portrayed the adolescents at the Morus School as the potentially violent minority purportedly revealed by the Heitmeyer study missed critical qualifiers. First, the term "parallel society" is a metaphor, not a fact. While the study authors do suggest that a parallel society could develop, they also emphasize the contingency of trying to predict future developments. Finally: the study authors build in a word of caution to the reader, asking them to remember that "inflammatory attitudinal patterns frequently develop long before political or violent sequences [of events]."[88] The authors could hardly have known in advance that their own concept of the parallel society would inflame just such a cultural debate, and be appropriated by sensational media coverage that mobilized the image of a parallel society to stoke fear among those Germans concerned that their culture could disappear. In many ways, this paradigm presages not the rise of a parallel society, but instead, of the integrative apparatus: attitudes towards guest workers and asylum seekers in the 1960s and 1970s prompted both the proliferation of government programs and political rhetoric known as integration politics, as well as multiple instances of right-wing nativist backlash. These attitudinal patterns are not merely discursive but exist parallel to action – the so-called nondiscursive practices that can become systemically discriminatory.

The media appropriation of the parallel society metaphor creates a discursive but mythical physical space in which the segregation of Muslims is not defined in terms of systemic exclusion, but rather as a personal choice to remain separate.[89] Such a metaphor in media reports ignores the importance of systemic integration for upward mobility, denies the effect of systemic discrimination and practices of inclusion, and overemphasizes the role of culture on the path towards assimilation.[90]

The media version of a parallel society sensationalizes a counterfactual underworld in which women and girls have no rights and men and boys adjudicate the rule of law based on religious practice and vigilante justice. Within but not of Germany, a parallel society in media coverage becomes the site of human rights abuses and remains beyond the reach of the German state and cultural norms. Because integration politics already marks the refusal to assimilate as a problematic behaviour, the main function of the parallel society trope is to portray ethnic neighborhoods as a threat to the nation and as the site at which integration must occur (but is also doomed to fail). The mobilization of the neighbourhood as a threat to the nation also reflects a metonymic approach to scale, in which small, local areas stand in as a proxy for the nation.[91] To refuse to acknowledge the necessity of integrating inhabitants of parallel societies is then depicted as a material and ideological abandonment of German values *and* German law and order. It is ultimately the mixed message of the parallel society trope (something must be done, but any attempt will surely fail) that facilitates its mobilization in integration politics.

Project Heroes

At the same time that integration rhetoric mobilizes the energy and outrage of scandal and purported failure, there is a concurrent media appetite for "feel-good" counternarratives, even if these narratives appear less frequently and can reinforce the negative or dehumanizing coverage by functioning as its foil. Within the integrative apparatus, the possibilities for complex or contradictory understandings of citizen and civic engagement are reduced: the aims and self-understandings of community or neighbourhood projects are often simplified and classified as either scandalous or redemptive. The media attention to Sürücü's murder is exemplary for spanning the breadth of this evaluative spectrum. For example, the founder of a so-called women's emergency assistance organization known as *Hatun und Can e.V.* (est. 2006) was later found to have embezzled nearly €700,000 for personal gain and was sentenced to over four years in prison.[92] In contrast to this obvious case of fraud, journalists often portray *Projekt Heroes*, the masculinities project I will examine in this section, as a community of exceptional young men who are single-handedly changing male gender roles in immigrant communities.[93] While the criminal activity of *Hatun und Can e.V.*'s founder is clear, *Projekt Heroes-Berlin* is a long-standing empowerment organization that is far more complex than the media reporting inherent to the integrative apparatus can portray. The organization has multiple goals that align with some of the best practices for violence prevention efforts that focus on young men: emotional articulation, group identity formation through shared goals and activities, and social recognition for the efforts of participants.[94] *Heroes* was both first conceived of and founded by European women but is an organization where the majority of staff come from the communities their programming purports to serve.

Projekt Heroes is routinely referred to as a *soziales Projekt* (social project). Many people call Berlin, where this organization was founded, a *"Stadt der Projekte,"* a city of projects. *Projekt Heroes* was co-founded in 2007 after a German and a Swedish social worker met at a conference and began to exchange ideas about how to institute programming in Germany inspired by the Swedish project *Hjältlar* (Heroes) under the umbrella of a Berlin nonprofit called *Strohhalm e.V.*[95] *Strohhalm*'s mission is to educate children about molestation and sexual assault through short scenes acted out by adults that give schoolchildren the vocabulary and narrative to understand inappropriate behaviour.[96] *Strohalm* recognized that there was a need for masculinities programming in Berlin and that it could serve as an institutional umbrella for such a project. *Hjältlar* offered one model for this kind of programming, although I suspect German staff at *Projekt Heroes* would all agree that *Heroes* became its own unique project and has changed over the past decade to meet their participants' needs.

Since 2010, *Projekt Heroes* has expanded to multiple franchises across Germany and Austria. *Projekt Heroes* – Berlin, the central and founding

branch, is staffed by people in various capacities: a project management team manages the finances and day-to-day operations, and a
group leader team runs the discussion groups with teenage boys and
young men and oversees trainings and school workshops. The definition of adolescence in Germany (*Jugend*) generally runs through about
age 25. Administrative staff tend to be women of either white German
or immigrant descent, and group leaders are generally men who share
an ethnic identity and immigration history with the younger men they
train. Since 2010, there has also been at least one female group leader,
but the organizational mission focuses on intracommunity knowledge
transmission and community development between men and boys
who share a marginalized ethnic or racial identity of some kind. All
group leaders and administrative staff must have a college degree. The
participants in the project, teenage boys and young men (the so-called
heroes), can lead school workshops only after they have advanced to
the position of peer educator. This step is marked by a ceremony for the
group in training after a 9–18-month period during which they have
learned discussion skills, been thematically educated about gender,
assault, and emotional awareness, and practised and memorized the
role-playing scenes used in school and public workshops. *Heroes*-Berlin
has trained 11 groups of peer educators as of 2021.

The structure of *Projekt Heroes* programming is twofold: the first step
is experiential. The boys and young men learn how to express themselves articulately in speech, how to talk about multiple social issues
with an emphasis on gender equality and human rights, and how to
practise the emotional regulation skills that they will need to run school
workshops for teens. German schools and cultural institutions place a
premium on articulate speech in ways that are far more demanding
than is common in the United States. The major exams that college
preparatory students take to indicate readiness for university study,
known in Germany as *Abitur*, include both written testing as well as
oral defences. College classes frequently require students to lead the
discussion of material through *Referate* (presentations and reports).
The long training period at *Heroes*, as the project is colloquially known,
takes place primarily in discussion sessions and shared activities so that
participants learn these dialogic skills, especially how to speak clearly
and think critically on their feet while running workshops. Most –
but not all – of the participants at *Projekt Heroes* are college preparatory students (*Gymnasiast*). The staff members with whom I have had
contact are all highly skilled at responding spontaneously to complex
dialogic needs due to the values of the project and the structure of their
interventions. *Heroes* has now been around for more than a decade and

has thus existed long enough that some group leaders have also gone through this training process themselves as former teenage participants in the program.

In addition to practising dialogic intervention and learning how to express themselves articulately and spontaneously, the heroes practise and develop short role-playing scene prompts that they use in workshops for public schools. Built on the forum theatre model of Agosto Boal, the skits used in workshops highlight issues of domestic violence as well as discrimination, and then ask school pupils to change what happens in those scenes for the better. Through the pupils' input, scenes are revised, repeated, and reworked in real time. School workshops focus on similar issues as the discussion-based training of workshop leaders: emotional regulation, assertive behaviour, gender roles, and human rights. Under a Facebook post on 22 December 2020 bearing the caption *"Das teilen wir auch gerne!* / Happy to share this, too!," *Heroes* staff shared a post of a photograph of what appears to be a British subway station on which someone painted the following in black on a red brick wall: ~~PROTECT YOUR DAUGHTER~~ / *EDUCATE YOUR SON*. The strikethrough on the black letters was applied in red paint.[97]

Legibility: How the Media Affects Social Work

As a non-profit founded in 2007, *Projekt Heroes* emerged during a time when European politics was deeply invested in the topics of so-called honour and balcony murders as criminal offences that were specifically racialized as a problem of Muslim immigrant communities. *Projekt Heroes* embraces the figure of Hatun Sürücü as the most extreme case of honour-related violence in Germany, and staff and participants have shown up at the yearly Sürücü memorials at the Oberlandgarten bus stop, as posts on their Facebook page illustrate.[98] The logic of cultural deficit was foundational in making a project like *Heroes* legible to various German audiences. Two staff members asserted in their responses to my survey questions that this framing in the media was frustrating to them, since it represents only a partial understanding of their work – revealing how aware staff are of the media framings of their project as well as the integrative logic in which discussions of the project are situated.[99] The project also routinely has to insist that they are not a Muslim project and that their participants have diverse religious affiliations, despite the fact that the media consistently labels the project as "Muslim."[100]

While the media attention to honour killings in Germany circulated tightly around the murders of women like Hatun Sürücü or Marwa

El-Sherbini, in Sweden there was a great deal of press attention to so-called balcony murders, where young women appeared to have died by suicide – but under further investigation had apparently been pushed by their families to their deaths from apartment balconies.[101] Similar discourses around a politics or culture of "honour" circulated in France, especially in the women's movement *Ni Putes Ni Soumises*, founded by French-Algerian activist Fadela Amara.[102] This political backdrop was not only the context for the production of native testimonial literature like the books of Necla Kelek, but has also been an ongoing topic of feminist theorizing and activist engagement for decades, if not a century.

Projekt Heroes is the first of the social programs I examine that exist within the integrative apparatus at the same time that they partially resist the dominant integrative narrative of compulsory assimilation. Social work projects offer compelling spaces for scholarly investigation because they exist at the nexus of political and journalistic articulations of problems. Because social workers are often critical of the obstacles created by any institutional apparatus, they are also a site of potential resistance to the apparatus itself, can represent attempts by nongovernmental organizations to fill the gaps created by government policy, or even serve to critique how journalism steers attention in the public sphere. Social work is not a panacea, and its interventions are both diffuse and varied. The terms "social work" or "social project" describe a whole host of activities, from youth political education to supportive programming designed to incorporate newcomers, people with disabilities, or those with chronic illness. It can also focus on bringing those who are coping with long-term unemployment back into the workforce. The labour of social work also includes multiple forms of counselling and other therapeutic interventions. Social work is nearly as broad in its sheer capacity to conceptualize and imagine intervention as integration politics itself is vague. It is neither inevitable that a social project will support the goals of the integrative apparatus, nor is it inevitable that a social work project will resist the political rhetoric of compulsory assimilation. Like all human activity, social intervention is complex. Because of that complexity, social labour shapes spaces in which we can observe people grappling with social constructs in real time. *Projekt Heroes* exists in a complicated space that is structured by intense media attention to and positive portrayals of the project, governmental recognition and praise for their programming, a struggle to secure long-term funding for the original office in Berlin, and the project's own day-to-day attempts to invest in their communities and create opportunities to empower young German men from immigrant families.

Early media coverage of *Projekt Heroes* focused primarily on the way that this project seemed to function as a corrective to discourses (and behaviours) of violent, Muslim men.[103] Part of that framing was inevitable given the timing of the origins of the project and the way that journalistic attention to gender had racialized these discussions and insisted that marginalized women needed saving.[104] As I argue elsewhere, the risk of publicity that cultural geographer Patricia Ehrkamp explored in her ethnographic analyses of the Turkish-German neighbourhood of Duisburg-Marxloh and the gendered use of public space applies also to the visibility of gendered and racialized subjects more broadly, especially when they enter the public sphere as participants. In order to assess how staff felt about their work in the context of the integrative apparatus, I conducted an online qualitative survey with staff members at *Projekt Heroes* during the summer of 2020. The pandemic made it impossible to conduct research in person, but *Heroes* staff were willing and amenable to participating in an online survey of nine questions about the goals of their work as well as questions about the definition of integration and integration politics writ large. I invited six staff members to participate anonymously in the survey and received four responses.

In 2007, the year *Heroes* was founded, there were already two projects for young women from immigrant families (*Madonna Mädchentreff* and *Szenenwechsel*) in the densely populated northern tip of Berlin-Neukölln, the neighbourhood where *Projekt Heroes* began and where they still have offices for the Berlin branch. I have not participated in any form of fieldwork with either of these organizations for girls, but both had offices and signs near many of the places I walked when I lived in the Boddinstraße between 2010 and 2012. The ornate, early twentieth century public swimming pool in Neukölln, where I swam regularly, was right by *Szenenwechsel*'s offices, and *Mädchentreff Schilleria* was not far away from the ice cream café that opened near the church at *Herrfurthplatz* a couple years later. *Madonna Mädchenclub* had offices in the same *AWO* building where the first *Projekt Heroes* offices were located until 2011. The *TIO* job-training project (*Treff- und Informationsort für türkische Frauen*), at whose Kreuzberg office activist Seyran Ateş had been shot in 1984 by a member of the Turkish nationalist group the Gray Wolves, has had a Neukölln office for job training in the *Schillerkiez* since 1994.[105] The number of projects for young women, especially women of colour, proliferate in this area of Berlin. There were no parallel projects in this neighbourhood that I have heard of during this time for young men.[106] In that sense, founding *Heroes* in 2007 filled a gendered gap in available youth programming. One staff member I surveyed confirmed that this gendered gap still exists: "The uniqueness of our work lies in the fact that in doing reflective gender work with boys, we specifically talk to young men with a family history of migration and serve as a complement to all the projects that are active in work with girls."[107]

I argue here and elsewhere that *Heroes* is a product of its time: media discussions about gendered violence rendered the project legible to a broader public – even if that legibility came through media reports that misunderstood the details of how the project worked and how much time was spent in training discussions with smaller groups of teens and young men.[108] Journalists focus intensely on one of the role-plays offered as part of the school workshop, in which a father demands that his son go get his sister who is hanging out too late. The son ends up slapping his sister to bring her home. This is a scene journalists frequently instrumentalize as evidence that the Muslim immigrant community in Germany clearly needs *Projekt Heroes'* programming. Similar to the coverage of Hatun Sürücü, these media portrayals miss the classical understanding of power and control common across various forms of domestic violence and control. The violence in this scene does not lead to murder but represents lower levels of still-problematic coercion and control.

Critics of *Projekt Heroes* argue – in line with the critiques of El-Tayeb, Yıldız and Weber – that the programming exaggerates the threat of honour killing and discourses of honour, and charges that the project perpetuates racist stereotypes of Muslim men through their focus on "coaching about the correct understandings of values."[109] One critique of the project published in 2013 in the online newspaper *Yeni Hayat/Neues Leben* asserted: "The majority of the young project participants were born and have grown up in Germany; they are social products of this country. To want to communicate 'correct values' in a project is a pathetic display for Germany (*ist ein Armutszeugnis für Deutschland*). For integration politics, for social politics, employment politics and educational politics."[110] The *Heroes* staff, however, turned out to share this critic's stance, complicating the conversation about discourse, aims and practices. In answers to my survey question about whether or not *Heroes* was an integrative project, the staff in 2020 were in universal agreement that their participants had been born and raised in Germany and thus were not in need of integration.[111] That staff and participants born and raised in Germany who attend German schools are seen as being in need of integration reflects the racist logic of integration politics and rhetoric. This overlap in rhetoric between staff and critics suggests to me that critics of the project may actually be unfamiliar with the day-to-day work of *Projekt Heroes* and that their critiques emerge primarily in response to media narratives about the project rather than engaging with the work of the project at all levels (private trainings and public workshops). After all, staff members are primarily representatives of marginalized groups who are also subjected to integrative rhetoric in their daily lives.

One of the things that I was most struck by in the media coverage of *Projekt Heroes* was the degree to which staff were quoted about training discussions that engage with questions of racism in German society.[112] A 2011 issue of *a tempo* magazine – the free periodical distributed at dm drugstores – did a six-page glossy spread about *Projekt Heroes* in which staff declared that at the start of the project, the heroes wanted to talk about their own experiences of discrimination in German institutions: schools, by the police, and in society more generally. When the reporter asks why the young men participate in the project when they could be out partying, an unnamed staff member declared: "Because we connect to their own experiences! Every one of them knows how exclusion and humiliation feels. Due to this they are capable of empathy."[113] The teenagers at *Heroes* also seemed to make natural connections between the in-group and out-group dynamics that Heitmeyer and his team had studied ten years earlier. One teen declared on a radio broadcast on 24 December 2008: "I mean, if someone wants to integrate, then they also need to have a feeling of belonging, but if they have [experienced] aversion from Germans – in the same way Turks do towards Germans like – 'You are outsiders' – then coexistence just becomes harder, and that's something I wanted to change." [114]

In 2021, as I draft this section, conversations about race and racism in Germany make it clear that a large amount of counterfactual information about what constitutes racist behaviour circulates in German public discourse. Charges of antiwhite racism are the most obvious example that frequently circulates. The discourse about antiwhite racism is counterfactual because it misunderstands the basic definition of racism, which is the presence of both discursive and non-discursive practices that essentialize group behaviour in order to systemically disenfranchise and exclude members of racialized groups from full participation in society. White Germans are neither essentialized nor systemically disenfranchised like people of colour. Charges of antiwhite racism are a false equivalency of the highest order and appropriate the language of marginalized struggle to serve the nationalistic goals of the right wing. And yet, those journalistic comments showing that staff were open about their discussions about race and culturalization – and that revealed how allowing youth to discuss discrimination produced empathy rather than aggression – were not sufficient to flip the media scripts that portrayed the project as integrative.

For *Projekt Heroes* to have been talking about the lived experiences of racial discrimination and colourism with teens a full decade before anti-Black racism became a global conversation after the death of George Floyd, before Germans started having these conversations and fighting about them in the most mainstream of public spaces, and for many of their discussions to have simply acknowledged that young men growing up in Germany whose families had immigrant histories were racialized in German society was both forward-thinking and progressive. *Projekt Heroes* partially acknowledged racism as a disadvantage in order to build empathy among their boys for the gendered discrimination of women; although academic conversations about specific identities tend to push back against this style of equivalence, pointing out the differences in the dynamics of racial, gender, and class differences, political approaches to solidarity building across groups frequently make these kinds of comparisons in precisely the manner the *Projekt Heroes* chose to employ. Pointing out that many different kinds of people struggle is the first step in building a coherent collective identity built upon a politics of solidarity. Every politics attempts to create a collective identity so groups can mobilize supporters under common cause. This is neither the purview of the right nor of the left. The techniques mobilized in order to do so, however, are qualitatively different. Comparisons at *Heroes* were designed to create opportunities for empathic response rooted in group identity that would permit a coalitional pursuit of goals. In contrast, as Daniel Koehler has shown, one technique used by violent extremists to bind disparate individuals together is to inflict trauma as a way to create shared social bonds.[115] The attention *Heroes* staff pay to the experiences of racism and discrimination felt by their participants reveals that they are aware of the contours of debates about racism in Germany and how their project is perceived from the outside, by politicians, white Germans, and by members of immigrant communities.

Finally, as the political conversations shifted over time, especially in light of ongoing discussions about sexual violence and racism in a German context, the work of *Project Heroes* seemed to grow into the intersectional paradigm now demanded by the public sphere around issues no longer relegated to immigrant concerns or honour killings, but rather to ongoing debates about gender equity and racism in a European context. The Twitter hashtags #MeToo (2017) and #MeTwo (2018) reflected an acknowledgment that the dynamics of domestic violence, sexual assault, and racism were all systemic problems in German society. The homophonic hashtag #MeTwo, attributed to writer, activist, and former asylum-seeker Ali Can, popped up in German digital spaces after soccer player and integration darling Mesut Özil resigned from the German national team due to racist discrimination perpetrated by the German Football League.[116] The hashtag, under which Germans of colour posted about their individual experiences of racism, introduced public audiences to different types of racist behaviour and the broad array of experiences – a critical corrective in a society where racism is primarily perceived only in anti-Semitic behaviour. This public conversation took place nearly ten years after *Projekt Heroes* was founded and after staff had long been discussing the effects of racism, sexism, and discrimination with their participants. The dynamics present in the Heitmeyer study, where the hostile, intolerant culture is not foreign, but rather very German, finds an echo in these conversations about race and racialization. Staff, in fact, even acknowledge that their goals are intersectional and use that language to express them. The English-language mission statement on the *Heroes* website declares in a section titled "Intersectionality": "The intersectional perspective of this anti-sexist and anti-racist project manifests on an individual level in the adolescents' (socio-)pedagogical care. The better part of the target audience, as well as people involved in the project, are directly affected by multiple forms of discrimination, especially concerning gender and migration. The project creates visibility for the intersectionality of discrimination and seeks to bridge the divide between these experiences of inequality."[117]

Projekt Heroes is – of course – inseparable from the demands of the integrative apparatus simply because the integrative apparatus has become such a prominent German cultural apparatus that many of its discursive and non-discursive practices and philosophies are currently inescapable. Citizens and residents can resist or not comply with the demands of integration politics, but the rhetoric of integration is socially and culturally pervasive. The responses I collected from staff about abstract notions of integration show very clearly how subjects implicated in the integrative apparatus have to perform complex feats of positioning and self-description in order to navigate the multiple valences and networks in which this type of social labour exists. The integrative apparatus in contemporary Germany exhibits connections between societal features such as a racialized underclass, political theatre that positions immigrants and their descendants in certain racialized categories or as players in cultural conflicts, as well as the resistance of those subjects implicated in such a structure to the discourses and rhetoric used to hail them.

Projekt Heroes and Staff Definitions of "Integration"

As *Projekt Heroes* garnered more attention, early observers began to classify their work as an integrative project. They won several integration prizes early in their tenure, and even as recently as 2016 were visited by then-Interior Minister Thomas de Maizière. The Interior Minister has frequently been the political position charged with integration policy at the level of the cabinet, even more so than the Commissioner of Integration (now called the *Integrationsminister*), which some scholars view as a highly symbolic post.[118]

While composing my survey questions, I was conflicted about the irritations that I knew I would provoke in order to ascertain how staff members felt about integration politics. In order to keep the survey short and easily completed during a time of intense global pandemic stress, I also knew that my questions would appear blunter and sharper than they likely would in a conversational setting, which is the format in which I have conducted all previous fieldwork. The answers I received to several questions implied that this was indeed the case. However, the survey did produce the kinds of responses that I needed to understand how staff members felt about the broader national discourses of integration and migration politics in which their work exists.

One of the contradictions present in staff survey responses appears in the disconnect between how *Projekt Heroes* staff in Berlin view their own work compared to the way that this work is assessed and interpolated within the integrative apparatus. When I asked staff members what the primary goals were for *Heroes-Berlin*, as well as the German and Austrian franchises, I received answers rooted in the day-to-day practice of working with and empowering teenage boys. Some of these were formulated in the language of therapeutic or educational interventions. Participant 1 declared that the goals of the project were "to move adolescents to question images – that are loaded with clichés – of gender, gender roles, and understandings of honour, violence and respect in order to grow into a mature person."[119] Participant 3 declared that the primary goals of the project were "to engage critically with values and traditions, for instance, if one feels limited by them, for instance in one's own actions, and simply cannot lead the life that one would like to (and with whom one would like to). Apart from that there are many smaller goals, like for instance encouraging democratic education and participation, etc."[120] The inclusion of the phrase "if one *feels* limited" [italics mine] by values and traditions suggests that staff are not explicitly involved in any push to change the cultural identities their participants have fashioned for themselves, as the 2013 critique suggested.

One thing that needs to be emphasized is that while compulsory assimilation within the integrative apparatus implies a level of coercion that I argue is intolerable in an anti-racist, democratic society, assimilation is still always and forever a choice – and surely an acceptable one, even if philosophies of assimilation are inherently debatable in multi-ethnic and multiracial societies.

Given the timing of my survey in the summer of 2020, two of the answers were also intensely practical and focused on the project's need for sustainable funding: Participant 2 articulated the primary goals as "surviving the coronavirus pandemic, and securing stable, long-term financing," while Participant 4 explained that "at the moment we are struggling financially to prevent *Heroes* from being closed, because we can only still fulfill the school workshops [*Schulkooperationen*] with our resources [*Kapazitäten*]."[121] While franchises in other cities have overwhelmingly been supported by funding from local governments, *Projekt Heroes-Berlin* has struggled for nearly a decade to find sustainable funding, despite the fact that they are positively regarded by political figures, initiated the franchise expansion in 2010, and continue to serve as the national organizational hub. In 2020, the situation was quite drastic, and staff marshalled the media to draw attention to their plight.[122]

Over the past decade, *Projekt Heroes* has won multiple integration awards. That "integration," an abstract, undefined cultural value, is something that can be "won" represents an opportunity for further theoretical study, since it is clearly functioning here as a social value that can be promoted and even purportedly produced by the correct programming. *Projekt Heroes* was awarded the third place *Hauptstadtpreis für Integration und Toleranz* in 2011, and the Rabbi Daniel Alter dedicated his Integration Bambi Award to *Heroes* in 2012. They also won the SPD's Otto-Wels Prize in 2018.[123] Right after the Integration Act was passed on 25 May 2016, Federal Interior Minister Thomas de Maizière visited the Berlin offices of *Projekt Heroes*, supposedly to show how integration should work "in practice."[124] De Maizière's politicization of a project that works with young German men, visiting *Heroes* merely one day after a law applicable to asylum seekers was passed, reveals how elite politicians reduce and racialize different histories and migration pathways through blanket classifications of refugees and Germans of colour as different from white Germans and in need of integrative interventions.

Projekt Heroes is a complex organization that performs social labour in the tense spaces between integration politics and the difficult and ongoing work of social incorporation that is part of all societies. A recent report about engaging with perpetrators as part of the European

ENGAGE project found that 23 per cent of all European women had experienced physical or sexual violence and 42 per cent of European women had experienced psychological violence.[125] A highly debated study by Prof. Monika Schröttle and Nadia Khelaifat from 2009 also reflected high rates of domestic violence across German, Russian immigrant, and Turkish immigrant populations, hierarchizing the smaller Turkish and Russian samples as quantifiably more violent than white German populations, which raised many questions about research design, oversampling marginalized groups in quantitative research, and hierarchies of abuse. What was not debatable was that women *in all three groups* experienced high rates of sexual and domestic violence.[126] The need for violence prevention across Europe is obvious when somewhere between one-quarter and one-half of the female population experiences some form of abuse.

One of the things *Projekt Heroes* emphasizes in their trainings is the need for young men of all cultural backgrounds to be able to articulate their ideas and feelings as a violence-prevention mechanism.[127] No less than Ayhan Sürücü expressed the same idea in an interview documentarians filmed in prison about his sister's murder:

> What I absolutely can suggest to young people, I mean, [those] with a migration background who are in a similar situation as I was, back then, [is] that they simply trust themselves and have the courage to talk about it openly, to open themselves to the outside, [and to do that] within the family as well as outside of it.[128]

That *Projekt Heroes* has existed for over 15 years reflects how community organizations performing incorporative labour that is deemed useful may initially become legible in the context of media scandals but can also persist in their work because their programming provides an opportunity that participants desire. Just because some members desire these opportunities does not mean that everyone will, and the desire for these sorts of labour can be critiqued by precisely the communities social workers intend to serve. *Projekt Heroes* manoeuvres in between and beyond discursive practices and is deeply aware of these critiques of their work. As Participant 1 articulated in response to the question of how the work has changed in the past ten years:

> the specific engagement with the topics of oppression in the name of honour has become very delicate. Through the emergence and the growth of the AfD, for instance, but also through repeated racist assaults and attacks on people with a migration background it has become more difficult to

speak critically about problems within immigrant communities. The talk is often of anti-Muslim racism or culturalization when we try to discuss our topics or present our work. These reproaches come partly from politics but also from other migrant projects/organizations. Mostly when they don't know us and our work or have only heard of it.[129]

Participant 4 echoed Participant 1's concerns: in spite of increased demand for and expansion of the project, political debates about "racism, anti-Muslim racism and religious extremism" made their work "more difficult."[130] *Projekt Heroes* is an organization that arose not only within but is subject to all of the stressors of the integrative apparatus.

Positioned within this complex web of praise and critique, I wanted to know how staff felt about the term "integration," about how they viewed integration policy more broadly, and whether they thought the work of *Projekt Heroes* fit into an integrative paradigm. I asked if their work was guided by a so-called *Integrationskonzept*, or a framework for integration, given the way that *Heroes* distinguishes their mission/format from other social work projects in the field. The answers were unambivalent: no. *Projekt Heroes* staff do not consider this work to be integrative. Their answers adeptly critiqued both how I formulated the question as well as integrative discourse more broadly.

- That it's not about "integrating outsiders" into a different society is something the question doesn't consider (*stellt sich die Frage nicht*).[131]
- Since we don't understand ourselves to be an integration project, we don't have such a framework. The boys and the children in the school classes are 99 per cent born and growing up here and, in our opinion, don't need to be integrated in the conventional sense.[132]
- I have a hard time with this term. The boys don't need to be integrated in my opinion, because they were born here and grew up here. Integration is thus not a goal of our work.[133]
- HEROES wouldn't describe itself as a political "integration project" because our goal is gender equality. Through our work there are obviously assumptions that foster a "cultural" integration in Germany, but that's not our goal. Our goal is to help the target group to become more independent and less [subject to] collective pressure, in order to awaken empathy for diverse cooperation and also for a freer life.[134]

The last contribution on this list positions an integrative argument in interesting ways while it simultaneously rejects the terms of the question: *Heroes* is not an integration project, but they admit that the focus in German society on integration is primarily on cultural integration and thus, *Heroes* can be read as a culturally integrative project by some observers. It is unclear to me whether "target group" refers to the peer educators in training or the children in school classrooms, or both. Either way, the respondent emphasizes that the project's focus is not on integration, but rather on fostering diverse multiplicities and cooperation: promoting *ein vielfältiges Miteinander* (togetherness in diversity).

A subsequent survey question asked whether the team itself viewed *Heroes* as an integration project, a question that was designed to make sure I captured the staff's perspective about the organization and its programming rather than merely a staff articulation of a position within integrative discourse. The answers here were also uniformly No. The definition of integration in these responses slipped in and out of what I would describe as a mix of integrative rhetoric and understanding a process of incorporation as a political praxis. One staff member stated, "no, but we experience that it has an integrative effect. Above all else for our boys [*Jungs*], who have an effect on society through their work at *Heroes*."[135] I read into this answer a subtextual redefinition of integration as a way to access participation, which is a common twist in German discourse to make "integration" sound both more democratic and more palatable. This twist also allows subjects who disagree with integrative discourse or rhetoric to reframe and rephrase the purported goals of integrative policy in language that is more acceptable and less offensive.

When I asked staff participants to define integration, it was clear to me that the discursive contours of the integrative apparatus and all the subtext that goes along with that apparatus in terms of viewing integration as a form of compulsory assimilation were clear to staff. In terms of political efficacy, this raises the question as to how or why political elites insist on continuing to mobilize a discourse that obviously does not describe how people think of themselves and their chosen or available forms of access to social, cultural, and political participation in German society. Two participants described integration as subsuming something small into something big. Pointedly, Participant 1 declared "integration means weaving something into something else – and therefore is useless as a policy for societies with real people."[136] I would be curious to have had the opportunity to continue a live conversation with this participant directly, which only would have been possible without the pandemic, to understand the metaphor of weaving. What I suspect is that the subtext of this statement implies that real people are far more complex than the discourse of integration allows, and thus speaking of people as in need of integration, integrable, or willing to integrate is so far removed from the realities of people's everyday lives that the concept does not have value outside of policy discourse.

In the additional three responses to the question asking staff members to define what integration meant, staff members also voiced that multiple, distinct opinions about this idea were present within the team, with Participant 2 declaring that questions like this are constantly under discussion at *Heroes*.[137] Participant 2 argued that integration is a process of participation for *everyone* who is part of a society, implicitly hailing white Germans within that paradigm. And Participants 2 and 3 both resisted definitions of integration as a form of assimilation or a way to render minorities invisible, with Participant 3 calling integration "out of date."[138] Finally, Participant 4 laid out a vision for both *Projekt Heroes* and what many progressive voices see as the best outcome for the true incorporation of both newcomers and marginalized people into societies: "Integration means making something small fit into something big. But we don't want to overwrite an identity with the majority identity, but instead create a space in which multiple identities, independent from majority and number, are at the same eye level."[139] This emphasis on equity appeared in the responses from staff that described how *Projekt Heroes* was invested in intersectional approaches of violence prevention as a form of civic engagement – that is, precisely the framing that had not yet become dominant in ongoing discussions of domestic violence as a cultural issue.

Hatun Sürücü's murder, the discourse of failed integration, the out-of-context appropriation of the parallel society trope, and media coverage that often conflicts with staff portrayals of *Projekt Heroes'* work are all examples of how social interactions and dynamics refract within the integrative apparatus. Discursive practices and media rhetoric limit the available interpretations of complex social practices and also render the similarities between white German and new German behaviours invisible or illegible. In narratives like these, the integrative *achievements* of the Sürücü family disappear, while the similarities between fundamentalist Muslim youth and right-wing German extremist youth are obscured. The need for all young men to be educated about both the dynamics of sexual assault and the assertive or emotional skills to prevent such behaviour becomes relegated to training the children of immigrants, who are then seen – in contrast to the desires of *Projekt Heroes* staff – as young people subjected to educational interventions rather than agents of their own educational and social pursuits. As we will see in chapter 3, these discourses of failure and insularity will take on new weight when combined with the economic and biological racism of Thilo Sarrazin's polemic thought.

Chapter Three

(Un)integrable Subjects: White Supremacy and Neoliberal Ideology

On 30 August 2010, the *Bundespressekonferenz*, or the Federal Press Conference, held a press event for Thilo Sarrazin, a German federal banker and member of the Social Democratic Party.[1] Sarrazin's first book, *Deutschland schafft sich ab* (Germany Abolishes Itself), went on sale that day. Many stores sold out by noon; the entire first printing of 25,000 copies sold out the first day.[2] Journalists filled the *BPK* for the press junket, sitting wall-to-wall in rows in front of the podium and taking notes. Others, pushed back to the edges of the room, stood next to television cameras or tried not to hit the boom operators holding pole mics and recording the audio feed with blank expressions. Practically pressed up against the table where Sarrazin sat were the print photographers, who pointed long lenses towards the author and clicked their shutters with frequencies usually reserved for sports stars. A camera feed of the event, available on YouTube, also pointedly offers some footage of other famous *Islamkritiker* like Henryk M. Broder, who also were in attendance.[3] Constant shuffling and whispering filled the video soundtrack as Necla Kelek stood at the podium to introduce Sarrazin's book. Sarrazin himself, with his trademark, exceptionally round, black glasses, sat silently behind the table during all the commotion, his arms crossed in front of his chest. Behind him, two giant covers of Sarrazin's book were hung against strikingly blue walls. Big black capital letters screamed out the book's title, typeset against a red background: "GERMANY ABOLISHES ITSELF: HOW WE ARE GAMBLING WITH OUR COUNTRY."

This was a big day: journalists had been waiting nearly a year to see what would happen to Thilo Sarrazin. In 2009, he had given an astonishing interview to the magazine *Lettre International*, in which he made several racist statements that garnered nationwide attention.[4] Sarrazin's arguments in both the *Lettre* interview and his book performed a specific function in the development of a contemporary integrative apparatus: he used blatantly racist language to criticize religion, culture, and socioeconomic status. Ironically, Sarrazin's racist rhetoric put both the intersectionality of integration debates and the contemporary diversity of immigrant populations in Germany on display. By couching his economic statements as a question of national sovereignty and failed integration, he managed to sidestep a debate about systemic exclusion and the costs of neoliberal economic policies for the poor – including white Germans in poverty. The publication and subsequent 24/7 media attention to Sarrazin's book is an example of how discursive practices about integration prompted a marked shift in which collective narratives about national identity moved to the right. Like Kelek, Sarrazin purportedly argued from a position on the centre-*left*, not the right: Sarrazin was a member of the Social Democratic Party. Holding stereotypically conservative positions while insisting that such views reflect a political position on the centre-left shows that the entire political spectrum has moved rightward. In an article about Sarrazin's press conference, journalist Andreas Kilb for the *Frankfurter Allgemeine* declared with resignation that Sarrazin had "set a new North Pole for the integration debate, to which the needle of the Berlin Republic's compass now points."[5]

While a great deal of attention has focused on Sarrazin's racial ideology, it's important to point out that neither race nor class is Sarrazin's primary concern. Intersectional analysis of this event requires not just the lenses of race, class, and gender, but also of national identity. Demonizing the poor required Sarrazin to mobilize a racializing structure in a specific national context. Outrage against Sarrazin's racism was also easier to articulate in the public sphere than it would have been to illuminate the neoliberal ideology in which Sarrazin's racism was steeped. Sarrazin's racism is inseparable from his distaste for poverty and striking adherence to severe fiscal restraint and austerity. His politics and bias emerge from an economic ideology that racializes and punishes the poor and justifies such moves by invoking the health of the national body politic. Sarrazin's celebrity serves as evidence that a racialized economic underclass exists in Germany that can be mobilized in political debates and that this intersection of race, class, and nation will have profound political consequences for the future. While Sarrazin portrays these consequences as the result of shifting demographics, these social and material realities are better framed by measuring access both to resources and opportunities for civic participation.

The Sarrazin debate strengthened connections between a variety of nodes on the integrative apparatus: white supremacy, overtly racist statements, and clearly articulated racial hierarchies; neoliberal fantasies of a *schlanker Staat* (trim state) as well as a blanket demoni-zation of the poor; and an insatiable PR machine more than willing to promote his platform. All of these nodes worked in concert to sharpen the contours of the integrative apparatus that were now visible to any-one who looked. The connections – as previous chapters have already shown – were already sketched out; the associations – however diffuse – already part and parcel of postwar and post-9/11 German culture. Sar-razin's celebrity and the massive financial success of his book made the politicized, contemporary definition of "integration" as a form of impossible compulsory assimilation concrete.

The effects of Sarrazin's rhetoric on integration politics writ large were to fuse biologically essentialist ideas about race and concurrent denigration of the poor to multiple philosophies and institutions within the integrative apparatus. This fusion expanded the reach of integra-tion politics in complex ways. First: the subtextual ethno-nationalism that undergirds a one-way understanding of integration was no longer subtext. Second: his tirades against poverty and the poor also made it clear that the social incorporation of both minorities and the white German poor is a task that implicates white Germans as much as it implicates minorities. This is what migration researcher Klaus Bade means when he describes true "integration politics" as "social politics for everyone" (*Gesellschaftspolitik für alle*).[6] Finally, the massive amount of press attention this scandal generated made the topic of integration commonplace in basic conversation. No debate about migration could escape platitudes about the failures of integration; the Sarrazin debate thus deeply politicized integration as a form of compulsory assimila-tion to white, Christian, middle-class German norms.

The tendency of some elite politicians to label Sarrazin as a truth teller, and as a "courageous" one at that, fused right-wing rhetoric with conspiratorial thinking. Arguments positing that limiting racist speech is either an assault on the "truth" or evidence of a government cov-er-up against those who want to "tell it like it is" show that far-right sympathies existed even in the large *Volksparteien*, or parties of the cen-tre (CDU/SPD). Furthermore, such debates revealed the tendency of "mainstream" German political actors to mobilize a narrative of major-ity persecution so common to the right wing. Sarrazin was neither courageous nor the first of his kind: the historical record shows that many of his ideas have a long cultural history in both German soci-ety and other industrialized nations. Without Sarrazin's celebrity and widespread public attention to his book, however, it is possible that the integrative apparatus would not have expanded to its current scale and scope.

Sarrazin's Interview in *Lettre International*

In early October 2009, Sarrazin gave an interview to the magazine *Lettre International*, which is primarily marketed at an intellectual elite. Titled *"Klasse statt Masse"* (best translated as "Quality, not Quantity"), this four-page interview made Sarrazin notoriously well known to the broader public. Two utterances from this interview appeared repeatedly in newspaper coverage about the outrage: "Turks are conquering Germany exactly how Kosovars conquered Kosovo: through a higher birthrate"; and, "I don't have to recognize anyone who lives off of the state, who rejects the state, who doesn't sufficiently take care of the education of his children and constantly produces new little headscarf girls."[7] The recourse to centuries-old images of the Turks (Ottomans) as a warring competitor threatening the gates of Vienna; denigration of another predominantly Muslim group (Kosovars) and biopolitical mobilization of arguments about birth rates; and the implication that Muslim fathers are negligent, welfare-dependent, and controlling of their daughters could not be a more derogatory collection of anti-Muslim stereotypes. Sarrazin's tone is also flippant and aggressive. Tropes of misogynist minorities with high birthrates are common elements of racist ideologies irrespective of ethnic background, and they often appear in societies with racialized socio-economic underclasses.[8] These stereotypes in particular are the cornerstones of anti-Muslim racialization as it appears today in Europe. The *Bild-Zeitung* – which one study found consistently perpetuated xenophobic reporting during the Sarrazin scandal – also reprinted the entire text of the *Lettre* article for its subscribers.[9] As the most-read daily newspaper in Germany, this interview that might have been relegated to the fringe became news for more than 2 million subscribers. *Bild* was later sued for damages by *Lettre*, which maintained that the *Bild-Zeitung* reprinted the article without permission.[10]

What Sarrazin's interview in *Lettre* brought to the forefront was the detailed racial hierarchy he mobilized in order to make his arguments about class and national identity. Alongside the two sentences that are most frequently cited, the printed interview includes an entire paragraph where he sketches out in remarkable detail which ethnic groups he considers capable of success and which ones he considers unintegrable. It's very clear that racial stereotypes fuel his hierarchy: Jewish people, through philosemitic assertions of their above average intelligence, occupy the highest rung; Eastern Europeans and Asians stay towards the top; people from the former Yugoslavia, as well as Turks, Arabs, and undereducated and poor white Germans, occupy the lowest rung.[11] I am aware of the dangers that come with reproducing Sarrazin's hierarchy; however, for North American readers and for the analysis of whiteness that I will undertake later, it is important to point out that many groups that maintain a high level of ethnic difference for Sarrazin would easily be assimilated as white in the United States or Canada. Sarrazin's detailed hierarchy also gives us a sense of which groups in German society hold proximity to whiteness, based on their location within the hierarchy. Sarrazin praises Asian immigrants, primarily Berlin's Vietnamese community, as model minorities, much like Asian immigrants from China and Japan who bear proximity to whiteness in North America. He does not mention Roma, Sinti, Latin Americans, Afro-Germans, or immigrants from Africa in this interview, which stands out precisely because he takes this opportunity to lay out the contours of his racial hierarchy for other parts of the world in such extreme detail. (His book, in contrast, does include passages about African immigrants).[12] The invisibility of Europeans of colour is upheld through this omission, and further strengthens Fatima El-Tayeb's argument that Europeans of colour remain largely invisible as participants, citizens, and creative agents in contemporary European countries.[13] Despite the fact that the largest number of immigrants to Germany come from countries in the European Union, Sarrazin also does not mention immigrants from any Western European nations (Italy, for instance), showing – through their absence – how the politics of belonging in Western Europe are constructed upon European whiteness as a matter of course.[14]

The unintended consequence – for Sarrazin, at least – of his racist statements is that they reveal the deep diversity of ethnic backgrounds and immigrant life in Germany. If activists and scholars often criticize the public sphere in the United States for the way that debates about social policy revolve around a Black-white binary, this binary in Germany is most often a German-Muslim one. By acknowledging, even incompletely, that German society is more diverse than political conversations give it credit for, Sarrazin's statements reveal that even white supremacists are aware that the racial politics of a Germany this diverse require multiple levels of colonial logic to pursue their nationalist aims, and he categorizes different groups of people in order to position them against each other.[15] Whiteness here serves as a powerful unifier, bringing together Germans, Western Europeans, Eastern Europeans of German descent and Jewish immigrants by marking these groups as assimilable, implicitly invoking decades-old extremist rhetoric about the eastern areas and the rights of ethnic Germans from across Eastern Europe to German citizenship. Including

Jewish people as assimilable to whiteness in such a hierarchy also allows Sarrazin to evade charges of anti-Semitism, perhaps the most taboo charge in postwar German culture, thereby recuperating his own identity as a post-war German aware of the past. Turkish- and Arab-Germans, who Sarrazin describes as groups in which "large portions are neither willing to integrate nor capable of integrating," are kept outside the boundaries of whiteness by his insistence on their cultural difference, evident in his references to headscarves and marriage practices. Of course, many Germans were not fooled by Sarrazin's rhetoric and saw in it the dangers of classifying German residents and citizens based on ethnicity, race, or religion.

The rhetoric of immigrants or their descendants showing an "unwillingness to integrate" or being considered "incapable of integrating" also reveals the parallels between a racial hierarchy and an integrative hierarchy. Within the integrative apparatus, levels of integrability can be linked with any number of ethnic or racial markers as well as with legal statuses that hierarchize people based on their identities. Various categories of access structured the institutionalization of so-called integration courses through legal reforms in 2005 and 2007. In 2016–17, when the first Integration Act took effect, legal categories related to the likelihood of asylum being granted (*Bleibeperspektive*) structured access to integrative programs based on asylum-seekers' nationalities, illustrating how racial, ethnic, and national identities still strongly affect contemporary integration policy.

Sarrazin's racist statements drove a good deal of the debate about integration in 2010. Discussions of Sarrazin's racism were ultimately damaging to public discourse about integration for two reasons. By stopping short of analysing how racism blocks access, and by focusing merely on whether Sarrazin's statements *were* racist, the public discussion worked as Sarrazin intended. Questioning whether Sarrazin's statements were racist frequently led journalists to try and fact-check his claims, which reproduced Sarrazin's focus on Muslim-Germans and the other racialized groups he denigrated. The emotional responses to racist speech acts obscured a more critical element of Sarrazin's economic philosophy: the rejection of the postwar class compromise and, in essence, of the welfare state. Obscuring Sarrazin's economic views meant that his racism just prompted more sensationalist coverage, instead of illuminating how perniciously Sarrazin's *actions* as a political official led to systematic exclusion and attacks on poor communities, whether immigrant or not.

Sarrazin's rhetoric reflects a libertarian ethos and deep fiscal conservativism, evidence of which can be found throughout his long history in government. Sarrazin served as the Berlin Senator for Finance from

2002–9, and his worldview is starkly authoritarian when it comes to the distribution of material resources. He portrays only upper-class white elites as capable of managing their resources. Amidst all that vitriol towards mismanagement of resources by the poor, it is at least curious to note that during his term as *Finanzsenator*, he was twice investigated for mismanagement of funds. (He was never charged by any court.)[16]

If an apparatus exists in the networks *between* discourses, philosophies, institutions, and legal mechanisms, notions of race *facilitate* some of the connections between discourses, philosophies, institutions, and legal mechanisms by serving as the discursive subtext for non-discursive practices. Notions of race are a fundamental element of the integrative apparatus and can inform how policymakers apportion resources such as welfare payments and educational opportunities like language classes. Racializing discourses in the public sphere are rarely as blatant as the comments made by someone like Sarrazin. A more precise description of how race enters the integrative apparatus would be to argue that racializing logic enters the apparatus through discursive means, and then discriminates against immigrants, refugees, and people of colour through forms of systemic exclusion that are uneven and erratic in practice. The individual experience of exclusion may be felt as random or logically inconsistent; systemic exclusion only becomes visible in the aggregate, when patterns emerge across the whole.

Sarrazin, Neoliberalism, and the Materiality of Race

Racism is an ideology of essentialism that justifies exclusionary social practices in order to limit access to material resources. The desire for social exclusion is never merely psychological nor ideological: racism exists in the material world and has material effects. At the heart of these social conditions are fights about access, which reflect any society's ideas about who is considered worthy of owning capital, whether social, cultural, civic (citizenship), or economic. Arguments both in favour of and against immigration frequently mobilize economic arguments as justification for their political stance. Far-right voters justify their anti-immigrant attitudes through an economic logic of competition that argues that immigrants take local jobs or drive down wages; left-wing arguments in favour of immigration argue that immigrants are drivers of economic growth, and that refugee migration leads to higher rates of consumption and entrepreneurship. The use of economic statistics and data can be used to justify nearly any political position on the spectrum – and accurate application of the data, as Sarrazin's faulty data science showed, is nearly useless as a predictor of successful political application. Using quantitative data to justify a political opinion also plays into the logic of rationalization and efficiency characteristic of neoliberal philosophies, which politicians on the right frequently deploy to argue against government measures seen as inefficient.[17] In particular, welfare or public education programs that require funding to provide services, humanitarian care, or a basic standard of living are frequent targets of budget hawks on either the centre-left or centre-right.

On 23 August 2010, a week before Sarrazin's book was published and the press conference took place at the BPK, *Der Spiegel* magazine and the *Bild-Zeitung* daily tabloid both printed an excerpt from *Deutschland schafft sich ab*.[18] The title of Sarrazin's book is somewhat odd, both in German and in English. The most common translation, "Germany Does Away with Itself," isn't an idiom, nor is it a common formulation. Perhaps a better translation would be "Germany Abolishes Itself," or an even more accurate attempt: "Germany is Making Itself Obsolete." The awkward title (alongside Sarrazin's awkward prose) cannot obscure his blunt message: if Germans want to preserve their cultural traditions and preserve an ethnic national community, they are going to have to fight for it. Not through warfare – no contemporary German would dare suggest such a thing. The coming fight will take place on the landscape of demographics and birth rates. Immigrant populations in Germany have more children than other groups, and if things continue as they are, he warns, soon white Germans will be in the minority.[19] Sarrazin hits all the high notes of a white supremacist identity politics based on resentment towards immigrants and globalization that became more sophisticated and blatantly nationalist in the decade that followed.[20] *Deutschland schafft sich ab* is a version of the Great Replacement Theory circulating in a German idiom of integration.

In addition to stoking white German fears of *Überfremdung* (foreign domination or infiltration), Sarrazin argues that Muslim populations (and other immigrant groups) are unfit to lead.[21] Their rise, he says, in no uncertain terms, will signal the decline of the nation: he insists that German society is becoming "dumber."[22] Using the logic of biological essentialism characteristic of racist theories, Sarrazin argues that immigrants – Muslims in particular – are neither smart nor hard-working enough to preserve the nation.[23] Their purported "culture" (code for both religion and race) makes it impossible for them to integrate into German society.[24]

Despite the blatant racism of such comments, German journalists were remarkably reluctant to label such statements "racist" during the ensuing debate.[25] Both German citizens and some politicians instead praised Sarrazin for breaking the silence about perceived social problems using rhetoric that had long been considered taboo in public. Joachim Gauck, at that time the former federal commissioner for the Stasi Records and future federal president of Germany, told the press that Sarrazin showed "courage" by publishing his book.[26] Multiple newspaper articles appeared in 2010 in various outlets with the title "What Sarrazin Gets Right."[27] Several politicians, however, also forcefully condemned his statements. Former Commissioner for Foreigners Barbara John declared: "What he says is derogatory, denigrative, destructive, and exclusionary."[28] In other statements, John even questioned his sanity, calling him a "therapy case" (*"ein Fall für die Couch"*),[29] a statement that perhaps was uttered for comic relief, but that in actuality twists a structural discussion of racism in Germany into a form of pathology that can be discursively contained by focusing on Sarrazin's actions.[30] On 25 August 2010, two days after the excerpt was printed, Chancellor Merkel expressed her irritation through her Press Secretary Steffen Seibert, who reported that Merkel had said that Sarrazin's statements could be interpreted as "extremely injurious, defamatory, and very polemically exaggerated" (*sehr polemisch zugespitzt*).[31]

Similar to Necla Kelek five years prior, Sarrazin insisted that his methods were scientific. The "scientific" quality of Sarrazin's work was supposedly due to his attempts to use statistical information to justify his illogical arguments. However, Sarrazin ignored or obscured much of the actual data about immigrant populations in Germany. He rejected established research findings on gains in social incorporation and educational achievement; a growing immigrant middle class; and the emerging class of primarily Turkish-German elites in positions of national prominence, especially in the media, culture, sport, and politics. Instead, as Klaus Bade argues, Sarrazin and his contemporaries claimed that their findings were based in research but, in reality, they simply revived decades-old stereotypes and legitimized populist and racist arguments about national self-preservation. Bade, a respected researcher who himself was targeted by both Kelek and Sarrazin, calls this form of public commentary *"Desintegrationspublizistik"* (disintegration media), and defines the effect of such journalistic behaviour on German society as a form of "negative integration":

> The result of this paradoxical tension is a dangerous surrogate debate (*Ersatzdebatte*) in place of that overdue discussion about a new identity in an immigrant society. [My] book describes this surrogate debate as negative integration: integration through partial segregation due to the aforementioned self-assurance of the majority by excluding a

large – Muslim – minority. The political sphere (*die Politik*) misreads the explosive nature of negative integration because it doesn't understand "integration politics" as social politics for everyone and doesn't learn to convey it in these terms.[32]

If Kelek's *Die fremde Braut* demonized Islam and gender roles, and the press coverage of the murder of Hatun Sürücü blamed a culture of honour for femicide by racializing a religious identity, Thilo Sarrazin's comments scapegoated and racialized an economic underclass to pursue explicitly nationalist and white supremacist aims. The intersectional elements of integration debates become clear when we take these three examples and lay them alongside each other – gender, race (also coded as culture, religion, or history) and class – are alternately moved into the foreground or background based on the specific example, but ultimately these categories are inseparable from each other. Gender, race, ethnicity, culture, class, and national identity mutually constitute each other based on their particular configuration.[33] The effects on the integrative apparatus would be the same no matter which examples were chosen: substitute another *Islamkritikerin* for Necla Kelek; another victim of domestic or family violence for Hatun Sürücü; or racist statements from a different economist invested in austerity politics for Thilo Sarrazin and many of the analytical conclusions about integration rhetoric would have similar contours.[34] The celebrity examples I include here are useful case studies due to the sheer media power these public figures held and because their identities served symbolic purposes on the national imaginary. But their argumentative contributions are rarely unique – it is their *celebrity* that makes the boundaries of their identity categories visible and allows them to foreground their identities in order to serve a representative function for German citizens who supposedly share their views.

Newspaper journalists were complicit in evading questions of race, and sidestepped the issue in subsequent interviews with Sarrazin.[35] Journalist Holger Schmale for the *Frankfurter Rundschau* summed up the ambivalent reaction of the press in his reporting about the BPK press conference: "Is he [Sarrazin] a racist, or even the anti-Semite that he appears to be to so many people – [if so,] then how can one create this kind of a forum for him? At Phoenix [German C-Span] they discussed this that morning, and then decided to broadcast the press conference live on TV."[36] One legal commentator even argued that Sarrazin's demonization of the ethnic German poor relativized his racist statements towards other groups, and thus demanded Sarrazin's comments be considered "in context." This commentator eventually concluded that Sarrazin could not be considered racist simply because he was also critical of the white German poor.[37] Yet, during the subsequent press tour, Sarrazin's own publisher had to issue an apology for some of his comments about Jewish people, and two local chapters of the SPD – Sarrazin's party – commissioned respected extremist researcher Gideon Botsch to compile a report that investigated whether or not Sarrazin's statements were racist. (Botsch found that they were).[38] Stopping short of analysing the rhetorical and political effects of such speech on German society, several newspaper articles found it sufficient merely to debate the question of whether or not these statements could be considered racist.[39]

Back in 2003, Sarrazin gave an interview to the left-leaning daily *die taz* about his work as Berlin's Finance Senator. In this interview, Sarrazin criticized the state for investing so much in education without quality returns; argued that unemployment and the de facto segregation of immigrants are unimportant factors when considering educational reforms; stated that there is no statistical correlation between classroom size and individual student successes (instead, students need simply to learn and study more); and bemoaned the fact that children in kindergarten aren't read to enough and are not familiar with the fairytales of the Brothers Grimm. In closing, he argued that his vision for educational reforms requires the state to impart "bourgeois values and orient teachers towards achievement" (*Leistung*). It is the state's responsibility, Sarrazin argues, to monitor student and teacher compliance with standards of achievement.[40] In this single interview, Sarrazin already revealed that he saw government funding as wasteful, rejected the possibility of systemic inequality, framed the problem of education as a question of individual effort, and saw familiarity with national cultural figures as the goal of early childhood education. At the same time that he implied that the government was throwing money away on ill-conceived programs, he also argued that the civil liberties of underprivileged children of immigrants require greater state control. By demanding the state enforce *Leistungsstandards* to ensure educational compliance, he suggested that education (and implicitly, integration) requires greater surveillance to secure middle-class German values and productivity standards.[41]

Sarrazin achieved his political goals through financial means. Political correspondent Heike Schmoll wrote an exposé in September 2010 for the *Frankfurter Allgemeine* about how Sarrazin made cuts to the educational system in Berlin in 2003 that turned into a self-fulfilling prophecy. State-financed kindergarten classes (*Vorklassen*) served 10,000 children in Berlin in 2003. Another 14,000 attended private kindergarten programs at that time. The primary group served by the free kinder-garten offerings were the children of immigrants who couldn't afford the course fees for private kindergartens.[42] During Sarrazin's time as finance senator of Berlin (2002–9), the salaries and working hours of early childhood educators were cut; at the same time, educators had to keep facilities open on the same schedule as before, thus earning "less money for the same number of working hours."[43] In addition, in order to prove the success of their programs, teachers were also now required to document the *daily* learning goals for *each child*. Schmoll pointed out that Berlin teachers were doubly burdened: they worked more hours for less money and started at atypically low entry-level salaries. Younger teachers, she writes, often tried as quickly as possible to move to another German state – where they, in contrast to Berlin, would also have the chance to become civil servants. Overall, the effect of cutting the public kindergarten option placed the task of school readiness on elementary school teachers – especially for those children of immigrants who had previously taken advantage of the free kindergarten option. They were forced to hold back many children for a third year of the two-year readiness curriculum, effectively taking on the burden of kin-dergarten instruction without compensation or reduction in class size.[44] As Schmoll pointedly notes: "In this manner, Sarrazin was responsible for his prophecy being fulfilled – the educational political struggle can hardly be won 'in a structure in which the number of those in need rises from year to year.'"[45] By compressing the number of available educa-tional options, elementary school teachers simply had to make do with less – and children from immigrant families bore the brunt of budget cuts. By 2009, right before Sarrazin switched to his position at the Fed-eral Bank, he also proposed that teacher salaries should be adjusted to a system in which 20 per cent of their wages would be dependent on their measurable successes in the classroom, effectively introducing a competitive wage structure into a profession previously defined as a civil service, a vocation, or a calling.[46]

Sarrazin's attempts to cut educational costs and his emphasis on the individualization of instruction reflect a neoliberal financial ideology. Many neoliberal practices remain unclearly articulated within the integrative apparatus. The broad acceptance for neoliberal policies across the globe and within the political centre of many parliaments around the world makes it difficult to approach the non-discursive practices of budget cuts and reduced welfare payments through discursive means. Even if we consider Germany's economy to be an ordoliberal system, Sarrazin's *rhetoric* is distinctly neoliberal and emphasizes deregulation, individualization, and privatization. The role that a state plays in a traditional social market economy is virtually absent from rhetoric that emphasizes efficiency, cost-saving, and the logic of productivity at the expense of the social contract. Rather than criticizing a system, commentators are more likely to criticize race, culture, or poverty.

Before his racist statements came to light in the *Lettre* interview, Sarrazin had also made multiple other statements that humiliated poor white Germans who received welfare benefits. Some of the more colourful statements he made included curiously specific budgeting schemes whereby welfare recipients should feed themselves on sausage and thereby spend less than 4 euros a day on food. (Sarrazin helpfully provided a precisely budgeted shopping list.)[47] Similarly erratic and categorically false remarks about welfare recipients using too much energy to heat their homes attempted to humiliate poor people for not being tough enough to survive the cold, but even that humiliation was counterfactual: welfare recipients *do not pay for heating costs* if they receive state financial assistance.[48] An interview between Sarrazin and journalist Matthias Lohre in the left-wing Berlin daily *die taz* from 2006 compiles a variety of Sarrazin's random public statements, including the opinion that Berliners wear more sweatpants (*Trainingsanzüge*) than anyone else in the world, and that Berlin would be fine if the numbers of opera houses and theatres were cut in half. Comments on fashion and limiting the number of cultural institutions are not only characteristic of a right-wing politics invested in projecting a "respectable" image of citizens, but also reflect a far-right attempt to limit forms of cultural expression.[49] Sarrazin consistently made public statements about the need for budget cuts to public institutions as well as uniquely specific critiques of how poor people spent their money. His statements, of which there are surely many more, reveal a functionary invested in austerity who portrays humanistic and aesthetic pursuits in the terms of cost-benefit analyses, rather than seeing aesthetics as a good unto itself.

In the same 2006 *taz* interview, journalist Lohre describes Sarrazin's reputation as that of a budgetary "hard ass" (*harter Hund*). Sarrazin responded, "But I hold back verbally. I only say what's necessary."[50] After the publication of his book, Sarrazin's reputation as a budgetary "hard ass" persisted – although by that time, no one could argue during the media frenzy that followed that Sarrazin had spared any words. During the press conference at the BPK, one journalist reported on a small protest against the event outside the building. One protestor held a much-photographed sign that consisted of a caricature of Sarrazin and two words: "Shut up!"[51]

Scholars of the German welfare state frequently note how cost-saving and *leistungsorientierte* (productivity) policies trap the poor in systems of economic and labour exploitation.[52] The emphasis on individual achievement works in a similar fashion, obscuring systemic disadvantages and the structural obstacles immigrants and asylum seekers face. Cuts to social welfare benefits or linking social welfare benefits to labour requirements (known as workfare in the US or colloquially as "One-Euro-Jobs" in Germany) do not promote independence and innovation among the poor. Instead, in order to keep their benefits, poor people are forced either into the black market and exploited as they provide additional labour below minimum wage to augment their benefits, or they are artificially kept in a cycle of poverty if the jobs they are trained for do not pay a wage any higher than their benefit checks.[53]

Rational efficiency in economic policies creates self-fulfilling social prophecies because it denies both the realities of systemic oppression and the need for funding social welfare benefits as a kind of class compromise that mitigates the income inequality between the business elites and the working poor. Neoliberal ideology denies the need for regulation of government and business, but increases the regulation of everyday lives, especially of the poor, limiting civil liberties for regular people while it expands the personal and commercial liberties of the business class.[54] Neoliberal philosophy also asserts a need for efficiency, but effectively thwarts the foundation of state-wide, governmental systems that could provide the fundamental national or even transnational regulatory structures to promote efficient, sustainable practices at scale. Neoliberal policies are critical to an integration apparatus because they are part of the centrifugal force that allows integration politics to expand. The proliferation of regulations imposed on everyday lives, coupled with sanctions and artificially created poverty, systematically thwarts the upward mobility that could negate the neoliberal rhetoric blaming the poor for their own poverty and result in broader, more diverse degrees of civic and labour participation.[55] If housing policy and segregation were the non-discursive practices that informed discourses of de facto segregation in German integration debates, budget cuts to state services served as one of the non-discursive policy decisions that fused the nodes of race and culture with class and locked those marked as unintegrable into positions of economic precarity by limiting their access to material resources.

In this model, the economic stagnation for all classes except the business elite creates an environment in which ethnic and racial prejudice can be mobilized in economic terms. An emphasis on competition and productivity creates conditions in which most workers are forced to fight for (artificially limited) resources.[56] German political scientist Christoph Butterwege articulates clearly how competition for resources leads to social exclusion:

> A "national state of competition" (*nationaler Wettbewerbsstaat*, Joachim Hirsch) that doesn't want to be a conventional welfare state bearing a comprehensive responsibility for social security and justice, exacerbates social inequality through its radical political economy of the market and in this manner prepares a sounding board for social processes of exclusion and ethnicization. The more competition found between state and human relationships, the easier it is for ethnic and cultural difference to take on political weight.[57]

Sarrazin's racialized class antagonism was set into motion through his power over budgetary matters for the city-state of Berlin, and his "achievements" in that position perform both functions: cuts promote competition and – by extension – create conditions of scarcity. Instead of promoting a collective responsibility for the state to distribute resources, financial matters are individualized, which simultaneously increases the distance between rich and poor.[58] The resulting economic exclusion from upward mobility creates an environment in which the poor, who are playing with a radically compromised hand, are humiliated for their station – and through Sarrazin's racist arguments – racialized as a group undeserving of economic or social mobility.

Sarrazin's book was spectacularly popular in 2010 *because* his ideas were not unique. Butterwege argues that Sarrazin managed to take discourses that had circulated for two decades in public life, such as debates about the threat to German prosperity through globalization, demographic shifts prompted by lower birth rates, and critiques of "*Sozialschmarotzer*" (welfare freeloaders), and successfully "connected, packaged, and exaggerated" them.[59]

Most importantly, what Butterwege's analysis reveals is how similar Sarrazin's logic is to other politicians in the German federal government who promote neoliberal policy. He compares Sarrazin's statements to those of Guido Westerwelle, the head of the FDP (Germany's equivalent to a libertarian party), who was serving as the vice chancellor in 2010. Butterwege argues that Westerwelle vehemently rejected charges that he was a neoliberal, preferring to call himself a "neosocial" politician – similar to Sarrazin's insistence that he was a Social Democrat.[60] But Butterwege also points out that Westerwelle used language similar to Sarrazin during debates about Hartz IV benefits (German long-term welfare). Westerwelle complained about "social criminality" among welfare recipients, advocated for a German form of trickle-down economics to support welfare cuts, requiring the German state to acquire wealth before paying out welfare benefits, and emphasized that because workers produce more, the employed should have a right to maintain a higher standard of living than those on welfare: "Productivity has to be worth it, and those who work have to have more than those who don't work."[61] Butterwege comments sarcastically that Westerwelle's statements could be used against him, since Westerwelle surely made more money from dividends in a single hour than millions of hard-working people in the Federal Republic make in a year.[62] For two politicians who promoted similar policies, it is contradictory to find evidence that Sarrazin and Westerwelle traded pointed political barbs. During reforms to the welfare benefit system in 2010, Sarrazin (!) even accused Westerwelle of "spiritual poverty" for being too cruel to welfare recipients.[63]

A cost-benefit analysis of immigrants and their productivity limits the ability of Germans to imagine a different form of national identity that could include immigrant participation at all levels of economic, social, political, and cultural life. Sarrazin's rhetoric about Muslim immigrants as an economic liability reveals that he perceives immigrants not as humans but rather as cogs in a capitalist machine, worthy of notice only if they are "productive." This rhetoric deliberately misreads the contributions of immigrants to society as a whole. Underclasses disproportionately labour in undesirable positions in ways that stabilize and promote the comfort of the white-collar and upper classes – something vividly on display during the COVID-19 pandemic – who generally garner wealth from the ability of capital to reproduce itself. If, as Bade argues, integration politics must be understood as social politics for all Germans, then critiques of the white German poor are just as indicative of self-fulfilling neoliberal prophecies as racist critiques of Turkish- and Arab-Germans as welfare "cheats" or as uneducated residents who are considered unfit to lead in the German public sphere.

Cuts to social programs and a lack of support for the welfare state are instrumental facets of Sarrazin's political history and his rhetoric, but they are not unique ideas: they exist across a wide section of the political spectrum, from the SPD to the FDP to the far right. The integrative apparatus requires immigrants prove they are both socially and systemically integrated. Sarrazin's book made social incorporation dependent upon the incorporation of immigrants into the market as "productive" forces. But these integrative demands were predicated on economic systems that actively worked against immigrants and the ethnic German poor gaining access to the employment market. While the racialized poor and white ethnic German poor are both unfairly targeted, each identity category – as Crenshaw argued in her early research on intersectional identities – captures different sociological effects. Poor white Germans are targeted and lack certain privileges that middle and upper-class Germans have. They are not, however, in danger of losing their citizenship, being discriminated against for having a foreign name during a job search and are unlikely to be attacked for their (white) appearance (unless they have a divergent gender identity, a disability, or for some other reason do not pass). This distinction between a racial underclass and a white German underclass is one of the effects of globalization on national identity, as a bifurcation of the lower class emerges that splits the lower class into multiple underclasses that are differently racialized. Anyone of any race can have any class identity, but the privileges of whiteness awarded in such a system are most likely to confine people of colour, immigrants, and refugees to a racialized underclass that exists alongside a white German working poor.[64]

Kelek and Sarrazin: Identity as Alibi

The integrative apparatus, as it exists in contemporary Germany under late capitalism, also requires celebrity. As the density of connections between various social structures increases, it becomes more and more difficult to view an apparatus in its entirety. An apparatus of security in the emerging societies of modernity, as Foucault explored in his lectures at the Collège de France, dealt with concrete changes on a small scale that emerged in societies that were only just discovering the art of governing.[65] In complex societies, existing structures of governmentality allow the density of nodes and networks to expand exponentially when there is enough energy to facilitate the creation of new connections. Celebrity serves a specific function within an apparatus because the concentration of attention directed towards one person or one event creates connections that extend out from celebrity into multiple directions. The emphasis in neoliberal ideology on individualism merges with the valorization of celebrity to elevate individuals as exceptional and deserving of concentrated media attention. The sheer volume of discursive attention offered by the media then connects celebrities with the structures that produce new philosophies, refine or reinvent discursive practices, influence the construction of ideology and, finally, garner economic power through the monetization of content. Celebrity and a 24-hour news cycle also produce a massive quantity of speech acts, effectively accelerating the entire process by which an apparatus expands.

It is therefore no surprise that Thilo Sarrazin asked Necla Kelek to introduce his book during the press conference at the *BPK* on 30 August

2010. Not only did Kelek's political views overlap with Sarrazin's, but the same identity contradictions that protected Kelek from charges of racism in her own work served to protect Sarrazin as well. Creating a media performance in which a German-Turkish woman absolved Sarrazin of the charges of racism that dogged the publication of his interview with *Lettre International* set the stage for Sarrazin to have a ready alibi for the inevitable charges of anti-Semitism and racism that accompanied the press coverage of his book.[66]

Kelek's remarks during the press conference feature pervasively stigmatizing language against Muslims. In her speech, Kelek summarizes Sarrazin's argument that "cultural impediments" will make it impossible for Muslims to become engineers and highly trained workers. She treats Sarrazin's opinion about the inheritability of intelligence as fact: when white German birth rates drop, she says, this drop will correspond to Germany "producing less techno-scientific intelligence."[67] Twelve minutes into her speech, Kelek fulfills her function as living alibi for Sarrazin's book, pointing out that her opinions about Islam confirm Sarrazin's depiction in *Deutschland schafft sich ab* and that any charges against Sarrazin as racist emerge from others' "ignorance": "Ladies and Gentlemen, you know that I don't just define Islam as a faith, but also as a political ideology and social system. And here is no race, but rather a cultural system that is also permitted to be criticized (*kritisiert*) and studied (*überprüft*) and re-thought (*überdacht*)."[68]

Kelek's speech maps out the political camps within integration politics. She includes Sarrazin as the author who has "quantitatively" proven the "qualitative" work of *Islamkritiker_innen* Seyran Ateş, Güner Balcı, Kirsten Heisig, Heinz Buschkowski, and Kelek herself. This move creates a parallel knowledge structure for *Islamkritik*, cementing the divide between researchers and polemic authors. Finally, she marks Sarrazin as merely a critic of mainstream integration politics, which she argues is a field of policy built upon a shaky foundation. Kelek ends her nearly 20-minute speech with a critique of mainstream politics, blaming the mainstream parties for ignoring the topics of integration and Islam since the federal election of 2009. I find this a rather cheeky admonishment given the extensive attention government officials paid to her books in 2005, as I explored in chapter 1.

Over the course of Kelek's introduction, she includes a number of statements that can be read as both neoliberal and as couched in right-wing rhetoric. Some of her most curious statements pretend to raise the question of whether Sarrazin should be considered right wing, a rather baffling train of thought, given her admission that Sarrazin is concerned about white people losing their majority and argues for limiting immigration from Muslim countries. These two topics are practically kindling for media attention to the right wing and illustrate the nativism characteristic of the right-wing party family. At the same time that Kelek argues against viewing Sarrazin as anything other than a Social Democrat, she mobilizes the rhetoric common to right-wing politicians who admit that they say horrible things, but argue that hateful speech is acceptable in the service of broader social goals: "My conclusion: a responsible citizen has drastically used his head to voice bitter truths and thoughts about Germany here [*hat sich um Deutschland einen Kopf gemacht*]. And, for these thoughts, Thilo Sarrazin is now obviously to be beheaded [*Und um diesen Kopf soll Thilo Sarrazin jetzt offensichtlich kürzer gemacht werden*]."[69] Finally, she pleads for all Germans to rebuild the country together: "We have to return to this – we have to learn to rebuild this country together, and above all things, to then permit critical thoughts. And [this is] so that we can find a common consensus."[70] From the vantage point of 2019, as I draft this chapter, it is impossible not to see the nationalistic connotation in any rhetoric about national renewal.

Cultural Rejection of Sarrazin – German Debates about Race

In the public debate that followed the publication of *Deutschland schafft sich ab*, journalists covering Sarrazin sidestepped the question of racism, politicians responded to Sarrazin with a mix of revulsion and enthusiasm, and the economic foundation of Sarrazin's arguments remained broadly uninterrogated. However, the cultural counteroffensive to Sarrazin's book from artists and public intellectuals was swift. Unsurprisingly, this counter-offensive was led by immigrants, their children, and Germans of colour. In *European Others*, El-Tayeb articulated in a trans-European context how the very notion of Europe is built upon whiteness. Building upon Avery Gordon's notion of "haunting," El-Tayeb queers European identities in order to "make [...] visible historical memory as a constantly (re)constructed process, shaped by interventions into the present that also always contest visions of the past."[71] European identity, she argues, still places people of colour outside European national and postnational communities, and racializing processes still haunt a Europe that insists it remains "untouched by the devastating ideology of race it exported all over the world."[72] European processes of racialization continue to place people of colour outside the limits of the new, supposedly inclusive, transnational community of Europeans. Proof that race and racialization haunt European society can be seen in Gordon's insistence that a haunted environment produces the specific urgency of "a something-to-be-done."[73] While this sense of urgency is similar to how an apparatus designates certain "problems" as "urgent," these two forms of urgency could not be more different. The something-to-be-done for El-Tayeb lies in the queered and performative responses by Europeans of colour to "Europe's silent racializations and ethnicizations" that highlight how social relationships are both situational and constructed. Within an apparatus, elites mark problems as urgent in order to manage a population, either by preserving inequitable social relations or compelling subjects into compliance through discipline or punishment. And it would be a mistake, in light of these responses, to simply accept that these methods of population management stemming from governmentality are always pervasive, sufficient, or successful.

By October 2010 – less than eight weeks after the publication of Sarrazin's book – the Berlin cultural organization *Werkstatt der Kulturen* had organized a three-part discussion series called "Playing in the Dark: Or the Racism Trap," featuring controversial TV journalist Michel Friedman as moderator. Host of *Studio Friedman*, a weekly program on N24 (a 24-hour news channel similar to CNN), Friedman is the son of Holocaust survivors and was one of the first people to accuse Sarrazin of racist ideas in the public sphere.[74] "Playing in the Dark," of course, is the title of Toni Morrison's critique of whiteness in literature. Consequently, I can only assume that the inter-textual reference chosen explicitly by the events' organizers was clear, broadcasting that these panel discussions would be rigorous and intellectually stimulating – and would not shy away from an interrogation of whiteness and white supremacy.

I attended all three of these panel discussions featuring well-known cultural figures and academic scholars from Germany. Each discussion had a packed house. Kien Nghi Ha, Naika Foroutan, Mekonnen Mesghena, Anetta Kahane, Maisha-Maureen Auma, Shermin Langhoff, Nadja Ofuatey-Alazard, Imran Ayata, and many other participants represented some of the most well-known cultural commentators, academics, and public intellectuals from marginalized groups across Germany. Many of these panelists were based in Berlin, which is not only the capital city but also home to multiple universities at which several panelists worked. For nearly two hours at a time, discussants answered questions that delved into their research projects, cultural anti-racist work, and theoretical framings of how racism functions. At the prompting of Friedman as moderator, many researchers were also encouraged to perform various types of affective labour about their own identities. Panelists engaged with the personal effects of how the

Sarrazin scandal affected their relationship to themselves, to their histories, and to their national identity as Germans.[75] Audience members were equally engaged, participating fully in back-and-forth negotiations about how different groups experience racist behaviour and what kinds of anti-racist efforts could further shape society.[76]

The educational function of these discussions, which offered to teach a local and general audience about the dynamics of racism and racist exclusion by inviting experts – not opinion commentators – to participate in discussions using conversational, and yet still theoretically acute language, provided a rigorous experience for the attendees. Thirteen years later, videos of these events are still available on YouTube – in fact, they were the first YouTube videos the WdK uploaded.[77] Thousands of people have watched them over a decade, which is rather remarkable for a panel discussion. A good number of the panelists continue to work on the topics of race, ethnicity, and national identity, such as Naika Foroutan, who now heads a prestigious excellence cluster at the Humboldt University of Berlin and published a book for academic audiences called *Die postmigrantische Gesellschaft* (The Postmigrant Society) in 2019.[78] Shermin Langhoff, a well-known theatre director who founded the Ballhaus Naunynstraße Theater and raised the theatre to international prominence before becoming the artistic director of the Maxim Gorki Theater, was awarded the Federal Medal of Honour in 2017 for her work on postmigrant theatre forms. On an editorializing note, I do not remember panelists in 2010 responding with any degree of resignation to the Sarrazin scandal. Instead, I had the impression that these events fit very much under the heading of what Gordon and El-Tayeb designate as "something to be done."

Only six months after the publication of *Deutschland schafft sich ab*, novelist and journalist Hilal Sezgin brought together 30 contributors who authored short essays, often autobiographical, that pushed back against stereotypical portrayals of immigrants that had become more common during the Sarrazin scandal. The book's title was a direct response to Sarrazin's book *Manifest der Vielen: Deutschland erfindet sich neu* (Manifesto of the Many: Germany Reinvents Itself). Germany was not making itself obsolete, the authors argued: it was reinventing itself. The release of this book took place at the Maxim Gorki Theater in Berlin. Ijoma Mangold, the literary critic for *Die Zeit*, remarked in his review of the book and event that many edited collections such as this one serve only to preach to the choir. But *Manifest der Vielen* struck a different chord after the Sarrazin scandal: "The Gorki Theater was filled to overflowing. The most varied milieus – from headscarves to pocket squares – were there. Everyone could feel it: there's a lot of catching up to do. We need to update our sense of reality."[79]

Cultural critics and artists continue to work in this vein, with some of the most recent examples coming from Jewish and Jewish refugee communities. Max Czollek and Sasha Marianna Salzmann, both writers and theatre artists, curated a festival called *Desintegration: Ein Kongress zeitgenössischer jüdischer Positionen* (Disintegration: A Congress of Contemporary Jewish Positions) that ran at the Gorki Theater in 2016. The next year, Salzmann published *Beside Myself*, their debut novel that follows the migration pathway of a refugee family from Russia. In 2018, Czollek published a book called *Desintegriert Euch!* (Disintegrate!), the same year that Salzmann contributed a collection of essays by Hengameh Yaghoobifarah and Fatma Aydemir in response to Horst Seehofer's renaming of the Interior Ministry the Homeland Ministry (*Heimatministerium*). The journalistic discourse is not all powerful, and arts organizations and other nonprofits are often the sources of both social and political critique.

In the early 2000s, Klaus Bade published an essay that laid out the terms for what he called a *"nachholende Integrationspolitik"* (catch-up integration politics).[80] While partially a concession to discourses that linked the contemporary lack of integration policy to a lack of early policy during the guest worker era, Bade made a compelling case in this essay for the notion that successful integration is both the norm in Germany as well as invisible. The entire field of integration politics is based on foregrounding integration *problems* rather than highlighting integrative *successes*. Seeing integration as an urgent problem sets the preconditions for an apparatus of integration to emerge. Loud insistence on the visibility of integrative problems, Bade argues, is how Sarrazin and Kelek kept a discussion going that not only was and is out of date, but which simultaneously furthered their own celebrity at the cost of stoking animosity and polarization within German society. In *Kritik und Gewalt*, Bade published a strikingly personal account of his role in the political discussions about integration during the time of Kelek and Sarrazin's rise. In 2010, he was the head of the *Der Sachverständigenrat deutscher Stiftungen für Integration und Migration* (The Council of Experts from German Foundations for Integration and Migration). The SVR, a think tank, published an evidence-based research report about integration in March 2010, merely a few months before the Sarrazin scandal broke. This report showed that German society was successfully integrating the large majority of immigrants and that education – precisely the sector that Sarrazin wanted to cut funding for and make more "productive" – was showing a particularly high level of improvement for immigrant children, especially after the PISA shock of 2001.[81] Part of Bade's desire to publish his account of the study's release just months before the Sarrazin scandal broke in 2010 is surely fuelled by his obvious outrage at Sarrazin's arguments as well as the outrage felt by researchers when the media gets a story wrong. Bade's book occupies a similar role in the Sarrazin scandal as the petition by 60 migration researchers published in *Die Zeit* after the rise of Kelek's star: Bade was a dismayed researcher trying to set things straight on a political landscape no longer able to evaluate claims to the truth.

After Sarrazin's book was published, the term "integration" was on everyone's lips: a sociological concept had fully arrived in every day speech. While all of the cultural responses to Sarrazin constituted attempts to educate Germans of all backgrounds about the dynamics at play about integration politics, none of these efforts could generate a response of sufficient counterweight to the press attention and economic success of Sarrazin's book and his ability to mobilize a journalistic machine. As a publicity stunt, journalist Güner Balci took Sarrazin on a tour through Kreuzberg in July 2011, where the reaction to Sarrazin in immigrant neighbourhoods and establishments was vicious. I lived in Berlin at this time and Sarrazin's "tour" through the "ghetto" was accompanied by a great deal of *Schadenfreude* and sarcastic laughter the next day at work. However, everyone had heard of Sarrazin's walk through Kreuzberg, but no one I knew had attended the WdK talks. The 8,000 views of an educational video on YouTube is but a speck of dust compared to the 1.1 million book copies sold of *Deutschland schafft sich ab* and the days and weeks of free media coverage about the book's publication. Unfortunately, the WdK was eventually starved of resources by the Berlin Senate and closed.[82] Sarrazin – in contrast – has published three more books and is a millionaire, despite having been finally kicked out of the SPD for his racist views in 2020.[83] Sales figures and the effect of commercial success on broader political conversations suggest that capital and its circulation through the commodification of content is a critical node of the integrative apparatus. The publishing industry – as an institution – provides material resources to elite political actors based on their discursive power. The commercial success of content fuels celebrity and provides elite actors with a platform through which media attention picks up and mobilizes discourse that informs both policies and legal measures. Sarrazin mobilized an ideology of white supremacy to do what white supremacy does best: assert privilege and keep undesired groups from claiming resources.

While Kelek's polemics appeared to cast gender, culture, and religion as the primary sociological problems for Germany, they also obscured her own class bias as an educated Turkish-German who places herself in the genealogy of secular politics beginning with Atatürk, the founder of the Turkish Republic. If Kelek's polemic rendered classism invisible to the general reader, what discussing Sarrazin's polemic revealed was that many of these "culturalized" conversations about race obscured the role that the welfare apparatus plays in integration politics. Sarrazin's statements were both racist and classist. He demonized white Germans of low socioeconomic status, but also used racist critique of immigrant communities and the construction of racial hierarchies to deflect from his distaste for poverty and inefficiency. The neoliberal framing of the welfare state and the subjects caught within it as insufficiently individualized, dependent, and a burden to society overlaps easily with integration rhetoric about marginalized groups who are seen as "victims" of collective cultural practices, dependent on financial support from the state, and who Sarrazin portrays as negatively affecting German social life. That all of these demographics may be German citizens, endowed with all the participatory rights German citizenship offers, is something both authors obscure. Kelek and Sarrazin working together as celebrities, pushing similar forms of right-wing rhetoric that deny certain groups full agency in the German political and public spheres, reflects how intersectional integration debates inherently are: gender, race, class, and national identity all act upon integrative rhetoric in ways that permit an integrative apparatus to expand across multiple identity categories, hailing more subjects than simply the descendants of guest workers or specific ethnic groups. In terms of the Sarrazin scandal, Sarrazin's rhetoric was designed to limit the agency and choices available to the German poor and did so by relentlessly racializing immigrants and their descendants as a class.

The real question embedded within the Sarrazin scandal, however, is less about *how* Sarrazin came to his conclusions and more about *why* he was able to find such a receptive audience for counterfactual ideas. If most immigrants to Germany adjust without difficulty, why – after nearly 50 years of state-sponsored migration – were so many people willing to believe the narrative about integration that Sarrazin peddled? The next four chapters will pull back from the immediacy of politicized media scandal in order to examine how historical continuities in migration policy and politics have been actively forgotten.

PART TWO

Historical Origins: The Emergence
of Integration Politics

Chapter Four

Integration and Ethnic Similarities

In order to understand how specific groups of immigrants and refugees are affected differently by the consolidation of integration policies in contemporary Germany, we need to return to the early policies of the postwar German state – decades before the start of the guest worker policies that are frequently marked in public discourse as the moment at which mass migration began. White subjects marked in some way as "German" have consistently been privileged in integration politics. Being marked as both "white" and "German" permitted various groups – from Eastern European expellees after 1945 to so-called late settlers from the collapsing Soviet Union nearly 50 years later – to gain access to German political and public spaces without being compelled to conform to the rhetoric of integration.

During the postwar chaos in Europe after 1945, millions of people were crossing the continent, many of them on foot. Two world wars had been fought to defend a variety of nationalist principles, and ethnic belonging still served as the foundation for national belonging. After the war, West Germans rebuilt their society as an exemplary social democracy, with one of the strongest economies in Europe. West Germans forged a new national identity founded on a sense of guilt for the destruction waged by the Nazi dictatorship and were committed to making their country both a democracy and a refuge for displaced peoples and the persecuted. The West German Basic Law (the place-holding document created in the context of the East-West division in 1949 that serves to this day as Germany's Constitution) included asylum as a basic right. Both Germans and international politicians largely understood this move to be a way to atone for imperial expansion and genocide under Nazi rule.

West German attitudes towards newcomers directly after the war and into the 1960s coalesced around two groups of people who played formidable roles in rebuilding the Federal Republic. One group is known by many different names: *Vertriebene* (expellees), *Aussiedler* (settlers), *Ausgewiesene* (deportees), *Umsiedler* (resettlers) or *Neubürger* (new citizens). All of these names describe more than 12 million people who were expelled from former German territory or from minority German communities in Eastern Europe after the Second World War as mandated by Article XIII of the Potsdam Agreement, signed by the leaders of the Soviet Union, the United States, and Great Britain in August 1945. Ethnic Germans were expelled from territories in Poland, Hungary, Yugoslavia, Czechoslovakia, Romania, and other states then part of the Soviet Union. While the French occupation forces, not having signed the Potsdam Agreement, largely resisted accepting them, by 1946 the British and American Occupied Zones had accepted nearly 6 million expellees; the Soviet Occupied Zone had accepted 3.6 million.[1] Those numbers rose into the early 1950s, and later included "refugees" (*Flüchtlinge*) from the Soviet Zone and the German Democratic Republic who moved into West Germany. The other group was colloquially known as guest workers.

The question of how we portray the successful social, economic, and political incorporation of newcomers lingers because local Germans in 1945 were loathe to view ethnic German expellees as equals. The devastation incurred by Nazi aggression was staggering. Despite ethnonationalism serving as the foundation for both territory and demography, local populations resisted the arrival of 12 million expellees into a territory a bit smaller than the state of Montana, where starvation, rape, and disease were everyday occurrences.[2] Historian Adam Seipp points out that while expellees thought they had a "clear claim to sympathy" and "chafed at the ambivalent welcome they received at the end of often harrowing treks," expellees "looked, sounded, and behaved as foreigners in existing German communities already facing occupation, urban refugees, and [...] large numbers of foreign DPs."[3] Seipp cites an ambivalent opinion column from the *Main-Post* from 29 December 1945, in which the author claimed expellees were "the driftwood of war, but they are German like us and so it is our duty to help them build a new future for themselves."[4] Ethnic belonging thus connected locals to expellees and served as the foundation for any gesture of solidarity, no matter how reluctantly given. In spite of this reluctant solidarity, ethnic German expellees were still subject to a process of downward mobility due to the conditions of their expulsion and the deprivations of the postwar period. There was no integrative apparatus to facilitate their incorporation into social relationships or the formal economy. However, the incorporation of the expellees is considered to be one of the success stories of the nascent Federal Republic, and the obstacles expellees faced have been forgotten in contemporary German cultural memory. The lack of an integrative apparatus served in critical ways to *facilitate* their incorporation, especially as many expellees either maintained or were granted access to German citizenship. It is the convergence of ethnic belonging and national belonging that made the incorporation of expellees easier to narrate, and this process stands in staunch contrast to the incorporation of foreign workers and other newcomers that I will take up later.

Despite the differences between capitalism and socialism, East Germany also incorporated expellees quickly and benefitted from their labour. Consequently, East German migration history shares some similarities with that of the Federal Republic and thus has relevance for understanding integration politics in united Germany today. One important difference, however, is that socialist discourse in the German Democratic Republic suppressed ethnic identity in favour of allegiance to a new collective worker identity.[5] Because ethnic German expellees to the German Democratic Republic were simply expected to adapt in the Soviet Occupied Zone in the years following the war, German historian Michael Schwartz argues that expellees underwent a process of "forced assimilation."[6] To acknowledge that *Umsiedler* (the initial bureaucratic term for expellees in the GDR) had been forcefully expelled from their homes would have required the Soviet Union to acknowledge the violence it had inflicted on both Poland and the German territories during and after the war.[7] Consequently, expellee identity was suppressed in East Germany.[8] Expellees were threatened with imprisonment if they attempted to organize based on their identity, and even singing songs well-known within the expellee community constituted an offence punishable by up to eight years in jail.[9] This suppression made it easier to ignore how expellees were incorporated into the GDR. The official party line simply reiterated that the expellees had been rapidly and seamlessly incorporated into the socialist collective.[10]

The Expulsion of Ethnic Germans from Eastern Europe

Between 1944 and 1950, 12.5 million ethnic Germans were expelled.[11] Some *Reichsdeutsche* (citizens of Nazi Germany) had already begun to flee west under Nazi orders as the Soviet forces advanced from the east at the end of the war.[12] Others were forced to abandon their homes and livelihoods, having lived in the east for generations.[13] State rhetoric in the 1960s in both Poland and East Germany argued that forced migration was an appropriate response to Nazi atrocities. To those ethnic

Germans whose families had lived in these places for generations, however, the expulsion surely felt like calculated revenge.[14]

The so-called Big Three (Roosevelt, Churchill, and Stalin) each had different opinions on the viability and usefulness of forcing millions of people to enter German territory after the war's end. The United States officially endorsed the concept of self-determination; for that reason, US officials supported minority ethnic groups' right to choose their national affiliation.[15] According to R.M. Douglas, however, the Americans abandoned their principles under the strain of "total war."[16] British Prime Minister Winston Churchill saw a need for what he had previously referred to as "population transfers," and there are many documents that attest to Churchill's support for expulsion.[17] Specifically, he suggested moving ethnic Germans into "rump Germany" (the FRG) as a way preserve the national identities of European nation-states without permitting Prussian militarism to re-emerge.[18] Stalin, perhaps unsurprisingly, was the most adamant supporter of forced migration under any conditions. Stalin had already grabbed land for Russia from Eastern Poland in 1939, expelling 2 million Poles in the process, and had no intention of giving up that recently acquired land to a newly independent Polish state.[19] Instead, he preferred to see Poland "compensated" for its losses by westward territorial expansion up to the natural borders created by the Oder and Neisse rivers, across territory long considered German.[20]

Without the underlying nationalist logic that touted ethnic homogeneity as the ideal demographic structure for nation-states, ethnic Germans might never have been expelled from Eastern Europe. As historians Rita Chin and Heide Fehrenbach put it, "By suggesting that 'mixture' was politically dangerous and destabilizing, the postwar political strategy of ethnic cleansing contributed to the cultivation of a culture of purity."[21] Today, various kinds of European "purists" continue to construct national identities through the language of ethnic belonging, and these identities are on vivid display among right-leaning Europeans who vehemently reject both economic and refugee migration in the twenty-first century.

During the postwar years, then, the expulsions almost certainly strengthened the notion that ethnic belonging determines national belonging. And yet, the Nazi empire itself – despite its racist rhetoric – had been multiethnic. The Nazi economy relied on foreign and slave labour to increase production, and transporting all of these groups mixed many European ethnic groups and cultures – as migration always does. Consequently, the collapse of the Nazi empire produced migration movements on a scale that is difficult to fathom. Migration studies scholar Barbara Dietz argues that Germany became "the most important immigration country in Europe" after the Second World War.[22] Expellees, refugees, asylum seekers, displaced persons, prisoners of war, concentration camp victims, and labour migrants all entered Germany after the war. Historian Klaus Bade suggests that the years 1939–45 may have seen 50–60 million refugees – 10 per cent of the European population – in transit across Europe.[23] As a point of contrast, consider that refugee movement into Europe over the years 2015–16 saw a bit more than five million people enter the entire continent.[24]

The expulsions were brutal. Millions of people died, and the testimonies of survivors, recorded in oral histories, recount over and over again stories of rape and sexual violence inflicted on women and girls.[25] The sheer scale of the trauma experienced by expellees would suggest that historians view the expulsions as a trans-European event with consequences for generations to come. And yet, by the early 1950s, political leaders and journalists in both Germanies celebrated the successful incorporation of all ethnic German expellees into East and West German society. Contemporary commentators still view the incorporation of 12 million ethnic Germans, especially in the Federal Republic, as a success story.[26] Telling this story of the expulsions portrays the German state as a competent and functioning entity capable of absorbing millions of assimilated immigrants without inflicting permanent damage on either its democracy or its economy.

This narrative of success also stands in dramatic contrast to how contemporary Germans demand immigrants, refugees, and people of colour integrate. In the Federal Republic, debates about the integration of foreign workers and their descendants have been front and centre in the national political arena for nearly half a century, while discussions of incorporating ethnic German expellees virtually disappeared within a decade. How was it possible for such a large number of immigrants to have been seamlessly absorbed into the German nation in such a short time? And why was a similar narrative of success unavailable to foreign workers and their descendants?

The Arrival of the Expellees

After the war, Stalin's unwillingness to permit the Soviet Occupied Zone to merge with the French, British, and American Occupied Zones effectively divided the German territory of 1937 into three parts: West Germany, the Soviet Occupied Zone (later East Germany), and the land now belonging to different countries (Poland, Czechoslovakia, Russia, and the Baltic states). These divisions separated West Germany, the industrial centre of the German empire, from a great deal of land in the east that had previously been used for agriculture. The eastern areas, which now belonged to Poland, had traditionally fed the West German industrial areas: East Prussia and Pomerania had been the breadbasket of Germany. Several states in the Soviet Zone (the areas that would become the German Democratic Republic), like Brandenburg, had also been traditionally agricultural – meaning their separation from the industrial centres of the West also profoundly disrupted the economy. The new German borders were thus just as disruptive to the West and East German economies as they were to German culture, since dividing a country into three parts raised many questions about both what a German state should be or produce and who should belong to it (or them). Against this backdrop of radical geographic change, pressing fears of famine emerged in the Western Occupied Zones. The practice of dismantling factories and other industrial property as a form of reparations paid to the Soviet Union also interrupted the production of goods and the reconstruction of housing and industry in the East for decades.

The lack of sanitation, housing, and industry made survival difficult and formal employment nearly impossible for almost everyone living in Occupied Germany. Despite the population losses created by war and genocide, the expulsion of ethnic Germans into the four occupied zones led to substantial population growth that increased population density and more than made up for soldier and civilian deaths. This population growth made the task of caring for expellees seem an impossible burden for locals to bear. The population of Schleswig-Holstein, the poorest and most rural state of West Germany, grew by a whopping 70 per cent between 1939 and 1948.[27] A decade later, 90 per cent of the population growth between 1950 and 1960 was attributed to the influx of refugees. As of 1960, 23.9 per cent of the total population of West Germany could be classified as either expellee or refugees from the German Democratic Republic.[28] The rapidity of the expulsions and utter material lack left little room for a calculated approach to incorporating the expellees. In the absence of a state, it is very difficult to speak of any coherent integration policy before 1949.

The *need* for some kind of policy, however, became evident as soon as the expulsions began. These early policy choices, which were strongly shaped by the ideologies and value systems of the military occupiers, reflect a policy of incorporation rather than the later insistence on integration which emerged in the 1970s in West Germany. The integrative apparatus requires a sense of historical urgency to justify a system of population management that promotes productivity at the same time that it neutralizes disintegrative potential; the integrative apparatus is therefore highly normative and encourages assimilation to social and political norms. But an apparatus exists in the networks between institutions, rather than in the institutions themselves, and in the immediate devastation that followed the war, these institutional networks had broken down. Integration politics under these conditions would not arise in an organized form. In the years of the occupation, expellees, displaced persons, returning soldiers, prisoners of war, local civilian populations, *and* the military occupiers were *all* concerned with survival and the provision of basic needs. The local population, however, increasingly viewed the expellees as second-class citizens who should not be entitled to aid at a moment when local Germans were also threatened by famine. It was under these circumstances that the military government – especially in the British and American Zones – tried to create measures to incorporate those who had been expelled.

Housing and employment were two of the most important and pressing issues for all residents. Since bombing had decimated urban housing stock, many expellees were crowded into rural areas, sometimes outnumbering the local village population. Mecklenburg-Vorpommern – which shared a border with the former eastern territories – was majority expellee as early as October 1945. Just five months after the war ended, expellees made up 56 per cent of the state's population.[29] Many were interned with rural local German families with extra space. As could be expected, forcing residents to share their private spaces created tensions and resentment, especially when the arrangements put strangers in such intimate spaces as kitchens, bathing areas, and laundries.[30]

Many locals also considered expellees to be a political threat. The occupiers and other elites expressed concerns that expellees would eventually agitate to take back their land; perhaps even organizing guerilla campaigns to reclaim the 1937 German borders.[31] The military occupiers effectively neutralized this threat by issuing prohibitions on political organizing by expellees and through the rapid recognition of the East German–Polish border by the GDR in 1950 (the Federal Republic did not formally recognize the border until the 1970s). During the early years after the war, especially before the military governments returned political sovereignty to the zones of occupation, fears of expellees becoming a radical element in German society were pervasive.

Locals often viewed expellees in more visceral terms: they saw expellees as parasites. A pastor in Lower Saxony described them as "'potato beetles' that devoured more than their fair share of resources in [an] already suffering region."[32] Other scholars have characterized this early period of resettlement as one during which conflicts between locals and newcomers were driven by "a spirit of class conflict."[33] In terms of employment, the overcrowding of rural locales meant that many expellees entered into the erratic and seasonal schedule of farm labour – whether or not they had previously worked in agriculture. This arrangement forced many expellees into dependent relationships with local farmers. Meanwhile, the speed of expellee arrivals, their rural housing placements, and the subsequent distance between potential expellee workers and industrial centres slowed the return of German industry.

West German industry had survived the war remarkably intact. According to prominent German historian Ulrich Herbert, "only 6.5 per cent of all machine tools in Germany [sic] industry had suffered any damage."[34] And yet, the recuperation of German industries stalled, because industrial centres had no place to house workers. In some large cities, up to 80 per cent of the residential areas had been destroyed.[35] Military campaigns had also all but destroyed local transportation networks, making commuting impossible. Industrial growth was fundamentally mismatched to patterns of settlement at this time, slowing reconstruction and exacerbating class conflict. Housing will continue to play a role in the integrative apparatus up to the present day.

Those expellees not housed by rural families were placed in camps where conditions were dire. The *Süddeutsche Zeitung* ran a story about the 30,000 to 50,000 children under ten years of age who were living in Bavarian camps in March 1946. More than half of the infants were suffering from rickets (a vitamin D deficiency resulting in softening of the bones). Somewhere between 45 and 60 per cent of the children were infected with measles. Mothers' breast milk had dried up, and they were feeding their infants as best they could with pre-chewed black bread. The chief pediatrician for the Swabian Hospital in Munich, Dr. Hussler [sic], commented on the conditions of utter lack:

> Without vigorous aid, these people will completely succumb to misery, and a psychic and physical collapse will provoke chaotic conditions (anarchy and lawlessness); because only a person whose physical needs are met can participate in a democratic sense [...] in the reconstruction of the world, which, after all, is in the interest of all the peoples on earth.[36]

Studies conducted by the American Military Government during the postwar occupation confirmed that local populations initially rejected the expellees. One study from March 1946 found that 20 per cent of the local Germans surveyed wanted to limit the political and economic rights afforded to expellees. Three out of four of those surveyed saw the expulsion of ethnic Germans as unjustified, and a crucial one in four of those surveyed didn't understand why the expellees (then often called refugees) had left their homes in the first place.[37] One military researcher reported that the most common epithet in his fieldwork area had rapidly changed from *Saupreuss* (damned Prussian) to *Sauflüchtling* (damned refugee).[38]

Hostility towards newcomers in the face of such misery arose partially from the suspicions local Germans held about the motives of those nations that had expelled the ethnic Germans. These suspicions included sending only criminals or withholding men. One of the early reports from the *Süddeutsche Zeitung* about trains transporting ethnic Germans arriving from Czechoslovakia to a Czech–Bavarian border town of Hof in December 1945 included the assurance that trains were inspected so Bavaria would not be forced to accept "Czechoslovakian elements" who were not entitled to residency (as opposed to Sudeten Germans, who were).[39] By January 1946, the American Zone already had 1.5 million expellees; Bavaria alone was supposed to accept an additional million.[40]

The German public's concerns about migration extended beyond border areas. The Social Ministry (*Sozialministerium*) of the state of North Rhine-Westfalia (in the western British Zone) also struggled with the arrival of expellees and "illegal" refugees (some of them simultaneously expellees and refugees) trying to escape from the Soviet Zone. The state's position as the centre of West German industry made it desperate for manpower, however, all immigrants were not treated equally. The Ministry divided "illegal" immigrants into two categories: those with training who were willing to work and those they described as "asocial." A report from the Social Ministry described asocial immigrants as "black market dealers of the kind one generally finds in large cities, like Düsseldorf."[41] They argued that it was of the utmost importance that "asocial" immigrants be rounded up into camps that were heavily patrolled by police.[42] Faced with descriptions like these, it is difficult to ignore the persistent skepticism and distrust with which societies treat immigrants and refugees, either in historical context or in the present.

Even as local Germans hoped that the ethnic Germans would soon return to their previous homes, many expellees largely understood that the migration they had been forced to undertake was permanent. Anecdotes from an ethnography conducted in the 1990s with postwar residents who had passed through an expellee camp in Freiburg-Bischofslinde show that some expellees arrived in their new locations ready to plan their futures. One farmer purportedly carried the official shaded map of his village with him on his exodus. As the village leader, this farmer was determined to find a suitable piece of land upon which he and his countrymen could rebuild an exact replica of their village. The group settled near Offenburg, but no one in the study could remember whether this group had succeeded in their plans to reconstruct their homes.[43] Even as they awaited housing and employment in crowded camps and were confronted by a hostile local population that did not understand why they were there, expellees like these were clearly preparing for their futures in the Federal Republic.

Demographic shifts related to religion also prompted anxiety, as Protestants flowed into traditionally uniform Catholic areas and vice versa. In Bavaria, a traditionally Catholic state, the shifts were quite noticeable. In 1939, more than 1,400 communities considered themselves "homogenous," that is, either all Catholic or all Protestant; by 1946, only nine such communities remained.[44] The British and American military governments also strictly prohibited expellees from founding political organizations until 1948. The policies in the Soviet Zone were especially repressive with regards to cultural identity, with various cultural practices criminalized.[45] But while both locations prohibited expellees from forming political organizations, at least the West allowed them to continue practising their religious beliefs. West German religious organizations played a significant role in helping expellees enter society by providing access to social services and aid.[46]

In the face of local hostility and extreme suffering, was successful incorporation even plausible? In the context of their forced expulsion, expellees themselves held widely differing opinions about the desirability of assimilating to their new surroundings. While many expellees understood early that their migration was permanent, as Yuliya Komska points out, Sudeten Germans who lived along the border between Bohemia and Bavaria had "political reasons to render this border uncertain or transient, even if [...] they did initially reinforce it. [...] [T]he divide appeared more irrevocable to some collectives than it did to others."[47] Many expellees wrote letters to Konrad Adenauer (CDU), the postwar mayor of Cologne who became the first chancellor of the Federal Republic in 1949. Some of them wrote to Adenauer for help finding their relatives or employment, and in his responses, he clearly uses his influence to help them where he could. Others sent Adenauer long argumentative theses as to why the German government should seize the eastern territories, Silesia, and the Sudetenland and return them to the German state. After the ban against political organizing for expellees was lifted in 1948, arguments like these would enter into German politics. Politicians from this era who were also expellees, such as the CSU politician Walter Rinke or the CDU functionary and later right-wing extremist Linus Kather, explicitly described incorporation into West German society as only a short-term goal, with a return to the German territorial borders of 1937 as the long-term project. Kather's slogan neatly summed up this notion: "Space to live in the West; Right to a Homeland in the East!"[48]

The policies of military government in all sectors were critically influential to expellee incorporation during the period before the founding of the two German states. In the face of animosity, the American Military Government doggedly pursued a policy of expellee assimilation.[49] British administrators also viewed the expulsions as permanent and acted accordingly.[50] The administration of expellee concerns – in contrast to those of concentration camp victims or displaced persons, who were under the care of the International Refugee Organization – was supposed to be a German responsibility. However, many local Germans in bureaucratic positions pursued these responsibilities half-heartedly and did not wish to recognize expellees as Germans.[51] The American Military Government rejected multiple German proposals they viewed as intending to segregate, rather than incorporate, the expellees. The Americans were emphatic that segregation was to be avoided at all costs – a curious position given the segregation policies in force for Black Americans.

In May 1946, for instance, while the expulsions were still in progress, the American Military Government of the state of Württemberg-Baden rejected a plan submitted by the provincial refugee commissioner because it was an emergency plan rather than a sustainable, long-term plan. In this case, both German administrators and expellees had suggested the construction of separate villages or ethnically distinct settlements (Prussians separate from Silesians, for example). The American Military Government rejected such proposals in order to "prevent the construction of residential ghettos (Wohnghettos)."[52] The Military Government objected:

3. The organization as outlined in the plans submitted, appears to be built somewhat on the principles of separation: separate budgets, separate staff, separate schools, separate sicities (sic) of settlers, separate industries. The basic principle approved by Military Government is one of assimilation, not separation. [...]

4. No part of the plan should establish a special category within the population. It is recommended that there be no special registration of expellee by the land.[53]

Faced with such staunch resistance on the part of the locals, three circumstances proved critical to successfully incorporating expellees. First, various legal measures that provided financial relief and citizenship rights acted as a relief valve and may be credited with preventing the radicalization of expellee populations. Second, the economic growth in West Germany spurred by the Marshall Plan and the ensuing *Wirtschaftswunder* eliminated the fierce competition for economic resources that had characterized the immediate postwar period. Finally, as historian Adam Seipp has convincingly demonstrated, the conflicts engendered by the military occupation pushed locals and expellees to come together in shared resistance against their foreign occupiers.[54] Against this backdrop, the "cultivation of a culture of purity" which Chin and Fehrenbach argue undergirded the nationalistic logic of the expulsions converged with the ability of expellees to become invisible based on both their ethnic identity and the concerns they shared with the local population that emerged against the backdrop of the Cold War.

Eingliederungspolitik: Incorporating Expellees

In nation-states with some degree of diversity, relationships between affinity groups can either facilitate newcomers' incorporation into society or fossilize hierarchical relationships based on access to or exclusion from power. When sanctioned by the state, hierarchical intergroup relationships can create permanent underclasses organized by identity (class, ethnicity, race, gender, education, caste, etc.). Public policy can play a role in making power relations more equitable between groups. In West Germany, a number of policy and political changes took place after 1948 that served to incorporate, rather than marginalize, expellees into the new Federal Republic.

This is not to say that social and economic policies uniformly helped the expellees, nor that expellees necessarily wanted to assimilate or be incorporated. In the years immediately following the war, many displaced persons and expellees scraped by in the informal economy. They bartered if they could not access formal employment or picked up erratic and undesirable jobs as day labourers. The Currency Reform of 1948 both dismantled unregulated economic activity and introduced the Deutsche Mark (DM) as a new currency. Christoph Buchheim, a German economic historian, argues that expellees were particularly hard-hit by the currency reforms. They were more likely to become unemployed during this time, and perhaps more importantly, new businesses they had founded were more likely to go bankrupt.[55]

The transition from RM to DM negatively affected small savers – the fixed-term savings account decision in October 1948 simply deleted the balance of such accounts, leading to many feeling that they had been dispossessed of their property (*enteignet*).[56] In terms of the shadow economy, Ludwig Erhard, the director of economics in the Bizone, lifted measures that had controlled both prices and the production of goods. As an effect of this deregulation, shopkeepers stopped hiding products away and returned them to shelves: "the black market virtually disappeared overnight."[57] The effect on the labour market was similar: those people who were engaged in some form of unregulated employment (*Scheinarbeitsverhältnis*) before the reform lost their source of income when money – and by extension, wage labour – once again held meaning and incentives for workers.[58] For expellees, the validity of wage labour did not necessarily lead to higher rates of employment: discrimination in the labour market was a fact of life in the postwar period. By the end of 1951, expellees had a long-term unemployment rate of 30 per cent with an additional 40 per cent working precarious jobs. The federal unemployment rate for West Germany as a whole in 1950 – considered the high point of unemployment – had only been 10.8 per cent.[59] One scholar describes the incorporation of expellees in the Federal Republic as an ongoing process of downward mobility (*Unterschichtungsprozeß*) well into the 1960s.[60]

And yet, these economic hardships were partially mitigated by reparations for expellees and those who had been harmed by the war. In 1948, the Frankfurt Economic Council (*Wirtschaftsrat*) – the Parliament of the Bizone and forerunner of the West German Parliament – initiated a broad sociopolitical discussion on various forms of assistance for the refugees and expellees moving into Germany. Ironically, the expellees themselves were largely excluded from these discussions because of the Military Government's prohibition against political organizing amongst expellees.[61] Nevertheless, expellees still benefitted from the process. In 1948, the Military Government began to work on the *Soforthilfegesetz*, or the Social Need Act, as drafted by the Economic Council. The law first took effect in August 1949, after the Federal Republic of Germany was founded. The *Soforthilfegesetz* provided a monthly pension of 70 DM to expellees, many of whom were also entitled to other forms of social aid.[62] Multiple scholars have described the *Soforthilfegesetz* as a release valve for social and psychological pressures among the expellee population, effectively eliminating the threat of radicalization.[63] Against the backdrop of the currency reform, however, this aid can also be read as a countermeasure to offset the negative economic environment for expellees.

Further policy changes initiated by the West German Parliament used financial benefit programs both to establish the new government's legitimacy and to minimize the threat of political radicalization. After the founding of the Federal Republic, Parliament replaced the *Soforthilfegesetz* with the *Lastenausgleichgesetz* of 1952, a massive, 400-paragraph legislative act that provided scaffolded levels of compensation for damages caused by the war. Not just expellees, but those who had lost their possessions or health due to bombs or violence, late-returning prisoners of war, refugees from the Soviet Zone, or those (with some limitations) who had been harmed by the currency reforms of 1948 could be granted individual subsidies – according to the text of the law – in the name of "social justice and economic opportunity."[64] Claimants could request compensation for up to 95 per cent of documented losses up to 5,000 *Reichsmark* with diminishing rates above that, topping off at 6.5 per cent of documented losses above 1 million RM.[65] Elderly persons and those unable to work were also afforded a pension as a way of extending some of the benefits of the *Soforthilfegesetz* to other groups in need.[66] Over the decades, this system of reparations paid more than 146 billion DM to those harmed by the war, including expellees. While one German scholar notes that "no one got rich" off their government payments, the measure is frequently invoked as an example of how the government used reparations to incorporate expellees into German society:

> In this way, the program of recompensation (*Lastenausgleich*) – above and beyond its economic significance – strongly contributed to constituting the sociopolitical legitimacy in postwar Germany that became extraordinarily meaningful in the face of the decline of the traditionally nationalistic [*nationalstaatlich*] mechanisms of integration.[67]

A fledgling democracy requires trust in the democratic process, but national pride could no longer provide the foundation for such trust in the aftermath of the Holocaust. The success of the *Lastenausgleich* encouraged Germans – new and longtime residents alike – to develop a sense of economic trust in their national government, thereby minimizing the threat of political radicalization.[68] When compared to the economic polarization pervasive across Europe today, the *Lastenausgleich* seems radical in its redistributive politics.

Robust economic growth was an important factor in the expellees' incorporation into German society. In fact, many the subsidies included in the *Lastenausgleich* were classified under the heading of *Eingliederungsdarlehen*, rather clumsily translated as "settling-in loans" or, more technically, as "incorporation loans." *Eingliederung* can be translated as "integration" or "incorporation" and was the preferred public policy term in the 1950s for what sociologists would call the systemic and social integration of expellees.[69] Economic stability makes willing participation in nearly any system more likely. In this vein, the Cold War likely contributed to a geopolitical climate in which West Germany benefitted both from the presence of US soldiers and from a defence industry that promoted economic growth.

In most locales in postwar Germany, local business owners decided which new businesses would be approved through municipal administrations that asked the local business owners to approve new businesses in their branch. As Ute Gerhardt and Birgitta Hohenester explain, this practice "systematically disenfranchised expellees and refugees and promoted locals," presumably by giving business owners the right to refuse the establishment of new businesses that could represent a competitive threat.[70] The American Military Government eventually declared – by decree – that starting in 1949, every state in the American Zone would permit free enterprise. New businesses emerged immediately in a period of drastic expansion, many owned and operated by expellees. In Bavaria alone, the number of businesses registered between the last quarter of 1948 and the first quarter of 1949 grew from 1,940 to 55,791.[71] The so-called Economic Miracle (*Wirtschaftswunder*) in the 1950s, largely driven by the Marshall Plan and later by the so-called Korea Boom due to the Korean War, accelerated expellee incorporation by producing wealth that could be shared across the German population and that promoted the emergence of a growing middle-class.[72] As Herbert so clearly articulates: "without the economic miracle, the integration of the refugees and *Ostvertriebene* would have been impossible; without the additional labor they provided, the economic miracle itself would have been an impossibility."[73]

As the military occupation of Germany came to an end, American troops didn't leave. Instead, the Korean War prompted the United States to expand its base operations in Germany and attempt to requisition even more land and extant buildings. These requisitions posed a threat to local businesses and farms. Seipp argues that the Korean War prompted locals and expellees in Hessen and Bavaria to find common cause by positioning themselves against a common foe: the American military. Expellees in particular were supposed to be protected by the German government and balked at the thought of being removed from their homes a *second* time.[74] These examples suggest that Germans of all backgrounds were frustrated by the continued presence of military "outsiders" and eventually worked together to protect their shared interests. As reparations and economic growth moved more locals and expellees alike into the middle class, and military occupiers became more of a nuisance for all German residents, the incorporation of expellees became both more likely and more common. Economic stability and solidarity with local populations, however, was only part of the puzzle. Expellees' access to citizenship and full political participation was also critical for incorporating them into every aspect of national life.

Citizenship, Political Participation, and Full Incorporation

It is impossible to *over*estimate how important citizenship rights are to immigrants. Expellees' rapid access to German citizenship – and with it, the right to participate in the political process – had long-lasting and positive consequences for the expellees' incorporation into both the West German state and German society. Although this fact should be obvious, it bears repeating: the essential benefit of citizenship is suffrage. Exercising the right to vote is both a civic duty and a privilege – and a basic requirement for social stability and just political representation in multicultural societies. Expellees who were German citizens exercised their right to vote from the very beginning of West Germany's history as a democracy, often in ways that affected the postwar political landscape. German political leaders soon came to understand that the expellee vote and expellee candidates could change a political party's fortunes.

The unique conditions of occupation after the end of the Second World War included some unfinished business when it came to territorial borders, with consequences for the boundaries of German citizenship. When the two German states were founded in 1949, the border between the German Democratic Republic and Poland had not yet been established. Technically, Poland had only been given the right to *administer* the eastern states – not to incorporate them into the Polish state. But this technicality quickly dissolved after the founding of the East German state. The German Democratic Republic recognized the Polish-East German border along the Oder-Neiße line hastily in 1950. The Federal Republic, however, refused to recognize the German Democratic Republic as a state until Chancellor Willy Brandt's famous genuflection before the Warsaw Ghetto in 1970. The open question as to Germany's territorial borders – and consequently, who should be a German citizen – was thus written into the founding documents of the Federal Republic. The West Germans viewed the Federal Republic as the only legitimate German state and drafted a so-called Basic Law rather than a constitution – a gesture that was supposed to prepare for the eventual incorporation of the Soviet Occupied Zone into the Federal Republic. The German Democratic Republic, as a Soviet satellite state, had no such plans.

Interestingly, the founding documents of both German states relied on the same definition of citizenship: the 1913 Nationality Law of the German Empire and States. This law defined future German citizenship through the principle of *jus sanguinis*, or bloodline descent, which linked ethnic identity to national belonging. As political scientists Karen Schönwälder and Triadafilos Triadafilopoulos argue, the 1913 definition of who was "German" had been explicitly designed to exclude Poles and Jewish people from citizenship in the early twentieth century.[75] When both German states reverted to the 1913 law after the war, it effectively created two countries – the German Democratic Republic and the Federal Republic of Germany – that shared a single definition of citizenship. In 1960, for example, East and West Germans competed together as a single national team in the Olympic Games on the premise that they held a shared citizenship as Germans.[76]

The construction of the Berlin Wall in 1961 separated the two countries and prohibited freedom of movement for East Germans. But it wasn't until 1967 that the East German government created a unique and limited category of citizenship in the German Democratic Republic.[77] For the first fifteen years after the war, the idea of "one German citizenship," defined by a shared German ethnicity, had been a political reality for two separate German states.

This historical artefact (that both German states could share citizenship) later facilitated the rapid unification of the two German states in 1990. Decades earlier, this logic of blood citizenship had accelerated the incorporation of ethnic German expellees into the postwar German states. The *Bundesvertriebenengesetz* (Federal Law on Expellees and Refugees) of 1953 granted citizenship to those persons of German descent who had been driven from their homes or subjected to persecution in the Eastern Bloc, made refugees who had been expelled *from* Germany after 1933 eligible to reacquire German citizenship, and made expellee status (and eligibility for benefits) inheritable. In the 1990s, this understanding of ethnic citizenship also permitted rapid naturalization of immigrants from Eastern Europe who had all but lost their connection to German culture – but could still prove ethnic German descent.

Ethnic German expellees certainly faced challenges in adjusting to their new lives – but for most, the fight to acquire citizenship was not one of them.[78] The majority of expellees from East Prussia, Silesia, or other territories east of the Oder-Neisse line who had lived within the boundaries of the German state in 1937 maintained their German citizenship, despite being forced from their homes. Even as local Germans questioned this sense of belonging, the expellees claimed their rights as citizens. In 1947, the Informational Control Division of the US Military found in a survey that only 55 per cent of the locals viewed expellees as citizens, while 88 per cent of expellees in that same survey reported that they *felt* like citizens of Germany.[79]

For different reasons, ethnic German expellees were quickly incorporated into the polity of both German states. In the case of the German Democratic Republic, however, it is difficult to trace exactly how that process of incorporation played out. Between the suppression of demographic information about expellees, the prohibition against identity-based politicking, and one-party rule, expellees do not usually appear as a group with a unique political identity in discussions of East German national belonging. Thus, by necessity, the remainder of my discussion of how expellees came to be incorporated into the German state focuses on the West German case.

By the mid-1950s, public and political opinion in West Germany generally considered expellees to have been successfully incorporated into German society. The myth of rapid and complete "integration" of *Vertriebene* was politically motivated: the West German state's ability to assimilate expellees was proof that it was a functional democracy that could be trusted to rule its own affairs after years of military occupation and limited sovereignty. Given those stakes, it was politically expedient, if not necessary, to smooth over any integrative difficulties faced by expellees in the 1950s. At least through the mid-1970s, researchers had limited opportunities to question this narrative: many historical and administrative documents were sealed for periods of 30 years as a matter of course.[80] In East Germany, communist ideology actively suppressed not only qualitative and interpretive social science research but also any identity-based movements that could have underscored and perpetuated social differences.[81]

It was only in the 1980s that researchers working in West Germany brought to light some of the difficulties that expellees faced in achieving full incorporation. Sociologist Paul Lüttinger, for instance, showed how expellees continued to fare worse than locals into the 1970s, especially when it came to home ownership, professional status, and educational achievements.[82] German historian Ulrich Herbert also argues that expellee incorporation was – at the very least – uneven. Considerable regional differences "led to a very uneven areal distribution of the various problems" that appeared in incorporating "the uprooted Germans from Eastern Europe."[83]

Invisibility can have both positive and negative effects. The documented financial and educational downward mobility of expellee populations in the early decades of the Federal Republic show that the claim that expellees were rapidly and successfully incorporated into the economy and structure of West German society is at least partially a myth.[84] At the same time, high rates of intermarriage suggest that the expellees *were* rapidly absorbed into broader German society.[85] Some estimates posit that nearly one quarter of the contemporary German population are direct descendants of expellees – a massive proportion of citizens who today are likely to identify simply as "German."[86]

For a certain kind of identity-based analysis, the relative invisibility of expellees, due to their lack of visible ethnic or racial difference, could be a considered an act of sociopolitical erasure that carries a negative connotation. At the same time, the cultural refrain that expellees were rapidly and successfully integrated into German society prevented discourses that portrayed the group as potentially resurgent Nazis, "parasites," competitors, or outsiders from persisting in mainstream discourse beyond a brief period following arrival. Over time, expellees blended into the broader population. Expellees needed policies to facilitate their incorporation into the Federal Republic, but a long-term and expansive integrative apparatus based on the notion of their difference did not emerge, in part because they entered the political sphere early on and were easily incorporated into a national identity category marked as "German." From the perspective of the present, this appears to be a luxury based on the intersection of ethnic German whiteness and the historical consequences of the reversion to the 1913 citizenship categories, as well as a sense of national belonging that existed in a single German citizenship across both German states until 1967. This luxury has not been afforded to foreign workers, their descendants, or contemporary immigrants and refugees.

Chapter Five

Constructing the Integrative Apparatus

The immediacy of the postwar German landscape made it difficult to imagine any kind of integrative apparatus for expellees simply because of overwhelming material lack in the postwar period. By the mid-1960s, however, West Germany faced quite different conditions. The Economic Miracle created material abundance in the Federal Republic. Founding the Federal Republic after occupation seemed to have proven that West Germany was a viable partner for transnational European integration and a willing participant in the democratic projects of the West during the Cold War. Between the late 1950s and early 1970s, nearly 14 million people were granted temporary work permits in the Federal Republic; 11 million returned home.[1] Three million – no small number, but certainly not even close to the majority – chose to settle permanently in the Federal Republic. As recruitment agreements for foreign workers rapidly expanded in the 1960s, politicized integration policies emerged that served as the foundation for the integrative apparatus.

West German society was caught within a web of contradictions: the Federal Republic desired a mobile labour force, but no permanent immigrants. The government wanted to pursue a process of European integration that would facilitate the circulation of goods and services but not necessarily a broad circulation of people. Finally, political actors in West Germany needed to promote a postwar identity as both a cooperative international partner and a nation that would not discriminate against minorities or violate human rights. By the mid-1960s, after the construction of the Berlin Wall and the West German consolidation of splinter parties along the far right, articulating a German national identity also faced multiple challenges. The division between East and West Germany was compounded by a neo-fascist minority in the West that sought a return to the German national borders of 1937, and many of these extremists had immigrated to Germany as expellees.

Conditions in the 1960s were thus ripe for an apparatus of integration to develop. Not only did new institutions exist by 1965 that structured society in ways that had been impossible under the deprivation of war and occupation, but these institutions had reached a level of sophistication that exhibited a complex mix of political conflicts, competing philosophies, and both discursive and non-discursive practices. Laying the foundation for the apparatus of integration unfolded in real time over the period of guest worker recruitment, as discursive practices worked alongside an emerging network of connections between institutions, philosophies, arguments, and policies. Considering the historical knowledge of how expellees and guest workers were socially incorporated into the Federal Republic, we can begin to trace how the specific technologies of power germane to the management of migration laid the groundwork for a culturally specific apparatus of integration to develop. A fair degree of the cultural specificity of a German integrative apparatus arises from the historical specificities found in a racialized hierarchy of immigrant subjects.

If expellees were "easily integrated" because the categories of ethnic identity and national belonging converged – as well as due to the simple truth that after the founding of the two German states, the German borders (and thus the expulsions themselves) became permanent – so-called guest workers confronted diametrically opposite conditions. They were ethnically and nationally different *and* their stay was envisioned as temporary. Such a simple formulation of these differences flattens the effects that discourses of ethnic difference and limited temporality had on guest workers' lives. But these discourses were not mere rhetoric: discourse is always intimately connected with subjectivity, and discourses and discursive practices fundamentally affected how guest workers interacted with German people, German employers, and German institutions.

Postwar approaches to incorporating expellees created a form of expellee invisibility that made assimilation the only and inevitable option. Why, then, could foreign workers and subsequent groups not access the same narrative of inevitable assimilation? It would seem plausible, after all, to consider the knowledge gathered from the experiences of incorporating nine million outsiders into West Germany (and an additional three million in East Germany) and to apply the knowledge thus gained to subsequent immigrant groups that came to Germany. From the beginning, however, how expellees and guest workers were granted access to residency, social participation, and citizenship was radically different. Many expellees were assured these rights and privileges, but the different expectations that governed the politics of guest worker recruitment withheld that foreign workers would be assimilated.[2] Schönwälder and Triadafilopoulos pointedly argue that the guest worker system "was purposefully designed to facilitate the exploitation of foreign workers while guarding against their social incorporation."[3] The Federal Republic of Germany was not the only agent here: sending nations also supported withholding social incorporation from guest workers. Turkey was particularly resistant in this regard and expected all Turkish citizens to return home.[4] While some of the realities of permanent settlement by guest workers were evident to municipal and regional authorities by the late 1950s and early 1960s, many politicians portrayed guest worker labour as temporary, impermanent, and a process to be guided by the myth of return. This tension between local realities and national political ideologies provided fertile ground for politicians and the media to instrumentalize guest workers as a problem for West German society.

From the late 1950s to the early 1970s, the presence of what would eventually become millions of guest workers (and their descendants) led to the development of institutions and systemic practices that formed the infrastructure upon which an apparatus of integration could be constructed. Some of these systemic practices, like housing patterns, arose from non-discursive practices (like segregation or legal codes) that later were given discursive form in debates about ghettos, parallel societies, and ethnic neighbourhoods. Other practices were discursive in essence, such as the development of the stereotype of the so-called Mediterranean Man, fears of which were easily sensationalized by the press. It is the mix of systemic, institutionalized, symbolic, discursive, and non-discursive practices that provide the conditions for an apparatus to develop in moments of perceived historical urgency. The sheer scale of guest worker immigration provided an impetus for viewing migration as a process worthy of broad attention by the press, state officials, and the broader public.

The globalization of labour as well as the construction of transnational institutions came with both long-term and short-term effects. The postwar project of European integration constituted an ongoing transnational process that informed how guest worker agreements both functioned as a tool of diplomacy available to the West German government and changed the demographic landscape of the Federal Republic. Germany's desire to be seen as a legitimate political partner in the European project led the government to leverage such agreements as a sign that West Germany's democracy was secure. But in the middle of the guest worker period (1966–7), the first recession since the war prompted both economic insecurity and criticism of guest workers.

By the global oil crisis of 1973, the guest worker program had ended in West Germany. Changes in the global political economy thus influenced the conditions for national political actors to mobilize anti-guest worker sentiment as a political issue, and both long-term and short-term processes underlay the sense of urgency that led to the development of an apparatus of integration.

The discursive and non-discursive practices that emerged after the war and into the 1970s had long-lasting effects on nearly every immigrant group that followed, as German policies and attitudes towards newcomers splintered, expanded, and shifted over time. In *A History of Foreign Labour in Germany, 1880–1980*, historian Ulrich Herbert realized as early as 1986 that "there was a kind of rupture in historical continuity and popular perception in dealing with foreign [guest] workers."[5] In fact, the experiences of incorporating expellees had been so starkly shaped by the unique conditions of the postwar period that "the integration of the *Ostvertriebene* [expellees] formed a sort of break in historical perception: an interposed chapter wedged between the deployment of *Fremdarbeiter* [foreign workers/slaves] under National Socialism and the resumption of massive employment of foreign labor [here: guest workers] in the Federal Republic."[6] Take as an example of this historical amnesia this declaration from a 1985 essay by Barbara John, then the foreigner commissioner of the Berlin Senate: "In the Federal Republic, because we have little to no experience incorporating foreign minorities into our existing society, it is difficult to assess the consequences of integrative [*integrationspolitischer*] decisions and policies."[7]

Political scientist Karen Schönwälder published a comparative study of British and German postwar migration policy in 2001. In *Einwanderung und ethnische Pluralität* (Immigration and Ethnic Plurality) she lays out in impressive detail how the governments of both countries developed policies to steer and manage postwar migration. I will draw heavily from her archival work over the next two chapters of secondary history, rereading this monograph in conversation with historians Ulrich Herbert, Karin Hunn, Julia Woesthoff, Rita Chin, Lauren Stokes, Jennifer A. Miller, and sociologist Ray C. Rist, in order to chart the changes that I argue led to the eventual construction of an integrative apparatus in contemporary Germany. Schönwälder admits that certainly none of the governmental debates or discussions into the late 1960s in West Germany were sophisticated or coordinated enough to earn the name "integration politics."[8] But as a project situated in the field of historical institutionalism, *Einwanderung und ethnische Pluralität* shows perhaps more than any other scholarly work about guest worker migration how power struggles between various governmental entities as well as non-governmental organizations in Germany laid the foundation for an apparatus of integration to emerge. Schönwälder's goal is to anchor questions about how processes of migration affect politics and society through comparison between Germany and Great Britain, but my interest in her work is that it offers a way to chart the early emergence of a network that becomes visible in the structures of institutions before an apparatus of integration was even possible.

Schönwälder points out that it is inevitable that migration will permanently change societies. These changes, she argues, are almost always unwanted by receiving countries.[9] Neither Great Britain nor Germany wanted to become a country of immigration, but postwar migration happened anyway.[10] Schönwälder raises several critical questions about this contradiction in particular: "Was it unclear what was happening, or did they not understand the consequences of migration processes? Did they want to intervene, but saw themselves unable to do so due to restrictions on action in the national and international contexts? Or was the desire not to become a country of immigration perhaps not the single, dominant orientation?"[11] Political developments are not inevitable. Instead, human actors make choices at every turn and, taken together, these choices represent processes of change.

In the context of the Federal Republic of Germany, treating foreign workers as temporary guests who would be difficult to incorporate into society is particularly striking given how enthusiastically Germans outwardly portrayed the successful incorporation of expellees. The West German government attempted both to limit permanent settlement as well as to set limits on foreigners' participation in political activities. Given that the expellees were more numerous and also often did not speak the same language(s), the attempts to limit the permanent settlement of guest workers can only be linked to the various ways that guest workers were repeatedly characterized and treated as something other than German.

Labour Policies as Diplomatic Tools

Faced with a severe labour shortage in the 1950s, many German industries wanted to import workers. In 1955, West Germany signed its first recruitment agreement with Italy. West Germany actively used these labour agreements – as well as their purported "success" in rapidly incorporating expellees, the few DPs that remained, and refugees from East Germany – as diplomatic tools. But West Germany had no intention of permitting permanent guest worker settlement: while authorities understood that forced expulsion of labourers would not be looked upon favourably, they used a variety of measures to make settlement difficult and preclude the possibility that workers would be treated similarly to Germans or ethnic German expellees.[12]

Guest worker programs brought millions of workers from countries in Southern and Eastern Europe, North Africa, and the Middle East to Germany between 1955 and 1973. Timing is an important factor when comparing guest workers to expellees: the first agreement to import labour was made merely two years after expellees were granted a pension and benefits through a legal measure called the *Lastenausgleichsgesetz* (Burden Equalization Act). From a present-day perspective, these two developments – the incorporation of expellees into the nation and the start of guest worker migration – were nearly simultaneous. The simultaneity of migratory flows is significant, not only because it shows the continuity of new arrivals to Germany but also because it highlights the differences in how German authorities responded to each group.

Between 1955 and 1968, the German government signed labour agreements with Italy (1955), Spain (1960), Greece (1960), Turkey (1961), Morocco (1963), South Korea (1963), Portugal (1964), Tunisia (1966), and Yugoslavia (1968). The term "guest worker" developed in colloquial speech. The formal designation for such workers was "*ausländische Arbeitnehemer*" or "foreign employees." Politicians intended for guest workers to supply German companies with a steady stream of unskilled workers on a rotational principle: they would work for a limited amount of time in Germany and then return to their countries of origin, perhaps with a new level of vocational training and experience. Nearly 80 per cent of guest workers did return. In this respect, the global labour migration system worked mostly as intended: German industry profited from young, healthy workers and Germany was not required to change its immigration or naturalization laws, which defined German citizenship through bloodlines. Labour migration alleviated unemployment for countries in the Global South by temporarily exporting part of their labour force to Europe – but this practice also led to brain drain in the sending countries. Both Germany and its global partners viewed labour migration and vocational education as a way to further industrial development in nations that were predominantly agricultural or subsistence economies.[13] While industrial development since 1950 has increased, it is highly unlikely that guest worker migration and subsequent knowledge transfer played a formidable role in the acceleration of development in the latter half of the twentieth century, despite the fact that remittances shored up the domestic economies of several sending nations.[14]

Despite the presence of early labour migration agreements with Italy, Spain, and Greece, "the number of foreign guest workers in Germany remained largely insignificant until 1961."[15] The construction of the Berlin Wall that year not only denied East German citizens freedom of movement but also denied West German employers a steady stream of East German employees.[16] From that point on, guest worker agreements expanded rapidly between West Germany and countries across Southern Europe and North Africa. By the early 1960s, the social changes wrought by migration were beginning to be cast as social problems. This critical discursive twist laid the groundwork for the integrative apparatus to emerge in the 1970s and 1980s, when the federal government both ended foreign labour recruitment programs and continued to portray immigrants' stay as temporary and impermanent.

During the period of active labour recruitment (1955–73), Germans debated the merits of foreign worker agreements in a variety of social arenas, from stereotypical representations in newspapers to interministerial conflicts at the local and national level. Many tropes or political arguments quickly solidified into discursive arguments, some of which persist virtually unchanged into the present day. The repetition of these tropes in contemporary debates about refugee migration and the integration of the descendants of foreign workers reveal how discursive shifts during the period of guest worker migration facilitated the emergence of an integrative apparatus. Non-discursive practices, such as the distribution of responsibilities for migration across governmental institutions and emerging interministerial conflicts, existed alongside discursive formations, such as the stereotypical treatment of guest workers in the press.

The guest worker problem (*Gastarbeiterproblem*) arose out of a specific configuration of discursive and non-discursive practices. Newspaper coverage of guest workers' lives created an atmosphere of social mistrust that may have informed the governmental desire to limit and police the movement and settlement of foreigners. Ambivalence across governmental institutions, which became particularly visible in tensions between regional governments, various ministries and the parliamentary bodies, obscured the positive effects of guest worker migration on the economy and exploited guest worker policy to thwart union efforts to shorten the workday. Finally, discursive formations used to describe assimilative behaviour shifted their vocabulary from *Eingliederung* (incorporation) to *Integration* (integration). This lexical shift revealed both the racist attitudes endemic to European societies and how the subtext of integration rhetoric often focused on limiting the political behaviour of immigrants and displaced persons.

Stereotypes and Mistrust

Labour practices intimately affect social life. Because of the West German labour shortage and the rapid pace of economic growth, guest workers easily filled a critical space in the labour force. Most worked in industries in which German nationals had no interest in participating: mining, assembly-line work, construction, and textiles.[17] Multiple historians have shown through careful historical analysis of West German newspapers how public debate about guest workers intensified in the mid-1960s as the numbers of guest workers rose rapidly.[18] Reports about Italian guest workers from the early 1960s introduced a West German audience to foreign workers and included in their coverage everything from details about their daily lives to explanations of how foreign labour agreements functioned.[19]

As the number of guest workers rose, journalistic reporting about guest workers increasingly associated foreigners with both criminality and sexual violence, contributing to a pervasive cultural mistrust of guest workers.[20] In 1960, about 200,000 guest workers were employed in West Germany. By September 1966, merely six years later, that number had reached over 1.3 million. Stereotypes of "southern" Europeans emerged during the period in which the number of guest workers and guest worker agreements were still growing (late 1960s); guest workers at this time were a heterogeneous group of nationalities.[21]

Guest workers were not the only group confronting cultural shifts. The mere presence of a low-skilled labour force also provided many lower-class Germans with a ready path to upward mobility.[22] Between 1960–70, the number of German white-collar workers increased by 2.3 million.[23] This upward mobility for Germans had profound effects on families and gender roles. Moving into white-collar employment raised Germans' salaries and consequently allowed German women to leave low-skilled work behind and remain at home "to focus on motherhood."[24] Through this female return to the home, the mere presence of a new, low-skilled labour force strengthened conservative social norms, particularly traditional bourgeois family structures in which German women stayed out of formal employment. This family structure had been disrupted during the war, and a return to bourgeois family life was part of a broader German nostalgia to return to the social and cultural practices of the past.[25]

At the same time that middle-class German women re-entered the private space of the home, many Germans began to perceive male guest workers as irritating or dangerous (a response potentially triggered by their presence in public spaces and reinforced by newspaper coverage linking foreigners to violence).[26] Several cities created cultural centres segregated by nationality to contain guest workers in spaces that provided options for fraternization, but still remained hidden from public view.[27]

Discursive connections between foreigners and criminality have been known to scholars researching the press attention to guest workers since Manuel Delgado's early study from 1972, published before active recruitment even ended.[28] Displaced persons, former prisoners of concentration camps, and slave labourers during Nazi rule were also broadly associated with criminality, showing continuity in the negative associations across multiple groups.[29] Descriptions of Turkish, Spanish, Italian, Greek, and Portuguese workers often included terms such as "hot-headed," described these workers as being of "childish character," and argued that guest workers distrusted authority. Historian Julia Woesthoff argues that these descriptors coalesced into a "Mediterranean" stereotype, effectively racializing guest workers.[30] Woesthoff also points out how stereotypes about a "Southern" temperament mixed essentialized cultural behaviours with the specifics of the guest worker experience living in Germany. This stereotype functioned as a way to explain the social behaviours German society saw as problematic: knife fights, higher numbers of German teenagers becoming pregnant by guest workers, and purported increases in sexual assaults and rates of prostitution and homosexual activity in West German cities.[31] Journalists portrayed most of these acts of violence as stemming from a childish disappointment in romantic relationships. Strangely, the impulsivity stemming from emotionality also rendered guest workers "a threatening competitor for female affection."[32] Focusing on guest workers' temperaments and masculinity created the preconditions for contemporary racializing tropes that stigmatize Muslims and men of colour.[33] While "sexual desire or jealousy were [labelled as] the primary reasons for most guest worker violence," Woesthoff argues that above all else, "it was the sexualization of *German* society that was at the root of this issue [italics in original]."[34] While some women were drawn back into the fold of traditional bourgeois life, other German women fully participated in the opportunities afforded to them by feminist movements and were thus seen as threats to German society.

Between 1955 and 1973, the nationalities of the guest workers went through multiple demographic shifts. Italian workers were the most numerous until the late 1960s, at which point Yugoslavians briefly overtook them before being outpaced by Turks. By 1972, Turkish guest workers were the largest group.[35] Stereotypes about "Mediterranean" guest workers visible in media portrayals in the mid-1960s turned out to be tropes that had a long shelf life. As the composition of the guest worker labour force changed into a labour force dominated by Turkish Muslims, the stereotypes previously applied to multiple nationalities coalesced over time into stereotypes about Turks.[36] This essentialized "southern" temperament prone to sexual violence portrayed guest workers (then Turks, then Muslims) as a civilizational burden to German society. The narrative of deficit and of a "hot-headed" proclivity to violence would later become crystallized in certain logics within integration politics, as we saw in chapter 2 in the case of the Sürücü murder and the media fallout that transformed students of multiple ethnicities into "three Turkish students."

In addition to stereotypes about southern European men, racial ideologies influenced how journalists interpreted the word "foreigner." No one was interested in the 120,000 (white) Dutch and Austrian citizens working in Germany by mid-1966.[37] Despite some mentions of Muslims or East Asians, hardly anyone was interested in Turks or in identifying guest workers based on their national identity, either. A darker skin colour, however, could become the primary characteristic worthy of journalistic attention, irrespective of nationality, showing that racialized hierarchies existed despite the fact that postwar West Germany tried to insist that processes of racialization (i.e., anti-Semitism) should be historically relegated to the recent past. An article Schönwälder cites from November 1966 with "N---r" as part of the headline accused Black American soldiers of sexual violence and assaults.[38] "The threatening foreigner could indeed be an American – if he were Black," Schönwälder comments.[39] By and large, however, the German press did not see continuities between the ethnic difference of guest workers and policies of racial discrimination in the United States or South Africa until the beginning of the 1970s.[40]

Racialized difference, however, was the constant subtext to debates about the presence of guest workers. Not only did federal ministries agree that workers were only to be recruited from Europe, but also that Asian and African countries were to be excluded from recruitment and that employers were to be prevented from hiring workers from these regions.[41] Nothing makes the racial foundations for selection clearer than the examples Schönwälder offers from a working group at the Federal Employment Agency. This working group told Portuguese authorities in 1965 that dark-skinned candidates for employment were unacceptable under the 1964 treaty, and that Germany would look elsewhere "should the Portuguese be uncooperative" in selecting workers according to their skin colour.[42] The point of this anecdote is hardly to single out German authorities for pursuing egregiously racist selection policies, which appear across the world in many different nations and in many different forms. Rather, this anecdote shows the degree to which guest workers were consistently seen as foreign and hierarchized based on their national, ethnic, and racial identities. The racial hierarchies that emerge in examples like these show a spectrum running from the most desirable (white, southern Europeans) to the least desirable (so-called Afro-Asians). Proximity to whiteness was critical. These hierarchies did not immediately mark various European groups that are often included within the boundaries of whiteness in the United States as different. But while southern Europeans were considered acceptable prospects for recruitment because they *were* white, they were *not* ethnically German. Some ethnic or religious identities (Turkish, Muslim) were later racialized and instrumentalized in integration debates about guest workers and their descendants; others were eventually permitted some assimilative privilege as white Europeans (for instance, Spaniards). Racialized hierarchies are mutable and that contributes to their longevity.

Within the social dynamics illuminated here, it is impossible to miss the intersectional effects of labour migration on society as a whole: the entrance of a new proletariat, which occupied the bottom rungs of the labour market, both permitted a return to conservative family life for those Germans who became upwardly mobile *and* exposed the gendered and classed ruptures caused by a transnational sexual revolution that empowered young (German) women. These reconfigurations of gender and social class within German society were both set into motion by a foreign labour force that permitted the German bourgeois family to retreat to private life and consequently prompted the development of an underclass that was subsequently racialized.

Stereotypes about foreigners as violent and their association with criminality can be traced from similar attitudes directed towards displaced persons after the Second World War; these attitudes were then directed towards each subsequent group of immigrants who arrived. Constructions of race and ethnicity are clearly one node of the integrative apparatus and how it revolves around a capacious category of foreigner that is easily adapted to different ethnic, racial, and national groups. It is important, however, to highlight the intersection of race, class, gender, and nationality and how these categories affected both the position of foreign workers on the social landscape of West Germany as well as the role white German women played in these debates. Woesthoff's conclusions about German feminism and Miller's arguments about gender relations and white German upward mobility show how the integrative apparatus implicates white Germans in debates about migration. Social workers tried to convince German women not to fall for or marry foreign men, and journalists critiqued young German women's expression of sexuality in the 1960s. These examples reveal how debates about race often mobilize a different debate about gender when one or the other is considered taboo. In this case, the debate about guest worker masculinity demonized foreign men and simultaneously attempted to police the behaviour of white women.

The AVPO and the 1965 Aliens Act (*Ausländergesetz*)

Associations of guest workers with criminality, however, were not just a theoretical subtext to journalistic coverage. These stereotypes affected how laws were conceived and applied. After the end of the occupation by the Allied powers, Germany re-instituted the *Ausländerpolizeiverordnung* (Foreigner Police Ordinance, AVPO), an "ordinance of the Nazi dictatorship," in the early 1950s.[43] This was not the only Nazi statute to be brought back. The Federal Republic re-appropriated a second instrument as well: the 1933 ordinance that had been used by the Nazis to police foreign labour.[44] In contrast to other scholars, Schönwälder argues that neither legal instrument was designed with application to the guest worker agreements in mind.[45] Instead, these instruments were used against former concentration camp inmates as well as displaced persons and stateless people in the 1950s, all of whom were subjected to the associations between criminality and asocial behaviour to which guest workers and refugees would later be subjected.[46] These associations took a long time to change. The Federal Criminal Police Office issued a warning as late as 1963 – nearly 20 years after the end of the Second World War – that stateless people (*heimatlose Ausländer*) were particularly inclined towards criminal activity.[47] The association of "foreigners" with criminality and violence thus *preceded* the establishment of guest worker agreements and influenced how politicians resuscitated lapsed legal instruments from the Nazi period designed to control the presence of foreigners in the Federal Republic.

Not everyone agreed that recuperating these regulatory instruments was acceptable in the new Republic. The interior minister of Schleswig-Holstein doubted the legality of these former Nazi instruments as early as 1949; however, many bureaucrats and politicians desired "to recover a customary, extensive discretionary power of the state over the presence of foreigners," a power that had previously been limited by the occupation forces.[48] In a 1951 letter sent from the Federal Ministry of the Interior to the Ministry of Labour, the FMI writes that only the AVPO would make it possible to control the flow of foreigners into the country. By 1956, then-Interior Minister Gerhard

Schröder tried to requisition budgetary funds to strengthen Germany's borders and declared that Germany needed to "protect itself 'against 10,000 stateless people' trying to claim asylum."[49] Bavaria, one of the most conservative states and a state positioned on multiple international borders, was particularly frustrated with the lack of options available to police foreigners.[50] In documents from the Bavarian Interior Ministry, bureaucrats portray the state of Bavaria as a modern-day Vienna, charged with protecting the gates to Germany from an influx of southeastern Europeans.[51] Schönwälder comments: "Many of the well-known patterns from later decades are already present here: the sweeping characterization of foreigners as a threat, the image of immigration as a constantly growing threat, as illegal 'infiltration' or 'flooding' and the attitude of victimization," she writes.[52] "These utterances show how strongly visions of threats and defensive attitudes against foreigners were, even before the implementation of a comprehensive labour migration [policy]."[53]

The Federal Ministry of the Interior chose in 1951 to reinstate a Nazi legal instrument rather than to begin a conversation about the appropriate mechanism for controlling foreign movement into a democratic state.[54] But at the regional political level, the federal states continued to push for a new Foreigner Law (*Fremdengesetz*) or at least, as Schönwälder notes, some "instructions" on implementing the AVPO.[55] In 1958, the Federal Cabinet decided it was not "pressing" to take up drafting such a law.[56] The conference of regional interior ministers in May 1959 once again insisted that a Foreigner Law needed to be proposed in the context of increasing immigration of foreigners into the Federal Republic.[57] It is interesting to note that the term "increasing immigration" comes from the minutes of the conference during which Bavaria, Hessen, and Saarland noted that Algerian, Arab, and Italian families had (already!) settled in their states.[58] Despite over ten years of discussion, the Federal Ministry of the Interior only began to work on a concrete draft of a new legal instrument to regulate foreigners in 1960. Politicians and officials now saw crafting a new law as sufficiently urgent. In the context of the Cold War, bureaucrats wanted to limit the left-wing political activities in which foreigners in the 1950s (especially those from Eastern Europe or Greece) could participate. What they hoped for was to create an instrument that could legally deport foreigners. In addition, the West German government also became concerned that decisions on asylum cases, especially for Eastern Europeans fleeing communist states, who were often seen as potential spies, were not uniform. They intended to develop a new law to better facilitate the asylum process.[59] That law would become the 1965 Aliens Act.

In contrast to the clear desire expressed in multiple communications across federal agencies that the government wanted the right to "apprehend, surveille and deport" foreigners, according to Schönwälder the first draft of the Aliens Act from 1960 was already being presented to the German public as "liberal and cosmopolitan."[60] This portrayal largely stemmed from a concerted campaign by German politicians to convince international partners that that topical controversies about the Nazi past were not indicative of Germany's future.[61] A wave of nearly 700 anti-Semitic acts (the so-called *Schmierwelle* during the winter of 1959/1960) took place alongside increased public criticism of former Nazis like Theodor Oberländer, who at that time held political and public offices in the Federal Republic. These events were front and centre in the international press and threatened to damage West Germany's postwar reputation as a democratic state. As Interior Minister Höcherl declared in 1964, "[the Aliens Act] should show the entire civilized world that the Federal Republic of Germany is committed to overcome the disastrous [events] of the past through positive regulations."[62]

Although the politicking behind the law included attempts to couch a conservative regulation trying to restrict permanent settlement in a discourse of liberal cosmopolitanism, the law as it was passed in 1965 *could have permitted* a more liberal engagement with foreigners, despite its genealogical origins in the Nazi dictatorship.[63] Because the Aliens Act, however, protects the rights of the state over the rights of the individual and gave agencies (*Behörden*) broad spaces within which to manoeuvre, the overall effect of the regulation was to work as a check on the liberalizing tendencies associated with trans-European integration. The most important political actors, however, were not European partners, but rather domestic politicians: "Although it was presented as a document of liberality, the draft [of the Aliens Act] was shaped by efforts of domestic politicians (and the agencies subordinate to them) to secure themselves the broadest possible instruments to counteract obviously unstoppable attempts to liberalize the freedom to travel and of employment markets [across Europe]."[64]

It was the most controversial element of the Aliens Act that provided the broadest check on liberalizing policies of movement as well as on political activities by foreigners. Paragraph 6 of the Aliens Act set limits on behaviours that posed a threat to public safety or to the "liberal democratic order of the Federal Republic of Germany."[65] The text of the law was deliberately left vague so that administrators could determine the practicable guidelines required for implementation. Dr. Fritz Franz, Councillor to the Higher Administrative Court in Berlin, pointed out that the primary danger of law lay in its vague statements about protecting national security. These concerns were being interpreted by judges as a reason to punish foreigners for behaviours that took place in private spaces. Writing in both a frustrated and somewhat sarcastic idiom, Franz lists off a series of cases in the late 1960s and early 1970s in which the Aliens Act neither facilitated foreign residency nor represented a "liberal and cosmopolitan foreign policy." A second generation German-Italian born to a German mother was deported to "his homeland" due to delinquency; that this young man had been born in Germany and did not speak Italian was not considered by the courts.[66] An Iranian citizen who drove drunk supposedly posed a security threat, because – as the legal brief argued – "whoever endangers traffic security endangers the domestic security of the state."[67] Domestic violence was treated with a similar logic: perpetrators of domestic violence should be punished with deportation for violent forms of conflict in private spaces.[68] The court opinions Franz cites about domestic violence include the argument that all guest workers have the right to behave according to their cultural "mentality"; however, these protections were not valid in public spaces [*in der Öffentlichkeit*] and certainly not for violent conflicts at home, where "public safety is endangered."[69] Domestic violence has long posed a challenge for legal philosophy: it is perhaps the key arena in which theorists weigh the benefits and limits of protection from the violence of the state versus protection from the violence of individual perpetrators. For that reason alone, domestic violence and sexual assault are complicated issues and still pose a challenge for courts. These theoretical debates notwithstanding, youthful delinquency, drunk driving, and domestic violence are all offences also committed by Germans and are not necessarily culturally motivated. There is very little substantive support for the idea that these offences – when enacted by foreigners – endanger the interests of the Federal Republic any more than such offences committed by German citizens, who cannot be deported. Ulrich Herbert took this argument further, suggesting that even permanent settlement could be considered a violation within this interpretation of the Aliens Act, which determined who could be granted which kind of residency permit.[70]

The Aliens Act of 1965 was formative in the development of the integrative apparatus for two reasons: one, it was used – partially because of the vague language about the needs of the Federal Republic and national security – to justify interventions by the state into private spaces and to use deportation as a way to thwart low-level criminal activity. The Aliens Act thus gave an emerging security apparatus permission to expand, adding mechanisms for deportation and limits on participation in the public sphere to the existing instrument of foreign labour agreements. Use of federal law to surveille, deport, and punish foreigners began to link institutions, philosophies, and discourses across multiple spaces of governing, contributing to the expansion of an apparatus designed to discipline large and diverse populations. Second, while the reforms that led to the 1965 law could have provided foreigners with some measure of political rights, whether that had been local voting rights, a pathway to permanent residency and eventually citizenship for foreigners and asylum seekers, or simply protect their human rights more robustly, the legal apparatus worked instead to prevent permanent settlement. Lawmakers set the conditions for this outcome by creating obstacles that required foreigners to secure both residency and employment permits separately and also by subjecting foreigners to stricter police discipline than German citizens.[71]

Housing and Segregation

The discursive practices embedded within the rhetoric of legal debates existed alongside the non-discursive practices of policies that limited settlement and isolated guest workers from other groups – a long-lasting sore spot in later integration debates. Structural isolation can be traced in part to the earliest ideas about guest workers as a group to be kept separate from German nationals.[72] Segregation was built into the guest worker agreements, and nowhere is segregation more evident than through housing practices and urban planning. The tendency of German institutional practice towards segregation is clear when one realizes that the barracks- or hostel-style housing offered to guest workers had successively housed *Fremdarbeiter* (Nazi slaves), expellees during their exodus, and then had been minimally repurposed to house guest workers during their temporary contracts. Historian Jennifer Miller argues that these housing placements limited the possibility of early experiences of contact with local German populations.[73] Rather than trying to facilitate the incorporation of workers, Miller argues that dormitory managers spent substantial amounts of energy trying to "control and judge workers, not to engage or integrate them."[74] She sees a direct line from conflicts between West German managers and guest workers in dormitory housing to the labour strikes of the 1970s and later integration debates of the 1980s.[75] Despite the fact that internment with local families was a highly problematic practice for expellees, the high rates of intermarriage between expellees and locals were likely influenced by proximity.

Dormitory housing was undoubtedly stressful for workers and ultimately paved the way for conflicts between segregated workers, their often paternalistic dorm managers, and society at large. In this context, it is unsurprising that workers might try and escape the stifling atmosphere of dormitories for the open space of the market or train station square. Segregation into dormitories, however, also had a stabilizing effect on society as a whole. At least in the late 1950s and early 1960s, segregation suppressed the visibility of guest workers until they became a group too numerous to hide.

In Germany, the lack of affordable and available housing persists into the present day, and the population density in cities is high. Guest workers were not necessarily forced to live in company-owned barracks, but guest worker agreements required proof of adequate housing before guest workers could bring their families to live with them – and "adequate housing" was difficult to find.[76] In the 1950s and 1960s, the struggle to find adequate housing applied to locals and guest workers alike, due to the long-term effects of the Second World War bombing raids on residential neighbourhoods. The difficulties were twofold for guest workers: they faced not only a lack of supply but also discrimination from landlords. Presumably, when they were unable to find adequate space for their families, many guest workers were relegated to dormitories by default. Legal debates about family togetherness in the context of European integration and the settlement of immigrant families in Germany were thus intimately linked to debates about housing. Political officials linked policies of family reunification with regulations about sufficient apartment sizes because they saw this regulation as an effective instrument with which to regulate permanent settlement.[77]

Family reunification was one means by which guest workers signalled their intent to settle permanently in Germany. Government ministries argued that once the entire family came, and leases in the country of origin lapsed or workers sold their homes in their countries of origin, it was unlikely that families would return "home." Interestingly, it is in the context of debates about family togetherness, permanent residency, and housing that integration rhetoric begins to shift into its contemporary register of both cultural assimilation and immigrants' need to meet certain demands. Schönwälder cites a 1962 report by the Federal Ministry of Labour that argues that due to the growing tendency of some guest workers to settle, special policies would be necessary to build apartments for foreign families in order to facilitate their "ultimate incorporation" (endgültige Eingliederung). Two years later, after a new regulation from the European Economic Community was passed in 1964 that strengthened the rights of foreign workers, permitting their families to join them in Germany, Interior Minister Schröder declared that apartments needed to be built for foreign workers and their families, but only "worthy" immigrants should be chosen to live in them: "'the enjoyment of these policies should only come to married workers and workers who have shown during a longer presence in Germany that they know how to adjust to German living conditions' and of whom it can be expected that they would stay longer in the Federal Republic."[78]

The establishment of ethnic neighbourhoods was both a solution to the necessity of finding private housing and the result of guest worker segregation from German populations. German developers, however, using methods common to anyone familiar with the planned neglect of American inner cities during the 1960s, often purchased housing they could rent to guest worker families while simultaneously choosing to actively neglect such properties.[79] When the condition of such housing fell below government standards, developers were able to secure permits which allowed them to destroy the older housing structures and construct far more profitable corporate structures like office buildings. In 2006, Germany finally passed civil rights legislation that included some protection for equal housing opportunity. In contrast, the political rights that could have disciplined slumlords were certainly not afforded to immigrants in the 1960s and 1970s.[80]

Despite the fact that Germans had actively promoted segregative practices since the beginning of guest worker labour recruitment, the development of ethnic neighbourhoods caused substantial public anxiety.[81] Immigrant neighbourhoods – as the sociological literature attests – are often a steppingstone to upward mobility rather than a blight on the urban landscape. Community-specific businesses and easy access to native speakers and cultural mediators facilitate the incorporation of the second and third generations by helping newcomers navigate the complexities of a new society. Immigrants stay in ethnic neighbourhoods only when they are unable to access mechanisms that promote their upward mobility.[82] Local and federal officials, however, did not see ethnic neighborhoods positively. Multiple political statements, documents, and journalistic reports from this period show that since the end of the war, Germans were deeply concerned with the emergence of "ghettos."[83] Several cities thus created settlement bans in the 1970s to inhibit the growth of ethnic neighborhoods. Officials closed the district of Berlin-Kreuzberg, along with Tiergarten and Wedding, to new immigrant settlement in 1975. In Berlin, all non-EEC citizens had their passports stamped with the new details of their residency permits. Stamps after 1 January 1975, included the clause "Settlement in the districts of Kreuzberg, Tiergarten and Wedding not permitted" above a seal showing the Berlin coat of arms.[84]

The development of ethnic neighbourhoods, however, was impossible to thwart. Berlin-Kreuzberg neighboured the district of Berlin-Neukölln. Both districts bordered the Berlin Wall and the active Tempelhof airport. For these reasons, the districts were undesirable to many middle- and especially upper-middle-class communities. When officials closed Kreuzberg to new immigrant settlement, immigrants just moved farther south, settling in the neighbourhood of North-Neukölln, which is within walking distance to Kreuzberg. Neukölln today includes residents of 160 different nationalities and is one of the most diverse districts in the city of Berlin.[85]

Zuzugssperren (local residency and settlement bans) – mostly lifted by 1980 – were ultimately ineffective for several reasons. First, they created strange conundrums that led to immigrant frustration, which historian Lauren Stokes has compellingly analysed. A father and his adult son who both worked at an Opel auto plant were prohibited from living together in the same apartment in Rüsselsheim (near Mainz) due to their different dates of arrival. The son was subject to the ban while his father was permitted to stay; ultimately, they had to secure separate apartments.[86] Families were sometimes told they had to move because they had an additional child or because their apartment was one square metre too small to be considered adequate.[87] Clauses about "adequate" housing even coerced immigrants into criminal behaviour. Immigrants, using their own agency to keep their families together or find affordable housing, sometimes forged or used counterfeit leases to secure or extend their residence permit.[88] In terms of the housing market, immigrants were hemmed in by both the simple reality of supply and demand *and* the added stress of excessive regulation and policing. Distrust of authority hardly seems like a personality flaw in this context: guest workers had reason to be skeptical of housing authorities in the face of such hardship.

The need for a structure to incorporate immigrants became clear to government officials in the context of new legal demands, such as the EEC agreements that guaranteed freedom of movement and longer residency permits for Italians, who were EEC members, as well as permission granted to guest workers to pursue family reunification. Both policies fuelled the need for permanent and adequate housing. The early shifts in the rhetoric of integration and incorporation, even if individual actors insisted that integration should permit guest workers or immigrants to return "home" and preclude "assimilation," shows a subtextual, tacit acceptance of long-term immigration processes and permanent settlement. The legal apparatus that guaranteed residency to those who met the requirements, either through the Aliens Act or the regulations of the EEC, were part of an early, skeletal integrative apparatus. The awkward attempts by public officials to develop a coherent discourse about how social incorporation and civic participation would follow patterns of permanent settlement illustrates how the discursive practices in this case lagged behind the development of this particular node of the integrative apparatus, which was primarily structured by regulations about legal residency and housing.

In 1965, the same year that the Aliens Act was passed, the Federal Ministry of Labour set up a new department called "The Department for the Coordination of All Policies for the Incorporation of Foreign Workers into the Economy and Society of the Federal Republic."[89] The Labour Ministry designed this department to collect information about workers' lives: they commissioned scholarly work, tracked rates of regular and irregular immigration and family togetherness, observed and watched whether Communists exerted influence on labour organizing, and collected criminality rates for foreigners. In short, they compiled any statistical and demographic information that would allow them to assess the social realities of the guest worker population and their families in a centralized governmental location.

Foucault theorizes that this kind of information gathering at the level of the population is characteristic of modern, complex states and forms the knowledge gathering arm of an apparatus. In his words, modern societies have "precisely" and appropriately termed this kind of knowledge gathering "'statistics,' meaning the science of the state."[90] Statistical knowledge about guest workers was not just compiled to understand how this new "population" lived, but rather constitutes an example of what he calls "a set of doctrinal principles concerning how to increase the power and wealth of the state."[91] The expansion of institutional apparatuses rooted in administrative policies, like the *Ausländergesetz*, or the regulations on housing and settlement, are to be expected as the government learns how to govern a more diverse society. But just as immigrant populations must be managed, so too is it necessary for governments to maintain a monopoly on power while managing political shifts.

The Emergence of a Consolidated Far Right

Several historical commentators writing about the beginnings of the guest worker programs in the Federal Republic mention, almost in passing, how the National Democratic Party emerged in the mid-1960s alongside the extra-parliamentary Left movements (feminist, ecological, liberatory sexual, and anti-capitalist movements) and that these political changes mobilized guest workers as a political issue.[92] The brief recession of 1966–7 and the end of the *Wirtschaftswunder* played a role in this mobilization, as did the first SPD-CDU Grand Coalition between the centrist parties, which provided space at the political margins for new forms of political opposition.[93] At each juncture in the history of migration to Germany, at each historical moment where migration begins to be viewed as a problem, there is a corresponding reactionary element in politics that emerges alongside changes to migration policy or to the demographic landscape. In the 1960s, the National Democratic Party emerged on a landscape that pitted two unique immigrant groups against each other: expellees and guest workers.

The development of the National Democratic Party (NPD) is not causally connected to the rise in the numbers of guest workers who entered West Germany in the early 1960s. In fact, the primary concern of far-right agitators in the 1960s was the unification of Germany and a return to the borders of 1937, including the eastern areas now belonging to Poland, from which ethnic Germans had been expelled. But the numbers of guest workers rapidly increased at the same time that far-right political actors consolidated their splintered efforts into a single party. Of interest for the study of integration politics is how some expellees, by virtue of their German identity, participated in far-right agitation that was nationalistic and xenophobic. NPD propaganda mobilized a German national identity by turning guest workers and immigrant families into scapegoats.[94] The centralization of far-right groups into a single party created a specific far-right node within the integrative apparatus that linked together nationalism, ethnonational identity, and anti-immigrant platforms and clearly positioned these rhetorical connections within a political party. The racial politics of the NPD, evident in their recuperation of Nazi biographies and fervent rejection of German responsibility for the Holocaust, shows how whiteness holds up the integrative apparatus.[95] Sarrazin, for instance, reproduced the links between Germans, German expellees, and "integrable" Eastern Europeans in starkly visible ways when he insisted on creating detailed racist hierarchies about the integrability of various groups. Debates about Eastern Europeans of ethnic German descent (*Spätaussiedler*) who immigrated in the 1990s following German unification are another point of reference for how whiteness serves as the foundation for German national identity. In the mid-1960s, however, this node was limited to alliances between neo-fascists, some extremist expellees, and policies that promoted the racialized recruitment of guest workers considered to be – or able to pass as – white.

As the military occupation of West Germany was coming to a close, a variety of smaller political parties with far-right platforms emerged as early as 1948. Far-right parties were essentially prohibited during the occupation, although the American occupiers seemed to be much more rigid in this respect than the French or the British. The Soviet occupiers were pursuing their own socialist political domination and moving towards one party rule – all political organizing outside of the Communist Party was suppressed. The founding myth of the German Democratic Republic as an anti-fascist state never would have granted legitimacy to a right-wing extremist political force. 1948 was also the year when the occupying powers in West Germany lifted bans on political activity for expellee populations.[96]

At the start of the 1950s, the far-right spectrum was dotted with small, primarily regional parties. The DRP (*Deutsche Reichspartei*), the BHE (*Bund der Heimatvertriebenen und Entrechteten*, the expellee party) and the SRP (*Sozialistische Reichspartei*) were various right-wing parties that stood for elections during the early years of the Federal Republic. The SRP was banned in 1952 for being undemocratic.[97] The GB/BHE succeeded in gaining representation in national parliament for the second electoral period (1953–7), but failed to top the newly instituted 5 per cent hurdle for the third electoral period.[98] Many politicians had also already defected from the BHE to the CDU by the time that the BHE failed to achieve representation at the national level, and Neubach points out that former BHE representatives joined the NPD in similar proportions to people from other parties, thus laying to rest the myth of the extremist expellee.[99] In 1961, the GB/BHE merged with the remnants of another splinter party, the DP (*Deutsche Partei*). In 1964, the National Democratic Party was formally founded through a merger of what was left of the DRP and the BHE/DP.[100] For the first time in West German postwar history, the far right had coalesced in a single party that achieved electoral representation in multiple regional elections.[101]

The National Democratic Party was explicitly ethnonationalist and also celebrated and tried to recuperate the Nazi pasts of many of its members and functionaries.[102] However, it is important to point out that while the NPD mobilized ethnonationalist slogans and occasionally scapegoated guest workers as a political tactic, the National Democratic Party emerged on a political landscape on which guest workers were neither seen as immigrants nor as potential heirs to German citizenship through naturalization. In this respect, the goals of the mainstream German government converged with those of the far right. Neither group planned for the permanent migration of guest workers. While guest workers could be mobilized as a political problem and targeted through rhetoric, there was no real political need for immigrants to be included into the (admittedly skeletal) NPD statements.

Both political commentators and NPD members asserted that the National Democratic Party lacked a coherent platform.[103] The most pressing issues for the NPD were territorial: members were deeply concerned with reclaiming the German territorial boundaries of 1937 and the unification of East and West Germany into a single German nation.[104] Other important issues for the NPD included the remilitarization of Germany, anti-corruption, and anti-foreign (i.e., American) investment, subventions for farmers to guarantee local agricultural production, an end to German foreign development aid (money sent from Germany to underdeveloped nations), anti-sexualization and a return to dignity for women, pro-natalist policies, a rejection of German guilt for the Holocaust, and reparations for widows and soldiers who served in the war.[105]

NPD members exhibited a strong anti-Americanist ideology and seethed about the postwar occupation and "Americanization" of West Germany.[106] In this way, the political desires of this neo-fascist party were primarily concerned with and reproduced the discourse of nationalist purity that had prompted some of the party members' own expulsion from the Eastern territories. For expellee members of the party as well as for former Nazis, their own history of expulsion and forced migration was inherently intertwined with the division of Germany and the fall of the Nazi Empire. Expellee identities and the historical formation of their subjectivity thus overlapped with far-right nationalist politics in unique way that most later immigrant groups could not access.[107] However, just because *some* expellees held political beliefs that overlapped with far-right political ideas, readers should not mistake this partial correlation for a blanket one. As Neubach suggests, it is most plausible that expellees were voting within the two large parties of the centre, and prominent members of the Federation of Expellees were primarily affiliated with the CDU. Most expellees had experienced the negative effects of fascist rule and lost everything on their exodus. After 1945, it was unlikely that the majority would have forgotten these traumatic events and joined a neo-fascist party, especially former members of the SPD.[108]

The success of the NPD in regional elections was both marked and brief. After reaching a high of 9.8 per cent in Bremen's provincial elections in 1968,[109] the party failed to meet the 5 per cent hurdle in the 1969 federal elections, thus hibernating until their resurgence as a regional party in the *Neue Länder* (new states in the East) after unification.[110] The reason it is important to connect guest worker migration with the founding of the National Democratic Party is to show how its electoral success (however brief) in the mid-1960s created a structural node adjacent to an emerging integrative apparatus through which racist and xenophobic ideas found political expression. The NPD's consolidating infrastructure was able to mobilize former Nazis, *some* expellees, and right-wing sympathizers into a group with shared concerns. The rhetoric and argumentation against foreigners and for an ethnonationalist state arose from the political centralization that brought together multiple far-right parties into an organized group. The NPD practically vanished from the mainstream political landscape after the 1969 Bundestag elections until unification. Despite going "underground," the consolidation of the far right into one party not only briefly mobilized a nationalist political campaign across West Germany, but also served as a kind of reservoir for neo-fascist and ethnonationalist ideas. Even during the decades when the NPD was unable to mobilize in a way that would secure political representation for the party, members and political actors kept political ideas alive, perhaps unintentionally providing rhetoric for future right-wing movements to emulate. The right wing was not yet – in the mid-1960s – connected to the emerging apparatus of integration. These developments remained separate until the late 1980s and accelerated around the time of German unification. But the construction of a nativist political constituency occurred alongside the construction of an apparatus concerned with the management of migration and the collection of information on foreign populations. Through the institutionalization of a party that became legible to the German public through the elections of the late 1960s, it would be possible for a later integrative apparatus to expand and incorporate the nativism characteristic of the far-right party family into integration politics.

Chapter Six

How the Integrative Apparatus Expands

The period of formal guest worker migration was merely 18 years, and this period neither represented consistent acceleration in foreign worker recruitment nor did the recruitment ban in 1973 signal the end of migration. During the recession of 1966–7, the number of foreign workers in West Germany dropped temporarily, only to grow exponentially after the economy picked back up in the late 1960s. A rapid expansion of foreign worker recruitment followed this short period of contraction, which ended abruptly with the recruitment ban of 1973. Fearing they would not be able to cross borders freely in the future, workers from countries outside the European Economic Community (EEC) began to send for their spouses and children after 1973, leading the number of foreign residents to rise moderately, even after formal recruitment ended.[1] As the number of foreign workers fluctuated, policies changed, and the massive postwar economic boom slowed. A different kind of migration overlapped with the end of the period of guestworker recruitment and became the most heatedly discussed migration issue in the 1970s and 1980s: refugee migration. Decolonization, war, civil unrest, and the impending collapse of the Soviet Union all created refugee movement, and Germany was a desirable destination for many reasons.

The debates about immigration and national identity that emerged after the recruitment ban persisted through German unification and are remarkably consistent with contemporary discursive debates, often even using the same terms and tropes (or slight variations thereof) that first emerged in the 1970s. Criminality and segregation persist as elements of the parallel society trope, as discussed in chapter 2. As permanent settlement became obvious and refugee movement from outside Europe strained the postwar West German understanding of national identity as ethnic identity, there was no broad consensus in the Federal

Republic – neither in Parliament, among Cabinet ministers, nor across a broader public – as to what role immigrants should play in society. Alongside "ambivalent" policy choices, debates about naturalization and national identity proliferated, neo-Nazi activity became more frequent, and a long-lasting economic downturn exacerbated ethnic divisions in the working classes. At the same time, we can also see evidence in the 1970s of immigrant participation in the public sphere and find an emerging consensus across foreign workers, their descendants, international students, and newly resettled refugee groups that newcomers wanted a say in shaping policies that affected both their daily lives and their German futures.

We can trace discussions of integration to this period, when the term began to appear in internal conversations across government institutions. These discussions reflected a need to manage increasingly complex modes of immigration and permanent settlement in the Federal Republic. Demographic, economic, and sociopolitical changes between 1966 and 1990 laid the groundwork for the various nodes of the integrative apparatus to become firmly established in German social, cultural, and political life. After all, "integration" can only become a politicized notion once countries are faced with and acknowledge the realities of permanent settlement. Just as workers began to express their intention to stay, the various networks, philosophies, and institutions that still guide contemporary integration policy and politics took root.

In the 1970s, the growing presence of foreign workers, their spouses, and their children in public space – as Stokes compellingly argues – prompted debates about "full integration," access to social benefits, and even local voting and citizenship rights for those who chose to settle in West Germany.[2] "Integration" became the leading rhetorical framework for debates about immigration and the incorporation of newcomers in the 1970s because it is in discussions about immigration and national futures that notions of *systemic* and *social* integration intersect. Citizenship is a form of incorporation into social, political, economic, and daily life. Citizenship rights can provide strong footing for minority groups who engage with distinct systems like education, employment, or housing, as well as to those who participate in more direct forms of civic action like voting, striking, and political lobbying. Engaging in forms of direct action like protests or strikes also constitutes a partially protected activity for citizens, who do not have to fear retaliation through deportation, as many foreign workers who participated in political activities like collective bargaining did. Consequently, rather than seeing systemic integration as relegated to the world of work, and social integration as assimilation to German cultural and linguistic norms, political participation requires both systemic integration into multiple systems, including the education level needed to understand the political process, as well as social integration into the cultural and procedural norms of political life. The SPD argued for a socially liberal foreign worker policy while it held the majority in Parliament (1969–82) and established the first bureaucratic office of the Commissioner of Integration for Foreign Workers and Their Families in 1978. But the conservative backlash across Europe in the 1980s – especially against refugee migration – prompted the CDU's return to power, and the party ran on a platform of controlling immigration in 1982. The CDU also pushed through incentives originally proposed by the SPD/FDP to entice former foreign workers to leave West Germany and return to their countries of origin (*Rückkehrhilfegesetz* [Act to Aid Return] of 1983).[3] The right wing may have been more adamant about return, but antagonism towards immigrants existed also on the left.

What are the benefits of reading the period between 1966 and 1990 as historically continuous? At first glance, this time period may seem willfully expansive. It includes recessions, multiple shifts in which parties held a political majority in Parliament, changing West German policy towards the USSR/East Germany, and the eventual fall of the Iron Curtain. For charting the emergence of an apparatus of integration, this volatility is beneficial rather than inhibiting. Polarization, backlash, and conflict reveal both opposing lines of argument as well as how those arguments bind to the non-discursive practices that structure the discursive reach of an apparatus. Especially important are events that illustrate immigrant desire: strikes, lobbying, and activism may not be concerned with integration as an ultimate goal. But in contrast to government skepticism about "assimilability" or "integrability," these activities provide ample evidence that immigrants wanted to stay and, above all else, wanted to participate in the public and private spaces that shaped their lives.

Both Foucault and Agamben argue that an apparatus emerges not in institutions or discourse per se, but rather exists in the spaces and networks *between* these various nodes. Rather than conceiving of conflict as singularly divisive, conflict can also represent a form of connection. Any dialectical method provides a framework for understanding that contradiction or opposing views offer the prospect of movement. But I want to be very clear that the notions of conflict and contradiction I have in mind, which serve as a form of connection or linkage between nodes in an apparatus, do not ascribe any linear progress narrative to contemporary integration policy. An apparatus of integration is not the inevitable telos of post-war German society. Government officials had

already acknowledged by the mid-1960s that permanent settlement
was taking place, even if 11 to 12 million of the 14 million foreign workers who at one point resided in Germany *did* return to their countries
of origin.[4]

Multiple scholars point out that there are many moments in the historical record where various immigration debates in Germany could
have changed direction and led to a different outcome than the contemporary reliance upon an integrative paradigm.[5] Conflict can be a form
of resistance and work against injustice or invisibility, but it can also be
a way to claim space and influence discursive or material conditions. It
is not purely antagonistic. Conflict can render conditions either visible
or invisible, irrespective of one's position on the political spectrum. At
its most reductive, conflict requires at least two parties with different
goals to exist in contact with one another. This basic understanding of
conflict reflects the friction necessary for an apparatus to emerge, which
requires society to cast a social development as a problem in need of an
urgent solution. Connecting various nodes between systems and
articulating discursive and non-discursive practices as social practices
requires spaces in which these conflicts can emerge and change. Conflict
both creates the connections between nodes and makes visible which
nodes are engaged at any point in time, offering a way to move beyond
binary relationships and into complex and complicated networks of
connection, engagement, and influence. The particularly positive connotation in Germany of a *Streitkultur* (a culture of debate) as essential
to healthy democracy also reveals the cultural relevance of conflict as a
political and cultural good.[6]

While the 1970s and 1980s are critical for understanding how a contemporary apparatus of governmentality developed around the notion
of "integration," this is also a period of German history that remains
under-researched. A good deal of scholarly energy focused first on
the arrival of foreign workers and later on the contemporary conflicts
between German and immigrant cultural norms.[7] In terms of integration politics, the 1970s–1990s are the foundational decades for understanding how discourses about permanent or temporary immigrant
settlement became intertwined with the construction of German
national identity and culture in its contemporary forms. They are also
the decades that thus need more scholarly attention.

This chapter will explore multiple conflicts that informed political
interventions about the incorporation of newcomers into German life
between the mid-1960s and unification in 1990. First, interministerial
conflict as well as fears of reproducing Nazi rhetoric and policy
thwarted more progressive policy choices that could have structured

the incorporation of foreign workers and asylum seekers and their families. Second, this widespread ambivalence about permanent settlement was both exacerbated and accompanied by what to call these processes. Lexical disagreement as to what these interventions and policy choices should be called also inhibited lawmakers' ability to imagine incorporation beyond the paradigms of assimilation or "forced Germanization." But citizens and foreign residents were not as hemmed in as lawmakers seemed to be, and both wildcat strikes in factories and nonprofit organizing by private citizens married to foreign residents shows that individuals were "integrated" to a far greater degree than the government acknowledged. Gender continued to play a significant role in how conflicts about immigration and national identity were managed, and guest worker and immigrant activism proves that people living in Germany wanted to participate fully in all areas of German social and political life. As more people were eligible for classification as refugees in the 1970s and 1980s, many Germans began to treat asylum seekers in particular with growing suspicion, especially their motives for seeking refuge. This suspicion both linked integration politics to racial hierarchies and laid the foundation for a securitization of migration discourse. Social frustration with immigrants claiming participatory rights as they lobbied for legal changes and organized wildcat strikes in factories appeared as a matter of course. Finally, the conservative backlash against foreign worker and refugee migration across Europe may have translated into broad support both for Helmut Kohl's four-term chancellorship as well as the public sentiment that foreign workers and immigrants had merely two options: to "integrate" or go home.

Federal Conflicts about the Incorporation of Foreign Workers

If, as I suggest, we consider the period between the 1966–7 recession and unification in 1990 as coterminous, it is the open debate about extending citizenship as an inevitable outcome of "full integration" for immigrants that makes such delimitation possible. Before the government could consider naturalization, however, it would need to engage with the central quandary for federal policymaking around foreign workers: a deep sense of ambivalence about whether foreign worker recruitment should use a policy of rotation or integration as its guiding principle.[8] In the 1970s and afterwards, this ambivalence would also surface in debates about how to limit or uphold the basic guarantee of asylum enshrined in the West German Basic Law.

Archival material proves that at the federal level, politicians understood as early as the mid-1960s that they were dealing with permanent immigration processes, found broad permanent settlement of foreign workers to be undesirable, and even discussed changing citizenship laws nearly 30 years before naturalization for foreigners in Germany became a reality.[9] However, politicians and cabinet officials offered no strong, singular vision for incorporating newcomers, much less could such a vision have succeeded politically. In the context of widespread political ambivalence, Schönwälder asks, "How can we explain a half-hearted policy that was neither consistently for nor against immigration?"[10]

First, the widely propagated narrative that the end of foreign labour recruitment was triggered by the 1973 oil crisis and that German politicians had been oblivious to processes of permanent settlement under foreign worker agreements does not hold up in light of historical scholarship.[11] The assumption that "[i]gnorance and the dominance of economic interests are [...] why German politicians allowed settlement but were unprepared for the emergence of a multiethnic German society" has become ingrained in the national narrative of foreign worker recruitment.[12] Characterizing the recruitment ban as a side-effect of the 1973 oil crisis also absolves German policymakers of their responsibility to create coherent policies to guide settlement. This narrative subtly justifies the ban as the logical outcome of a supply chain crisis stoked by Middle East politics, taking politicians' statements at face value, instead of acknowledging that the oil crisis gave policymakers a convenient justification for ending recruitment cast in the terms of an economic downturn. Several scholars now argue that the factors leading to the recruitment ban were multiple, and included frustration with foreign worker strikes, security concerns after the 1972 Olympic bombing in Munich, as well as the political need to seem in "control" of large-scale migration movements during the conservative turn across Western Europe.[13]

If foreign worker recruitment agreements were used as a tool of foreign policy in the 1950s and '60s, domestic politics in the 1970s and '80s were critical in shaping how the integrative apparatus arose. Some of the ambivalence in immigration policy arose from how conflicts about managing foreign workers mapped onto institutional structures. The Federal Ministry of Labour and the Federal Ministry of the Interior competed with each other for control over the jurisdiction of foreign workers and for the power to set the terms of *Ausländerpolitik* (foreigner politics/policy).[14] The discrepant goals of the Minister of the Interior and the Minister of Labour, alongside the ambivalent lexical choices to discuss immigration to Germany and social integration, reflect the ambivalence of public opinion in the early 1970s. Westhoeff shows that newspaper coverage was similarly ambivalent, with progressive papers criticizing the German government for missteps while conservative outlets put forth arguments designed to neutralize charges of discrimination or German guilt.[15] But as Schönwälder notes, "among the wider public, neither a harsher restrictionist course nor a consistent policy of integration was likely to find unequivocal support, and the government feared major conflicts."[16] It was partially a fear of societal conflict that impacted the ability of policymakers to craft a clear and inclusive vision for the future. In order to acknowledge the reality of permanent settlement, the government needed to articulate a vision of the good life for foreign workers and their descendants. Against the backdrop of nearly 20 years of recruitment, which had partially garnered public acceptance for guest workers by insisting on the myth of return, it was clear conflict would emerge once demographic change became visible. In order to bridge the gap between discourse and demography, politicians embraced a contradictory policy of "'return-oriented integration' as the *Süddeutsche Zeitung* described it in 1973, a self-contradictory and inconsistent policy which tried to combine the incompatible aims of both integrating and getting rid of the migrants."[17] The integrative apparatus expanded in debates that far exceeded the mere management of refugee or foreign worker immigration to Germany. Ambivalent policy choices that neutralize, ignore, or simply permit the persistence of conflict increase the severity of the backlash, especially among the far right and conservative parties, who can then blame the left for inaction during their time controlling the government. The conservative backlash that desired to limit and integrate immigration also arose from the various *successes* foreign workers experienced by claiming their rights in West Germany through strikes and changes to citizenship law – in short, due to foreign workers' success in leveraging their political power to achieve their goals.

While the Federal Ministry of the Interior was responsible for questions of citizenship and administering foreigner law (*Ausländerrecht*), the Federal Ministry of Labour had actively claimed responsibility since August 1965 for coordinating responses to the (growing) concerns of immigrants, even creating a special section in 1971 to coordinate various tasks around questions of foreign employment and the economics of family settlement.[18] In the late 1960s, the Ministry of Labour had no desire to end recruitment. Multiple scholars describe the discussions between 1969 and 1971 at the Ministry of Labour about future foreign recruitment as "optimistic" and maintain that bureaucrats foresaw both continued foreign recruitment and also recognized a high assimilative potential among foreign workers and their families.[19] Some scholars argue that this optimism arose from the fact that the 1966–7 recession had been quickly reversed, "thus demonstrating the possibility that the government could step in effectively and steer the economy."[20] Conversations within the *Sozialpolitische Gesprächsrunde* (Sociopolitical Forum), a federal consulting group that included "major actors in civil society," strongly rejected any suggestion that the foreign workforce should be reduced.[21] In October 1973 (just one month before the recruitment ban was issued!), the Economic Ministry estimated that 2.5 million foreign workers were necessary to maintain the labour force and "did not call for a recruitment stop."[22] Even the foreign secretary did not support a recruitment ban, noting that based on conversations during his visits abroad, reducing the number of foreign workers would have negative diplomatic effects on the relationships between West Germany and sending countries.[23] This "optimistic" approach also appeared at the regional level: the labour ministers of various West German states had already agreed that they wanted to pursue a politics of incorporation and vowed to intensify their cooperative efforts in 1969.[24] Around the start of the 1970s, then, politicians and bureaucrats asserted that West Germany simply *required* foreign labourers to maintain a fully functioning economy. Labour Minister Walter Arendt even declared in 1971 that foreign workers contributed to economic growth and should be recognized for their value rather than being thought of as a burden.[25]

Despite broad economic optimism, conflict at the federal level arose from divergent conceptualizations of the structure of foreign worker agreements. Given the premise that foreign worker recruitment must continue, debates after the 1966–7 recession centred mainly around whether continued recruitment should be based on a policy of rotation or a policy of integration.[26] While rotation would be a "potentially effective" strategy to prevent immigration, integration would eventually lead to both permanent settlement and, taking this policy option to its logical conclusion, "full" integration would have to include naturalization.[27] The Interior Ministry rejected a policy of reduction through rotation not only because – as the Labour Ministry and the Employment Agency also feared – putting limits on foreign recruitment would "require an allocation mechanism reminiscent of the Nazis' forced labour system," but also because the Interior Ministry found it "unfeasible" to use expulsions as a disciplinary measure to make sure the limits on a maximum stay in Germany held.[28]

Interior Minister Genscher (FDP, 1969–74) was the first elite politician who publicly favoured a policy of naturalization for permanent immigrants.[29] In the lead up to the federal elections in October 1972, Genscher gave a now widely cited interview to the *Westdeutsche*

Allgemeine Zeitung.[30] In *Becoming Multicultural*, Triadafilos Triadafilopoulos neatly sums up Genscher's comments:

> Hans-Dietrich Genscher attracted significant press coverage by proposing a two-pronged response to Germany's migration-membership dilemma. On the one hand, Genscher argued that Germany had reached the "limits of receptiveness" and should therefore scale down its foreign recruitment policies; on the other hand, he wondered whether it would not make sense to formulate a "real immigration policy" that offered migrants who had effectively cut off ties to their former countries a "real chance at integration in our country."[31]

This two-pronged policy of limiting entry and integrating permanent immigrants would become the dominant migration paradigm across Western Europe by the 1980s.[32] During a meeting of the *Innenausschuss* (Home Affairs Select Committee) in February 1973, Genscher laid out "quite elaborate guiding principles for (*Grundkoordinaten*), alternatives to and the problems of a future foreigner politics (*Ausländerpolitik*)."[33] Genscher also argued that Germany had become a "country of immigration" and therefore needed a comprehensive "immigration policy."[34] This rhetoric seems unique to Genscher, since the Interior Ministry had long supported the notion that Germany was not a country of immigration, nor was an immigration policy evident in the revisions to naturalization guidelines completed in 1971.[35] Genscher ultimately could not find sufficient cabinet support for such a policy.[36] Neither of the two policy documents subsequently composed in March and June 1973 on this issue were taken up for debate in their respective committees.[37]

Integration was a hard sell to the Ministry of Labour due to fears that foreign workers posed a competitive threat to German workers, as well as Labour Minister Walter Arendt's personal opposition to naturalization.[38] While Genscher asked his colleagues to "opt for a 'true immigration policy with full integration,'" Arendt was not in favour of such a plan.[39] So, despite the Ministry's rejection of a policy of rotation, the Labour Minister also did not support a policy of "full" integration, thereby positioning the political views of the Labour Minister against the Minister of the Interior. Genscher was even out of step with his own ministry, his party *and* the broader public on this issue, given that the Interior Ministry did not favour offering a path to citizenship, either.[40] Genscher's statements hardly dissolved the competition between the Ministries of Labour and the Interior, and both continued to work on separate plans for German *Ausländerpolitik* between 1972 and 1973.[41]

That Genscher advocated for full integration while the Interior Ministry continued to insist that Germany was not a country of immigration reflects the diffuse and multiple points of discursive and ideological conflicts in government at this time. Schönwälder pointedly asserts that in cabinet conversations, the conflicts between the Ministry of Labour and the Ministry of the Interior about rotation and integration reflected an environment where "no one wanted to be the villain," nor did either want to be responsible for limiting foreign recruitment or preventing permanent settlement.[42] She views the choice to strengthen residency rights as a way "to honour the government's commitment to a policy of integration" and thus to represent a "compromise between restrictionism and integration."[43] Given the contemporary outcomes of integration politics, I argue that attempts to neutralize conflicts are a form of stasis that in this case pushed the decision-making process into an even more conflict-ridden future.

The ambivalence of foreign worker politics at this time is inseparable from the difficult process of Germans attempting to come to terms with the past. Both the expulsion of foreign workers and offering naturalization as an option were seen as policies reminiscent of Nazi demographic politics (Bevölkerungspolitik): Parliamentary State Secretary at the Ministry of Interior Wolfram Dorn (FDP) argued in 1971 that "'in light of an earlier, expansive politics of naturalization, the impression of mass naturalization programs [should] be avoided.'"[44] The weight of the fascist past inhibited many government officials from being able to envision a progressive future in which a multicultural Germany where naturalization was an option would not resemble the forced migration politics and segregation of the past. Part of this may be due to philosophical contradictions policy-makers created for themselves. Sociologist Rist's assessment of European worker policy, published in 1979, was particularly damning:

> The immigrant countries appear to be opting for the creation of a stable migrant worker population committed to long-term residency. It is in this sense that the countries of the North are speaking of the "integration" of the migrant workers, an integration of expedience that will allow the sizable group to function at a minimal level of effort within the host country. It is not an integration that aims at the enhancement of either assimilation or pluralism, but rather a process to institutionalize marginality.[45]

Furthermore, Rist also pointed out that it was already clear that the refusal to make clear decisions about exclusion, expulsion, and limiting immigration across Western Europe was producing social conflicts that could lead to violence: "Rotterdam experienced an anti-Turkish riot in 1972; race riots broke out in Marseilles in 1973 that left six Algerians dead; bombs exploded at a Turkish bank and the Turkish Consulate office in Zürich in May 1976. From all sides has come the evidence that to treat the consequences of the south to north migration with benign neglect courts further schism and more intransigent difficulties."[46]

In the period after the 1966–7 recession during which recruitment expanded, acceptance of permanent settlement occurred in a wide variety of contexts. In 1971, representatives from the *Arbeiterwohlfahrt* (AWO, worker's welfare organization, politically left) declared at a federal conference that Germany had become a country of immigration, acknowledging the reality of permanent settlement. That same year, the Christian Democrats' Committees for Social Affairs (*Sozialausschüsse*, politically right), also "declared Germany a de facto country of immigration" at the party's convention.[47] Accepting that immigration had occurred was the first step towards designing systems that could incorporate immigrants into all aspects of German daily life, and both right and left seemed to agree that permanent settlement was just that: permanent.

While the Ministry of Labour and the Ministry of the Interior fought for dominance in setting the terms of federal immigration politics, broader conversations about immigrant incorporation took place across the federal Cabinet and in Parliament, as well as in the broader public sphere. Schönwälder points out that as early as 1971, churches, journalists, and other social circles publicly demanded new (integrative) policies that would permit naturalization: "According to a widespread consensus in the newspapers, the government's rejection of rotation and its declared policy of integration could hardly mean anything but the eventual naturalization of the long-term immigrants. What else could it mean, if differences between Germans and immigrants were to be abolished?"[48] It is doubtful, however, that most elite actors wanted to "abolish" the differences between Germans and immigrants. The widespread notion that foreign workers should function as a kind of "industrial reserve army" – a phrase repeated by nearly every scholar after its utterance by Willy Brandt in 1973 – suggests that many Germans still preferred a foreign workforce that would remain invisible and return home when no longer needed. As Rist wrote presciently in 1979: "Migrants from the peripheral countries are to remain on the periphery in the host countries, save for the manner in which they offer their labour."[49]

Lexical Conflicts: Assimilation, Integration, Incorporation, Adjustment

Genscher's proposed policy of "full integration" for immigrants, which would have included naturalization, was unsuccessful at drumming up Cabinet-level support, but the eventual dominance of "integration" as the term to describe multiple processes of immigrant incorporation shows that Genscher's perspective eventually became the dominant one. In the 1970s, "assimilation" (*Assimilation*) was strongly associated with fascism, and "incorporation" (*Eingliederung*) was strongly associated with the postwar exodus of ethnic German refugees. "Integration" (*Integration*) emerged in the 1970s as a relatively neutral alternative and was primarily applied to foreign workers. Other words used to describe parts of these processes include *Aufnahme, Einfügung, Einordnung,* and *Anpassung* (acceptance, inclusion, placement, and adaption).

Discourse provides the necessary scaffolding for an apparatus, and the discursive scaffolding for the integrative apparatus is clearly visible in early rhetorical conflicts that position integration as completely separate from assimilation, in addition to the ensuing rhetorical manoeuvres that were required to portray "full integration" as somehow stopping short of citizenship rights.[50] Politicians and bureaucrats in the 1970s are inconsistent in their lexical choices because the language around immigrant incorporation was and is historically and politically charged.

The long history of assimilation debates in Germany reaches back through multiple centuries, and includes philosophical treatises about Jewish assimilation, Prussian relationships with Polish subjects and the ever-changing borders of Poland, and the forced labour practices and genocide of the Second World War. In the eighteenth century, philosophers were deeply concerned with Jewish emancipation, naturalization, and their incorporation into a German nation-state. Johann Gottfried Herder, an 18th century German philosopher, held conflicting views on both Jewish "integration" and multinational states, seeing the former as inevitable in Europe and the latter as an abomination. Johann Gottlieb Fichte, known for his "Speeches to the German Nation," viewed Jewish people as incapable of assimilating into any state.[51] After successive phases of legal emancipation granted to Jews in various principalities after 1848 and after Prussian unification in 1871, Jewish people were granted access to citizenship rights. The question of assimilation followed emancipation and constituted a rich range of processes that took place unevenly across Europe, as Jewish people both migrated from the village to the urban centre and debated the secular behaviours they desired to take up.[52] This openness to Jewish assimilation ended with Hitler's rise to power in 1933. The question of assimilation is thus contextually bound to Jewish exclusion and genocide over multiple centuries. Political invocation of "assimilation" in the 1970s was carefully avoided or chosen against the backdrop of this history.

One of the terms that was flat-out rejected during this period was the notion of Germanization. Germanization had been the name for land-grabbing policies pursued during the Nazi territorial expansion into Eastern Europe, as well as for social policies described under the same name.[53] These policies created complicated and often tense hierarchies between ethnic groups who might now all be described as "ethnic German."[54] In Eastern Europe, subsumed under the term "Germanization" were also brutal policies of kidnapping "phenotypically pleasing Polish, Czech, and Yugoslavian children" to be brought up in German families.[55] Historian Tara Zahra argues that in and of itself, the word "Germanization" has a long history in the borderlands of Eastern Europe, reaching as far back as the Hapsburg Empire, and that this long history is critical for a scholarly understanding of the broad swath of policies that can be historically included under the term.[56] In the context of postwar German history, however, the Nazi connotation of "Germanization" surfaced repeatedly in political conversations about immigrant incorporation, and was vehemently rejected by postwar politicians and bureaucrats. The mention of "Germanization" primarily surfaces as a defensive manoeuvre: politicians define integration, incorporation, or assimilation as a process that has little to do with "Germanization" before they are even accused of advocating "Germanizing" policies. Internal governmental discussions about permanent settlement thus tended to insist that assimilation (sometimes called "forced Germanization") as a top-down policy was not a desirable goal. But not everyone agreed that naturalization was essential for "full integration," either.[57]

Historians like Karin Hunn have laid out how getting caught in a lexical conflict can limit policymakers' effectiveness as well as their ability to assert a strong political vision for the future. In the spring of 1969, at a meeting of ministerial undersecretaries (*Staatssekretärbesprechung*), West German bureaucrats discussed various approaches towards the social incorporation (*Eingliederung*) of foreign workers. The themes of this meeting would eventually appear in what is often thought of as the first document of integration politics, the April 1970 memo "Grundsätzen zur Eingliederung ausländischer Arbeitnehmer" (Principles for the Incorporation of Foreign Employees).[58] In order that foreign workers could become more productive workers, the undersecretaries agreed to support policies geared towards the acquisition of the German language as well as job training, which they hoped would also make foreign workers more "independent in work and social life."[59] Beyond broader agreement on the skills necessary for increasing productivity and independence, however, this meeting did not produce consensus on what it would mean to "integrate" workers nor to what degree such an incorporation should take place.[60] At this meeting, notions of loyalty to the German state or some form of "assimilation" that could be demanded of foreign workers were both rejected. Because these terms are fluid, and actors use various euphemisms and substitutions to express themselves in these conversations, the historical record of a single meeting reflects how perplexing the language used to describe the incorporation of immigrants could be. In particular, this lexical conflict shows that there are multiple outcomes from conflict. Some conflicts illustrate connection, others are destructive, and some lead to impasse.

At this meeting of *Staatssekretäre*, representatives actively negotiated the discursive field, trying to find a name for the social processes that accompany immigration. The ideological values in conflict in debates about assimilation became clear in an exchange between State Secretaries Kattenstroth (Labour) and Harkort (Foreign Service). Harkort insisted during this conversation that it was a fact that no one "could belong to two cultures" (*Kulturkreise*).[61] But Kattenstroth argued that incorporation should be pursued to prevent de facto segregation in national community centres – at the same time he insisted that incorporation did not mean assimilation. Kattenstroth also felt it necessary to clarify an earlier mention of *Eingliederung* (incorporation) insisting "that also the Federal Ministry of Labour in no way was interested in assimilation."[62] While Harkort's views are simply false, Kattenstroth's rhetorical moves ultimately trap him in a lexical knot. It is unclear to me what Kattenstroth's preferred vision of "integration" might be, other than an option with no connotations of assimilation – which then raises the question of why he sees any incorporation policy as necessary.

The inability of bureaucrats to move beyond word choice and evaluate what kinds of policy choices might lie beyond the immediate, knee-jerk reactions to specific, politically charged words, comes through in Hunn's descriptions of this meeting of undersecretaries. The exchange about incorporation, integration, and assimilation prompted rhetorical compromise but no operational policy vision. The statement upon which the *Bundesressorts* (federal ministries) could agree argued that federal government policy should in no way represent an attempt to assimilate foreign workers. Instead, foreigners should maintain their differences in order to return to their countries of origin.[63] The federal ministries at this meeting did nothing remarkable: they agreed merely on a negative statement and did not come down clearly on the side of integration *or* rotation.

The rejection of assimilation as a purported goal of integration policy, as well as the general imprecision of this case of compromise and rhetorical disagreement do not just represent lexical or rhetorical distinctions. In these internal government discussions, there was no consensus about some of the most fundamental questions for continued foreign worker recruitment, which Hunn neatly sums up: How long could workers expect to stay? What were the terms of linguistic, professional, and social integration into "the German milieu," as Kattenstroth called it? To what degree would such an integrative practice impact foreign workers' ability to return (*Rückkehrfähigkeit*) or their will to do so?[64] An inability to decide on a clear vision for the future also illustrates that the lack of agreement on terminology reflected a misunderstanding of the scale of recruitment and inhibited pragmatic policymaking. At this 1969 meeting, the various stakeholders assumed that the number of foreign workers would reach 1.88 million by 1980. But that number was reached by 1970 – merely *months* after this conference took place.[65]

These lexical debates were pervasive and ongoing. An internal paper of the German Trade Union Confederation (DGB) stated that: "The GTUC is of the opinion that the Federal Republic is not a country of immigration (i.e., no politics of assimilation)."[66] The Workers' Welfare Association (AWO) argued similarly: "on behalf of the foreign workers, an 'identification with the German people or also a national assimilation [...] is very rarely intended.'"[67] Resistance to the terms "assimilation" and "forced Germanization" had a long shelf life. In 1979, ten years after the meeting of undersecretaries depicted above, the first Commissioner for Integration, Heinz Kühn (SPD), published a surprisingly progressive memo about the German futures of immigrants and their descendants. While proposing that the second and third generations of immigrants to Germany "must be offered unconditional and permanent integration" – which included citizenship as one of the primary demands – Kühn still felt it necessary to assert that integrating "children and adolescents" into mainstream classrooms posed "no risk of 'forced Germanization,'" thereby effectively accommodating and preserving the lexical variants used to describe the processes of immigrant incorporation.[68]

If incorporation or integration was seen by some as too closely related to assimilation to be practicable in a German context, it is worth looking at how integration could simultaneously be defined as culminating in or stopping short of access to citizenship rights and naturalization. If German media and politicians today frequently label immigrants or refugees as *"integrationsfähig"* (capable of integrating) or *"integrations(un)willig"* ([un]willing to integrate), we can see similar formulations in the 1960s and '70s in the context of debates about naturalization, in which immigrants are expected to be *"assimilierungsfähig"* (capable of assimilating) or *"assimilierungswillig"* (willing to assimilate). The rhetoric about naturalization thus reflects some lexical consistency with contemporary integration politics and discourse and points to conceptual overlap between assimilation and integration. If, however, policymakers like the *Staatssekretäre* or Integration Commissioner Kühn were loathe to suggest that foreign workers assimilate, when it came to naturalization, there was little resistance to seeing assimilation as the prerequisite to becoming a German citizen.[69]

As early as 1968, a department head at the Ministry of the Interior referred to as Dr. Lechner had asserted in a memo to the Parliamentary Committee of the Interior "that the organization (*Verband*) of [our] own citizens can expand only with people both inherently willing to [assimilate] and capable of assimilating."[70] Lechner's subordinate, Eckhart Schiffer, later published a 1973 article that argued against large-scale naturalization due to Germany's high population density – a peculiar argument – but also acknowledged that the state should not prohibit foreign workers from naturalizing "if they fulfilled certain conditions (*Voraussetzungen*)."[71] This argument attempts to neutralize charges of exclusion by maintaining access to naturalization for certain kinds of foreign workers. Despite Schiffer's ambivalence as to who would be permitted to naturalize, his insistence on assimilation was nonnegotiable: "Requirement of naturalization certainly should remain 'assimilation.' This requires a readiness 'to live as a German among Germans,' the sheer will to be incorporated (*Einfügung*) into the state community (*Staatsvolk*) does not suffice."[72]

That naturalization was discussed at all in the 1960s and 1970s reflects the fact that many Germans understood that foreign worker recruitment would lead to inevitable permanent settlement and that permanent settlement would require citizenship to be separated from ethnic identity. Adolf Arndt, a politician for the SPD who served in Parliament for twenty years, initiated a strikingly prescient discussion about citizenship in 1967 as part of the SPD working group on legal affairs. Arndt describes the German process of naturalization as in need of "demythologizing" and as strangely determined by "very mystical notions."[73] He also criticized *jus sanguinis* (bloodline citizenship): "It is often assumed that granting citizenship simultaneously represents an 'inclusion into the German people'."[74] This distinction did not just represent the ideological position of the centre-left SPD: the Catholic Bureau – hardly a bastion of left-wing thought – declared in 1969 that the draft revision of the citizenship law should demand that immigrants adhere to the constitutional order rather than require "getting into line with German popular and cultural life [*Einordung in das deutsche Volks- und Kulturleben*]," which was the phrase included in the revision of the law.[75] Rather than take up the suggestions made by the Catholic Bureau, the next draft of the law simply included a more neutral version of the original formulation, demanding that those who were willing to naturalize "position themselves within German standards of living [*sich in die deutschen Lebensverhältnisse einordnen*]."[76]

Schönwälder argues that this formulation still required those wishing to naturalize to prove they had met the standard of cultural and social assimilation – and it represents yet another instance of bureaucrats attempting to set the terms required for immigrant incorporation without engaging in a deep negotiation of conflict and contradictions inherent to their lexical choices and demands. It is worth asking whether the desire to avoid conflict could be better summed up as white German resistance to sharing power. Indeed, this line of argument was already clear to some functionaries in 1968. Schönwälder notes that someone in the the Working Group for Legal Policy (*Arbeitskreis Rechtspolitik*) in the SPD – perhaps, she wonders, Martin Hirsch? – made commentary in the margins of Dr. Lechner's memo. At the point where he declared that it would be impossible to relax citizenship law because the state would lose the ability to select only those future citizens willing to assimilate, this reader wrote "likely means race" in the margins.[77]

Curiously, various actors created programs during this time designed to help foreign workers "adjust" (*Hilfe zur Anpassung*), which would purportedly ease "the adjustment to German standards of living" – presumably also to prevent conflict.[78] In spite of claims by the Ministry of Labour that they were in charge of overseeing the social aspects of workers' lives, historian Rita Chin argues that the tasks of managing foreign workers were structured around "a strict (though largely unspoken) division of labour" between government and private organizations.[79] The Ministry of Labour limited its tasks to bureaucratic procedures: hiring and matching workers to employers, medical tests and conducting screenings.[80] "To the extent that government officials registered any social component to recruitment," Chin comments, "they generally off-loaded this responsibility to the company that actually hired the foreign labourers" or to the religious NGOs and unions who helped workers access services and adapt.[81] One scholar argues that it was thus churches and outside organizations that can be considered the "earliest practitioners of integration."[82] The decision to grant employers and NGOs local control – rather than drafting a federal integration policy – meant that efforts at social incorporation were also regionally specific and thus decentralized.

Schönwälder argues that these adjustment programs conceived of a one-sided adjustment coming *from* foreign workers moving *into* German society, rather than framing incorporation and adjustment as a two-way process.[83] The Sachs company, for instance, provided Turkish skilled workers with lessons in "general behaviour" that included lessons on cultural differences; how they should behave with respect to German women; eating habits, punctuality, using the toilet; and company behavioural norms.[84] *"Anpassung"* was also clearly expected by the president of the German Caritas Association, who argued that whether or not foreign workers liked German norms and customs, he expected their adherence to them.[85] This subtext continues in contemporary "integration" initiatives that sanction immigrants and refugees for perceived noncompliance (such as absences during integration courses).[86]

Both the demands these programs made of their participants and claims of program effectiveness remained vague.[87] The conversational argument that the German government just didn't understand they were dealing with permanent settlement may be a popular interpretation of the absence of coherent policy and clear objectives for policies of integration stemming from this particular constellation of government (in)action.

Naturalization could have served as a clear policy objective, but neither the DGB nor the AWO saw citizenship as a necessary goal for foreign workers. The AWO in particular argued that social integration was more important than acquiring citizenship, and declared that political debates about immigration and naturalization reflected *"Scheinprobleme"* (pseudo-problems).[88] Eberhard de Haan, who was in charge of foreign affairs for the AWO, described cultural incorporation as separate from and less pressing than the urgency of "vocational, linguistic [and] civilizing inclusion."[89] This statement represents a quite different approach from de Haan's argument from 1966, when he argued against assimilation: "Measured against the European perspective, 'the question of assimilation loses its meaning. As a category, it stems from nationalistic thought, the overemphasis of supposedly national values.'"[90] Furthermore, the AWO declared in 1973 that "[t]he sociopolitical task with which these people and their families are confronted is not their naturalization, but rather their social and societal integration."[91] The attempt to draw a clear line between social and societal integration and citizenship – as well as the assumption that foreign workers needed to be 'civilized' – is flabbergasting: Schönwälder asks "Why? And what was the motive for insisting on this distinction?"[92]

Power was clearly in play. As Rist argued in 1979, "National policy makers appear to have little choice between two courses – either exploitation and structural marginality or integration and structural equality for the immigrants."[93] From the vantage point of the present, especially after naturalization has been an option for nearly 20 years, the only plausible interpretation for why these lexical conflicts seemed so important is because they could camouflage attempts to exclude immigrants – whose presence and permanent settlement could no longer be denied – from claiming access to all the rights and duties of citizenship and from sharing the power these rights and privileges bestow.

In the 1960s and '70s, acceptance for a national public sphere in which growing minority groups could participate in shaping the national future was scattershot – and would remain so for decades to follow.[94] The lexicon that emerged in Germany to talk about this process is, in some ways, uniquely German, and represents an outcome of coming to terms with the politicized language of a fascist past. Debates about the meaning of integration and segregation; between incorporation, assimilation, and naturalization; about contradictory ideas held about the limits of participation and inclusion; as well as rhetoric that portrayed foreign workers as guests who merely came to Germany for temporary labour – all of these conflicts shifted, morphed, and competed for rhetorical prominence against the demographic backdrop of increasing permanent settlement. The term "integration" was fully intertwined with the concepts of naturalization, citizenship, and the participatory qualities of democracy from the start, no matter how emphatically bureaucrats tried to keep citizenship out of the conversation.

Guest Worker and Immigrant Activism

The West German federal government struggled to decide both how it wanted to *manage* migration (rotation or integration) as well as which vocabulary it needed to *talk* about migration (assimilation, integration, incorporation, inclusion, adjustment), often choosing – in the face of conflicts – just not to decide. But newcomers, pressured by the reality of daily life, did not wait for discursive clarity to act. Throughout the 1970s, citizens and residents participated in various political campaigns to improve their legal status, their working conditions, or their children's futures. Wildcat strikes in factories in the early 1970s, as well as the campaign for citizenship parity in marriage and family law, were two arenas in the Federal Republic where participatory, direct action illustrates how the integrative apparatus expands through non-discursive practices. Refugee politics and repatriation would become additional arenas that reached maturity as political issues in the 1980s and early 1990s. Whether or not "full integration" was defined as including citizenship rights, these participatory practices indicated that people both saw a future for themselves and their families in Germany and were also sufficiently "integrated" to pursue their goals. Furthermore, pursuing their goals offered German citizens and immigrants the opportunity to see each other as groups with shared goals, whether that be a higher wage or access to citizenship rights.

Immigration at this point, however, had become a political concern that was increasingly governed – especially after the Munich massacre during the 1972 Olympics – by discourses of securitization. The discourses about "the Mediterranean Man" that Woesthoff documents as well as the later concerns after 9/11 of terrorism and fundamentalism bookend the turn to securitization as a domestic German reaction to migration, as well as a global shift in the attitudes of highly developed countries towards Africa and the Middle East in particular.

The Munich massacre prompted the SPD to campaign on a platform of "getting tough" on immigration, and widespread deportation by West Germany of Palestinian immigrants after the hostage-taking and murder of Israeli athletes prompted German women married to Palestinian men to organize in order to secure changes to citizenship law.[95] Worried their husbands could be deported and their families disadvantaged by the gendered double standard in citizenship law, most of the discussions about citizenship rights that prompted changes in the 1970s came through German women advocating for their full rights (rather than from immigrants or foreign workers organizing a strong lobby). This organizing was likely legible due to the widespread topical concern with gender parity, the visibility of second-wave feminism, and was surely buoyed by the broader extra-parliamentary social movements of the New Left stemming from the student protests of 1968. The conflicts between state and citizen desires can help us plot how debates about citizenship that had been circulating in philosophical modes in the press and in bureaucratic conversations about foreign worker recruitment appeared in a different mode as German women lobbied for their full citizenship rights and the right of their children to inherit German citizenship.

The nexus around citizenship, binational marriages, and immigration – like the debates about lexical choices – also links integration politics to the global effects of the Holocaust and the founding of Israel as a state that engages in land-grabbing practices in the Palestinian territories (Israeli settlers began to occupy the West Bank and Gaza not at the moment of its founding in 1948, but first in 1967). It was in this context – similar to the foreign policy implications of the original guest worker recruitment agreements and the revisions to the *Ausländergesetz* (AuslG) in 1965 – that it became clear "how deeply the federal West German foreigner politics was also always defined as a politics of policing and security."[96]

Although Genscher's public statements on citizenship as the outcome of "full integration" make him seem ahead of his time, Genscher was already convinced in November of 1969 that stricter policies were needed to surveille immigrant organizations and thereby thwart criminality.[97] By 1972, 219 foreigner associations had been classified as "*sicherheitsgefährdend*" (a danger to security, a term that was not synonymous with criminal or terrorist activity, Schönwälder notes).[98] By 1970, the Ministry of the Interior had already discussed Parliament amending the 1965 Foreigner Law so that surveillance of the political activities of foreigners could come under the purview of the *Verfassungsschutz* (intelligence services). The amendment to the law did not manifest, but Schönwälder reads these plans as an indication that the left/libertarian SPD/FDP coalition tried to take a hard line on matters of immigration.[99] The justification for the amendment declared "that the FRG is no longer willing to take on this increasingly radical political behaviour of individual foreigners in the Federal Republic at the cost of its international relations and its international reputation."[100] As Schönwälder notes, the reaction of the Federal Government to Palestinian political actors who attacked Jewish people and Israeli institutions presented a tense topic for foreign relations: "[t]hat the Federal Republic was not permitted to become a 'stomping ground for competing groups of foreigners' was one of the standard statements of the Interior Minister, who certainly also emphasized that he did not want to express a 'xenophobic attitude' nor articulate 'a general suspicion of criminality.'"[101]

The Federal Government's reaction to the Israeli athletes and coaches who were taken hostage by Palestinian terrorists and subsequently killed during a failed attempt to free them in Munich in 1972 was to increase border patrols and issue sweeping deportation orders for Arab immigrants perceived as even vaguely pro-Palestinian. They also prohibited two Palestinian organizations. Both actions were later criticized in court.[102] Despite Genscher's frequent assertion that he didn't want to stoke xenophobic attitudes, the deportations and organizational bans were widely seen as doing just that in the name of projecting a

tough stance on immigration.[103] Amidst the backdrop of rising inflation and citizen concerns about domestic security, the CDU/CSU tried
even harder to portray themselves as tougher on immigration than the
SPD.[104]

Support for the integration of immigrants could retreat quickly in
the face of security concerns. When Willy Brandt later appeared at a
convention with SPD representatives in the Hessen-South district in the
run-up to the 1972 election, he declared: "A large party is not permitted
to ignore what moves 'the people' ('Menschen dieses Volkes'); demands
to liberalize foreigner policy (Ausländerrecht) was 'unworldly' (welt-
fremd). Instead what mattered was (es gelte) taking a hard line against
those who wanted 'to make the Federal Republic a hotbed of violent
activity.'"[105] It was in this political atmosphere ripe with conflict that
German women married to foreign men lobbied to change German
citizenship law. Integration was not their goal, but participation and
incorporation certainly were. It is in spaces of tension like this that the
apparatus expands.

As early as 1966, the UN had criticized Germany's citizenship policy
for German women married to foreign men.[106] Until 1972, only German
men had the right to acquire German citizenship for their foreign wives
through marriage. German women had no such option. Until 1975,
children of a German mother and foreign father could only hold their
father's citizenship – effectively stripping German mothers of their
full citizenship rights. Children of foreign fathers were not German citizens by birth, not even through the logic of jus sanguinis (bloodline
citizenship).

Bureaucrats regularly defended this double standard for binational
marriages. The department leader at the Ministry of the Interior for
questions of marriage and citizenship – Dr. Lechner – found that while
foreign wives would generally adjust to "the German lifestyle pre-
scribed through the German partner," naturalizing foreign men would
have "unwanted consequences."[107] The threat of the unintegrated foreign man is an unmistakable subtext here, revealing both the depth
of German misogyny as well as long-standing discriminatory stereotypes against foreign men.[108] These notions were not just bureaucratic:
Christian churches in Germany – in particular when confronted with
German women marrying Muslim men – held various concerns about
these marriages, including fears of cultural and ethnic mixing, perceptions of domestic abuse as widespread among foreign men, and an
acknowledgment that these women were making their right to legal
residency precarious, especially if they were later to divorce and face
custody battles.[109]

West Germany had a history of questionable treatment of children from interracial and binational partnerships: famed Afro-German poet May Ayim was born to a Ghanian father and German mother in 1960 under circumstances that granted biological fathers of illegitimate children no rights. After being put up for adoption by her biological mother, she was adopted by a white family and maintained she had an unhappy and abusive childhood.[110] Heide Fehrenbach notes that in the case of occupation children conceived between Black American GIs and German women, racial bias made marriage nearly impossible, "rendering most Black occupation children 'illegitimate,' and also foreclosing the possibility of German mothers emigrating through marriage."[111]

Against the backdrop of a growing feminist movement, German women were positioned in a state of relative privilege to foreign workers and their families given that they knew the law, knew how to assert their rights through legal challenges, could access legal counsel, and founded organizations to lobby for their rights. Their husbands were also more likely to have been international students rather than foreign workers, likely signalling both better language fluency in German as well as a higher educational level than foreign workers.[112] By far the most famous binational marriage activist was Rosi Wolf-Almanasreh, whose husband at the time was Palestinian. Fearing her husband might be one of the many Palestinians to be deported after the 1972 massacre, she founded an organization called the IAF (*Interessengemeinschaft der mit Ausländern verheirateten deutschen Frauen*, Interest Group of German Women Married to Foreigners) in September 1972.[113] This three-step process – the terrorist attack, the blanket deportation of Palestinians, and the subsequent founding of a non-profit lobby – shows how an international event created conditions under which the apparatus for domestic integration politics expanded. Later, Wolf-Almanasreh would serve as the director of Frankfurt's well-known NGO called AmkA (*Amt für multikulturelle Angelegenheiten*, Office of Multicultural Affairs), revealing how the connections between political activism, social work projects, and the persistence of political concerns around immigration politics remained relevant from the 1970s into the present and how progressive politics in reaction to regressive policy are critical for understanding how an apparatus of integration influences all German subjects.

The success of a multipronged organizational activist strategy led to various legal changes that slowly and belatedly brought parity of access to citizenship for the children of binational partnerships. Sabine Kriechhammer-Yağmur, the executive director of the IAF in 1989, described the political work of the IAF as taking place across multiple levels:

We drummed up support (*getrommelt*) at many different levels and of course not only about the topic of racism – but also emphasized it (*aber eben auch dazu*). We drummed on – in a metaphorical sense – the politicians, the parties, the ministries, the judges, the unions, in order to make people aware of our situation. We also drummed up support among women's initiatives, migrant initiatives, and in groups that dealt with human or civil rights in the broadest sense. [...] We got a lot done.[114]

As of 1 January 1975, children were finally granted the right to inherit German citizenship from either parent, and in 1983, the German Supreme Court declared the area of international private law requiring the subordination of women's rights to the legal realm of their husband's country of origin to be unconstitutional. Parity in this instance was eventually achieved with new legal measures in 1986.[115] The raced, classed, and gendered facets of binational marriages provided a different node beyond the concerns of foreign workers through which German women applied sufficient pressure to change citizenship law. While mainstream feminist organizations rejected the work of the IAF at its founding, the organization created the possibility for white German women married to foreign residents to join with the foreign women who actively looked to the IAF for information, attended their activities, and turned out to be critical instigators in the push to eventually change the IAF's name to the Association of Bi-national Families and Partnerships (*Verband binationaler Familien und Partnerschaften*).[116] Individual citizen and resident participation is critical for an apparatus to expand its reach. The activities of the IAF and other social projects represent a form of political participation that engaged in feminist politics and built solidarity with foreign women through consciousness raising to successfully lobby for legal changes that benefitted both spouses in a binational partnership.

Union organizing in the 1970s was another arena in which participatory direct action affected both factory conditions and public policy as well as the discursive portrayal of foreign workers. Unions were a particular site where conflict and contradiction took centre stage: "unions confront a difficult dilemma: choosing between nationalistic and working-class sentiments which would propel them to resist the importation of foreign labour, and recognition of the fact that the guestworkers [sic] enhance the economic well-being of the same union workers."[117] As early as 1973, scholars were aware that conflict within the working class was splitting along national and ethnic lines. While foreign workers facilitated upward mobility among European workers, foreign workers themselves remained segregated on the factory floor, were relegated to unskilled or semi-skilled positions, and were pushed into substandard housing.[118] Sociologists Castles and Kosack understood that creating a class of underskilled workers effectively divided the working class into a racialized underclass of foreign workers and a white working class they describe as indigenous to Europe. Unions were particularly aware of this conflict.[119] The division between a white German and a racialized working class persists into the present. It is the precondition required for polemics like Kelek's and Sarrazin's that demonize the working class and those in poverty at the same time that they stoke and cement racialized difference.

These racialized class conflicts came to the fore in the wildcat strikes in various auto plants common in the 1970s. Striking is a tried and true method of protest for claiming rights within a state apparatus. German unions at this time had long supported treating foreign workers in the same manner as German workers because they understood that wage suppression would make it far more difficult for German workers to earn a living wage – as would an increase in undocumented or non-union labourers, who companies could hire in order to suppress wages.[120] As Grassler, Miller, and Rist all argue, participation in strikes and other forms of protest serve to illustrate how foreign workers were already integrated into institutional structures and intended to make their futures in West Germany.[121] Lacking citizenship and an effective lobby, "there [were] few other institutional channels [other than unions] through which to make their [foreign workers'] needs and concerns known."[122] Union participation was also higher among foreign workers (22 per cent) than it was among German workers (17 per cent).[123] Political organizing was not without risk: it could open up unionized workers to the dangers of deportation, dismissal, or harassment by police. Three *IG Metall* (metalworkers union) members from Spain were arrested in Remscheid, and they were held for three days but not charged. Another Spanish trade unionist in Hannover was arrested, held for two days, and dismissed from work before legal action initiated by the union restored his position.[124]

The famous strike at the Ford plant in Cologne in 1973 shows how union organizing fuelled a growing backlash against labour. Three hundred Turkish workers who, for the second time, had returned to work late from their annual four-week vacation in Turkey, were promptly fired upon return without a grace period. The strict reaction of the management prompted anger since Turks had been demanding extensions in unpaid vacation days for years so that they could undertake the strenuous return journey from Germany to Turkey.[125] The combination of inflation and merely modest gains in salaries, as well as a factory floor pace that was too fast, also contributed to the strikes. In Cologne, the Ford strike prompted conflicts between those Turkish workers who had returned on time and those who had come back late as well, since the final assembly steps were nearly all staffed by Turkish foreign workers, and those who returned early felt the pressure created by their colleagues' absence on the line.[126]

The protest that began on the afternoon of Friday, 24 August 1973, started from the end of the line (*Endmontage*). Over the weekend, factory management and the union "considerably underestimated the willingness among the foreign workers to strike."[127] Despite rumours of leftist Turks leading the strike, Hunn points out that this was unlikely and that a broad coalition of left-wing, secular, conservative, and religious Turks were all represented among those striking – and German colleagues as well as members of the workers' council (*Betriebsräte*) joined the effort.[128] Hunn suggests that the cause for the protest was simple: workers of the Ford plant were working under poor conditions, and they felt they were being handled unfairly.[129] The broad coalition of foreign and German workers who had initially started the strike dwindled to mostly foreign workers after five days, as management offered workers a cost of living allowance of 280 marks, and offered to pay them for their days spent striking. But the Turkish workers did not see their demands being met and saw the end of the strike as a defeat: while trying to organize those working the night shift, fights broke out, and police immediately intervened, threatening foreign workers participating in the strike with deportation. Rather than changing vacation policies, restoring the jobs of those who had come back late, and honouring the right to strike for foreign workers, "dozens of workers were fired immediately because of their active participation in the strike and a larger number of workers took up the dubious suggestion of management" and decided to voluntarily resign rather than suffer being fired.[130]

Hunn interprets the conditions leading to the strike as stemming from class divisions that were becoming more pronounced because of the segregation of foreign workers from their German peers: "the obvious tendency towards racialized downward mobility [*ethnische Unterschichtung*] [led] to [the fact] that German and foreign employees could hardly develop common interests."[131] She also asserts that the strikes both garnered workers more public attention as well as revealed to unions that they needed to pay more attention to workers' needs. But extensive media coverage of the strikes prompted broad segments of the German population to ask whether continued worker recruitment was still necessary or desirable.[132]

An article from *Die Zeit* published a week after the strike put this antagonism on display: "We sat in the foreman's office and hid under the desk as the Turks made their way through the warehouse," the article begins, followed by the journalist's dramatic commentary: "Even now, fear seems to linger in this worker's body."[133] Portrayal of the strike as a kind of violence rather than labour organizing makes it possible to link participatory action to discourses of security. Despite including a great deal of factual material about the difficult working conditions and the segregation of Turkish workers into the most difficult and worst compensated jobs, ultimately this journalist frames the strike as foreign ("not a German strike"), and marks the Ford strike as the cause of "resentment about the foreigners' 'rabble rousing'."[134] Articles like this had the potential to perpetuate segregation between German and Turkish workers by cultivating fear and mistrust. This particular article ends with a call to end or at least revise recruitment, declaring that it is "high time" for the union and factory management "to take a close look at their guest worker policies."[135] This kind of media coverage hardly awakened public sympathy for the indignities suffered by Turkish workers. Federal Chancellor Willy Brandt declared that the strike at the Ford plant in Cologne was no longer even a strike – it was a movement. The management at the Ford plant replied to Brandt's speech with wry sarcasm: "over the years, we have discovered that foreigners came to us with a much too highly developed [sense of] confidence."[136] Brandt's commentary passive-aggressively acknowledges the political power of collective action while casting the unionized foreign workers as illegitimately wielding their labour power.

The so-called women's strikes at the Pierburg Auto Parts Factory near Düsseldorf both preceded and were much more successful than the 1973 Ford strike in Cologne, precisely because "they were spearheaded by foreign women, achieved full participation by all employees, and successfully challenged the federally mandated wage system."[137] The Pierburg strikes were wage-based conflicts between 1970 and 1973 where workers struck multiple times to eliminate the gendered "light-wage" categories that kept women's salaries low by classifying a variety of tasks as "light" work.[138] The five "light wage" categories developed after 1955 were a workaround to maintain low wages for work done primarily by women, despite the reality that some of it demanded both physical strength and stamina.[139] The 1973 Pierburg strike was also not supported by the union, which viewed it as illegal.[140] And yet – in a large part due to solidarity across the female workers – the strike achieved most of its goals. Quoting an eyewitness, Miller comments: the solidarity between foreigners and Germans "was a real blow to the management who had hoped to break the strike through the loyalty of the German workers [...] From that moment the strike was won."[141] Striking workers in Pierburg won the support of both German and foreign workers and achieved a pay raise and the elimination of light-wage category II, as well as a cost-of-living bonus.

Strikes showed just how systemically integrated foreign workers already were, the kind of political power they could wield, and also how critical foreign workers had become to the West German economy. But political direct action could be twisted to show that immigrants were a "social liability."[142] Miller points out that "labour militancy still had an impact" on the end of labour recruitment:[143] "These strikes called into question who belonged to the category German citizen or German worker, long before foreign populations dominated public political debates."[144]

Conservative Backlash in the 1980s

On 13 October 1982, newly elected Federal Chancellor Helmut Kohl gave his first speech to the *Bundestag*.[145] He had been elected by Parliament as chancellor less than two weeks before, following a vote of no-confidence that ousted Chancellor Helmut Schmidt (SPD) on 1 October. Kohl would remain chancellor until 1998, eventually overseeing unification and holding the position of chancellor longer than any other postwar leader until Angela Merkel. His first speech to the *Bundestag* lays out some of the issues that would resurface in the federal election of 1983, when Kohl ran on a platform of limiting immigration. Until now, I have categorized the invocation of integration rhetoric as a lexical workaround or the sign of bureaucratic attempts to avoid conflicts. Kohl's political mobilization of the term, however, reveals how conservative politics linked restrictive immigration policy, the rhetoric of integration, and debates about the right to asylum with conservative, centre-right nationalism.

If integration rhetoric had previously been uttered across the political spectrum, the shift to political debates in which integration became the primary demand made of immigrants cemented integration as a cornerstone of conservative immigration politics. Policymakers simultaneously attempted to restrict immigration as they expanded the reach of the integrative apparatus by positioning conservative policy makers as both champions of integration and defenders of national interests. This stance correlates with increasingly antagonistic rhetoric about immigrants, former guest workers and their families, asylum seekers, and refugees, often expressed through debates either about security or economic costs and benefits. It is not implausible to connect this shift in tone with exclusionary policies and, especially after 1990, increasing violence against immigrants and their descendants.

In his first speech as chancellor, Kohl declared that his aims for immigration policy were threefold: to integrate foreigners, to continue to restrict immigration, and to assist immigrants living in Germany with a return to their homeland. Kohl declared:

> integrating the foreigners living with us is an important goal of our foreigner politics. Integration means not the loss of one's own identity but rather *the most frictionless coexistence possible* between foreigners and Germans. Integration will be possible only if the number of foreigners living with us does not continue to increase. It is crucial to avoid an unbridled and uncontrolled immigration.[146] (italics mine)

The language used in this speech sets up the rhetoric of integration as a form of compulsory assimilation. The subtext of integration rhetoric in the 1980s emerges from phrases like "frictionless coexistence" and the binary choice between return versus integration. Assimilation *à la* integration seems to be cast as the easiest pathway to "frictionless coexistence" (which does not exist in any society). Those who choose not to assimilate and potentially cause "problems" for German society – like "abusing" the right to asylum – can then be told that they can go home if they do not want to assimilate.[147] But Kohl hardly acknowledged that white Germans still held the power to determine which behaviours counted as assimilated and could still control when and how those criteria might shift.[148] "Foreigners in Germany should be able to decide freely, but they must decide if they want to return to their country or stay here and integrate," Kohl asserted.[149] Finally, Kohl declared that the CDU "will do everything to prevent the abuse of the right to asylum."[150]

In her study of European multiculturalism, Rita Chin points out that the broad strokes of a two-pronged policy to integrate foreign workers and restrict further immigration held across all of the Western European countries (France, Great Britain, Germany, and the Netherlands): every country ended foreign labour recruitment in the 1970s and then pursued this double strategy. Crucial to my argument is her assertion that all of these countries also saw a concomitant rise in anti-immigrant right-wing activity in the decade to follow.[151] Whether all of these countries also witnessed the development and expansion of something we could call an integrative apparatus would require knowing to what degree this rhetoric is part of daily cultural and political life in each location. In contrast, Jürgen Fijalkowski argues that the two-pronged strategy [*Doppel-Strategie*] of "Integration plus Delimitation" was a calculated political move by the CDU/CSU and merely extended the two-pronged policy first developed by the SPD/FDP. He considers this double strategy to have purportedly offered both the most "realistic chance of [integrative] success" as well as to represent the strategy most likely "to limit the risk of regression into aggressive ethnonationalism."[152] While some interpreted the CDU's approach towards foreigner politics as pragmatic, archival material made public in the early 2000s shows that Kohl had told Margaret Thatcher that he wanted to reduce the number of Turks in Germany by a whopping 50 per cent – precisely because he considered them unassimilable.[153] Whether this remark constitutes a *shift* in or instead represents a *continuity* in ethnonational beliefs clearly present among some Germans is indiscernible. Many scholars and political commentators fall on the side of continuity.[154]

Either way, Kohl's attitudes can hardly be considered unique – and should lay to rest the idea that the German government in 1982–83 was just being pragmatic or neutral in their foreigner politics. Public acceptance of guest workers was moving in an antagonistic direction before the early 1980s. Attitudinal surveys found that 39 per cent of respondents showed a "preference for guest workers to return home rather than be integrated" in 1978. By 1982, that proportion had risen to 68 per cent.[155] Woesthoff notes that the German desire for foreign workers to return "home" continued to increase. In 1983, that proportion had reached 80 per cent. The rate of those Germans who supported return had doubled in merely five years.[156]

The popular desire to reduce the number of foreign workers and their families in the Federal Republic of Germany arose from a variety of social pressures that later found their expression in governmental policy. The program known as the *Rückkehrhilfegesetz*, which took effect in December 1983, created a legal pathway for predominantly Turkish workers to return home by paying them one lump sum to compensate them for their German retirement benefits and pensions, and was the brainchild of the social liberal coalition in the 1970s. Before 1982, when Kohl became chancellor, the social liberal coalition had both proposed and also disagreed about the merits of return. However, this policy idea garnered broad consensus after the CDU became the ruling party and chose, with the help of the FDP as coalition partner, to pursue a tougher course on foreigner politics.[157] In a short article published in 1982, sociologist Heinz Harbach argued that it was "surprising" that "a basic consensus existed between the politically influential groups," pointing out that despite the progressive suggestions made by Heinz Kühn in his

1979 memo, the federal government's plan to further develop *Auslän-derpolitik* in 1980 was "disappointing" to scholarly critics, and treated "skeptically" if also basically accepted by the AWO.[158] Hunn points out that foreign policy played an additional role in making return less plausible for Turks specifically, since the Turkish economy was in freefall, there had just been a military coup, and the Turkish government did not really want to repatriate 1 million workers into an economy that was barely functional.[159]

In 1983, the Kohl government passed plans for such a repatriation scheme called the *Rückkehrhilfegesetz* (Act to Aid Return). Overall, proportionally few workers took a buyout and returned home. The Federal Government's public declaration that 300,000 workers participated in the program, Hunn says, should be "treated skeptically," since other studies place the number of participants between 120,000 and 133,000 in total.[160] Of those later surveyed, not a single Turkish returnee who had hoped to establish a business upon their return to Turkey had done so, even one year after return.[161] However, even though the policy was taken advantage of by an almost laughably small number of foreign workers living in Germany, the cost-benefit ratio of the scheme ended up balancing the coffers of the social services, and thus was considered a symbolic success by the CDU.[162] The CDU could cite the balanced budget as proof of effective policy without having to reference the limited reach of this policy and the extremely modest effect it had on the demographics of permanent settlement. To some degree, the Act to Aid Return served to politically tie up the ends of guest worker recruitment ten years after the recruitment stop: by offering incentives – however flimsy – to return and balancing the social services budget in a way that could leverage the Act as successful, the era of foreign worker recruitment could now be seen as having come to a close.

Overall, the changes in immigration policy between the first postwar recession in 1966, the election of the SPD as the leading party for the first time in West German history, immigrant engagement in participatory politics like striking and lobbying, and the conservative backlash under the Kohl Chancellorship, which reflected a broader conservative turn across Europe, can be read together as evidence that the apparatus of integration expanded during this time period. Foreigner politics first moved towards integration as the preferred neutral term for immigrant incorporation, but later used integration as a way to maintain limits on immigration and demand assimilative behaviour from those who stayed.[163]

There are two takeaways from this attempted survey of a broad swath of historical material. The first is how difficult Germans still found it to engage with ethnic, racial, and cultural difference during the period of exponential increases in the number of guest workers residing in Germany between 1967 and 1972. The second is how difficult it was to acknowledge that the conflicts of labour organizing and family law were actually proof of guest worker and immigrant "integration." The inconsistent and incoherent policy choices bureaucrats made under the pressure of coming to terms with the Holocaust, which made any decisive engagement with a diverse population of immigrants moving towards naturalization quite difficult, if not impossible, inhibited politicians and civil organizations from being able to envision what Germany could become if immigrants were allowed to naturalize. Conservative politicians missed the fact that increasing access and sharing political power would preserve the very liberal democracy they purported to protect through limiting immigration and demanding integration. Rather than viewing the history of immigration to Germany as a history of political negligence, the evidence I cite here interprets purportedly "neutral" decision-making as a form of avoidance that perpetuated exclusionary social structures. In post-Holocaust Germany, the widespread belief that immigrant incorporation would be too similar to "forced Germanization" to be practicable was a philosophical obstacle that partially inhibited the development of successful policies of immigrant incorporation and participation. After Chancellor Kohl was elected in 1982, a broader trans-European conservative backlash against increasing diversity and the visible agency of striking workers and German women married to foreigners prompted a contradictory response. Instead of praising them for civic participation, the government instead instituted financial incentives for workers to return home. That this suspicion is informed by racializing beliefs that hierarchize different ethnic groups based on their purported "integrability" or "willingness to integrate" (expressed at this historical moment in terms of assimilability) is clear.

As the economic downturn in Germany persisted and the CDU held on to power for four terms, extreme right-wing political activity in Germany increased. East Germany – whose history has been noticeably absent from the past two chapters – also saw similar growth in extremism and coordination with West German extremist actors before the fall of the Wall. Despite the fact that the NPD did not succeed at garnering federal representation in 1969, new right-wing parties that existed to the right of the CSU emerged in fragmented ways across the right-wing spectrum. The NPD tried to revitalize its political activity in the early 1980s, and immigration was the cornerstone issue for several independent protest movements connected to the NPD: *Bürgerinitiative Ausländerstopp* (1980, Citizens' Initiative to Stop Immigration, NRW),

Kieler Liste für Ausländerbegrenzung (Kiel List to Limit Foreign Immigration, 1982, SH), and *Hamburger Liste für Ausländerstopp* (1982, Hamburg List to Stop Foreign Immigration, HH) all propagated exclusionary ideas.[164] The *Republikaner*, a party founded in 1983, embraced many of the issues previously seen as important to the *Bund der Heimatvertriebenen und Entrechteten* (BHE) in the early '50s. They were frustrated by détente and the new politics towards East Germany that subsidized and recognized the GDR as a state, and were partially inspired by the right-wing populism of the French *Front Nationale*.[165] Among the extreme right actors of the time, Gerhard Frey, a "multimillionaire media czar" who acquired multiple right-wing newspapers and nationalist monthlies, founded the *Deutsche Volksunion* e.V. in 1971, a nonprofit that initially did not hold a licence to function as a political party. This umbrella organization consisted of a complicated mix of action groups and politicized organizations. In 1986, Frey founded his own extremist political party called the *Deutsche Liste*, which by the early 1990s was known as the *Deutsche Volksunion*.[166] In the 1980s, most of these parties had limited, if any, political success in contesting elections.

The broader conservative turn in the early 1980s did not go far enough for those who – along an admittedly fragmented right-wing spectrum after the failure of the NPD to reach the federal level in 1969 – participated in the numerically small but significantly active organization of the extreme right into multiple parties. The violence associated with extreme right-wing actors existed before unification and grew alongside the early expansion of the integrative apparatus for immigrants, as the socially liberal policy under the SPD/FDP prompted a conservative, CDU-led backlash built on notions of Turkish unassimilability, rejection of immigrant participation in political activity, security concerns and demands that immigrants to "integrate or go home." Given that a long-term right-wing goal had been the unification of Germany, it is hardly surprising that right-wing nationalist violence increased exponentially after unification.

Chapter Seven

One German State, One (Integrated) German Nation

The attacks in Hoyerswerda (Saxony) began on Tuesday, 17 September 1991 at the *Marktplatz*. Vietnamese traders, selling untaxed cigarettes, were attacked by eight skinheads.[1] The skinheads' choice of target may have been influenced by "a highly publicized raid" in Hoyerswerda in early July 1991, during which 120 police officers – a shocking number to me – arrested 19 Vietnamese citizens and one Turkish citizen at the marketplace.[2] The day after skinheads attacked the Vietnamese traders, schoolchildren continued the assault by engaging in petty violence, shattering windows of the dormitory where Vietnamese and African workers lived.[3] By Thursday, 19 September, two days after the initial *Marktplatz* attack, a crowd had gathered outside the dormitory for workers in the *Albert-Schweitzer-Straße*. Young people were the primary perpetrators, but they had the "moral support of their elders," who cheered them on as they threw rocks, bottles, and Molotov cocktails at the building. These events continued over the next day, and by 21 September, the workers in the dormitory were eventually evacuated.[4] However, the evacuation of the dormitory in the *Albert-Schweitzer-Straße* was not the end of the violence; instead, the crowd moved to an asylum home (*Asylheim*) in the *Thomas-Müntzer-Straße* and continued their assaults. The movement from place to place reveals the conflation of the categories of contract workers and refugees as groups both bearing differences worth targeting by the right wing.

As part of a 30-year retrospective on the violence in Hoyerswerda in May 2021, the MDR (Central German Broadcasting) posted archival video footage of broadcasts from 1991 filmed during the riot. While reporters in 1991 conducted serious interviews, small blond children playfully tried to get on television by crowding behind them, reflecting the "festival" type atmosphere of a community event for which the children themselves may have had little understanding. One video from 22 September 1991 shows activists purportedly from the Berlin autonomous scene (*Autonomenszene*) creating a third front on the street holding large signs made of cotton fabric that were painted with slogans. Another photograph shows Asian residents of the *Asylheim* hoisting their own fabric banner while Black residents stand behind them, presumably in support of their efforts: "Why do you hate us? SOS! We want to return to the West. Only West Germany – Germany."[5]

Local residents watched the commotion by congregating on the street, and residents of the *Asylheim* crowded into windows above, waiting to see what would happen. The counterdemonstration from the left led to an escalation in violent behaviour. Police officers clad in olive green riot gear used plastic shields and attack dogs when the groups engaged in fistfights. In addition to the now infamous chants of "Ausländer raus!" (Foreigners out!), the MDR footage shows counterprotesters yelling "Ausländer bleiben!" (Foreigners stay!).[6]

Army vehicles moved into town on Monday, 23 September, "taking over responsibility for public order from the police," who were reluctant to intervene and whose reticence prompted reporters to describe the events as a "pogrom."[7] Two-thirds of the asylum seekers were eventually evacuated by bus on 23 September. The army attempted to keep onlookers away, but nearly 300 people cheered the asylum seekers' departure. Residents threw stones at the bus, shattering windows and injuring at least one person severely.[8] On 24 September, after the asylum seekers had been evacuated to Dresden, Saxony's Governor (*Ministerpräsident*) Kurt Biedenkopf declared at a press conference that he had spoken with federal authorities about whether the new states could be expected, under the social and economic stress of unification, to continue to participate in the FRG quota system for the distribution of asylum seekers.[9] Following the attacks in Hoyerswerda, other attacks occurred in Freiburg im Breisgau (Baden-Württemberg), Saarlouis (Saarland), Hünxe (NRW), and Greifswald (Mecklenberg-Vorpommern). A similar riot took place in Rostock (Mecklenburg-Vorpommern) in 1992. That attack was grouped together in media coverage with two arson attacks in the West German cities of Mölln (Schleswig-Holstein) in 1992 and Solingen (NRW) in 1993 in which multiple members of Turkish-German immigrant families lost their lives.

Media coverage in 1991 stumbled trying to make sense of the events in Hoyerswerda. On 29 September, *Der Spiegel* magazine made the violence in Hoyerswerda their lead story. The cover story featured a confusing collection of photographs of riot police, Black, Vietnamese, and Rom_nja victims, neo-Nazi graffiti, infographics about asylum claims and attacks on foreigners, as well as stock press photos of refugee arrivals and deportations in Italy and France. Alongside these images, the main story jumps from questions of racism to right-wing parties to statements by politicians to survey data, all supposedly confirming the persistence and reemergence of East German racism.[10] Racist quotes from residents of Hoyerswerda are printed in the commentary section of the title story alongside humanizing statements made by asylum seekers, all wrapped up together in a patronizing tone of West German judgment.[11]

In one of the stranger media spectacles I have ever seen, the ARD (state run media) broadcast an episode of the program *im Brennpunkt* after the events in September 1991 from Hoyerswerda. That episode has since been uploaded to YouTube as part of the 2012 campaign "Rassismus-tötet!" (racism kills).[12] A TV crew filmed a conversation between Saxony's State Interior Minister Rudolf Krause and an ARD reporter on the *Marktplatz*, the site of both the July 1991 police raid and the September 1991 attack on Vietnamese cigarette sellers. Surrounded by community members and filmed after dark, the special begins with an eight-minute montage about the events of the past two weeks, featuring footage presumably filmed in Hoyerswerda by a crew earlier that day. The film montage ends with a TV reporter asking a Black resident if he will come to the live broadcast at 7:30 at the *Marktplatz*. "I won't come to the *Marktplatz*. That would be like suicide," he says. At this point, the broadcast feed cuts to dismissive laughter from the crowd gathered at the *Marktplatz*, indicating that this montage was screened outdoors to those who came to the filming.[13] The first question the reporter poses to Interior Minister Krause cuts to the chase: "Did the constitutional state capitulate [to the racists]?"[14] The program ends with interviews in the crowd. As the "Rassismus-tötet!" account explains in their summary of the posted YouTube video, this version of a town hall put German antagonism to migration on display:

> From the prominent politicians, who clearly distinguished themselves from the mob standing around them through their knowledge of High German, but [in whom one] could hardly recognize a difference in their attitudes towards the "Asylum Question," calls of "Foreigners Out!" can also be heard. For example, Edmund Stoiber [CSU] is scared of the rest of the inhabitants of the globe, whose collective goal is supposedly to migrate to Germany. "Globally, we have millions of potential asylum seekers and we cannot manage them in the manner we currently are."[15]

The focus on both racism and economic deprivation as sources of the violent behaviour in Hoyerswerda courses through both scholarship and media coverage.[16] The *Spiegel* article and the ARD program both quote statements from residents of Hoyerswerda that link racist attitudes to the rhetoric of white deprivation: "They live better than we do. We pay for them and then they take away jobs from us Germans." "I believe they are having a miserable time (*es denen dreckig geht*), but right now we are up first." "They have the money. And we don't."[17] While these statements may reflect how people felt, it is important to note that employment rates in Hoyerswerda were actually higher – on average – than in other similar locations in the former East. In this case, actual deprivation is not quantifiable, even if the affect of disadvantage ran rampant.[18]

If the initial attack on Vietnamese cigarette traders had not escalated to a riot, the events in Hoyerswerda would simply fit within the pattern of violent acts committed by individual perpetrators motivated by racist ideas across all 16 states in the Federal Republic. In fact, there had been multiple other attacks in August 1991, both on those perceived to be foreign and on homes for asylum seekers, inÜckermunde (Mecklenburg-Vorpommern), Aschersleben (Saxony-Anhalt), Leisnig (Saxony), Wurzen (Saxony), Zittau (Saxony), Chemnitz (Saxony), Tambach-Dietharz (Thuringia), and Halberstadt (Saxony-Anhalt). The asylum home in Achersleben, where according to the parliamentary record, "Romanians" lived – perhaps code for Roma – was attacked three times in two weeks.[19] Despite this list of Eastern attacks, right-wing racist events took place that month in West Germany as well. Twenty skinheads attacked a group of Turks and Germans socializing at a city festival in Lower Saxony on 18 August. That same day approximately 1,300 neo-Nazis marched under police protection through the city of Wunsiedel in Bavaria to honour Rudolph Hess, Hitler's right-hand man, and intimidated onlookers through the use of the Hitler salute and phrases like "Ausländer raus!" The events recounted in this paragraph are merely a partial list from 1–18 August 1991. It would take too much space here to recount the 33-page report later submitted as documentation of the violence by Representatives Ulla Jelpke, Dr. Gregor Gysi, and PDS/Die Linke to the *Bundestag* in 1992.[20]

Scholars, journalists, politicians, and critics, alongside German citizens and residents, narrate the unification of the two German states in 1989/1990 in as many registers and from as many perspectives as one could possibly imagine. The process of bringing together the Eastern and Western *Länder* to form a new state with an old name (the Federal Republic of Germany) has been portrayed as everything from an inevitable historical outcome, foreseen even in the drafting of the German Basic Law (ratified 1949), to a colonizing land grab by which the

Federal German government and Western companies swooped in and corporatized the Eastern states.[21]

The changes wrought by unification that are relevant to the integrative apparatus reflect two primary themes: migration and racist, right-wing violence. Unification accelerated the growth of the integrative apparatus on several levels: it strengthened (but was not the source of) nationalist assumptions about the overlap between race, ethnicity, and nationality.[22] It imagined a nostalgic community of Germans that was homogenous, culturally uniform, and claimed to have a primordial right to be considered a single nation, even though an examination of German history reveals multiple German empires, national states, and ethnicities rather than one easily defined nation. Cultural studies scholar Peggy Piesche argues that attention to the protest chants that accompanied the *Wende* (unification) reflect a contradictory – but easily legible – transition from populist solidarity (We are the people!) to a popular desire for an ethnonational community (We are one people!) to nationalist slogans (Germany for the Germans!) to nationalist violence (Foreigners out!). Violence, indeed, was one significant outcome of the so-called Peaceful Revolution.[23] Finally, unification prompted multiple groups to renegotiate their relationship to the nation. West, East, and "new" Germans – in all of their various intersections – took on new and layered meanings in the context of German politics and culture after 1990.

It is undeniable that unification was a critical event in the history of integration politics writ large for both Germanies. The levels at which some degree of sociological integration took place in 1989–90 were multiple: the Federal Republic took over or dissolved East German institutions and economic systems; multiple groups of newcomers – from East German citizens to immigrants, refugees, and their descendants – entered or moved within the now unified state; and the new Federal Republic was engaged in an ongoing process of so-called integration into the European Union. It was a moment of massive territorial, economic, cultural, political, and demographic change.

Unification in a German context is a global event with both domestic and regional consequences. The unification of two previously separate states, however, is not necessarily a uniquely German experience. National borders frequently shift, and states have separated and unified since the end of the Second World War. India/Pakistan, Yugoslavia and the subsequent Balkan states, Vietnam, Korea, Ethiopia/Eritrea, Sudan/South Sudan; Ukraine, Crimea, and the Donetsk/Luhansk Republics: geopolitical shifts that translate into territorial division or unification are frequent. The types of sociological questions that are critical for organizing society – how to provide people access to employment, education, social and civic opportunities, as well as cultural and political participation in the public sphere – absolutely apply to the incorporation of the citizens of the former German Democratic Republic. The right-wing argument that former East German citizens also need their own integration politics has some elements of truth.[24] That German ethnicity – rather than their own humanity – entitles them to this politics is the part that is counterfactual.

Multiple scholars point to the overlapping topical frames of migration and right-wing extremism during and after unification. Political historian Oliver Schmidtke examines the intersection between migration and political transition, arguing that unification not only created the conditions for new migration patterns, but also prompted a need for "recalibrating" the political elements that could unify citizens.[25] Sociologist Hermann Kurthen and political scientist Michael Minkenberg point out that not only were profound political shifts among the so-called West German New Left *and* New Right underway before unification, but also that division had thus far protected West Germany from "a large East-West migration."[26] Nevim Çil argues that retired Turkish guest workers and Turkish-Germans of the second generation found themselves newly confronted with exclusionary, ethnonational Germanness in ways that were more explicit after 1990 than ever before.[27] Following the work of sociologist Elçin Kürsat-Ahlers, Çil explains that West Germany positioned itself as having treated its immigrants more "democratic[ally]" than the East, and in this configuration, immigration to the West and notions of East German "xenophobia" helped West Germany both ignore violent acts against immigrants in the FRG *and* polish up their *Wir-Bild* (self-image) as a superior society to the German Democratic Republic.[28] Unification therefore raised the question of who was considered German anew, both because of the incorporation of the East *and* because of long-term and new migration patterns into the expanded Federal Republic.[29] The German Basic Law granted ethnic German populations in Eastern Europe the right of return, and the collapse of the Soviet Union finally made return possible for multiple groups. Those known as *Spätaussiedler* and Russian-Jewish *Kontingentflüchtlinge* became the first large groups to migrate to Germany from Eastern Europe since the expulsions.[30]

At this time, an intense asylum debate was also running in West Germany, shaped strongly by the ruling CDU's insistence under Chancellor Kohl that Germany was not a country of immigration. Kurthen and Minkenberg in particular draw attention to how debates about political systems in transition are intimately related to debates about immigration and asylum, as both the right and the left use immigration as an issue to promote their values.[31] Critical for understanding how Germany's integrative apparatus constructs a form of governmentality that mobilizes conservative and often nationalist ideas that are deeply embedded within discourses of integration and assimilation therefore requires that we turn some attention to the German nationalist rhetoric and anti-immigrant violence that garnered substantial press attention after unification.

One of the dominant interpretations of East-West unification was that the process of unification itself prompted a rebirth of nationalism that manifested in attacks on immigrants, Jewish people, and racial minorities in both Western and Eastern states, in large part due to the purportedly widespread and blatant racism of people in the Eastern states.[32] Unification, so it goes, gave nationalists the justification to act out their fantasies of an ethnonational state. Nationalist politics, however, was ascendant in both East and West Germany years before unification was even seen as a possibility – and this nationalist expansion existed alongside a growing *acceptance* of diversity across the German population.[33] Çil uses ethnographic interviews, however, to reveal that unification starkly changed the relationship between immigrants and the West German state. Alongside the conservative turn of the 1980s, discussions of local voting rights for immigrants and growing acceptance of diversity had led many descendants of guest workers to identify with what Çil calls the "established West German society" – that is, the white German majority. Unification and the violence in the Western cities of Mölln and Solingen changed all that.[34] The youngest generation of Turkish-Germans interviewed in Çil's study articulated their experiences of moving through a process of exclusion as media attention to the arson attacks accentuated social and ethnic difference in new ways. Rather than be considered West German, as they had been in 1990, her Turkish-German subjects had suddenly become foreigners ("Ich war jetzt ein Ausländer").[35] Theories of the essentially "brown [fascist] East" or the argument that Nazism had gone underground before it re-emerged during unification are too reductive for understanding the complexity of the changes at hand.[36] Rather than viewing unification as an event that spontaneously prompted violent attacks on immigrants and people of colour, it is important to understand that the nationalist violence that accelerated after unification had long-standing historical origins, was part of a broader trans-European turn to the right, and was also shaped by local factors, including whether citizens could access options for social and political participation.

Integration politics is an apparatus whose scaffolding is provided by discourse, but whose fully complex and interconnected form has non-discursive and material effects. CDU rhetoric that Germany was not a country of immigration and that the right to asylum could be "abused" provided right-wing extremists in multiple places with rhetoric that could be invoked against immigrants, and a lack of condemnation or swift response by law enforcement suggested that extremists could act without punishment.[37] Conflicts between West Germans with privilege and East Germans who came up short after unification also created resentments on nationalist grounds: if all Germans were now citizens of the Federal Republic, and German ethnicity determined who was considered German, why were East Germans being treated as if they were not "fully" German?

Former citizens of both the Federal Republic and the German Democratic Republic who advocated for unification through the logic of an ethnonational state used an intersectional identity of European whiteness, national German identity, and Germanness as an ethnic identity to justify white Germans as worthy of federal aid, solidarity, and the entitlements given to citizens, like voting rights or full state pensions. At the same time, those white identities split between East and West Germans, with whiteness alone to offer no guarantee of protection against West German privilege. And while nationalism was hardly new in a postwar German context, the incorporation of the Eastern states and ensuing racist violence cemented long-standing disputes between white Germans, Germans of colour, immigrants, and their descendants as to which groups could justify their claim to material and social resources, as well as find access to the public sphere *as participants*.

Right-wing groups require this construction of white Germanness in order to make political claims. PEGIDA and the Alternative for Germany party (AfD) both emerged from longer historical struggles about citizenship, who is entitled to it, and the relationship between national and ethnic identity as justification for being considered worthy of all the privileges of state and national belonging. These conflicts about whiteness, in turn, reveal the racializing and racist ideologies present in both East and West Germany before and after unification.

Integrating Socialists: Different Kinds of Whiteness?

A critical element for the construction of contemporary white Germanness and a white identity politics rooted in resentment was the inequality after unification between white Germans from the West and white Germans from the East. This division between more and less privileged subjects who were considered both white and German prompted a multiplicity of social resentments along the lines of class, the ability to speak High German rather than dialect, as well as proximity to democratic socialization. After 1989, I am aware of no other Eastern European post-Soviet state that was incorporated into an existing Western European state in which such a distinction was possible. If integration debates and rhetoric in the Federal Republic before 1989 had focused on foreign workers, asylum seekers, and their descendants, for a brief period following unification, the incorporation of former socialists into a democratic state was also a national concern. Those divisions (and concerns) persist into the present.

Both proximity to whiteness and intersectional distinctions between different kinds of whiteness are critical for understanding some of the tensions within unified Germany that are both separate from – and connected to – migration politics. Granted immediate citizenship, former East German citizens were still treated as inferior by their democratizing West German counterparts. Attention to reintegration programs for civil servants, the collapse of the East German army, and shifting conditions for community activists show some of the prejudices and power dynamics between East and West German citizens during the process of unification.

In his study of one high school in East Berlin, labour relations scholar Martin Upchurch laid out some of the workplace inequities between East German and West German teachers between 1993 and 1996. The Federal Republic required East German teachers trained in "ideologically tainted" fields such as history, social studies, or Russian as a foreign language to fully retrain in order to keep their jobs.[38] East German teachers who did not retrain and take the West German praxis exam were paid at 80 per cent of the western salary irrespective of their seniority, and there were further pay discrepancies between teachers recruited from West Germany and those who had been trained in the East.[39] These conditions prompted a fair degree of resentment, clearly illustrated by a participant in the study, who said, "I have been teaching English for 20 years and I have a degree from one of East Germany's good Universities [sic] yet I am paid less than this western teacher in our school who has only taught for half the time."[40] Upchurch also describes teacher resentment about the investigation of all teachers for past *Stasi* connections, especially since many of the teachers employed in the school "had involved themselves directly in opposition activity during the buildup to the event of 1989."[41] Merely one teacher in a school of nearly 60 employees had been found to be a *Stasi* informer.[42] Further differences emerged around collective bargaining rights. Many East German teachers rejected the fact that they would lose collective bargaining rights if they pursued *Beamte* (lifetime civil servant) status, making the pursuit of such an appointment primarily an interest of Western teachers.[43] Involvement in opposition activity and a desire to maintain collective bargaining rights suggests that East German teachers understood the process of democratic civic engagement quite well, and likely did not need much retraining after unification.

Another institution starkly affected by unification was the East German army, known as the National People's Army (NVA). In his ethnography of East German army officers, anthropologist Andrew Bickford explains the sources of resentment among NVA officers who were unable to "integrate" into the West German *Bundeswehr*. Bickford also points out two perplexing contradictions that NVA officers faced. First, members of the NVA were classified in *Bundeswehr* terminology as members of a foreign army or "foreign veterans," thereby essentially marking them as non-German.[44] Second, members of the NVA are not permitted to use their military rank, claim academic titles earned in the GDR, nor are they permitted the honour of a state burial.[45] Their pensions – for 16 years after unification – were also merely "between 30 and 65 per cent of that of a West German officer," prompting the colloquial term *Strafrente* (lit. "pension of punishment.")[46] In stark contrast, former Nazi soldiers who had a history of serving in the SS or the *Wehrmacht* and later served in the West German army were still permitted to use their official titles and could receive a full pension and a state burial. NVA officers took umbrage at this double standard, pointing out that they neither participated in genocide nor an expansionist military regime and demanded recognition as Germans and German soldiers. As Bickford strikingly summarizes:

> Throughout my field work, former officers stated that they wanted to be treated as "Germans among Germans," as equal citizens, not as "second-class" citizens. This was a call for inclusion in the German state as well as the German "Volk," the German nation; they demanded full acceptance and treatment as German citizens. This feeling of being "inferior" or "non-Germans," sets the stage for political anomie, disengagement, distrust in the democratic process, and a possible move towards nativist politics, the extreme right, and xenophobia, engendered, as they see it, by West German rules, laws, and practices of exclusion.[47]

Military traditions that recognize former members of the *Wehrmacht* and the SS also seemed to confirm to former NVA members – in concordance with the founding myth of the GDR – that the Federal Republic was merely an extension of the fascist German state.[48] Bickford argues that this case study of military integration should serve "as a cautionary tale of how state actors should and should not design 're-unification' or reintegration strategies for former soldiers, unless, of course, the desired goal is social and political marginalization."[49] These two case studies illustrate that whiteness or German ethnicity is not always a guarantee of privilege. Class, former professional status, and East/West distinctions are critical factors in the construction of whiteness in German society, especially right after 1989–90.

Finally, after unification, the options for citizen participation in the public sphere changed radically, especially the relationship between activists and the media. Samirah Kenawi, an East German lesbian activist who had engaged in gay liberation struggles since the early 1980s, recounted in the documentation project *Labor89* that adjusting to both West German media practices and the West German women's movement was so difficult that it prompted disillusionment. For GDR activist groups, *Stasi* surveillance had taken on a media-like role. Despite admitting her ambivalence to *Stasi* observation, Kenawi states "it produced a ... feeling of being taken seriously and of [our] own political importance."[50] In contrast, if the media didn't cover an event in the West, it didn't exist: "What didn't appear [in the press], didn't happen."[51] Kenawi felt pushed to the periphery, mostly because she and her East German colleagues did not understand the new media landscape. At the same time, she argues, the situation for women and homosexuals in the East had actually been better than it was in 1989–90 in the West, something Western women's movements denied or were unable to acknowledge.[52] According to Kenawi, these complex experiences led to a form of political apathy and disempowerment:

> the disillusionment set in accordingly quickly. It showed that we were running behind the short-term political events, were being overtaken by them, and couldn't act at all. [...] New realities were constantly being produced: lickety-split and to some degree with a kind of brutality that left us stunned. With that, the dream of being able to shape society was as good as over.[53]

If we think about integration in sociological terms as the incorporation of people into systems and institutions, it is clear that East German citizens required incorporative measures that would help people not just adjust, but also gain access in equitable ways to participate in shaping society. The incorporative process after unification did not run smoothly and led to feelings or resentment or disappointment for many East German citizens.[54]

Decades after unification, there is a different relationship between East and West Germans. As Katharina Warda recounts, the youngest generation of former East German citizens who grew up in in unified Germany during the 1990s were taught to "pass" by schoolteachers who marked them down for using dialect in the classroom and discouraged school pupils from taking Russian as a foreign language.[55] Much of the GDR gerontocracy has since passed and former East German identities are frequently invisible in unified Germany. A complex hierarchy of integrability has emerged: race, ethnicity, access to citizenship, and historical connection to the pre-Nazi German state matter. Compared to East Germans, ethnic German *(Spät-)Aussiedler*, and *Kontingentflüchtlinge* from the former USSR – all of whom were immediately granted citizenship in the Federal Republic in or after 1990 – immigrants, asylum seekers, and their descendants from countries of origin outside of Europe had to wait another ten years before they (but primarily their children) could be easily naturalized.[56] The white German identities that had previously been positioned against each other can be mobilized today as one unified white identity to take up populist and nativist politics against people of colour, immigrants, refugees, and their descendants, who are viewed as the primary threat to German national cohesion. Both subtle and obvious to those who look at this process of consolidating German whiteness is that also it requires the erasure of narratives of and by East Germans of colour.

Erasure of East Germans of Colour from Narratives of the East

In an autobiographical essay for the *Journal der Künste,* scholar and journalist Katharina Warda (b. 1985) describes the media representation of East Germans in the 1990s as a "site of projection of all unwelcome qualities and subjects. The site from which one can distance themselves to the greatest degree. A kind of evil twin of the West."[57] The intersecting pressures she feels as a Black East German shape her self-image, she writes, which is overwhelmingly determined by others: "As a victim of racism, I am automatically a 'foreigner' *(Ausländerin)*, even though that's not what I am. I'm Eastern *(Ossi)*, and what that means is something I find out about from the West. I am 'asocial' *(asozial)*, as if our precarious life were not already difficult enough."[58] She coped as a teen in the 1990s by joining a punk clique, where she felt understood for the first time.[59]

Peggy Piesche (b. 1968) narrates her experiences growing up in the GDR in a different idiom that still arrives at similar conclusions. In an oral history interview for the exhibit *Anderen wurden es schwindelig* (Others Became Dizzy) on display at the Anne Frank House in Frankfurt from November 2019 to March 2020, Piesche points out how, in the

GDR, the myth of socialist brotherhood was still constructed within a frame of white hegemonic power:

> As a child, also as a Black child, to grow up in the GDR, in a small town, meant: this international connection gestured towards a point of identification. It was a possibility, one of the very few possible forms of being offered a chance to identify. But it was a relatively indecent offer [of identification] that I received, or that all Black people or people of colour received in the GDR. [...] That the GDR offered solidarity, that there was a language for international solidarity: this language was not to be expected at all in the 1960s and '70s in the Federal Republic of Germany. [... But] then it very quickly became clear that there is a very clear hierarchy within solidarity [...]. That there were clear power relations, attributions, and markings. [...] So international solidarity assumed that of course, the international socialist revolution would come from Europe, the Soviet Union and the GDR. That's where the knowledge is, that's where the expertise is. Today we would translate that as: everything is, of course, generated from whiteness.[60]

The conflict of intra-German whiteness was able to work in concert with "real existing" racism in the GDR and the FRG, both to erase certain narratives from the historical record, hierarchize relationships based on a racialized discourse of solidarity (Quinn Slobodian calls this "socialist chromatism"), and maintain relationships of dominance that stemmed from the purported superiority of whiteness.[61]

White dominance can be facilitated in many social situations because of the presence – rather than the absence – of difference. The German Democratic Republic led a variety of educational exchange and guest worker programs with countries that spanned the range of socialist republics, from Korea and Vietnam to Angola and Mozambique. Many of those workers and exchange students – given the suddenness of the collapse of the GDR – were still residents of East Germany when the Wall fell. Some were deported, some stayed through the early 1990s finishing up their work contracts, and some settled permanently in the new Federal Republic. Many had to fight to be granted permission to remain.[62] About 1.2 per cent of the GDR population was foreign in 1989, not counting the nearly 400,000 Soviet troops also stationed in the country.[63] The GDR framed interaction and contact with both international students and foreign workers as a gesture of internationalist cooperation within a network of solidarity among socialist states.[64]

Although labour recruitment certainly accelerated after 1970, Nigerian international students came to East Germany as early as 1951, and by 1965, there was already an organization called the Union of African students in the GDR.[65] Short term contracts for foreign labourers began in 1967 between the East German government and Hungary. In the 1970s, Poland, Algeria, Cuba, and Mozambique entered into labour agreements, and that group expanded to include Vietnam, Mongolia, China, and Angola in the 1980s.[66] By June of 1989, 150,400 foreign workers lived in the GDR, working predominantly in low-skilled jobs in factories, construction, and mining.[67] In other words, the German Democratic Republic employed foreign labour in similar capacities as did the Federal Republic – just on a smaller scale.

The GDR government also used these labour agreements in ways similar to their use in the Federal Republic: as diplomatic agreements. Sara Pugach argues that the German Democratic Republic used educational exchange agreements to challenge the Hallstein doctrine, which the Federal Republic used until 1972 to "punish any state that recognized the GDR's political existence by threatening to sever diplomatic and economic ties with the offender."[68] Crafting agreements with African nations, especially those recently decolonized, became a tool by which the "GDR thus challenged the doctrine and asserted itself as a legitimate political entity."[69]

While the Federal Republic attempted to exclude Afro-Asian immigrants during the period of postwar labour recruitment, the relationships across socialist states meant that immigrant labour from African and Asian countries to East Germany was common. The mere presence of African and Asian international students and labourers as welcome participants in a global network of socialist brotherhood, however, does not necessarily constitute an anti-racist politics. Quinn Slobodian, building on the work of Toni Weiss, echoes Peggy Piesche's statements: even if the notion of race in East Germany

> broke definitively with the Third Reich's hierarchical associations between phenotype and ability [...] the visual repertoire of race and racism in the GDR reproduced many of the exaggerated and even offensive stereotypical depictions of people of color. The right of representation also remained in the hands of white Germans, producing the effect, arguably subconsciously, of either prioritizing of the white leadership role or the presentation of the nonwhite person as icon rather than individual.[70]

Jeanette Sumalgy, the daughter of the (likely) first Black locomotive engineer in the GDR and an activist historian in her own right, recounts in

Labor89 with substantial anger the amount of everyday racism that she experienced personally as a Black East German, a narrative echoed by Warda and Piesche.[71] The aggression towards Sumalgy only increased when she attempted to marry her partner, with whom she had two children and led a long term relationship despite not being permitted to marry. He had come to the GDR as a foreign worker from Mozambique, and it was falsely assumed by the *Stasi* that Sumalgy's petition for marriage was an attempt to escape the GDR.[72]

In fact, it was the similarities between East and West Germany that had historically influenced the degree to which both Germanies were attractive to foreign workers, international students, and people seeking asylum. In their respective geopolitical contexts, East Germany had a high standard of living and "technological prowess," just like West Germany.[73] Consequently, while post-unification economic resentment clearly played a role in how East Germans perceived the distribution of resources, the notion that East German citizens were antagonistic towards people of colour and susceptible to racism and nationalistic hate because they lacked experience with ethnic difference does not fully hold up against the historical record, just as Barbara John's 1985 statement that the West lacked experience integrating foreigners cited previously is also historically inaccurate.

While it is true that East Germans were kept separate from foreign labourers through segregating housing arrangements that relegated foreign workers to dormitories, nearly 1,000 children were born to relationships between East Germans and Mozambicans alone.[74] Zambian officials complained as early as 1967 that multiple Zambian students living in the German Democratic Republic had chosen to or wanted to marry East German women.[75] Jennifer Miller describes multiple relationships between Turkish workers living or working in West Berlin who married or dated in the East.[76] East Germans thus clearly participated in cross-cultural and interracial relationships. Pugach states that, "archival records also indicate that relationships between African male students and East German women were fairly commonplace. Many personal files from the KMU [Karl Marx University] in Leipzig reveal such relationships," including the existence of an illegal abortion ring run by a Nigerian international student and German doctors in the early 1960s, pointing perhaps in the crassest of terms to ongoing and unexceptional contact between Germans and contract workers.[77] The East German government tried to prevent these abortions by arguing that biracial children had citizenship rights, a stark contrast to discourses of multiracial identities in the West, where white mothers were often convinced or forced to give up their Black children, or were unable to pass FRG citizenship to their children if they married foreign men.[78] International labour agreements required Mozambican women who became pregnant to return home and banned marriage between East German women and Mozambican or Vietnamese citizens.[79] Despite the prohibitions on legal marriage, marriage was possible if couples could obtain permission.[80] By the end of the 1980s, 323 marriages had taken place between East Germans and Vietnamese citizens residing in the GDR despite bureaucratic challenges.[81] Simultaneously, 1 per cent of all Vietnamese contract workers in the GDR returned to Vietnam each year because they became pregnant.[82] Considering these numbers, it is clear that claims to a white German identity politics across large swaths of the political spectrum in the present requires the erasure of East Germans of colour from the historical narrative. And yet, how does one explain violence against immigrants and people of colour as a trans-German phenomenon if the historiography of East Germany barely acknowledges the presence of people who had long been targets?

Mary Fulbrook's study of daily life and leisure in the GDR includes two short mentions of foreign workers in a monograph of 350 pages, as well as one picture each of a Black nursing student from 1973 and a visiting youth delegation from Korea.[83] Konrad Jarausch's study of the political machinations that unification required mentions nothing of the role socialist migration between allies played in East German society – nor the role such agreements played in keeping the East German economy afloat.[84] Migration into the GDR remains absent until the final three pages of Jarausch's text, where, in spite of this omission he still argues that the role of neo-Nazi violence and the question of refugee arrivals in the East were the dominant historical questions in the early 1990s.[85] In light of these scholarly silences, both Warda and Piesche's works on unification explicitly articulate the desire to remember and reflect narratives of East German history that include all of its subjects.[86]

Racist Attacks before and after Unification

Dresden, Eberswalde, Berlin, Hoyerswerda, Rostock: the names of East German cities where attacks and murders took place have become metonymic markers for post-unification violence. Taken at face value as signs of deep-seated East German racism, media coverage of these violent acts demonized East German citizens as backward or more racist than those in the West. However, racist violence and the spread of conservative ideologies had been on the rise in both Germanies since the 1970s: while racist attitudes are pervasive, the conditions that prompt widespread racist violence like the riot in Hoyerswerda are complex.

The persistence of white supremacist ideologies since the Enlightenment also requires us to admit the contradictory ways in which racist ideology simultaneously mutates and seems immutable.

Multiple West German researchers argue that racist violence arose in the East after unification and then spread to the West.[87] Statements such as these overlook the persistence of violently racist acts in West and East Germany before unification. Even if the most extreme riots seem to be correlated with unification and white German resentment, violence was neither sudden nor were racist attacks unheard of in either country. In 1987, an Iranian political refugee named Kiomars Javadi, merely twenty years old, was strangled to death in Tübingen. Supposedly 20 onlookers watched without intervening to stop the murder. His purported offence? He may have tried to steal food to supplement his 2,30 DM per diem as an asylum-seeker receiving welfare benefits (the facts are disputed).[88] In 1988 alone, *thirteen* asylum or *Aussiedler* housing units experienced arson attacks in West Germany.[89] A teenage right-wing extremist in Schwandorf (Bavaria) set fire to a house in 1988 in which multiple Turkish-German residents lived. Osman Can (49), Fatma Can (43), Mehmet Can (11), and Jürgen Hübener (47) died.[90] The similarity here to the arson attacks in Mölln and Solingen five years later is striking. This is merely a short list. Racist and right-wing violence, especially acts by individuals or small groups of perpetrators, took place in both East and West Germany in the decade leading up to unification.[91] Except for sustained, multi-day rioting, the methods here are sadly quite similar to the violence that would follow unification and persist into the twenty-first-century crimes of the National Socialist Underground: murder, assault, arson. The targets were consistent across all the states of the contemporary Federal Republic: those who could not pass as white, those who were read as foreign, or those who were read as part of the left wing. The timing shows similarities across Germany and aligns with a broader conservative turn across Europe in the early 1980s. It is thus quite difficult to argue that racist acts could spread to West Germany from somewhere else. There is no denying that racist violence was already there.

Even a willingness to deny the presence of neo-Nazi, fascist, and racist acts – what Bade calls being "blind in [the] right eye" – turned out not to be a Western quality.[92] The East German government ignored the growth of a violent skinhead scene that began around 1982 or 1983 and became both more political and antiauthoritarian starting around 1985–6, choosing to attribute skinhead violence to adolescent behaviour, a desire for attention, or isolated incidents stemming from corrupt and imported Western ideologies rather than being a result of right-wing radicalization.[93] By the time the *Stasi* compiled its first report in December 1987, the GDR already had 800 skinheads between age 16 and 25, and 38 different skinhead groups, mostly in Berlin and Potsdam.[94] Skinheads targeted "foreigners, especially those with a dark skin, gays, Goths, punks, disabled persons, and younger members of the Army and police with contacts with the youth; even 'ordinary' people were not spared."[95] Between 1983 and 1987, scholars estimate that right-wing extremist violence in the East increased by nearly 500 per cent.[96]

In both East and West, commentators blamed the rise in violence on theories of spread or, in the East, "the import thesis." Neither wanted to label themselves the site of origin. The *Stasi* portrayed right-wing extremism as an import of the West rather than a product of East German society. Multiple East German studies comparing punks and skinheads or analysing criminal proceedings and over 1,200 transcripts of formal questioning between October 1987 and November 1989, however,

> largely support the contention that skinheads and members of right-wing extremist groups were not socially marginalized, did not have a deprived family background and were not losers in East German style socialist modernization (Ross 200: 104, 106, Engelbrecht 2008: 102–4). They also underscore the thesis of Konrad Weiss that the skinheads were "our children" raised in the country's own kindergartens and schools. Indeed, two of the GDR's leading right-wing extremists came from the ranks of the GDR "establishment," including officers in the Armed Forces.[97]

The only clear markers of majority were age and gender: it was young men who were most likely to be skinheads or militants.[98]

Against this backdrop, three revisions need to be made to narratives of unification. First, it is nearly impossible to describe the GDR as an ethnically homogenous society. Hundreds of thousands of East German residents and citizens were either immigrants, citizens of colour, or Soviet troops. Second, we cannot necessarily determine that East Germans were *more* racist than West Germans nor that white disadvantage was the site of origin for right-wing violence. Anti-Blackness, anti-Ziganism, anti-Semitism, resentment of foreign workers, violence towards refugees and asylum seekers, and the inability to name right-wing extremism as the threat it clearly was, all represent a collection of widely held attitudes about the construction of race and national identity. Third, these two conditions – despite the different Cold War economic and political ideologies – were shared across the whole territory of unified Germany.

Although right-wing violence clearly existed before unification, the quantity of violent incidents increased after 1990. Some attribute the increase in 1991 to the events that took place in Hoyerswerda (Saxony). As I laid out in the beginning of this chapter, the event known as "Hoyerswerda" was a series of events with various groups of perpetrators, and according to historian Panikos Panayi, these events "sparked off the enormous explosion of violence in the following six weeks."[99] Panayi strikingly reports: "It is difficult to offer a full description or explanation of the events in Germany in the first two weeks of October 1991. Morning news broadcasts simply began by listing the attacks which had taken place the previous evening."[100]

In this section about the overlap between right-wing ideologies and migration politics following the unification of East and West Germany, I do not have sufficient space to address the particularities of each violent act. The events in the Eastern cities of Hoyerswerda and Rostock rightly deserve some attention because of the scale of compounding violence over several days and the focus on victims who were visibly different. For the purposes of this section, I will explore just the events in Hoyerswerda in order to compare the media attention and popular conversations about the events with comparative research from political science that suggests that political participation and police response to right-wing violence may have played a much larger role than the simple existence of racist ideas.

Political scientist Roger Karapin offers an analysis that moves beyond economic competition and resentment or resurgent racist nationalism as explanatory theses. In a deeply compelling comparative study between the events in Hoyerswerda and a similar East German locality named Riesa, Karapin works out multiple hypotheses about the causes of the violence in Hoyerswerda. Ethnographic interviews and newspaper coverage suggest to Karapin that ethnic competition and national anti-asylum discourses were less important as causal factors for violence than local democratic conditions.[101]

In terms of the effects of unification on the expansion of the integrative apparatus, Karapin's comparative argument brings critical context about political participation and access to the public sphere into a conversation about racist violence. Pointing out the similarities between the locations like Hoyerswerda and Riesa, which were both towns that were industrial centres with significant groups of foreign workers and asylum seekers, as well as an active right-wing skinhead scene, Karapin raises the question as to why shocking levels of violence took place in Hoyerswerda while Riesa saw very little violence at all.

The primary differences between the two locations come from varying responses by police, the presence of tacit support for anti-immigrant positions by elites that seemed to condone violence or removal, as well as the channelling of political participation into nonviolent forms.[102] Riesa, he notes, saw *seven* attempted riots by large numbers of youth in 1991, but "Riesa's police acted decisively against right-wing youths almost every time they engaged in violence. In particular, police did not allow skinheads to employ vigilantism or to dominate the streets during any period."[103] This stands in stark contrast to Hoyerswerda, where residents had come to view neo-Nazi groups as civil actors more effective than either police or politicians, who were both seen as negligent.[104] Most importantly, Karapin points out that when it mattered (especially in solving murder cases and suppressing right-wing crime), local police in Riesa were willing to be transparent with the press, admit their mistakes, and cooperate with the public.[105] The most important difference Karapin highlights between the locations was the simple access residents of Riesa had to what he calls "nonviolent channels of participation."[106] There were 17 "hearings and discussions on a wide range of local public policy issues" held in 1990 in Riesa, more than four times the amount held in Hoyerswerda (where there were merely four).[107] In Hoyerswerda, "county and city authorities were passive and inattentive towards the issue of foreigners." They had not addressed the cultural conflicts that had preceded the riot by many years. Acting Mayor of Hoyerswerda Klaus Naumann (SPD) even used one of the rare 1991 public meetings to consider "the possibility of removing the asylum seekers from the neighbourhood even as he was trying to channel residents' participation into negotiations and legal channels rather than violence."[108] Similar events among politicians and citizens in Rostock, the site of a 1992 riot, may have given the impression "that the asylum seekers could be forced out violently."[109]

Indeed, alongside statements from residents that confirmed the presence of racist attitudes, citizens of Hoyerswerda interviewed by MDR on 23 September 1991, voiced the same the critiques of their city that Karapin raises. One adolescent boy declared: "If it doesn't work with political means, then it just has to arise with violence." A man in his late 20s or early 30s also stated, "The city and everyone can talk, but that takes forever, but when you enter with violence, then it happens within one, two weeks."[110] Violence in these statements characterizes force as the only effective method of dealing with conflict.

Right-Wing Intersections with Integration Politics

The relationship between unification and integration politics exists on multiple planes. First, there is the question of citizenship in the FRG. Foreign workers, asylum seekers, and international students studying in West Germany who held primary citizenship in a country outside of Europe were disadvantaged in their pursuit of German citizenship compared to East German citizens (including East German citizens of colour), Eastern European immigrants of ethnic German background, and Jewish refugees from the East, who were immediately incorporated into the citizenship regime after unification in 1990. Second, the conservative insistence that Germany was not a country of immigration or that East German citizens had no experience with foreigners when all facts pointed to the contrary were important discursive components of a broader turn to right-wing politics. This rhetoric could justify taking ethnonationalist ideas to their extreme as right-wing actors used violent methods like murder, arson, and riots to pursue their politics. Third, divisions between West Germans with certain privileges and East Germans who felt themselves to be treated like second-class citizens and subjected during the *Wende* to various forms of disintegration created divisions between Germans bearing different types of whiteness or Germans with multiple intersecting identities. Both the discrepancies between the power and privilege of West German and East German citizens directly following unification as well as both groups' use of ethnonationalist rhetoric to justify their claims to German identity facilitated how right-wing movements could harness the resentments of Germans who felt they had been left behind into political participation that prioritized either violent rhetoric or violent acts.

Many of the methods used in 1991 to force asylum seekers out of Hoyerswerda and Rostock would be mobilized in 2015 against those who entered Germany on foot and sought asylum. At that time, political organizations like PEGIDA would channel political participation in their movements into violence, using much of the same rhetoric to justify their actions as the crowd in Hoyerswerda in 1991. Similar to the debates between Kelek, Sarrazin, and researchers of migration, the examples gathered in this chapter – especially the work of Roger Karapin – illustrate that we have evidence-based interpretations of violence that do not reproduce popular rhetoric about fear as the cause of violence. Active forgetting does not just apply to the memory of the nation, its demographics, and the desire of marginalized people to participate in national life. Actively forgotten – or never internalized – are also the scholarly analyses of the events themselves.

PART THREE

2015: Refugee Resettlement
and Right-Wing Extremism

.

Chapter Eight

"Muslims Who Integrate Themselves": Integration and the Extreme Right[1]

On 16 April 2016, Lutz Bachmann arrived at the first day of his trial for *Volksverhetzung* (lit. "incitement of the people") in Dresden.[2] Born in 1973, the year the *Anwerbestopp* effectively ended postwar foreign worker recruitment, Bachmann became famous in late 2014 as the front man and co-founder of a right-wing organization called PEGIDA: Patriotic Europeans against the Islamization of the West. A group of Saxons who had been active in conservative local politics founded the organization in the fall of 2014, starting their efforts initially through a Facebook group Bachmann founded.[3] Within weeks, thousands of people were attending their rallies on the *Schlossplatz* in Dresden's historic city centre, participating in the ritual of gathering in public space, listening to speeches, and walking along the roads that form a ring around the city centre. PEGIDA's rhetoric at these events was both racist and nationalist. More importantly, however, was how the rhetoric that came from functionaries and adherents of the PEGIDA "movement" conceived of political participation and agitation as a right only afforded to white German citizens. To be precise, Bachmann and those organizing with him found any notion of refugee agency to be odious. To them, contemporary migration policy represented a failure of government because it failed to appropriately regulate asylum-seeker migration, even if PEGIDA participants could not correctly distinguish between immigrants, refugees, and asylum seekers.

At his trial in 2016, Bachmann arrived wearing a unique set of sunglasses that looked like the black censor bar editors place across photographs in order to protect people's identities (*Zensurbalkenbrille*).[4] He also visibly stuck a toothbrush in the front pocket of his trademark jean jacket, supposedly signalling to his supporters that he was willing to "resist" the state and go to prison for his actions that evening if necessary, being thus prepared to spend the night in jail.[5] While Bachmann appeared to be styling himself through these visual cues as a victim of state suppression, he had already spent 14 months in prison a decade prior for charges related to multiple robberies, assault, failure to pay child support, and drug trafficking.[6] Outside the Dresden Courthouse, supporters from PEGIDA secured a permit to protest until early afternoon, and by 8:55 a.m., counterdemonstrators from the left were already camped out in front of the courthouse alongside PEGIDA supporters and TV reporters.[7] Both journalistic interest and the need for security were high, and the judge consequently banned all recording equipment, including smart phones, from the courtroom.[8]

The charges against Bachmann stemmed from events that took place in September 2014. On Facebook, Bachmann had posted comments under an article from the *Süddeutsche Zeitung* about housing conditions for asylum seekers that a "Facebook friend" had shared. Bachmann's comments used language many people viewed as dehumanizing and derogatory, and after he posted these comments, the "friend" blocked him on the platform.[9] A printed copy of the conversation was eventually leaked to a journalist, who submitted the comments to the authorities.[10] Bachmann was then charged in 2015 with incitement of the people (*Volksverhetzung*), a charge used to prevent the kinds of dehumanizing rhetoric that was a fundamental part of anti-Semitic Nazi politics.[11] There are many translations of this specific crime in the English-language media coverage of Bachmann's trial, from "incitement" to "incitement of hatred" or "incitement to racial violence."[12] For North American readers, what is important about this particular charge is that it cannot be committed against generic identities, like one's profession – it only applies to racial, ethnic, religious or otherwise essentialized categories of difference. The charge is essentially that of a racialized hate crime, targeting dehumanizing speech that would likely be protected in an American context.[13] In Bachmann's case, this means that his actions and rhetoric – and by extension, that of PEGIDA operatives – are marked as racist, a designation about which there is much hemming and hawing in a German context, since the charge is socially severe. Bachmann was found guilty in 2016 of *Volksverhetzung* and faced subsequent court charges in 2016, 2017, and 2018 for additional crimes that often took the form of speech acts, including additional charges of *Volksverhetzung*.[14]

After a second day of trial proceedings and sentencing, Bachmann was required to pay €9.600 ($11,000) in fines.[15] Before the 2016 trial, the prosecution had sought a seven-month jail term. That jail term was not required under the terms of sentencing, unless Bachmann couldn't or wouldn't pay, at which point he would spend four months in jail. One commentary in *Die Zeit* praised both the verdict and the sentence as *"hart und mutig"* (harsh and courageous), pointing out that the judge had walked a finely balanced line between punishing Bachmann and not giving his supporters a reason to protest:

> And the judge sentenced thoughtfully. Bachmann seems to be punished harshly, but he will not become a martyr. A prison sentence, however, would have given the Pegidists of Dresden an opportunity to march through their city on Mondays for months and to send a signal of solidarity to their leader in prison. Now it won't come to that. [16]

PEGIDA was founded just one month after Bachmann posted the dehumanizing Facebook comments about asylum seekers. (I will try to distinguish in this chapter between actual human beings seeking asylum ["asylum seekers"] and more widespread politicized resentment towards the generic category of "refugees"). For a brief period in 2014–15, Bachmann and PEGIDA were able to mobilize thousands of Germans to take "walks" around the perimeter of Dresden as a protest against both immigration and the ruling political elites. By January of 2015, 25,000 people were reported in attendance at PEGIDA rallies, although police may have inflated that number.[17] By the late winter of 2015, organizational infighting prompted a shift in participants, revealing a core group that had become more radical – and that was much, much smaller. Attempts to increase attendance at the rallies were erratic in spring 2015, and by the summer, PEGIDA was implicated in a three-day riot against a hotel-turned-asylum-seeker-housing complex in the Saxon town of Freital, a 15-minute train ride from Dresden. Lutz Bachmann both called for participation in the riot on Facebook and was in attendance.[18]

PEGIDA's politics were decisively populist, and its rhetoric at rallies was racist. Speakers often railed against the state and demonized Chancellor Angela Merkel. Surveys of supporters found that those who chose to participate in the rallies primarily were dissatisfied with politics, rather than immigration or asylum policy per se.[19] Racist, nationalist rhetoric, however, is politically expedient and functioned as a way for PEGIDA to mobilize populist frustration with political elites. As a political movement, PEGIDA never succeeded in translating those frustrations with political elites into a political party that could contest elections or send representatives to Parliament. Instead, the PEGIDA actions were primarily speech acts or media spectacles that made use of striking visual forms: through photos of thousands of people gathered at the *Schlossplatz* waving various eye-catching flags, rallies followed by city walks as an orderly and participatory ritual, racist and anti-statist speeches, and the circulation of conspiracy theories both at rallies and on social media, PEGIDA used its power to make speech acts previously considered taboo common in public space. While their rallies were not violent, PEGIDA's actions led to the formation of violent splinter groups and also served to facilitate the entry of the far-right party *Alternative für Deutschland* into the EU Parliament. (The AfD was founded in 2013, nearly the same time as PEGIDA).[20] In 2021, seven years after its founding, the participants in the movement who remain – including Lutz Bachmann – are radicalized to such a degree that the state of Saxony finally declared the group to be extremist and placed it under state surveillance.[21] Bachmann responded to the announcement by thanking the government for their free publicity, and posted photos of TV headlines about the new classification (where else?) on Facebook.[22]

Lutz Bachmann, PEGIDA, and the AfD represent multiple forms of extreme right mobilization indicative of contemporary debates and German social relations. Using social media as a tool to facilitate political mobilization, the contemporary German extreme right welds nativist ideology to a sense of resentment towards refugees and Germans of colour, especially when members of these groups exert their own agency. Opposed to further migration, the organizational leadership insists that assimilation to German norms and values must be compelled, lest German culture, traditions, and national identity disappear under the pressure of so called Islamization. The differences between PEGIDA, the Alternative for Germany (AfD) party, and the long-standing right-wing extremist splinter groups organized by the NPD primarily revolve around their willingness to turn rhetorical violence into physical violence, and their success at accessing other networks of far-right actors with whom they can cooperate.[23]

How extreme right actors succeed or fail in accessing traditional channels of power varies. A symbiotic relationship exists between sensationalistic coverage of extreme right scandals from which journalistic outlets profit.[24] Mainstream coverage can also be a way for right-wing actors to use alternative and digital media strategies to critique whatever coverage they have been afforded and thereby amplify mainstream coverage by creating multiple loops around the same story. Far right actors simultaneously profit from mainstream media attention at the same time that they sow doubt among their supporters as to the veracity of mainstream news and information, preferring conspiratorial messaging that inculcates both fear and a sense of knowing superiority among their supporters. Broad media attention to scandal, in turn, prompts broader social acceptance for radical ideas through this twisted and complex series of steps.[25]

For scholars, extreme right parties and politics are neither exceptional nor unpredictable. Especially across conservative political groups in Germany, suspicion of newcomers, the insistence on bloodline (rather than birthright) citizenship, and difficulty reconceptualizing both political participation and national identity to accommodate multiple ways of being German have long been domestic political struggles. Post-unification and globalizing economic systems are surely implicated in these cultural constructs: political scientists Herbert Kitschelt and Terri Givens argue that experiences in the labour market (rather than class identity or gender alone) influence the attractiveness of voting for the radical right, especially when considering the relationships workers have to globalizing pressures.[26] At the same time, political struggles are not necessarily indicative of voter behaviour or party affinity. Thilo Sarrazin was a registered Social Democrat. A larger portion of German citizens are sympathetic to the views of groups like PEGIDA or the AfD than would vote for them, and support for racist, nationalist, or authoritarian ideas stretches far beyond the arena of participatory politics.[27] Critical for my study is how racist and nativist attitudes function both as a core ideology of the far right and as an "ideological glue" that can be used in times of so-called crisis to galvanize support for authoritarian politics.[28] These attitudes intersect with immigration when politicians rely on a discourse of integration as an explanatory paradigm for the process of immigrant incorporation. Late-stage integration discourse prompts policymaking that underestimates the desire of immigrants, refugees, and their descendants to participate in shaping German society and infuses the discourse of integration with the subtext of compulsory assimilation. This chapter will focus on the right-wing desire to limit refugee agency as a critical component of the kinds of political rhetoric that invoke "integration" in ways that lead to violence.

Asylum is an issue deemed so important that it was given its own article in the German Basic Law and thereby functions as a constitutionally protected right. After unification, integration politics, asylum and migration movement, and far-right rhetoric converged at an apex of the integrative apparatus, each influencing the other in turn. My focus here will be on the PEGIDA movement because frontman Lutz Bachmann fulfills a media function similar to celebrities such as Necla Kelek and Thilo Sarrazin. Finally, the massive amount of media attention to the PEGIDA protests helped to prepare the ground for the right-wing party Alternative for Germany to succeed in elections and also prompted a small group of violent right-wing terrorists known as the *Gruppe Freital* to engage in violent acts. The ideas PEGIDA circulated "in the streets" – especially in terms of frustration with, distaste for or blatant rejection of any notion of participatory refugee agency – lowered the threshold of taboos for right-wing rhetoric before critical European and German parliamentary elections in which the AfD successfully passed federal representational hurdles. Those ideas were connected to the attempted murder of both asylum seekers and left-wing politicians.

An Evening Stroll

On 8 June 2015, I took a four-hour train ride from Berlin to Dresden to observe a PEGIDA demonstration.[29] After having watched the media coverage of PEGIDA become a global event, spilling into US media and even prompting the US State Department to issue a travel advisory for American citizens telling us to avoid protests, I wanted to observe this movement in public space.[30] Dresden had held its election for senior mayor the day before, and as I travelled, the N24 headline broadcast across train TV read: "PEGIDA reaches almost 10 per cent."[31] The headline was somewhat misleading: PEGIDA is not a political party and merely endorsed one of the candidates, Tatjana Festerling. Festerling had also been endorsed by the neo-Nazi National Democratic Party (NPD). But previous polls had predicted that only 2–3 per cent of the voters would cast votes for Festerling, so the final tabulation of 9.6 per cent (~21,000 votes) for her was indeed a surprise.[32]

When I arrived in Dresden, about an hour before the demonstration started, the first thing I noticed was a strong police presence. Seven police vans had already assembled at the *Schlossplatz*, and the organizers huddled together in the centre of the square, waiting for the arrival of the covered flatbed truck that would serve as a stage. Compared to reports of a limited or delayed police presence at actual violent events, especially at asylum-seeker housing units, the response to PEGIDA seemed profligate to me. Typical for early June in Central Germany, the weather was horrible – rain alternated between a drizzle and a downpour – and even though it was almost summer, the temperature was cold enough for everyone to be wearing zipped-up jackets and coats. My feet, in tennis shoes, were soaking wet for most of the evening. I saw some of the prominent PEGIDA members previously profiled in *New York Times Video* indeed *live* (in person), recognizing one due to his trademark jacket, from my perch on Brühl's Terrace, the famous stone steps along the river near the *Schlossplatz*.[33]

Despite the bad weather, the square was soon filled with a variety of demonstrators waving brightly coloured flags that stood out against

the soot-covered historical stone architecture of the surrounding buildings, all of us standing under dark clouds inching towards the incipient
twilight. A tourist from Japan came up to one of the security marshals
PEGIDA provided to keep the peace and wanted to know if the stage
setup meant that there would be music. The *Ordner* tried to explain that
this was a political organization and that the tourist should stay and
see what it's all about. I watched this interaction take place in middling
English with amusement, being quite perplexed as to how this demonstration would be legible in any way, shape, or form if the tourist didn't
speak German.[34]

The rhetoric, ritualistic walk, and visual field of the demonstration
read more like a disparate collection of right-wing visual symbols than
a coherent and focused tactical campaign. Political scientists Vorländer,
Herold, and Schäller confirm this assessment of PEGIDA's political
platform: sentiments at rallies were xenophobic, not out of step with
German public attitudes at large, and demonstrators were motivated
by populist sentiment, criticizing parties and politicians for an "inadequate 'closeness to the public,' insufficient feedback related to the genuine wishes and opinions of citizens (responsivity) as well as a relatively
low degree of confidence in parties and politicians."[35] A clear majority
of the demonstrators neither identified with a political party, nor did
they confidently position themselves along the political spectrum.[36]
Most of the participants at this demonstration were over 45. Many
spoke *Sächsisch*. The federalism of the German Republic was on display
through the many, many flags, with demonstrators waving the state
flags of Saxony (green and white), Saxony-Anhalt (red and white) and
Bavaria (blue and white). These three states in particular, two in the former East and one in the former West, are conservative electoral strong-
holds. Flags I had never seen before were also common, especially a
combination of the white-blue-red of the Russian Federation lined up
along a diagonal split against the black-red-yellow of the Federal Republic of Germany.[37] One flag used the German national colours in the
design of a black Nordic cross outlined in yellow and placed on a bright
red background. This flag is known as the Wirmer flag and was proposed in 1944 by anti-Nazi resistance member Josef Wirmer. PEGIDA
supporters and other right-wing extremists have appropriated the flag
to style themselves as "the resistance."[38] The German Defense League
and HoGeSa (Hooligans against Salafists), both extreme right organizations that are offshoots of the English Defence League, use either
the Wirmer flag or invert the colours by placing a yellow Nordic cross
with red trim against a black background. The Wirmer flag is not prohibited by statute in Germany like the Nazi flag or the *Reichskriegsflagge*

(imperial war flag), which means it is available for appropriation by the right wing to signal their nationalist politics in a visual form different from the current German national flag. The yellow Identitarian flag was also common.

After speeches by Tatjana Festerling and Hans-Joachim Müller, a former member of the Leipzig *Neues Forum* and a current Q-Anon/*Querdenker* supporter, it was time to walk.[39] We took a peaceful stroll over the river to Neustadt, walked along the riverbanks, and then crossed back over two blocks later. I remember being surprised watching a couple over 50 hold hands, as if they were on a date for a city walking tour. Maybe they were. As we returned to the *Schlossplatz*, people stood up on the steps of Brühl's Terrace and applauded at our return while supporters in cars honked their horns as they drove by.[40]

The protest in Dresden was orderly and controlled. In late June or July 2015, I attended a Bärgida (Berlin) offshoot demonstration that was both smaller and clearly more extreme (an assessment I made based on the participants' blatantly neo-Nazi clothing and the presence of undercover cops with earpieces who were watching the event). A counter demonstration by *Die Linke* in Berlin-Mitte that I attended was infinitely more raucous due to drum circles and other noisemakers but was also a scene where families brought small children along, illustrating the wide range of protest activity taking place across the country that summer. I attempted to attend one of the larger Legida rallies in Leipzig, but that rally was cancelled for reasons I no longer remember.[41]

As with many protests, the outdoor speeches were difficult to hear and difficult to follow, but video of that rainy Dresden demonstration on 8 June 2015 is available in full on YouTube.[42] Most of the speeches that evening centred around rallying supporters to prevent a local red-red-green coalition from coming to power, urging the participants to first vote for the FDP, and then – once it became clear that the organizational team was also divided about this advice – to vote for either the FDP or the CDU in the run-off. At various times, the crowd called Angela Merkel a traitor. Müller ended his speech by arguing that Germany was a "shitty state" and was subject to a *Parteidiktatur* (a dictatorship of the party). While Festerling's and Bachmann's speeches focused on the election and urged supporters to use their votes to prevent a left coalition from taking local power, Müller provided the nativist ideological glue by arguing that Merkel was using Islam as a "divide and conquer" strategy to control the population and dropped in a comment about "1.5 million Africans" who want to come to Germany. After the speeches, the YouTube documentation video also included several minutes of footage showing hundreds of people crossing the bridge across the river. This image functioned both as documentary filler for the 20–30 minutes during which we walked around the city, and made a visual argument for the size and strength of the movement. The essence of Bachmann's final comments about voting for CDU, FDP, or really, just anyone but the left, suggests that the goals of such a demonstration are primarily affective, and offer an emotional appeal through which PEGIDA positions itself against contemporary developments and thus channels this antagonism without having to be particularly specific about policy.[43] The one thing that surveys of demonstrators repeatedly make clear is the anti-immigrant nativism of the demonstrators, which Vorländer, Herold, and Schäller attribute to "the impression of power-lessness" and "fears of being socially disadvantaged compared to the 'foreigners.'"[44]

Lutz Bachmann and PEGIDA

As the infamous celebrity founder of a right-wing "citizens' initiative" (*Bürgerinitiative*), Lutz Bachmann's criminal backstory provides endless opportunities for sensationalist media coverage, and his continued inability to behave appropriately in public space and frequent legal troubles make it possible for him, especially as a white, ethnic German man, to serve as an example of how the right wing perceives and constructs narratives of its own victimization to justify its dehumanizing rhetoric about refugees. Especially between 2013 and 2015, Bachmann consistently pushed the limits of his own celebrity – and not only through the comments on Facebook that later landed him in court. Facebook, however, aided his ability to reach a wide audience, serving as a way to amplify Bachmann's voice.[45] In January 2015, Bachmann posted a selfie in which he posed like Hitler. He attempted to brush the selfie off as satire when the image prompted public outrage and organizational chaos.[46] While he was forced to resign for posting the picture, less than eight weeks later the PEGIDA board and membership reelected him as their chairperson.[47] He did not face real consequences: those were left up to the courts and the monetary fines they could impose.

As a right-wing celebrity, Bachmann consistently refuses to take responsibility for his behaviour and public statements. This behaviour is also common with other right-wing extremists, who frequently give interviews to the press, appear to seek out attention, and yet remain evasive when asked to simply articulate and claim their own politics.[48] During his 2016 trial for charges of *Volksverhetzung*, Bachmann did not give a statement in court. Instead Bachmann's lawyer chose the rather bizarre strategy of trying to contest that Bachmann had even posted the comments, arguing that his Facebook profile could have been hacked. This argument – itself an extreme attempt to evade responsibility through conspiratorial narrative – failed due to its own implausibility when the judge admitted a video from a PEGIDA rally as evidence. In this video, Bachmann conceded in public to having expressed the ideas represented by the Facebook comments. The judge consequently called the video an admission of guilt.[49] Such comments were hardly out of context with PEGIDA's rhetoric: nearly every newspaper article about the trial also included an explanatory sentence about PEGIDA's public rhetoric, calling PEGIDA a "German anti-immigrant movement" (*New York Times*), "islam- und fremdenfeindlichen Protestinitiative" (an Islamophobic and xenophobic protest initiative, *Tagesspiegel*), a movement that "macht Stimmung gegen Muslime, Flüchtlinge, Politiker und Medien" ("stirs up resentment against Muslims, refugees, politicians and media," *Süddeutsche Zeitung*), or simply the declarative sentence: "PEGIDA organizes regular demonstrations against Islam and asylum seekers" (*BBC*).[50] This assessment of PEGIDA's essential character was widespread: PEGIDA espoused racist ideas and clearly occupied a position on the extreme right of the political spectrum.

At the height of PEGIDA's visible organizing success, members were also notorious for criticizing the media, refusing to give interviews, and calling journalists members of the "*Lügenpresse*," or "lying press."[51] This term has Nazi connotations, although it has circulated in German-language journalism and propaganda since the early twentieth century.[52] In December 2014, however, right at the beginning of the PEGIDA movement, Bachmann did give an interview to the *Bild-Zeitung*, a tabloid paper with right-wing leanings. This interview is critical because it lends some insight into the motivations Bachmann had for founding the organization and shows how affectively charged and simultaneously vague Bachmann's political project was from the start. The interview begins abruptly:

> BILD: How did you actually come up with the idea of a protest?
> BACHMANN: "After a protest by PKK adherents on Prague Street, we wanted to do something. There [at that protest] weapons were demanded for the unconstitutional and prohibited PKK – I'm against that. So we founded a Facebook group. I never thought that it would be such a success." [quotation marks only for Bachmann in original][53]

The primary goal of the protest on Prague Street in Dresden was to draw attention to the Yazidi genocide during the Siege of Kobanî, and the demonstration was part of a larger wave of demonstrations taking

place at this time across Europe.[54] Yazidis have their own religion and
are not typically Muslim, which is why they were targeted by ISIL.
The slippage between resentment of this protest and PEGIDA's name
(Patriotic Europeans against *Islamization*) shows Bachmann's lack of
understanding of immigrant and refugee heterogeneity. The PKK is a
Kurdish paramilitary organization designated as a terrorist organization in Germany and the United States, but some protestors in Dresden
were calling for its decriminalization.[55] The protests were not about
immigration to Germany, but rather about the politics of Kurdistan,
which was lost on Bachmann. The interviewer then asked Bachmann
what PEGIDA wants, and he says, "a change of thought in politics."
The interviewer follows up, presumably to clarify what kind of change
Bachmann desires: "Regarding the topic of asylum?" Bachmann reacts
defensively to this follow-up, declaring that PEGIDA adherents are not
against asylum and would readily grant it to anyone fleeing war. They
do not, however, support the immigration of so-called *Wirtschaftsflüchtlinge* (economic refugees).[56] The interview continues in a rapid back and
forth in which Bachmann makes it sounds like he supports progressive
causes, while the interviewer points out the presence of multiple right-
wing groups like hooligans and neo-Nazis at PEGIDA rallies:

> BILD: Are you playing on people's fears?
> BACHMANN: "Those fears are already there! Due to a misguided politics
>   of asylum. When the Interior Minister says there are higher rates
>   of criminality surrounding asylum-seekers' housing, that's okay. But
>   if I say it, we are immediately pegged as Nazis and brown crackpots
>   (*braune Spinner*)."
> BILD: Then what should politics change?
> BACHMANN: "We need faster processing and the integration of those who
>   are allowed to stay. Decentralized housing instead of asylum-seekers'
>   homes that are partly inhumane."
> BILD: Now you're starting to sound like a Pro-asylum-organization!
> BACHMANN (laughs): "We're not really that different from each other!"[57]

To be clear, the refugee advocacy organization known as ProAsyl and
PEGIDA could not have politics that are more different. How Bachmann
narrates his decision to found PEGIDA, however, matches the reasons
survey participants gave for why they took part in PEGIDA protests
in late 2014 and early 2015. While participants were primarily secular (eliminating the possibility of ties to organized religion) and had
weak ties to party affinity (likely a clue as to the broad early interest
across the spectrum in PEGIDA's politics), demonstrators frequently

expressed two primary motivations for participating. First, they were critical of the political process and antagonistic to the political elite. Second, while participants rarely expressed fears of so-called Islamization, they frequently expressed the opinion that German refugee, immigration and integration policies were all inadequate.[58] In his study on right-wing terrorism in Germany, Daniel Koehler pointed out that most of the violent acts in 2015 and beyond were committeed by "individuals with no ties to the extreme right-wing movement but who were deeply embedded in these [PEGIDA, NPD, *Der Dritte Weg*] right-wing anti-immigration protest movements."[59]

As PEGIDA attracted more adherents, the German media covered the movement with reports and opinion articles that seemed to all ask the same question: How had PEGIDA succeeded in attracting so much support? Media in previously stable democracies with post-industrial, service economies tend to respond in similar ways to right-wing movements. Coverage ranges from sensationalist and alarming reports about how dangerous these movements could be to clickbait that feeds attention to the movement through a mutually beneficial relationship between revenue and coverage, or by simply posing the same question over and over again, as if authoritarian politics were an unknown entity about which we know relatively nothing.

While the press or the public may have been caught off guard, scholars certainly were not. Research about right-wing politics reaching back into the 1990s reflects that the specific attitudes driving participation in PEGIDA were not only unsurprising, but also confirm that we have long had the tools to interpret right-wing movements. Anti-statist views characteristic of populist protest movements often arise, especially along the radical right, when left and right parties of the centre are no longer seen as substantially different.[60] This certainly applies to the German context after 2013, since the CDU and SPD ruled the federal government as a so-called Grand Coalition until 2021, and this context was also likely behind the rise of the NPD in the 1960s.[61] While it is unclear *exactly* how racism, ethnocentrism, and xenophobia function in terms of voter turnout, especially within parliamentary democracies like Germany in which there are now six major parties, it is impossible to find a right-wing party without racist views. Political scientists essentially concur that racism and nativism are essential to right-wing politics. Cas Mudde argues that nativism may function as the core ideological component of the far right, and Herbert Kitschelt suggests that racism may ideologically facilitate whatever changes leadership calls for, especially in times of "crisis." Dietrich Thränhardt pointed out in a comparative study of English, French, and German politics that "conservative parties have successfully manipulated xenophobic issues against social democratic governments" in all three locations, and that anti-immigrant or racist campaigning rhetoric often dies down after an election has successfully deployed the strategy to gain power.[62] Vorländer, Herold, and Schäller's comparative study of early research on PEGIDA confirms that the group is indoubtably "ethnocentric" and uses racist language.[63] Finally, Terri Givens found that "attitudes toward political issues, particularly immigration, [have] a disproportionate impact on the probability of voting radical right," but in the 1990s, a German mainstream right party (CSU) was outmaneuvering the radical right on the issue of immigration.[64] It remains unclear as to whether racism is a core ideology of the right wing that leads to a white supremacist politics, or if racism and white supremacy are simply so widespread that they can be invoked to grow the size of a movement and affect electoral futures. Racism, however, is clearly a critical motivating factor for participation in a variety of conservative political actions and parties.

In terms of an anti-refugee politics, it is also important to maintain an intersectional perspective in which both systemic racism and socioeconomic status play a role as explanatory factors. But not because of theories that paint PEGIDA supporters as economic losers: the majority are neither poor nor undereducated.[65] Rather, the kind of welfare chauvinism that facilitates anti-asylee and anti-immigrant sentiment is critically intertwined with the electoral success of the far right and its implication as a component of the integrative apparatus: when PEGIDA supporters say that they support war refugees but not "economic" ones, they are reflecting back the individualist rhetoric of pro-capitalist economic ideologies, which makes individuals – rather than markets or systems – personally responsible for their class position. Kitschelt had already argued in 1995 that electoral successes of the New Radical Right in Western Europe required NRR parties to meld authoritarian positions with an embrace of libertarian (neoliberal) economics.[66] In his study, only NRR parties that took a pro-capitalist stance were electorally successful.[67] While PEGIDA is not a party, Kitschelt's research and the welfare chauvinism of PEGIDA supporters reveal that PEGIDA's rhetoric and attitudes of demonstrators follow the playbook of the New Radical Right.

Finally, the slippage between left and right that occurred in the interview that Bachmann gave to *Bild* is representative of how the far right appropriates a variety of political tactics and strategies from its opponents, if not only to disguise their political intent, then also to make it more socially palatable. Part of this appropriative behaviour can be explained if we understand far right movements as countermovements that may not have an original strategic vision. As sociologists Kathleen M. Blee and Kimberly A. Creasap explain succinctly in their literature review of conservative and right-wing movements:

> Rightist movements tend to be known for what they are against, not what they support (Durham 2007, Lo 1982). Anti-gay movements are mobilized by LGBT gains. The antiabortion movement fights legal abortion. Anti-immigrant movements are fueled by the advances of immigrants. As counter-movements, their rhetoric and tactics are influenced by opposing movements.[68]

This model fits well with those who argue that the New Radical Right is, above all else, a response to the New Left movements that have slowly become culturally dominant since 1968.[69] Concern for the environment, acknowledgement of diverse genders and sexualities, reforms to citizenship and immigration policy, and revisions to performative German memory culture all arose from this collection of extra-parliamentary movements that later found parliamentary representation after the Green Party was founded in the FRG in 1983. The extraparliamentary movements of the late 1960s also occurred alongside the political groundwork that led to the integrative apparatus, as I argued in chapter 6. The politics of the New Left and the New Right emerged alongside integration discourse and policy and are inextricably linked to the integrative apparatus.

Antagonism to Refugee Agency

If xenophobia and racism are part of the ideological glue around which right-wing supporters can be galvanized, it is important for us to understand how PEGIDA mobilized and what specific form of racialized antagonism was at play when PEGIDA was at its height. Bachmann narrates the founding of PEGIDA as a countermovement to marginalized people who organized their own protests. The comments that landed Bachmann in court in 2016 have not been published in their entirety, but involved equating refugees with animals in ways the court later found injured the dignity of people seeking asylum and thereby threatened the public peace.[70] Bachmann's comments were posted under an article from the *Süddeutsche Zeitung* that dealt with "the conditions in refugee housing in Frankish Zirndorff."[71] The SZ and the *Abendzeitung München* published multiple articles beginning in late August 2014 about the difficulties Bavaria was having in housing increasing numbers of asylum seekers, illustrating that the topic was getting a fair amount of press local to Bavaria about a year before the so-called refugee crisis began.[72]

This context is important: a refugee crisis did not suddenly develop in the fall of 2015. The number of people seeking asylum in Europe stayed both low and fairly steady between 2004 and 2011.[73] But numbers began to rise slowly in 2012 and rose beyond the level of moderate variation in 2013 and 2014 before jumping markedly in 2015. Numbers only returned to 2014 levels in 2020, which I presume was due to movement restrictions instituted during the COVID-19 pandemic.[74] In Germany, a protest movement led by asylum seekers existed alongside a rise in asylum applications between 2012 and 2014. The protests started in 2012, when 50 teenagers in a Bavarian barracks undertook a 13-day hunger strike to protest the use of security personnel instead of social workers during the night shift, their exclusion from schools and apprenticeships, and the fact that the majority of the teenagers had been living in the barracks longer than the 90 day period permitted by law due to a lack of space in more permanent housing designed to serve children and teenagers.[75] Of all the migration pathways, asylum seekers are disproportionately young and male. Sociologist Peter Schimany writes: "In terms of age, asylum seekers are by far the youngest amongst all migrant groups in Germany."[76] Two-thirds of all asylum applications in Germany in 2012 were filed by people under 30.[77] No other form of migration is so heavily dominated by men.[78] Both youth and male privilege make intuitive sense: treacherous journeys are rarely undertaken by people who know they will risk more by trying to complete them than by staying put.

Between 2012 and 2014, additional groups of asylum seekers protested the conditions of their housing, provisions, and forced immobility through hunger strikes, political protests, public journeys on foot, and the threat of suicide.[79] At first, a number of unconnected political actions arose spontaneously after multiple asylum seekers caught in bureaucratic struggles did die by suicide. Most of these protests originated in Bavaria, where the official policy on asylum seekers is deterrence, formulated in the rhetoric of "nichtintegration" (non-integration).[80] Two actions received the most press: the first was the protest walk that began on 20 September 2012, in Würzburg, where 15 to 20 people seeking asylum walked the 600 kilometres from Bavaria to Berlin in protest of the German *Residenzpflicht*, which did not allow asylum seekers to leave the district in which they were registered. The group arrived in Berlin on 5 October 2012. Newspapers published articles focusing on their progress fairly frequently between September and October, meeting up with those walking, especially as other organizations or locals walked alongside them for parts of the journey.[81] The visual imagery of the walk was also eerie in its foreshadowing, as over a million refugees would cross the continent on foot during the spring and summer of 2015.

The second protest action emerged from the first, as refugees built up a tent city at Oranienplatz in Berlin-Kreuzberg and organized multiple protests against the conditions they faced in terms of housing, freedom of movement, and employment or schooling. Some 6,000 people attended a protest on 13 October 2012 in Berlin to advocate for the rights for refugees and asylum seekers.[82] The next day, ten activists, including six Nigerian citizens who had been housed not in Bavaria, but rather in Baden-Württemberg, occupied the Nigerian embassy and protested a practice known as "embassy hearings" (*Botschaftsanhörungen*), during which asylum seekers whose nationality cannot be determined are subjected to dialect analysis in order to determine the country to which they should be deported.[83] A smaller group of refugees protested near the Brandenburg Gate by camping at *Pariser Platz* at the end of October, hoping to meet with parliamentary politicians (*Bundestagsabgeordnete*).[84] Asylum seekers in Munich began a hunger strike in June 2013, and especially during the summer of 2013, protests took place in Bitterfeld, Hamburg, Eisenberg, Eisenhüttenstatt, Stuttgart, and Würzburg.[85] The tent city on Oranienplatz as well as other protest walks that started after the first one in 2012 often faced police raids or were thwarted from continuing their protest by police.[86]

By 2014, the protest movement itself had fractured.[87] While broader attention to some of the more obscure effects of the laws and policies governing the lives of asylum seekers had brought positive changes in terms of the benefits given to asylum seekers as they waited for their cases to be decided, the stresses put on state and local governments to fund these benefits – combined with the visibility of refugee agency – was more than enough to prompt broad public antagonism.

Visible agency is not merely a form of resistance that produces empowerment: visibility brings risks as well as rewards. Patricia Ehrkamp's ethnographic work in the neighbourhood of Duisburg-Marxloh posits: "Becoming public bears the risk of being represented in ways that are different from, and sometimes counterproductive to, the intention of why groups became public in the first place. The notion of public space as space of risk appears as a useful lens through which to examine social relations in immigrant-receiving societies."[88] In terms of the founding of PEGIDA, media coverage of protests led by marginalized groups certainly seems to have prompted a minority of Germans to then make their aggression and antagonism visible in public space.

Writing during the Trump presidency, US literary historian Koritha Mitchell gave a name to the aggression that visibility prompts:

> know-your place aggression [is] the flexible, dynamic array of forces that answer the achievements of marginalized groups such that their success brings aggression as often as praise. Any progress by those who are not straight, white, and male is answered by a backlash of violence – both literal and symbolic, both physical and discursive – that essentially says, *know your place!* [italics in original][89]

Mitchell was writing specifically about race, gender, class, and ability in a US context, but her work holds relevance for German social dynamics between white Germans and the descendants of "guest workers" in particular:

> the category "citizen" still refers to a particular demographic, and all others are treated like guests whose membership cards can always be revoked. When "guests" feel like they belong, that small victory will often inspire hostility.
>
> Know-your-place aggression comes in many forms – from microaggressions to assault, to murder – but the message is the same: certain people do not belong. They should be grateful if they are tolerated but never presume decent treatment to be their birthright.[90]

Asylees seeking humanitarian protection are not exempt from being considered a type of guest. As anthropologist Damani Partridge argues:

> "pity" is necessary for the initial welcome, but also [...] "pity" differentiates the citizen from the noncitizen "guest." Hospitality [...] sustains the hierarchical position of the citizen in this relationship. Even while he, she or they welcome(s), he, she or they also sustain(s) a morally superior position in a relationship in which reciprocity seems impossible.[91]

Lest critics believe that agency that prompts backlash is a formulation imported from scholars working in the United States, it is important to note that the demand for gratefulness from immigrant and refugee populations appears frequently in German popular literature written by German public intellectuals.[92] Journalist Ferda Ataman, as of July 2022 the Independent Federal Commissioner for Antidiscrimination, starts her humorous rant for general audiences at precisely this juncture. The title page to the first section of *Ich bin von hier. Hört auf zu fragen!* (I am from here. Stop asking!) reads: "MIGRANTS DON'T OWE

GERMANY ANYTHING. TO THE CONTRARY!"[93] Ataman argues that being subjected to the demand for gratefulness can even be inherited: "What still holds today: they should toil like labourers, but hold back like guests. Don't dare to make any demands. This expectation for people 'with a migration background' is even inherited. I am also supposed to be grateful that I am allowed to live here and should not – pretty please – criticize politics or call out the shift rightwards. A grateful migrant does not complain."[94]

What all of these critical texts point to is that the place for immigrants and refugees lies outside the realm of both participatory politics and a culture of participation – i.e., a demand (*Forderung*) for passivity rather than the encouragement (*Förderung*) to exercise agency and initiative. Not only did Lutz Bachmann consistently frame his motivation for starting PEGIDA as a response to a visible protest organized by a marginalized group: through the *Volksverhetzung* court case and subsequent rhetorical acts, we have evidence that Bachman was deeply antagonistic to refugee migration. Surveys of PEGIDA supporters reproduce know-your-place aggression most clearly when they capture the distinctions made between war refugees and so-called economic refugees. The division into those who are deserving of resettlement and those who are not is simply a cover for broader know-your-place aggression expressed in a vocabulary that attempts to avoid the social cost of charges of racism and comparisons to National Socialists. But covering up or evading blatantly taboo language reveals its performative nature when right-wing actors engage in violence. The discrepancy between word and deed renders any rhetorical cover nonsensical. In Saxony, the attacks by the *Gruppe Freital* revealed how PEGIDA's politics of refugee antagonism culminated in explosive attacks with homemade incendiary devices against both asylum seekers and left-wing politicians.

Freital

For a short time, PEGIDA succeeded in achieving what had long been part of the political program of the NPD: to make racist, xenophobic, and nationalistic rhetoric so common in public space that these kinds of rhetoric would no longer prompt outrage.[95] Think of it as a kind of exposure therapy for right-wing, authoritarian ideas: the more frequently citizens heard such arguments, the easier it would be for the public to simply classify these extreme ideas as a political ideology like any other. The continuity of this rhetoric from native testimonials, through debates about parallel societies, the tirades of Thilo Sarrazin, and into PEGIDA rallies points to nearly a decade of unabated media attention to cultural narratives about the various and vague dangers that purportedly stem from immigration.[96]

No matter how orderly PEGIDA rallies were, violence against asylum seekers and those perceived to be refugees continued. Beginning in March 2015, citizens of Freital, a city about 15 minutes from Dresden, began protesting the presence of asylum seekers in the city. Freital had a sprawling hotel complex called the Hotel Leonardo that could be easily repurposed for asylum seeker housing. By late June 2015, these protests reached their peak, culminating in a three-day altercation between right-wing demonstrators, protestors showing solidarity with asylum seekers, and police. Germany was already resettling a growing number of asylum seekers in 2014 and 2015, months before Chancellor Merkel opened the southern German border to permit the free movement of people who had travelled mostly on foot into Europe through the Balkan Route. Despite local resistance to asylum seekers being housed in Freital, as well as the fact that public fora that past March had been cancelled due to security concerns, the state government decided to house asylum seekers in Freital due to overflow near Chemnitz.[97] In Chemnitz an untenable situation had already developed in which hundreds of people were living in tents due to a lack of proper housing.[98] Some Freital residents felt like the decision to house people at the Hotel Leonardo had been made overnight, against their wishes, and by politicians who had not transparently communicated with them.[99] Some of the frustrations Roger Karapin pointed out as critical factors leading to the riots in Hoyerswerda are relevant in the case of Freital nearly 25 years later, especially a broad frustration with the political elite and the feeling that critical decisions were being made without community input.

Lutz Bachmann, who at that time lived in a neighbouring town, encouraged supporters to go out and protest in Freital's streets.[100] The *Tagesspiegel* reported that Bachmann "incited" (*hetzte*) supporters, by posting – again, where else? – on Facebook:

> ... he agitated (*hetzte*) against the "surprise attack" ("*Überrumpelungsaktion*") during which "150 asylum seekers" had been "carted in" ("*angekarrt*"). [Bachmann wrote:] "This must come to an end! Into the streets! Defend yourselves!"[101]

Bachmann also commented that asylum was a big, corrupt business and called refugees "*Glücksritter*" from Africa, a term that translates either as adventurer or mercenary/soldier of fortune.[102] That Black people served an ideological function as a spectre rather than as a group whose real presence prompts backlash is clear when we look at the demographics of refugee migration. Between 2003–12, not a single African state was represented among the ten states from which the majority of asylum seekers originated.[103] The rhetoric of refugees as crusaders was even invoked by politicians, revealing a stark anti-Black racism that exists alongside Islamophobic rhetoric across the right wing.

Other Facebook groups had popped up several months prior and served as critical incubators for Germans who held right-wing ideas and who rejected refugee resettlement in Freital. The group most often cited was specific to the cause and called *"Freital wehrt sich – Nein zum Hotelheim"* (Freital Defends Itself: No to the Hotel Home).[104] Pages like "Freital Watch" and *"Perlen aus Freital"* (Pearls from Freital) were launched as an object lesson by counterprotestors to put the racist rhetoric of the right wing on display. The Amadeu-Antonio-Stiftung criticized this doxxing tactic as inappropriate for prevention work across the political spectrum: "We reject this method of ridicule (*Pranger*), a denunciation that is used in exactly the same way by the right."[105] PEGIDA also had an active offshoot group in Freital known as *"Frigida,"* without which it might have been difficult to generate a large turnout among protestors.

For three days, beginning 23 June 2015, right-wing demonstrators gathered in the street in front of the Hotel Leonardo to protest use of the complex for asylum-seeker housing. About 100 people protested while 15 to 20 people stood in solidarity with the asylum seekers.[106] Bachmann supposedly called the people supporting refugees the *"SAntifa-Einsatzstaffel."*[107] The capitalized "SA" stands for *"Sturmabteilung,"* a reference to the Nazi paramilitary organization.[108] The numbers of those participating fluctuated from day to day, and the next night nearly 200 people protested in solidarity with asylum seekers against about 80 right-wing demonstrators. Both sides were kept separate by police.[109] On the third night, a bus with 40 additional asylum seekers arriving in Freital for the first time had to find a detour because the police had blocked off the street leading to the hotel due to the protest.[110] The press attention drops off markedly by 26 June 26. In the night of 26–27 June, violent right-wing extremists detonated a bomb in a local politician's car, causing massive damage. Michael Richter had been a Freital city council member for *Die Linke* and had engaged affirmatively with asylum and resettlement policy.[111] He eventually left both government and the State of Saxony due to the stress of being targeted by extremists.[112] The bombing seemed to put an end to the protest activity outside the hotel, but what followed was even more sinister: a violent right-wing extremist group known as the *Gruppe Freital* had formed. The group engaged in multiple bombings of politician's cars, attempted to murder politicians, and threw incendiary devices similar to small splinter bombs into refugee housing units while people slept.[113]

Members of the group were later charged with attempted murder, and at the conclusion of a 73-day trial, the perpetrators were sentenced to stark jail time, with both ringleaders receiving terms of 9.5 or 10 years in prison.[114]

The overall argument of this book is that there are complex networks of actors, discourses, and institutional logics that create – in their diffuse and networked form – conditions for right-wing activity, racism, and a pressure to assimilate to flourish and proliferate. In this kind of apparatus, there are not direct causative lines that point from origins to outcomes, but rather a moving, interconnected field in which certain behaviours and actions become possible. The mere existence of PEGIDA did not lead directly to the *Gruppe Freital*. PEGIDA, however, was a critical factor in the expansion of right-wing activity because of the way their rallies provided opportunities for ideas to circulate and also created a way for extremists to organize and network in public space.

In terms of the protests around Freital and their links to PEGIDA, there are several points that are critical. First, the rhetoric circulating during the protest and uttered by members of the *Gruppe Freital* bears the hallmark features of resentment of refugee agency. An article in the *Nordwestzeitung* from 25 June 2015 cited a protestor in Freital named Sebastian who justified his protest by declaring: "We have nothing against civil war refugees. These are economic refugees, who think they can do whatever they want here."[115] This distinction between refugee groups, while common in German daily life, is factually specious. Peter Schimay argues: "in individual cases, it probably isn't clear whether voluntary or compulsory [movement] prevails, when people react to adverse political, economic, social, demographic, and ecological conditions with migration. According to Castles (2003), a division between economic migrants and refugees is difficult because 'weak economies' and 'weak states' generally emerge together."[116] After the *Gruppe Freital* was arrested, the ARD television show *Panorama* ran a segment in which they interviewed Patrick Festing, one of the *Gruppe Freital* leaders, who expressed the same idea as Sebastian: "Just because I have a problem with asylum policy, *ne*? And that I don't necessarily agree that every foreigner can come in here as he likes, and can do what he wants, doesn't mean that I'm necessarily a Nazi."[117] The rhetorical denial of Naziism surfaced in various and coded ways in statements from politicians during the period of protests, which also matches up with Karapin's analysis of subtle or unintended state support for right-wing ideas as a critical correlate to riotous behaviour.

Anti-refugee statements from politicians were consistently linked with references to integration, the suspicion that integration policy was insufficient, and a sense that the desire to integrate among refugees was limited. In the document titled "19 Theses" that PEGIDA published in December 2014 as a kind of position paper, seven of the 19 positions mention refugees or asylum policy, confirming the inordinate role that refugee resettlement played in their political positions. Two, however, also mention integration: one suggests the constitution should be amended to include a duty to integrate. The second declares that PEGIDA has no critique of "Muslims who live here and are integrating themselves."[118]

As Karapin argued in the case of Hoyerswerda, political officials and their rhetoric were critical for understanding why some considered violence to be justifiable. Matthias Meisner and Lars Radau from *Der Tagesspiegel* commented that Freital's Senior Mayor Uwe Rumberg (CDU) "regularly provided those opposed to asylum [*Asylgegner*] with arguments":

> The CDU senior mayor elected at the beginning of June, Uwe Rumberg, doubted the will to integrate of the majority of asylum seekers after he was elected. "It must be more clearly distinguished between those who really are in need of help, and those so-called soldiers of fortune [*Glücksritter*] who are coming to Germany to lead a carefree life on the cost of the community without service in return [*Gegenleistung*].[119]

Alexander Kraus of the CDU fraction in the Saxon state Parliament positioned himself on 29 June – merely two days after the rioting in Freital – as against an asylum housing arrangement in the city of Schneeberg, declaring: "Whoever doesn't have papers or has forgotten his name should immediately be put in jail. Just like in Switzerland. The experiences there show: a stay behind bars encourages the ability to remember to an enormous degree. We have to know more quickly: Who may stay? And then start with a reasonable integration."[120] Whether the traumatic experience of incarceration can serve as the first step towards a "reasonable integration" is dubious. Instead, prison or jail represent the ultimate limit the state can exercise on human agency.

While the vocabulary can exhibit moderate tonal shifts depending on whether the statement comes from a state official or a protestor, what is important is that all of these affective registers constitute a resentment towards or rejection of refugee agency. Whether an asylum claim is considered valid is determined by a long, complicated, and possibly re-traumatizing process run by the Federal Agency for Migration and Refugees (BAMF). The external determination as to whether someone's choice to flee is justified is already a basic limit on the kinds of agency asylum seekers can exercise in the first place. That refugee movement is essentially exploitative, dangerous, and risky brings to mind the famous poem "Home" by Warsan Shire, which includes a line quoted so often that it itself has become a meme: "you have to understand, / that no one puts their children in a boat / unless the water is safer than the land."[121] Preventing refugees from "doing what they want" is ultimately a fantasy of authoritarian power: every citizen and resident in a democracy is permitted to live how they wish so long as no laws are broken and respect remains for the monopoly on violence exercised by the state. Right-wing extremists who commit violent acts, however, violate both democratic tenets.

And yet, local residents in Freital had a remarkably difficult time accepting that limiting the agency of refugees through violence constituted antidemocratic and extremist activity. The *Panorama* segment about the *Gruppe Freital* included an interview with a local man of about 50 years old, who – when asked about the group's violent crimes – flippantly rejected the idea that its members could be terrorists:

> RESTAURANTEUR: Well, they aren't right wing. I mean, that's what I think. [...]
> INTERVIEWER: When you say, they aren't right wing, but also they have overwhelmingly attacked refugees and leftists – what are they, if they aren't right wing?
> RESTAURANTEUR: Attacking refugees: is that right wing? I dunno.[122]

1993 *Asylkompromiss* (Asylum Compromise)

Historian Lauren Stokes has written that large-scale refugee migration into the Federal Republic is not "a situation without precedent." Instead, since its founding, there has been a permanent refugee crisis in the FRG. Stokes even portrays "ongoing migration" as a "structural feature of the Federal Republic." Delving deeply into the historical record, Stokes makes a compelling argument that "the official reception of forced migrants has been structured by a categorical distinction between genuine refugees and ersatz 'economic refugees'."[123] Asylum law has been regularly reinterpreted since the first resettlement legislation took effect in 1953.[124] The Asylum Compromise in 1993, however, was the outcome of a tense, public debate before, during, and after unification that eventually changed the German constitution. The 1993 changes both limited how asylum was granted and brought German domestic law into compliance with new EU agreements like the Schengen Treaty and the Dublin Regulations. Colonial subjects had been explicitly excluded from recognition as refugees in the Geneva Convention to appease colonial powers in Europe, especially Great Britain and France, at the time of the UN's founding.[125] The debates around the 1967 Protocol that amended the Geneva Convention extended into German domestic politics. As Germany debated the right to asylum enshrined in the Basic Law in the 1970s, historian Patrice Poutrus notes that only as of 1975 did West German courts finally agree that the right to seek asylum had no "intrinsic limits" (*immanenten Schranken*).[126]

Integration politics at this juncture begins to reveal two characteristics that are critical for charting the increasing complexity of the integrative apparatus. First, the portrayal of various groups as easily assimilated or unassimilable began to be attached to race or ethnicity. The group of refugees in the early 1980s who received the most media and political attention were those from Vietnam. However, there were many groups seeking asylum in the '70s and '80s, including political exiles from the Pinochet regime in Chile, Eastern European refugees from Yugoslavia, Hungary, and East Germany, as well as both Turks and Kurds fleeing the tense political situation in Turkey.[127] Germany ultimately accepted 35,000 refugees from Southeast Asia.[128] But in contrast to Chilean refugees who were primarily left-wing and viewed as a Communist security threat, Vietnamese refugees were positively received across the political spectrum as victims of Communism.

Second, the integrative hierarchies of the present reproduce and aggregate years of stereotypical assertions. Vietnamese refugees were marked in the 1980s as "easily integrated." But this stereotype says very little about ethnic difference and reveals a lot more about systemic advantage. Whatever truths existed within the myth of "easy integration" obscured the fact that Vietnamese integration was facilitated by broad political agreement on their right to enter Germany, as well as a variety of funding and programmatic initiatives that assisted them with finding housing, learning how to speak German, and incorporating into the host society.[129] This divide-and-conquer logic that racializes ethnic groups and pits them against each other is characteristic of what Fatima El-Tayeb calls the logic of neoliberal multiculturalism, in which dominant society pushes the responsibility of assimilation onto various ethnic groups while maintaining the right to determine the criteria and rules under which "integration" is seen as possible.[130] That Vietnamese refugees and their descendants continue to function as a model minority in racialized hierarchies – when many Vietnamese foreign worker communities pre-date Vietnamese refugee arrival by a full generation – reveals how the lack of programmatic assistance for incorporation into society negatively affects perceptions of "integrability."[131] Descendants of other immigrant groups who did not have access to similar programs are still frequently marked as unwilling to integrate, showing that integration policy is not neutral.

Refugee studies scholar B.S. Chimni has studied the difference between how refugees from postwar and communist countries were treated differently during the Cold War than people fleeing the Global South in the 1970s and 1980s.[132] While Chimni points out that politicians and journalists evoked a number of "novel features" to cast refugees after 1960 as intrinsically different from European refugees; for the German debate, the most important element on his list is the suspicion with which asylum claims from "Third World" countries were subjected: "in contrast to refugees from Europe, most of the asylum claims made by non-Western asylum seekers were [seen as] spurious, representing a thinly disguised movement of economic migrants rather than political refugees."[133] Then-mayor of West Berlin Heinrich Lummer made precisely this style of argument in an editorial published in 1985 in *Die Zeit*: "Everyone familiar with the issues," he claimed, "understands that a large percentage of asylum seekers are coming to our country not because of 'political persecution' (Article 16 of the Basic Law) but for economic reasons and because the drawn-out legal process allows them to receive social-welfare assistance for many years, thanks to German taxpayers."[134] In this 1985 editorial, Lummer goes on to connect asylum seekers with violent crime, drug offences, prostitution, and dealing heroin.

The domestic political debate in the 1980s and early 1990s asked what the limits of German refugee resettlement in a European context would be at the same time that racist attacks and a (growing right-wing political scene) weaponized migration as a political issue. The distinction between "economic" and "war" refugees also shaped right-wing notions of welfare chauvinism and racial exclusion. Those distinctions were not new: PEGIDA frequently repeated rhetorical structures invoked during the debates about the Asylum Compromise. The changes instituted in 1993 were not minimal: the Asylum Compromise amended the German Basic Law and fundamentally limited future refugee migration. That refugees might "abuse" the right to asylum (*Asylmißbrauch*) is the subtext of any specious division between "economic" and "war" refugees invoked by contemporary right-wing protestors. This rhetorical formulation – the purported distinction between economic and war refugees, as well as the suspicion of abuse – was also common in the 1990s, when levels of post-Soviet migration were comparable to the number of refugees who entered Germany in 2015. It had been clear before the Asylum Compromise was passed that the only way to limit the right of political asylum in Germany would be through a constitutional amendment.[135] Of the 3.3 million people who filed asylum applications between 1953 and 2012, nearly 73 per cent of the applications were filed in or after 1990.[136] Still, the changes made to the German Basic Law did reduce the numbers of asylum seekers entering Germany, since the amendments limited the right to asylum in multiple ways. First, it was no longer permitted for citizens of the European Union to seek asylum in a different European country, which would later affect Rom_nja and Sint_ezze attempting to leave Eastern Europe.[137] Second, the German government was allowed to determine which countries were seen as sufficiently upholding the terms of the Geneva Convention, which also would negate a claim to asylum for citizens of countries who were compliant. Finally, those who entered a transit country that upheld the Geneva Convention were required to seek asylum in the land of first entry, which effectively stopped the flow of asylum seekers overland into Germany until 2015.[138]

In Germany in the early 1990s, the same kinds of conflicts that had circulated around foreign workers, especially conflicts between the local and the federal level of government, circulated following unification. Ursula Münch argues that asylum and immigration policy held multiple conflicts of interest between the federal and the local governments. The cost of housing asylum seekers is borne by municipalities or the states, not by the federal government – but the right to asylum is a right at the federal level.[139] This conflict is critical for understanding how asylum policy is taken up by politicians, especially conservative ones, because states would try to escape the costs of hosting asylum seekers and could do so through politicking in the *Bundesrat* (upper house, like the US Senate). Münch writes: "The dynamic of how opinions formed about political processes of asylum was regularly characterized by the fact that it was always the states, and here primarily the states governed by union parties [CDU/CSU-jsc], out of which the various initiatives for policies to accelerate processing *and limit abuse* came."[140] (italics mine). The state senators of Baden-Württemberg, Berlin and Bavaria – even under Social Democratic leadership – consistently and persistently argued for asylum law to become stricter – presumably, according to Münch, to avoid costs.[141]

The rhetoric of the far right at PEGIDA-led protests or in the press, where Lutz Bachmann or protestors like "Sebastian" argue that asylum is being misused or that the demands of the far right are simply humane (in favour of faster processing or faster deportation, for example), mirrors the political rhetoric of the CDU/CSU in the 1990s. Münch continues:

> The states and state governments, respectively, thereby took up the protests from the local communities and evaluated them in the context of their own interests. That Bavaria and Baden-Württemberg were the states that stood out in front for many decades is not only to be attributed to the fact that these states attracted more asylum seekers compared to structurally weak regions because of their attractive economies. It seems more important that both states, without exception, had governors with federal ambitions ... .[142]

In short, conservative politicians used anti-refugee politics as a strategy to fuel their political careers.

The discursive paradigm of asylum abuse informed integration politics. The subtext of deceit at the centre of the rhetoric of asylum abuse translates nearly directly into the language of integration, with its varied hierarchies of populations considered unwilling to integrate, resistant to integration, or unintegrated. That this rhetoric circulates nearly unchanged across the right wing and can be successfully channelled into integration rhetoric at the level of government reveals historical continuities in the reception of asylum seekers and immigrants more broadly. Potentially, we could argue that this continuity suggests that for many Germans, the 1993 constitutional amendment was hardly a compromise, but rather a line drawn in the sand.

Lucy Mayblin, a historian of refugee migration to Britain who builds upon B.S. Chimni's research, argues that the Geneva Convention was written with the figure of a refugee fleeing communism in mind.[143] Münch points out that Article 16 of the German Basic Law had no such delimitation and was designed to be an individual right. Until 1967, when the Geneva Convention was revised to include refugee subjects beyond those fleeing communism, the West German public basically saw Article 16 and the Geneva Convention as synonymous and limited the perception of refugees to those fleeing communism (rather than anyone seeking refuge, as Article 16 implied): "The initial restriction of an actually limitlessly valid basic right to asylum to Eastern Bloc refugees represents one of the roots of the perception of asylum abuse."[144] Those who didn't fit the picture of a Soviet refugee were not perceived as in need of protection.

Once the narrative of deceit and abuse had been established, it could be further expanded to accommodate policy changes. The decision in March 1975 to grant asylum seekers immediate access to work as their applications were processed was interpreted by many as a way for Turks to "abuse" the system by providing a workaround for those seeking to immigrate after the recruitment ban of 1973.[145]

> Getting around the recruitment ban became incredibly easy: instead of applying from the country of origin in the context of a recruitment process (Herbert and Hunn 2007a, 705ff.), one just filed an application for asylum upon entry to Germany. From the point of view of those willing to enter, this distinction was hardly of consequence; from the point of view of politicians – especially against the backdrop of completely different economic conditions – this fulfills the conditions of an offence of "abuse" of the right of asylum.[146]

But later changes to refugee policy that took away the right to work did not succeed in changing narratives about refugee deceit. Ulrich Herbert writes:

> Eventually, in order to prohibit immigration through this path, asylum seekers were put into group housing [*Sammellager*]. At the same time, they were prohibited from working in order to inhibit a "silent integration." The asylum seekers who were forced to be lazy, often for years, were in this way presented to the public as do-nothings and freeloaders [*Nichtstuer* and *Schmarotzer*], and the high percentage of rejections, above all else with respect to civil war refugees, soon held as proof [...] that they were "economic asylum seekers," who in reality were not politically persecuted, but rather had come to Germany solely for social reasons [*aus sozialen Gründen*].[147]

Local and federal politicians leading up to the 1990 elections frequently campaigned on the notion that the majority of asylum seekers were supposedly being seduced by the social benefits Germany offered: "with asylum seekers it was primarily about tricksters and frauds [*Schwindler* and *Betrüger*]."[148] Herbert's analysis of media discourse includes examples from 1990 before the election, from several days after the Hoyerswerda attacks in 1991, and from 1992 as Germans debated accepting Bosnian war refugees.[149]

The metaphor of asylum abuse does two things: first, the backlash against refugee agency and suspicion of deceit and abuse reveals a form of welfare chauvinism that maps out easily onto white supremacist or ethnonationalist lines.[150] Second, after the Sarrazin scandal, it is important to point out that the notion of *Wirtschaftsflüchtlinge* also maps onto a neoliberal discourse that punishes anyone who struggles to become financially independent and socially and culturally self-sufficient. The backlash against refugee agency thus brings together three interwoven strands of new radical right-wing politics: racism/nativism, welfare chauvinism (the idea that resources should be spent on white German citizens first), and authoritarian notions of political participation (that only certain groups should be permitted to participate in shaping German society). These three nodes may well be the most important intersections within the integrative apparatus, since they represent both access to systems and limits on social incorporation, especially political agency. In terms of governmentality and the methods through which states manage their demography, it is worth pointing out that issue ownership of all three areas falls to conservative politicians and parties, who often fashion themselves as both just and justifiably strict gatekeepers invested in the sovereignty and persistence of state, nation, and culture.

Chapter Nine

The 2016 Integration Act

"That's ridiculous," the Facebook comment read. "Are you saying that you want to prohibit entry for women with children out on a green meadow using armed force?"[1] On 30 January 2016, Beatrix von Storch had posted on Facebook that refugees crossing the border could be considered assailants (*Angreifer*).[2] When she saw the above comment under her post, the deputy leader of the Alternative for Germany party responded simply to the commenter's outrage: "Yes." Two letters – *Ja.* – followed by a period, starkly framed by the blue and white Facebook colour scheme, repeated the message that already flowed within and across right-wing political movements: refugee agency was intolerable in the context of national sovereignty. Under such conditions, humanitarian assistance was portrayed as a farce; deadly force as a calculated, rational decision.

It is difficult to *underestimate* the power right-wing ideas found through their circulation on Facebook and other social media platforms in 2015 and 2016. Not only images, but a sheer proliferation of right-wing chatter was made possible by the format and algorithms of the platform.[3] Frauke Petry, then the press spokeswoman for the AfD, had given a similar statement about the use of force to the *Mannheimer Morgen* a couple of days earlier, saying that, of course, as last resort, defending the border through the use of armed force was legally acceptable, a point of view echoed by Petry's then lover and now husband Marcus Pretzell, a representative to EU Parliament for the AfD.[4] Von Storch's original Facebook post expressed a bewildering mix of affective outrage at the desecration of the memory of those shot by border guards along the inner German border with specious legal argumentation that simply crossing the border was an act of violence. Finally, it wasn't just politicians who were using social media to agitate for border policing and deportation – these debates were constant among elites and popular voices alike in 2015–16.

Coverage of this social media "event" – meaning, traditional news outlets publishing coverage of yet another polemic conversation on Facebook – was of interest only because of the celebrity of the people posting. The backlash against von Storch and Petry's commentary was rapid and swift, with headlines like "AfD-Vice Chair Wants to Permit Police to Even Shoot at Children"[5] and "[Use] Guns against Refugees? Women Yes, Children No," the latter of which covered Beatrix von Storch's half-hearted attempt to qualify the statements she had made in her post.[6]

In addition to brutally callous commentary, the summer of 2015 was a season of images, and all media with visual elements (Facebook, newspapers, magazines, TV news) circulated images of refugees fleeing. Journalists captured photographs from the sea, the forest, the sky, and up close. This visuality, like the rhetoric of integration, revealed to discerning observers the historical memory of past migration movements and linked the historical iconography of past refugee movement to the present. Photographs of the infamous *Vlora* freighter that docked in Italy in 1991, carrying thousands of Albanian citizens fleeing Eastern Europe, resembled the Greek ferry *El Venizelos* in 2015, which carried people who had landed on the Greek outlying islands into Athens.[7] Drone images in 2015 captured wavy lines of mostly young men walking through Balkan forests, modern replicas of *Vertriebene* walking west through the *Ostgebiete* in the winter of 1945, or Bosnian refugees fleeing Srebrenica in 1993, who had been flanked by UN soldiers in their trademark blue helmets.[8] Images of refugees camping at the Keleti train station in Budapest brought to mind East German refugees camping on the grounds of the East German embassy in Prague in 1989; and the euphoria of German citizens welcoming refugees on trains from Hungary arriving in Munich in 2015 seemed similar to the euphoria of thousands of East German citizens crossing from Prague back through East German territory in transit to asylum in the Federal Republic. East German asylum seekers stuck their hands out of train windows in nearly uniform blue jacket sleeves and waved at the East German crowds cheering, clapping, and waving at them as the trains travelled *back* through eastern stations to get to the West.[9]

The right-wing responses to refugee movement in 2015 and 2016 reflect both the far-right's hatred of Angela Merkel, the reliance of the new radical right on migration as both a scapegoat and a polarizing issue, as well as the consistent public appetite for sensationalist media spectacles about human beings in distress. If the demands of integration rhetoric – to integrate oneself into society, to sanction those considered unwilling to integrate, to talk incessantly of integration as if it were more concrete and shorter than the long-term, abstract process that it is – all constitute a lexicon of cultural terms and ideas particular to the German context of integration politics, the so-called refugee crisis of 2015 represented a new synthetic consolidation of multiple networks within the integrative apparatus. I call this consolidation the late-stage apparatus of integration. The first network to consolidate was one of racialization, primed both by previous scandals and the sheer diversity of people walking along the Balkan Route in the summer and early fall of 2015. Stereotypes of the "Mediterranean" guest worker in the 1960s that had consolidated into post 9/11 Islamophobic fears of veiling and racialized masculinities were able to combine in 2015 with racist colonial fantasies about Blackness and the fear so frequently voiced at right-wing rallies that African immigration would negatively affect German society. Sarrazin's racialized hierarchy was a constant cultural subtext to debates about refugee identity and the respective integrability of various national identities.

The second node consolidated around economics, legal status, and class. The sheer scale of funding social services for such a large number of people and the need for a new legal apparatus to channel that funding harkened back to previous periods of accelerated refugee movement and their attendant legal changes. The logic of neoliberal efficiency, however, also lent a strange cadence to debates about funding, since the Federal German Republic at that moment was flush with cash and would have had no trouble appropriately funding such measures. (Refugee resettlement also tends to spur economic growth in the areas with large refugee communities.)

The third node of critique is always present but not always audible. The past half century of immigration to Germany – which had transformed Germany into a truly diverse, multiracial, and multiethnic liberal democracy long before 2015 – did not only result in conservative integrative rhetoric and right-wing backlash against immigration. There was a critical presence of centre-left and left-wing voices across many decades who welcomed refugee movement and immigration and pushed back against the racialization of immigrants and refugees so prominent across the right. The social workers whose voices appear in this section and who served refugee populations before and after 2015 represent a critical population in Germany – those who welcome immigration of nearly all kinds as a way to strengthen not only the cultural richness of Germany, or the financial contributions to the social welfare system with sufficient workers, but also the political and social participation of a diverse citizenry.

The late-stage integrative apparatus bears multiple contradictions. In spite of the fact that integration politics is formally considered a local concern, the 2016 Integration Act at the federal level responded to local frustrations, to state-based integration laws that preceded the federal legislation, and to a so-called crisis facilitated by questions of freedom of movement, security, and border policing at the discretion of the chancellor and the interior minister in 2015. The late-stage integrative apparatus has become increasingly federal with the passage of multiple laws, policies, and consultation structures by the federal government after 2005, which is the starting point for this book.[10] Klaus Bade declared that around this time "the state awakened like a sleeping giant" to the need for federal management of migration and immigrant incorporation.[11] These changes overlap with the acceleration of globalization and the rhetoric of economic efficiency that followed the collapse of the Soviet Union, which is inseparable from late capitalism and has also had profound effects on migration globally. The chronology of when the integrative apparatus entered this "late stage" of development overlaps with the sixteen years of the Merkel chancellorship, but it is important to note that the steps to extend and fortify this apparatus began in Gerhard Schroeder's chancellorship with the Hartz Reforms and the new German citizenship regulations that took effect in 2000. The 2005 Immigration Act, its amendment in 2007, and the consultation structures of the German Integration Summits and German Islam Conference, both of which began in 2010, are all evidence that a late-stage apparatus has been fortified over time. The expansion of the integrative apparatus will also certainly continue after the federal elections of 2021 and refugee resettlement from Ukraine in 2022.

The 2016 Integration Act was not unpredictable and reveals continuities over time within the discursive metaphors of integration in German society and cultural discourse. The 2016 legislation also illustrates how different identities continue to be portrayed as more or less deserving of humanitarian assistance and social attention depending on national origin, religious background, racial or ethnic identity, and sexual orientation (in the case of queer/trans asylum seekers). These hierarchies show that racialization has always been a critical component of the integrative apparatus. Especially after Sarrazin's polemic garnered so much attention, his recapitulation of racialized hierarchies made it seem both normal and acceptable to create lists of deserving and less deserving populations as a way to manage a large population. The Federal Integration Act of 2016 was not simply a top-down legislative exercise, but followed in the wake of multiple state-level integration laws passed in states with large immigrant populations, such as Baden-Württemberg and North-Rhine Westphalia. The movement of legislative impulses from the state to the federal levels also shows how a late-stage integrative apparatus incorporates ideological movement and influence from multiple directions, since the content of the federal integration law differs starkly from the focus of state integration laws.

This chapter will focus on both levels of the late-stage integrative apparatus: first, I will attend to the passage of the 2016 Integration Act as a synthetic outcome of the integrative apparatus thus far, in which politicians strengthened the discursive connections between various philosophies, ideologies, and non-discursive practices. The Integration Act itself was also a discursive object that documents the linkages between various other pieces of legislation from previous periods of refugee migration. If we needed any proof that an apparatus is not a device nor itself the name for a network of connected institutions, but rather a construct which exists in the spaces between institutions, discourses, and ideologies, the table of contents for the Integration Act of 2016 provides the equivalent of a logical proof through its list of updates to policies linked across a variety of federal bureaucratic locations.

I also ask: What is the work of incorporation that can be done within the context of a late-stage integrative apparatus? I conducted several months of fieldwork at a nonprofit called *beramí*, located in Frankfurt am Main, in the summer and fall of 2017, both in the lead up to and early months after the federal elections in September of that year. *Beramí* is a large and well-respected social work organization in a superdiverse city in the state of Hessen that has served the needs of immigrants and refugees trying to access suitable and upwardly mobile employment since the 1990s. Through participant observation in six different programs and interviews with seven staff members running these programs and training courses, I explore the stresses of this work for which there is both obviously great need and also insufficient funding and staffing. Finally, I will try to connect the rhetoric of resentment that conservative politics not only stokes but also validates by analysing speeches by politicians who demand that refugees fulfill their "duties" and hold up the economic bargain of migration.

Integration politics, even at this late stage, is neither all-encompassing nor static. Instead, it is a sufficiently powerful force to be correlated with a wide variety of social outcomes, from right-wing violence to successful attempts to care for newcomers.

The 2016 Integration Act

After widespread outrage, Beatrix von Storch and Frauke Petry quickly walked back their comments about using armed and lethal force at the border. This walking back, however, took place in the idiomatic context of the right wing, which almost always requires politicians to double down on the essence of their message while attempting to communicate some level of humanitarian concern. Von Storch simply admitted that children should not be shot but did not retreat from the argument that Germany had a right to defend its border through the use of armed force.[12] Petry insisted her comments had been taken out of context, despite having approved the final text of the interview with the *Mannheimer Morgen* before publication.[13]

Both politicians' comments were made in January 2016, several weeks after the scandal of the Cologne train station, where hundreds of women reported being groped, harassed, or – in rare cases – raped during the chaos of New Year's Eve, a holiday marked by public excess. This event was interpreted culturally as a referendum on Merkel's open doors policy. After the excitement of the so-called culture of welcome of the early fall, the literal turn to winter brought with it a metaphorical coldness towards the chancellor, those seeking asylum, and the refugee policy for which Merkel was compelled to take responsibility. In the early spring, the Grand Coalition (CDU/CSU/SPD) released its first working paper. These ideas would become the Federal Integration Act. On 14 April 2016, party leaders Chancellor Angela Merkel (CDU), Horst Seehofer (CSU), Sigmar Gabriel (SPD), and Interior Minister Thomas de Maizière (CDU) gave a press conference to introduce this issue paper to the public, and by late May, the German Cabinet met at the chancellor's palace in Meseberg to discuss the new legislation.[14]

On 3 June 2016, German Parliament took up the first reading of the Integration Act in session. Thomas De Mazière, as the interior minister, introduced the legislation to the *Bundestag* with a speech about integration as a federal task that reproduced all of the high points of integrative discourse. Starting by declaring that "insights into successful and unsuccessful integration" should inform decisions about how to proceed with the integration of refugees, he then transitioned into a dichotomy between what he called the "two realities" of integration, dividing immigrants into those who had used their chance to move up in society, and those who enter German society "barely or not at all." This succinct summary of integrative discourse in the context of crafting the first Federal Integration Act deserves to be quoted in full, since it both divides people into "good" and "bad" immigrants, invokes the social topics of concern that have circulated in media coverage for years, and repeats a narrative of failed integration that contradicts research evidence, but confirms narratives about German national identity as a construct in need of defence.

But there is also another reality: in some places in Germany people with foreign roots live who barely participate actively in our country, or don't do so at all. They live a life among themselves, almost without contact with Germans and without incorporation into [*ohne Einbindungen in*] our society. They hardly speak German or don't want to and also have no formal employment. Some young men among them commit crimes strikingly frequently. Many shut themselves off, some through religion, others through odd notions of honour, or through both. The teachers in schools in those areas often do not succeed in compensating for the lacking German language skills of the children, to say nothing of the communication of values and educational prospects.

These insights about both realities in our country hurt, also because part of this development has to do with mistakes from our own past: languorous visions of difficult integrative tasks, the formation of ghettos in cities and towns, too many scattered desires, and too few clear expectations. Let us do everything we can so that such mistakes do not repeat themselves.[15]

This description of the task of integration makes immigrants and refugees responsible both for their degree of contact with German citizens, who may reject them, as well as their ability to speak German or to find appropriate work. It demonizes, subtextually but specifically, Muslim men who stay unintegrated due to "religion" or inappropriate "understandings of honour," essentializing these men as bearing a higher level of aggression and misogyny than German men. It relieves teachers from the task, described here as nearly impossible, of successfully teaching children to speak German while simultaneously blaming them for not being able to achieve what is purportedly impossible. The emphasis on the transmission of values hints at the discourse around *Leitkultur*, which is the point at which a discourse of integration and compulsory assimilation intersects most strongly.

Finally, the second paragraph of the quotation above reveals just how powerfully narratives about the failure of integration have entered into political discourse despite the fact that this continues to be a sociological untruth. Systemic and social integration is the norm, not the exception; immigrant neighbourhoods and communities promote both incorporation and upward mobility; the primary mistake of previous incarnations of integration politics has been precisely the ideological divisions between "us" and "them" that make political notions of integrative duties, requirements, and legal sanctions causes of backlash. The rhetoric of those fleeing abusing the right to asylum that was so common in both the lead up to the 1993 Asylum Compromise and the formation of right-wing groups like PEGIDA or the *Gruppe Freital* resurfaces in the metaphorical comparisons de Maizière offers for the insistence that immigrants and refugees have a "duty" to integrate. Near the end of his introduction, he compares the duty to integrate to other duties such as compulsory schooling and the demand that parents care for their children (*Schulpflicht* and *Pflicht zur elterlichen Sorge*).[16] These two duties in particular exist in order to protect dependent children from abuse. The "duty to integrate" offers no such protection (neither to refugees nor to the state) and is also not comparable: instead, this paternalistic comparison subtextually implies that refugees are not deserving of care due to the conditions of their flight, but rather that those seeking protection are required to earn their keep and prove that they have not "abused" the chance to seek humanitarian assistance in Germany. A "duty to integrate" was also part of the rhetoric of the 2005 Immigration Act that established the integration course system.[17]

When de Maizière declared in this speech that, together with Andrea Nahles (SPD), he would present a draft of the first Integration Act for Germany, and that this legislation represented "a decisive turning point for our country," he missed the fact that he had both succinctly summarized and recapitulated integrative discourse, but also that this legislation more likely represented an extension of the policies passed and enacted by the federal government since the 1990s. Rather than a turning point, the Integration Act of 2016 is a culminating event. As he wrapped up his introduction of the new legislation, de Maizière declared

> We must position ourselves together against those who want to establish open or hidden xenophobia as social politics. (Applause from the CDU/ CSU and the SPD.) Populists have never brought our country forward by even a centimeter. They are the opposite of the culture upon which our political and human orientation should be based. The integration of people who are allowed to stay lies in our own, I [dare] say: in our national interest. [...] We don't just do this for people with the prospect of staying: we do this for ourselves; we do it for Germany.[18]

The direct and yet half-hearted reference to racism (which he calls xenophobia) and the lukewarm rejection of populist rhetoric, when compared to the conservative rhetoric invoked earlier in his speech that mirrors many of the same right-wing talking points about immigrants and refugees mobilized and uttered by PEGIDA supporters and AfD politicians, reveal an ambivalent nationalism that is particularly hard to ignore upon close reading. Although tempered here, the utterances across the spectrum of the political right tend to invoke German culture and society as an arena subject to various threats and thus in desperate need of protection.

Previous Integration Laws at the State Level

Between 2010 and 2016, three states had passed legislation with titles that invoked the label "integration act." Berlin was the first, with a "Participation and Integration Act" in 2010; North-Rhine Westphalia followed in 2012 with an "Act to Encourage Societal Participation and Integration"; and Baden-Württemberg passed a "Participation and Integration Act" in early December 2015.[19] All three states focused heavily in their integration legislation on what in North America would currently be termed "diversity, equity, and inclusion" (DEI) efforts: creating institutional structures designed to facilitate the representation of marginalized people in state government, business, and other areas in which systemic integration is required for full incorporation. While "integration and participation" efforts (the German parlance for DEI), are, of course, related to the discursive social demand that immigrants integrate through assimilative behaviour, the elements of participatory representation included in early integration laws at the state level are primarily nondiscursive practices that exist as part of symbolic order made visible in and through the discourse of integration.[20] More precisely, in these DEI-style efforts, activist re-interpretations of the term "integration" have been appropriated within an integrative discourse by translating "integration" into "participation" – without fully doing away with the language of integration.

Strikingly, both Berlin and North-Rhein Westphalia's laws focus more on non-discursive practices than on recapitulating integration discourse. Non-discursive practices frequently bear meaning within an apparatus relative to the degree that such practices are taken up as symbolic practices that are both related to or "within" discourse and are in some way able to enter into the space of institutional, everyday life. Non-discursive practices are more tightly related to actions, rather than to speech, rhetoric, or discourse.[21] Calls to make sure that people deemed to have a "migration background" are represented in institutional bodies through the structures created by "participation and integration" laws; are represented by and have advocates in the multiple commissioners of integration at the level of the district, Senate, and State; and the broad demand for all German citizens and residents to participate in practices of "intercultural opening up" are some examples of the non-discursive practices described and legislated in "participation and integration" laws.

The 2016 Integration Act is qualitatively different from these state-level statutes. Interculturality or representation are not the primary concerns of the federal legislation. Instead, the law cobbles together adjustments to a variety of other legal instruments designed to facilitate asylum seekers into employment. The Act also describes how the federal government will pay for a variety of programming needs in order to provide both job training and language instruction. The table of contents of the Integration Act is quite literally a list of seven articles that each propose changes to the *Sozialgesetzbuch* (Social Welfare Code), the *Asylbewerberleistungsgesetz* (Asylum-Seeker Welfare Act), the *Aufenthaltsgesetz* (Residency Act), the *Asylgesetz* (Asylum Act), and the *Ausländerzentralregister-Gesetz* (Central Foreigner Registry Act), most of which was legislation previously amended in the early 1990s to adapt to post-unification refugee and immigrant movement.[22]

Before the proposed law was drafted, the left-wing opposition parties *Die Linke* and *Bündnis 90/Die Grünen* submitted petitions (*Anträge*) to Parliament that laid out the structural conditions that they argued inhibited the integration of asylum seekers into the workplace and society and laid out their suggestions for changes to previous policy. These proposals both emphasized the structural obstacles asylees faced in entering the workforce, especially through exploitative working conditions (*Lohndumping*), as well as the obstacles to other forms of integration that overlap in the space between social and systemic incorporation, like medical care and language courses. Both proposals heavily emphasized the need to support refugee agency, and did so in the language of citizenship:

> Refugees [*Flüchtlinge*] need to be supported in their rights. As citizens [*Bürger und Bürgerinnen*] with equal rights they can make important contributions to the well-being of this society.[23]

> Integration is a process moving towards a life [lived] within the framework of the legal system with equal social opportunities and cultural self-determination. The foundation for [this definition] is the claim of refugees [*Geflüchteten*] to participation and to establish a vision for the future: from refugee to co-citizen, on the basis of an Integration Act. The Integration Act further develops the legal foundations for integration created in 2005.[24]

Both proposals also advocate for funding nondiscursive practices (language courses, subsidies, access to vocational training and work, appropriate housing), which constitutes an expansion of the integrative apparatus, and reveals how fortified integration politics has become as a form of governmentality positioned within the federal government and Parliament.

The introductory paragraphs to the Draft Legislation laid out by the CDU and the SPD reveal, however, the logic undergirding integration politics that was also reflected in De Maziere's introductory speech and is more characteristic of a conservative approach to integration, whether centre left or centre right. With some similarities to the economic logic of achievement and efficiency that shaped how Sarrazin constructed a racial hierarchy rooted in a distaste for the poor, the draft of the 2016 Integration Act justifies changes not in humanitarian terms, but rather in the logic of cost savings and sanctions. An entire paragraph justifies reducing the paper used to communicate asylum decisions in order to save nearly €165,000 in postage costs. This change would also reduce the workforce assigned to producing these letters, thereby further reducing costs by cutting five staff members in middle management, saving €234,000 per year.[25] While it is clear that for proposed legislation, parliaments obviously have to provide budgeting information about how the proposed policy changes will be paid for, there still seems to be an existential absurdity to the proposal's emphasis on cost-sharing through postage given that the yearly costs for various other budgets at the Ministry of Labour to serve asylum seekers are listed in the range of €93 million in 2016 and up to €215 million in 2017, with the most expensive years being between 2016 and 2019.[26] Another policy proposal was to reduce welfare benefits for those who do not comply with integration programs. The CDU/CSU/SPD declared:

> The introduction of new reductions in social welfare benefits due to dereliction of a duty to cooperate with administrative procedures (§ 1a Section 5 Asylum-Seekers Benefits Act) as well as due to unwillingness to participate in refugee integration policies (§ 5a ASBA) or unwillingness to attend integration courses (§ 5a ASBA) means certain groups of people will only receive minimal benefits that serve to secure their livelihood. The service provider can save costs through this provision.[27]

Later, however, the lawmakers admit that many of these costs are actually unquantifiable:

> The designated requirement to participate in Integration Courses in §5b ASBA and the following decisions here about sanctions to social benefits if the demands are not followed will create additional costs for the offices of the states and municipalities in an unquantifiable sum. The same holds for the cooperation and surveillance duties linked to these decisions.[28]

Rather than evaluate these statements on the basis of whether or not the accounting is correct, which are questions for which I neither have data nor would I be mathematically capable of solving such an equation, what I want to point out are the rhetorical absurdities of how politicians and policy makers justify their decisions to compel integration. Is sanctioning refugees for non-participation in the integrative apparatus ultimately justifiable if surveillance requires increased costs and budgets balanced on the backs of welfare recipients? Furthermore, if those costs at the time of law-making will either increase or are unable to be quantified, why are these policy choices justified in the language of investment, efficiency, and cost savings? Why not focus on how to get the majority to succeed instead of developing methods to punish the minority who might fail?

Critiques

Critiques of the federal legislation were many. Five days before the Cabinet met to discuss the proposed legislation, members of a working group composed of ProAsyl, the Association for Social Equality, the Diaconia, and the Council for Migration protested the Act. The common refrain from researchers and advocates working in the realm of integration politics – that political decision makers were ignoring research evidence as to how integration works and portraying refugees as unwilling, unable, or resistant to integration – was once again articulated in various ways. They also critiqued the hierarchical divisions within the act as to which groups of asylum seekers would be designated as having "good chances to remain" (*gute Bleibeperspektiven*) versus those seen to have limited chances of having their claim for asylum accepted. These categories had material effects: how someone was categorized determined whether or not they had access to services like state-funded language courses.[29] But the category of *Bleibeperspektive* tried to maintain a boundary that was, in fact, quite difficult to hold: Afghans, for example, were not designated in 2016 as a national group with "good chances to remain." By 2017, however, Afghan nationals had a 61 per cent positive asylum application rate; in 2016, the rate had been over 51 per cent.[30] Despite the high rate of acceptance, Afghans were ineligible for state-sponsored language and integration courses because they had been classified as unlikely to remain. I delve into the treatment of Afghan nationals in particular here because I think this case illustrates well how national and ethnic categorizations function within the apparatus, despite an individual right to asylum. If Sarrazin singled out various national, racial, and ethnic groups for dehumanizing vilification, marking certain groups as incapable of integrating, it is important to pay attention to this style of hierarchical categorization when it shows up in policy. There are structural consequences to categorizing asylum cases based on nationality (as opposed to individual circumstances), and these hierarchical categorizations become structural constraints when they are linked to and then absorbed into the apparatus.

Finally, the decision to link integration "achievements" to "sanctions" that reduce benefits was vilified in both the evaluations of the law issued by consulting organizations that are submitted to Parliament as part of the legal process of crafting new legislation and in the media.[31] This type of societal head-shaking meant that despite Thomas de Maizière's rhetoric, most Germans did not accept the rhetoric of integration as a duty to be sanctioned for non-compliance. Instead, many people recognized that access to systems – language instruction, employment, school enrollment, medical care, and suitable housing – was the primary concern for most refugees and asylum seekers and that providing this access would be integrative.

While politicians were fighting about national identity and the "duties" of integration, there were people living all over Germany who actively needed, desired, and requested services to help facilitate their systemic integration into schools and workplaces, and who needed help navigating sometimes unbearable social conditions, such as mass dormitories or housing in cheap hotels where late-night noise was such a hindrance that people couldn't wake up on time for work or integration courses. This section will incorporate multiple periods of fieldwork that I conducted in 2017 with staff members at a nonprofit called *beramí* in Frankfurt am Main. From identifying possible sites to conducting interviews and participant observation, I conducted this work over a period of about 15 months, four of which were spent on site in Frankfurt am Main (June 2016, June–July 2017, and November 2017). In 2017, I observed multiple projects designed to facilitate the entry into the workforce in various ways. I watched individual counselling sessions where people seeking work – some newly arrived in the summer or fall of 2015, some who had been in Germany for a decade or more – spoke with an adviser about their dreams and the realities of their personal situation. I conducted participant observation at a week-long, nearly 20-hour course known as the Employment Orientation Course, which was one of multiple courses designed to prepare people for a job search. This course served a mix of asylum seekers, immigrants, and long-term residents looking to change jobs. I also observed two educational sessions with a project for international college students who were likely to remain in Germany and that were designed to facilitate civic participation in a democracy. Finally, I attended a German language course designed to reach participants who were not granted access to a formal, state-sponsored integration course. I conducted seven one-on-one qualitative interviews of 30–70 minutes with individual staff members and spent time in multiple conversations with an eighth staff member that were not recorded. I obviously had conversations with people seeking asylum or seeking to permanently immigrate to Germany over the course of these activities, but I want to be clear that in this study of integration politics, my interest lies in how policy and programming are implemented. I did not interview people seeking asylum, nor will their stories be recounted here. There will be some scholars who will critique this approach as insufficiently taking into account the lives of those who are most affected by these policies; I argue that to do so would be a very different project than the study of governmentality, migration, and the far right. I also want to reiterate that the majority of social workers that I interviewed for this book project are themselves of immigrant background and came to Germany as immigrants or are the descendants of immigrant and/or refugee parents. They are thus themselves often hailed in integrative discourses. European data protection laws prevent me from this level of individual subject identification, preferring anonymized interview data, but my sample demographics overall are important to note. As far as I know, only one-third of the total number of social work professionals interviewed or surveyed for this book are of white German descent, although the conclusions I have drawn based on visuality and naming may also be flawed (meaning in this context that the proportion of white social workers may be lower). Based on research by Birgit Rommelspacher and multiple comments in my interview transcripts, this reflection of the field of social workers and ethnic or racialized identity is atypical: immigrants and their descendants continue to be underrepresented in the fields of social work and counselling services.[32]

berami: *berufliche Integration* (Vocational Integration)

berami is a large career counselling organization that provides myriad services to those newcomers seeking advice about how best to systemically integrate into the job market in Germany. They have 56 salaried employees and more projects than I was able to observe, some of which bring on additional contract labourers.[33] The cornerstones of their work lie in preparing people to conduct a job search, finding a job that will meet their skills and their desires, and helping newcomers orient themselves throughout all the various stages of these activities. While *berami* often serves a highly educated segment of the immigrant and refugee population, offering courses for doctors to recertify in Germany, mentoring programs for white-collar college graduates, and political education seminars for international students, many of the basic offerings – like individual job counselling sessions – serve a wide range of people with varying degrees of education and professional training. The sheer breadth of their offerings include programs that also offer skills training to people who may be illiterate or semiliterate in their first language or who have merely a grade school education. The basic philosophy of *berami*'s services is that those seeking advice must be able to participate fully in finding employment: jobs and careers will be sustainable if people are given a choice as to what kinds of employment they take up, under what conditions they work, and – most critically in an age of rationalized efficiency and neoliberal financing – maintain control over the pace of life transitions, whether that means how long it takes to achieve B2 German proficiency or how much extra support one might need to master the math problems on an apprenticeship exam.

This emphasis on newcomer agency at *berami* runs counter to the rhetoric of duties and sanctions that infused the political rhetoric surrounding the 2016 Integration Act. That is not to say that the 2016 Act was ineffectual or useless: for multiple groups, social conditions in Germany improved after the 2016 Act was passed. However, as one of my participants commented as we discussed the legislation, this improvement was not equitable across the spectrum of asylum seekers: "Yes, so to that degree, of course the situation has basically improved. That was a huge improvement. But for many people the situation still remains precarious. There's the rub."[34]

In this section about *berami*'s work, I examine three main themes that surfaced in all my interviews. First, definitions of integration in this context were markedly different from the definitions commonly invoked in everyday integration rhetoric. The immediacy of watching and facilitating the work of incorporation in actual exchange and contact with living, breathing people makes clear why the social workers at *berami* would not fall back on tired tropes that were so easily uttered by journalists and politicians. They have intimate insight into the obstacles and challenges immigrants and refugees both encounter and the skills they carry with them. Second, what was nearly unanimous in the interviews I conducted was the acknowledgment that ideologies of individualized, rationalized efficiency were hurting the work. Financing came up again and again: if Germans were so proud to pay taxes and have those taxes fund a welfare state, why were politicians so reluctant to fully fund integrative praxis, such as language courses and integration projects? Finally, both racism and a lack of contact between white Germans and immigrant and refugee communities came up often enough in conversation to be of note.

Defining Integration

With an object that is as slippery as the term "integration," I needed to make sure that I understood what people meant when we talked about integration, whether that was the focus on *berufliche Integration* (vocational integration) in *berami's* programming or the general opinions of the social workers themselves. When I asked the people I interviewed to define integration, the definitions they offered were in line with both the definition of integration as a form of social and systemic integration in the sociological context as well as the revisions to the reductive, colloquial use of the term that have been common in community work over the past twenty years. Many people have begun to redefine the social goals of incorporation as better articulated through the notion of full participation in German society rather than in the language of "integration."

One social worker who was working on building an immigrant consulting network that would offer coaching about professionalization to organizations that had previously been run solely by volunteers declared the goals of her project to be: "Participation in general, moving away from this term 'integration.'"[35] But state government, which funded the project, shared this interpretation of integration, she added: "And one has to say that this is also quite clear to the governmental department (*Ministerium*). The thought isn't: you have to integrate yourselves. Instead, it's about: we all belong together. [...] And we are all important stakeholders in this area. And each one fulfills, so to speak, his role and function."[36]

One of the constant refrains in interviews was also the subtextual understanding that integration meant different things in different contexts. This participant made sure to add, "I'm not totally solid or familiar with this whole topical, academic debate about integration/inclusion."[37] Despite this participant's hesitancy to commit to a theoretical understanding of the term, another project coordinator who preferred abstraction in her answers came up with virtually the same definition:

PARTICIPANT: It is important to me that [participants] receive the support for what they can do professionally here in Germany. That is – for integration into our contemporary society, into majority society – that they find a place where they don't feel sorted out. That they don't feel excluded. And that they can simply participate in this society. Or simply be.
JSC: Is the goal of integration participation, then?
PARTICIPANT: Yes.[38]

This same participant also noted that integration was the opposite of assimilation: "It means that things coexist with one another. Right? And absolutely something new, [something] hybrid can probably develop out of that, right?"[39]

Another program that focused primarily on finding mentors for college-educated immigrants (mentors who could facilitate their entry into the job market and build networking opportunities) stayed very close to the definition of integration as systemic integration into employment: "So: Integration now in this mentoring project means vocational integration into the German labour market."[40] This social worker also viewed integration as a two-part process, whereby systemic integration would facilitate later social integration:

> and seen conversely: when they then enter into this process [of seeking employment] once again and it works, vocational integration works, [...] then social integration is also easier because she is then also – a content wife and mother and neighbour, and all the things she is – [she is then] able to, of course, affect this society more than if she is sitting at home and frustrated, right? And I often hear – there are really moving phrases – [...] one of them said once, "now I remember that I can do more than speak bad German."[41]

The emphasis on agency as a critical element of successful incorporation – knowing that the person seeking advice has skills they can put to use as they desire – circulated through multiple interviews, even if social workers rejected commenting on the broader effects of successful incorporation beyond the systemic arena of employment: "Ok, vocational integration – I can say something about that," one participant said after I had limited the discussion terms:[42] "We understand under the heading of vocational integration that the people who come here and have experienced migration, can enter into the German labour market (into German professional life) with adequate qualifications according to their desires. And again, [that they do this] with adequate qualifications and in a self-determined way. That is vocational integration."[43] As this participant described the multiple steps and emotional facets of integration processes, the definition of integration in this interview and others consistently came back to the relationship between incorporation as a process that necessarily must take desire (an illustration of agency) into account.

The emphasis on integration as a process appeared in nearly every interview. One social worker who works extensively with new arrivals and refugees described also the sheer number of tasks that can be considered essentially integrative: "Hmmm, so: we count various things as integrative achievements. There are larger and smaller integrative achievements, right?"[44] These integrative achievements were hardly just individual acts that could be completed or sanctioned for lack of completion, as Thomas de Maizière implied in his speech to Parliament: they required the interplay of individual effort, temperament, *and* legal status. For this social worker, the multiple skill sets and conditions required to come together in this way for success was clear. The individual ability to learn a language – an ability that arose from a lack of traumatic experiences interfering with concentration, an understanding of how to systematically acquire new information, and quiet and appropriate places to study and complete homework – was influenced or made possible by having a recognized asylum application (*ein anerkanntes Asylverfahren*) and the correlated legal status transfer from the *Asylbewerberleistungsgesetz* into the *SGB-II (Sozialgesetzbuch II)*. All of these conditions needed to be met for successful systemic integration.[45]

This process was long and complicated: "But then it finally moves forward. And then they can attend an integration course and can be guided in a German course up to B2, right? And then it's easier. When the people are through the asylum process. Yeah, that sometimes took months. Until they had their hearings here."[46] Only after these needs were met, she said, might a new arrival look around and declare, "so, now as far as I'm concerned, I have B1 [language proficiency level]" and then if this person then looked around and started looking for a job, integration certainly could be successful, she asserted.[47] At this point, she further clarified what she meant by integration: "integration into the labour market. But the hurdles up to that point are individual."[48] Part of these individual hurdles also related to the status of an asylum seeker's family members: this social worker noted how difficult it was for individuals to concentrate or focus on finding a job when their family members were still in danger and the German state would not permit them to be reunited (for instance, in cases where asylees had been granted only subsidiary – i.e., partial and individual – protection). Contrary to elite political demands that integration begin on the day of arrival, what this social worker was describing was a process of integration as a long and tedious path into German society. And yet – despite the fact that integration, especially integration into employment and broader society – could only ever *begin* after a whole host of other issues had been clarified, this participant articulated the notion that individuals were ready for more integration, but the legal system and society as a whole were not:

    JSC: There are prerequisite things that need to be cleared up; it can take
    years until someone is even ready to start with integration at all.
    PARTICIPANT: Exactly. *They* are ready well before that. The society here isn't
    ready. We aren't ready due to our laws.[49]

One of the participants I interviewed also subtly inverted the terms of
integration discourse, describing the elite politicians as "unintegrated"
and *beramí* – due to its high proportion of social workers of colour – as
a "parallel society," both inversions that not only gave her a way to
escape the strictures of integration discourse but also permitted her
to flip the perception of integration as an immigrant problem on its
head.[50] It took me multiple readings of this participant's transcript
and listening to the interview recording twice to realize that she was
purposefully making a joke, since the overall tone of the interview
was critically serious. This participant was deeply engaged in an-
swering my questions, and these subtle moments went over my head
due to the stressful attention and the demand to be present that is
required of live interviews. Realizing that she had been subtly teas-
ing me at multiple points was funny and a welcome respite from the
intensity with which these conversations take place in a German context. For a term that reads as bland in a North American context, it
is difficult to explain how heated, controversial, and defensive conversations about integration can be. The understanding that racial
dynamics are embedded within an integrative paradigm may give
North American readers a pathway into understanding what these
conversations also *feel* like: discussions of race, racism, and white supremacy in the United States can prompt a similar range of affective
responses, which to me confirms not the universality of affect within
conversations about difference, but rather the degree to which such
conversations throw members of the majority off balance by requiring them to consider social conditions from a position different from
their own.

These definitional exercises revealed a core understanding of
integration among the social workers at *beramí*. Incorporating
immigrants, refugees, and other newcomers requires a *process*, is
individually directed – both regarding the temperament of the person
who has arrived, the spaces and places in which they desire to work,
as well as their individual care responsibilities – and is either facilitated
or hindered by their *legal* status. As two participants also signalled,
political and discursive conditions often served as the primary obstacle
to people's incorporative needs: the will was there, but legal status and
systemic obstacles often got in the way.

Rational Efficiency and the Neoliberal Hurdle

If integration is a process, with different outcomes depending on the subject's individual situation and their legal status, it makes sense to identify what kind of obstacles interfere with this process of incorporation. One of the primary themes that surfaced in multiple interviews – something I discovered in the field and was surprised by in 2017 – was the omnipresence of financing and funding regimes that structured the success or lack of success in integrative policymaking. These concerns have been present since the first National Integration Plan was finalized in 2007: as Elisabeth Musch points out, migrant associations "expressed concerns [...] that they lack[ed] the financial means needed to fulfill" the voluntary commitments agreed upon as part of the 400-point federal integration plan.[51] In social work, funding regimes affected the timely financing of integrative projects as well as the sustainability of that funding and the growing expectation that integration policies would be rational and efficient. While the truism that social work and social engagement are underfunded in industrialized, liberal democracies is certainly relevant, what was more surprising to me was how specifically marketized both the integration course system and the funding schemes for integration projects had become. The class animosity and logic of efficiency and efficacy that were both racialized in the context of the Sarrazin scandal appear as a constant subtext in my interviews with social workers who lead or run projects designed to incorporate immigrants and refugees through language-learning, career counselling, or professional development programs. Whether the cost matches the purported achievement level at the end of the program and how much investment is considered to have a high likelihood of increasing returns were themes that appeared in most interviews.

During the Hartz Reforms under Chancellor Schröder, *beramí* had been negatively affected by the shifts in federal funding priorities, prompting staff and leadership to later pay more attention to political change. From one day to the next, the Hartz Reforms shifted the economics of subsidies and grants in such a way that *beramí* had to file for bankruptcy because its funding structure had been rendered moot.

One of the social workers described how one of the first retraining programs *beramí* organized was a program to train immigrant women who were customer service representatives to move into wholesale sales positions. This training program was funded by a program that targeted certain groups for support – a German version of affirmative action designed to remedy inequity by funnelling money to certain groups. This program was both successful and sustainable, and *beramí* graduated hundreds of higher-skilled saleswomen in a short amount of time who were trained to work in wholesale environments. The Hartz reforms, however, eliminated all targeted group funding schemes in favour of mixed groups. The social worker I spoke to found this incredibly frustrating because the changes did not make the services they could offer *more* effective:

> And the target group grants were eliminated through the Hartz reforms. There wasn't just Hartz IV, but there was also Hartz II, Hartz I, Hartz III. That wasn't so well-known. So: there were four Hartz Acts. [...] And Hartz II – that's where this [grant] belonged – [declared]: now we don't need a target group grant anymore, everyone is equal.[52]

She pointed out that the effect of these changes was basically to return to a logic of Darwinian selection. While *beramí* still offered vocational retraining programs, they were forced to change their structure: "(A) they aren't allowed to run so long, (B) they are very, very, very poorly funded, and (C) they no longer are looking to target certain groups but rather, migrants are in these retraining programs, right? So: they are mixed groups. And – well – then we're back to natural selection: the best rise to the top [*kommen nach vorne*] and those who simply aren't able to follow, they get stuck."[53]

The ideologies behind these changes to political financing schemes were purported to be more "efficient" and "effective," but this social worker bemoaned the fact that such plans forgot what people really needed in order to move up: "This is a really important point in that one measures success differently, right? It's – [they] attempt to make it really effective, efficient, i.e., the consulting firms are somehow raking in the cash from LEAN-Management and how you can have all that and save [...] and, and, and, and metrics and metrics auditing and monitoring, and, and, and, and, and – but in the whole process they forget the person. That he needs his process."[54]

After the Hartz Reforms, *beramí* changed its funding structure, got out of bankruptcy and is now an organization that pays all of the social workers I spoke with a salaried wage. (Teachers of German courses and workshop or training leaders are most often paid per course.)[55] However, social workers still were frustrated by and complained about the reality of their budgets, described how they made do with the project funds they had, and criticized the perception by political elites that it would somehow be possible to always do more with less. One participant called this cost-benefit analysis "*Projektplastik*": "And then we have to look [... at] the budget. What is doable with that?"[56] An additional social worker emphasized that funders demanded they do more with less, pointing to her own workload as evidence. Ten years ago she was responsible for one program. Now she oversaw three.[57] Another declared more forcefully that the grant budget she received indicated that integration was not really the goal: "But with these, with these budgets no one can really mean integration."[58] The implication is that these funding schemes were performative rather than effective.

The negotiations around questions of financing tended to centre around three themes: many social workers sought to invert how the discourse of investment in integration could be framed, pointing out that in addition to *Leistung* (achievement, productivity) and investment, there were different forms of human capital that also constituted a form of investment, including maintaining the energy for reproducing civil society through parenting or civic engagement, preventing depression or mental illness, and confronting the kinds of rhetoric that rendered immigrant contributions invisible.[59] Second, several social workers pointed out that to use the language of rational efficiency as the ultimate goal of a successful integration politics really resulted in a Darwinian process through which those who were young, dynamic, and perhaps already college-educated rose to the top while those who needed more assistance (especially in learning German) raced to the bottom.[60] The affective costs of this neglect were considered to be great, both for the social workers trying to serve the people who came to them for help and for those staff trying to stay sane in a job that brought multiple pressures. Most upsetting were the concerns staff had for those newcomers who sought help who also reported feeling – as a side-effect of such pressures – like they were worthless to German society.[61] Finally, many social workers critiqued the state of affairs by pointing out the way that German citizens were proud of certain economic conditions considered integral to their national identity, namely state wealth and the social welfare system that had the ability to redistribute wealth through tax collection. German social workers who referenced the stereotypes of Germans as proud tax-payers or deficit hawks humorously suggested that Germans start living up to the stereotypes of German national identity ... and fund social programs.[62]

These conversations about money were intrinsically bound to affect. At the end of interviews, I always ask participants if they would like to add anything I didn't ask about. Frequently participants say no and then tack on another conversation in spite of this demurral, like Participant 1, who declared that one of the important topics for *berami* was the question of organizational health and survival, which also included the workloads of the social workers employed in what she called the "integration machinery," and whether or not they could survive the demands this work made of them.[63]

Identity was also an important consideration linked to this question of funding and the commitment to the work: "I think that also has something to do with the fact that many of us are also migrants, i.e., we also act – how should I say this, hmmm. There are […] these different levels that act upon it, and then there's also this outward level, these compulsory levels: we have to be fast, we have to be diverse, we have to be professional because we have little security in terms of planning. Because we are financed per project and have that pressure that also affects us internally."[64] As we continued talking, she confirmed that the stress of doing such work was "extreme" and joked, "I've always said for myself: we are building a house and simultaneously running a marathon."[65] When I commented that that was surely unsustainable, she described the process as "burnout at thirty."[66]

For *beramí*, one of the discursive constants was the emphasis nearly all social workers placed on immigrant, refugee, and newcomer agency. Agency – the ability to gather the skills needed in order to transition into a job or career a specific person chose for themselves – was considered the key to successful incorporation into both society and the workplace. Compulsion, force, punishment, or sanctions were bound to see little success. The demands of German workplace culture are cultural norms that need to be communicated and likely adhered to in order to be successful. The emphasis on training and vocational education in a German context is also quite rigid – jobs like that of cashier (considered unskilled labour in the US) require training certificates in Germany. But obstacles to access are not insurmountable when people are supported through an orientation process to German systems and processes.

Rigid application processes where typos are intolerable, employers resist accommodating myriad differences, and new financing schemes restrict the ability to target groups who need specific forms of support all reveal the overlap between the logic of rational efficiency and the systemic obstacles social workers would gladly see abolished. The reduction of the welfare state and the limiting of training programs by time and funding amount to cost-saving measures that reflect strictures on refugee agency, most particularly as it relates to time. The result of creating competition schemes within integration politics (only those who complete their tasks rapidly are rewarded) has negative effects on how refugees and immigrants can view their ability to contribute to society. This works in contradiction to the purported goals of integration policy: by punishing and disciplining subjects through legal sanctions or limits on pacing, funding, or access, integration discourses and measures create the affective backlash they purportedly attempt to prevent.

Race and Racism

Whether described as racism or culturalization; ethnicity or culture; systemic bias or hate, notions of essentialized difference came up often enough in interviews to be of note. The idiomatic contours of a discussion of difference are unique to the spaces and places in which they take place. In this particular context, racism was acknowledged by the social workers I spoke to as a real, material obstacle that influenced people's lives. One of the first conversations I had with the staff member at *berami* who facilitated my interview scheduling across the organization was about how Germany's societal needs were limited by the presence of anti-Black racism in villages and small towns. The particular conditions about which we spoke dealt with the shortage of doctors in rural and semi-rural areas that could have been remedied by the medical professionals currently completing the course *berami* offered to help doctors who had trained elsewhere pass the German medical licensing exam. This social worker, however, exclaimed something in conversation that resembled the following: I'm certainly not going to send an African doctor into a rural Eastern state to set up a private practice. The implication, if I remember correctly, was that the situation would be untenable: not only would residents possibly refuse to accept services from a Black doctor, but for the doctor that placement might also be deadly.[67]

Many of the social workers I spoke with were involved in their children's schools. Certainly, in terms of temperament, this is hardly atypical for members of the helping professions: civic engagement mirrors the ways people prefer to engage across the board. But schools and apprenticeships were also marked as an institutional hurdle, especially for coping with essentialized, racialized, or culturalized difference. One of the social workers I spoke with was quite open about how the racism she faced at school had been a motivating factor for her professional success: "It's like this: I absolutely wanted to study social work, of course. Even back then [as a teen]. (laughs) And ... whereas I came to Germany [as a pre-teen], I also had my problems, right, my difficulties with German. And ... the teachers were – some of them – very racist. They didn't encourage us migrant kids at all. To the contrary. 'You all [*ihr*] won't accomplish anything anyway.' [...] Of course, that had a different effect on me."[68] What bothered this participant deeply was that the same arguments used against her as a child were popping up at her own child's school in the twenty-first century. The historical continuation of anti-immigrant discourse was something she found intolerable, for obvious reasons.

Two participants discussed what is more specifically called "cultur-alization" in a German context – i.e., the invocation of culture as justi-fication for behaviour or aptitude. While both recognized the potential of culturalizing discourses to cause harm, their work at the intersection of arrival and incorporation showed that especially for new arrivals, acculturation to German cultural norms was impossible to dispense with. Germany was a unique place with unique practices and behav-iours into which newcomers had to be incorporated, and that process of incorporation needed to be explicit. One participant told a story about a professional development seminar she had been leading recently, noting that this particular encounter had stuck with her and given her cause to think. The question posed during the seminar was: What is intercultural competence? She described the framing of this discussion as follows: "There's also this academic discussion, about this – or di-versity competencies – as well and always [this idea about] how much is culture taken up […] as an explanatory model. For people. And: to what degree is that [culture] also rejected. And, we always say, ok: there's a framework. So – especially for newcomers – this – let's say 'culture' or 'cultural codes' or something – is still important. Because it offers a framework for action."[69] Within the space in which interpreta-tion of cultural behaviour is individual and specific, this social worker argued that Germans also had a cultural framework to be explained and communicated. In essence, she was arguing against the invisibil-ity of traditionally white German majority norms. "So," she said, "we can't avoid that cultural socialization also here in Germany provides us, often, with the frame in which we move. Or in which we act or feel or whatever. But it is, of course, always dependent on my individual interpretation of it [the frame]."[70] She rejected the notion that these cul-tural differences should be treated reductively or used in culturalizing ways. But she also argued for more rigour in attending to the presence of difference at all:

> PARTICIPANT: You can't say: you are [this nationality] and these are the culturalizing values someone attributes to you.
> JSC: No.
> PARTICIPANT: That's not ok. But at the same time, we need it [this framework]. And I think that this discussion […] there's also very little – or in this differentiation – there's very little […] possibility for description.[71]

The need for more description to be able to narrate clearly what happened in such encounters also required, in her opinion, an overall reduction of social fear and tension.

So, we all need a certain kind of ease [*Entspanntheit*] in this topic area. [...] I find [unintelligible] speaking politically correctly to be important and in any case correct, but [...] – for me, it's always also [about] people's intentions. [...] [She references in what follows an earlier anecdote where someone commented on her appearance – jsc]. She didn't say that because she wanted to hurt me. So: one can be a bit more relaxed and say, it's ok. Or start conversations with people when you want to – if not, then don't. But to throw everything together, to me – to me personally that just isn't productive [*bringt es nichts*]. [...] Because I can just as easily – so to speak – have a similarly limited view of other minorities, or have little experience [with that group]. That can happen to me in exactly the same way.[72]

By pointing out that having a marginalized identity herself didn't necessarily mean that she was free of bias towards identities about which she had less knowledge, this social worker described an approach to managing difference that included space for cross-identity solidarity, attention, and ease instead of a hierarchy of oppression.

On the other hand, one social worker insisted that racism was not the social obstacle she faced in trying to run her project. As she tried to make connections with organizations and partners in the community, rejection was part and parcel of such work. But she declared quite clearly that I should not assume that racism was the reason for such rejections on behalf of the community partners with whom she worked. I struggled with how to interpret this comment: was a fear of naming racism part of the motivation for this statement? Many of the community critiques of this particular project were based on a broader German social rejection of the idea that college graduates might need help in making the transition to employment after immigration: "But why [we] have to give college graduates – who have, for some reason, not been able to do it by themselves, but who actually have a great foundation – why [we] now also ha[ve] to support *them* with government funding was something we also had to listen to as critique at the beginning. On the other hand, it is of course true – [... it] doesn't cost much money to give them this information because a lot of volunteer engagement goes into it. And when then they become integrated into our system and pay taxes, then that all immediately comes back."[73] It is probable that in this particular circumstance, the social worker with whom I spoke was trying to emphasize class bias, especially how a neoliberal ideology in which individuals are required to carry their own burdens without assistance surfaced in her work. Immigrants and refugees who came to Germany with a university diploma still faced many of the same hurdles as less-educated immigrants and refugees. The individualization of these hurdles was different for those with college diplomas than it was for those without an education, but the solution – to pull yourself up by your bootstraps despite systemic obstacle – was experienced by both groups. The idea that integration was ultimately systemic and that taxes were a kind of ultimate integrative achievement surfaced in many rhetorical contexts, including this interview.[74]

Finally, multiple social workers also pointed out that *beramí* served a more educated clientele than some other agencies because of the programs that they offered: job preparation workshops, courses to prepare for medical licensure, processing foreign university degrees and transcripts for state recognition, mentoring projects for white collar jobs, and 90-minute career counselling appointments were services that could apply and cater to professionals.[75] Understanding difference was part and parcel of those conversations: when I asked a social worker what kinds of competencies asylum seekers carried with them into German society as an attempt to counter a narrative of deficit, this social worker insisted on rigorous distinctions based on life experience: "and one also can't say – if a person for example, comes from Eritrea – that he inherently has a lot or little education. It depends on what area of Eritrea. There are people who have hardly any education and there are some who have little education and there are some who have a high degree of education. We have determined that here at *beramí* – perhaps also due to the emphasis on recognizing foreign degrees – [… that] maybe the people who have higher levels of education are also more likely to find us."[76] She began to list the professional backgrounds of the asylum seekers she had served: teachers, doctors, IT specialists, a professor, oil and gas engineers, TV journalists. She also emphasized that *beramí* served a large group of people with applied skill sets: people who were working in freight shipping, who drove 18-wheelers, who had worked in security services or other organizations, partly due to the German security presence in Afghanistan that had employed Afghan citizens in these capacities. This interview also explicitly addressed the topic of the "abuse" of asylum:

PARTICIPANT: [...] they don't leave their country voluntarily.
JSC: OK.
PARTICIPANT: And that [...], that's twisted by some populists here in Germany.
JSC: Yes.
PARTICIPANT: They claim, for instance, that they are economic refugees. That's nonsense covered in sauce, right? [...] It's completely unobjective [...] and usually, they also don't know anyone [any refugees], I think. They have never spoken with anyone, otherwise they wouldn't claim that.[77]

While she later asserted that "racists exist everywhere" (meaning in every nation in the world), she vehemently disputed the notion that refugee migration was something to fear: "Yes, but the crazy thing is, ok: what is one afraid of?"[78] She called such fears unrealistic and humorously added that Germany had not fully descended into anarchy: "No refugee is going to show up, open the door and say, 'so, you don't need this [touches her jacket] anymore, it's cold, I'm going to take it with me [...].'"[79] As the conversation continued, she referred back to her experiences serving people seeking asylum in Germany and asserted that the majority were "very polite" and even stood up when you spoke to them or entered the room, a sign of respect she was familiar with in the context of her own childhood interactions with elders.[80] This final move, to see similarity across the categories of difference, is an empathic one that recognizes and relativizes cultural experiences as a way to humanize people different from oneself.

Conclusion

Conservative ideas formed the background against which many of my interviews with social workers took place. Whether racism, neoliberal funding regimes, the rhetoric of productivity and achievement, demands made of the "duty" to integrate, or simply nativist ideas, there was no way to escape how starkly the social welfare state had been shaped by conservative talking points while in discussion with social workers engaged in the day-to-day work of immigrant and refugee incorporation.

Integration politics as an apparatus of governmentality is a form of policymaking deeply concerned with people management. Given that reality, there is no reason to believe that this apparatus will disappear, but it most certainly will continue to shift over time. As may be apparent by now, despite the fact that the integrative apparatus has become dominated by conservative ideas about German national identity, I do not view an apparatus itself as a politicized construct. The petitions submitted by both the Green and the Left parties before the Integration Act was drafted and passed by the Grand Coalition of the CDU/CSU/SPD were equally invested in the expansion of the apparatus, but argued for this expansion based on different priorities of party ownership, primarily access to services and representation, honouring refugee agency, limiting economic exploitation, and expanding the services offered. Political ownership of the integrative apparatus primarily comes down to the political ownership of certain value-based ideologies: which subjects can Germans "trust" to be democratic? How much agency are citizens given to shape the state in which they live? Finally, what adjustments need to be made to national identity in order both to preserve a democratic state and to make sure all citizens can access democratic participation and representation?

Epilogue: Subjectivity within the Integrative Apparatus

Ich glaube, es gibt diese eine gelebte Lebenswirklichkeit.
Und dann gibt es noch mal die Art und Weise, wie wir darüber reden.

I believe there's this lived [version] of real life.
And then, there's also the way that we talk about it.

– Social worker, *berami*[1]

Understanding how the discourse of integration, its attendant non-discursive practices, and the networks between the multiple social, political, economic, and cultural arenas in which these discursive and non-discursive practices exist and together constitute an apparatus of governmentality that uses the term "integration" to manage German-ness and German subjects is a highly abstract task. Any discussion of an apparatus is incomplete without a subsequent discussion of subjectivity: an apparatus produces subjects because it acts on subjects through all of the discursive and non-discursive processes attended to in this book. Discourse shapes subjectivity; discourse also shapes all of the practices and institutions that build the networks that constitute an apparatus. And if an apparatus produces subjects, one of the issues we need to discuss is how being talked *about* in politics and the media shapes subjectivity. Integration rhetoric facilitates how German citizens and residents think and talk about national identity and national subjectivities. Discourses about the question of refugee agency and white German attempts to limit refugee and immigrant agency are just one example of how the apparatus of integration also shapes and influences the frameworks available for thinking about difference – different lives, different lived realities, and different subjectivities. The colourism and racialized hierarchies inherent to the integrative apparatus is another.

In a democracy, political participation is the primary form of agency that brings with it the chance to act within and upon power. In Europe, national sovereignty and national politics are not the only arena in which this happens: European parliamentary processes present an arena in which political agency can also be exercised, although that arena has remained mostly unexamined in this book. Even in the context of the European Union, however, the primacy of the national arena for immigration and integration policy is undisputed. People's lives, both those of German citizens and German residents, are highly dependent on and shaped by the institutions with which they interact, the citizenship regimes that provide options for naturalization, and the taxation policies that fund the German social welfare state. To deny the still-present power of national politics in post-national Europe, especially at a moment in which populist nationalism has reasserted the importance of the national arena, would be a mistake.

National politics, in particular, shapes the opportunities for immigrant and refugee agency in specific ways. The political agency afforded to citizens – either naturalized or born into citizenship rights – who participate in politics proper or, especially in Germany, in community engagement through the *Verein* system, is a critical element of integrative politics and reveals not only how the political spectrum maps on to questions of agency for people of colour, immigrants, and refugees, but also how notions of power-sharing and representation achieved through equitable access pose a discursive way out of the trap of integration discourse.

When I was conducting fieldwork at *beramí*, one of the projects that I observed was a political education project designed to teach international university students how to participate successfully in German civic life. This type of project has a long history in Germany under the rubric of "political education," for which there is even a national clearinghouse of educational materials called the *Bundeszentrale für politische Bildung* (Federal Center for Political Education). I was able to attend two events organized by this project, one about gender identity and gender roles, and the other about unions and collective bargaining. Frankfurt in particular has a long history of collective industrial bargaining. The offices of the *IG Metall*, the largest metalworkers union in Europe, are located in downtown Frankfurt. *Beramí* even provides job counselling in the *IG Metall* building through a partnership with the refugee drop-in centre known as *Der Laden* (The Storefront).

One of the goals of the political education project *beramí* offers is making clear to participants how Germans structure civic life and conceptualize civic responsibility. In my interview with one of the leaders of the project, she explained the difference between how civic engagement as a moralistic paradigm of charity or helping – certainly the dominant paradigm in the United States – was common in many of the participants' countries of origin. But civic engagement in Germany was a wholly different notion, she said, rooted in the idea that citizens have a duty to engage, and that this duty must be regularly exercised. Conceptualizing integration as a "duty" is an echo from this broader understanding of the civic duties German citizens supposedly hold. The *Verein* structure is also different from club structures such as the Rotary Club or Kiwanis Club – two long-standing US civic clubs. *Vereine* are recognized, official organizations that require regular participation from volunteers who take on specific responsibilities in order to make sure the events and activities run smoothly. It wasn't enough, she emphasized, to show up occasionally and do something good. Participation in Germany – even as a volunteer – required a commitment.

As I have said, many of the social workers I interviewed *were* active in this way outside of work and told me about some of the activities in which they participated. Whether leading language school on Saturdays for a heritage group, participating as a parent on a school board, or engaging politically in community organizations, this group of social workers in particular was especially civically active. One social worker tried to express to the people who came to her for career counselling that a great way to simultaneously learn German *and* advocate for your children was to participate in "Parents' Evenings" at school.[2] Two social workers expressed that the need for empowerment work – which I translate as community support for individual agency – was required for integration to truly take on the desired connotations of participation in a democratic context. Not just everyday knowledge (how do I use a computer, buy stamps, open a bank account?), but the kinds of literacy necessary for civic participation (how do I avoid exploitation at work, or learn to read my employment contract?) were critical skills for all immigrants.[3] Finally, the question of politics was never far from these discussions, especially when they focused on political education as a form of empowerment. And yet, their frustration with the options available for participation was palpable. One social worker declared:

In the [political] parties, . . . I have already talked with politicians and the will is not there. The will is definitely not there, it's just political. It's just – said politically correctly, of course – we want more migrants in the parties; that would be nice. Everything representative and everything that one wants, but in reality, the parties have not opened themselves and [...] they will not open themselves up. And that is a conscious decision, because that would mean sharing power. Maybe in East Germany we have gotten to that place, but here in Frankfurt, we're [POC/immigrants] 52 per cent [of the population] – i.e., if there were actually a lot more Turks and a lot more other migrants in the parties, then one would also vote for them. At least those who have citizenship would vote for them, and not only for the most progressive: also the very conservative and fundamentalist [candidates] would be voted for as well, i.e., some people would be elected, and that would mean one has to share power and that is something they don't want and they know perfectly well that if it should come to that, that would happen. Because in the meantime we have very few [candidates of colour], but we [do] have the Turks who stand for election, and they are elected.[4]

Hilfe zur Selbsthilfe – helping people to help themselves – was a phrase that surfaced in multiple interviews and that reflects the empowerment activities in which various social projects engage across the country. Embracing agency is the critical foundation of democratic and civic engagement. And participation writ large – including whether people fight for those opportunities, for the *interkulturelle Öffnung* so highly touted in professional development seminars and "Integration and Participation Acts" – will be the marker of whether or not Germany retreats into authoritarian posturing or takes responsibility for providing opportunities to the people politicians have already recognized that Germany will depend upon to maintain its status as a wealthy, industrialized nation and to fund its social programs and pensions.

As I write this epilogue, the new German cabinet under Chancellor Olaf Scholz (SPD) has just been announced. Of 16 ministers, just one – Cem Özdemir – comes from an immigrant family. Based on Germany's own statistical recordkeeping, 27.2 per cent of the population has a "migration background."[5] To have representative participation in the cabinet would require at least four Cabinet ministers from marginalized groups, including people with disabilities. In their book *Gemeinschaft der Ungewählten*, feminist theorist Sabine Hark took up the question of what it would take to envision a different national imaginary – one that is neither homogenous nor uniform, but one that can cope with difference and provide opportunities for participation to everyone who wishes to do so. Central to their theory of democratic engagement are the juxtaposed notions of "brute" and "tender" citizenship, ideas inspired by the Polish novelist Olga Tokarczuk. Brute citizenship is polarizing and essentially authoritarian. Tender citizenship has nothing romantic about it, but rather incorporates a sense of civic responsibility that earns its name because it requires care: care for democracy, for ourselves, and for each other.[6]

Not just civic responsibility is a form of care: simple access to citizenship and the privilege of naturalizing is critical. The German citizenship reforms undertaken in 1999–2000 were important for changing the state of play regarding the naturalization of immigrants and refugees. By making naturalization easier and providing citizenship to those born on German soil – rather than reserving the right of citizenship for those who could prove German ancestry – the reforms fundamentally shifted how Germans could engage civically and politically. For the refugees and immigrants who arrived in Germany after this shift, the change may be imperceptible – but it is certainly material. Without citizenship rights, there are reduced opportunities for participation. This was abundantly clear to one of the social workers I interviewed, who spoke about the college graduates she mentored as likely to naturalize not because of an affective German identity, but rather out of a sense of practicality. Mentees generally understand, she said, "that citizenship is not a question of feelings, but rather a question of pragmatism, and that you, with the rules that are valid in this country, simply cannot totally participate socially or politically without citizenship. Because we – as people from non-EU countries – we have no local voting rights, i.e., you might have already decided, ok, I *would* vote for the SPD, but I'm not allowed to vote, *ja*?"[7]

But as citizenship becomes an invisible or private status, one of the outcomes of an integrative discourse and integrative apparatus is that visual features, clothing, names, or identity take on increased importance. Decoupled from – admittedly racist – notions of who looks or sounds German, integrative discourses that demonize Muslims, Afro-Germans, people of colour, people wearing headscarves, or people with accented speech perpetuate the racializing hierarchies that opening up access to citizenship had purportedly rendered insignificant. When one can no longer "see" citizenship, what *is* left visible are socially extant notions of race. It is this particular intersection between essentialized difference and racialization that buttresses the right-wing nativist agitation that leads to either violent rhetoric or violent acts.

However, none of the social workers I spoke to believed that perpetual exclusion was inevitable. German society is already in flux; integration rhetoric is the potentially maddening and certainly desperate attempt both to maintain discursive power and to deny the shifts that are already in motion. At the same time, one of the things I have attempted to do in this book is to show, through the chapter sequences that reflect both on the present and the past, how attention to what has come before is critical for understanding what is happening now. As I revise my drafts of this section, current events change more quickly than

I can adjust my prose. The United States has withdrawn all troops from Afghanistan, creating a new need for refugee migration that is affecting the United States and Germany alike. Refugees on the Polish-Belorussian border are freezing and starving to death in the forests; thousands hope to enter Germany while the German government attempts to limit access. The ongoing COVID-19 pandemic has created high infection rates during the second pandemic winter and talk in Germany about an additional lockdown is ever-present. In nearly all societies, people of colour and marginalized immigrant groups are most likely to suffer and die from the disease. Russia invaded Ukraine and displaced millions of Ukrainian citizens in 2022. Race plays a role in all refugee movement: white Ukrainian asylum seekers have refused to be housed together with Ukrainian Rom_nja in German asylum homes. There were also multiple media reports merely weeks after the invasion of Ukraine that were quick to point out the discrepancies between how German law treated Ukrainian refugees versus those from Syria and Afghanistan.[8] One report even framed Syrians and Ukrainians as victims of the same violence, describing both as fleeing from "Putin's bombs."[9] (Russia continues to conduct missile strikes in Syria, even in 2023). The racializing logics of state policies are not obscured in the ways they might have been merely a decade ago during the Sarrazin scandal, but the AfD is still in Parliament, and will soon be granted access to nearly €80 million in state funding that is simply a cultural perk for each political party represented in government. Such funding exists to fund a party foundation for political outreach that will basically spread right-wing extremist rhetoric with taxpayer funds. Various scandals about a right-wing infiltration of military organizations or other institutions emerge frequently in German news coverage, prompting the disbanding of special forces units in addition to revised and better funded federal anti-extremist education efforts. Facebook, Twitter, Instagram, and other social media platforms continue to circulate misinformation, leading in the pandemic to deep skepticism of vaccines and of government itself. This can be seen most visibly in the conspiracy theories of the *Querdenker* movement (the German interpretation or incarnation of the *QAnon* conspiracy). The characteristics of this discourse are even transnational. When Erdoğan was reelected in 2023, my friend Ela snapped a photo of a *Tagesspiegel* advertisement on 31 May in Berlin. The headline read: "German-Turks for Erdogan: Integration Failed?" While the identity category itself has shifted since 2005 (German-Turks as a hyphenate then would have been extremely uncommon), the ultimate message has stayed the same. "Turks" (read: immigrants) will resist integration and fail to become part of the German nation.

Finally, in late September 2023, as refugee movement from Africa and the Middle East accelerated and fuelled yet another period of scandalous debate about migration in European media, the cover for *Der Spiegel* featured an image of migrants arriving on Lampedusa infused with the visual tropes and colour palette of a popular anti-Semitic postcard that had circulated in the early twentieth century in Austria and Hungary. Due to the sharp perception of Dr. Amy Passmore, a German Studies scholar who tweeted both images in juxtaposition, the historical memory of refugee rejection went moderately viral, with several thousand people engaging with a tweet viewed over half a million times.[10] The original postcard image features Eastern European orthodox Jews migrating on foot in long lines into Vienna.[11] The postcard was created during a time when Vienna's mayor was openly anti-Semitic and anti-immigrant. Despite the voices that would insist upon forgetting, comparing similarities over and across time is a necessary activity that allows us to remember in context.

Incorporative work is difficult. Whether trying to get young people into the work force or higher education, or to facilitate the desires of adults attempting to transition into new lives in a new place, a new language, and a new job, the work of incorporation requires both effort and commitment. Incorporation is not just work demanded of immigrants and refugees: it is an ongoing process of engagement and inclusion, *as well as* the exclusion (or re-integration) of those – such as extremists – who refuse to abide by the terms of a democratic agreement. As Klaus Bade declared, integration politics in its most holistic definition is social politics. For everyone.

Notes

Introduction: Integration Politics

1 Stephan Löwenstein, "Integrationsgipfel: Merkel: 'Fast ein historisches Ereignis,'" *Frankfurter Allgemeine Zeitung*, July 14, 2006, accessed June 15, 2023, https://www.faz.net/aktuell/politik/inland/integrationsgipfel-merkel-fast-ein-historisches-ereignis-1357015.html.

2 "Integrationsgipfel: 'Zuwanderung gezielt nutzen,'" *Frankfurter Allgemeine Zeitung*, July 12, 2006, accessed June 15, 2023, https://www.faz.net/aktuell/politik/inland/integrationsgipfel-zuwanderung-gezielt-nutzen-1353214.html.

3 "Integrationsgipfel: 'Zuwanderung gezielt nutzen.'"

4 "Integrationsgipfel: Merkel: 'Fast ein historisches Ereignis.'"

5 Demokratie Spiegel, "Integrationsgipfel 2006," July 13, 2007, accessed June 15, 2023, http://www.demokratie-spiegel.de/printable/archiv/politik/integrationsgipfel2006.html; Sabine am Orde, "Ausländerpolitik: Integrationsgipfel ohne Migranten?" *Die Tageszeitung*, July 4, 2007, accesed June 15, 2023, https://taz.de/!5198505/; "Integrationsgipfel: Merkel: 'Fast ein historisches Ereignis'."

6 Jörg Säuberlich, "Merkel 'außerordentlich zufrieden,'" *Der Tagesspiegel*, July 14, 2006, accessed July 15, 2023, https://www.tagesspiegel.de/politik/integrationsgipfel-merkel-ausserordentlich-zufrieden/731042.html.

7 Deutscher Bundestag, *Antwort der Bundesregierung auf die Kleine Anfrage der Abgeordneten Siylle Laurischk, Hartfrid Wolff (Rems-Mur), Cornelia Pieper, weiterer Abgeordneter und der Fraktion der FDP*, DRS 16/3758, Berlin: Deutscher Bundestag, 2006. PDF, accessed June 15, 2023, https://dserver.bundestag.de/btd/16/037/1603758.pdf (accessed June 15, 2023).

8 "Integrationsgipfel: Merkel: 'Fast ein historisches Ereignis.'"; phw/dpa/AFP, "Integrationsgipfel: 'Ein fast historisches Ereignis,'" *Der Spiegel*, July 14, 2006, accessed June 15, 2023, https://www.spiegel.de

/politik/deutschland/integrationsgipfel-ein-fast-historisches-ereignis
-a-426823.html; Säuberlich, "Merkel 'außerordentlich zufrieden.'"

9   Säuberlich, "Merkel 'außerordentlich zufrieden.'"

10 For critiques of this plan, see: Helmuth Schweitzer. "Durch periodisches
Wiegen wird die Sau nicht fetter," *Sozial Extra* 36, no. 7 (2012): 27–30.
https://doi.org/10.1007/s12054-012-0081-z.

11 Katharina Schuler, "Nun aber mal konkret," *Zeit Online*, July 14, 2006,
accessed February 20, 2024, https://www.zeit.de/online/2006/29
/Integrationsgipfel.

12 AFP, "Spitzentreffen: Gehen dem Integrationsgipfel die Migranten aus?,"
Der Tagesspiegel, July 5, 2007, accessed June 15, 2023, https://www.
tagesspiegel.de/politik/spitzentreffen-gehen-dem-integrationsgipfel-die
-migranten-aus/978700.html; am Orde, "Ausländerpolitik: Integrationsgipfel
ohne Migranten?"

13 AFP, "Spitzentreffen: Gehen dem Integrationsgipfel die Migranten aus?,";
am Orde, "Ausländerpolitik: Integrationsgipfel ohne Migranten?"

14 "Deutscher Integrationsgipfel," *Wikipedia*, last modified, March 10, 2021,
https://de.wikipedia.org/w/index.php?title=Deutscher
_Integrationsgipfel&oldid=209660511.

15 dpa/AFP/AP/cn, "Integrationsgipfel: Merkel freut sich über 'Meilenstein,'"
Die Welt, July 12, 2007, accessed June 15, 2023, https://www.welt
.de/politik/article1021724/Merkel-freut-sich-ueber-Meilenstein.html.

16 Website of the Federal Government, "13th Integration Summit with
Chancellor Angela Merkel," accessed June 15, 2023, https://www
.bundesregierung.de/breg-en/news/13th-integration-summit-1875236.

17 Karin Hunn, *"Nächstes Jahr kehren wir zurück–": die Geschichte der türkischen "Gastarbeiter" in der Bundesrepublik* (Göttingen: Wallstein Verlag,
2005), 13. It's no coincidence that Lauren Stokes has titled her book
about this period *Fear of the Family* (New York: Oxford University Press,
2022).

18 Hunn, *"Nächstes Jahr kehren wir zurück,"* 13. Here: "unverzichtbar."

19 Burkart Holzner, "The Concept 'Integration' in Sociological Theory,"
The Sociological Quarterly 8, no. 1 (1967): 51–62, https://doi
.org/10.1111/j.1533-8525.1967.tb02273.x.

20 Rita Chin, *The Guestworker Question in Postwar Germany* (New York:
Cambridge University Press, 2009), 171.

21 Paul Mecheril, "Wirklichkeit schaffen: Integration als Dispositiv," *Aus
Politik und Zeitgeschichte: 50 Jahre Anwerbeabkommen mit der Türkei* 61,
no. 43 (2011): 50, 53–4, accessed June 15, 2023, https://www.bpb.de
/system/files/pdf/P6W6D1.pdf. I was unaware of Mecheril's short
essay when I published this article in 2017: Johanna Schuster-Craig,
"Integration Politics as an Apparatus," *German Studies Review* 40, no. 3

(2017), https://doi.org/10.1353/gsr.2017.0096. That we came to virtually the same idea separately (to see integration as a Foucauldian apparatus of governmentality that limits how one could imagine a future society) suggests to me that the frame Foucault offers has value when used to analyse German integration politics.

22 Mecheril, "Wirklichkeit schaffen," 49–50. See also Serhat Karakayli, "Ambivalente Integration," *Heinrich-Böll-Stiftung*, accessed June 15, 2023, https://heimatkunde.boell.de/2007/11/18/ambivalente-integration.

23 Fatima El-Tayeb, *European Others: Queering Ethnicity in Postnational Europe* (Minneapolis: University of Minnesota Press, 2011), xxxi.

24 Kiên Nghị Hà, "Deutsche Integrationspolitik als koloniale Praxis," in *re/visionen: Postkoloniale Perspektiven von People of Color auf Rassismus, Kulturpolitik und Widerstand in Deutschland*, eds. Kiên Nghị Hà, Nicola Lauré al-Samarai, and Sheila Mysorekar (Münster: Unrast Verlag, 2007), 113–28.

25 Triadafilos Triadafilopoulos and Karen Schönwälder, "How the Federal Republic Became an Immigration Country: Norms, Politics and the Failure of West Germany's Guest Worker System," *German Politics & Society* 24, no. 3 (2006), 1.

26 Viktor Steiner and Johannes Velling, "Re-Migration Behavior and Expected Duration of Stay of Guest Workers in Germany," in *The Economic Consequences of Immigration to Germany* (Physica, Heidelberg, 1994), 101–19, https://doi.org/10.1007/978-3-642-51177-6_6.

27 Thomas de Maziére (CDU) and Andrea Nahles (SPD) were insistent on the need for an integration law to prevent "ghetto formation" in 2016. phoenix, "Integrationsgesetz: Thomas de Maizière und Andrea Nahles geben Pressekonferenz am 25.05.16," YouTube, 40:04, May 25, 2016, accessed June 15, 2023, https://www.youtube.com/watch?v=Lt_3SrCXTH8. The symbolic function of "ghetto" in German debates about integration has been addressed by many scholars, including Ayşe S. Çağlar, "Constraining Metaphors and the Transnationalisation of Spaces in Berlin," *Journal of Ethnic and Migration Studies* 27, no. 4 (2001): 601–13, https://doi.org/10.1080/13691830120090403; and Maria Stehle, "White Ghettos: The 'Crisis of Multiculturalism' in Post-Unification Germany," *European Journal of Cultural Studies* 15, no. 2 (2012): 167–81, https://doi.org/10.1177/1367549411432025.

28 Jens S. Dangschat, "Residentielle Segregation nach Nationalität – ein Diskurs voller Widersprüche," *Österreichische Zeitschrift für Soziologie* 41, no. 2 (2016): 81–101, https://doi.org/10.1007/s11614-016-0225-7. See also Wolf-Dietrich Bukow et al., *Was heißt hier Parallelgesellschaft?: Zum Umgang mit Differenzen* (Wiesbaden: Verlag für Sozialwissenschaften, 2008).

29 Kirsten Heisig, *Das Ende der Geduld: Konsequent gegen jugendliche Gewalttäter* (Freiburg: Herder, 2010); Freia Peters, "Araber in Berlin haben

ihren eigenen Richter," *Die Welt*, January 15, 2011, accessed June 15, 2023, www.welt.de/politik/deutschland/article12176488/Araber-in-Berlin -haben-ihren-eigenen-Richter.html; Claudia Keller, "Familien-Union: Die Clanchefs bitten zum Tee," *Der Tagesspiegel*, February 26, 2011, accessed June 15, 2023, www.tagesspiegel.de/berlin/familien-union-die -clanchefs-bitten-zum-tee/3887376.html.

30 Paul Lüttinger and Rita Rossmann, *Integration der Vertriebenen: Eine empirische Analyse* (Frankfurt: Campus Verlag, 1989).

31 Lüttinger and Rossmann, *Integration der Vertriebenen*, 30.

32 Roger Cohen, "Germany Makes Citizenship Easier for Foreigners to Get," *The New York Times*, May 22, 1999, accessed June 15, 2023, https://www .nytimes.com/1999/05/22/world/germany-makes-citizenship -easy-for-foreigners-to-get.html; "Germany Unveils Citizenship Reforms," *BBC News*, January 13, 1999, accessed June 8, 2018, http:// news.bbc.co.uk/2/hi/europe/254688.stm.

33 Karen Schönwälder and Triadafilos Triadafilopoulos, "A Bridge or Barrier to Incorporation? Germany's 1999 Citizenship Reform in Critical Perspective," *German Politics and Society* (30), no. 1 (2012): 52–70.

34 Lamya Kaddor, "Nicht nur Flüchtlinge brauchen Demokratieunterricht," *T-Online*, May 11, 2018, accessed June 15, 2023, https://www.t-online.de /nachrichten/deutschland/id_83755144/nicht-nur-fluechtlinge-brauchen -demokratieunterricht.html; Heike Klovert, "Kritik an Unionsplänen: Brauchen geflüchtete Kinder einen eigenen Werteunterricht?," *Spiegel Online*, May 8, 2018, accessed June 15, 2023, http://www.spiegel.de /lebenundlernen/schule/wertekunde-fuer-fluechtlingskinder-macht-das -sinn-a-1206763.html; SZ.de/dpa/Reuters/gal/dit, "Unionsfraktionschefs fordern Wertekunde-Unterricht für Flüchtlingskinder," *sueddeutsche.de Süddeutsche Zeitung*, May 7, 2018, accessed June 15, 2023. http://www .sueddeutsche.de/politik/union-wertekunde-unterricht -fluechtlingskinder-1.3970311. Ulrike Davy argues for a unique and legal definition of integration that does not really enter the discourse: that integration can be achieved through legal instruments that attempt to narrow "the gap between the (inferior) status of immigrants and the status of nationals, at least to some extent." This article was published at the same time that the new *Zuwanderungsgesetz* 2005 had been discussed and passed. Ulrike Davy, "Integration of Immigrants in Germany: A Slowly Evolving Concept," *European Journal of Migration and Law* 7 (2005): 129.

35 Interestingly, this approach to democratization has some parallels in the (one-sided) re-education programs East German civil servants were required to undergo after unification in 1990. See Jennifer A. Yoder, *From East Germans to Germans?: The New Postcommunist Elites* (Durham: Duke University Press, 1999), 93. See also Necla Kelek's anecdote about

teaching such a course in *Die fremde Braut: ein Bericht aus dem Inneren des türkischen Lebens in Deutschland* (Cologne: Kiepenheuer & Witsch, 2005), 265–7.

36 Mecheril, "Wirklichkeit schaffen," 50.

37 This slogan "to encourage and demand" (*fördern und fordern*) is also used for welfare recipients receiving Hartz IV benefits (long-term unemployment benefits), showing the connection between how the government treats both the German poor and a racialized underclass. Katharina Belwe, "Editorial: Aus Politik und Zeitgeschichte: Arbeitsmarktreformen." Bundeszentrale für politische Bildung 16 (2005): 2, accessed June 15, 2023, https://www.bpb.de/system/files/pdf/R74OJH.pdf.

38 I address these critiques of integration policy in "Integration Politics as an Apparatus." A representative from the German Diaconia criticized the proposed Integration Act in 2016 during a comment meeting run by the Committee for Labor and Social Concerns of the German Bundestag as a law that "alleges [of refugees] a lack of a will to integrate" Deutscher Bundestag, Ausschuss für Arbeit und Soziales, *Wortprotokoll der 82. Sitzung*. Protokoll-Nr. 18/82, Berlin: Deutscher Bundestag, 2016. PDF, https://www.bundestag.de/resource/blob/428440 /01b6d5f50e4d0837e3a48095ca650421/82_wortprotokoll-data.pdf, 1345 (accessed February 22, 2024). See also the expert letter of protest from the left-leaning NGO *ProAsyl*: Prof. Dr. Rolf Rosenbrock et al., "Referentenentwurf zu einem Integrationsgesetz vom 29.04.2016," ProAsyl, last modified May 19, 2016, accessed February 22, 2024, https:// www.proasyl.de/wp-content/uploads/2015/12/2016-05-19-Brandbrief -an-Bundesregierung-zum-Integrationsgesetz.pdf.

39 In June 2016, a representative for BAMF told the German Parliamentary Committee for Labour and Social Concerns that between October 2015 and June 2016, 211,000 people signed up to take integration courses (Ausschuss für Arbeit und Soziales, *Wortprotokoll der 82. Sitzung*, 1341.) courses. BAMF releases its integration course statistics yearly on its website, where five years of statistics are open to the public: "Integrationskurszahlen," BAMF: Bundesamt für Migration und Flüchtlinge, April 25, 2018, accessed June 30, 2023, https://www.bamf.de/DE /Themen/Statistik/Integrationskurszahlen/_functions/inge-bund-suche -link-table.html?nn=284810. The lack of available spots in integration courses is a long-running media topic: Journalists have blamed austerity politics (Anna Reimann, "Integrationskurse: Sparwut der Regierung bremst Einwanderer aus," *Spiegel Online*, September 22, 2010, accessed June 30, 2023, http://www.spiegel.de/politik/deutschland/integrationskurse -sparwut-der-regierung-bremst-einwanderer-aus-a-718855.html) and rising immigration rates (Jan Bielicki, "Nicht einmal jeder Zweite

bekommt einen Platz im Integrationskurs," *Süddeutsche Zeitung*, September 22, 2016, accessed June 30, 2023, http://www.sueddeutsche. de/politik/migranten-run-auf-deutschkurse-1.3174463). In 2017, BAMF released information that refugees were waiting an average of 12.5 weeks to take an integration course rather than the approved six-week waiting period. See AFP, "Flüchtlingsamt BAMF: Lange Wartezeit für Integrationskurse," *Frankfurter Allgemeine Zeitung*, accessed December 20, 2021, https://www.faz.net/aktuell/politik/inland/fluechtlingsamt -bamf-lange-wartezeit-fuer-integrationskurse-15357225.html.

40 The left-wing party *Die Linke* noted in their proposal from November 10, 2015 that 98% of tolerated persons (refugees without an asylum decision) are excluded from integration courses, and that asylum seekers from the Balkans have to wait 24 months to participate (Deutscher Bundestag, *Antrag: Flüchtlinge auf demWeg in Arbeit unterstützen, Integration befördern und Lohndumping bekämpfen*, Die Linke. Drucksache 18/6644. Berlin: Deutscher Bundestag, 2015. PDF, http://dipbt .bundestag.de /dip21/btd/18/066/1806644.pdf (accessed June 30, 2023). In June 2016, a representative for the Commissariat of German Bishops told the German Parliamentary Committee for Labor and Social Concerns that other obstacles that prevent the success of integration courses are that teachers face a long training period and then are not paid well after they are qualified to teach the courses. (Ausschuss für Arbeit und Soziales, *Wortprotokoll der 82. Sitzung*, 1342.)

41 Mecheril, "Wirklichkeit schaffen."

42 In German *Desintegration* has two definitions: one is the synonym to disintegration in English – to fall apart. The other definition, sometimes translated as de-integration, is a political call to resist the demand to integrate. When talking about social theories of integration and its opposites, I mean "disintegration."

43 Peter Imbusch and Dieter Rucht, "Integration und Desentegration in modernen Gesellschaften," in *Integrationspotenziale einer modernen Gesellschaft*, eds. Wilhelm Heitmeyer and Peter Imbusch (Wiesbaden: Verlag für Sozialwissenschaften, 2005), 14–15.

44 Silke Hans, "Theorien der Integration von Migranten: Stand und Entwicklung," in *Einwanderungsgesellschaft Deutschland*, eds. Heinz Ulrich Brinkmann and Martina Sauer (Wiesbaden: Verlag für Sozialwissenschaften, 2016), 25.

45 Hans, "Theorien der Integration," 25–6; Imbusch and Rucht, "Integration und Desentegration," 14.

46 Hans, "Theorien der Integration," 25.

47 Imbusch and Rucht, "Integration und Desentegration," 62–3.

48 Hans, "Theorien der Integration," 25. See also Hartmut Esser, *Die Konstruktion der Gesellschaft* (Frankfurt/Main: Campus Verlag, 2002), 261–306.

49 Chin, *Guestworker*, 86–140. Chin summarizes here how the discourse of integration emerged.
50 Chin, *Guestworker*, 96.
51 Chin, *Guestworker*, 96.
52 Chin, *Guestworker*, 96.
53 Chin, *Guestworker*, 96–7.
54 Hans, "Theorien der Integration," 27, 35–7. See also Richard Alba and Victor Nee, *Remaking the American Mainstream: Assimilation and Contemporary Immigration* (Boston: Harvard University Press, 2009).
55 Hartmut Esser, "Does the 'New' Immigration Require a 'New' Theory of Intergenerational Integration?" *IMR* 38, no. 3 (2004): 1130–2.
56 Hans, "Theorien der Integration," 27.
57 The phrase active forgetting has a long history of application in memory studies. Fatima El-Tayeb uses this term in *European Others* to talk about the way Europeans obscure their role in the creation of post-Imperial racism (xxiv) and Yasemin Yıldız employs it to reference both El-Tayeb's notion of racial amnesia in *Undeutsch* and as part of her analysis of racial discrimination in Yade Kara's novel *Selam Berlin*. See Yasemin Yıldız, "Reading Racialization: Yadé Kara's Selam Berlin," *German Studies Review* 46, no. 1 (2023): 97–115 and Aleida Assmann, "Canon and Archive," in *Cultural Memory Studies*, eds. Astrid Erll and Ansgard Nünning (Berlin: De Gruyter, 2008), 97–108. https://doi. org/10.1515/9783110207262.2.97. Many thanks to Yasemin Yıldız for pointing me to this resource.
58 Michel Foucault, *Security, Territory, Population: Lectures at the Collège de France 1977–1978*, ed. Michel Senellart, trans. Graham Burchell (New York: Picador, 2007); Foucault, *The Birth of Biopolitics: Lectures at the Collège de France, 1978–1979*, ed. Michel Senellart, trans. Graham Burchell (New York: Picador, 2010).
59 Foucault, *Security*, 193–203.
60 Andrea D. Bührmann and Werner Schneider, *Vom Diskurs zum Dispositiv: Eine Einführung in die Dispositivanalyse* (Bielefeld: transcript Verlag, 2008), 50.
61 Bührmann and Schneider, *Diskurs*, 49.
62 Bührmann and Schneider, *Diskurs*, 61, 106.
63 Or "hailed" in the words of Louis Althusser, "Ideology and State Ideological Apparatuses," in *Lenin and Philosophy and Other Essays* (New York: Monthly Review Press, 2001), 85–126.
64 Kim McKee, "Post-Foucauldian governmentality: What does it offer critical social policy analysis?" *Critical Social Policy* 29, no.3 (2009): 468, https://doi.org/10.1177/0261018309105180.
65 Schuster-Craig, "Integration Politics," 609.
66 See Chapter Three, §44a, "Verpflichtung zur Teilnahme an einem Integrationskurs" of the 2005 Immigration Act. Germany, Deutscher

Bundestag, *Gesetz zur Steuerung und Begrenzung der Zuwanderung und zur Regelung des Aufenthalts und der Integration von Unionsbürgern und Ausländern (Zuwanderungsgesetz)*, July 30, 2004, Chapter 3, §44a, https://www.bmi.bund.de/SharedDocs/gesetzestexte/DE/Zuwanderungsgesetz.pdf (accessed February 23, 2024).

67 Deutscher Bundestag, *Beschlussempfehlung und Bericht des Ausschusses für Arbeit und Soziales (11. Ausschuss) a) zu dem Gesetzentwurf der Fraktionen der CDU/CSU und SPD [...]*, Ausschuss für Arbeit und Soziales. Drucksache 18/9090. Berlin: Deutscher Bundestag, 2016. PDF, https://dserver.bundestag.de/btd/18/090/1809090.pdf (accessed February 23, 2024).

68 Nell Irvin Painter, *The History of White People* (New York: W. W. Norton & Company, 2011), 16.

69 Fatima El-Tayeb, *Undeutsch: die Konstruktion des Anderen in der postmigrantischen Gesellschaft* (Bielefeld: transcript Verlag, 2016).

70 Leigh Gilmore, *Autobiographics: A Feminist Theory of Women's Self-Representation* (Ithaca, NY: Cornell University Press, 1994).

71 El-Tayeb, *European Others*, xv.

72 El-Tayeb, *European Others*, xv–xvi.

73 El-Tayeb, *European Others*, xiv.

74 El-Tayeb, *European Others*, xvii.

75 For one example, see Celia Parbey, "Was als normal gilt, wird von weißen Cis Männern bestimmt," *Zeit.de: Ze.tt*, February 15, 2021, accessed June 15, 2023, https://www.zeit.de/zett/politik/2021-02/emilia-roig-why-we-matter-gerechtigkeit-rassismus-sexismus-politikwissenschaft-buch/komplettansicht.

76 Marco Berger, "Statement – Maisha Maureen Auma," Zentrum für transdisziplinäre Geschlechterstudien, 2021, accessed June 15, 2023, https://www.gender.hu-berlin.de/en/diverses-en/2021_en/statement_auma_en; Christoph David Piorkowski, "'Nur tagsüber sind Universitäten weiße Institutionen'," *Der Tagesspiegel*, December 18, 2020, accessed June 15, 2023, https://www.tagesspiegel.de/wissen/struktureller-rassismus-an-deutschen-hochschulen-nur-tagsueber-sind-universitaeten-weisse-institutionen/26730214.html.

77 Sara Ahmed, "A Phenomenology of Whiteness," *Feminist Theory* 8, no. 2 (2007): 149–68, https://doi.org/10.1177/1464700107078139; Matthew W. Hughey, "The (Dis)Similarities of White Racial Identities: The Conceptual Framework of 'Hegemonic Whiteness,'" *Ethnic and Racial Studies* 33, no. 8 (2010): 1289–309, https://doi.org/10.1080/01419870903125069.

78 Black feminist power, "Statement von Adefra e.V. – Anlässlich der aktuellen Förderzusage des Bundestages an das Deutsche Zentrum für Integrations- und Migrationsforschung (DeZIM), mit insgesamt neun Millionen Euro zur Stärkung der Rassismus-Forschung in Deutschland,"

Generation ADEFRA, accessed March 11, 2021, http://www.adefra.com
/index.php/blog/87-statement-von-adefra-schwarze-frauen-in
-deutschland-e-v-anlaesslich-der-aktuellen-foerderzusage-des-bundestages
-an-das-deutsche-zentrum-fuer-integrations-und-migrationsforschung
-dezim-mit-insgesamt-neun-millionen-euro-zur-staerkung-der-rassismus
-forschung.

79 Hengameh Yaghoobifarah, "Blicke," in *Eure Heimat ist unser Albtraum*,
ed. Fatma Aydemir and Hengameh Yaghoobifarah (Berlin: Ullstein,
2019), 69–81.

80 Tiffany M. Florvil, *Mobilizing Black Germany: Afro-German Women and the
Making of a Transnational Movement* (Urbana: University of Illinois Press,
2020), 48.

81 Tina Marie Campt, *Other Germans: Black Germans and the Politics of Race,
Gender, and Memory in the Third Reich* (Ann Arbor: University of Michigan
Press, 2009).

82 Cas Mudde, *Populist Radical Right Parties in Europe* (Cambridge:
Cambridge University Press, 2007), 19.

83 Ruth Wodak et al., *The Discursive Construction of National Identity*
(Edinburg: Edinburgh University Press), 2009.

84 Hans-Georg Betz, "Nativism across Time and Space," *Swiss Political
Science Review* 23, no. 4 (2017): 337, https://doi.org/10.1111/spsr.12260.

85 Schuster-Craig, "Integration Politics as an Apparatus," 611–2.

1 Demanding Integration

1 Sandra Dassler, "11. September Terrorist Mohammed Atta arbeitete in
Neuruppin," *Der Tagesspiegel*, 11 September 2016, accessed 15 June 2023,
http://www.tagesspiegel.de/berlin/11-september-terrorist-mohammed
-atta-arbeitete-in-neuruppin/14530830.html.

2 "Anschlag vom 11. September 2001: Terrorist Mohammed
Atta arbeitete als Bauzeichner in Neuruppin," *Berliner Zeitung*,
September 9, 2016, accessed June 16, 2023, https://www.berliner-zeitung.
de/mensch-metropole/anschlag-vom-11-september-2001-terrorist
-mohammed-atta-arbeitete-als-bauzeichner-in-neuruppin-li.67816.

3 Arne Lichtenberg, "9/11 – Die Hamburger Zelle," *Deutsche Welle*,
September 11, 2011, accessed June 16, 2023, http://www.dw.com/de/9-11
-die-hamburger-zelle/a-15349371.

4 Many thanks to Mihri Özdoğan for sending me this reference:
Werner Schiffauer, "Der unheimliche Muslim: Staatsbürgerschaft und
zivilgesellschaftliche Ängste," in *Konfliktfeld Islam in Europa*, eds. Monika
Wohlrab-Sahr and Levent Tezcan (Baden-Baden: Nomos, 2007), 111–34.

5 Many thanks to Reviewer 1 for suggesting this tool.

6 Schiffauer, "Der unheimliche Muslim;" Almut Zwengel and Gudrun
  Hentges, "Einleitung," *Migrations- und Integrationsforschung in der
  Diskussion: Biografie, Sprache und Bildung als zentrale Bezugspunkte*
  (Wiesbaden: Verlag für Sozialwissenschaften, 2008), 14.
7 Daniel Koehler, *Right-Wing Terorrism in the 21st-Century: The 'National
  Socialist Underground' and the History of Terror from the Far-Right in
  Germany* (New York: Routledge, 2017), 157.
8 Carol J. Williams, "Emerging from Darkness, Shrouded in Doubt,"
  Chicago Tribune, January 30, 2002, accessed January 26, 2018, http://
  articles.chicagotribune.com/2002-01-30/features/0201300033_1_burqa
  -taliban-afghanistan; Jürgen Hein, "Afghanistan: Verband afghanischer
  Frauen befürchtet neue Unterdrückung," *Frankfurter Allgemeine
  Zeitung*, November 25, 2001, accessed February 23, 2024, http://www
  .faz.net/1.37404.
9 Robert Jervis, "Understanding the Bush Doctrine," *Political Science
  Quarterly* 118, no. 3 (2003): 365–88.
10 Necla Kelek, "Die Braut als Schnäppchen," *Die Zeit*, January 27,
  2005, 10.
11 Gayle Rubin, "The Traffic in Women," in *Literary Theory: An Anthology*,
  eds. Julie Rivkin and Michael Ryan (Malden, MA: Blackwell, 2004),
  770–94.
12 "Die fremde Braut – Necla Kelek," *Kiepenheuer & Witsch*, accessed June
  26, 2023, https://www.kiwi-verlag.de/buch/necla-kelek-die-fremde
  -braut-9783462034691.
13 Kelek, *Die fremde Braut*, 254–67.
14 Ute Rasche, "Smear Campaign against German-Turkish Female Activists,"
  Qantara.de, April 26, 2005, accessed June 16, 2023, https://en.qantara.de
  /content/german-edition-of-hurriyet-newspaper-smear-campaign
  -against-german-turkish-female-activists. Cem Özdemir even defended
  the authors in an opinion piece for *Die Zeit* on 9 June 2005. Cem Özdemir,
  "Alles Verräter," *Die Zeit*, 9 June 2005, accessed July 13, 2023, https://
  www.zeit.de/2005/24/H_9frriyet-t_9frk_Medien.
15 Otto Schily, "Integration: 'Alarmierender Einblick'," *Der Spiegel*, no. 4,
  2005, 59–60.
16 Jörg Lau, "Wie eine Deutsche," *Die Zeit*, February 24, 2005, accessed
  February 23, 2024, http://www.zeit.de/2005/09/Hatin_S_9fr_9fc_9f_09;
  Rainer Grell, "Dichtung und Wahrheit: Die Geschichte des Muslim-Tests
  in Baden-Württemberg," *DocPlayer*, January 2017, accessed June 16, 2023,
  http://docplayer.org/33102620-Dichtung-und-wahrheit-die-geschichte
  -des-muslim-tests-in-baden-wuerttemberg-30-fragen-die-die-welt
  -erregten-nicht-nur-die-islamische.html.
17 Necla Kelek, *Die verlorenen Söhne: Plädoyer für die Befreiung des türkisch-
  muslimischen Mannes* (Cologne: Kiepenheuer & Witsch: 2006).

18   "Necla Kelek, 49, Best-Selling Author," *The New York Times*, December 1, 2005, accessed June 16, 2023, http://www.nytimes.com/2005/12/01 /news/necla-kelek-49-bestselling-author.html.

19   Tobias Betz, Sonja Pohlmann, and Carsten Volkery, "Islam-Konferenz: Schäuble wünscht sich 'deutsche Muslime'," *Spiegel Online*, September 27, 2006, accessed June 16, 2023, http://www.spiegel.de/politik/deutschland /islam-konferenz-schaeuble-wuenscht-sich-deutsche-muslime-a-439389.html.

20   "Mercatorprofessur 2006," Universität Duisburg-Essen, last modified July 1, 2014, accessed June 16, 2023, https://www.uni-due.de/de/mercatorprofessur/2006.shtml.

21   Kelek, "Die Braut als Schnäppchen," 10.

22   Kelek, "Die Braut als Schnäppchen," 10.

23   Patrick Bahners, *Die Panikmacher: die deutsche Angst vor dem Islam: eine Streitschrift* (Munich: C.H.Beck, 2011), 136.

24   Ian Buruma, *Murder in Amsterdam: Liberal Europe, Islam, and the Limits of Tolerance* (New York: Penguin Books, 2007).

25   Kelek, *Die fremde Braut*, 12.

26   Margot Badran, *Feminists, Islam, and Nation* (Princeton: Princeton University Press, 1996); Chandra Talpade Mohanty, "Under Western Eyes: Feminist Scholarship and Colonial Discourses," *Boundary*, 2, no. 12/13 (1984): 333–58; Anne McClintock, *Imperial Leather: Race, Gender, and Sexuality in the Colonial Contest* (New York: Routledge, 1995); Shahrzad Mojab, "Tracing Dollars, Mapping Colonial Feminism: America Funds Women's 'Democracy' Training in Iraq," in *Arab Feminisms: Gender and Equality in the Middle East*, eds. Jean Said Makdisi, Noha Bayoumi, and Rafif Rida Sidawi (London: I.B. Tauris Publishers, 2014), 379–88.

27   Gayatri Spivak, "Can the Subaltern Speak?," in *Marxism and the Interpretation of Culture*, eds. Cary Nelson and Lawrence Grossberg (Champaign, IL: University of Illinois, 1988), 296.

28   Birgit Rommelspacher, "Feministinnen und Rechte: Ungebrochene Selbstidealisierung," *Die Tageszeitung*, January 18, 2010, accessed June 16, 2023, http://www.taz.de/!5149236/.

29   Saba Mahmood, "Feminism, Democracy, and Empire: Islam and the War on Terror," in *Women's Studies on the Edge* (Durham, N.C.: Duke University Press, 2008), 81–114.

30   Rommelspacher, "Ungebrochene Selbstidealisierung."

31   Mahmood, "Feminism," 83, 93.

32   Seyran Ateş, *Große Reise ins Feuer* (Berlin: Rowohlt, 2003); Fadela Amara and Sylvia Zappi, *Breaking the Silence: French Women's Voices from the Ghetto* (Berkeley: University of California Press, 2006); Irshad Manji, *The Trouble with Islam: A Muslim's Call for Reform in Her Faith*, (New York: St. Martin's Press, 2004); Serap Çileli, *Serap: Wir sind eure Töchter, nicht eure Ehre!* (Michelstadt: Neuthor Verlag, 2002).

33 Bahners, *Panikmacher*, 155.

34 "Erwerb der deutschen Staatsangehörigkeit," Auswärtiges Amt, November 4, 2021, accessed June 16, 2023, https://www.germany.info /us-de/service/staatsangehoerigkeit/erwerb/1216790.

35 "Six Decades of Quality Journalism: The History of der Spiegel," *Spiegel Online*, October 5, 2011, accessed June 16, 2023, http://www.spiegel.de /international/six-decades-of-quality-journalism-the-history-of-der -spiegel-a-789853.html.

36 Otto Schily," 'Alarmierender Einblick': Bundesinnenminister Otto Schily über die Darstellung der türkischen Parallelgesellschaft in Necla Keleks Buch *Die fremde Braut,*" *Der Spiegel* 4 (2005), January 23, 2005, 59, accessed February 23, 2024, https://www.spiegel.de/politik/alarmierender -einblick-a-2d58049f-0002-0001-0000-000039080827.

37 Schily, "Alarmierender Einblick," 60.

38 Deutscher Bundestag, *Entwurf eines ... Strafrechtsänderungsgesetzes §§ 180b, 181 StGB (... StÄndG)*, Joachim Stünker et al. Drucksache 15/3045, Berlin: Deutscher Bundestag, 2004. PDF, https://dserver.bundestag.de /brd/2004/0846-04.pdf (accessed July 13, 2023). The text of this document does not explicitly address marriage, but does address forced helplessness connected with residency permits, which is the condition into which *Die fremde Braut* attempts to intervene.

39 Schily, "Alarmierender Einblick," 60.

40 Schily, "Alarmierender Einblick," 59.

41 *Gesetz zur Steuerung und Begrenzung der Zuwanderung und zur Regelung des Aufenthalts und der Integration von Unionsbürgern und Aus- läendern (Zuwanderungsgesetz)*, Chapter 3, §44a.

42 *Gesetz zur Steuerung und Begrenzung der Zuwanderung und zur Regelung des Aufenthalts und der Integration von Unionsbürgern und Aus- läendern (Zuwanderungsgesetz)*, Chapter 3, §44a.

43 *Gesetz zur Steuerung und Begrenzung der Zuwanderung und zur Regelung des Aufenthalts und der Integration von Unionsbürgern und Aus- läendern (Zuwanderungsgesetz)*, Chapter 2, §9.

44 Deutscher Bundestag, Vermittlungsausschuss, *Beschlussempfehlung des Vermittlungsausschusses zu dem Gesetz zur Steuerung und Begrenzung der Zuwanderung und zur Regelung des Aufenthalts und der Integration von Un- ionsbürgern und Ausländern (Zuwanderungsgesetz)*, Hans-Joachim Hacker and Peter Müller. Drucksache 15/3479, Berlin: Deutscher Bundestag, 2004. PDF, http://dipbt.bundestag.de/dip21/btd/15/034/1503479.pdf (accessed February 23, 2024).

45 *Gesetz zur Steuerung und Begrenzung der Zuwanderung und zur Regelung des Aufenthalts und der Integration von Unionsbürgern und Ausläendern (Zuwanderungsgesetz)*, Chapter 1, §1.

46 Necla Kelek, "Der Individuationsprozess der muslimischen Frau in der Moderne," *Fachtagung Integration und Islam* (Nürnberg: Bundesministerium für Migration und Flüchtlinge, 2006), 102–19.

47 "Geschwister-Scholl-Preis," accessed June 16, 2023, https://geschwister -scholl-preis.de/geschwister-scholl-preis/.

48 All dissertations in Germany must be published for students to complete the requirements of the PhD.

49 Necla Kelek, *Islam im Alltag: Islamische Religiosität und Ihre Bedeutung in der Lebenswelt von Schülerinnen und Schülern türkischer Herkunft* (Münster: Waxmann, 2002), 172–91.

50 Klaus J. Bade, "Versäumte Integrationschancen und nachholende Integrationspolitik," in *Nachholende Integrationspolitik und Gestaltungsperspektiven der Integrationspraxis*, eds. Klaus J. Bade and Wolfgang Schäuble (Göttingen: V& R Unipress, 2007); Schiffauer, "Der unheimliche Muslim."

51 "Necla Kelek: 'Sarrazins Gegner haben ihr Ziel erreicht'," *DiePresse.com*, January 16, 2019, accessed June 16, 2023, diepresse.com/home/schaufenster /salon/1334649/Necla-Kelek_Sarrazins-Gegner-haben-ihr-Ziel-erreicht.

52 Yasemin Karakaşoğlu and Mark Terkessidis, "Integration: Gerechtigkeit für die Muslime!," *Die Zeit*, February 1, 2006, accessed June 16, 2023, http://www.zeit.de/2006/06/Petition.

53 Karakaşoğlu and Terkessidis, "Integration: Gerechtigkeit für die Muslime!"

54 Necla Kelek, "Integration: Entgegnung," *Die Zeit*, February 2, 2006, updated February 8, 2006, accessed 16 June 2023, http://www.zeit.de /online/2006/06/kelek_replik.

55 Werner Schiffauer, *Die Migranten aus Subay: Türken in Deutschland, Eine Ethnographie* (Stuttgart: Klett-Cotta, 1991). If you compare the chapter structure and overall organization of *Die fremde Braut* with *Die Migranten aus Subay*, it is obvious that Kelek admires and enjoys Schiffauer's work. *Die fremde Braut* imitates his writing style and Schiffauer's chapter structure.

56 Yasemin Yıldız, "Governing European Subjects: Tolerance and Guilt in the Discourse of 'Muslim Women,'" *Cultural Critique* 77 (2011): 77. https://doi.org/10.1353/cul.2011.0002.

57 Matthias Wulff, "Werte-Test für Muslime: Der strittige Fragenkatalog aus Baden-Württemberg," *Welt Online*, January 8, 2006, accessed June 16, 2023, https://www.welt.de/print-wams/article137162/Werte-Test-fuer -Muslime-Der-strittige-Fragenkatalog-aus-Baden-Wuerttemberg. html. The *taz* made fun of the test questions by posing them to Muslim celebrities and printing their answers. Kerstin Speckner, "Mach den Muslim-Test!," *Die Tageszeitung*, January 6, 2006, accessed June 16, 2023, http://www.taz.de/!493413/

58 Christine Jähn, "Integration: Kein Muslimtest mehr," *Die Zeit*, April 1, 2009, accessed June 16, 2023, http://www.zeit.de/online/2006/04/bundestag_fragebogen.

59 Deutscher Bundestag, *Antrag: So genannter Muslimtest in Baden-Württemberg – Verfassungsrechtlich problematische Gesinnungstests beenden*, Renate Künast et al. Plenarprotokoll 16/11, Berlin: Deutscher Bundestag, 2006, 754D-769D. PDF, https://dserver.bundestag.de/btp/16/16011.pdf (accessed June 16, 2023). Sitzung." (Plenarprotokoll 16/11, Berlin, 2006). 754D-769D. https://dserver.bundestag.de/btp/16/16011.pdf. (accessed June 16, 2023).

60 Statistische Berichte Baden-Württemberg, Endgültige Ergebnisse der Wahl zum 15. Landtag von Baden-Württemberg am 27. März 2011. Artikel-Nr. 4232 11001, Stuttgart: Statistisches Landesamt Baden-Württemberg, 2011. PDF, https://www.statistischebibliothek.de/mir/servlets/MCRFileNodeServlet/BWHeft_derivate_00015783/4232_11001.pdf (accessed February 23, 2024). AFP/segi. "'Gesinnungstest' für Ausländer vor dem Aus," *Süddeutsche Zeitung*, July 25, 2011, accessed February 23, 2024, https://www.sueddeutsche.de/politik/baden-wuerttemberg-gesinnungstest-fuer-auslaender-vor-dem-aus-1.1124496.

61 Rainer Grell, *Dichtung und Wahrheit: Die Geschichte des Muslim-Tests in Baden-Württemberg. 30 Fragen, die die Welt erregten (nicht nur die Islamische)*, DocPlayer, 2006, accessed February 23, 2024, https://docplayer.org/33102620-Dichtung-und-wahrheit-die-geschichte-des-muslim-tests-in-baden-wuerttemberg-30-fragen-die-die-welt-erregten-nicht-nur-die-islamische.html.

62 Grell, *Dichtung und Wahrheit*, 6.

63 Grell, *Dichtung und Wahrheit*, 75.

64 Grell, *Dichtung und Wahrheit*, 75.

65 Deutscher Bundestag. *16. Wahlperiode – 54. Sitzung*. Plenarprotokoll 16/54, Berlin: Deutscher Bundestag, 2006, 5148–9. PDF, https://dserver.bundestag.de/btp/16/16054.pdf (accessed July 11, 2023).

66 Deutscher Bundestag, *16. Wahlperiode - 54. Sitzung*, 5148–9.

67 Deutscher Bundestag, *16. Wahlperiode - 54. Sitzung*, 5149A.

68 Deutscher Bundestag, *16. Wahlperiode - 54. Sitzung*, 5164D.

69 Deutscher Bundestag, *16. Wahlperiode - 54. Sitzung*, 5156B.

70 Kelek, *Die fremde Braut*, 20.

71 Deutscher Bundestag, *16. Wahlperiode - 54. Sitzung*, 5152A.

72 Kelek, *Die fremde Braut*, 226.

73 Deutscher Bundestag, *16. Wahlperiode - 54. Sitzung*, 5162C.

2 Failed Integration

1 Basdorf et al., Urteil vom 28. August 2007 in der Strafsache gegen 1. [Blank] 2. [Blank] wegen Mordes u.a., 5 StR 31/07 (5. Strafsenats 2007).

2 "Urteil," 6.

3 "Urteil," 4.
4 "Urteil," 4.
5 "Urteil," 5. "… wegen ihres von ihm als ehrlos empfundenen Lebenswandels…".
6 "Urteil," 5.
7 "Urteil," 3.
8 "Urteil," 3.
9 "Urteil," 10; "Bundesgerichtshof hebt Freisprüche im sogenannten Ehrenmordprozess auf," Mitteilung der Pressestelle Bundesgerichtshof, Nr. 117/2007, August 28, 2007, accessed February 23, 2024, https://juris.bundesgerichtshof.de/cgi-bin/rechtsprechung/document.py?Gericht=bgh&Art=pm&Datum=2007-8&Sort=3&nr=41045&pos=4&anz=8. Jan Müller, "Ehrenmord-Prozess: Verdächtige SMS – Bundesrichter kippen Sürücü-Urteil," *Spiegel Online*, August 28, 2007, accessed June 21, 2023, http://www.spiegel.de/politik/deutschland/ehrenmord-prozess-verdaechtige-sms-bundesrichter-kippen-sueruecue-urteil-a-502533.html.
10 Sabine Beikler, "Hatuns Bruder will sich neuem Prozess doch nicht stellen," *Der Tagesspiegel*, January 20, 2008, https://www.tagesspiegel.de/berlin/polizei-justiz/fall-sueruecue-hatuns-bruder-will-sich-neuem-prozess-doch-nicht-stellen/1145286.html. –, "Fall Sürücü kommt zu den Akten," *Der Tagesspiegel*, February 2, 2009, https://www.tagesspiegel.de/berlin/kriminalitaet-fall-sueruecue-kommt-zu-den-akten/1434286.html. Both accessed June 21, 2023.
11 dpa/cpa, "Nach Beschwerde der Türkei: Berliner "Ehrenmord"-Prozess gegen Sürücü-Brüder wird neu aufgerollt," *Die Welt*, February 22, 2018. https://www.welt.de/vermischtes/article173865433/Nach-Beschwerde-der-Tuerkei-Berliner-Ehrenmord-Prozess-gegen-Sueruecue-Brueder-wird-neu-aufgerollt.html.
12 Matthias Deiß, "Sürücü-Mörder in die Türkei abgeschoben," *rbb24*, July 4, 2014, accessed June 21, 2023, https://www.rbb24.de/politik/beitrag/2014/07/hatun-sueruecue-bruder-ayhan-in-die-tuerkei-abgeschoben.html.
13 In an embarrassing situation for the German embassy, Ayhan Sürücü was found to be working for a Turkish security firm and was dispatched as a substitute worker to provide security for the German ambassador on two separate occasions in 2015 before the situation was remedied. cke, "Hatun Sürücü: Ihr Mörder arbeitete für den deutschen Staat," *Welt Online*, July 29, 2015, accessed June 21, 2023, https://www.welt.de/vermischtes/article144606108/Hatuns-Moerder-arbeitete-fuer-deutschen-Botschafter.html.
14 Beverly Weber, *Violence and Gender in the "New" Europe, Islam in German Culture.* (New York: Palgrave MacMillan, 2013), 66. Katherine Pratt Ewing and Joan Scott have made similar arguments about Germany and France,

respectively. See Ewing, *Stolen Honor: Stigmatizing Muslim Men in Berlin.* (Stanford: Stanford University Press, 2008), 190–9, and Scott, *The Politics of the Veil* (Princeton: Princeton University Press, 2010), 151–74.

15 Werner Schiffauer, *Die Gewalt der Ehre: Erklärungen zu einem deutsch -türkischen Sexualkonflikt* (Frankfurt am Main: Suhrkamp, 1983).

16 Leti Volpp, "Framing Cultural Difference: Immigrant Women and Discourses of Tradition," *Differences* 22, no. 1 (2011): 90–110. https://doi.org/10.1215/10407391-1218256.

17 El-Tayeb, *European Others.* Yıldız, "Governing European Subjects." See also Yasemin Yıldız, "Turkish Girls, Allah's Daughters, and the Contemporarz German Subject: Itinerary of a Figure," *German Life and Letters* 62, no. 4 (2009): 465–81.

18 El-Tayeb, *European Others*, 81–2.

19 Weber, *Violence and Gender*, 61–76. Ewing, *Stolen Honor*, 151–79.

20 Weber, *Violence and Gender*, 61.

21 dpa/cpa, "Nach Beschwerde der Türkei."

22 tsp/ddp, "Gedenktafel für ermordete Hatun Sürücü," *Der Tagesspiegel*, June 11, 2008, accessed June 21, 2023, https://www.tagesspiegel.de/berlin /ehrenmord-gedenktafel-fuer-ermordete-hatun-sueruecue/1253802.html. Full inscription available at "File:Gedenktafel Oberlandgarten 1 (Temp) Hatun Sürücü.JPG - Wikipedia," July 2, 2010, accessed June 21, 2023, https://commons.wikimedia.org/wiki/File:Gedenktafel_Oberlandgarten_1 _(Temp)_Hatun_S%C3%BCr%C3%BCc%C3%BC.JPG.

23 Der Tagesspiegel, "10 Jahre Gedenken an Hatun Sürücü in Berlin," YouTube video, 2015, no longer available, https://www.youtube.com /watch?v=qzyouxBpn5c. Aviva Redaktion, "Gedenkfeier für Hatun Sürücü am damaligen Tatort im Oberlandgarten 1 in Tempelhof-Schöneberg am 7. Februar 11:00 Uhr," Aviva - Online Magazin und Informationsportal für Frauen, last modified May 2, 2016, accessed June 21, 2023, https://www.aviva-berlin.de/aviva/Druck.php?id=14191724; Kerstin Hense, "Integrationsprojekt erinnert an getötete Hatun Sürücü, *Der Tagesspiegel*," February 7, 2013, accessed June 21, 2023, https://www .tagesspiegel.de/berlin/gedenkfeier-fuer-deutsch-kurdin -integrationsprojekt-erinnert-an-getoetete-hatun-sueruecue/7746166.html.

24 Lama Abu Odeh describes "a paradigmatic example of a crime of honour" as "the killing of a woman by her father or brother for engaging in, or being suspected of engaging in, sexual practices before or outside marriage." Lama Abu Odeh, "Crimes of Honour and the Construction of Gender in Arab Societies," *Feminism and Islam: Legal and Literary Perspectives*, ed. Mai Yamani (New York: New York University Press, 1996), 141, quoted in Lynn Welchmann and Sara Hossain, eds., *'Honour': Crimes, Paradigms and Violence against Women* (London: Zed Books, 2005), 5. Ewing also calls the Sürücü murder "paradigmatic," *Stolen Honor*, 153.

25 Johanna Schuster-Craig, "The Demands of Integration," (PhD Diss., Duke University, 2012), 244.

26 Güner Yasemin Balci, *Arabboy: eine Jugend in Deutschland, oder, Das kurze Leben des Rashid A* (Frankfurt am Main, Fischer-Taschenbuch-Verlag, 2010). —. *ArabQueen oder der Geschmack der Freiheit* (Fankfurt am Main: Fischer-Taschenbuch-Verlag, 2012). Heisig, *Das Ende der Geduld.* Sineb El Masrar, *Muslim Girls: Wer wir sind, wie wir leben* (Frankfurt am Main: Eichborn, 2010). I examine the books by Heisig and El Masrar in more detail here: Johanna Schuster-Craig, "Mass-Market Paperbacks and Integration Politics," *German Politics and Society* 39, no. 2 (2021): 22–46.

27 Jörg Lau, "Wie eine Deutsche," *Die Zeit*, February 24, 2005, accessed June 12, 2023, https://www.zeit.de/2005/09/Hatin_S_9fr_9fc_9f_09. Stefan Theil and Sarah Sennott, "The Barbarians Within," *Newsweek* March 28, 2005, accessed July 11, 2023, https://www.newsweek.com/barbarians-within-114557. Anna Reimann, "Ehrenmord: Sorgerechts-Gezerre um Hatun Sürücüs Sohn," *Spiegel Online*, February 5, 2007, https://www.spiegel.de/panorama/justiz/ehrenmord-sorgerechts-gezerre-um-hatun-sueruecues-sohn-a-464439.html. Freia Peters, "Mord ohne Reue," *Welt Online*, July 27, 2011, https://www.welt.de/print/die_welt/politik/article13509815/Mord-ohne-Reue.html. Sabine Beikler, "Wir konnten ihr Leben nicht tolerieren," *Der Tagesspiegel*, July 25, 2011, https://www.tagesspiegel.de/berlin/der-fall-sueruecue-wir-konnten-ihr-leben-nicht-tolerieren/4430780.html. Sarah Borufka, "Sie musste sterben, weil sie leben wollte," *Berliner Zeitung*, February 7, 2015. https://www.bz-berlin.de/berlin/sie-musste-sterben-weil-sie-leben-wollte. Kemal Hür, "Zehn Jahre nach Mord an Hatun Sürücü: Nichts ist vergessen," *Deutschlandfunk Kultur*, February 7, 2015, https://www.deutschlandfunkkultur.de/zehn-jahre-nach-mord-an-hatun-sueruecue-nichts-ist-vergessen-100.html. All accessed June 22, 2023.

28 Matthias Deiß and Jo Goll, *Verlorene Ehre: Der Irrweg der Familie Sürücü*, TV Documentary (Rbb, WDR, ARD, 2011), accessed June 24, 2023, https://youtu.be/1A4hk8gduxU, In their nonfiction book that was released the same year as their documentary, authors Deiß and Goll comment that Mutlu's German is "not quite fluent" (*nicht ganz so flüssig*). Matthias Deiß and Jo Goll, *Ehrenmord: Ein deutsches Schicksal*, (Hamburg: Hoffmann und Campe Verlag, 2011). 103.

29 Deiß and Goll, *Ehrenmord*, 135–70.

30 Ferda Ataman, "Fünf Jahre danach: Die verlorene Ehre der Familie Sürücü," *Potsdamer Neuste Nachrichten*, February 6, 2010, accessed October 22, 2019, https://www.pnn.de/brandenburg/die-verlorene-ehre-der-familie-sueruecue/22176562.html. Deiß und Goll, *Ehrenmord*, 86. Deiß and Goll report that after the murder, this brother finished his university degree, but the press attention and loss of his sister had a negative effect on him. He

apparently will not tell the press where he lives in Germany. Both sources here report that this brother is attempting to change his name due to stigma.

31 Melek A. was awarded fifth place in the "Most Important Berliner of the Year" contest by the *Berliner Morgenpost*. Cited in Deiß and Goll, *Ehrenmord*, 163.

32 Werner Schiffauer, "Der unheimliche Muslim,"111.

33 Peter Schneider, "The New Berlin Wall," *The New York Times Magazine*, December 4, 2005, accessed June 22, 2023, https://www.nytimes .com/2005/12/04/magazine/the-new-berlin-wall.html. "Wie Ayhan Sürücü seine Schwester tötete," *Berliner Morgenpost*, accessed July 17, 2019, https://www.morgenpost.de/vermischtes/article105052837 /Wie-Ayhan-Sueruecue-seine-Schwester-toetete.html. "Blutsverwandte – der Fall Sürücü," *Der Tagesspiegel*, February 2, 2016, accessed June 22, 2023, https://www.tagesspiegel.de/gesellschaft/blutsverwandte-der -fall-surucu-4869850.html. Katja Füchsel, "Der Tod und die Mädchen," *Der Tagesspiegel*, October 12, 2005, accessed June 22, 2023, https://www .tagesspiegel.de/berlin/der-tod-und-die-madchen-1264705.html. Deiß and Goll, *Ehrenmord*, 15.

34 Sonia Phalnikar, "Die Freiheit war ihr Todesurteil," *DW.COM*, 25 February 2005, accessed June 23, 2023, https://www.dw.com/de /die-freiheit-war-ihr-todesurteil/a-1499642; Schneider, "The New Berlin Wall;" Deiß and Goll, *Ehrenmord*, 15–17, 54.

35 In addition to all the other sources cited above, see the description of Hatun Sürücü in the prize created by the Green Party: "Hatun-Sürücü-Preis 2019," Grüne Fraktion Berlin, November 12, 2018, accessed June 23, 2023, https://gruene-fraktion.berlin/kampagne/hsp/.

36 *Urteil*, 4. Stefan Theil and Sarah Sennott, "The Barbarians Within." Michael Mielke, "Warum Hatun Sürücü sterben musste," *Berliner Morgenpost*, February 7, 2010, accessed June 23, 2023, https://www .morgenpost.de/berlin/article103961528/Warum-Hatun-Sueruecue -sterben-musste.html. Deiß and Goll, *Ehrenmord*, 17.

37 Deiß and Goll, *Ehrenmord*, 61, 66.

38 Weber, *Violence and Gender*, 66. Joan Scott makes similar claims about France in *The Politics of the Veil*, 151–74.

39 Weber, *Violence and Gender*, 63. Weber is quoting Tanja Laninger and Dirk Banse, "Mord an einer Türkin–Ermordet, weil sie frei sein wollten," *Berliner Morgenpost*, Feb. 16, 2005: 20 and "Ehrenmord-Prozess: Die Frage der Ehre," *Zeit Online*, Aug. 28, 2007.

40 Deiß and Goll, *Verlorene Ehre. Ehrenmord*, 77.

41 Deiß and Goll, *Ehrenmord*, 101–2. Deiß and Goll point to possible incestuous abuse of Hatun by her brother Alparslan, one of the three tried for her murder. One of Hatun's friends declared as an early witness during the murder trial that Alparslan had molested Hatun. Alparslan Sürücü

was acquitted due to lack of evidence. He lives in Turkey. See also Henning Kober, "Ehre vor Gericht," *Die Welt*, April 1, 2006, accessed February 23, 2024, https://www.welt.de/print-wams/article140501/Ehre-vor-Gericht.html.

42 "Urteil," 5.

43 Deiß and Goll, *Verlorene Ehre*; Deiß and Goll, *Ehrenmord*, 87–9. Michael Mielke, "Warum Hatun Sürücü sterben musste," Jörg Lau, "Wie eine Deutsche."

44 Deiß and Goll, *Ehrenmord*, 73–4.

45 Deiß and Goll, *Ehrenmord*, 74.

46 Purna Sen, "'Crimes of Honor,' Value and Meaning," in *"Honour": Crimes, Paradigms, and Violence against Women*, eds. Lynn Welchman and Sara Hossain (London: Zed Books, 2005), 42–63.

47 Lama Abu-Odeh, "Comparatively Speaking: The Honor of the East and the Passion of the West," *Utah Law Review* 1997, no. 2 (1997): 289. https://scholarship.law.georgetown.edu/facpub/1401.

48 L. Heise, M. Ellsberg, and M. Gottmoeller, "A Global Overview of Gender-Based Violence," *International Journal of Gynaecology and Obstetrics* 78, no. 1 (2002): S8. https://doi.org/10.1016/S0020-7292(02)00038-3.

49 Klaus Theweleit, *Male Fantasies: Volume 1*, trans. Stephen Conway, Erika Carter, and Chris Turner (Minneapolis: University of Minnesota Press, 1987). See also Mary L. Knight, "(L)earned Monsters: Psychopathic Masculinities in Contemporary German Film and Fiction," *Colloquia Germanica* 46, no. 1 (2013): 4–20.

50 R.G. Grose and S. Grabe, "The Explanatory Role of Relationship Power and Control in Domestic Violence Against Women in Nicaragua: A Feminist Psychology Analysis," *Violence Against Women* 20, no. 8 972–93. https://doi.org/10.1177/1077801214546231.

51 Certainly, recent studies in the US about perceived higher pain tolerance of Black people and greater maternal health dangers for Black women shows that this underestimation of pain is prevalent in multiracial societies with racial hierarchies. Mary Beth Flanders-Stepans, "Alarming Racial Differences in Maternal Mortality," *The Journal of Perinatal Education* 9, no. 2 (2000): 50–1. https://doi.org/10.1624/105812400X87653. Ronald Wyatt, "Pain and Ethnicity," *AMA Journal of Ethics* 15, no. 5 (2013): 449–54. https://doi.org/10.1001/virtualmentor.2013.15.5.pfor1-1305.

52 Wolfram Pfreundschuh, "Kulturalisierung," *Kulturkritik*, accessed February 23, 2024, https://kulturkritik.net/begriffe/begr_txt.php?lex=kulturalisierung. Multiple scholars have built upon Etienne Balibar's notion of cultural racism that has some shared content with *Kulturalisierung*. For my purposes, what may be most salient is the work of Geraldine Heng, who methodically tracks how culturalization leads to a concept of race and has done so since the Middle Ages. Her introductory examples of Jewish populations in England

before 1300 are instructive. See Geraldine Heng, *The Invention of Race in the European Middle Ages* (Cambridge: Cambridge University Press, 2018), 15–27.

53 Inderpal Grewal, and Caren Kaplan, "Global Identities: Theorizing Transnational Studies of Sexuality," *GLQ: A Journal of Lesbian and Gay Studies* 7, no. 4 (2001): 663–79. https://doi.org/10.1215/10642684 -7-4-663. Chandra Talpade Mohanty, "Under Western Eyes: Feminist Scholarship and Colonial Discourses," *Boundary 2* 12/13 (1984): 333–58. https://doi.org/10.2307/302821. Lila Abu-Lughod, *Do Muslim Women Need Saving?* (Cambridge, MA: Harvard University Press, 2013). See also Volpp, "Framing Cultural Difference."

54 Katrin Osterloh and Nele Westerholt, "Kultur," in *Wie Rassismus aus Wörtern spricht: (K)Erben des Kolonialismus im Wissensarchiv deutscher Sprache – ein kritisches Nachschlagewerk*, eds. Susan Arndt and Nadja Ofuatey-Alazard, (Münster: Unrast-Verlag, 2011), 412–16.

55 Anna C. Cöster, *Ehrenmord in Deutschland* (Marburg: Tectum Wissenschaftsverlag, 2009), 30.

56 It is difficult to confirm the exact date of the counselling session. Most press attention does not include the date of the press release, and the largest number of articles appear between February 17–19, 2005, accessed February 23, 2024, Annette Kögel, "Mut zur Öffentlichkeit," *Der Tagesspiegel*, February 19, 2005. https://www.tagesspiegel.de /berlin/mut-zur-oeffentlichkeit/586364.html. Regina Köhler, "Schule hat viel zu wenig Einfluß," *Die Welt*, February 19, 2005, accessed February 23, 2024, https://www.welt.de/print-welt/article471295 /Schule-hat-viel-zu-wenig-Einfluss.html. Andrea Hömke, and Michael Pagel, "Schüler der Thomas-Morus-Oberschule freuten sich über Ermordung der schönen Hatin [*sic*] und beleidigten Mädchen ohne Kopftuch," *BZ*, February 18, 2005, accessed February 23, 2024, https:// www.bz-berlin.de/artikel-archiv/schueler-der-thomas-morus -oberschule-freuten-sich-ueber-ermordung-der-schoenen-hatin-und -beleidigten-maedchen-ohne-kopftuch.

57 "'Ehrenmord' an Hatin [*sic*] Sürücü: Bundespräsident Köhler dankt couragiertem Schulleiter." *Spiegel Online*, August 12, 2005, accessed February 23, 2024, https://www.spiegel.de/lebenundlernen/schule /ehrenmord-an-hatin-sueruecue-bundespraesident-koehler-dankt -couragiertem-schulleiter-a-369481-2.html. Steffens's letter says "behaved" (benommen); other media sometimes says "lived" (gelebt). Both are used in this article. Colloquially, I hear "gelebt" more often when talking about Hatun Sürücü.

58 Tanja Buntrock, "Gedenken mit Hilferuf," *Der Tagesspiegel*, February 23, 2005, accessed February 23, 2024, https://www.tagesspiegel.de /berlin/gedenken-mit-hilferuf/587420.html.

59 Sabine Deckwerth and Frank Nordhausen, "Eine Mahnwache für die getötete Türkin Hatin Sürücü [sic]," *Berliner Zeitung*, February 23, 2005.
60 "'Ehrenmord' an Hatin [sic] Sürücü." In 2015, when Ayhan Sürücü was released from prison, *Die Welt* asserted that the perpetrator himself had made such a statement. cke, "Ihr Mörder."
61 Lau, "Wie eine Deutsche." Phalnikar, "Die Freiheit war ihr Todesurteil."
62 Ewing, *Stolen Honor*, 152.
63 Volker Steffens, "Der offene Brief des Schulleiters nach dem Mord und das Dankschreiben von Bundespräsident Köhler," *Spiegel Online*, August 18, 2005, accessed June 24, 2023, https://www.spiegel.de/lebenundlernen /schule/ehrenmord-an-hatin-sueruecue-bundespraesident-koehler -dankt-couragiertem-schulleiter-a-369481-2.html.
64 Deckwerth and Nordhausen, "Eine Mahnwache." Hömke and Pagel, "Schüler." Peter Kirschey, "Mord ist keine Ehre – ein Verbrechen," *neues deutschland*, February 23, 2005, accessed February 24, 2024, https://www .neues-deutschland.de/artikel/67911.mord-ist-keine-ehre-ein-verbrechen. html. Jörg Lau, "Kulturbedingte 'Ehrenmorde,'" *Die Zeit*, March 3, 2005, accessed February 23, 2024, https://www.zeit.de/2005/10/Ehrenmorde; —, "Wie eine Deutsche"; "Rektor: 'Kollegen haben mir den Rücken gestärkt,'" *Berliner Morgenpost*, February 18, 2005, accessed February 23, 2024, https:// www.morgenpost.de/printarchiv/berlin/article104159781/Rektor-Kollegen- haben-mir-den-Ruecken-gestaerkt.html. Sabine Am Orde, "'Sprechen Sie mit den Jungs!'" *Die Tageszeitung*, February 22, 2005, accessed February 23, 2024, https://taz.de/Sprechen-Sie-mit-den-Jungs/!641168/. Am Orde, "Zehn Punkte gegen Gewalt," *Die Tageszeitung*, February 26, 2005, accessed February 23, 2024, https://taz.de/Zehn-Punkte-gegen-Gewalt/!639768/; Florian Peil, "Mahnwache für ermordete Türkin: 'Alles Liebe in einer anderen Welt,'" *Spiegel Online*, February 22, 2005, accessed February 23, 2024, https://www .spiegel.de/panorama/mahnwache-fuer-ermordete-tuerkin-alles -liebe-in-einer-anderen-welt-a-343155.html; Phalnikar, "Die Freiheit war ihr Todesurteil." Jörg Steinert, "Mahnwache für Hatin [sic] Sürücü," Press Release, LSVD-Landesverband Berlin-Brandenburg, February 18, 2005, accessed February 23, 2024, https://www.lsvd.de/bund/presse/0502180.html. Till Stoldt, "'Die war halt zu Deutsch,'" *Welt am Sonntag*, February 20, 2005 accessed June 25, 2023, https://www.welt.de/print-wams /article123850/Die-war-halt -zu-deutsch.html. Buntrock, "Gedenken mit Hilferuf."
65 Bauer, "Hinter der Schulfassade," *Die Tageszeitung*, March 9, 2005 accessed July 13, 2023, https://taz.de/!636694/. lvt/kög, "Wowereit: Muslime müssen sich integrieren." *Der Tagesspiegel*, February 22, 2005, accessed July 13, 2023, https://www.tagesspiegel.de/berlin/wowereit -muslime-mussen-sich-integrieren-1195681.html. Lau, "Kulturbedingte 'Ehrenmorde.'" Deiß and Goll, *Ehrenmord*, 173.

66 Jörg Lau's article "Kulturbedingte 'Ehrenmorde'" asserts that Sürücü was the sixth victim of honour-related violence in four months. I have never been able to confirm this count. Sabine am Orde asserts that there were five honour killings between October 2004 and February 2005. In a group interview for *taz*, am Orde presents this to a group of Turkish-German community members, and Hüseyin Midik of DİTİB pushes back, by saying, "I don't know if in all five cases it was about honour." Am Orde, "'Sprechen Sie mit den Jungs!'." The *Bundeskriminalamt* commissioned a study of honour killings between 1996–2005, published in 2011. For the entire year of 2005, they mark five deaths and two survivals. They categorize those deaths as three honour murders and four cases of murder of an intimate partner that may or may not have been motivated by notions of honour. Dietrich Oberwittler and Julia Kasselt, *Ehrenmorde in Deutschland 1996–2005*, ed. Bundeskriminalamt, Kriminalistisches Institut. (Cologne: Luchterhand, 2011), 217–18, accessed July 13, 2023, https://www.bka.de/SharedDocs/Downloads/DE/Publikationen/Publikationsreihen/PolizeiUndForschung/1_42_EhrenmordeInDeutschland.html.

67 "Demo gegen Gewalt," *Die Tageszeitung*, March 3, 2005, accessed July 13, 2023, https://www.taz.de/!638397/. Steinert, "Mahnwache für Hatin [*sic*] Sürücü."

68 Seyran Ateş, *Große Reise ins Feuer*, 144–65.

69 "Demo gegen Gewalt." Steinert, "Mahnwache für Hatin [*sic*] Sürücü."

70 Peil, "Mahnwache für ermordete Türkin."

71 Weber, *Violence and Gender*, 49–61.

72 While this book will not focus on education, this is an arena deserving of more future research. The PISA shock of 2001 and the Rütli School scandal of 2006 both showed that conflicts within German schools are a critical element of German cultural debates and deserve to be and have been taken up by researchers in more detail than I can here. See, as an example: Raphaela Schlicht, *Determinanten der Bildungsungleichheit* (Wiesbaden: Verlag für Sozialwissenschaften, 2011), https://doi.org/10.1007/978-3-531-92626-1. Aladin El-Mafaalani's book for general audiences on this topic *Mythos Bildung: Die ungerechte Gesellschaft, ihr Bildungssystem und seine Zukunft* was published by Kiepenheuer and Witsch – Necla Kelek's publisher in Cologne – in 2020.

73 Schönwälder argues that political discussions about *Überfremdung* in Switzerland influenced the discussion in Germany. In the mid-1960s, however, German officials did not think that "foreign infiltration" was a pressing danger, although they acknowledged that in urban centres with large foreign worker populations there could come a time where fears of *Überfremdung* increased. Karen Schönwälder, *Einwanderung und ethnische*

*Pluralität: politische Entscheidungen und öffentliche Debatten in Grossbritan-
nien und der Bundesrepublik von den 1950er bis zu den 1970er Jahren* (Essen:
Klartext, 2001), 333.

74 John Hooper, "Anti-Islamic Italian Author in New Legal Fight," *The
Guardian*, July 12, 2005, accessed June 25, 2023, https://www.theguardian
.com/world/2005/jul/13/books.italy. Kelek, *Die fremde Braut*, 211–13.

75 Schiffauer, *Gewalt*, 65. Schiffauer defines this notion of honour in a
Turkish village context as a line marking the distinction between public
and private, two concepts that I argue have morphed in a parallel society
trope to fit a German cultural context.

76 Ewing, *Stolen Honor*, 82. Ewing's book *Stolen Honor* is broadly accurate
in that she identifies and analyses how Muslim masculinity is stigma-
tized in Germany. But I am shocked by its subtle errors. She argues that
Heitmeyer and his colleagues "in a book on Islamic 'fundamentalism' in
Germany accused Turks of resisting integration because of their involvement in Islam," and states that in her interviews, leaders of Islamic
organizations were "outraged at the book's conclusions." This description does not describe the book I read, which is a rigorous collection
of survey instruments and interview excerpts that is transparent in its
methodology, and aruges for the emergence of Islamic fundamentalism
as a reaction against German discrimination of Turks. Heitmeyer's book
consistently argued that Turkish adolescents desired more contact with
Germans, not less. Why naming this discrimination in particular would
infuriate leaders of Islamic organizations is unclear, unless these
leaders are relying – like Ewing clearly does – on secondhand information rather than their own reading of the study. See also Markus C.
Schulte von Drach, "Existieren Parallelgesellschaften in Deutschland?,"
Süddeutsche Zeitung, August 10, 2016, accessed June 25, 2023, https://
www.sueddeutsche.de/politik/muslime-und-migranten-gibt-es
-parallelgesellschaften-in-deutschland-1.3012266. Wilhelm Heitmeyer,
"Für türkische Jugendliche in Deutschland spielt der Islam eine wichtige
Rolle," *Die Zeit*, August 23, 1996 accessed June 25, 2023, https://www
.zeit.de/1996/35/heitmey.txt.19960823.xml/komplettansicht.

77 Wilhelm Heitmeyer, Joachim Müller and Helmut Schröder, *Verlockender
Fundamentalismus* (Frankfurt am Main: Suhrkamp Verlag, 1997).

78 Heitmeyer, Müller and Schröder, *Verlockender Fundamentalismus*, 162.

79 Heitmeyer, Müller and Schröder, *Verlockender Fundamentalismus*, 253.

80 Heitmeyer, Müller and Schröder, *Verlockender Fundamentalismus*, 31, 53–6,
143, 162–3, 179, 183.

81 Heitmeyer, Müller and Schröder, *Verlockender Fundamentalismus*, 162–3.

82 Heitmeyer, Müller and Schröder, *Verlockender Fundamentalismus*, 53–5.
Patricia Ehrkamp, "Risking Publicity: Masculinities and the Racialization

of Public Neighborhood Space," *Social & Cultural Geography* 9, no. 2 (2008): 117–33. https://doi.org/10.1080/14649360701856060.

83 Heitmeyer, Müller and Schröder, *Verlockender Fundamentalismus*, 130.

84 Heitmeyer, Müller and Schröder, *Verlockender Fundamentalismus*, 192.

85 Heitmeyer, Müller and Schröder, *Verlockender Fundamentalismus*, back cover.

86 Heitmeyer, Müller and Schröder, *Verlockender Fundamentalismus*, 192.

87 Heitmeyer, Müller and Schröder, *Verlockender Fundamentalismus*, 192.

88 Heitmeyer, Müller and Schröder, *Verlockender Fundamentalismus*, 192.

89 Werner Schiffauer, *Parallelgesellschaften*: Wie viel Wertekonsens braucht unsere Gesellschaft. Für eine kluge Politik der Differenz (Bielefeld: transcript Verlag, 2008), 7–8.

90 Schiffauer, *Parallelgesellschaften*, 7–10. See also Wolf-Dietrich Bukow, et al., eds. *Was heißt hier Parallelgesellschaft?: Zum Umgang mit Differenzen* (Wiesbaden: Verlag für Sozialwissenschaften, 2007).

91 Susan Ruddick, "Constructing Difference in Public Spaces: Race, Class, and Gender as Interlocking Systems," *Urban Geography* 17, no. 2, 132–51. https://doi.org/10.2747/0272-3638.17.2.132.

92 Strikingly, the fraud was discovered by Alice Schwarzer, who donated half a million Euros to the project after winning "Who Wants to Be a Millionaire?" and later wanted to know what *Hatun und Can e.V.* had done with the money. Alice Schwarzer, "Hatun & Can: Die bittere Wahrheit," *Emma*, July 1, 2010. https://www.emma.de/artikel/hatun-can-die-bittere -wahrheit-265142; "Lange Haft wegen Spendenbetrugs," *BZ*, September 21, 2011, https://www.bz-berlin.de/artikel-archiv/lange-haft-wegen-spendenbetrugs; hut/dpa/dapd, "Spendenbetrug: Fast fünf Jahre Haft für Gründer von Hatun & Can," *Der Spiegel*, September 21, 2011, https://www.spiegel.de/panorama/justiz/spendenbetrug-fast-fuenf-jahre-haft -fuer-gruender-von-hatun-can-a-787680.html. All accessed June 25, 2023.

93 Johanna Schuster-Craig, "'Well-Integrated Muslims'and Adolescent Anti-Violence Activism in Berlin," German Life & Letters 68, no. 1 (2015): 125–44. https://doi.org/10.1111/glal.12072.

94 "HEROES – gegen Unterdrückung in Namen der Ehre – Ein Projekt für Gleichberechtigung von Strohhalm e.V," Projekt Heroes, accessed June 25, 2023, https://www.heroes-net.de/.

95 Schuster-Craig, "'Well-Integrated Muslims' and Adolescent Anti-Violence Activism in Berlin," German Life & Letters 68, no. 1 (2015): 125–44. https://doi.org/10.1111/glal.12072. 127.

96 As a graduate student, I worked as an intern at Project Heroes for 15 months while I was a German Chancellor Fellow of the Alexander from Humboldt Foundation. This section, however, is based on data gathered through a Qualtrics survey in 2020.

97 Kim Able (née Allen), "Will keep sharing," Facebook post, November 17, 2020, https://www.facebook.com/photo/?fbid=10157562337978053 &set=a.10151180610098053. This post has since been deleted.

98 HEROES-Gegen Unterdrückung im Namen der Ehre, 2021. "Heute gedenken wir Hatun Sürücü," Facebook post, February 7, 2021. https://www.facebook.com/123509897767344 /photos/a.3628681887250110/3632766670174965/. HEROES-Gegen Unterdrückung im Namen der Ehre, "-at Sonnenallee Berlin-Neukölln," Facebook post, February 5, 2021, https://www.facebook.com/HEROES -Gegen-Unterdr%C3%BCckung-im-Namen-der-Ehre-123509897767344 /photos/pcb.3628681917250107/3628681733916792/.

 99 Participants 1 and 3, online survey, 2020.
100 Schuster-Craig, "'Well-Integrated Muslims'," 128–9.
101 "'Suicides' Really Honour Killings?" *Sveriges Radio*, October 18, 2011, accessed March 5, 2024, accessed March 5, 2024, https://sverigesradio. se/artikel/4771356; Anna Åberg, "Falldöd misstänkt hedersmord," *Svenska Dagbladet*, July 6, 2009, accessed June 25, 2023, https://www.svd .se/falldod-misstankt-hedersmord.
102 Fadela Amara and Sylvia Zappi, *Ni putes ni soumises* (Paris: Découverte, 2003); Amara and Zappi, *Weder Huren noch Unterworfene* (Berlin: Orlanda Frauenverlag, 2005); Amara and Zappi, *Breaking the Silence: French Women's Voices from the Ghetto* (Berkeley: University of California Press, 2006).
103 Schuster-Craig, "'Well-Integrated Muslims'."
104 Schuster-Craig, "Mass-Market Paperbacks and Integration Politics."
105 Seyran Ateş, *Große Reise ins Feuer*, 136. "Selbstdarstellung," *TIO-Beratung-sprojekt*, accessed June 26, 2023, https://www.tio-berlin.de/tio-e-v/ selbstdarstellung/
106 Werner Schiffauer's *Die Gewalt der Ehre* (1984) describes his work in the early 1980s with a youth centre that seems to be predominantly for young men, but also had coeducational events or programs. This is one of the earliest discourses of toxic masculinity in an immigrant community, since there was a spectacular case of gang rape committed by many of the young men who attended this youth centre. Schiffauer's analysis suggests that cultural difference can be blamed for this intensely violent act, but when I read his account, I was more likely to see this behaviour as indicative of male bonding through the act of rape. Multiple-perpetrator rape exists in many locations as a social phenomenon; thus, we have little evidence that this behaviour has a cultural explanation. Miranda A.H. Horvath and Jessica Woodhams, *Handbook on the Study of Multiple Perpetrator Rape: A Multidisciplinary Response to an International Problem* (London: Taylor & Francis, 2013); Amber Aubone and Juan Hernandez, "Assessing Refugee Camp Characteristics and The Occurrence of Sexual Violence: A Preliminary Analysis of the Dadaab Complex," *Refugee Survey Quarterly* 32, no. 4 (2013): 22–40, https://doi.org/10.1093/rsq/hdt015; Werner Schiffauer, *Die Gewalt der Ehre: Erklärungen zu einem deutsch-türkischen Sexualkonflikt* (Frankfurt: Suhrkamp Press, 1983), 136–42. *Aufbruch Neukölln*

has an intercultural men's group that seems targeted at fathers. See "Männerarbeit," *Aufbruch Neukölln e.V.*, accessed June 25, 2023, https://www.aufbruch-neukoelln.de/anleitung/.

107 Participant 3, Online survey, 2020. "Die Besonderheit unserer Arbeit besteht darin, dass wir in der geschlechterreflektierten Jungenarbeit gezielt junge Männer mit familiärer Migrationsgeschichte ansprechen und als Ergänzung zu allen Projekten dienen, die in der Mädchenarbeit tätig sind."

108 Schuster-Craig, "'Well-Integrated Muslims,'" 139–40.

109 Ali Candemir, "Heroes – doch zu viel des Guten?," May 13, 2013, accessed June 25, 2023, https://yenihayat.de/heroes-doch-zu-viel-des-guten/.

110 Candemir, "Heroes – doch zu viel des Guten?"

111 Participants 1–4, Online survey, 2020. Participant 3, online survey, 2020. "Die Besonderheit ist, dass keiner von ihnen migriert ist und somit auch nicht integriert werden muss, sondern ist."

112 Schuster-Craig, "Well-integrated Muslims," 137–8.

113 Ralf Lilienthal and Wolfgang Schmit, "Kiez-Helden: Das Berliner Projekt 'Heroes – Gegen Gewalt im Namen der Ehre'," *A tempo*, October 2011, 13.

114 Jenny Breidenstein, ed. *Heroes: Dokumentation des ersten Jahres*, 22. Internal document.

115 Daniel Koehler, "Violent Extremism, Mental Health and Substance Abuse among Adolescents: Towards a Trauma Psychological Perspective on Violent Radicalization and Deradicalization," *Journal of Forensic Psychiatry and Psychology*, 31, no. 3 (2020): 455–72, https://doi.org/10.1080/14789949.2020.1758752.

116 "Ali Can: The Two-Hearted Man," *Politico EU*, December 4, 2018, accessed March 5, 2023, https://www.politico.eu/list/politico-28-class-of-2019-the-ranking/ali-can/; Riham Alkousaa, "German and Something Else: Minorities Say #metwo after Ozil Quits," *Reuters*, July 27, 2018, no longer available, https://www.reuters.com/article/us-soccer-germany-ozil-migration-idUSKBN1KH20E; Yassin Musharbash, "#MeTwo: Einfach mal zuhören!," *Zeit Online*, July 27, 2018, accessed March 5, 2023, https://www.zeit.de/gesellschaft/zeitgeschehen/2018-07/metwo-deutschland-migrationshintergrund-erfahrungen-rassismus-alltag-grosszuegigkeit; Ijoma Mangold, "#MeTwo: Was ist Rassismus? Und was ist keiner?," *Zeit Online*, August 1, 2018, accessed March 5, 2024, https://www.zeit.de/2018/32/metwo-rassismus-alltag-twitter-diskussion. Tom Bryant, "Mesut Özil walks away from Germany Team citing 'Racism and Disrespect'," *The Guardian*, July 23, 2018, accessed March 5, 2024, https://www.theguardian.com/football/2018/jul/22/mesut-ozil-retires-german-national-team-discrimination. "Mesut Özil tritt aus Nationalmannschaft zurück," *tagesschau.de*, July 23, 2018, accessed September 24, 2021, https://www.tagesschau.de/sport/oezil-ruecktritt-101.html, accessed September 24, 2021.

117 "Concept – English Translation, accessed June 25, 2023, " https://heroes-netzwerk.de/wp-content/uploads/2021/09/HEROES_Concept_EnglishTranslation.pdf. Heroes-Duisburg also uses "intersectionality" as a tag for various events: *Mein Test Gelände: Das Gender Magazin*, Heroes-Duisburg, accessed June 25, 2023, https://www.meintestgelaende.de/author/heroes_neu/.

118 Elisabeth Musch, "Consultation Structures in German Immigrant Integration Politics: The National Integration Summit and the German Islam Conference," *German Politics* 21, no. 1 (2012): 76, https://doi.org/10.1080/09644008.2011.653342.

119 Participant 1, Online survey, 2020. "Jugendliche dazu zu bewegen, klischeebeladene Bilder von Geschlecht, Geschlechterrollen und Vorstellungen von Ehre, Gewalt und Respekt zu hinterfragen, um so zu einer mündigen Person heranzuwachsen."

120 Participant 3, Online survey, 2020. "… sich kritisch mit Werten und Traditionen auseinanderzusetzen, z.B., wenn man sich durch sie eingeschränkt fühlt, z.B. im eigenen Handeln und eben nicht das Leben führen kann, was man möchte (und mit wem man möchte). Ansonsten gibt es viele Unterziele wie z.B. demokratische Bildung und Partizipation fördern etc."

121 Participant 2, Online survey, 2020. "Die Corona-Zeit zu überstehen, stabile langfristige Finanzierungen zu sichern." Participant 4, Online survey, 2020. "Zur Zeit kämpfen wir finanziell, dass HEROES nicht zugemacht wird, den[n] wir können mit unseren Kapazitäten nur noch die Schulkooperationen erfüllen."

122 Nina Kugler and Philipp Siebert, "'Was der Bruder gemacht hat, ist absolut ehrlos,'" *Berliner Morgenpost*, February 2020, accessed March 5, 2024, https://www.morgenpost.de/berlin/article228356687/Was-der-Bruder-gemacht-hat-ist-absolut-ehrlos.html; Heroes Team, Email to the author, June 18, 2020. Funding had been secured only from August – December 2020.

123 "Hauptstadtpreis für Integration und Toleranz," In *Wikipedia*, May 14, 2020 accessed June 25, 2023, https://de.wikipedia.org/w/index.php?title=Hauptstadtpreis_f%C3%BCr_Integration_und_Toleranz&oldid=19994643. "SPD vergibt Otto-Wels-Preis." *Berliner Woche*, March 22, 2018, accessed June 25, 2023, https://www.berliner-woche.de/neukoelln/c-soziales/spd-vergibt-otto-wels-preis_a146229. Press Release, *Jüdische Gemeinde zu Berlin*, "Rabbiner Alter widmet seinen Integrations-Bambi dem Projekt Heroes," December 9, 2012, accessed June 25, 2023, http://www.jg-berlin.org/beitraege/details/rabbiner-alter-widmet-seinen-integrations-bambi-dem-projekt-heroes-i613d-2012-12-09.html.

124 Bundesministerium des Innern, für Bau und Heimat, "Wie aus jungen Männern 'Helden' werden," Government Website, May 26, 2016 accessed June 25, 2023, https://www.bundesregierung.de/breg-de/service/wie-aus-jungen-maennern-helden-werden-756508.

125 Heinrich Geldschläger et al. European Network for the Work with
Perpetrators of domestic violence (WWP EN), "ENGAGE: Roadmap for
Frontline Professionals Interacting with Male Perpetrators of Domestic
Violence and Abuse," Rights, Equality and Citizenship Programme,
European project REC-VAW-2016/776919, European Union, 2019,
4, accessed March 5, 2024, https://www.work-with-perpetrators.eu
/fileadmin/WWP_Network/redakteure/Projects/ENGAGE/Final
_roadmaps/engage_EN_191127_web.pdf.
126 Monika Schröttle and Nadia Khelaifat, "Gesundheit – Gewalt –
Migration," Kurzfassung, (Rostock: Bundesministerium für Familie, Senioren, Frauen und Jugend, 2009), https://www.bmfsfj.de/bmfsfj/service
/publikationen/gesundheit-gewalt-migration/80598. See also the 2004
study Ursula Müller et al., "Lebenssituation, Sicherheit und Gesundheit von Frauen in Deutschland: Eine repräsentative Untersuchung zu
Gewalt gegen Frauen in Deutschland. Zusammenfassung zentraler Studienergebnisse," Bundesministerium für Familie, Senioren, Frauen und
Jugend, Summer 2004 accessed March 5, 2023, https://www.bmfsfj.de
/blob/84316/10574a0dff2039e15a9d3dd6f9eb2dff/kurzfassung-gewalt
-frauen-data.pdf.
127 Communication and emotional self-regulation (two skills *Projekt Heroes*
training sessions target) are critical skill sets required for male partners
who perpetrate intimate partner violence to change their behaviour.
Whether or not individuals implement those skills or whether or not
people comply with treatment depend on a multiplicity of factors across
individuals and their treatment protocols. See O. Gilbar, C. Taft, and
R. Dekel, "Male Intimate Partner Violence: Examining the Roles of
Childhood Trauma, PTSD Symptoms, and Dominance," *Journal of Family
Psychology*, Advance online publication, accessed April 30, 2020, http://
dx.doi.org/10.1037/fam0000669 and Casey T. Taft et al., "Process and
Treatment Adherence Factors in Group Cognitive–Behavioral Therapy for
Partner Violent Men," *Journal of Consulting and Clinical Psychology*, 71,
no. 4, 812–20, https://doi.org/10.1037/0022-006X.71.4.812.
128 Doku Gönner, "EHRENMORD? Wenn die türkische Tochter für ihre
Integration büßen muss," YouTube, 2017, accessed June 25, 2023, https://
www.youtube.com/watch?v=1A4hk8gduxU.
129 Participant 1, Online survey, 2020. "…die spezifische Beschäftigung mit
dem Thema Unterdrückung im Namen der Ehr[e] sehr heikel geworden.
Durch die Entstehung und den Wachstum der AfD z.B. aber auch durch
wiederlholte [sic] rassistische Angriffe und Attentate auf Menschen mit
Migrationshintergrund ist es schwieriger geworden Probleme innerhalb
der migrantischen Communities kritisch anzusprechen. Die Rede ist
oft von antimuslimischem Rassismus oder Kulturalisierung wenn

wir versuchen unsere Themen zu Diskutieren oder unsere Arbeit zu präsentieren. Diese Vorwürfe kommen zum Teil aus der Politik aber auch aus anderen migrantischen Projekten/Organisationen. Meist wenn sie uns und unsere Arbeit nicht kennen und nur davon gehört haben."

130 Participant 4, Online survey, 2020. "…die Arbeit [ist] an sich schwieriger geworden, durch mehrere politische Debatten in der Öffentlichkeit wie Rassismus, antimuslimischer Rassismus und religiöser Extremismus."

131 Participant 1, Online survey, 2020. "Da es nicht darum geht, 'Außenseiter' in eine andere Gesellschaft zu 'integrieren', stellt sich die Frage nicht."

132 Participant 2, Online survey, 2020. "Da wir uns nicht als Integrationsprojekt verstehen haben wir kein solches Konzept. Die Jungs und die Kinder in den Schulklassen sind zu 99 Prozent hier geboren/aufgewachsen und müssen unserer Meinung nach nicht in dem herkömmlichen Sinne integriert werden."

133 Participant 3, Online survey, 2020. "Ich tue mich mit dem Begriff schwer. Die Jungs müssen meiner Meinung nach [nicht] integriert werden, denn sie sind hier geboren und aufgewachsen. Integration ist somit nicht das Ziel unserer Arbeit."

134 Participant 4, Online survey, 2020. "HEROES würde sich nicht als politisches "Integrationsprojekt" bezeichnen, da unser Ziel Geschlechtergleichberechtigung ist. Durch unsere Arbeit entstehen natürlich Voraussetzungen die eine 'kulturelle' Integration in Deutschland fördern, sie sind aber nicht unser Hauptziel. Unser Ziel ist es, die Zielgruppe zu mehr Selbstbestimmung und weniger kollektiven Druck zu verhelfen, für ein freieres Leben und so auch die Empathie für ein vielfältiges Miteinander zu wecken."

135 Participant 2, Online survey, 2020. "Nein, wir erleben aber, dass es integrative Wirkung hat. Vorallem für unsere Jungs, da sie durch ihre Arbeit bei Heroes in der Gesellschaft mitwirken."

136 Participant 1, Online survey, 2020. "Integration bedeutet das Einflechten von etwas in etwas anderes – und ist deshalb als Konzept für Gesellschaften mit echten Menschen unbrauchbar."

137 Participant 2, Online survey, 2020. "Wir sind innerhalb unseres Teams und auch unter den verschiedenen Teams immer am diskutieren und haben oft unterschiedliche Meinung."

138 Participant 3, Online survey, 2020. "Der Begriff ist ziemlich veraltet."

139 Participant 4, Online survey, 2020. "Integration bedeutet das 'Kleine' in das 'Große' passend zu machen. Wir möchten aber nicht eine Identität mit der Mehrheitsidentität überschreiben, sondern einen Raum schaffen, in der mehrere Identitäten, unabhängig von Mehrheit und Größe, dieselbe Augenhöhe haben."

3 (Un)integrable Subjects: White Supremacy and Neoliberal Ideology

1 The BPK (Federal Press Conference) is a non-profit cooperative of political journalists who must be German citizens and primarily report on politics, economics, and culture. Founded in 1949, the BPK holds government press conferences every Monday, Wednesday, and Friday, to which they invite important cultural or political figures. Press conferences are open only to dues-paying members of the BPK. Bundespressekonferenz, "Bundespressekonferenz: Information in English," Federal Press Conference, accessed July 7, 2023, https://www.bundespressekonferenz.de/information-in-english. See also Holger Schmale, "Der Tag des Provokateurs," *Frankfurter Rundschau*, August 31, 2010, accessed July 7, 2023, https://www.fr.de/panorama/provokateurs-11461356.html; Andreas Kilb, "Sarrazins Buchvorstellung: erst mal lesen, dann gratulieren," *Frankfurter Allgemeine Zeitung*, August 31, 2010, accessed July 7, 2023, https://www.faz.net/aktuell/feuilleton/sarrazin/das-buch/sarrazins-buchvorstellung-erst-mal-lesen-dann-gratulieren-11024362.html.

2 Stein notes that the DVA (Sarrazin's publisher) has not released the total number of copies sold, but the first printing of 25,000 copies sold out the first day. Christina Stein, *Die Sprache der Sarrazin-Debatte: Eine diskurslinguistische Analyse* (Marburg: Tectum Wissenschaftsverlag, 2012), 1, 33; B. von Stuckrad-Barre, "Ortstermin: Thilo Sarrazin kritisiert türkischstämmige Fußballfans," *Die Welt, I*, October 9, 2010, accessed March 5, 2024, https://www.welt.de/politik/deutschland/article10179969/Thilo-Sarrazin-kritisiert-tuerkischstaemmige-Fussballfans.html. This chapter cites from the 18th hardback printing. Thilo Sarrazin, *Deutschland schafft sich ab: Wie wir unser Land aufs Spiel setzen*, 2011 (Munich: Deutsche Verlags-Anstalt, 2010). Michael Meng, "Silences about Sarrazin's Racism in Contemporary Germany," *The Journal of Modern History* 87, no. 1 (2015): 102–35, https://doi.org/10.1086/680259. According to Meng, 1.3 million people bought the book (104).

3 Bon Sneyder, *Necla Kelek stellt Sarrazins Buch vor 1/2*, YouTube, uploaded 30.08.10, accessed July 7, 2023, https://www.youtube.com/watch?v=nQnSfxlsUsw&t=21s.

4 Frank Berberich, "Klasse statt Masse," *Lettre International*, Fall 2009, accessed July 7, 2023, https://www.lettre.de/content/frank-berberich_klasse-statt-masse.

5 Kilb, "Sarrazins Buchvorstellung."

6 Klaus J. Bade, *Kritik und Gewalt: Sarrazin-Debatte, "Islamkritik" und Terror in der Einwanderungsgessellschaft* (Schwalbach/Ts: Wochenschau Verlag, 2013), 14.

7 Berberich, "Klasse statt Masse." Stefan Berg et al., "Politik der
   Vermeidung," *Der Spiegel*, no. 42, October 11, 2009, accessed July 10,
   2023, https://spiegel.de/politik/politik-der-vermeidung-a-f96b
   4be5-0002-0001-0000-000067282817. Thomas Hüetlin, "Blut, Schweiß,
   Weißwein," *Der Spiegel*, no. 51, December 13, 2009, accessed March 5,
   2023, https://www.spiegel.de/panorama/blut-schweiss-weisswein-a
   -c23b72e9-0002-0001-0000-000068167770. phw/AP/dpa, "Debatte um
   Ausländerschelte: Ökonom fordert Integrationsministerium," *Spiegel
   Online*, October 11, 2009, accessed March 5, 2024, https://www.spiegel
   .de/politik/deutschland/debatte-um-auslaenderschelte
   -oekonom-fordert-integrationsministerium-a-654465.html; Fatina
   Keilani and Annette Kögel, "Sarrazin ist nah dran und doch daneben,"
   Der Tagesspiegel, October 8, 2009, accessed July 7, 2023, https://www
   .tagesspiegel.de/berlin/umstrittene-aeusserungen-sarrazin-ist-nah-dran
   -und-doch-daneben/1611714.html, "Kalt duschen ist viel gesünder,"
   Süddeutsche Zeitung, March 10, 2010, accessed March 5, 2024, https://
   www.sueddeutsche.de/politik/thilo-sarrazin-ein-mann-und-seine
   -sprueche-1.592750-4; "Die Türken erobern Deutschland," *Berliner
   Morgenpost*, October 2, 2009, accessed July 7, 2023, https://www
   .morgenpost.de/printarchiv/berlin/article104594137/Die-Tuerken
   -erobern-Deutschland.html; Jörg Lau, "Sarrazin-Debatte: unter
   Deutschen," *Die Zeit*, October 8, 2009, accessed July 7, 2023, https://
   www.zeit.de/2009/42/01-Sarrazin-Integration, Sieglinde Geisel,
   "Vergiftete Analyse," *Neue Zürcher Zeitung*, October 12, 2009, https://
   www.nzz.ch/vergiftete_analyse-1.3855379, Jasper Barenberg, "Dieser
   Mensch ist verwirrt," *Deutschlandfunk* October 7, 2009, accessed July 7,
   2023, https://www.deutschlandfunk.de/dieser-mensch
   -ist-verwirrt.694.de.html?dram:article_id=67668.
8 As an example, see Eric Tang, *Unsettled: Cambodian Refugees in the New York
   City Hyperghetto* (Philadelphia: Temple University Press, 2015), 146–56.
9 Thomas Eppinger, a blogger, hosts what looks like a print-to-pdf copy
   of the *Bild* reprint of Sarrazin's interview on his blog "S t a n d p u
   n k t e," S t a n d p u n k t e, accessed July 7, 2023, https://eppinger.
   wordpress.com/.Thilo Sarrazin, "Thilo Sarrazin im Gespräch mit
   'Lettre International,'" *Bild.de*, October 8, 2009, accessed March 5, 2024,
   https://eppinger.files.wordpress.com/2009/10/klasse-statt-masse.pdf.
   Cangrande, "Canabbia: Volltext des Interviews von Lettre International
   (Frank Berberich) mit Thilo Sarrazin: ausgerechnet die Bild-Zeitung
   publiziert den Gesamttext!." *CANABBAIA* (blog). October 2009, https://
   beltwild.blogspot.com/2009/10/volltext
   -des-interviews-von-lettre.html. The original *Bild* posting is no longer
   accessible.

10 can/ddp, "'Lettre'-Magazin fordert Schadenersatz von 'Bild,'" *Spiegel Online*, October 27, 2009, accessed March 5, 2024, https://www.spiegel.de/kultur/gesellschaft/sarrazin-interview-lettre-magazin-fordert-schadenersatz-von-bild-a-657626.html.

11 Sander L. Gilman, *New German Critique* 117, vol. 39, no. 3 (2012): 48; Sarrazin, *Deutschland schafft sich ab*, 58–9.

12 Sarrazin, *Deutschland schafft sich ab*, 59.

13 El-Tayeb, *European Others*, 17–36.

14 Bundesinstitut für Bevölkerungsforschung, "Bevölkerung mit Migrationshintergrund und ausländische Bevölkerung nach den 10 häufigsten Herkunftsländern," Bundesinstitut für Bevölkerungsforschung, 2021, accessed July 7, 2023, https://www.bib.bund.de/DE/Fakten/Fakt/B95-Bevoelkerung-mit-Migrationshintergrund-Auslaend-Bevoelkerung-Herkunftslaender.html.

15 I first understood this concept through Mekonnen Mesghena's comments during the WdK panel. Johanna Schuster-Craig, "Resisting Integration: Neukölln Artist Reponses to Integration Politicsi" in *Cultural Topographies of the New Berlin*, eds. Karin Bauer and Jennifer Ruth Hosek (New York: Berghahn Books, 2018), 242–3.

16 Kerstin Gehrke and Matthias Oloew, "Letzter Akt in der Tempodrom-Affäre," *Der Tagesspiegel*, January 8, 2008, accessed July 11, 2023, https://www.tagesspiegel.de/berlin/polizei-justiz/prozessbeginn-letzter-akt-in-der-tempodrom-affaere/1135838.html. "Eichel kritisiert Mißbrauch von Aufbau-Ost-Geldern," *Die Welt*, November 27, 2004, accessed July 11, 2023, https://www.welt.de/politik/article355153/Eichel-kritisiert-Missbrauch-von-Aufbau-Ost-Geldern.html.

17 For more on neoliberal efficiency, see Wendy Brown, *Undoing the Demos: Neoliberalism's Stealth Revolution* (Brooklyn: Zone Books, 2015), and Elizabeth Popp Berman, *Thinking Like an Economist: How Efficiency Replaced Equality in U.S. Public Policy* (Princeton: Princeton University Press, 2022).

18 Bade, *Kritik und Gewalt*, 89; Egbert Jahn, "The Offences and Repudiation of Thilo Sarrazin: Are There Limits to Freedom of Political Opinion in Germany?," in *German Domestic and Foreign Policy: Political Issues Under Debate – Vol. 2*, ed. Egbert Jahn (Berlin: Springer Verlag, 2015), 17–42, Stein, *Die Sprache der Sarrazin-Debatte*, 33.

19 Sarrazin, *Deutschland schafft sich ab*, 331–408.

20 Alexandra Minna Stern, *Proud Boys and the White Ethnostate: How the Alt-Right Is Warping the American Imagination* (Boston: Beacon Press, 2019).

21 Bade, *Kritik und Gewalt*,13–14.

22 Sarrazin, *Deutschland schafft sich ab*, 57–84, 90–102.

23 Gilman, "Thilo Sarrazin," 52. Sarrazin, *Deutschland schafft sich ab*, 262, 264–5, 267–81.
24 Berberich. Sarrazin, *Deutschland schafft sich ab*, 172–5.
25 Meng, "Silences about Sarrazin's Racism in Contemporary Germany." Andrea Seibel, Joachim Fahrun und Hajo Schumacher, "Thilo Sarrazin – 'Ich bin kein Rassist,'" *Berliner Morgenpost*, August 28, 2010, accessed July 10, 2023, https://www.morgenpost.de/berlin-aktuell/article104530856 /Thilo-Sarrazin-Ich-bin-kein-Rassist.html.
26 "Integrationsdebatte: Joachim Gauck – Politiker können von Sarrazin lernen," *Die Welt*, December 30, 2010, accessed July 10, 2023, https://www.welt.de/politik/deutschland/article11902962 /Joachim-Gauck-Politiker-koennen-von-Sarrazin-lernen.html. Antje Sirleschtov and Stephan Haselberger, "Gauck attestiert Sarrazin 'Mut,'" December 30, 2010, accessed July 10, 2023, https://www.tagesspiegel.de /politik/integration-gauck-attestiert-sarrazin-mut/3685052.html.
27 Ralph Giordano, "Wo Thilo Sarrazin recht hat," *Die Welt*, September 19, 2010, accessed July 10, 2023, https://www.welt.de/welt_print/debatte /article9733057/Wo-Thilo-Sarrazin-recht-hat.html. Volker ter Haseborg, "Wo Thilo Sarrazin recht hat," *Hamburger Abendblatt*, September 17, 2010, accessed July 7, 2023, https://www.abendblatt.de/hamburg /article107854160/Wo-Thilo-Sarrazin-recht-hat.html. Norbert Wallet, "Bosbach: Thilo Sarrazin hat recht," *Stuttgarter Nachrichten*, September 2, 2010, July 10, 2023, https://www.stuttgarter-nachrichten.de/inhalt.bosbach -thilo-sarrazin-hat-recht.b40a6051-90b1-4357-ad95-9250f395439e.html.
28 Bade, *Kritik und Gewalt*, 44.
29 Bade, *Kritik und Gewalt*, 91. Ulrich Zawatka-Gerlach, Sandra Dasslef, and Mariz Hubschmid, "Sarrazin stellt seine Weltsicht vor," *Der Tagesspiegel*, August 31, 2010, accessed March 5, 2023, https://www.tagesspiegel.de /berlin/pressekonferenz-sarrazin-stellt-seine-weltsicht-vor/1914788.html.
30 Many thanks to Reviewer 1 who helped clarify this point.
31 Bade, *Kritik und Gewalt*, 91. "Umstrittene Thesen zu Migration: Merkel entrüstet über Sarrazin," *Spiegel Online*, August 25, 2010, accessed March 5, 2023, https://www.spiegel.de/politik/deutschland/umstrittene-thesen-zu-migration-merkel-entruestet-ueber-sarrazin-a-713752.html; dpa, "Integrationspolitik: Kanzlerin empört über Sarrazins Polemik," *Die Zeit*, August 25, 2010, accessed March 5, 2023, https://www.zeit.de/politik /deutschland/2010-08/sarrazin-merkel.
32 Bade, *Kritik und Gewalt*, 14. Klaus Bade is a long-standing researcher of integration who has deep connections with the German government and has attempted to work together with policymakers for decades. His research is often critical of the mistakes made by government authorities who are either ignorant of or have not sufficiently understood

evidence-based research. Bade wrote a book about Kelek and Sarrazin that confirms many of the political ideologies represented in the public response to these figures. It is important to note that Bade's monograph about these political developments is sharply pointed and deeply emotional due to his own long political involvement in German integration debates. And yet, his narrative confirms many arguments against the integration rhetoric celebrities like Kelek and Sarrazin use.

33 Kimberlé Crenshaw, "Demarginalizing the Intersection of Race and Sex: A Black Feminist Critique of Antidiscrimination Doctrine, Feminist Theory and Antiracist Politics," *University of Chicago Legal Forum*, Article 8 (1989): 139–67.

34 As an example of how these debates are not specific to individuals, note the effects of Henryk Broder's Islamophobic, Sarrazin-like rhetoric on this Swiss pastor: Benjamin Rosch, and Jonas Hoskyn, "Denn sie weiss, was sie tut: Islamgegnerin neu im Basler Kirchenrat," *Aargauer Zeitung*, September 7, 2019, accessed July 8, 2023, https://www.aargauerzeitung.ch/schweiz/denn-sie-weiss-was-sie-tut-islamgegnerin-neu-im-basler-kirchenrat-135581135.

35 Meng, 116.

36 Schmale, "Der Tag des Provokateurs."

37 Mehrdad Payandeh, "Die Entscheidung des UN-Ausschusses gegen Rassendiskriminierung im Fall Sarrazin: Chancen und Grenzen des menschenrechtlichen Individualbeschwerdeverfahrens aus der Perspektive der deutschen Rechtsordnung," *Juristen Zeitung* 68, no. 20 (2013): 980–90.

38 Gideon Botsch, "'Es fehlte der Wille, sich deutlich abzugrenzen,'" interview by Hans Hermann Kotte, *Mediendienst Integration*, August 26, 2013 accessed March 5, 2023, Gideon Botsch, "Gutachten im Auftrag des SPD-Kreisverbandes Spandau und der SPD-Abteilung Alt-Pankow zur Frage: 'Sind die Äußerungen von Dr. Thilo Sarrazin im Interview mit der Zeitschrift Lettre International (deutsche Ausgabe, Heft 86) als rassistisch zu bewerten?'" Report. Berlin, December 22, 2009, accessed March 5, 2024, https://www.tagesschau.de/inland/gutachtensarrazin100.pdf.

39 Berg et al., "Politik der Vermeidung." Zawatka-Gerlach et al., "Sarrazin stellt seine Weltsicht vor." Richard Rother, "Nach Migranten-Kritik: Bundesbank entmachtet Sarrazin," *Die Tageszeitung*, October 13, 2009 accessed July 10, 2023, https://taz.de/!5154460/.

40 Robin Alexander, "'Acht Stunden Verwahrung,'" *Die Tageszeitung*, July 18, 2003, accessed March 5, 2024, https://taz.de/!739709/.

41 The German word *Leistungsfähigkeit* is difficult to translate into English. English speakers use different words in different contexts for this idea, whereas *Leistungsfähigkeit* has broad reach into multiple areas of German society. It can mean productivity, performance ability,

achievement potential, efficacy, or capacity. Germans use the term to describe schoolchildren's academic performance as well as the productivity of a particular industrial sector. Germans also talk of a *Leistungsgesellschaft*, which can denote both a meritocracy as well as an "achievement-oriented" society, i.e., a society based on competition. The underlying connotation of *Leistung* in political economy emphasizes efficient productivity and the ability of a society, in the service of capital, to harness such productivity from its workforce.

42 Heike Schmoll, "Bildung in Berlin: Sarrazin gab den Sparkommissar." *Frankfurter Allgemeine Zeitung*, September 13, 2010, accessed July 7, 2023. https://www.faz.net/1.1040135. Cited in Bade, *Kritik und Gewalt*, 43.

43 Schmoll, "Bildung in Berlin."

44 Schmoll, "Bildung in Berlin."

45 Schmoll, "Bildung in Berlin."; also cited in Bade, *Kritik und Gewalt*, 43.

46 Schmoll, "Bildung in Berlin."

47 Bade, *Kritik und Gewalt*, 44. Gilbert Schomaker, "Essen für 4,25 Euro: Sarrazin entwickelt Hartz-IV-Speiseplan," *Die Welt*, 8 February 8, 2008, accessed July 10, 2023, https://www.welt.de/politik/article1649762 /Sarrazin-entwickelt-Hartz-IV-Speiseplan.html. Antje Hildebrandt, "So gesund ist Sarrazins Hartz-IV-Diät," November 20, 2008, accessed July 10, 2023, https://www.morgenpost.de/vermischtes/article103236011 /So-gesund-ist-Sarrazins-Hartz-IV-Diaet.html, accessed July 10, 2023. Henning Onken, "Sarrazin: So sollten Arbeitslose einkaufen," *Der Tagesspiegel*, February 11, 2008, accessed July 10, 2023, https://www .tagesspiegel.de/berlin/landespolitik/hartz-iv-menue-sarrazin-so -sollten-arbeitslose-einkaufen/1164148.html.

48 jof/dpa/ddp/mim/hed, "Sarrazin empfiehlt zum Energiesparen warme Pullis," *Berliner Morgenpost*, 29 July 2008, accessed July 10, 2023, https://www .morgenpost.de/berlin/article102243278/Sarrazin-empfiehlt-zum -Energiesparen-warme-Pullis.html. "Soziale Kälte: Empörung über Sarrazins Pulli-Provokation," *Spiegel Online*, July 29, 2008, accessed July 10, 2023, https://www.spiegel.de/politik/deutschland/soziale-kaelte -empoerung-ueber-sarrazins-pulli-provokation-a-568833.html.

49 Cynthia Miller-Idriss, "The Rise of Fascist Fashion: Clothing Helps the Far Right Sell Their Violent Message," *Salon*, April 21, 2018, accessed July 8, 2023. https://www.salon.com/2018/04/21/the-rise-of-fascist-fashion -clothing-helps-the-far-right-sell-their-violent-message/. See also Cynthia Miller-Idriss, *The Extreme Gone Mainstream: Commercialization and Far Right Youth Culture in Germany* (Princeton: Princeton University Press, 2018).

50 Matthias Lohre, "'Wenn ich komisch bin, dann meist unfreiwillig,'" *Die Tageszeitung*, 4 March 2006, accessed July 10, 2023, https://taz .de/!466257/.

51 Kilb, "Sarrazins Buchvorstellung"; Zawatka-Gerlach et al., "Sarrazin stellt seine Weltsicht vor." A paragraph about Sarrazin in the *Spiegel Chronik* for 2009 picked up this sentiment and called Sarrazin a "Lästermaul" (literal translation: a compound word made of the words "tattle" or "slander" combined with "mouth" or "yap"; figurative translation – complainer, big mouth). "Sarrazins Schelte," *Spiegel Chronik*, December 9, 2009, accessed July 10, 2023, https://www.spiegel .de/politik/sarrazins-schelte-a-95ddd1fc-0002-0001-0000-000068105096.

52 See Christoph Butterwegge, "Standortnationalismus, Rechtsextremismus und Zuwanderung." *Widerspruch: Beiträge zu Sozialistischer Politik* 21, no. 41 (2001): 53–62, https://doi.org/10.5169/seals-652173 and Christoph Butterwegge, Rudolf Hickel, and Ralf Ptak, *Sozialstaat und Neoliberale Hegemonie: Standortnationalismus als Gefahr für die Demokratie.* (Berlin: Elefanten Press, 1998).

53 Tang, *Unsettled*, 77–94. mbe, "Alleinerziehende mit Mindestlohn verdienen weniger als Hartz-IV-Empfänger," *FOCUS Online*, December 12, 2018, accessed July 10, 2023, https://www.focus.de/finanzen/news /bundesregierung-ermittelt-selbst-in-vollzeit-alleinerziehen- de-mit-mindestlohn-verdienen-weniger-als-hartz-iv-empfaenger_id _10031493.html. AFP/KNA/jr, "Bundesregierung: Alleinerziehende mit Mindestlohn haben weniger Geld als Hartz IV," *Die Welt*, December 6, 2018 accessed July 10, 2023, https://www.welt.de/politik/deutschland /article185107758/Bundesregierung-Alleinerziehende-mit -Mindestlohn-haben-weniger-Geld-als-Hartz-IV.html.

54 Harvey, *A Brief History of Neoliberalism*, 82–4.

55 Harvey, *A Brief History of Neoliberalism*, 77.

56 Vandana Shiva, *Stolen Harvest: The Hijacking of the Global Food Supply* (University Press of Kentucky, 2016), 16–17.

57 Butterwegge, "Standortnationalismus," 53.

58 Ptak points out in his historical overview of the German welfare state (*Sozialstaat*) that the first efforts to provide social support emerged as part of a mercantilist, absolutist welfare state in which social welfare benefits were only available to those who were given workfare assignments in public institutions or were bound to proof of formal residency status. Ptak, "Verordnet – geduldet – erledigt? Zur Entwicklung des deutschen Sozial- staates im historischen Kontext," in *Sozialstaat und neoliberale Hegemonie: Standortnationalismus als Gefahr für die Demokratie*, eds. Christoph Butter- wege, Rudolf Hickel, and Ralf Ptak (Berlin: Elefanten Press, 1998), 19.

59 Christoph Butterwegge, "Die Demontage des Sozialstaates: Arme und Migrant/Innen im Visier von Guido Westerwelle, Thilo Sarrazin et al.," *Widerspruch: Beiträge zu sozialistischer Politik* 30, no. 59 (2010): 88, https:// doi.org/10.5169/seals-652446.

60 Butterwegge, "Demontage," 88.
61 Butterwegge, "Demontage," 87–8.
62 Butterwegge, "Demontage," 87.
63 ler/apn, "Hartz-IV-Debatte: Sarrazin attestiert Westerwelle geistige Armut," *Spiegel Online*, March 1, 2010, accessed July 7, 2023, https://www.spiegel.de/politik/deutschland/hartz-iv-debatte-sarrazin-attestiert-westerwelle-geistige-armut-a-680976.html. It's also important to note that Barbara John, who mercilessly criticized Sarrazin's book, also promoted the idea of workfare, arguing against providing welfare benefits for those between age 16 and 30. Her argument against providing welfare benefits for younger people was based on the argument that such provisions would foster dependency on the state, which sounds remarkably similar to Sarrazin's argument about how the state has lost sight of individual responsibility. jof/sh, "Sarrazin ist für mich ein verbaler Triebtäter," *Berliner Morgenpost*, March 21, 2010, accessed March 5, 2024, https://www.morgenpost.de/berlin-aktuell/article104049999/Sarrazin-ist-fuer-mich-ein-verbaler-Triebtaeter.html.
64 Butterwegge, "Standortnationalismus," 54. See Castles and Kosack for a prescient early analysis of this side effect of guest worker migration across Western Europe and Great Britain, as well as Hoffman-Nowotny for similar conclusions in a Swiss context. Stephen Castles and Godula Kosack, *Immigrant Workers and Class Structure in Western Europe* (London: Oxford University Press, 1973). Hans-Joachim Hoffmann-Nowotny, *Soziologie des Fremdarbeiterproblems* (Stuttgart: Enke, 1973).
65 Foucault, *Security, Territory, Population.*
66 In the forward to *Manifest der Vielen*, novelist Christoph Peters views the events similarly, remarking sardonically that instead of bringing in "knowledgeable, rigorous and reflective Muslims" into the conversation, "a sociologist of Turkish descent who was illiterate in Arabic and largely ignorant of the history of the Islamic humanities [*Geisteswissenschaften*] was paraded [*gejagt*] through the German talk shows as the key witness for the general backwardness and unconstitutionality of Islam." The sociologist referred to here can only be Kelek. Hilal Sezgin, ed., *Manifest der Vielen: Deutschland erfindet sich neu* (Berlin: Blumenbar, 2011), 8.
67 The syntax in German is just as idiosyncratic as my translation. "Statistisch gesehen wird Deutschland weniger technisch-wissenschaftliche Intelligenz produzieren." See the video of the talk: "Necla Kelek stellt Sarrazins Buch vor 2/2," YouTube, August 31, 2010, accessed July 7, 2023, https://www.youtube.com/watch?v=6ypBu9k4oGw&t=12s.
68 "Necla Kelek stellt Sarrazins Buch vor 2/2."
69 By 2019, the right wing had forced a discursive conflict about the meaning of the terms "concerned citizen" and what kind of rhetoric

counts as "civic" (*bürgerlich*). "Necla Kelek stellt Sarrazins Buch vor 2/2."
Schmale, "Der Tag des Provokateurs." See Malte Lehming, "Wenn ein
Schimpfwort zum Ehrbegriff wird," *Der Tagesspiegel*, September 3, 2019,
accessed July 10, 2023, https://www.tagesspiegel.de/politik/ist-die-afd
-buergerlich-wenn-ein-schimpfwort-zum-ehrbegriff-wird/24975010.html.
"AfD: Was bedeutet 'bürgerlich'?," *hr-Info Aktuell*, accessed November 8,
2019, https://podcasts.apple.com/us/podcast/afd-was-bedeutet-
b%C3%BCrgerlich/id1080275660?i=1000448440040. No longer available.
Jasper von Altenbockum, "AfD: unheimlich bürgerlich," *Frankfurter
Allgemeine Zeitung*, 12 September 2019, accessed July 10, 2023, https://
www.faz.net/1.6379477. Eric Gujer, "'Der andere Blick': Warum die AfD
keine bürgerliche Partei ist," *Neue Zürcher Zeitung*, September 13, 2019,
accessed July 10, 2023, https://www.nzz.ch/meinung/der-andere-blick
/die-afd-ist-keine-buergerliche-partei-aber-auch-cdu-und-spd-machen
-propaganda-ld.1508195, Nils Minkmar, "AfD nennt sich 'bürgerlich':
Das ist Bürgerbeleidigung," *Spiegel Online*, September 3, 2019, accessed
July 10, 2023, https://www.spiegel.de/kultur/gesellschaft
/afd-nennt-sich-buergerlich-das-ist-buergerbeleidigung-debattenbeitrag
-a-1285112.html.
70 "Necla Kelek stellt Sarrazins Buch vor 2/2."
71 El-Tayeb, *European Others*, xx.
72 El Tayeb, *European Others*, xv.
73 Gordon 1997, xvi, cited in El-Tayeb, *European Others,* xix.
74 "Rechthaber oder Rechtsausleger – Deutschland streitet über Sarrazin."
    Hart aber Fair, News, Talk-Show, 2010. Cited in Meng, FN 53.
75 Schuster-Craig, "Resisting Integration."
76 "8. Spieglein, Spieglein an der Wand, wer ist der Integrierteste im ganzen
    Land?," YouTube, accessed July 7, 2023, https://www.youtube.com
    /watch?v=ad04Dnvk2Nk&list=PLAE43F26246ED6586.
77 "WERKSTATT DER KULTUREN - Diskussion," YouTube, 2010,
    accessed July 7, 2023, https://www.youtube.com/channel
    /UC2GFAmAfvDnnXX-GldoGBAw.
78 Naika Foroutan, *Die postmigrantische Gesellschaft: Ein Versprechen der
    pluralen Demokratie*. (Bielefeld: transcript Verlag, 2019).
79 Ijoma Mangold, "'Manifest der Vielen': Seht ihr uns?," *Die Zeit*,
    March 3, 2011, accessed March 5, 2023, https://www.zeit.de/2011/10
    /Manifest-gegen-Sarrazin.
80 Klaus J. Bade and Wolfgang Schäuble, eds., *Nachholende Integrationspolitik
    und Gestaltungsperspektiven der Integrationspraxis*, (Göttingen: V & R
    Unipress, 2007).
81 Sachverständigenrat deutscher Stiftungen für Integration und Migration
    (SVR), *Einwanderungsgesellschaft 2010: Jahresgutachten 2010 mit Integra-
    tionsbarometer* (Berlin: SVR, 2010).

82 Susanne Memarnia, "Nachfolger der 'Werkstatt der Kulturen': Der misslungene Neustart," *Die Tagezeitung,* March 13, 2020, accessed July 14, 2023, https://taz.de/!5667538/.

83 SZ.de/dpa/jobr, "Sarrazin wird aus der SPD ausgeschlossen," *Süddeutsche Zeitung,* July 31, 2020, accessed July 7, 2023, https://www .sueddeutsche.de/politik/sarrazin-ausschluss-spd-1.4985099. "Oberstes SPD-Gericht bestätigt Parteiausschluss Sarrazins," *tagesschau.de,* July 31, 2020, https://www.tagesschau.de/inland/spd -sarrazin-ausschluss-105.html.

4 Integration and Ethnic Similarities

1 Wolfgang Schulz, "Deutsche Künstlerinnen und Künstler aus dem Osten: Bewahrung der kulturellen Traditionen in der Bundesrepublik Deutschland als Elemente einer frühen Verständigung mit den Nachbarn," in *Die Bundesrepublik Deutschland und die Vertriebenen: Fünfzig Jahre Eingliederung, Aufbau und Verständigung mit den Staaten des Östlichen Europa,* eds. Christof Dahm and Hans-Jakob Tebarth (Bonn: die Kulturstiftung der deutschen Vertriebenen, 2000), 68.

2 Consider as well that in addition to 12.5 million expellees, another 10–12 million displaced persons with upwards of 20 nationalities who spoke 35 different languages were on the move. This does not include other categories of people migrating across Europe at that time, including returning soldiers, former forced workers for the Nazis, and evacuees moved out of German cities to escape bombing. See Klaus J. Bade and Jochen Oltmer, "Mitteleuropa: Deutschland," in *Enzyklopädie Migration in Europa: vom 17. Jahrhundert bis zur Gegenwart,* eds. Klaus J. Bade et al. (Paderborn: Schöningh Verlag, 2007), 157.

3 Adam R. Seipp, *Strangers in the Wild Place: Refugees, Americans, and a German Town, 1945-1952* (Bloomington: Indiana University press, 2013), 119.

4 None, "200,000 Flüchtlinge kommen nach Mainfranken," *Main-Post,* December 29, 1945. Cited in Seipp, *Strangers,* 119.

5 Michael Schwartz, "Vertriebene im doppelten Deutschland: Integrations- und Erinnerungspolitik in der DDR und in der Bundesrepublik," *Vierteljahrshefte für Zeitgeschichte* 1 (2008): 104.

6 Schwartz, "Vertriebene," 101.

7 Schwartz, "Vertriebene," 102.

8 Schwartz, "Vertriebene," 117; Ute Schmidt, "Vom Flüchtling zum 'Neubürger': Die Vertriebenen in der SBZ und in der DDR vor dem Hintergrund 'verordneter' Verständigung mit dem Osten," in *Die Bundesrepublik Deutschland und die Vertriebenen: Fünfzig Jahre Eingliederung, Aufbau und Verständigung mit den Staaten des Östlichen Europa,* eds. Christof Dahm and Hans-Jakob Tebarth (Bonn: die Kulturstiftung der deutschen Vertriebenen, 2000), 76–8.

9 Schwartz, "Vertriebene," 105.

10 Schmidt, "Vom Flüchtling zum Neubürger," 76.

11 Klaus Bade, *Migration in European History*, trans. Allison Brown (Malden, MA: Blackwell Publishing, 2003), 214.

12 Bade, *European History*, 213–14; Betty Barton, "The Problem of 12 Million German Refugees in Today's Germany" (Philadelphia: American Friends Service Committee, May 1949), 6–7.

13 Barton, "The Problem," 6–9.

14 Warsaw Press Agency, *Transfer of the German Population from Poland: Legend and Reality* (Warsaw: Western Press Agency, 1966). R.M. Douglas, *Orderly and Humane: The Expulsion of the Germans after the Second World War* (New Haven, CT: Yale University Press, 2012).

15 Douglas, *Orderly and Humane*, 28, 73, 86. Alfred M. de Zayas,. *Nemesis at Potsdam: The Anglo-Americans and the Expulsion of the Germans: Background, Execution, Consequences.* (London: Routledge, 1977), 81–2.

16 Douglas *Orderly and Humane*, 73.

17 Douglas *Orderly and Humane*, 84–5.

18 Matthew Frank, *Expelling the Germans: British Opinion and Post-1945 Population Transfer in Context* (Oxford: Oxford University Press, 2007), 75, 81–2, 116–18.

19 Douglas *Orderly and Humane*, 82.

20 Douglas *Orderly and Humane*, 82.

21 Rita Chin and Heidi Fehrenbach, "Introduction: What's Race Got to Do with It? Postwar German History in Context," in *After the Nazi Racial State: Difference and Democracy in Germany and Europe* (Ann Arbor: University of Michigan Press, 2010), 26.

22 Barbara Dietz, "Aussiedler in Germany: From Smooth Adaptation to Tough Integration," in *Paths of Integration: Migrants in Western Europe (1880–2004)*, eds. Leo Lucassen, David Feldman, and Jochen Oltmer (Amsterdam: Amsterdam University Press, 2006), 118.

23 Bade, *Migration in European History*, 204–5.

24 "Refugee Crisis in Europe: Aid, Statistics, and Relief Efforts," *USA for UNHCR: The UN Refugee Agency*, 2018, accessed July 7, 2023, https://www.unrefugees.org/emergencies/refugee-crisis-in-europe/.

25 *The Savage Peace*, directed by Peter Molloy, (2015; London, BBC Two), Netflix. Peter Molloy, *The Savage Peace*. Documentary, History. BBC Two, Netflix, 2015. Schwartz, "Vertriebene," 102.

26 Bernd Ulrich, "Flüchtlinge: Naivität des Bösen" *Die Zeit* (41), October 8, 2015, accessed July 7, 2023, https://www.zeit.de/2015/41/fluechtlinge-krise-deutschland-zaun-angela-merkel.

27 Barton, "The Problem," 16.

28 Ulrich Herbert, *A History of Foreign Labor, in Germany, 1880–1980: Seasonal Workers, Force Labourers, Guest Workers*, trans. William Templer (Ann Arbor: University of Michigan Press, 1990), 196.

29 Schmidt, "Vom Flüchtling zum Neubürger," 75.

30 Franz J. Bauer, "Aufnahme und Eingliederung der Flüchtlinge und Vertriebenen: Das Beispiel Bayern 1945–1950," in *Die Vertreibung der Deutschen aus den Osten: Ursachen, Ereignisse, Folgen*, ed. Wolfgang Benz (Frankfurt am Main: Fischer Verlag, 1985), 165.

31 Falk Wiesemann, "Fluchtlingspolitik in Nordrhein-Westfalen," in *Die Vertreibung der Deutschen aus den Osten: Ursachen, Ereignisse, Folgen*, ed. Wolfgang Benz, (Frankfurt am Main: Fischer Verlag, 1985), 173. Lüttinger, *Integration der Vertriebenen,* 14 Helmut Neubach: "Heimatvertriebene in den politischen Parteien", in Die Bundesrepublik Deutschland und die Vertriebenen: Fünfzig Jahre Eingliederung, Aufbau und Verständigung mit den Staaten des östlichen Europa, eds. Christof Dahm and Hans-Jakob Tebarth (Bonn: Kulturstiftung der deutschen Vertriebenene, 2000), 37.

32 Seipp, Strangers, 9.

33 A. Grosser, *Geschichte Deutschlands seit 1945: Eine Bilanz* (Munich: dtv, 1982), 273. Cited in Paul Lüttinger, "Der Mythos der schnellen Integration: eine empirische Untersuchung zur Integration der Vertriebenen und Flüchtlinge in der Bundesrepublik Deutschland bis 1971," *Zeitschrift für Soziologie* 15, no. 1 (02/01/1986): 20, https://doi.org/10.1515/zfsoz-1986-0102.

34 Herbert, *A History of Foreign Labor*, 193.

35 Herbert, *A History of Foreign Labor*, 193.

36 "Das Kinderelend der Ausgewiesenen," *Süddeutsche Zeitung*, March 15, 1946, 3.

37 Uta Gerhardt and Birgitta Hohenester, "Beruf und Kultur: Zum gesellschaftstheoretischen Verständnis der Integration von Vertriebenen/Flüchtlingen in Westdeutschland nach 1945," *Soziale Welt* 48, no. 3 (1997): 262.

38 Gerhardt and Hohenester, "Beruf und Kultur," 261.

39 W. Maschner, "Die Vorhut einer Million," *Süddeutsche Zeitung*, December 21, 1945, 4.

40 France, "Flüchtlingszentrale Hof," *Süddeutsche Zeitung*, February 1, 1946, 4.

41 Falk Wiesemann, "Flüchtlingspolitik," 179.

42 Wiesemann, "Flüchtlingspolitik," 179.

43 Hans-Werner Retterath, "Vom Barackenlager zum Übergangswohnheim: Volkskundliche Anmerkungen zur Aufnahme von Vertriebenen im Freiburger Stattteil Bischofslinde," in *Flucht und Vertreibung: 50 Jahre danach*, ed. Gottfried Habenicht (Freiburg: Johannes-Künzig-Institut für ostdeutsche Volkskunde, 1996), 82. Herbert also argues that it was already clear in 1948 that "there was simply no practicable alternative to their permanent and complete integration" (*A History of Foreign Labor*, 200).

44 Bauer, "Aufnahme und Eingliederung," 160.

45 Schwartz, "Vertriebene," 104–5. The Soviets also prevented expellees from even being mentioned in any government statistics or reports after 1949, an

act of data suppression which both prevented debate and political organizing, and which also created great difficulties for conducting research about this group later on. See Schmidt, "Vom Flüchtling zum Neubürger," 77.

46 Hermann Weiss, "Die Organisationen der Vertriebenen und Ihre Presse," in *Die Vertreibung der Deutschen aus dem Osten* (Frankfurt am Main: Fischer Verlag, 1985), 193–7.

47 Yuliya Komska, *The Icon Curtain: The Cold War's Quiet Border* (Chicago: University of Chicago Press, 2015), 18–19.

48 Schwartz, "Vertriebene," 124.

49 Gerhardt and Hohenester, "Beruf und Kultur," 263.

50 Frank, *Expelling the Germans*, 275–6.

51 Gerhardt and Hohenester, "Beruf und Kultur," 261.

52 Gerhardt and Hohenester, "Beruf und Kultur," 265. Contemporary integration policies for refugees and immigrants in Germany use the same logic as the American Military in 1946: the Integration Law of 2016 was also purportedly crafted to prevent the construction of refugee "ghettos." "Integrationsgesetz: Thomas de Maizière und Andrea Nahles geben Pressekonferenz am 25.05.16," Filmed May 2016. YouTube, accessed June 15, 2023. Posted May 25, 2016, https://www.youtube.com/watch?v=Lt_3SrCXTH8.

53 OMGUS RG 260, 12/63-1/7, Letter from June 22, 1946 by William W. Dawson, Governor of the Württemberg-Baden Military Government (OMGWB) to Minister President Dr. Reinhold Maier, State Ministry of Stuttgart, "Plan for German Expellees and Refguees" cited in Gerhardt and Hohenester, "Beruf und Kultur," 265.

54 Seipp, Strangers, 181–222.

55 Christoph Buchheim, "Die Währungsreform 1948 in Westdeutschland," *Vierteljahrshefte für Zeitgeschichte* 36, no. 2 (1988): 228. See also Wiesemann, "Flüchtlingspolitik," 181.

56 Buchheim, "Währungsreform," 228.

57 "Occupation and the Emergence of Two States (1945–1961): Currency Reform (June 20, 1948)," German History in Documents and Images (GHDI), *German Historical Institute*, accessed July 10, 2023. http://germanhistorydocs.ghidc.org/sub_image.cfm?image_id=1018.

58 Buchheim, "Währungsreform," 222.

59 Rolf Messerschmidt, "Vertriebene und Flüchtlinge in der unmittelbaren Nachkriegszeit. Erkenntnisse der jüngeren Zeitgeschichtsforschung," in *Die Bundesrepublik Deutschland und die Vertriebenen: Fünfzig Jahre Eingliederung, Aufbau und Verständigung mit den Staaten des Östlichen Europa*, eds. Christof Dahm and Hans-Jakob Tebarth (Bonn: die Kulturstiftung der deutschen Vertriebenen, 2000), 27–8.

60 Wiesemann, "Flüchtlingspolitik," 181.

61 Reinhold Schillinger, "Der Lastenausgleich," in *Die Vertreibung der Deutschen aus den Osten*, ed. Wolfgang Benz (Frankfurt am Main: Fischer Verlag, 1985), 184.
62 Schillinger, "Lastenausgleich," 184.
63 Lüttinger and Rossmann, *Integration der Vertriebenen*, 166. Schillinger, "Lastenausgleich," 184–5.
64 "Präambel LAG – Einzelnorm," *Gesetze im Internet*, accessed July 10, 2023, https://www.gesetze-im-internet.de/lag/pr_ambel.html.
65 Schillinger, "Lastenausgleich," 189.
66 Schillinger, "Lastenausgleich," 189.
67 Schillinger, "Lastenausgleich," 190–1. Ute Schmidt also notes that most expellees recouped about 22% of their property losses – a fairly modest percentage ("Vom Flüchtling zum Neubürger," 93).
68 Schillinger, "Lastenausgleich," 185.
69 The term persisted into the mid-1960s when it was occasionally still used in the context of foreign worker migration. The Latin term, *Integration*, eventually became the preferred form after the rapid uptick of sociological studies about migration commissioned in the 1970s. *Eingliederung* is still used by the government in the context of (re)incorporating workers who have been injured or sick into the workplace.
70 Gerhardt and Hohenester, "Beruf und Kultur," 265.
71 Gerhardt and Hohenester, "Beruf und Kultur," 266.
72 Seipp, *Strangers*, 198–99. Bauer, "Aufnahme und Eingliederung," 172.
73 Herbert, *A History of Foreign Labor*, 195.
74 Seipp, *Strangers*, 202.
75 Triadafilos Triadafilopoulos and Karen Schönwälder, "Became an Immigration Country," 5.
76 Ingo Von Münch, *Die deutsche Staatsangehörigkeit: Vergangenheit – Gegenwart – Zukunft* (Berlin: Walter de Gruyter, 2011), 90.
77 Von Münch, Staatsangehörigkeit, 90–1.
78 Von Münch, Staatsangehörigkeit, 78.
79 Gerhardt and Hohenester, "Beruf und Kultur," 263.
80 Messerschmidt, "Vertriebene und Flüchtlinge," 10.
81 Messerschmidt, "Vertriebene und Flüchtlinge," 12–13. See also Schwartz, "Vertriebene."
82 Lüttinger, and Rossman, *Integration der Vertriebenen*, 77–230.
83 Herbert, *A History of Foreign Labor*, 195.
84 Lüttinger, "Der Mythos der schnellen Integration."
85 Richard D. Alba and Victor Nee, *Remaking the American Mainstream: Assimilation and Contemporary Immigration* (Cambridge, MA: Harvard University Press, 2005). Leo Lucassen and Charlotte Laarman, "Immigration, Intermarriage and the Changing Face of Europe in the Post War Period," *The History of the Family* 14, no. 1 (2009): 54.

86 Jenny Lindner, "Jeder Zweite in Deutschland mit Migrationshintergr-
und?," *Mediendienst Integration*, January 7, 2015, accessed July 7, 2023,
https://mediendienst-integration.de/artikel/kermani-rede-jeder-zweite
-hat-migrationshintergrund.html.

5 Constructing the Integrative Apparatus

1 Marcel Berlinghoff, "Geschichte der Migration in Deutschland,"
Bundeszentrale für politische Bildung, May 14, 2018, accessed July 7,
2023, http://www.bpb.de/gesellschaft
/migration/dossier-migration/252241/deutsche-migrationsgeschichte.
2 I will use the words guest worker and foreign worker interchangeably for
ausländische Arbeitnehmer in this book. Neither term is preferable – both
are considered in various contexts to be offensive. "Foreign Worker
/Employee" is the literal translation of *ausländische Arbeiter/Arbeitnehmer*,
but it restricts the frame of reference to the workplace and sounds much
like the Nazi-era *Fremdarbeiter* when translated into English.
3 Triadafilopoulos and Schönwälder, "How the Federal Republic Became
an Immigration Country," 4.
4 Hunn, *"Nächstes Jahr kehren wir zurück,"* 59. See also Yilmaz Özkan,
"Stabilisierungsfaktor oder revolutionäres Potential? Politische Sozialisation
der Gastarbeiter" (PhD diss., Free University of Berlin, 1975), 214.
5 Herbert, *A History of Foreign Labor,* 201.
6 Herbert, *A History of Foreign Labor,* 201.
7 Barbara John, "Ausländerpolitik für Inländer – Zur konzeptionellen
Weiterentwicklung der Integrationspolitik," *Zeitschrift für Ausländerrecht
und Ausländerpolitik* 1 (1985): 3.
8 Karen Schönwälder, *Einwanderung und ethnische Pluralität: politische
Entscheidungen und öffentliche Debatten in Grossbritannien und der Bundesrepublik
von den 1950er bis zu den 1970er Jahren* (Essen: Klartext, 2001), 366.
9 Schönwälder, *Einwanderung,* 12.
10 Great Britain had postcolonial migration as well as voluntary labour
migration. Stephen Castles, "The Guest-Worker in Western Europe – An
Obituary – Stephen Castles, 1986," *International Migration Review* 20, no. 4
(1986), https://doi.org/10.1177/019791838602000402.
11 Schönwälder, *Einwanderung,* 13.
12 Herbert, *A History of Foreign Labor,* 232–3. Schönwälder, *Einwanderung,*
157–366.
13 Ray C. Rist, "Migration and Marginality: Guestworkers in Germany and
France," *Daedalus* 108, no. 2 (1979): 103.
14 Ray C. Rist, *Guestworkers in Germany: The Prospects for Pluralism* (New
York: Praeger, 1978), 42–7.

15 See also Herbert, *A History of Foreign Labor,* 207; Rist, *Guestworkers in Germany,* 10.

16 Herbert, *A History of Foreign Labor,* 209.

17 Rist, *Guestworkers in Germany,* 111; Bade, *Migration in European History,* 229.

18 Chin, *Guest Worker Question,* 41–52, Schönwälder, *Einwanderung,* 157–364. Woesthoff's primary data set for her dissertation is a comparative journalistic analysis. See Julia Woesthoff, "Ambiguities of Antiracism: Representations of Foreign Laborers and the West German Media, 1955–1990" (Dissertation, Michigan State University, 2004). See also Deniz Göktürk, Anton Kaes, and David Gramling, eds., Germany in Transit: Nation and Migration 1955–2005, (Berkeley: University of California Press, 2007).

19 Schönwälder, *Einwanderung,* 161–2.

20 Schönwälder, *Einwanderung,* 202, 230, 238, 245.

21 Woesthoff, "Ambiguities of Antiracism," 28–127. See Chin, "Gender and Incommensurable Cultural Difference," *Guest Worker Question,* 141–90, Ewing, Weber, *Stolen Honor,* and "'We Must Talk about Cologne': Race, Gender, and Reconfigurations of 'Europe,'" *German Politics and Society* 34, no. 4 (2016): 68–86, https://doi.org/10.3167/gps.2016.340405.

22 Bade, *Migration in European History,* 230.

23 Herbert, *A History of Foreign Labor,* 217.

24 Miller, *Turkish Guest Workers,* 7.

25 See Rist, *Guestworkers in Germany,* 179–80, for an example of similar nostalgia likely motivated the return to the tripartite schooling system (and that was unable to adapt to the needs of guest workers' children). See also Miller, *Turkish Guest Workers,* 7.

26 Schönwälder, *Einwanderung,* 187–96, Woesthoff, "Ambiguities of Antiracism," 47–55.

27 Mark E. Spicka, "Cultural Centres and Guest Worker Integration in Stuttgart, Germany, 1960–1976," *Immigrants & Minorities* 33, no. 2 (2015) 122, https://doi.org/10.1080/02619288.2014.904639.

28 Jésus Manuel Delgado, *Die Gastarbeiter in der Presse: eine inhaltsanalytische Studie* (Opladen: Leske Verlag, 1972), cited in Schönwälder, *Einwanderung,* 187 and Ulrike Irrgang, "Beyond Sarrazin? Zur Darstellung von Migration in deutschen Medien am Beispiel der Berichterstattung in SPIEGEL und BILD," *Global Media Journal: German Edition* 1, no. 2 (2011), https://www.globalmediajournal.de/index.php/gmj/article/view/127.

29 Schönwälder, *Einwanderung,* 222. Seipp, *Strangers,* 120, 229–30.

30 Woesthoff, "Ambiguities of Anti-Racism," 44–6.

31 Woesthoff, "Ambiguities of Anti-Racism," 55.

32 Schönwälder, *Einwanderung,* 188.

33 These tropes are not new. See Ewing, *Stolen Honor* and Weber, "Cologne."

34 Woesthoff, "Ambiguities of Anti-Racism," 56.
35 Gottfried E. Voelker, "More Foreign Workers – Germany's Labor Problem No. 1?," in *Turkish Workers in Europe 1960–1975: 1960–1975 a Socio-Economic Reappraisal*, ed. Nermin Abadan-Unat (Leiden: Brill, 1976), 332–3.
36 Gokçe Yurdakul, *From Guest Workers into Muslims: The Transformation of Turkish Immigrant Associations in Germany* (Newcastle upon Tyne: Cambridge Scholars Publishing, 2009).
37 Schönwälder, *Einwanderung*, 191.
38 Schönwälder, *Einwanderung*, 191.
39 Schönwälder, *Einwanderung*, 192.
40 Schönwälder, *Einwanderung*, 192.
41 Karen Schönwälder, "Why Germany's Guestworkers Were Largely Europeans: The Selective Principles of Post-War Labour Recruitment Policy," *Ethnic and Racial Studies* 27, no. 2 (March 2004): 249, https://doi .org/10.1080/0141987042000177324.
42 Schönwälder, "Why Germany's Guestworkers Were Largely Europeans," 250. The same anecdote appears in Schönwälder, *Einwanderung*, 269.
43 Schönwälder, *Einwanderung*, 218.
44 Schönwälder, *Einwanderung*, 218. *Verordnung über ausländische Arbeitnehmer vom 23. Januar 1933*, Juridical document, *Deutsch: Scan aus dem Deutschen Reichsgesetzblatt 1933, Teil 1*, accessed October 23, 2019, https://commons.wikimedia.org/wiki/File:Deutsches _Reichsgesetzblatt_33T1_005_0026.jpg.
45 Schönwälder, *Einwanderung*, 218.
46 Schönwälder, *Einwanderung*, 220.
47 Schönwälder, *Einwanderung*, 222.
48 Schönwälder, *Einwanderung*, 219.
49 BT 151. Sitzung/3. WP, 21.6.1956, S. 8075, cited in Schönwälder, *Einwanderung*, 223, see FN 256. The digitized archive starts in the 4th Electoral period.
50 Schönwälder, *Einwanderung*, 224.
51 Schönwälder, *Einwanderung*, 224.
52 Schönwälder, *Einwanderung*, 224.
53 Schönwälder, *Einwanderung*, 223–4.
54 Schönwälder, *Einwanderung*, 230.
55 Schönwälder, *Einwanderung*, 231.
56 Schönwälder, *Einwanderung*, 231.
57 Schönwälder, *Einwanderung*, 231–2.
58 Schönwälder, *Einwanderung*, 232, FN291.
59 Schönwälder, *Einwanderung*, 222–7.
60 Schönwälder, *Einwanderung*, 231, 233–4.
61 Schönwälder, *Einwanderung*, 234.

62 Cited in Schönwälder, *Einwanderung*, 234 from *Ausländer in der Bundesrepublik Deutschland*, 1190.

63 Schönwälder, *Einwanderung*, 238.

64 Schönwälder, *Einwanderung*, 239.

65 Bundesrepublik Deutschland, Bundesministerium der Justiz, Bundesamt der Justiz, Bundesgesetzblatt Teil 1, Z1997a, May 8, 1965, Paragraph 6, 345.

66 Fritz Franz, "Kritik am Ausländergesetz von 1965," *Jahrbuch für internationales Recht* 15, no. 1 (1971): 330.

67 Franz, "Kritik," 331.

68 Franz, "Kritik," 332.

69 Franz, "Kritik," 332.

70 Herbert, *A History of Foreign Labor*, 214–15.

71 Frantz, "Kritik," 334.

72 Woesthoff, "Ambiguities of Anti-Racism," 37.

73 Miller, *Turkish Guest Workers*, 79, 82.

74 Miller, *Turkish Guest Workers*, 79.

75 Miller, *Turkish Guest Workers*, 80.

76 Lauren K. Stokes, "'Fear of the Family': Migration and Integration in West Germany, 1955–2000" (PhD diss., University of Chicago, 2016), 115.

77 Miller, *Turkish Guest Workers*, 103, Rist, *Guestworkers in Germany*, 80, 87, 151, 174, Schönwälder, *Einwanderung*, 286, Stokes, "Fear of the Family," 114.

78 Schönwälder, *Einwanderung*, 293.

79 Herbert, *A History of Foreign Labor*, 238.

80 Antidiskriminierungstelle des Bundes, Allgemeines Gleichbehandlungsgesetz (AGG), Bundesgesetzblatt I, 2006, adapted 2022, *Antidiskriminierungstelle des Bundes*, accessed July 14, 2023, https://www.antidiskriminierungsstelle.de/SharedDocs/downloads/DE/publikationen/AGG/agg_gleichbehandlungsgesetz.pdf

81 Schönwälder, *Einwanderung*, 162, 286, 314–23.

82 Wolf-Dietrich Bukow et al., eds. *Was heißt hier Parallelgesellschaft?:Zum Umgang mit Differenzen* (Heidelberg: Verlag für Sozialwissenschaften, 2007) 12, 60–1.

83 Gerhardt and Hohenester, "Beruf und Kultur," 265; Rist, *Guestworkers in Germany*, 116; Stokes, "Fear of the Family," 112.

84 Udo Gößwald and Kerstin Schmiedeknecht, eds. *Wie zusammen Leben: Perspektiven aus Nord-Neukölln*. (Berlin: Museum Neukölln, 2009), 17.

85 Gößwald and Schmiedeknecht, *Wie zusammen Leben*, 5.

86 Stokes, "Fear of the Family," 146.

87 Stokes, "Fear of the Family," 130–1.

88 Stokes, "Fear of the Family," 127.

89 Finding a formal English translation for this department has not been possible: "Referat zur Koordinierung aller Maßnahmen zur

Eingliederung ausländischer Arbeitnehmer in die Wirtschaft und
Gesellschaft der BRD." Schönwälder, *Einwanderung*, 305.

90 Foucault, *Security*, 100–1.

91 Foucault, *Security*, 101.

92 Chin, *Guest Worker Question*, 60–1, Schönwälder, *Einwanderung und
Pluralität*, 184–5, Woesthoff, "Ambiguities of Anti-Racism," 90–3.

93 John David Nagle, *The National Democratic Party: Right Radicalism in the
Federal Republic of Germany* (Berkeley: University of California Press,
1970), 41, 44, 46–7. Chin, *Guest Worker Question*, 60.

94 Nagle, *The National Democratic Party*, 88–9, Fred H. Richards, *Die NPD:
Alternative oder Weiderkehr?* (Munich: Olzog, 1967), 49–50.

95 Nagle, *The National Democratic Party*, 4, 15, 34–5. El-Tayeb, *European Others*,
xxi–xxix. Susan Arndt, "Weißsein. Die verkannte Strukturkategorie Europas und Deutschlands," in *Mythen, Masken und Subjekte: kritische Weissseinsforschung in Deutschland* (Münster: Unrast, 2005), 24–8; Peggy Piesche,
"Der 'Fortschritt' der Aufklärung," in *Mythen, Masken und Subjekte: kritische
Weissseinsforschung in Deutschland* (Münster: Unrast, 2005), 30-9.

96 The three *Lizenzparteien* (SPD, CDU/CSU, and FDP) were permitted to
organize. The Communist Party had been permitted by the occupiers as a
fourth party before being banned in the Federal Republic in 1956.
Nagle, *The National Democratic Party*, 16.

97 Nagle, *The National Democratic Party*, 49.

98 Nagle, *The National Democratic Party*, 42, Werner Smoydzin, *NPD:
Die Geschichte und Umwelt einer Partei* (Pfaffenhofen A.D. ILM: Ilmgau
Verlag, 1967), 133–4. Neubach, "Heimatvertriebene," 42.

99 Neubach, "Heimatvertriebene," 42, 54; Nagle, *The National Democratic
Party*, 24.

100 Smoydzin, *NPD*, 13, Nagle, *The National Democratic Party*, 25–33,
Richards, *Die NPD*, 41.

101 Nagle, *The National Democratic Party*, 9, 42–9, 62–8. Stuart Drummond,
"West Germany: Land Elections, the NPD, and the Grand Coalition,"
World Today, 1 September 1967. 385–95.

102 Nagle *The National Democratic Party*, 34–5.

103 Smoydzin, *NPD*, 180. Smoydzin argues that the lack of a formal program
doesn't mean the NPD lacked ideology. Nagle argues that nothing would
have prohibited the NPD from turning their basic propaganda into a program. Nagle, *The National Democratic Party*, 69.

104 Nagel, *The National Democratic Party*, 70, Schönwälder, *Einwanderung*, 184.

105 Richards, *Die NPD*, 100–6.

106 Nagle, *The National Democratic Party*, 88.

107 *Spätaussiedler* from the Soviet Union are an exception to this rule, but
many at that point were no longer familiar with the German language,
even if their political sympathies were right wing.

108 Neubach , "Heimatvertriebene," 38.
109 Nagle, *The National Democratic Party*, 66.
110 "Wahlergebnisse – Bundestag (Bundestagswahl)," accessed October 14, 2019, http://www.wahlrecht.de/ergebnisse/bundestag.html.

6 How the Integrative Apparatus Expands

1 Chin, *The Guestworker Question*, 93–4; Hunn, *"Nächstes Jahr kehren wir zurück,"* 343. Schönwälder, *Einwanderung*, 496. These questions were already being discussed more than a year before the ban: Der Bundesminister für Arbeit und Sozialordnung, "Politik der Bundesregierung gegenüber den ausländischen Arbeitnehmern in der Bundesrepublik Deutschland," Drucksache 6/3085, 6. WP, January 31, 1972.
2 Stokes, "'Fear of the Family'" Hunn, *"Nächstes Jahr kehren wir zurück"*: 210–11.
3 Hunn, *"Nächstes Jahr kehren wir zurück,"* 451–77.
4 Göktürk, Gramling and Kaes, *Germany in Transit*, 499. Schönwälder, *Einwanderung*, 505–7.
5 Bade, "Versäumte Integrationschancen." Rist, "Migration and Marginality," 95–108; and Schönwälder, *Einwanderung*.
6 Deutscher Bundestag, "Rede von Bundestagspräsidentin Bärbel Bas zum Tag der Deutschen Einheit 2022," October 2022, accessed March 6, 2024, https://www.bundestag.de/parlament/praesidium/reden/2022/20221003-912680.
7 Castles and Kosack, *Immigrant Workers*. Schiffauer, *Die Gewalt der Ehre*.
8 Karen Schönwälder, "The Difficult Task of Managing Migration: The 1973 Recruitment Stop," in *German History from the Margins*, eds. Neil Gregor, Nils Roemer, and Mark Roseman, (Bloomington, IN: Indiana University Press, 2006), 252–67. Schönwälder, *Einwanderung*, 496–515, 612–26; Hunn, *"Nächstes Jahr kehren wir zurück,"* 371–99.
9 Schönwälder, "The Difficult Task," 252–4; Schönwälder, *Einwanderung*, 500; Hunn, *"Nächstes Jahr kehren wir zurück,"* 278.
10 Schönwälder, "The Difficult Task," 253.
11 Schönwälder, "The Difficult Task," 253–5; Schönwälder, *Einwanderung*, 595–601; Ulrich Herbert and Karin Hunn, "Guest Workers and Policy on Guest Workers in the Federal Republic: From the Beginning of Recruitment in 1955 until Its Halt in 1973," in *The Miracle Years: A Cultural History of West Germany, 1949–1968*, ed. Hanna Schissler (Princeton: Princeton University Press, 2001), 210. Hunn, *"Nächstes Jahr kehren wir zurück,"* 328–38; Rist, "Migration and Marginality 95–108. Philipp Gassert, *Bewegte Gesellschaft: Deutsche Protestgeschichte seit 1945* (Stuttgart: W. Kohlhammer GmbH, 2018), 9.
12 Schönwälder, "The Difficult Task," 252.

13 Schönwälder, "The Difficult Task," 252–67; *Einwanderung*, 595–601. Miller, *Turkish Guest Workers*, 163–7, Rita Chin, *The Crisis of Multiculturalism in Europe: A History* (Princeton: Princeton UP, 2017). 75–9, Patrice Poutrus, *Umkämpftes Asyl: Vom Nachkriegsdeutschland is in die Gegenwart* (Berlin: Ch. Links Verlag, 2019), 63–4.
14 Schönwälder, "The Difficult Task," 256–9.
15 Woesthoff, "Ambiguities of Antiracism," 60–4.
16 Schönwälder, "The Difficult Task," 261.
17 Schönwälder, "The Difficult Task," 262.
18 Schönwälder, *Einwanderung*, 505–6; Herbert and Hunn, "Guest Workers and Policy" 201.
19 Schönwälder, *Einwanderung*, 507, Hunn, *"Nächstes Jahr kehren wir zurück,"* 278.
20 Herbert and Hunn, "Guest Workers and Policy," 204.
21 Schönwälder, "The Difficult Task," 259.
22 Schönwälder, "The Difficult Task," 259.
23 Schönwälder, "The Difficult Task," 259–60.
24 Schönwälder, *Einwanderung*, 505.
25 Schönwälder, *Einwanderung*, 502.
26 Hunn, *"Nächstes Jahr kehren wir zurück,"* 210, 277, Schönwälder, "The Difficult Task," 256, *Einwanderung*, 513–15.
27 Schönwälder, "The Difficult Task," 256–8, Hunn, *"Nächstes Jahr kehren wir zurück,"* 210, Schönwälder, *Einwanderung*, 500. For a description of how political parties avoided the discussion of citizenship rights, see Chin, *Multiculturalism*, 130–1.
28 Schönwälder, "The Difficult Task," 260.
29 Schönwälder, "The Difficult Task," 257–8.
30 Chin, *Multiculturalism*,126–7; Schönwälder, "The Difficult Task," 257; Schönwälder, *Einwanderung*, 548.
31 Triadafilos Triadafilopoulos, *Becoming Multicultural: Immigration and the Politics of Membership in Canada and Germany* (Vancouver: UBC Press, 2012), 82.
32 Chin, *Multiculturalism*, 135; Hunn, *"Nächstes Jahr kehre wir zurück,"* 303; Schönwälder, "The Difficult Task," 258, Schönwälder, *Einwanderung*, 548. Musch, "Consultation Structures," 77.
33 Schönwälder, *Einwanderung*, 574.
34 Schönwälder, *Einwanderung*, 522
35 Schönwälder, *Einwanderung*, 522.
36 Schönwälder, "The Difficult Task," 259.
37 Schönwälder, *Einwanderung*, 574–5.
38 Schönwälder, "The Difficult Task," 258.
39 Schönwälder, "The Difficult Task," 257–8.

40 Schönwälder, *Einwanderung*, 561.
41 Schönwälder, *Einwanderung*, 506.
42 Schönwälder, "The Difficult Task," 259–60.
43 Schönwälder, "The Difficult Task," 260.
44 Schönwälder, *Einwanderung*, 563.
45 Rist, "Migration and Marginality," 105.
46 Rist, "Migration and Marginality," 103.
47 This is most astonishing given that later, the CDU would coin the famous slogan, "Germany is not a country of immigration" (*Deutschland ist kein Einwanderungsland*.) Schönwälder, "The Difficult Task," 258.
48 Schönwälder, "The Difficult Task," 258.
49 Schönwälder, "The Difficult Task," 257. Rist, "Migration and Marginality,"104. See also Hunn, *"Nächstes Jahr kehren wir zurück,"* 220 and Herbert, *A History of Foreign Labor*, 214.
50 I will do my best to attend to language here, but because of the imprecision in these debates, slippage will occur.
51 Sander L. Gilman, "Aliens vs. Predators: Cosmopolitan Jewish people vs. Jewish Nomads," *European Review of History: Revue Européenne d'histoire* 23, no. 5–6 (2016): 784–96, https://doi.org/10.1080/13507486.2016.1203870.
52 Marion Kaplan, "Redefining Judaism in Imperial Germany: Practices, Mentalities, and Community." *Jewish Social Studies* 9, no. 1 (2002): 1–33.
53 Alan E. Steinweis, "Ideology and Infrastructure: German Area Science and Planning for the Germanization of Eastern Europe, 1939–1944," *East European Quarterly* 28, no. 3 (1994): 335–47.
54 Rachel O'Sullivan, "Integration and Division: Nazi Germany and the 'Colonial Other' in Annexed Poland," *Journal of Genocide Research* 0, no. 0 (2020): 1–22, https://doi.org/10.1080/14623528.2020.1757904.
55 Heidi Fehrenbach, "Black Occupation Children and the Devolution of the Nazi Racial State," in *After the Nazi Racial State: Difference and Democracy in Germany and Europe* (Ann Arbor: University of Michigan Press, 2009), 30.
56 Tara Zahra, "Looking East: East Central European 'Borderlands' in German History and Historiography," *History Compass* 3, no. 1 (2005): 1–23, https://doi.org/10.1111/j.1478-0542.2005.00175.x.
57 Italy still does not offer naturalization for second-generation immigrants. Angelica Marin, "This Liberian Italian Beatmaker Uses Music to Tackle Racism in Italy," *The World from PRX* June 29, 2020, accessed July 10, 2023, https://www.pri.org/stories/2020-06-29/liberian-italian-beatmaker-uses-music-tackle-racism-italy.
58 Hunn, *"Nächstes Jahr kehren wir zurück,"* 283.
59 Hunn, *"Nächstes Jahr kehren wir zurück,"* 282.
60 Hunn, *"Nächstes Jahr kehren wir zurück,"* 283.
61 Hunn, *"Nächstes Jahr kehren wir zurück,"* 283.

62 Hunn, *"Nächstes Jahr kehren wir zurück,"* 282–3.
63 Hunn, *"Nächstes Jahr kehren wir zurück,"* 283.
64 Hunn, *"Nächstes Jahr kehren wir zurück,"* 283–4.
65 Hunn, *"Nächstes Jahr kehren wir zurück,"* 284.
66 Schönwälder, *Einwanderung*, 523.
67 Schönwälder, *Einwanderung*, 524.
68 Heinz Kühn, "The Present and Future Integration of Foreign Workers and Their Families in the Federal Republic of Germany," Memorandum of the Federal Government Commissioner, September 1979, 1, 2, 25.
69 Schönwälder, *Einwanderung*, 523.
70 Schönwälder, *Einwanderung*, 516–17.
71 Schönwälder, *Einwanderung*, 522.
72 Schönwälder, *Einwanderung*, 522.
73 Schönwälder, *Einwanderung*, 518.
74 Schönwälder, *Einwanderung*, 518.
75 Schönwälder, *Einwanderung*, 518.
76 Schönwälder, *Einwanderung*, 518. *Einordnen* is yet another synonym for integration, meaning "to classify or to align with."
77 Schönwälder, *Einwanderung*, 516–17 and 517, FN 71. Schönwälder cites these arguments in the context of a longer excursus about policy memos about changing naturalization law for foreign men to have access through marriage to citizenship.
78 Schönwälder, *Einwanderung*, 506.
79 Chin, *Multiculturalism*, 128.
80 Chin, *Multiculturalism*, 127.
81 Chin *Multiculturalism*, 127–8.
82 Brett Klopp, *German Multiculturalism: Immigrant Integration and the Transformation of Citizenship*. Westport, CT: Praeger Publishers, 2002. 63. Quoted in Chin, *Multiculturalism*, 128, endnote 151.
83 Schönwälder, *Einwanderung*, 506.
84 Hunn, *"Nächstes Jahr kehren wir zurück,"* 291–2.
85 Hunn, *"Nächstes Jahr kehren wir zurück,"* 291.
86 Deutscher Bundestag, CDU/CSU/SPD, "Entwurf eines Integrationsgesetzes," DS 18/8615, accessed July 10, 2023, https://dserver.bundestag.de/btd/18/086/1808615.pdf.
87 Schönwälder, *Einwanderung*, 507, 510.
88 Schönwälder, *Einwanderung*, 523.
89 Hunn, *"Nächstes Jahr kehren wir zurück,"* 291.
90 Schönwälder, *Einwanderung*, 524.
91 Schönwälder, *Einwanderung*, 523.
92 Schönwälder, *Einwanderung*, 523.
93 Rist, "Migration and Marginality," 99.
94 Chin, *Multiculturalism*, 132.

95 Schönwälder, *Einwanderung*, 529–30.
96 Schönwälder, *Einwanderung*, 527.
97 Schönwälder, *Einwanderung*, 527.
98 Schönwälder, *Einwanderung*, 527.
99 Schönwälder, *Einwanderung*, 528.
100 Schönwälder, *Einwanderung*, 529.
101 Schönwälder, *Einwanderung*, 529.
102 Schönwälder, *Einwanderung*, 530.
103 Schönwälder, *Einwanderung*, 530.
104 The fears about domestic security were also related to the activities of the Red Army Faction, which committed three bombings in May of 1972, escalating in other attacks into 1977. Fears about immigrant terrorists were likely scapegoats for domestic terrorists who murdered upwards of thirty people. Fatima El-Tayeb points out how this projection functions by comparing right-wing and Islamic terrorisms in *Undeutsch*, 10–11.
105 Schönwälder, *Einwanderung*, 531.
106 Schönwälder, *Einwanderung*, 516.
107 Schönwälder, *Einwanderung*, 516n68.
108 This bias would become visible in spectacular ways after the events at the Cologne train station of 2015 and 2016. One of the first books to examine this conflict nearly a century earlier is Tina Campt's *Other Germans*, which begins with the figure of the "Rhineland Bastard," children of Black French soldiers who were born after the French occupation of the Rhineland after the First World War. See Tina Campt, *Other Germans: Black Germans and the Politics of Race, Gender, and Memory in the Third Reich* (Ann Arbor: University of Michigan Press, 2004).
109 Julia Woesthoff, "'Foreigners and Women Have the Same Problems': Binational Marriages, Women's Grassroots Organizing, and the Quest for Legal Equality in Post-1968 Germany," *Journal of Family History* 38, no. 4 (2013): 426, https://doi.org/10.1177/0363199013504386.
110 Silke Mertins, "Was sollen die letzten Worte sein," *Die Tageszeitung*, December 23, 1997, accessed July 10, 2023, https://taz.de/Was-sollen -die-letzten-Worte-sein/. accessed July 10, 2023. Natasha Kelly, "May Ayim," Digitales Deutsches Frauenarchiv, 2018, accessed July 10, 2023, https://www.digitales-deutsches-frauenarchiv.de/akteurinnen /may-ayim. May Ayim/Opitz, "Aufbruch," in *Farbe Bekennen: Afro-Deutsche Frauen auf den Spuren ihrer Geschichte*, eds. May Ayim, Katharina Oguntoye, and Dagmar Schultz. (Berlin: Orlanda Frauenverlag, 2020 (1986)). Kindle. Locations 3995–4119 of 4670.
111 Fehrenbach, "Black Occupation Children," 37.
112 Julia Woesthoff, "'When I Marry a Mohammedan': Migration and the Challenges of Interethnic Marriages in Post-War Germany," *Contemporary European History* 22, no. 2 (2013): 205.

113 Julia Woesthoff, "'When I Marry a Mohammedan'," 222. Shirin Daftari, *Fremde Wirklichkeiten: Verstehen und Missverstehen im Fokus bikultureller Partnerschaften* (Münster: LIT Verlag, 2000), 158.
114 Daftari, *Fremde Wirklichkeiten*, 159.
115 Daftari, *Fremde Wirklichkeiten*, 159.
116 Woesthoff, "'Foreigners and Women Have the Same Problems,'" 435.
117 Rist, "Migration and Marginality," 101.
118 Castles and Kosack, *Immigrant Workers*, 7, 57, 74, 93, 98, 119–25. Friedrich K. Kurylo, "The Turks Rehearsed the Uprising," in *Germany in Transit: Nation and Migration 1955–2005*, eds. Deniz Göktürk, Anton Kaes, and David Gramling, trans. David Gramling (Berkeley: University of California Press, 2007), 42–4.
119 Castles and Kosack, *Immigrant Workers*, 127–8.
120 Castles and Kosack, *Immigrant Workers*, 129.
121 Gassert, *Bewegte Gesellschaft*, 254; Miller, *Turkish Guest Workers*, 136, 160; Chin, *Multiculturalism*, 77.
122 Rist, "Migration and Marginality," 102.
123 Rist, "Migration and Marginality," 102.
124 Castles and Kosack, *Immigrant Workers*, 126.
125 Hunn, "*Nächstes Jahr kehren wir zurück*," 243.
126 Hunn, "*Nächstes Jahr kehren wir zurück*," 244.
127 Hunn, "*Nächstes Jahr kehren wir zurück*," 245.
128 Kurylo, "The Turks Rehearsed the Uprising," 44; Hunn, "*Nächstes Jahr kehren wir zurück*," 244–6.
129 Hunn, "*Nächstes Jahr kehren wir zurück*," 249.
130 Hunn, "*Nächstes Jahr kehren wir zurück*," 252.
131 Hunn, "*Nächstes Jahr kehren wir zurück*," 275.
132 Hunn, "*Nächstes Jahr kehren wir zurück*," 276.
133 Kurylo, "The Turks Rehearsed the Uprising," 42.
134 Kurylo, "The Turks Rehearsed the Uprising," 44.
135 Kurylo, "The Turks Rehearsed the Uprising," 44.
136 Miller, *Turkish Guest Workers*, 159.
137 Miller, *Turkish Guest Workers*, 146.
138 Miller, *Turkish Guest Workers*, 150–3.
139 Miller, *Turkish Guest Workers*, 147.
140 Miller, *Turkish Guest Workers*, 152.
141 Miller, *Turkish Guest Workers*, 155.
142 Miller, *Turkish Guest Workers*, 159.
143 Miller, *Turkish Guest Workers*, 160.
144 Miller, *Turkish Guest Workers*, 161.
145 The German Parliament is not dissolved after a successful vote of no confidence. Kohl was first elected by Parliament to hold the position

of Chancellor. He then forced a successful vote of no confidence to dissolve Parliament and prompt snap elections so that his position as Chancellor could be legitimized through a national vote. James M. Markham, "Bonn Parliament Votes out Schmidt and Elects Kohl," *The New York Times*, October 2, 1982, sec. 1, pg. 1, accessed March 6, 2024, https://www.nytimes.com/1982/10/02/world/bonn-parliament-votes-out-schmidt-and-elects-kohl.html.

146 Helmut Kohl, "Coalition of the Center: 'For a Politics of Renewal,'" in *Germany in Transit: Nation and Migration 1955–2005*, eds. Deniz Göktürk, Anton Kaes, and David Gramling, trans. David Gramling (Berkeley: University of California Press, 2007), 46. Helmut Kohl, "Regierungserklärung von Bundeskanzler Kohl in der 121. Sitzung des Deutschen Bundestages." *Konrad-Adenauer-Stiftung*, October 13, 1982, accessed July 7, 2023, https://www.bundeskanzler-helmut-kohl.de /seite/erklaerungen-1/.

147 Kohl, "Coalition of the Center," 46.

148 El-Tayeb, *Undeutsch*, 15, 17.

149 Kohl, "Regierungserklärung." Translation my own: "Die Ausländer in Deutschland sollen frei entscheiden können, aber sie müssen sich auch entscheiden, ob sie in ihre Heimat zurückkehren oder ob sie bei uns bleiben und sich integrieren wollen."

150 Kohl, "Coalition of the Center, 46. "Regierungserklärung."

151 Chin, *Multiculturalism*, 80–191.

152 Jürgen Fijalkowski, "Nationale Identität versus multikulturelle Gesellsachft. Entwicklungen der Problemlage und Alternativen der Orientierung in der politischen Kultur der Bundesrepublik in den 80er Jahren," in *Die Bundesrepublik in den achtziger Jahren: Innenpolitik, Politische Kultur, Außenpolitik* (Opladen: Leske und Budrich, 1991), 249.

153 Woesthoff, "'Foreigners and Women Have the Same Problems'," 441, FN 81.

154 El-Tayeb, *Undeutsch; European Others*; Ferda Ataman, *Ich bin von hier. Hört auf zu fragen!* (Frankfurt am Main: S. Fischer Verlag, 2019); Kiên Nghị Hà, et. al., *re/Visionen*.

155 Herbert, *A History of Foreign Labor,* 243–4.

156 Woesthoff, "'Foreigners and Women Have the Same Problems'," 432.

157 Hunn, *"Nächstes Jahr kehren wir zurück,"* 453, 471–3.

158 Heinz Harbach, "Konzepte der Ausländerpolitik in der Bundesrepublik Deutschland 1955–1982," *Institut für Höhere Studien* 6 (1982): 235, 242.

159 Hunn, *"Nächstes Jahr kehren wir zurück,"* 515.

160 Hunn, *"Nächstes Jahr kehren wir zurück,"* 486–7.

161 Hunn, *"Nächstes Jahr kehren wir zurück,"* 489.

162 Hunn, *"Nächstes Jahr kehren wir zurück,"* 487.

163 Hunn, *"Nächstes Jahr kehren wir zurück,"* 451.

164 Cas Mudde, *The Ideology of the Extreme Right* (Manchester: Manchester University Press, 2013), 29.
165 Mudde, *Ideology*, 32.
166 Mudde, *Ideology*, 60–2.

7 One German State, One (Integrated) German Nation

1 Panikos Panayi, "Racial Violence in the New Germany 1990–93," *Contemporary European History* 3, no. 3 (1994): 267; Roger Karapin, "Antiminority Riots in Unified Germany: Cultural Conflicts and Mischanneled Political Participation," *Comparative Politics* 34, no. 2 (2002), https://doi.org/10.2307/4146935.
2 Karapin, "Antiminority Riots," 160.
3 Panayi, "Racial Violence," 267.
4 Panayi, "Racial Violence," 267–8.
5 MDR, "Hoyerswerda 1991: Nach drei Jahrzehnten aufeinander zugehen," *Mitteldeutscher Rundfunk*, May 15, 2021, accessed May 25, 2021.
6 MDR, "Hoyerswerda 1991."
7 Panayi, "Racial Violence," 268.
8 Matthias Matussek, "Jagdzeit in Sachsen," *Der Spiegel*, September 29, 1991, 41–51; MDR, "Hoyerswerda 1991."
9 MDR, "Hoyerswerda 1991."
10 The title story / section is a collection of three articles. "Lieber sterben als nach Sachsen," *Der Spiegel*, September 29, 1991, 30–8.
11 Matussek, "Jagdzeit in Sachsen."
12 Rassismustoetet, "Pogrom Hoyerswerda – 'Ausländerjagd Rassismus im neuen Deutschland?'" YouTube, 2012 accessed May 26, 2021, *Im Brennpunkt*, Hoyerswerda: ARD, 1991, https://www.youtube.com/watch?v=0gjFyPnCQnU&t=544s.
13 Rassismustoetet, "Pogrom Hoyerswerda."
14 Rassismustoetet, "Pogrom Hoyerswerda."
15 Rassismustoetet, "Pogrom Hoyerswerda."
16 See Panayi, "Racial Violence," and Klaus J. Bade, "Immigration and Social Peace in United Germany," trans. Lieselotte Anderson. *Daedalus* 123, no. 1 (1994): 85–106.
17 Rassismustoetet, "Pogrom Hoyerswerda."
18 Karapin, "Antiminority Riots," 154.
19 PDS/Die Linke, "Kleine Anfrage der Abgeordneten Ulla Jelpke und der Gruppe der PDS/Linke Liste: Ausländerfeindliche Übergriffe und rechtsextremer Terror," Ulla Jelpke and Dr. Gregor Gysi. DS 12/2086, Berlin: Deutscher Bundestag, 1992. PDF, https://dipbt.bundestag.de/doc/btd/12/020/1202086.pdf (accessed March 6, 2024), 3.
20 Jelpke and Gyisi, "Ausländerfeindliche Übergriffe," 1–4.

21 Georg Wiessala, "Problems of Nationalism, Neo-fascism and National Identity in Post-unification Germany," *Journal of Area Studies* 5, no. 10 (1997): 68–72, 75–8, 77, https://doi.org/10.1080/02613539708455797. Wiesenthal 1992 cited in Martin Upchurch, "Institutional Transference and Changing Workplace Relations in Post Unification East Germany: A Case Study of Secondary Education Teachers," *Work, Employment and Society* 12, no. 2 (1998): 198, https://doi.org/10.1177/0950017098122001.

22 Many thanks to Michael Rothberg for pointing me to this citation. Nevim Çil, *Topographie des Aussenseiters* (Berlin: Verlag Hans Schiler, 2007), 11.

23 Azadê Peşmen, "Nicht-weißer Blick auf die Wende – Das neue 'Wir' ohne uns," Deutschlandfunk Kultur (Berlin: Deutschlandfunk, November 6, 2019), accessed June 15, 2023, https://www.deutschlandfunkkultur.de /nicht-weisser-blick-auf-die-wende-das-neue-wir-ohne-uns.976.de. html?dram:article_id=462792, accessed June 15, 2023. Çil, *Topographie des Aussenseiters*, 142.

24 Petra Köpping, *"Integriert doch erst mal uns!" Eine Streitschrift für den Osten* (Berlin: Ch. Links Verlag, 2018).

25 Oliver Schmidtke, "Reinventing the Nation: Germany's Post-Unification Drive Towards Becoming a 'Country of Immigration,'" *German Politics* 26, no. 4 (2017): 501, https://doi.org/10.1080/09644008.2017.1365137.

26 Hermann Kurthen and Michael Minkenberg, "Germany in Transition: Immigration, Racism and the Extreme Right," *Nations and Nationalism* 1, no. 2 (1995): 178, https://doi.org/10.1111/j.1354-5078.1995.00175.x.

27 Çil, *Topographie des Aussenseiters*, 11–13.

28 Çil, *Topographie des Aussenseiters*, 143.

29 Wiessla, "Problems of Nationalism," 82, Bade, "Immigration and Social Peace," 92–106.

30 Schmidtke, "Reinventing the Nation," 501.

31 Kurthen and Minkenberg, "Germany in Transition," 188, 192–3.

32 Daniel Koehler, *Right-Wing Terrorism in the 21st Century: The "National Socialist Underground" and the History of Terror from the Far-Right in Germany* (New York: Routledge, 2018), 7–21, 85–6, 94–5. Koehler offers the most intensive analysis of how and when the government "counts" crimes as extremist.

33 Kurthen and Minkenberg, "Germany in Transition," 186. Çil, *Topographie des Aussenseiters*, 142–50.

34 Çil, *Topographie des Aussenseiters*, 181–7.

35 Çil, *Topographie des Aussenseiters*, 196–7.

36 Norbert Madloch, "Rechtsextremistische Tendenzen und Entwicklungen in der DDR, speziell in Sachsen, Bis Oktober 1990," in *Rechtsextremismus und Antifaschismus: Historische und aktuelle Dimensionen*, eds. Klaus Kinner and Rolf Richter (Berlin: Dietz, 2000), 65.

37 Karapin, "Antiminority Riots," 150.

38 Upchurch, "Institutional Transference," 203. David Phillips, "The Legacy of Unification," in *Education in Germany since Unification*, edited by David Phillips (Cambridge: Symposium Books, 2000), 9.

39 Upchurch, "Institutional Transference," 203, 207. Stephanie Wilde, "A Study of Teacher's Perceptions in Brandenburg *Gesamtschulen*," *Education in Germany since Unification* (Cambridge: Symposium Books, 2000), 143, 149.

40 Upchurch, "Institutional Transference," 208. Phillips, "Legacy, " 10.

41 Upchurch, "Institutional Transference," 212.

42 Upchurch, "Institutional Transference," 203–4.

43 Upchurch, "Institutional Transference," 208.

44 Andrew Bickford, "Soldiers, Citizens, and the State: East German Army Officers in Post-Unification Germany," *Comparative Studies in Society and History* 51, no. 2 (2009): 271.

45 Bickford, "Soldiers," 271–2.

46 Bickford, "Soldiers," 278.

47 Bickford, "Soldiers," 275. Çil also mentions briefly that in the discursive space following unification, the East German regime was often equated with Naziism. See Çil, *Topographie des Aussenseiters*, 143 and FN 199.

48 Bickford, "Soldiers," 272.

49 Bickford, "Soldiers," 284.

50 Peggy Piesche, ed., *Labor89: intersektionale Bewegungsgeschichte*n aus West und Ost.* (Berlin: Verlag Yilmaz-Günay, 2019), 37.

51 Piesche, *Labor89*, 37.

52 Piesche, *Labor89*, 39.

53 Piesche, *Labor89*, 41.

54 Bade, "Immigration and Social Peace," 91–2.

55 Katharina Warda, "Dunkeldeutschland: Fünf Erinnerungen aus dem gesellschaftlichen Unbewussten," *Journal der Künste* 12 (2020) 26.

56 The similarities to the political mobilization of expellees versus displaced persons are worthy of future comparative consideration. There are also groups who continue to lack a pathway to citizenship despite decades of residence.

57 Warda, "Dunkeldeutschland," 25.

58 Warda, "Dunkeldeutschland," 25. Edward Said makes similar arguments in "Orientalism" between East and West (i.e., the Orient and Europe) through his concept of imaginative geographies. Edward W. Said, "Orientalism," *The Georgia Review* 31, no. 1 (1977): 162–206, www.jstor.org /stable/41397448. Çil, quoting sociologist Kürsat-Ahlers makes similar arguments about the East as a surface onto which the West could project its self-image. Çil, *Topographie des Aussenseiters*, 143.

59 Warda, "Dunkeldeutschland," 25.

60 Bildungsstätte Anne Frank, "Peggy Piesche im Interview / Teil der Ausstellung 'Anderen wurde es schwindelig,'" YouTube, 14:34, September 28, 2020, https://www.youtube.com/watch?v=zEujgzFsfTw&t=142s. Translation from video adjusted.

61 Quinn Slobodian, "Socialist Chromatism: Race, Racism, and the Racial Rainbow in East Germany," in *Comrades of Color: East Germany in the Cold War World*, ed. Quinn Slobodian (New York: Berghahn Books, 2015), 24.

62 Karin Weiss, "Zwischen Rückkehr in die Heimatländer und Existenzsicherung vor Ort," bpb.de, Bundeszentrale für politische Bildung, March 5, 2021, accessed June 15, 2023, https://www.bpb.de/themen /deutsche-einheit/migrantische-perspektiven/325194/zwischen -rueckkehr-in-die-heimatlaender-und-existenzsicherung-vor-ort/.

63 If this percentage seems small or negligible, keep in mind that the Jewish population in Germany in 1933 was 0.75% of the population. The Indigenous population of the United States in 2010 was 1.7% (identification as American Indian or Alaskan Native alone). The number of people in the United States with a PhD is nearly 2%. These proportions represent millions of people; in East Germany – a very small country – the population in 1989 was a mere 16.4 million people, with 191,000 of those being classified as foreign. See United States Holocaust Museum Memorial, "Germany: Jewish Population in 1933," *Holocaust Encyclopedia*, accessed June 15, 2023, https://encyclopedia.ushmm.org/content/en/article /germany-jewish-population-in-1933. National Congress of American Indians, "Demographics," June 1, 2020 accessed June 15, 2023, https:// www.ncai.org/about-tribes/demographics. Reid Wilson, "Census: More Americans Have College Degrees Than Ever Before," *The Hill*, April 3, 2017, accessed June 15, 2023, https://thehill.com/homenews /state-watch/326995-census-more-americans-have-college-degrees-than -ever-before Statista, "Population of East and West Germany 1950–2016," accessed June 15, 2023. https://www.statista.com/statistics/1054199 /population-of-east-and-west-germany/. In addition to the nearly 200,00 foreign students, workers, and business people, Madloch lists 500,000 Soviet troops as stationed in the GDR in 1989, Madloch, "Rechtsextremistische Tendenzen," 63–145, 84. Mike Dennis and Norman LaPorte, *State and Minorities in Communist East Germany* (New York: Berghahn Books, 2011), 87. Knurthen und Minkenberg, "Germany in Transition," 178.

64 Dennis and LaPorte, *State and Minorities*, 107.

65 Sara Pugach, "African Students and the Politics of Race and Gender in the German Democratic Republic," in *Comrades of Color: East Germany in the Cold War World*, ed. Quinn Slobodian (New York: Berghahn Books, 2015), 131–56, 138–9.

66 Dennis and LaPorte, *State and Minorities*, 88.

67 Dennis and LaPorte, *State and Minorities*, 89.
68 Pugach, "African Students, " 132.
69 Pugach, "African Students, " 132.
70 Slobodian, "Socialist Chromatism,"33.
71 Warda, "Dunkeldeutschland," 24–6, Bildungsstätte Anne Frank, "Peggy Piesche."
72 Piesche, *Labor89*, 97, 99.
73 Slobodian, "Introduction," in *Comrades of Color: East Germany in the Cold War World*, ed. Quinn Slobodian (New York: Berghahn Books, 2015), 3.
74 Dennis and LaPorte, *State and Minorities*, 109.
75 Pugach, "African Students," 131.
76 Miller, *Turkish Guest Workers*, 107–34.
77 Pugach, "African Students," 133.
78 Pugach, "African Students," 145–6.
79 Dennis and Laporte, *State and Minorities*, 109. Göktürk et al., "Agreement on the Procedures concerning Pregnancy among Vietnamese Laborers in the GDR," *Germany in Transit*, 88.
80 Pugach describes the meeting between East German officials and representatives from Zambia as unambivalent: GDR officials would not hinder marriages at the Zambians' request. (Pugach, "African Students," 131; Dennis and Laporte, *State and Minorities*, 109–10.) To the contrary, Jeanette Sumalgy was not granted permission decades later to marry her partner, a Mozambican contract worker. (*Piesche, Labor 89*, 99). In an oral history video filmed by the Digitalen Deutschen Frauenarchiv in 2020, Mai-Phuong Kollath described the prohibitions on pregnancy for Vietnamese workers. She recounts the high financial costs of paying to be released from her foreign work contract in order to remain in the DDR and get married. Esra Karakaya, "DDF-Talk: 30 Jahre geteilter Feminismus," YouTube, 1:18:58, September 30, 2020, https://www.youtube.com/watch?v=NdLTqjoc8tw&t=2763s.
81 Dennis and LaPorte, *State and Minorities*, 110.
82 Dennis and LaPorte, *State and Minorities*, 111. Göktürk et al. included the "Agreement on the Procedures concerning Pregnancy among Vietnamese Women Laborers in the GDR in their compendium *Germany in Transit*: "Vietnamese women who do not avail themselves of contraception or abortion must report at a predetermined time for their premature return to Vietnam, upon being cleared by a doctor to travel. In the case of a refusal to leave the country, the embassy of the Socialist Republic of Vietnam in the GDR will take immediate, necessary steps toward the execution of the deportation order and will be responsible for all costs incurred in the process." The document goes on to say the under special circumstances mothers and children can remain in the GDR until it is safe to travel. Göktürk et al., *Germany in Transit*, 88.

83 Mary Fulbrook, *The People's State: East German Society from Hitler to Honecker* (New Haven, CT: Yale University Press, 2005), 218, 266–7.

84 Dennis and Laporte, *State and Minorities*, 90–1.

85 Konrad Jarausch, *The Rush to German Unity* (Oxford: Oxford University Press, 1994), 208–10.

86 Warda, "Dunkeldeutschland," 26, Piesche, *Labor89*, 5–9.

87 Dietrich Thränhardt, "Germany: An Undeclared Immigration Country." *Journal of Ethnic and Migration Studies* 21, no. 1 (1995): 32, https://doi.org/1 0.1080/1369183X.1995.9976470. Bade, "Immigration and Social Peace," 85.

88 "Tod umsonst," *Der Spiegel* 36 (August 30, 1987), accessed June 15, 2023, https://www.spiegel.de/politik/tod-umsonst-a -e9e0faa0-0002-0001-0000-000013526485. "Kiomars Javadi – TUEpedia," Tüpedia: Stadtwiki Tübingen, August 20, 2020 accessed March 7, 2024, https://www.tuepedia.de/wiki/Kiomars_Javadi.

89 Deutscher Bundestag, "Schriftliche Fragen mit den in der Woche vom 22. Januar 1990 eingegangenen Antworten der Bundesregierung," DS 11/6323, Berlin: Deutscher Bundestag, 1990. PDF, http://dipbt.bundestag.de/doc /btd/11/063/1106323.pdf (accessed March 7, 2024), 4–5.

90 uh mit Stadt Schwandorf/Pressemitteilung, "Schwandorf gedenkt Opfer des Brandanschlages von 1988 – 'kein Platz für Gewalt und Extremismus'," *Wochenblatt*, December 15, 2018, last modified January 10, 2021, accessed June 15, 2023, https://www.wochenblatt.de/archiv /schwandorf-gedenkt-opfer-des-brandanschlages-von-1988-kein-platz -fuer-gewalt-und-extremismus-268777.

91 Koehler, *Right-Wing Terrorism*, 82–4.

92 Bade, "Immigration and Social Peace," 95. Madloch. "Rechtsextremis- tische Tendenzen," 79.

93 Dennis and LaPorte, *State and Minorities*, 173.

94 Dennis and LaPorte, *State and Minorities*, 170.

95 Dennis and LaPorte, *State and Minorities*, 171.

96 Dennis and LaPorte, *State and Minorities*, 172.

97 Dennis and LaPorte, *State and Minorities*, 182–3.

98 Dennis and LaPorte, *State and Minorities*, 183.

99 Panayi, "Racial Violence," 266.

100 Panayi, "Racial Violence," 268.

101 Karapin, "Antiminority Riots," 148.

102 Karapin, "Antiminority Riots," 158–60.

103 Karapin, "Antiminority Riots," 158.

104 Karapin, "Antiminority Riots," 157–9.

105 Karapin, "Antiminority Riots," 158–9.

106 Karapin, "Antiminority Riots," 159.

107 Karapin, "Antiminority Riots," 159, 157.

108 Karapin, "Antiminority Riots," 160.

109   Karapin, "Antiminority Riots," 160.
110   MDR, "Hoyerswerda 1991."

8 "Muslims Who Integrate Themselves": Integration and the Extreme Right

1   There are different uses of far right, extreme right, and radical right, depending on the context. Think of the far right as a container category that includes everything from conservative ideologies to the rejection of democracy. The extreme right rejects democracy and can be violent. The radical right prefers an illiberal form of democracy. The Anti-Defamation League in the US sees all three terms as essentially synonymous. See: Cas Mudde, *The Far Right Today* (Cambridge, UK: Polity Press, 2019), and ADL, "Extreme Right: Defining Extremism," *Anti-Defamation League*, accessed July 7, 2023, https://www.adl.org/resources/glossary-term/extreme-right-radical-right-far-right.

2   Sven Eichstädt, "Prozessbeginn: Lutz Bachmann inszeniert sich vor Gericht," *Die Welt*, April 17, 2016, accessed July 7, 2023, https://www.welt.de/politik/deutschland/article154444813/Bachmann-macht-sich-ueber-Strafprozess-lustig.html.

3   Maximillian Popp and Andreas Wassermann, "Where Did Germany's Islamophobes Come From?" *Spiegel Online*, January 12, 2015, accessed July 7, 2023, https://www.spiegel.de/international/germany/origins-of-german-anti-muslim-group-pegida-a-1012522.html.

4   Eichstädt, "Prozessbeginn," Agence France Presse. "Head of German Anti-Islam Group on Trial for Hate Speech," *The Guardian*, April 19, 2016, accessed July 12, 2023, https://www.theguardian.com/world/2016/apr/19/head-of-german-anti-islam-group-pegida-trial-hate-lutz-bachmann dpa, AFP, "Prozess gegen PEGIDA-Gründer: Anwältin von Lutz Bachmann fordert Einstellung des Verfahrens," *Der Tagesspiegel*, April 19, 2016, accessed July 12, 2023, https://www.tagesspiegel.de/politik/prozess-gegen-PEGIDA-gruender-anwaeltin-von-lutz-bachmann-fordert-einstellung-des-verfahrens/13467984.html.

5   AFP, "Head of German Anti-Islam Group on Trial for Hate Speech," SZ/lex, "Ereignisprotokoll: Der erste Tag im Bachmann-Prozess," *Sächsische Zeitung*, April 19, 2016, accessed July 12, 2023, https://www.saechsische.de/ereignisprotokoll-der-erste-tag-im-bachmann-prozess-3375694.html.

6   Bachmann's original sentence was for 3 years and 8 months, but he was released early. Eichstädt, "Prozessbeginn" SZ.de/dpa/dayk, "Lutz Bachmann: Geldstrafe wegen Volksverhetzung," *Süddeutsche Zeitung*, May 3, 2016, accessed July 12, 2023, https://www.sueddeutsche.de/politik/pegida-gruender-bachmann-geldstrafe-wegen-volksverhetzung-1.2979363, accessed July 12, 2023.

7   dpa, AFP, "Prozess gegen PEGIDA-Gründer" SZ/lex, "Ereignisprotokoll."
8   SZ/lex, "Ereignisprotokoll."
9   SZ/lex, "Ereignisprotokoll."
10 SZ.de/dpa/dayk, "Geldstrafe wegen Volksverhetzung." pr/adi, "Prozess gegen PEGIDA-Gründer - Bachmann wegen Volksverhetzung verurteilt," *Deutschlandfunk Kultur,* May 3, 2016, accessed July 12, 2023, https://www.deutschlandfunkkultur.de/prozess-gegen-PEGIDA-gruender-bachmann-wegen.1895.de.html?dram:article_id=353211.
11 SZ/lex, "Ereignisprotokoll."
12 AFP, "Head of German Anti-Islam Group on Trial for Hate Speech," *The Guardian,* April 19, 2016, accessed July 12, 2023, https://www.theguardian.com/world/2016/apr/19/head-of-german-anti-islam-group-PEGIDA-trial-hate-lutz-bachmann; "German Far-Right PEGIDA Founder Bachmann Guilty of Race Charge," *BBC News,* May 3, 2016, accessed July 12, 2023, https://www.bbc.com/news/world-europe-36199739. Kate Brady, "PEGIDA Founder Lutz Bachmann Found Guilty of Inciting Hatred," DW.COM, May 3, 2016, accessed July 12, 2023, https://www.dw.com/en/PEGIDA-founder-lutz-bachmann-found-guilty-of-inciting-hatred/a-19232497.
13 Benedikt Rohrßen, *Von der "Anreizung zum Klassenkampf" zur "Volksverhetzung" (§ 130 StGB): Reformdiskussion und Gesetzgebung seit dem 19. Jahrhundert* (Berlin: De Gruyter, 2009).
14 Bernhard Honnigfort, "Lutz Bachmann nutzt Spendenkasse," *Frankfurter Rundschau,* October 25, 2016 accessed July 12, 2023, https://www.fr.de/politik/lutz-bachmann-nutzt-spendenkasse-11050550.html. "Lutz Bachmann," Wikipedia, May 9, 2023, accessed July 15, 2023, https://de.wikipedia.org/w/index.php?title=Lutz_Bachmann&oldid=233566848.
15 Brady, "PEGIDA Founder Lutz Bachmann Found Guilty of Inciting Hatred"; Honnigfort, "Lutz Bachmann nutzt Spendenkasse," Melissa Eddy, "German Anti-Immigrant Leader Fined over Facebook Post," *The New York Times,* May 3, 2016, accessed July 12, 2023, https://www.nytimes.com/2016/05/04/world/europe/lutz-bachmann-PEGIDA-fined-germany.html.
16 Tilman Steffen, "Bachmann wird weiter hetzen," *Zeit Online,* May 3, 2016, accessed July 12, 2023, https://www.zeit.de/gesellschaft/zeitgeschehen/2016-05/pegida-gruender-lutz-bachmann-volksverhetzung-geldstrafe.
17 Hans Vorländer, Maik Herold, and Steven Schäller, *PEGIDA and New Right-Wing Populism in Germany* (Cham, Switzerland: Palgrave Macmillan, 2018), 4–5; "Record PEGIDA Rally in Dresden Sparks Mass Rival Protests," *BBC News,* January 12, 2015, accessed July 12, 2023, https://www.bbc.com/news/world-europe-30777841, accessed July 12, 2023. Eddy, "German Anti-Immigrant Leader Fined Over Facebook Post."

18 Süddeutsche Zeitung/AFP/dpa/sks/anri, "Pegida-Hochburg – Proteste gegen Flüchtlingsheim in Freital bei Dresden," *Süddeutsche Zeitung*, June 24, 2015, accessed July 15, 2023, https://www.sueddeutsche.de/politik /wohnort-von-pegida-gruender-lutz-bachmann-proteste-gegen -fluechtlingsheim-in-freital-bei-dresden-1.2535171.

19 Vorländer, Herod, and Schäller, *PEGIDA*, 87.

20 Vorländer, Herold, and Schäller, *PEGIDA*, 137, 197, 202.

21 Editorial Board, "Der Sächsische Verfassungsschutz ist auf den Hund gekommen – PEGIDA nun offiziell 'rechtsextrem,'" *Alternative Dresden News: Solidarische Berichterstattung aus Dresden* (blog), May 13, 2021 accessed July 12, 2023, https://www.addn.me/nazis/der-saechsische -verfassungsschutz-ist-auf-den-hund-gekommen-PEGIDA-nun-offiziell -rechtsextrem/. MDR Sachsen, "Landesverfassungsschutz stuft PEGIDA als extremistisch ein," MDR.de, May 7, 2021, https://www .mdr.de/nachrichten/sachsen/verfassungsschutz-stuft-PEGIDA-als -exteremistisch-ein-100.html. No longer available.

22 Lutz Bachmann, "Lutz Bachmann Profiles," Facebook, May 7, 2021, https://www.facebook.com/public/Lutz%20Bachmann. This profile is either no longer active, has increased its privacy restrictions, or the post has been deleted.

23 Vorländer, Herold, and Schäller, *PEGIDA*, 66–8. Because of access to EU Parliamentary networks, the AfD succeeded in building these networks, but PEGIDA was left to networking with fringe and small groups. Fabian Virchow, "The Groupuscularization of Neo-Nazism in Germany: The Case of the Aktionsbüro Norddeutschland," *Patterns of Prejudice* 38, no. 1 (2004): 56–70, https://doi.org/10.1080/0031322032000185587.

24 Pavel Lokshin, "AfD und die Medien: 'Ein symbiotisches Verhältnis,'" *Mediendienst Integration*, September 22, 2016, accessed July 12, 2023, https://mediendienst-integration.de/artikel/ein-symbiotisches -verhaeltnis.html. Kai Hafez, "Doku Leipzig (Teil 2): Wie die Medien zur Ausbreitung des Rechtsradikalismus beitragen … Grimme Lab," accessed July 21, 2021, https://www.grimme-lab.de/2019/12/19 /doku-leipzig-teil-2-wie-die-medien-zur-ausbreitung-des -rechtsradikalismus-beitragen/. Helga Druxes, "Manipulating the Media: The German New Right's Virtual and Violent Identities," in *Digital Media Strategies of the Far Right in Europe and the United States*, (London: Lexington Books, 2015), 123–40.

25 Whitney Phillips, "The Oxygen of Amplification," *Data and Society*, May 22, 2018, accessed July 12, 2023, https://datasociety.net/library /oxygen-of-amplification/.

26 Herbert Kitschelt, *The Radical Right in Western Europe* (Ann Arbor: University of Michigan Press, 1995), 8–10; and Terri E. Givens, *Voting Radical*

Right in Western Europe (Cambridge: Cambridge University Press, 2005), 46; "The Radical Right Gender Gap," *Comparative Political Studies* 37, no. 1 (2004): 36–9.

27 Cas Mudde, "The Populist Radical Right: A Pathological Normalcy," *West European Politics* 33, no. 6 (2010): 1178, https://doi.org/10.1080/01402382.2010.508901.

28 Kitschelt, *The Radical Right*, 3, 20–4, 31–2, 61. Mudde, "Pathological Normalcy," 1173.

29 This research trip was funded by a re-invitation grant from the Alexander von Humboldt Foundation in 2015.

30 Overseas Security Advisory Council, "Security Message for US Citizens: Berlin (Germany), Demonstration Notice," US Department of State, January 26, 2015; dpa/epd/fp, "State Department warnt vor Pegida-Demos," *Die Welt*, January 28, 2015, accessed July 7, 2023, https://www.welt.de/politik/article136867558/State-Department-warnt-vor-Pegida-Demos.html.

31 Fieldwork notes, June 8, 2015.

32 "Oberbürgermeisterwahl Dresden 2015 – Erster Wahlgang Am 07.06.2015," *Dresden.de*, last modified February 26, 2021, http://wahlen.dresden.de/2015/OBW/index.html. Results from 2015 are no longer listed due to the amount of time that has passed since the elections. heb, "Dresden OB-Wahl: NPD Unterstützt PEGIDA-Frau Festerling," *Der Spiegel*, April 21, 2015, accessed July 8, 2023, https://www.spiegel.de/politik/deutschland/dresden-ob-wahl-npd-unterstuetzt-PEGIDA-frau-festerling-a-1029656.html. Bernhard Honnigfort, "Unterstützung von den Hetzern," *Frankfurter Rundschau*, June 9, 2015 accessed March 7, 2024, https://www.fr.de/politik/unterstuetzung-hetzern-11178651.html. This race used runoff voting, so Festerling withdrew after the first round and eventually Dirk Hilbert (FDP) won the second round of voting on July 5, with 54 per cent of the vote. Hilbert was later re-elected in 2022. "Oberbürgermeisterwahl 2022 – Zweiter Wahlgang," *Dresden.de*, accessed July 8, 2023, https://wahlen.dresden.de/2022/obwzwg/index.html.

33 Erik Olsen and Melissa Eddy, "Video Feature: PEGIDA Movement Divides Germany," *The New York Times*, February 11, 2015, accessed July 8, 2023, https://www.nytimes.com/2015/02/12/world/europe/PEGIDA-movement-divides-germany.html.

34 Fieldwork notes, June 8, 2015.

35 Vorländer, Herold, and Schäller, 118, 137–9, at 139.

36 Vorländer, Herold, and Schäller, *PEGIDA*, 142.

37 PEGIDA rejected sanctions imposed by Germany against the Russian occupation of the Ukraine, declaring that conflict with Russia in "a proxy

war" was both unwanted and potentially catastrophic. Daniel Schrödel, "AfD und Pegida demonstrieren Hand in Hand in Dresden," *MDR Sachhsen*, MDR.de, February 25, 2023, accessed July 7, 2023, https:// www.mdr.de/nachrichten/sachsen/dresden/dresden-radebeul /ukraine-jahrestag-krieg-afd-pegida-100.html.

38 Ned Richardson-Little, "From Stauffenberg to PEGIDA: How the Far Right Adopted the Flag of the Anti-Hitler Resistance," *Superfluous Answers to Necessary Questions* (blog), July 20, 2017, accessed July 7, 2023, https://historyned.blog/2017/07/20/from-stauffenberg-to -PEGIDA-how-the-far-right-adopted-the-flag-of-the-anti-hitler -resistance/. Many thanks to Kira Thurman for sending me this link.

39 Henrik Merker, "Antisemiten kapern Corona-Proteste, *Störung-smelder (blog), Die Zeit,*" May 14, 2020, https://blog.zeit.de/ stoerungsmelder/2020/05/14/antisemiten-kapern-corona-proteste_29718.

40 Fieldwork notes, June 8, 2015.

41 Headnotes, June 8, 2015.

42 AfD in Sachsen und Dresden – Die Dokumentation, "Ungekürzt in HD: PEGIDA 8. Juni 2015, 50:02, June 9, 2015, accessed July 7, 2023," https:// www.youtube.com/watch?v=SAAI7yk4PqI&t=1267s.

43 Vorländer, Herold, and Schäller, *PEGIDA*, 184.

44 Vorländer, Herold, and Schäller, *PEGIDA*, 146.

45 Koehler, *Right-Wing Terrorism*, 114. Koehler spends some time exploring the development since the mid-1990s of the neo-Nazi concept of the "leaderless resistance," in which dynamic networks of smaller groups and individuals function "as 'incubators' and hubs aggregating knowl-edge, structural capabilities, ideological foundations and a pool of human resources." I can think of no better description of the function of social media like Facebook.

46 Kate Connolly, "Photograph of Germany's PEGIDA Leader Styled as Adolf Hitler Goes Viral," *The Guardian*, January 21, 2015 accessed July 8, 2023, https://www.theguardian.com/world/2015/jan/21/pegida -leader-styled-adolf-hitler-lutz-bachmann-german-islamist-terrorists -facebook; accessed July 8, 2023. No author, "Germany PEGIDA: Protest Leader Quits amid Hitler Row," *BBC News*, January 21, 2015 accessed July 8, 2023, https://www.bbc.com/news/world-europe-30920086 "Lutz Bachmann: PEGIDA-Gründer spielt Hitler," *Frankfurter Allgemeine Zeitung,* January 21, 2015, https://www.faz.net/aktuell/politik /inland/lutz-bachmann-PEGIDA-gruender-spielt-hitler-13382531.html; accessed July 8, 2023. AFP/dpa/fp, "Bild Mit Hitlerbart: Herbst vs. Bachmann – 'Habe Keine Facebook-Seite,'" *Die Welt*, January 21, 2015, accessed July 8, 2023, https://www.welt.de/politik/deutschland /article136626463/Herbst-vs-Bachmann-Habe-keine-Facebook

-Seite.,html; Cf/lsc/hjv, "PEGIDA-Chef Lutz Bachmann: Hitler-Foto und Ausländer-Beleidigungen bei Facebook," *Bild.de*, January 21, 2015, https://www.bild.de/politik/inland/PEGIDA/chef-lutz-bachmann -hitler-foto-und-auslaender-beleidigungen-bei-facebook-39430448.bild. html; Alison Smale, "German Anti-Immigrant Leaders Resign," *The New York Times*, January 28, 2015, accessed July 8, 2023, https://www.nytimes. com/2015/01/29/world/europe/pegida-german-protest-group -announce-resignatons.html; accessed July 8, 2023. dpa/UM/mkl, "Ex-PEGIDA-Chefs planen offenbar neues Bündnis," *Die Welt*, January 29, 2015, accessed July 8, 2023, https://www.welt.de/politik /deutschland/article136906332/Ehemalige-PEGIDA-Chefs -gruenden-neues-Buendnis.html; stb, "Kathrin Oertel macht jetzt was Eigenes," *Stern*, January 29, 2015 accessed July 8, 2023, https://www .stern.de/politik/deutschland/kathrin-oertel-will-nach-PEGIDA-neues -buendnis-gruenden-3462168.html.

47 Melissa Eddy, "German Who Posed as Hitler Returns to Position in Anti-Immigrant Group PEGIDA," *The New York Times*, February 24, 2015, accessed July 8, 2023, https://www.nytimes.com/2015/02/25/world /europe/lutz-bachmann-PEGIDA.html; tsp/AFP, "Lutz Bachmann ist wieder PEGIDA-Chef," *Der Tagesspiegel*, February 23, 2015, accessed July 8, 2023, https://www.tagesspiegel.de/politik/anti-islam-bewegung-lutz- bachmann-ist-wieder-PEGIDA-chef/11408898.html; Zeit Online, dpa, sk. "PEGIDA: Lutz Bachmann wieder im Vorstand von PEGIDA," *Die Zeit*, February 23, 2015 accessed July 8, 2023, https://www.zeit.de /gesellschaft/zeitgeschehen/2015-02/pegida-lutz-bachmann-zurueck- im-vorstand; Ben Knight, "PEGIDA Head Lutz Bachmann Reinstated after Furore over Hitler Moustache Photo," *The Guardian*, February 23, 2015 accessed July 8, 2023, https://www.theguardian.com/world/2015 /feb/23/pegida-head-lutz-bachmann-reinstated-hitler-moustache-photo.

48 Katrin Bennhold et al., "Franco A," *Day X*, June 16, 2021, accessed July 15, 2021. https://www.nytimes.com/2021/06/16/podcasts /franco-a-trial-germany-terrorism.html; ARD/Robert Bongen, et al., "'Lausbuben': Wie man in Freital Terroristen verharmlost," YouTube, 12:19, December 15, 2017, accessed March 8, 2024, https://www.youtube .com/watch?v=dtpQ5FzEr_c. See also Stern's references to "plausible deniability" as a tactic reinforced by the anonymity of digitality, *Proud Boys*, 75, 95.

49 "German Far-Right PEGIDA Founder Bachmann Guilty of Race Charge," *BBC News*, 3 May 2016, accessed July 8, 2023, https://www.bbc.com /news/world-europe-36199739.

50 "German Anti-Immigrant Leader Fined over Facebook Post;" dpa/AFP, "Anwältin von Lutz Bachmann fordert Einstellung des Verfahrens;" AFP,

"Head of German anti-Islam group on trial for hate speech;" SZ.de/dpa /dayk; "PEGIDA-Gründer Bachmann erhält Geldstrafe wegen Volksverhetzung;" "German Far-Right PEGIDA Founder Bachmann Guilty of Race Charge."

51 Critique of the media was the second most frequent motivation given for participating in PEGIDA rallies by those surveyed. Vorländer, Herold and Schäller, *PEGIDA*, 87.

52 Rainer Blasius, "Unwort des Jahres: Von der Journaille zur Lügenpresse," *Frankfurter Allgemeine Zeitung*, January 13, 2015, accessed July 8, 2023, https://www.faz.net/aktuell/gesellschaft/unwort-des-jahres-eine -kleine-geschichte-der-luegenpresse-13367848.html.

53 Christian Fischer,"PEGIDA-Erfinder: Wir hören erst auf, wenn die Asyl-Politik sich ändert!" *Bild.de*, January 12, 2014, accessed July 8, 2023, https://www.bild.de/regional/dresden/demonstrationen/PEGID A-erfinder-im-interview-38780422.bild.html, accessed July 8, 2023.

54 Kurdish residents were protesting in Dresden (and across Europe) against the Islamic State's genocide of ethnic Kurds, but Bachmann attributed this demonstration as an action to support the PKK, or the Kurdistan Workers Party, a group designated as terrorist in Germany. While there are links between the organizations, the situation for Kurds in Northern Iraq and Syria at this time was dire. In June 2014, the Islamic State had designated itself as a caliphate, and was increasingly successful in its campaign of brutal expansion. The siege of Kobani took place in summer of 2014. By late summer and early fall, the Islamic State was attempting to control Sinjar province, and cut off Yazidi Kurdish communities from escape. The PKK and the YPG worked together with support from US forces in Sinjar province (500 km from Kobani, to give one a sense of the territorial expansion of ISIL) to free Yazidi through the creation of a safe corridor, through which thousands of Yazidis were able to flee ISIL. The UN found that ISIL perpetrated genocide against Kurdish Yazidi communities in Northern Iraq.

    Christian Fischer, "PEGIDA-Erfinder"; "ISIL/Da'esh Committed Genocide of Yazidi, War Crimes against Unarmed Cadets, Military Personnel in Iraq, Investigative Team Head Tells Security Council," *UN Security Council*, May 10, 2021, accessed March 8, 2024, https://www.un.org /press/en/2021/sc14514.doc.htm; Editorial Board, "Kobanê ist überal," *Alternative Dresden News: Solidarische Berichterstattung aus Dresden*, (blog), October 10, 2014, accessed July 12, 2023, https://www.addn.me/news /kobane-ist-ueberall/, accessed July 12, 2023; "Pro-kurdische Proteste: Mehr als ein Dutzend Tote," *Kurier*, October 8, 2014, accessed July 12, 2023, https://kurier.at/politik/ausland/europas-kurden-fordern-hilfe -mehr-als-ein-dutzend-bei-pro-kurdischen-protesten/89.766.076; "Kurds

Stage Major Kobani Protest in Düsseldorf," *Deutsche Welle*, October 11, 2014, accessed July 12, 2023, https://p.dw.com/p/1DTY1; Popp and Wassermann, "Where Did Germany's Come from?"

55 Editorial Board, "Kobanê ist überall."

56 Fischer, "PEGIDA-Erfinder."

57 Fischer, "PEGIDA-Erfinder."

58 Vorländer, Herold and Schäller compiled multiple surveys of PEGIDA participants that were conducted during the first year of PEGIDA's existence. Overall, these multiple surveys come to similar conclusions: antagonism to immigration, critique of the media and distrust of the political system were the primary attitudes present amongst demonstrators. *PEGIDA*, 99–167.

59 Koehler, *Right-Wing Terrorism*, 111.

60 Kitschelt, *The Radical Right*, 25, Givens, *Voting Radical Right*, 39.

61 The first Merkel cabinet between 2005–2009 was also a grand coalition.

62 Dietrich Thränhardt, "The Political Uses of Xenophobia in England, France and Germany," *Party Politics* 1, no. 3 (July 1, 1995): 323–45. https://doi.org/10.1177/1354068895001003002. Quote at 325; see also 328 and 338. Mudde, Cas. *The Far Right Today*. Cambridge: Polity Press, 2019. Kitschelt, Herbert, in collaboration with Anthony J. McGann, *The Radical Right in Western Europe: A Comparative Analysis*. Ann Arbor: University of Michigan Press, 1995, 61–63.

63 Why Vorländer, Herold and Schäller use these two terms is unclear to me unless the researchers are presuming a scale of whiteness within xenophobia. Given the limited theoretical interest in whiteness in German political science, I find this unlikely and suspect it is due to hesitation around the employment of the language of race and uneasiness about labelling PEGIDA supporters "racist." See Vorländer, Herold and Schäller, *PEGIDA*, 117–37.

64 Givens, "The Radical Right Gender Gap"; 50; *Voting Radical Right*, 85.

65 Vorländer, Herold, and Schäller, *PEGIDA*, 80.

66 Kitschelt, *The Radical Right*, 20, 31, 47.

67 Kitschelt, *The Radical Right*, 47, 66. The one exception to pro-market attitudes can be found in state-subsidy protections for agriculture. Givens, *Voting Radical Right*, 38–9.

68 Kathleen M. Blee and Kimberly A. Creasap, "Conservative and Right-Wing Movements," *Annual Review of Sociology* (2010) 36: 271.

69 See Kitschelt, *The Radical Right*; Kurthen and Minkenberg, "Germany in Transition."

70 *epd*, "PEGIDA-Gründer Lutz Bachmann verurteilt: Neuer Strafbefehl gegen Bachmann," *Frankfurter Allgemeine Zeitung*, May 3, 2016, accessed July 12, 2023, https://www.faz.net/aktuell/politik/inland/wegen

-volksverhetzung-PEGIDA-gruender-lutz-bachmann-verurteilt-14214054.
html; pr/adi, "Prozess gegen PEGIDA-Gründer – Bachmann wegen
Volksverhetzung verurteilt," *Deutschlandfunk Kultur*, May 3, 2016, accessed
July 12, 2023, https://www.deutschlandfunkkultur.de/prozess-gegen
-PEGIDA-gruender-bachmann-wegen.1895.de.html?dram:article_id=353211.

71 SZ/lex, "Ereignisprotokoll."

72 Katja Auer, "Asylbewerber in Bayern – Zufluchtsort Kaserne," *Süddeutsche
Zeitung*, September 10, 2014 accessed July 12, 2023, https://www
.sueddeutsche.de/bayern/asylbewerber-in-bayern-zufluchtsort
-kaserne-1.2122233; Olaf Przybilla, "Zirndorf – Menschenwürdig ist
das nicht," August 28, 2014, accessed July 12, 2023, https://www
.sueddeutsche.de/bayern/fluechtlinge-in-zirndorf-menschenwuerdig
-ist-das-nicht-1.2108279; dpa, "Immer mehr Flüchtlinge in
Aufnahmeeinrichtung Zirndorf," August 26, 2014, accessed 12
July 2023, https://www.abendzeitung-muenchen.de/bayern/
immer-mehr-fluechtlinge-in-aufnahmeeinrichtung-zirndorf-art-249375.

73 Peter Schimany, "Asylmigration nach Deutschland," in *20 Jahre Asylkompromiss*, eds. Stefan Luft and Peter Schimany (Bielefeld: transcript verlag,
2014), 55.

74 "Asylum Statistics," Eurostat: Statistics Explained, April 27, 2021,
accessed July 12, 2023, https://ec.europa.eu/eurostat/statistics
-explained/index.php?title=Annual_asylum_statistics.

75 "Hungerstreik Bayernkaserne – Bayerischer Flüchtlingsrat." Bayerischer
Flüchtlingsrat, accessed July 12, 2023, https://archiv.fluechtlingsrat
-bayern.de/hungerstreik-bayernkaserne.html, accessed July 12, 2023.

76 Schimany, "Asylmigration," 57.

77 Schimany, "Asylmigration," 57.

78 Schimany, "Asylmigration," 58.

79 Damani J. Partridge, "Articulating a Noncitizen Politics: Nation-State Pity
vs. Democratic Inclusion," in *Refugees Welcome?: Difference and Diversity
in a Changing Germany*, eds. Jan-Jonathan Bock and Sharon Macdonald
(New York: Berghahn Books, 2019): 278; Lea Hampel, "Iranische Flüchtlinge protestieren: Hungern für die Normalität," *Die Tageszeitung*, April 4,
2012, accessed July 7, 2023, https://taz.de/!5096782/.

80 Hampel, "Iranische Flüchtlinge."

81 Patrick Guyton, "Der lange Marsch der Flüchtlinge," *Süddeutsche Zeitung*,
September 24, 2012, accessed July 12, 2023, https://www.tagesspiegel.
de/politik/asylpolitik-der-lange-marsch-der-fluechtlinge/7173520.html;
"Protestmarsch von Asylbewerbern – Würzburger Flüchtlinge erreichen
Berlin," *Süddeutsche Zeitung*, October 5, 2012, accessed July 12, 2023,
https://www.sueddeutsche.de/bayern/protestmarsch-von
-asylbewerbern-wuerzburger-fluechtlinge-erreichen-berlin
-1.1488037; N. Schreiter, "Demo für mehr Flüchtlingsrechte:

'Das war Berlin, jetzt kommt Europa.'" *Die Tageszeitung*, October 14, 2012, accessed July 12, 2023, https://taz.de/!5081849/.

82 N. Schreiter, "Demo für mehr Flüchtlingsrechte."

83 Johannes Wendt, "Protest gegen Anhörungen: Flüchtlinge besetzen Botschaft," *Die Tageszeitung*, 15 October 2012, accessed July 12, 2023, https://taz.de/!5081767/.

84 Barbara Galaktionow, "Flüchtlinge demonstrieren am Brandenburger Tor-Aktivisten empört über Polizei," *Süddeutsche Zeitung*, October 29, 2012, accessed July 12, 2023, https://www.sueddeutsche.de/politik /fluechtlinge-demonstrieren-am-brandenburger-tor-aktivisten -empoert-ueber-polizei-1.1508793; Thomas Gerlach, "Flüchtlingsprotest in Berlin: "Sie sollen uns ernst nehmen!" *Die Tageszeitung*, November 2, 2012, accessed July 12, 2023, https://taz.de/!5080317/; Konrad Litschko, "Flüchtlingsprotest in Berlin: Wieder im Hungerstreik," *Die Tageszeitung*, November 16, 2012, July 12, 2023, https://taz.de/!5079274/.

85 Kristiana Ludwig, "Flüchtlinge protestieren: Ein Camp auf der Verkehrsinsel," *Die Tageszeitung*, May 21, 2013, accessed July 12, 2023, https://taz.de/!5066959/, accessed July 12, 2023; "Asylsuchende in München: Hungerstreik für die Anerkennung," *Süddeutsche Zeitung*, June 24, 2013, accessed July 12, 2023, https://www.sueddeutsche.de /muenchen/demonstration-am-rindermarkt-hungern-fuer-ein-besseres -leben-1.1703402; Mareen Ledebur, "Münchner Asylbewerber im Trinkstreik: 'Wir gehen bis zum Ende,'" *Die Tageszeitung*, June 26, 2013, accessed July 12, 2023, https://taz.de/!5064541/; Marlene Halser, "Kommentar Hungerstreik: Bis einer stirbt!" *Die Tageszeitung*, June 27, 2013 accessed July 12, 2023, https://taz.de/!5064415/; Patrick Guyton, "Hungerstreikgebiet, bitte nicht betreten," *Der Tagesspiegel*, June 28, 2013, accessed July 12, 2023, https://www.tagesspiegel.de/politik /asylbewerber-protestieren-in-muenchen-hungerstreikgebiet-bitte -nicht-betreten/8421734.html; "Vom großen Gefängnis ins kleine," *Der Tagesspiegel*, July 11, 2013 accessed July 12, 2023, https://www .tagesspiegel.de/politik/asylbewerber-vom-grossen-gefaengnis-ins -kleine/6862636.html; Christian Jakob, "Kommentar Flüchtlingscamps: Rückfall in trennende Konzepte." *Die Tageszeitung*, August 8, 2013, accessed March 8, 2023, https://taz.de/!5061706/.

86 Kerstin Vogel, "Protestmarsch von Asylsuchenden: Polizei stoppt Flüchtlinge," *Süddeutsche Zeitung*, September 1, 2013, accessed July 12, 2023, https://www.sueddeutsche.de/muenchen/freising /einkesselte-fluechtlinge-schimpfende-demonstranten-unmittelbarer -zwang-1.1760048; Daniela Martens, "Nach Besetzung der nigerianischen Botschaft-Flüchtlinge klagen Berliner Polizei an," *Der Tagesspiegel*, November 10, 2012, accessed July 12, 2023, https://www.tagesspiegel .de/berlin/nach-besetzung-der-nigerianischen-botschaft-fluechtlinge

-klagen-berliner-polizei-an/7372032.html. Many thanks to my research assistant Dan Nemeth who assisted me in gathering articles about these protests in 2020. See also Olivia Landry, "'Wir sind alle Oranienplatz'! Space for Refugees and Social Justice in Berlin," *Seminar: A Journal of Germanic Studies* 51, no. 4 (2015): 398–413.

87   Occasional attempts were made to revive the movement. See Julia Haak, "Vor der Europa-Wahl: Flüchtlinge wollen zu Fuß nach Brüssel," *Berliner Zeitung*, May 16, 2014, accessed July 12, 2023, https://www.berliner-zeitung.de/mensch-metropole/vor-der-europa-wahl-fluechtlinge-wollen-zu-fuss-nach-bruessel-li.66636.

88   Patricia Ehrkamp, "Risking Publicity: Masculinities and the Racialization of Public Neighborhood Space." *Social & Cultural Geography* 9, no. 2 (2008): 120, https://doi.org/10.1080/14649360701856060.

89   Koritha Mitchell, "Identifying White Mediocrity and Know-Your-Place Aggression: A Form of Self-Care." *African American Review* 51 no. 4 (2018) : 253, https://doi.org/10.1353/afa.2018.0045. 253.

90   Mitchell, "Indentifying White Mediocrity," 258.

91   Partridge, "Non-Citizen Politics," 266.

92   This demand was also part of my orientation sessions while I was a teenage exchange student: we were taught to be grateful of the opportunities the exchange scholarship offered us, but what was also demanded of us was that we be grateful and uncritical of our host families, even when the housing situations in which we were placed deserved critique. This kind of nationalist attitude towards difference thus even applies to spaces of relevant privilege when foreignness is at work.

93   Ferda Ataman, *Ich bin von hier. Hört auf zu fragen!* (Frankfurt am Main: S. Fischer Verlag, 2019).

94   Ataman, *Ich bin von hier*, 25–6.

95   Virchow, "Groupuscularization," 59, 63.

96   This rhetoric in its most generic form absolutely spans more than a decade: what I am pointing to specifically are the kind of shifts that have taken place in contemporary media coverage following September 11, 2001. See Gizem Arslan et al., "Forum: Migration Studies," *The German Quarterly* 90, no. 2 (2017): 212–34. Many thanks to Ela Gezen for drawing my attention to this forum.

97   SZ/wei, "Asylforum in Freital abgesagt," *Sächsische Zeitung*, March 12, 2015, accessed June 16, 2021, https://www.saechsische.de/asylforum-in-freital-abgesagt-3056177.html; Matthias Meisner, "'Besorgte Bürger' brüllen Asyl-Aktivisten nieder," *Der Tagesspiegel*, July 7, 2015, accessed July 12, 2023, https://www.tagesspiegel.de/politik/freital-besorgte-buerger-bruellen-asyl-aktivisten-nieder/12020774.html.

98 Süddeutsche.de et al., "Pegida-Hochburg – Proteste gegen Flüchtlingsheim in Freital bei Dresden," *Süddeutsche Zeitung*, June 24, 2015, accessed July 12, 2023, https://www.sueddeutsche.de /politik/wohnort-von-pegida-gruender-lutz-bachmann-proteste-gegen -fluechtlingsheim-in-freital-bei-dresden-1.2535171.

99 SZ/wei,"Asylforum in Freital abgesagt"; Zeit Online/dpa/mp, "Tumulte bei Bürgerversammlung in Freital," *Die Zeit*, July 7, 2015, accessed March 8, 2024, https://www.zeit.de/politik /deutschland/2015-07/freital-buergerversammlung-tumulte; Doreen Reinhard, "Freital: Lust auf Lynchen," *Die Zeit*, July 7, 2015, accessed July 12, 2023, https://www.zeit.de/politik/deutschland/2015-07/freital -fluechtlinge-buergerversammlung; Cornelius Pollmer, "Auftritt der pöbelnden Schaummünder," *Süddeutsche Zeitung*, July 7, 2015, accessed July 12, 2023, https://www.sueddeutsche.de/politik/freital-ausdauernd -aufgeheizt-1.2554805, accessed July 12, 2023. Vorländer, Herold, and Schäller, *PEGIDA*, 139.

100 "PEGIDA-Gründer macht gegen Asylantenheim" *NWZonline.de*, June 25, 2015, accessed July 12, 2023, https://www.nwzonline.de/panorama /PEGIDA-gruender-macht-gegen-asylantenheim-mobil_a_29,0,2401981158 .html

101 The reference to herds of cattle implied by "angekarrt" is a particularly chilling invocation of the Holocaust and transports to concentration camps. Matthias Meisner and Lars Radau, "Vergleiche mit Hoyerswerda sind angebracht," *Der Tagesspiegel*, June 23, 2015, accessed July 12, 2023, https://www.tagesspiegel.de/politik/anti-asyl-proteste-in-freital -vergleiche-mit-hoyerswerda-sind-angebracht/11955918.html.

102 Doreen Reinhard, "Freital: Rassismus als Happening," *Zeit Online*, June 25, 2015 accessed July 12, 2023, https://www.zeit.de/politik /deutschland/2015-06/freital-fluechtlingsheim-proteste-stellungskrieg.

103 Schimany, "Asylmigration," 56.

104 Ulrike Nimz and Cornelius Pollmer, "Freital: Wo der Hass regiert," *Süddeutsche Zeitung*, June 25, 2015, accessed July 12, 2023, https://www.sueddeutsche.de/politik/ proteste-gegen-fluechtlinge-in-freital-wo-der-mob-skandiert-1.2537601.

105 Jonas Jansen,"Rassistische Kommentare: 'Die kannst du nur erschlagen.'" *Frankfurter Allgemeine Zeitung*, August 7, 2015 accessed July 12, 2023, https://www.faz.net/aktuell/gesellschaft/kriminalitaet /perlen-aus-freital-tumblr-sammelt-rassistische-kommentare -13691724.html.

106 Jansen, "Rassistische Kommentare."

107 Meisner and Radau, "Vergleiche mit Hoyerswerda sind angebracht."

108 This is an example of discursive DARVO: Deny-Attack-and-Reverse-Victim-and-Offender, which is a fairly common abusive tactic among right-wing extremists who attempt to gaslight their antagonists.

109 Süddeutsche.de et al., "PEGIDA-Hochburg – Proteste gegen Flüchtlingsheim in Freital bei Dresden."

110 Nimz and Pollmer, "Freital: Wo der Hass regiert."

111 Hans Pfeifer, "Right-Wing Terror Trial Stirs up Violent Memories in Germany's Freital," *Deutsche Welle*, July 9, 2020 accessed July 12, 2023, https://www.dw.com/en/germany-freital/a-54818274.

112 Richter moved to Bavaria, lives on a farm, and now tries to remain distant from politics. See Pfeifer, "Right-Wing Terror,"

113 ARD/ Robert Bongen et al., "'Lausbuben'"; Zeit Online/dpa/sk, "Freital: Polizei nimmt Rechtsextremisten in Sachsen fest," *Zeit Online*, November 5, 2015, accessed July 12, 2023, https://www.zeit.de /gesellschaft/zeitgeschehen/2015-11/freital-razzia-buegerwehr -mitglieder.

114 What constitutes a harsh sentence in Germany is different from the United States. Life sentences in Germany are a minimum of 15 years.

115 "PEGIDA-Gründer macht gegen Asylantenheim mobil."

116 Schimany, "Asylmigration," 37.

117 ARD/Robert Bongen, "'Lausbuben.'"

118 "Positionspaper der PEGIDA," December 10, 2014, accessed July 12, 2023, https://www.menschen-in-dresden.de/wp-content/uploads/2014/12/ PEGIDA-positionspapier.pdf. See also Vorländer, Herold, and Schäller, *PEGIDA*, 12–16 for more information about origins of PEGIDA policy positions. The text sections related to integration are points 2 and 10: "2. PEGIDA ist FÜR die Aufnahme des Rechtes auf und die Pflicht zur Integration ins Grundgesetz der Bundesrepublik Deutschland (bis jetzt ist da nur ein Recht auf Asyl verankert)!" and "10. PEGIDA ist FÜR den Widerstand gegen eine frauenfeindliche, gewaltbetonte politische Ideologie aber nicht gegen hier lebende, sich integrierende Muslime!" Translation: 2. (PEGIDA is FOR the acceptance of a right and the duty to integrate into the Basic Law of the Federal Republic of Germany (until now only anchored in a right to asylum)! 10. PEGIDA is FOR resistance against a misogynist, violent political ideology but not against those Muslims who live here and integrate themselves!

119 Meisner and Radau, "Vergleiche mit Hoyerswerda sind angebracht." Part of Rumberg's statement was also cited in Matthias Meisner, "PEGIDA, Freital, Meißen...: ... und die CDU. In Sachsen ist was faul," *Der Tagesspiegel*, June 29, 2015, accessed July 12, 2023, https://www.tagesspiegel .de/politik/-und-die-cdu-in-sachsen-ist-was-faul-4416304.html.

120 Meisner, "PEGIDA, Freital, Meißen."

121 "'Home' by Warsan Shire," Facing History & Ourselves, last updated May 4, 2022, accessed June 26, 2023, https://www.facinghistory.org /resource-library/home-warsan-shire.

122 ARD/ Robert Bongen et al., "'Lausbuben.'" Gastronom: "Also, rechts sind die nicht. Also: behaupte ich jetzt."

123 Lauren Stokes, "The Permanent Refugee Crisis in the Federal Republic of Germany, 1949–," *Central European History* 52 (2019): 19, https://doi .org/10.1017/S0008938919000025.

124 Poutrus, "Asylum in Postwar Germany," 132.

125 Lucy Mayblin, "Colonialism, Decolonisation, and the Right to Be Human: Britain and the 1951 Geneva Convention on the Status of Refugees," *Journal of Historical Sociology* 27, no. 3 (2014): 423–41, https://doi .org/10.1111/johs.12053.

126 Patrice Poutrus, *Umkämpftes Asyl: Vom Nachkriegsdeutschland bis in die Gegenwart* (Berlin: Ch. Links Verlag, 2019), 70–71.

127 Poutrus, *Umkämpftes Asyl*, 61–102.

128 Göktürk, Kaes, and Gramling, *Germany in Transit*, 501.

129 Poutrus, *Umkämpftes Asyl*, 87–9.

130 El-Tayeb, *Undeutsch*, 17–19.

131 Vietnamese contract workers had been part of the foreign workforce in the GDR before unification, which was an additional pathway through which Vietnamese citizens came to Germany.

132 Mayblin, "Colonisation"; B.S. Chimni, "The Geopolitics of Refugee Studies: A View from the South," *Journal of Refugee Studies* 11, no. 4 (1998): 350–74, https://doi.org/10.1093/jrs/11.4.350-a.

133 Chimni, "Geopolitics," 356.

134 Heinrich Lummer, "Victims of Freeloaders?," in *Germany in Transit: Nation and Migration 1955–2005*, eds. Deniz Göktürk, Anton Kaes, and David Gramling, trans. Tess Howell (Berkeley: University of California Press, 2007), 113–14.

135 Ulrich Herbert, "'Asylpolitik im Rauch der Brandsätze' – der zeitgeschichtliche Kontext," in *20 Jahre Asylkompromiss*, eds. Stefan Luft and Peter Schimany (Bielefeld: transcript verlag, 2014): 91.

136 Schimany, "Asylmigration," 33.

137 Ayşe Çağlar, "Displacement of European Citizen Roma in Berlin: Acts of Citizenship and Sites of Contentious Politics," *Citizenship Studies* 20, no. 5 (2016): 647–63.

138 Luft 14, Herbert, "Asylpolitik," 100–1.

139 Ursula Münch, "Asylpolitik in Deutschland - Akteure, Interessen, Strategien," in *20 Jahre Asylkompromiss*, eds. Stefan Luft and Peter Schimany, (Bielefel: transcript Verlag, 2014), 72.

140 Münch, "Aylpolitik," 74.
141 Münch, "Asylpolitik," 74.
142 Münch, "Asylpolitik," 74.
143 Mayblin, "Colonialism," 429–32.
144 Münch, "Asylpolitik," 77.
145 Münch, "Asylpolitik," 72. Stokes, "The Permanent Refugee Crisis," 35.
146 Münch, "Asylpolitik," 73.
147 Herbert, "Asylpolitik," 90.
148 Herbert, "Asylpolitik," 92–3.
149 Herbert, "Asylpolitik," 93–100.
150 Figuring out which of these dynamics are at work is difficult. Anti-Black, anti-Roma or Islamophobic racism appears in these statements, especially in 2014. Racism, built as it is on the foundational ideology of white supremacy, is the only appropriate term for those statements. But proximity to whiteness also matters. Aihwa Ong and Eric Tang have explored how certain South Asian minorities, especially Cambodian or Laotian refugees, undergo a process of ideological blackening in an American context. Given the prevalence of anti-African and anti-Black rhetoric when Germans talk about refugees, future work must explore how processes of blackening occur after unification in Germany and which groups benefit from proximity to whiteness. See Aihwa Ong, *Buddha Is Hiding: Refugees, Citizenship, the New America* (Berkeley: University of California Press, 2003), and Tang, *Unsettled.*

9 The 2016 Integration Act

1 nto./Reuters,"AfD-Vizechefin will Polizei auf Kinder schießen lassen," *Frankfurter Allgemeine Zeitung*, January 31, 2016, accessed July 12, 2023, https://www.faz.net/aktuell/politik/fluechtlingskrise/beatrix -von-storch-afd-vizechefin-will-polizei-sogar-auf-kinder-schiessen -lassen-14044186.html.
2 nto./Reuters, "AfD-Vizechefin will Polizei auf Kinder schießen lassen."
3 Kevin Roose, produced by Andy Mills, Julia Longoria, and Sindhu Gnanasambandan, edited by Larissa Anderson and Wendy Door. *Rabit Hole*. April 22, 2020. Podcast, MP3, 8 episodes. https://www.nytimes. com/2020/04/22/podcasts/rabbit-hole-prologue.html, https://www .nytimes.com/column/rabbit-hole.
4 Zeit Online, afp, ces, "Frauke Petry: AfD will Flüchtlinge notfalls mit Waffengewalt stoppen," *Die Zeit*, 30 January 2016, accessed July 12, 2023, https://www.zeit.de/politik/deutschland/2016-01/frauke-petry-afd- grenzschutz-auf-fluechtlinge-schiessen; Justus Bender and Alexander Haneke, "AfD-Chefin Frauke Petry fodert Schießbefehl an Grenze,"

Frankfurter Allgemeine Zeitung, January 31, 2016, accessed July 12, 2023, https://www.faz.net/aktuell/politik/inland/afd-chefin-frauke-petry -fodert-schiessbefehl-an-grenze-14044672.html; "Flüchtlinge an deutschen Grenzen: Petry für Schusswaffeneinsatz," *Die Tageszeitung,* January 30, 2016, accessed July 12, 2023, https://taz.de/!5274430/.

5 nto./Reuters, "Beatrix von Storch: AfD-Vizechefin will Polizei sogar auf Kinder schießen lassen."

6 "Schießen auf Flüchtlinge: Frauen ja, Kinder nein, *tagesschau*," January 31, 2016, accessed July 12, 2023, https://www.tagesschau.de/inland /afd-schusswaffen-103.html.

7 While the Italian crack down on the Albanians aboard the Vlora descended into violence and deportation, Syrian refugees aboard El Venizelos were transported to Athens for processing. "Vlora (Ship)," in *Wikipedia,* August 11, 2021, July 12, 2023, https://en.wikipedia. org/w/index.php?title=Vlora_(ship)&oldid=1038289918; Gregory Pappas,"Government-Chartered Ferry Eleftherios Venizelos Shuttling Thousands of Refugees Daily Off Greek Islands to Mainland," *The Pappas Post* (blog), August 31, 2015, accessed July 12, 2023, https://pappaspost. com/government-chartered-ferry-eleftherios-venizelos-shuttling -thousands-of-refugees-daily-off-greek-islands-to-mainland/.

8 Margot Litten, "Vertriebene – Ablehnung und Verachtung für Landsleute aus dem Osten," *Zeitfragen,* Deutschlandfunk Kultur, August 24, 2016, accessed July 12, 2023, https://www.deutschlandfunkkultur. de/vertriebene-ablehnung-und-verachtung-fuer-landsleute-aus-100. html; Aviral Goenka, "Bosnia's Srebrenica Genocide 25 Years On," *The Wire,* July 28, 2020, accessed July 12, 2023, https://thewire.in/world/ srebrenica-genocide-25-years-later.

9 "Vor 30 Jahren: Ausreise aus der Prager Botschaft," Bundeszentrale für politische Bildung, September 27, 2019, accessed July 12, 2023, https:// www.bpb.de/politik/hintergrund-aktuell/297704/prager-botschaft; Rebecca Harms, "English: Refugees at Budapest Keleti Railway Station," Wikimedia Commons, September 4, 2015, accessed July 12, 2023, https:// commons.wikimedia.org/wiki/File:Refugees_Budapest _Keleti_railway_station_2015-09-04.jpg; "München und die Flüchtlinge 2015: 'Ich kämpfte kurz mit den Tränen,'" tagesschau.de, September 5, 2020, no longer available, https://www.tagesschau.de/fluechtling-shelfer-muenchen-2015-101.html.

10 Schuster-Craig, "Integration Politics as an Apparatus."

11 Bade and Schäuble, eds., *Nachholende Integrationspolitik,* 54; Schus-ter-Craig, "Integration Politics as an Apparatus," 613.

12 Zeit Online, "AfD: Beatrix von Storch will doch nicht auf Kinder schießen," *Die Zeit,* January 31, 2016, accessed July 12, 2023, https://

www.zeit.de/politik/2016-01/alternative-fuer-deutschland-beatrix-von
-storch-petry-schusswaffen; syd, dpa, "AfD: Beatrix von Storch nimmt
Äußerung über Schüsse auf Flüchtlinge zurück," *Der Spiegel*, February 10,
2016, accessed July 12, 2023, https://www.spiegel.de/politik/deutschland
/afd-beatrix-von-storch-nimmt-aeusserung-ueber-schuesse-auf-fluechtlinge
-zurueck-a-1076757.html.

13 Walter Serif and Steffen Mack, "Sie können es nicht lassen!" *Mannheimer
Morgen*, January 29, 2016 accessed July 12, 2023, https://www.
mannheimer-morgen.de/politik_artikel,-politik-sie-koennen-es
-nicht-lassen-_arid,751556.html; Alexander Becker, "Frauke Petry vs.
Mannheimer Morgen: Schusswaffen-Interview wird zum Fall für den
Presserat," *MEEDIA* (blog), February 8, 2016, no longer available,
https://meedia.de/2016/02/08/frauke-petry-vs-mannheimer-morgen
-schusswaffen-interview-wird-zum-fall-fuer-den-presserat/; Katharina
Hamberger, "Reaktionen auf Petry-Äußerungen – 'Kein deutscher
Polizist würde auf Flüchtlinge schießen,'" Deutschlandfunk, January
30, 2016 accessed July 12, 2023, https://www.deutschlandfunk.de
/reaktionen-auf-petry-aeusserungen-kein-deutscher-polizist
-100.html, accessed July 12, 2023.

14 Schuster-Craig, "Integration Politics as an Apparatus," 611.

15 Deutscher Bundestag, *Deutscher Bundestag Stenografischer Bericht 174. Sitzung*.
Plenarprotokoll 18/174, Berlin: Deutscher Bundestag, 2016. PDF, https://
dserver.bundestag.de/btp/18/18174.pdf, 17185D, (Accessed July 10, 2023).

16 Deutscher *Bundestag, Stenografischer Bericht 174. Sitzung*.

17 Bundesamt für Migration und Flüchtlinge, "Konzept für einen
bundesweiten Integrationskurs Überarbeitete Neuauflage – April 2015,"
accessed July 10, 2023, https://www.bamf.de/SharedDocs/Anlagen
/DE/Integration/Integrationskurse/Kurstraeger/KonzepteLeitfaeden
/konz-f-bundesw-integrationskurs.pdf.

18 *Deutscher Bundestag Stenografischer Bericht 174. Sitzung*, 17187A.

19 Die Landesregierung Nordrhein-Westfalen, *Gesetz zur Förderung der gesellschaftlichen Teilhabe und Integration in Nordrhein-Westfalen (Teilhabe-
und Integrationsgesetz)*. Pub. L. No. GV. NRW. S. 97, Berlin Düsseldorf:
Landesregierung Nordrhein-Westfalen, 2012. Website, https://recht.nrw
.de/lmi/owa/br_bes_text?sg=0&menu=0&bes_id=47273&aufge
hoben=N&anw_nr=2, (Accessed July 12, 2023); Landesregierung Berlin,
Partizipations- und Integrationsgesetz des Landes Berlin, Pub. L. No. GVBl
S. 842, 850–2 PartIntG, Berlin: Landesregierung Berlin, 2010. Website,
https://gesetze.berlin.de/bsbe/document/jlr-PartIntergrGBErahmen
(Accessed July 12, 2023);

Landesregierung Baden-Württemberg, "Neues Gesetz folgt dem
Grundsatz, 'Fordern und Fördern,'" Baden-Württemberg.de, December

4, 2015 accessed July 12, 2023, https://sozialministerium.baden-
wuerttemberg.de/de/integration/partizipations-und-integrationsgesetz/.
Bavaria passed such a law only after the federal Integration Act had taken
effect: Bayerische Staatskanzlei, *Bayerisches Integrationsgesetz (BayIntG)*,
Horst Seehofer. Pub. L. No. GVBl. S. 335, BayRS 26-6-I Munich: Bayerische
Staatskanzlei, 2017. Website, https://www.gesetze-bayern.de/Content
/Document/BayIntG (Accessed July 12, 2023).

20 Bührmann and Schneider, *Diskurs*, 47.
21 Bührmann and Schneider, *Diskurs*, 49–50.
22 CDU/CSU/SPD, Deutscher Bundestag, *Entwurf eines Integrationgesetzes*,
CDU/CSU and SPD. DS 18/8615, Berlin: Deutscher Bundestag, 2016.
PDF, https://dserver.bundestag.de/btd/18/086/1808615.pdf, (Accessed
July 10, 2023).
23 Deutscher Bundestag, Die Linke, *Antrag: Flüchtlinge auf dem Weg in
Arbeit unterstützen, Integration befördern und Lohndumping bekämpfen*,
Sabine Zimmerman (Zwickau) et al. DS 18/6644, Berlin: Deutscher
Bundestag, 2015. PDF, https://dserver.bundestag.de
/btd/18/066/1806644.pdf, 4 (Accessed July 10, 2023).
24 Deutscher Bundestag, Bündnis 90/ Die Grünen, *Antrag: Integration ist gelebte Demokratie und stärkt den sozialen Zusammenhalt*, Luise Amtsberg et al.
DS 18/7651. https://dserver.bundestag.de/btd/18/076/1807651, Berlin:
Deutscher Bundestag, 2016. PDF, 1, (Accessed July 10, 2023).
25 CDU/CSU/SPD, *Entwurf eines Integrationsgesetzes*, 29.
26 CDU/CSU/SPD, *Entwurf eines Integrationsgesetzes*, 28.
27 CDU/CSU/SPD, *Entwurf eines Integrationsgesetzes*, 29.
28 CDU/CSU/SPD, *Entwurf eines Integrationsgesetzes*, 29.
29 Cordula Eubel, "Integration durch Sprache: Afghanen dürfen nicht in
Deutschkurse," *Der Tagesspiegel*, November 16, 2015, accessed March 8,
2024, https://www.tagesspiegel.de/politik/afghanen-durfen-nicht-in-
deutschkurse-5200177.html.
30 Fabio Ghelli et al., "Zehn Fragen zu afghanischen Flüchtlingen,"
Mediendienst Integration, August 17, 2021, accessed July 8, 2023, https://
mediendienst-integration.de/artikel/zehn-fragen-zu-afghanischen
-fluechtlingen.html. See Thomans Ruttig, "Afghan Exodus: Afghan
Asylum Seekers in Europe (3) – Case Study Germany," Afghanistan
Analysts Network, Reliefweb, February 17, 2017, accessed July 8, 2023,
https://reliefweb.int/report/germany/afghan-exodus-afghan-asylum
-seekers-europe-3-case-study-germany, 1, 6. Part of the mismatch
between how Afghans were designated in 2016 arose from how the
German government calculates the proportion of positive asylum
decisions and when those proportions were calculated. The 2013, 2014,
and 2015 proportion was lower than the number of Afghans who arrived

in 2016, when the number of positive cases increased. Afghans being classified as "second class asylum seekers" is due to poor data (i.e., the government using out of date statistics).

31 Schuster-Craig, "Integration Politics as an Apparatus," 615–18, 621–3; DW Deutsch / ShababTalk, "Politiker und Flüchtlinge diskutieren über das neue Integrationsgesetz," ShababTalk, *Deutsche Welle*, 2016. YouTube, 44:33, May 20, 2016, https://www.youtube.com/watch?v=ADUEi2sv2gk.

32 Birgit Rommelspacher, "Kulturelle Grenzziehungen in der Sozialarbeit: Doing and undoing differences," in *Diversität und soziale Ungleichheit: Analytische Zugänge und professionelles Handeln in der sozialen Arbeit*, eds., Herbert Effinger, et al., *(Leverkusen: Verlag* Barbara Budrich, 2012), 43–55.

33 Personal communication, January 24, 2023.

34 Participant 6, in discussion with the author, November 2017. "Ja, also insofern, natürlich hat das die Situation in Grund verbessert. Das ist ein großer Fortschritt gewesen. Aber für viele Menschen bleibt die Situation halt nach wie vor prekär. Das ist es halt nur."

35 Participant 1, in discussion with the author, July 2017. "… Partizipation im Allgemeinen, weg von diesem Integrationsbegriff."

36 Participant 1, in discussion with the author, July 2017. "Und da muss man sagen, auch dass das von dem Ministerium sehr klar ist. Dass der Gedanke, das ist nicht: ihr müsst euch integrieren. Sondern, es geht darum, wir gehören alle zusammen. [...] Und wir sind alle wichtige Akteure in diesen, in dieser Thematik. Und jeder erfüllt, sozusagen seine Rolle und Funktion."

37 Participant 1, in discussion with the author, July 2017. "…ich bin jetzt nicht so firm oder vertraut mit dieser ganzen aktuellen wissenschaftlichen Debatte von Integration/Inklusion."

38 Participant 6, in discussion with the author, July 2017. "[...] Es ist für mich wichtig, dass die [Teilnehmer …] diese Unterstützung bekommen, für das, was sie beruflich machen können, hier in Deutschland. Das ist, für die Integration in dem hiesigen Gesellschaft, die Mehrheitsgesellschaft, dass sie einen Platz finden, dass sie sich auch nicht aussortiert fühlen. Dass sie sich nicht ausgegrenzt fühlen. Und dass sie einfact ein Teilhabe von dieser Gesellschaft nehmen können. Also, oder sein können.
JSC: Ist dann das Ziel von Integration Teilhabe?
P: Ja."

39 Participant 6, in discussion with the author, November 2017. "Es [Integration] bedeutet, also, dass Dinge miteinander koexistieren. Ja? Und durchaus sich vielleicht auch was Neues, Hybrides daraus entwickeln kann. Ja?"

40 Participant 2, in discussion with the author, July 2017. "Also: die Integration jetzt in diesem Mentoringprojekt heisst berufliche Integration in den deutschen Arbeitsmarkt."

41 Participant 2, in discussion with the author, July 2017. "… und das andersrum gesehen: wenn die dann eben in diesen Prozess wieder einsteigen und es klappt, mit der beruflichen Integration [...] dann ist auch die soziale Integration einfacher, weil sie ja dann auch-, ähm, ja dann also eine glückliche Ehefrau und Mutter und Nachbarin und, was sie alles ist, kann natürlich in dieser Gesellschft viel mehr bewirken, als wenn sie zuhause sitzt und frustriert ist, ja? Und ich höre dann auch oft so, es gibt da ganz bewegende Sätze [...] eine [hat] auch mal gesagt, jetzt weiss ich wieder, dass ich mehr kann als nur schlechtes Deutsch."

42 Participant 3, in discussion with the author, July 2017. "Ok, berufliche Integration, da kann ich was dazu sagen."

43 Participant 3, in discussion with the author, July 2017. "Unter beruflichen Integration verstehen wir, dass die Menschen, die hierher kommen und einer Migrationserfahrung haben, Qualifikationsadäquat und nach ihren Vorstellungen auf den deutschen Arbeitsmarkt in das deutsche Berufsleben einmunden und zwar: Qualifikationsadäquat und selbstbestimmt. Das ist berufliche Integration."

44 Participant 5, in discussion with the author, July 2017. "Mmmm, also, wir zählen zu Integrationsleistungen verschiedene Sachen. Das gibt größere und kleinere Integrationsleistungen, ja?"

45 Participant 5, in discussion with the author, July 2017.

46 Participant 5, in discussion with the author, July 2017. "Aber dann geht's endlich voran. Und dann können sie ein Integrationskurs besuchen, also gesteuert in 'nem Deutschkurs bis B2 kommen, ja? Und dann ist es einfacher. Wenn die Leute durch's Asylverfahren sind. Na, das hat ja teilweise Monate gedauert. Bis sie überhaupt ihre Anhörungen hatten hier."

47 Participant 5, in discussion with the author, July 2017. "[...] so, jetzt hab' ich meinentwegen B1 [...]."

48 Participant 5, in discussion with the author, July 2017. "…eine Integration in den Arbeitsmarkt. Aber, die Hurden bis dahin sind individuell."

49 Participant 5, in discussion with the author, July 2017. "JSC: Es gibt vorläufige Sachen, die geklärt werden müssen, es kann Jahre dauern, bis jemand bereit ist, überhaupt mit der Integration anzufangen.
    Participant: Genau. Die sind vorher schon bereit. Die Gesellschaft ist hier nicht bereit. Wir sind von unseren Gesetzen her nicht bereit."

50 Participant 7, in discussion with the author, July 2017.

51 Musch, "Consultation Structures," 80.

52 Participant 3, in discussion with the author, July 2017. "Und die Zielgruppenförderung wurde durch die Hartz-Reformen abgeschafft. Es gab ja

nicht nur Hartz IV, sondern es gab auch Hartz II, Hartz I, Hartz III. Das war nicht so bekannt. Also, es gab vier Hartz-Gesetze. Und Hartz IV kennen alle, alle, so, und Hartz II – da gehörte diese, wir brauchen jetzt auch keine Zielgruppenförderung mehr, alle sind gleich."

53 Participant 3, in discussion with the author, July 2017. "… a) dürfen sie nicht mehr so lange gehen, b) sind sie sehr, sehr, sehr schlecht finanziert. Und c) haben sie keine Zielgruppenförderung vor Augen, sondern also MigrantInnen sind in diesen Umschulungen, ja? Also, sie sind gemischte Gruppen. Und, naja, da sind wir wieder beim Selektionsgesetz: die besten kommen nach vorne und die, die eben nicht mitkommen, die bleiben hängen."

54 Participant 3, in discussion with the author, July 2017. "Das ist ein ganz wichtiger Punkt, in dem man Erfolg anders misst. Ja? Es wird also, man versucht es wirklich effektiv, effizient, also die Beraterfirmen sind irgendwie, verdienen sich dum und dämlich an dem, wie kann man das LEAN-Management und auch was da alles haben und sparen und zusammen und Effizienz und Effektivität und, und, und, Kennzahlen und Kennzahlenüberprüfung und Monitoring, und und und und und, bei dem ganzen vergisst man aber den Menschen. Dass der seinen Prozess braucht."

55 Personal communication, email, January 24, 2023.

56 Participant 1, in discussion with the author, July 2017. "Und dann müssen wir gucken, wie ist, sozusagen, das Budget? Was ist davon machbar?"

57 Participant 4, in discussion with the author, November 2017.

58 Participant 7, in discussion with the author, July 2017. "Aber, mit solche, mit solche Budgets … kann man Integration nicht wirklich meinen."

59 Participants 2 and 7, in discussion with the author, July 2017.

60 Participants 3, 5 and 6 in discussion with the author, July 2017.

61 Participants 2 and 3, in discussion with the author, July 2017; Participant 4, in discussion with the author, November 2017.

62 Participants 2 and 7, in discussion with the author, July 2017.

63 Participant 1, in discussion with the author, July 2017. "… die Anforderungen an Organisationen in dieser Integrationsmaschinerie. Zu überleben."

64 Participant 1, in discussion with the author, July 2017. "… ich glaube, das hat auch etwas damit zu tun, dass viele von uns auch MigrantInnen sind, also wir agieren, auch wie soll ich sagen: so. Das sind diese verschiedene, also diese verschiedenen Ebenen, die auch da einwirken, und dann gibt es aber so diese äußere Ebene, diese Zwangsebenen, wir müssen schnell sein, wir müssen vielfältig sein, wir müssen professionell sein, weil: wir haben wenig Planungssicherheit. Weil wir diese Projektfinanzierung haben und welchen Druck, das auch wirklich nach innen auswirkt."

65 Participant 1, in discussion with the author, July 2017. "...ich habe
    früher immer gesagt, zum Thema Professionalisierungsprozesse, ich
    hab' für mich immer gesagt, wir bauen ein Haus und laufen gleichzeitig
    Marathon."

66 Participant 1, in discussion with the author, July 2017. "Burnout auf dreißig."

67 Head notes, discussion with Participant 8, July 2017.

68 Participant 4, in discussion with the author, November 2017. "... es ist so,
    ich wollte unbedingt Sozialarbeit studieren, natürlich. Das schon damals.
    [lacht] Und .. wo ich [als Kind] nach Deutschland gekommen bin, habe
    ich ja auch meine Probleme, Schwierigkeiten gehabt, was Deutsch betrifft.
    Und ... Die Lehrer und Lehrerinnen waren, also manche, sehr rassistisch.
    Die haben uns Migrantenkinder gar nicht gefördert. Im Gegenteil. Ihr
    schafft sowieso nichts. [...] Das hat bei mir natürlich anders gewirkt."

69 Participant 1, in discussion with the author, July 2017. "Da gibt's ja auch
    so diese wissenschaftliche Diskussion, auch so von dieser, oder Diversi-
    ty-Kompetenz, und immer so, wie viel wird Kultur sozusagen hergenom-
    men, oder diese kulturelle, ethnische, Hintergrund als Erklärungsmuster.
    Für die Menschen. Und: wie sehr wird das auch abgelehnt. Und, wir
    sagen immer so, naja, es gibt einen Rahmen. Also, gerade, für Neuzuge-
    wanderte ist dieses, sage ich mal Kultur oder kulturelle Codes oder sonst
    irgendwie, ist immer noch wichtig. Weil das gibt ihren Handlungsrah-
    men vor."

70 Participant 1, in discussion with the author, July 2017. "Also wir können
    das nicht vermeiden, dass die kulturelle Sozialisation uns auch hier in
    Deutschland, uns vorgibt, häufig, in welchem Rahmen wir uns bewegen.
    Oder, indem wir handeln oder fühlen oder was auch immer. Aber, es
    kommt natürlich immer auf meine individuelle Interpretation dessen
    an."

71 Participant 1, in discussion with the author, July 2017. "Man kann nicht
    sagen, du bist die [se Nationalität], und das sind die kulturalisierenden
    Werten, die man jemandem zuschreibt.
        JSC: Nein.
        Participant: Das geht gar nicht. Aber gleichzeitig braucht man es. Und
    ich finde, in dieser Diskussion, [...] da gibt es sehr wenig, oder in dieser
    Ausdifferenziertheit, das gibt wenig [...] Beschreibungsmöglichkeiten."

72 Participant 1, in discussion with the author, July 2017. "[...] Also wir
    brauchen alle eine gewisse Entspanntheit in diesem Themenbereich. [...]
    Ich bin, ich finde [unintelligible] wichtig politisch korrekt zu reden auf
    jeden Fall richtig, aber [...] für mich ist es immer auch, die Intention von
    Menschen, [...]. Aber die Person [...] sagt das nicht, weil sie mich ver-
    letzen möchte. Also, da kann man ein bisschen auch relaxter sein, und
    zu sagen, ist o. k. Oder mit den Menschen ins Gespräch kommen, wenn

man Lust hat, wenn nicht, dann nicht. Aber, ich finde das alles so auf die, auf die [Bandscheibe?] zu werfen, mir, mir, mir persönlich bringt es nichts. [...] Weil: ich kann genauso gut sozusagen andere Minderheiten gegenüber genauso 'ne eingeschränktere Sichtweise haben, oder wenig Erfahrung haben. Das kann mir genauso gehen."

73 Participant 2, in discussion with the author, July 2017. "Aber warum man jetzt die Akademiker, die es aus irgendwelchen Gründen nicht alleine schaffen, aber eigentlich ein tolles Fundament haben, warum man *die* jetzt auch noch mit staatlichem Geld unterstützen muss, müssten wir uns am Anfang als Kritik anhören. Wiederum ist es aber natürlich so [...] es braucht nicht wirklich, es kostet nicht wirklich viel Geld, ihnen diese Informationen zu geben, weil da ja sehr viel ehrenamtliches Engagement dabei ist. Und wenn die dann erst mal wieder in unserem System integriert sind und Steuern bezahlen, dann kommt das ja sofort wieder zurück."

74 Thomas de Maizière made this connection in two different rhetorical forms on an episode of the talk show *Anne Will* to discuss the Integration Act in 2016. Schuster-Craig, "Integration Politics as an Apparatus," 618.

75 Participants 5 and 6, in discussion with the author, July 2017.

76 Participant 5, in discussion with the author, July 2017. "Und man kann auch nicht sagen, wenn ein Mensch zum Beispiel aus Eritrea kommt, der hat grundsätzlich viel oder wenig Bildung. Es kommt darauf an, aus welchem Gebiet von Eritrea. Da gibt es Menschen, die haben wenig Schulbildung, und es gibt welche, die haben eine hohe Schulbildung. Wir haben festgestellt, dass hier bei beramí vielleicht auch durch Schwerpunkt Thema Anerkennung ausländischer Abschlüsse [...]. Vielleicht die Leute, die höher ausgebildet sind, auch eher zu uns finden."

77 Participant 5, in discussion with the author, July 2017.

   PARTICIPANT: Ja? Und, ähm, das sind: die verlassen ihren Land nicht freiwillig.
   JSC: Ok.
   PARTICIPANT: Und das [...] von manchen Populisten hier in Deutschland wird das umgedreht.
   JSC: Ja.
   PARTICIPANT: Behaupten zum Beispiel, dass es Wirtschaftsflüchtlinge sind. Das ist Quatsch mit Soße, ja? [...] Das ist völlig unsachlich, die haben – und meistens kennen die auch niemanden [no refugees], behaupte ich. Die haben noch mit niemanden gesprochen, sonst würden sie das nicht behaupten.

78 Participant 5, in discussion with the author, July 2017. "Ja, aber das Verrückte ist, ja, wovor hat man Angst?"

79 Participant 5, in conversation with the author, July 2017. "Da kommt doch kein Geflüchteter und macht die Türen auf und sagt, so, du brauchst jetzt hier den nicht, es ist kalt, ich nehme ihn jetzt mit [...] ?"

80 Participant 5, in discussion with the author, July 2017."... sehr höflich."

Epilogue: Subjectivity within the Integrative Apparatus

1 Participant 1, in discussion with the author, July 2017.
2 Participant 4, in discussion with the author, November 2017.
3 Participant 4, in discussion with the author, November 2017 and Participant 6, in discussion with the author, July 2017.
4 Participant 7, in discussion with the author, July 2017. "In den Parteien, und da habe ich schon mit dem Politiker geredet, und: da ist der Wille nicht da. Da ist der Willen definitiv nicht da, es ist nur politisch, es ist nur so political korrekt gesagt, jaja, wir wollen mehr MigrantInnen in den Parteien; das wäre schon schön. Alles repräsentative und alles, was man will, aber in der Wirklichkeit, haben sich die Parteien nicht geöffnet und [...] die öffnen sich das nicht. Und das ist eine bewusste Entscheidung., weil das würde bedeuten, Macht zu teilen.Vielleicht in Ostdeutschland, sind wir noch so weit, aber hier in Frankfurt, wir sind 52 % – d. h., wenn es hier tatsächlich ganz viele mehr Türken und ganz viele mehr andere MigrantInnen in den Parteien wären, dann würde man die auch wählen. Mindestens, die schon die Staatsangehörigkeit haben, würden die wählen, und zwar nicht nur die Progressivesten, auch die sehr Konservativen und Fundamentalisten, die würde man auch wählen, also einige Leute werden gewählt, und das würde bedeuten, man muss Macht teilen, und das wollen sie nicht und sie wissen ganz genau, wenn es, falls es dazu kommen sollte, dass wird passieren. Weil: mittlerweile haben wir wenig, aber wir haben die Türken, die kandidieren, die werden gewählt."
5 "Gut jede vierte Person in Deutschland hatte 2021 einen Migrationshintergrund," Statistisches Bundesamt, April 12, 2022, accessed July 8, 2023, https://www.destatis.de/DE/Presse/Pressemitteilungen/2022/04/PD22_162_125.html.
6 Sabine Hark, *Gemeinschaft der Ungewählten: Umrisse eines politischen Ethos der Kohabitation* (Berlin: Suhrkamp Verlag, 2021), 121–7, 214–24.
7 Participant 7, in discussion with the author, July 2017."[...] dass die Staatsangehörigkeit keine Sache der Gefühle ist, sondern eine Sache des Pragmatismus, und dass du, mit denen Regeln, die hier in diesem Land gelten, einfach ohne die Staatsangehörigkeit, ähm, nicht total sozial oder politisch teilhaben kannst. Weil wir als Drittländer, als, als, als Menschen, der aus dritten Ländern, wir haben keine kommunales Wahlrecht, d. h., du kannst sogar schon entschieden haben, ok, ich würde die SPD wählen, nur ich darf nicht wählen, ja?"
8 Michael Köhler, "Integrationsforscherin Edele – 'Es könnte eine Zweiklassengesellschaft unter Geflüchteten geben,'" *Deutschlandfunk*,

March 26, 2022, accessed July 8, 2023, https://www.deutschlandfunk.
de/vieles-ist-diesmal-einfacher-integrationsforscherin-aileen-edele-dlf
-eefcc300-100.html.

MDR Exactly / mpö, "Afghanistan oder Ukraine: Deutschland
behandelt nicht alle Geflüchtete gleich," *MDR.DE*, last modified May 14,
2022, accessed January 1, 2023, no longer available, https://www.mdr.de
/nachrichten/deutschland/gesellschaft/ukraine-syrien-fluechtlinge
-deutschland-unterschied-100.html; Luise Sammann, "Eine EU
-Richtlinie und ihre Auswirkungen - Unmut über ungleiche Behandlung
von Kriegsflüchtlingen," *Deutschlandfunk*, last modified May 6, 2022,
accessed July 8, 2023, https://www.deutschlandfunk.de/zwei-klassen
-gefluechtete-100.html; NDR. "Flüchtlinge aus der Ukraine: Kritik an
unterschiedlicher Behandlung," *NDR.DE*, last modified April 1, 2022,
accessed July 8, 2023. https://www.ndr.de/nachrichten/hamburg
/Fluechtlinge-aus-der-Ukraine-Kritik-an-unterschiedlicher
-Behandlung,ukraine2524.html.

9   "Geflüchtete aus der Ukraine und Syrien: unterschiedlich Willkommen
in Deutschland?" *Monitor*, ARD, 2022, accessed July 8, 2023, https://
www.youtube.com/watch?v=TVYZk8RfIWs.

10   Personal email, September 28, 2023.

11   Ashley Passmore (@golatschen), "What's old is new again: left is 2023
and the right, 1901. A political campaign to create panic over refugee
Jews coming to Vienna under the antisemitic mayor, Karl Lueger, Tweet,
September 23, 2023, https://twitter.com/golatschen
/status/1705634612381093928?s=20.

Bibliography

Ethnographic Interviews and Field Notes

beramí, Participants 1, 2, 5, 6, 7, Interview, July 2017.
beramí, Participants 3, 4, Interview, November 2017.
Projekt Heroes, Participants 1–4, Online Survey. 2020.
Fieldwork and Headnotes, July 8, 2015, Dresden.
Fieldwork Notes, Werkstatt der Kulturen, *Playing in the Dark* Event Series,
Attendance, 2010–11.

Secondary Sources

Åberg, Anna. "Falldöd misstänkt hedersmord." *Svenska Dagbladet*, July 6,
2009. https://www.svd.se/falldod-misstankt-hedersmord.
Abu-Lughod, Lila. *Do Muslim Women Need Saving?* Cambridge, MA: Harvard
University Press, 2013.
Abu-Odeh, Lama. "Comparatively Speaking: The 'Honor' of the 'East' and the
'Passion' of the 'West.'" *Utah Law Review* 287, no. 2 (1997): 287–307.
AfD in Sachsen und Dresden – Die Dokumentation. "Ungekürzt in HD: Pegida
8. Juni. 2015 mit Lutz Bachmann und Tatjana Festerling." June 9, 2015,
YouTube, 50:02. https://www.youtube.com/watch?v=SAAI7yk4PqI&t
=1267s.
"AfD: Beatrix von Storch will doch nicht auf Kinder schießen." *Die Zeit*,
January 31, 2016. https://www.zeit.de/politik/2016-01/alternative
-fuer-deutschland-beatrix-von-storch-petry-schusswaffen.
AFP. "Flüchtlingsamt BAMF: Lange Wartezeit für Integrationskurse."
Frankfurter Allgemeine Zeitung, December 24, 2017. https://www.faz.net
/aktuell/politik/inland/fluechtlingsamt-bamf-lange-wartezeit-fuer
-integrationskurse-15357225.html.

AFP. "Head of German Anti-Islam Group on Trial for Hate Speech." *The Guardian*, April 19, 2016. https://www.theguardian.com/world/2016/apr/19/head-of-german-anti-islam-group-pegida-trial-hate-lutz-bachmann.

AFP/KNA/jr. "Bundesregierung: Alleinerziehende mit Mindestlohn haben weniger Geld als Hartz IV." *Die Welt*, December 6, 2018. https://www.welt.de/politik/deutschland/article185107758/Bundesregierung-Alleinerziehende-mit-Mindestlohn-haben-weniger-Geld-als-Hartz-IV.html.

Agamben, Giorgio. *"What Is an Apparatus?"and Other Essays*. Palo Alto: Stanford University Press, 2009.

Ahmed, Leila. *Women and Gender in Islam*. New Haven, CT: Yale University Press, 1992.

Ahmed, Sara. "A Phenomenology of Whiteness." *Feminist Theory* 8, no. 2 (2007): 149–68. https://doi.org/10.1177/1464700107078139.

Alba, Richard, and Victor Nee. *Remaking the American Mainstream: Assimilation and Contemporary Immigration*. Cambridge, MA: Harvard University Press, 2009.

Alexander, Robin. "'Acht Stunden Verwahrung.'" *Die Tageszeitung*, July 18, 2003. https://taz.de/Acht-Stunden-Verwahrung/!739709/.

Alkousaa, Riham. "German and Something Else: Minorities Say #metwo after Ozil Quits." *Reuters*, July 27, 2018. https://www.reuters.com/article/us-soccer-germany-ozil-migration-idUSKBN1KH20E.

Althusser, Louis. *Lenin and Philosophy and Other Essays*. New York: Monthly Review Press, 2001.

Am Orde, Sabine. "Ausländerpolitik: Integrationsgipfel ohne Migranten?" *Die Tageszeitung*, July 4, 2007. https://taz.de/!5198505/.

–. "'Sprechen Sie mit den Jungs!'" *Die Tageszeitung*, February 22, 2005.

–. "Zehn Punkte gegen Gewalt." *Die Tageszeitung*, February 26, 2005.

Amara, Fadela, and Sylvia Zappi. *Breaking the Silence: French Women's Voices from the Ghetto*. Oakland: University of California Press, 2006.

–. *Ni putes ni soumises*. Paris: Découverte, 2003.

–. *Weder Huren noch Unterworfene*. Berlin: Orlanda Verlag, 2005.

ARD. "Geflüchtete aus der Ukraine und Syrien: Unterschiedlich Willkommen in Deutschland?" *Monitor*. ARD, April 11, 2022, YouTube, 8:53. https://www.youtube.com/watch?v=TVYZk8RfIWs.

Arndt, Susan. "Weißsein. Die verkannte Strukturkategorie Europas und Deutschlands." In *Mythen, Masken und Subjekte: kritische Weissseinsforschung in Deutschland*, 24–8. Münster: Unrast, 2005.

Arslan, Gizem, Brooke Kreitinger, Deniz Göktürk, David Gramling, B. Venkat Mani, Olivia Landry, Barbara Mennel, Scott Denham, Robin Ellis, and Roman Utkin. "Forum: Migration Studies." *The German Quarterly* 90, no. 2 (Spring 2017): 212–34.

Assmann, Aleida. "Canon and Archive." In *Cultural Memory Studies*, edited by Astrid Erll and Ansgard Nünning, 97–108. Berlin: De Gruyter, 2008. https://doi.org/10.1515/9783110207262.2.97

"Asylsuchende in München – Hungerstreik für die Anerkennung." *Süddeutsche Zeitung*, June 24, 2013. https://www.sueddeutsche.de/muenchen/demonstration-am-rindermarkt-hungern-fuer-ein-besseres-leben-1.1703402.

Ataman, Ferda. "Fünf Jahre danach: Die verlorene Ehre der Familie Sürücü." *Potsdamer Neuste Nachrichten*, October 22, 2019. https://www.pnn.de/brandenburg/die-verlorene-ehre-der-familie-sueruecue/22176562.html.

–. *Ich bin von hier. Hört auf zu fragen!* Frankfurt am Main: S. Fischer Verlag, 2019.

Ateş, Seyran. *Große Reise ins Feuer*. Berlin: Rowohlt, 2003.

Aubone, Amber, and Juan Hernandez. "Assessing Refugee Camp Characteristics and The Occurrence of Sexual Violence: A Preliminary Analysis of the Dadaab Complex." *Refugee Survey Quarterly* 32, no. 4 (2013): 22–40. https://doi.org/10.1093/rsq/hdt015.

Auer, Katja. "Asylbewerber in Bayern – Zufluchtsort Kaserne." *Süddeutsche Zeitung*, September 10, 2014. https://www.sueddeutsche.de/bayern/asylbewerber-in-bayern-zufluchtsort-kaserne-1.2122233.

Aufbruch Neukölln e.V. "Männerarbeit." Accessed June 25, 2023. https://www.aufbruch-neukoelln.de/anleitung/.

Auswärtiges Amt. "Erwerb der deutschen Staatsangehörigkeit." November 4, 2021. https://www.germany.info/usde/service/staatsangehoerigkeit/erwerb/1216790.

Ayim/Opitz, May. "Aufbruch." In *Farbe bekennen: Afro-deutsche Frauen auf den Spuren ihrer Geschichte*, edited by May Ayim, Katharina Oguntoye, and Dagmar Schultz, 2nd Edition, Location 3995–4114. Berlin: Orlanda Frauenverlag, 2020 (1986).

Bade, Klaus J. *Enzyklopädie Migration in Europa: vom 17. Jahrhundert bis zur Gegenwart*. Paderborn: Wilhelm Fink Verlag, 2007.

–. "Immigration and Social Peace in United Germany." Translated by Lieselotte Anderson. *Daedalus* 123, no. 1 (1994): 85–106.

–. *Kritik und Gewalt: Sarrazin-Debatte, "Islamkritik" und Terror in der Einwanderungsgessellschaft*. Schwalbach am Taunus: Wochenschau-Verlag, 2013.

–. *Migration in European History*. Translated by Allison Brown. Malden, MA: Blackwell Publishing, 2003.

Bade, Klaus J., and Wolfgang Schäuble, eds. "Versäumte Integrationschancen und nachholende Integrationspolitik." In *Nachholende Integrationspolitik und Gestaltungsperspektiven der Integrationspraxis*. Göttingen: V & R Unipress, 2007.

Baden-Württemberg.de. "Neues Gesetz folgt dem Grundsatz 'Fordern und Fördern'." December 4, 2015. https://sozialministerium.baden-wuerttemberg.de/de/integration/partizipations-und-integrationsgesetz/.

Badran, Margot. *Feminists, Islam, and Nation*. Princeton: Princeton University Press, 1996.

Bahners, Patrick. *Die Panikmacher: Die deutsche Angst vor dem Islam*. Munich: C.H. Beck, 2017.

Balcı, Güner Yasemin. *Arabboy: eine Jugend in Deutschland, oder, das kurze Leben des Rashid A*. Frankfurt am Main: Fischer Taschenbuch Verlag, 2010.

–. *ArabQueen oder der Geschmack der Freiheit*. Frankfurt am Main: Fischer Taschenbuch Verlag, 2012.

Barenberg, Jasper. "Dieser Mensch ist verwirrt." *Deutschlandfunk*, October 7, 2009. https://www.deutschlandfunk.de/dieser-mensch-ist-verwirrt-100.html.

Barton, Betty. "The Problem of 12 Million German Refugees in Today's Germany." Philadelphia: American Friends Service Committee, May 1949.

Basdorf, Gerhardt, Raum, Schaal, and Jäger. "Urteil vom 28. August 2007 in der Strafsache gegen 1. [Blank] 2. [Blank] wegen Mordes u.a." 5StR 31/07. 5. Strafsenats 2007.

Bauer, Franz J. "Aufnahme und Eingliederung der Flüchtlinge und Vertriebenen. Das Beispiel Bayern 1945–1950." In *Die Vertreibung der Deutschen aus den Osten: Ursachen, Ereignisse, Folgen*, edited by Wolfgang Benz, 158–72. Frankfurt am Main: Fischer Verlag, 1985.

Bauer, Patrick. "Hinter der Schulfassade." *Die Tageszeitung*, March 9, 2005.

Bayerischer Flüchtlingsrat. "Hungerstreik Bayernkaserne." January 17, 2012. https://archiv.fluechtlingsrat-bayern.de/hungerstreik-bayernkaserne.html.

Bayerische Landesregierung. *Bayerisches Integrationsgesetz (BayIntG)*. Horst Seehofer. Pub. L. No. GVBl. S. 335, BayRS 26-6-I. Munich: Bayerische Landesregierung, 2017. Accessed June 4, 2024. https://www.gesetze -bayern.de/Content/Document/BayIntG.

Beikler, Sabine. "Hatuns Bruder will sich neuem Prozess doch nicht stellen." *Der Tagesspiegel*, January 20, 2008. https://www.tagesspiegel.de/berlin /polizei-justiz/fall-sueruecue-hatuns-bruder-will-sich-neuem-prozess -doch-nicht-stellen/1145286.html.

–. "'Wir konnten ihr Leben nicht tolerieren'." *Der Tagespiegel*, July 25, 2011. https://www.tagesspiegel.de/berlin/der-fall-sueruecue-wir-konnten-ihr -leben-nicht-tolerieren/4430780.html.

Beikler, Sabine, and Anette Kögel. "Fall Sürücü kommt zu den Akten." *Der Tagesspiegel*, February 2, 2009. https://www.tagesspiegel.de/berlin /kriminalitaet-fall-sueruecue-kommt-zu-den-akten/1434286.html.

Belwe, Katharina. "Editorial." *Aus Politik und Zeitgeschichte: Arbeitsmarktreformen* 16 (2005). https://www.bpb.de/system/files/pdf/R74OJH.pdf.

Bender, Justus, and Alexander Haneke. "AfD-Chefin Frauke Petry fodert Schießbefehl an Grenze." *Frankfurter Allgemeine Zeitung*, January 31, 2016. https://www.faz.net/aktuell/politik/inland/afd-chefin-frauke-petry -fodert-schiessbefehl-an-grenze-14044672.html.

Bennhold, Katrin, Lynsea Garrison, Clare Toeniskoetter, Kaitlin Roberts, Larissa Anderson, and Mike Benoist. "Franco A." Produced by Lynsea Garrison, Clare Toeniskoetter and Kaitlin Roberts. *Day X*, June 16, 2021. Podcast, MP3, 37:14. https://www.nytimes.com/2021/06/16/podcasts/franco-a-trial-germany-terrorism.html.

Berberich, Frank. "Klasse statt Masse." *Lettre International*, 86 (2009). Accessed March 10, 2024. https://www.lettre.de/content/frank-berberich_klasse-statt-masse.

Berg, Stefan, Thomas Darnstädt, Katrin Elger, Konstantin von Hammerstein, Frank Hornig, and Peter Wensierski. "Politik der Vermeidung." *Der Spiegel* 42, November 11, 2009. Accessed March 10, 2024. https://www.spiegel.de/politik/politik-der-vermeidung-a-f96b4be5-0002-0001-0000-000067282817.

Berger, Marco. "Statement – Maisha Maureen Auma." Zentrum für transdisziplinäre Geschlechterstudien. February 2, 2021. https://www.gender.hu-berlin.de/en/diverses-en/2021_en/statement_auma_en.

Berlinghoff, Marcel. "Geschichte der Migration in Deutschland." Bundeszentrale für politische Bildung. May 14, 2018. http://www.bpb.de/gesellschaft/migration/dossier-migration/252241/deutsche-migrationsgeschichte.

Berman, Elizabeth Popp. *Thinking Like an Economist: How Efficiency Replaced Equality in U.S. Public Policy*. Princeton: Princeton University Press, 2022.

Betz, Hans-Georg. "Nativism Across Time and Space." *Swiss Political Science Review* 23, no. 4 (2017): 335–53. https://doi.org/10.1111/spsr.12260.

Betz, Tobias, Sonja Pohlmann, and Carsten Volkery. "Islam-Konferenz: Schäuble wünscht sich 'deutsche Muslime.'" *Spiegel Online*, September 27, 2006. http://www.spiegel.de/politik/deutschland/islam-konferenz-schaeuble-wuenscht-sich-deutsche-muslime-a-439389.html.

Bickford, Andrew. "Soldiers, Citizens, and the State: East German Army Officers in Post-Unification Germany." *Comparative Studies in Society and History* 51, no. 2 (2009): 260–87.

Bielicki, Jan. "Nicht einmal jeder Zweite bekommt einen Platz im Integrationskurs." *Süddeutsche Zeitung*, September 22, 2016. http://www.sueddeutsche.de/politik/migranten-run-auf-deutschkurse-1.3174463.

"Bild mit Hitlerbart: Herbst vs. Bachmann – 'Habe keine Facebook-Seite'." *Die Welt*, January 21, 2015. https://www.welt.de/politik/deutschland/article136626463/Herbst-vs-Bachmann-Habe-keine-Facebook-Seite.html.

Bildungsstätte Anne Frank. "Peggy Piesche im Interview. Teil der Ausstellung *Anderen wurde es schwindelig*." September 28, 2020. YouTube, 14:35. https://www.youtube.com/watch?v=zEujgzFsfTw&t=86s.

bka. "CSU-Vorstoß: Migranten sollen zu Hause Deutsch sprechen." *Spiegel Online*, December 5, 2014. http://www.spiegel.de/politik/deutschland/csu-in-bayern-migranten-sollen-im-wohnzimmer-deutsch-sprechen-a-1006904.html.

Blasius, Rainer. "Unwort des Jahres: Von der Journaille zur Lügenpresse." *Frankfurter Allgemeine Zeitung*, January 13, 2015. https://www.faz.net /aktuell/gesellschaft/unwort-des-jahres-eine-kleine-geschichte-der -luegenpresse-13367848.html.

Blee, Kathleen M., and Kimberly A. Creasap. "Conservative and Right-Wing Movements." *Annual Review of Sociology* 36, no. 1 (2010): 269–86. https:// doi.org/10.1146/annurev.soc.012809.102602.

Bloemraad, Irene, and Karen Schönwälder. "Immigrant and Ethnic Minority Representation in Europe: Conceptual Challenges and Theoretical Approaches." *West European Politics* 36, no. 3 (2013): 564–79. https://doi.org /10.1080/01402382.2013.773724.

Bongen, Robert, Thomas Datt, Philipp Hennig, and Johannes Jolmes. "'Lausbuben': Wie man in Freital Terroristen verharmlost." *Panorama*. ARD: NDR. December 14, 2017. YouTube, 12:19. https://www.youtube.com /watch?v=dtpQ5FzEr_c.

Borufka, Sarah. "Sie musste sterben, weil sie leben wollte." *Berliner Zeitung*, February 7, 2015. https://www.bz-berlin.de/berlin/sie-musste-sterben -weil-sie-leben-wollte.

Botsch, Gideon. "Gutachten im Auftrag des SPD-Kreisverbandes Spandau und der SPD- Abteilung Alt-Pankow zur Frage: 'Sind die Äußerungen von Dr. Thilo Sarrazin im Interview mit der Zeitschrift Lettre International (deutsche Ausgabe, Heft 86) als rassistisch zu bewerten?'" Report. Berlin, December 22, 2009. https://www.google.com/search?q=About+https:// www.tagesschau.de/inland/gutachtensarrazin100.pdf.

Brady, Kate. "PEGIDA Founder Lutz Bachmann Found Guilty of Inciting Hatred." *DW.COM*, May 3, 2016. https://www.dw.com/en/pegida -founder-lutz-bachmann-found-guilty-of-inciting-hatred/a-19232497.

Breidenstein, Jenny, ed. *Heroes: Dokumentation des ersten Jahres*, 22. Internal document.

Brown, Wendy. *Undoing the Demos: Neoliberalism's Stealth Revolution*. Brooklyn: Zone Books, 2015.

Bryant, Tom. "Mesut Özil Walks Away from Germany Team Citing 'Racism and Disrespect.'" *The Guardian*, July 23, 2018. https://www.theguardian .com/football/2018/jul/22/mesut-ozil-retires-german-national-team -discrimination.

Buchheim, Christoph. "Die Währungsreform 1948 in Westdeutschland." *Vierteljahrshefte für Zeitgeschichte* 36, no. 2 (1988): 189–231.

Bührmann, Andrea D., and Werner Schneider. *Vom Diskurs zum Dispositiv: Eine Einführung in die Dispositivanalyse*. Bielefeld: transcript Verlag, 2008.

Bukow, Wolf-Dietrich, Claudia Nikodem, Erika Schulze, and Erol Yildiz, eds. *Was heißt hier Parallelgesellschaft?: Zum Umgang mit Differenzen*. Wiesbaden: VS Verlag für Sozialwissenschaften, 2007.

Bundesamt für Migration und Flüchtlinge. "Inhalt und Ablauf." Accessed December 10, 2021. https://www.bamf.de/DE/Themen/Integration /ZugewanderteTeilnehmende/Integrationskurse/InhaltAblauf/inhaltablauf -node.html.

–. "Integrationskurszahlen," April 25, 2018. http://www.bamf.de/DE/Infothek /Statistiken/InGe/inge-node.html.

Bundesgerichtshof, Mitteilung der Pressestelle. *Bundesgerichtshof hebt Freisprüche im sogenannten Ehrenmordprozess auf.* 117/2007. Karlsruhe: Bundesgerichtshof, 2007. Accessed March 10, 2024. https://www.bundesgerichtshof.de /SharedDocs/Pressemitteilungen/DE/2007/2007117.html.

Bundesinstitut für Bevölkerungsforschung. "Bevölkerung mit Migrationshintergrund nach den häufigsten Herkunftsländern/-Regionen (2016)." Accessed October 9, 2019. https://www.bib.bund.de/DE /Fakten/Fakt/B48-Bevoelkerung-mit-Migrationshintergrund-Herkunft .html?nn=9992206.

Das Bundesministerium des Innern, für Bau und Heimat. "Wie aus jungen Männern 'Helden' werden." May 26, 2016. http://www.bmi.bund.de /SharedDocs/kurzmeldungen/DE/2016/05/bundesinnenminister-besucht -projektheroes.html.

Der Bundesminister für Arbeit und Sozialordnung. *Politik der Bundesregierung gegenüber den ausländischen Arbeitnehmern in der Bundesrepublik Deutschland.* Antwort auf Kleine Anfrage DS 6/2897, DRS 6/3085 IIc-68/29. Berlin: Der Bundesminister für Arbeit und Sozialordnung, 1972. Digitized photocopy.

Bundespressekonferenz. "Bundespressekonferenz: Information in English." October 9, 2019. https://www.bundespressekonferenz.de/information -in-english.

Die Bundesregierung. "13th Integration Summit with Chancellor Angela Merkel." Accessed October 15, 2021. https://www.bundesregierung.de /breg-en/news/13th-integration-summit-1875236.

Buntrock, Tanja, and Annette Kögel. "Gedenken mit Hilferuf." *Der Tagesspiegel*, February 23, 2005. https://www.tagesspiegel.de/berlin/gedenken-mit -hilferuf/587420.html.

Buruma, Ian. *Murder in Amsterdam: Liberal Europe, Islam, and the Limits of Tolerance.* New York: Penguin Books, 2007.

Buschmann, Rolf, Alexandra Farrensteiner, and Ulrike Plesser. "Integration per Gesetz – Wer soll zu Deutschland gehören?" Produced by NDR. *Anne Will.* May 8, 2016. Podcast, MP3 audio, 1:01:36. https://podcasts.apple .com/de/podcast/das-erste-anne-will/id277698119.

Butterwegge, Christoph. "Die Demontage des Sozialstaates: Arme and Migrant/Innen im Visier von Guido Westerwelle, Thilo Sarrazin et al." *Widerspruch: Beiträge zu sozialistischer Politik* 30, no. 59 (2010): 85–95. https:// doi.org/10.5169/seals-652446.

–. "Standortnationalismus, Rechtsextremismus und Zuwanderung." *Widerspruch: Beiträge zu sozialistischer Politik* 21, no. 41 (2001): 53–62. https:// doi.org/doi.org/10.5169/seals-652173.

Butterwegge, Christoph, Rudolf Hickel, and Ralf Ptak. *Sozialstaat und neoliberale Hegemonie: Standortnationalismus als Gefahr für die Demokratie.* Berlin: Elefanten Press, 1998.

Çaglar, Ayşe S. "Constraining Metaphors and the Transnationalisation of Spaces in Berlin." *Journal of Ethnic and Migration Studies* 27, no. 4 (2001): 601–13. https://doi.org/10.1080/13691830120090403.

–. "Displacement of European Citizen Roma in Berlin: Acts of Citizenship and Sites of Contentious Politics." *Citizenship Studies* 20, no. 5 (2016): 647–63.

Campt, Tina Marie. *Other Germans: Black Germans and the Politics of Race, Gender, and Memory in the Third Reich.* Ann Arbor: University of Michigan Press, 2009.

Can, Ali. "The Two-Hearted Man." *Politico EU,* 2019. https://www.politico .eu/list/politico-28-class-of-2019-the-ranking/ali-can/.

can/ddp. "'Lettre'-Magazin fordert Schadenersatz von 'Bild.'" *Spiegel Online,* October 27, 2009. https://www.spiegel.de/kultur/gesellschaft/sarrazin -interview-lettre-magazin-fordert-schadensersatz-von-bild-a-657626 .html.

Castles, Stephen. "The Guest-Worker in Western Europe – An Obituary." *International Migration Review* 20, no.4 (1986). https://doi.org/10.1177/0197 91838602000402.

Castles, Stephen, and Godula Kosack. *Immigrant Workers and Class Structure in Western Europe.* London: Oxford University Press, 1973.

Cf/lsc/hjv. "Pegida-Chef Lutz Bachmann: Hitler-Foto und Ausländer -Beleidigungen bei Facebook." *Bild.de,* January 21, 2015. https://www.bild .de/politik/inland/pegida/chef-lutz-bachmann-hitler-foto-und -auslaender-beleidigungen-bei-facebook-39430448.bild.html.

Chimni, B.S. "The Geopolitics of Refugee Studies: A View from the South." *Journal of Refugee Studies* 11, no. 4 (1998): 350–74. https://doi.org/10.1093 /jrs/11.4.350-a.

Chin, Rita. *The Crisis of Multiculturalism in Europe: A History.* Princeton: Princeton University Press, 2017.

–. *The Guestworker Question in Postwar Germany.* New York: Cambridge University Press, 2009.

Chin, Rita, Heide Fehrenbach, Geoff Eley, and Atina Grossmann. *After the Nazi Racial State: Difference and Democracy in Germany and Europe.* Ann Arbor: University of Michigan Press, 2009.

Çil, Nevim. *Topographie des Aussenseiters.* Berlin: Verlag Hans Schiler, 2007.

Çileli, Serap. *Serap: Wir sind eure Töchter, nicht eure Ehre!* Michelstadt: Neuthor Verlag, 2002.

cke. "Hatun Sürücü: Ihr Mörder arbeitete für den deutschen Staat." *Die Welt*, July 29, 2015. https://www.welt.de/vermischtes/article144606108/Hatuns -Moerder-arbeitete-fuer-deutschen-Botschafter.html.

Cohen, Roger. "Germany Makes Citizenship Easier for Foreigners to Get." *The New York Times*, May 22, 1999. https://www.nytimes.com/1999/05/22 /world/germany-makes-citizenship-easier-for-foreigners-to-get.html.

Connolly, Kate. "Photograph of Germany's Pegida Leader Styled as Adolf Hitler Goes Viral." *The Guardian*, January 21, 2015. http://www.theguardian .com/world/2015/jan/21/pegida-leader-styled-adolf-hitler-lutz-bachmann -german-islamist-terrorists-facebook.

Cöster, Anna C. *Ehrenmord in Deutschland*. Marburg: Tectum Wissenschaftsverlag, 2009.

Crenshaw, Kimberlé. "Demarginalizing the Intersection of Race and Sex: A Black Feminist Critique of Antidiscrimination Doctrine, Feminist Theory and Antiracist Politics." *University of Chicago Legal Forum*, 8, no. 1 (1989): 139–67.

Daftari, Shirin. *Fremde Wirklichkeiten: Verstehen und Missverstehen im Fokus bikultureller Partnerschaften*. Münster: LIT Verlag, 2000.

Dangschat, Jens S. "Residentielle Segregation nach Nationalität – ein Diskurs voller Widersprüche." *Österreichische Zeitschrift für Soziologie* 41, no. 2 (2016): 81–101. https://doi.org/10.1007/s11614-016-0225-7.

Davy, Ulrike. "Integration of Immigrants in Germany: A Slowly Evolving Concept." *European Journal of Migration and Law* 7, no. 2 (2005): 123–44.

Deckwerth, Sabine, and Frank Nordhausen. "Eine Mahnwache für die getötete Türkin Hatin [sic] Sürücü." *Berliner Zeitung*, February 23, 2005.

Deiß, Matthias, and Jo Goll. *Ehrenmord: Ein deutsches Schicksal*. Hamburg: Hoffmann und Campe Verlag, 2011.

–. *Verlorene Ehre: Der Irrweg der Familie Sürücü*. TV Documentary. Rbb, WDR, ARD, 2011. (Video no longer available because YouTube terminated the account.) https://www.youtube.com/watch?v=JCf_l3wZ31U.

Delgado, Jésus Manuel. *Die Gastarbeiter in der Presse: eine inhaltsanalytische Studie*. Düsseldorf: C.W. Leske Verlag, 1972.

"Demo gegen Gewalt." *Die Tageszeitung*, March 3, 2005.

Demokratie Spiegel. "Integrationsgipfel 2006." July 13, 2007. http://www .demokratie-spiegel.de/printable/archiv/politik/integrationsgipfel2006 .html.

Dennis, Mike, and Norman LaPorte. *State and Minorities in Communist East Germany*. New York: Berghahn Books, 2011.

Deutsch: Scan aus dem Deutschen Reichsgesetzblatt 1933, Teil 1; English: Scan from the Imperial Law Gazette of Germany, 1933, Part 1. Scanned by user. Accessed October 23, 2019. https://commons.wikimedia.org/wiki/File:Deutsches _Reichsgesetzblatt_33T1_005_0026.jpg.

Deutscher Bundestag. "16. Wahlperiode – 54. Sitzung." Plenarprotokoll 16/54. Berlin: Deutscher Bundestag, September 28, 2006. Accessed July 11, 2023. https://dserver.bundestag.de/btp/16/16054.pdf.

–. *Allgemeines Gleichbehandlungsgesetz (AGG)*. BGBl. I S. 1897 §. Berlin: Deutscher Bundestag, 2006 (last amended 2022). Accessed March 10, 2024. https://www.gesetze-im-internet.de/englisch_agg/englisch_agg.html.

–. *Antwort der Bundesregierung: auf die Kleine Anfrage der Abgeordneten Siylle Laurischk, Hartfrid Wolff (Rems-Mur), Cornelia Pieper, weiterer Abgeordneter und der Fraktion der FDP*. DRS 16/3758 Berlin: Deutscher Bundestag, 2006. PDF, https://dserver.bundestag.de/btd/16/037/1603758.pdf. Date from text.

–. Ausschuss für Arbeit und Soziales. "Beschlussempfehlung und Bericht des Ausschusses für Arbeit und Soziales (11. Ausschuss)." Tobias Zech. DS 18/9090. Berlin: Deutscher Bundestag, 2016. Accessed date from text. https://dserver.bundestag.de/btd/18/090/1809090.pdf.

–. *Entwurf eines Integrationsgesetzes*. CDU/CSU/SPD. DS 18/8615. Berlin: Deutscher Bundestag, 2016. Accessed March 10, 2024. https://dserver. bundestag.de/btd/18/086/1808615.pdf.

–. *Entwurf eines ... Strafrechtsänderungsgesetzes – §§180b, 181 StGB (... StRÄndG)*. Joachim Stünker et al.. Drucksache 15/3045. Berlin: Deutscher Bundestag, 2004. Accessed July 13, 2023. https://dserver.bundestag.de/btd/15/030 /1503045.pdf.

–. Die Grünen. *Antrag: Integration ist gelebte Demokratie und stärkt den sozialen Zusammenhalt*. Luise Amtsberg, Volker Beck, Kerstin Andrae, Annalena Baerbock, and Ekin Deligöz, et al. DS 18/7651. Berlin: Deutscher Bundestag. Accessed February 24, 2016. https://dserver.bundestag.de/btd/18/076 /1807651.pdf.

–. *Kleine Anfrage der Abgeordneten Ulla Jelpke und der Gruppe der PDS/Linke Liste Ausländerfeindliche Übergriffe und rechtsextremer Terror*. Ulla Jelpke and Dr. Gregor Gysi. DS 12/2086. Berlin: Deutscher Bundestag, 1992. Accessed March 13, 2024. https://dipbt.bundestag.de/doc/btd/12/020/1202086.pdf.

–. Die Linke. *Antrag: Flüchtlinge auf dem Weg in Arbeit unterstützen, Integration befördern und Lohndumping bekämpfen*. Sabine, Zimmerman, Ulla Jelpke, Jutta Krellmann, Matthias W. Birkwald, Sevim Dagdelen, and Die Linke. DS 18/6644. Berlin: Deutscher Bundestag, 2015. Accessed date from text. https://dserver.bundestag.de/btd/18/066/1806644.pdf.

–. "Rede von Bundestagspräsidentin Bärbel Bas zum Tag der Deutschen Einheit 2022." October 3, 2022. https://www.bundestag.de/parlament /praesidium/reden/2022/20221003-912680.

–. *Schriftliche Fragen mit den in der Woche vom 22. Januar 1990 eingegangenen Antworten der Bundesregierung*. DS 11/6323. Berlin: Deutscher Bundestag, 1990. Accessed March 7, 2024. http://dipbt.bundestag.de/doc/btd/11/063 /1106323.pdf.

–. Vermittlungsausschuss. *Beschlussempfehlung des Vermittlungsausschusses zu dem Gesetz zur Steuerung und Begrenzung der Zuwanderung und zur Regelung des Aufenthalts und der Integration von Unionsbürgern und Ausländern (Zuwanderungsgesetz) – Drucksachen 15/420, 15/522, 15/955, 15/1365.* Hans-Joachim Hacker and Peter Müller. DS 15/3479. Berlin: Deutscher Bundestag, 2004. Accessed March 10, 2024. http://dipbt.bundestag.de/dip21/btd/15/034/1503479.pdf.

–. "Deutscher Bundestag Stenografischer Bericht 174. Sitzung." Plenarprotokoll 18/174. Berlin: Deutscher Bundestag, June 3, 2016. Accessed July 10, 2023. https://dserver.bundestag.de/btp/18/18174.pdf.

Dietz, Barbara. "Aussiedler in Germany: From Smooth Adaptation to Tough Integration." In *Paths of Integration: Migrants in Western Europe (1880–2004),* edited by Leo Lucassen, David Feldman, and Jochen Oltmer, 116–36. Amsterdam: Amsterdam University Press, 2006.

Doku Gönner. *[DokuHD] EHRENMORD? Wenn die türkische Tochter für ihre INTEGRATION büßen muss.* December 5, 2017. YouTube, 43:31. https://www.youtube.com/watch?v=1A4hk8gduxU.

Douglas, R.M. *Orderly and Humane: The Expulsion of the Germans After the Second World War.* New Haven: Yale University Press, 2012.

dpa. "Ausländer: Muslime: Sarrazins Buch Kampfansage an Demokratie." *Die Zeit,* August 30, 2010. https://www.zeit.de/news-nt/2010/8/30/iptc-bdt-20100830-474-26176586xml.

–. "Flüchtlinge an deutschen Grenzen: Petry für Schusswaffeneinsatz." *Die Tageszeitung,* January 30, 2016. https://taz.de/!5274430/.

–. "Immer mehr Flüchtlinge in Aufnahmeeinrichtung Zirndorf." *Abendzeitung,* August 26, 2014. https://www.abendzeitung-muenchen.de/bayern/immer-mehr-fluechtlinge-in-aufnahmeeinrichtung-zirndorf-art-249375.

–. "Integrationspolitik: Kanzlerin empört über Sarrazins Polemik." *Die Zeit,* August 25, 2010. https://www.zeit.de/politik/deutschland/2010-08/sarrazin-merkel.

dpa/AFP. "Prozess gegen Pegida-Gründer: Anwältin von Lutz Bachmann fordert Einstellung des Verfahrens." *Der Tagesspiegel,* April 19, 2016. https://www.tagesspiegel.de/politik/prozess-gegen-pegida-gruender-anwaeltin-von-lutz-bachmann-fordert-einstellung-des-verfahrens/13467984.html.

dpa/AFP/AP/cn. "Integrationsgipfel: Merkel freut sich über 'Meilenstein.'" *Die Welt,* July 12, 2007. https://www.welt.de/politik/article1021724/Merkel-freut-sich-ueber-Meilenstein.html.

dpa/cpa. "Nach Beschwerde der Türkei: Berliner 'Ehrenmord'-Prozess gegen Sürücü-Brüder wird neu aufgerollt." *Die Welt,* February 22, 2018. https://www.welt.de/vermischtes/article173865433/Nach-Beschwerde-der-Tuerkei-Berliner-Ehrenmord-Prozess-gegen-Sueruecue-Brueder-wird-neu-aufgerollt.html.

dpa/epd/fp. "State Department warnt vor Pegida-Demos." *Die Welt*, January 28, 2015. https://www.welt.de/136867558.

dpa/UM/mkl. "Ex-Pegida-Chefs planen offenbar neues Bündnis." *Die Welt*, January 29, 2015. https://www.welt.de/politik/deutschland /article136906332/Ehemalige-Pegida-Chefs-gruenden- neues-Buendnis. html.

Dresden.de. "Oberbürgermeisterwahl Dresden 2015 – Erster Wahlgang am 07.06.2015." February 26, 2021. http://wahlen.dresden.de/2015/OBW /index.html.

Druxes, Helga. "Manipulating the Media: The German New Right's Virtual and Violent Identities." In *Digital Media Strategies of the Far Right in Europe and the United States*, edited by Patricia Anne Simpson and Helga Druxes, 123–40. London: Lexington Books, 2015.

DuBois, Laurent. *Soccer Empire*. Oakland: University of California Press, 2010.

DW Deutsch. *Politiker und Flüchtlinge diskutieren über das neue Integrationsgesetz*. ShababTalk. Deutsche Welle. May 30, 2016. YouTube, 44:33. https://www .youtube.com/watch?v=ADUEi2sv2gk.

Eddy, Melissa. "German Anti-Immigrant Leader Fined over Facebook Post." *The New York Times*, May 3, 2016. https://www.nytimes.com/2016/05/04 /world/europe/lutz-bachmann-pegida-fined-germany.html.

–. "German Who Posed as Hitler Returns to Position in Anti-Immigrant Group Pegida." *The New York Times*, February 24, 2015. https://www.nytimes .com/2015/02/25/world/europe/lutz-bachmann-pegida.html.

"'Ehrenmord' an Hatin Sürücü: Bundespräsident Köhler dankt couragiertem Schulleiter." *Spiegel Online*, August 12, 2005. https://www.spiegel.de /lebenundlernen/schule/ehrenmord-an-hatin-sueruecue-bundespraesident -koehler-dankt-couragiertem-schulleiter-a-369481-2.html.

"Ehrenmord-Prozess: Die Frage der Ehre," *Die Zeit*, August 28, 2007. https:// www.zeit.de/online/2007/35/revisionsverfahren-ehrenmord.

Ehrkamp, Patricia. "Risking Publicity: Masculinities and the Racialization of Public Neighborhood Space." *Social & Cultural Geography* 9, no. 2 (2008): 117–33. https://doi.org/10.1080/14649360701856060.

"Eichel kritisiert Mißbrauch von Aufbau-Ost-Geldern." *Die Welt*, November 27, 2004. https://www.welt.de/politik/article355153/Eichel-kritisiert -Missbrauch-von-Aufbau-Ost-Geldern.html.

Eichstädt, Sven. "Prozessbeginn: Lutz Bachmann inszeniert sich vor Gericht." *Die Welt*, April 17, 2016. https://www.welt.de/politik/deutschland /article154444813/Bachmann-macht-sich-ueber-Strafprozess-lustig.html.

El-Maafalani, Aladin. *Mythos Bildung: Die ungerechte Gesellschaft, ihr Bildungssystem und seine Zukunft*. Cologne: Kiepenheuer & Witsch, 2020.

El Masrar, Sineb. *Muslim Girls: Wer wir sind, wie wir Leben*. Frankfurt am Main: Eichborn AG, 2010.

El-Tayeb, Fatima. *European Others: Queering Ethnicity in Postnational Europe.* Minneapolis: University of Minnesota Press, 2011.

–. *Undeutsch: die Konstruktion des Anderen in der postmigrantischen Gesellschaft.* Bielefeld: transcript Verlag, 2016.

"'Es fehlte der Wille, sich deutlich abzugrenzen.'" Interview by Hans Hermann Kotte. *Mediendienst Integration*, August 26, 2013. https://mediendienst-integration.de/artikel/sarrazin-rassismus-gutachten-gideon-botsch.html.

Esra Karakaya. "DDF-Talk 30 Jahre geteilter Feminismus." Berlin: Deutsches Digitales Frauenarchiv, September 30, 2020. YouTube: 1:18:58. https://www.youtube.com/watch?v=NdLTqjoc8tw&t=2763s.

Esser, Hartmut. "Does the 'New' Immigration Require a 'New' Theory of Intergenerational Integration?" *The International Migration Review* 38, no. 3 (2004): 1126–59.

–. *Die Konstruktion der Gesellschaft.* Frankfurt am Main: Campus Verlag, 2002.

Esslinger, Detlef. "Deutsch-Pflicht der CSU – erstens plausibel – und zweitens verrückt." *Süddeutsche Zeitung*, January 15, 2015. http://www.sueddeutsche.de/bayern/deutsch-pflicht-der-csu-erstens-plausibel-und-zweitens-verrueckt-1.2255213.

Eubel, Cordula. "Integration durch Sprache: Afghanen dürfen nicht in Deutschkurse." *Der Tagesspiegel*, November 16, 2015. https://www.tagesspiegel.de/politik/afghanen-durfen-nicht-in-deutschkurse-5200177.html.

Eurostat: Statistics Explained. "Asylum Statistics." April 27, 2021. https://ec.europa.eu/eurostat/statistics-explained/index.php?title=Asylum_statistics.

Ewing, Katherine Pratt. *Stolen Honor: Stigmatizing Muslim Men in Berlin.* Stanford: Stanford University Press, 2008.

Facing History and Ourselves. "'Home' by Warsan Shire." Accessed December 16, 2021. https://www.facinghistory.org/standing-up-hatred-intolerance/warsan-shire-home.

Fahrun, Andrea Seibel, Hajo Schumacher, and Joachim Fahrun. "Ich bin kein Rassist." *Die Welt*, August 29, 2010. https://www.welt.de/welt_print/politik/article9263576/Ich-bin-kein-Rassist.html.

Faist, Thomas, and Christian Ulbricht. "Von Integration zu Teilhabe?" *Working Papers: Center on Migration, Citizenship and Development*, no.130 (2014): 35. https://www.uni-bielefeld.de/fakultaeten/soziologie/fakultaet/arbeitsbereiche/ab6/ag_faist/downloads/WP_130.pdf.

Federal Republic of Germany, Commissioner for the Encouragement of the Integration of Foreign Workers and their Family Members. Beauftragten zur Förderung der Integration der ausländischen Arbeitnehmer und ihrer Familienangehörigen. Heinz Kühn. Memorandum of the Federal Government Commissioner P710909. Berlin: September 1979. Digitized photocopy from the Library of the German Parliament.

Fehrenbach, Heidi. "Black Occupation Children and the Devolution of the Nazi Racial State." In *After the Nazi Racial State: Difference and Democracy in Germany and Europe*, edited by Rita Chin, Heidi Fehrenbach, Geoff Eley and Atina Grossman, 30–54. Ann Arbor: University of Michigan Press, 2009.

Fijalkowski, Jürgen. "Nationale Identität versus multikulturelle Gesellschaft. Entwicklungen der Problemlage und Alternativen der Orientierung in der politischen Kultur der Bundesrepublik in den 80er Jahren." In *Die Bundesrepublik in den achtziger Jahren: Innenpolitik, politische Kultur, Außenpolitik*, edited by Werner Süß, 235–52. Opladen: Leske und Budrich, 1991.

Fischer, Christian. "PEGIDA-Erfinder: Wir hören erst auf, wenn die Asyl-Politik sich ändert!" *Bild.de*, January 12, 2014. https://www.bild.de/regional /dresden/demonstrationen/pegida-erfinder-im-interview-38780422.bild .html#fromWall.

Flanders-Stepans, Mary Beth. "Alarming Racial Differences in Maternal Mortality." *The Journal of Perinatal Education* 9, no. 2 (2000): 50–1. https:// doi.org/10.1624/105812400X87653.

Foroutan, Naika. *Die postmigrantische Gesellschaft: Ein Versprechen der pluralen Demokratie*. Bielefeld: transcript Verlag, 2019.

Förster, Andreas. "9/11: Mohammed Atta – vom Neuruppiner Bauzeichner zum Terroristen." *Berliner Zeitung*, September 9, 2016. http://www.berliner -zeitung.de/berlin/brandenburg/9-11-mohammed-atta---vom-neuruppiner -bauzeichner-zum-terroristen-24712050.

Foucault, Michel. *Birth of Biopolitics: Lectures at the College de France, 1978–1979*, edited by Michel Senellar. Translated by Graham Burchell. London: Picador, 2010.

–. *Discipline and Punish: The Birth of the Prison*. Translated by Alan Sheridan. New York: Vintage Books, 1995.

–. *The Order of Things: An Archaeology of Human Sciences*. New York: Knopf Doubleday Publishing Group, 2012.

–. *Security, Territory, Population: Lectures at the Collège de France 1977–1978*, edited by Michel Senellar. Translated by Graham Burchell. New York: Macmillan, 2009.

France. "Flüchtlingszentrale Hof." *Süddeutsche Zeitung*, February 1, 1946.

Frank, Matthew. *Expelling the Germans: British Opinion and Post-1945 Population Transfer in Context*. Oxford: Oxford University Press, 2007.

Franz, Fritz. "Kritik am Ausländergesetz von 1965." *Jahrbuch für internationales Recht* 15, no. 1 (1971): 319–35.

Füchsel, Katja. "Der Tod und die Mädchen." *Der Tagesspiegel*, October 12, 2005. https://www.tagesspiegel.de/berlin/der-tod-und-die-maedchen/649928 .html.

Fulbrook, Mary. *The People's State: East German Society from Hitler to Honecker*. New Haven: Yale University Press, 2005.

Galaktionow, Barbara. "Flüchtlinge demonstrieren am Brandenburger Tor-Aktivisten empört über Polizei." *Süddeutsche Zeitung*, October 29, 2012. https://www.sueddeutsche.de/politik/fluechtlinge-demonstrieren-am-brandenburger-tor-aktivisten-empoert-ueber-polizei-1.1508793.

Gassert, Philipp. *Bewegte Gesellschaft: deutsche Protestgeschichte seit 1945.* Stuttgart: Verlag W. Kohlhammer, 2018.

Gehrke, Kerstin, and Matthias Oloew. "Letzter Akt in der Tempodrom-Affäre." *Der Tagesspiegel*, January 8, 2008. https://www.tagesspiegel.de/berlin/polizei-justiz/prozessbeginn-letzter-akt-in-der-tempodrom-affaere/1135838.html.

Geisel, Sieglinde. "Vergiftete Analyse." *Neue Zürcher Zeitung*, October 12, 2009. https://www.nzz.ch/vergiftete_analyse-1.3855379.

Gerhardt, Uta, and Birgitta Hohenester. "Beruf und Kultur: zum Gesellschaftstheoretischen Verständnis der Integration von Vertriebenen /Flüchtlingen in Westdeutschland nach 1945." *Soziale Welt* 48, no. 3 (1997): 253–75.

Gerlach, Thomas. "Flüchtlingsprotest in Berlin: 'Sie sollen uns ernst nehmen!'." *Die Tageszeitung*, November 2, 2012. https://taz.de/!5080317/.

"German Far-Right Pegida Founder Bachmann Guilty of Race Charge." *BBC News.* May 3, 2016. https://www.bbc.com/news/world-europe-36199739.

German History in Documents and Images (GHDI). "Currency Reform (June 20, 1948)." Accessed February 6, 2019. http://germanhistorydocs.ghi-dc.org/sub_image.cfm?image_id=1018.

"Germany Pegida: Protest Leader Quits amid Hitler Row." *BBC News*, January 21, 2015. https://www.bbc.com/news/world-europe-30920086.

"Germany Unveils Citizenship Reforms." *BBC News*, January 13, 1999. http://news.bbc.co.uk/2/hi/europe/254688.stm.

Geschwister-Scholl-Preis. "Geschwister-Scholl-Preis." Accessed January 26, 2018. http://www.geschwister-scholl-preis.de/preistraeger_2000-2009/2005/index.php.

Gesetze im Internet. "Präambel LAG – Einzelnorm." Accessed January 14, 2019. http://www.gesetze-im-internet.de/lag/pr_ambel.html.

Ghelli, Fabio, Carsten Janke, Andrea Pürckhauer, and Antonia Hafner. "Zehn Fragen zu afghanischen Flüchtlingen." *Mediendienst Integration*, August 17, 2021. https://mediendienst-integration.de/artikel/zehn-fragen-zu-afghanischen-fluechtlingen.html.

Gilbar, O., C. Taft, and R. Dekel. "Male Intimate Partner Violence: Examining the Roles of Childhood Trauma, PTSD Symptoms, and Dominance." *Journal of Family Psychology.* Advance online publication (2020). http://dx.doi.org/10.1037/fam0000669.

Gilman, Sander L. "Aliens vs. Predators: Cosmopolitan Jewish people vs. Jewish Nomads." *European Review of History: Revue Européenne d'histoire* 23, no. 5–6 (2016): 784–96. https://doi.org/10.1080/13507486.2016.1203870.

–. "Thilo Sarrazin and the Politics of Race in the Twenty-First Century." *New German Critique* 117, vol. 39, no. 3 (2012): 47–59.

Gilmore, Leigh. *Autobiographics: A Feminist Theory of Women's Self-Representation.* Ithaca: Cornell University Press, 1994.

Giordano, Ralph. "Wo Thilo Sarrazin Recht hat." *Die Welt*, September 19, 2010. https://www.welt.de/welt_print/debatte/article9733057/Wo-Thilo -Sarrazin-recht-hat.html.

Givens, Terri E. "The Radical Right Gender Gap." *Comparative Political Studies* 37, no. 1 (2004): 30–54. https://doi.org/10.1177/0010414003260124.

–. *Voting Radical Right in Western Europe.* Cambridge: Cambridge University Press, 2005.

Goenka, Aviral. The Wire. "Bosnia's Srebrenica Genocide 25 Years On." July 28, 2020. https://thewire.in/world/srebrenica-genocide-25-years-later.

Göktürk, Deniz, Anton Kaes, and David Gramling, eds. *Germany in Transit: Nation and Migration 1955–2005.* Oakland: University of California Press, 2007.

Gößwald, Udo, and Kerstin Schmiedeknecht, eds. *Wie zusammen leben: Perspektiven aus Nord-Neukölln.* Berlin: Museum Neukölln, 2009.

Grell, Rainer. "Dichtung und Wahrheit: Die Geschichte des Muslim-Tests in Baden-Württemberg. 30 Fragen, die die Welt erregten (nicht nur die Islamische)." DocPlayer, Accessed June 16, 2023. http://docplayer. org/33102620-Dichtung-und-wahrheit-die-geschichte-des-muslim-tests -in-baden-wuerttemberg-30-fragen-die-die-welt-erregten-nicht-nur-die -islamische.html.

Grewal, Inderpal, and Caren Kaplan. "Global Identities: Theorizing Transnational Studies of Sexuality." *GLQ: A Journal of Lesbian and Gay Studies* 7, no. 4 (October 1, 2001): 663–79. https://doi.org/10.1215/10642684-7-4-663.

Grimme Lab. "Doku Leipzig (Teil 2): Wie die Medien zur Ausbreitung des Rechtsradikalismus beitragen." Accessed July 21, 2021. https://www.grimme -lab.de/2019/12/19/doku-leipzig-teil-2-wie-die-medien-zur-ausbreitung-des -rechtsradikalismus-beitragen/

Grose, Rose Grace and Shelly Grabe. "The Explanatory Role of Relationship Power and Control in Domestic Violence Against Women in Nicaragua: A Feminist Psychology Analysis." *Violence Against Women* 20, no. 8 (2014), 972–93. https://doi.org/10.1177/1077801214546231

Grüne Fraktion Berlin. "Hatun-Sürücü-Preis 2019," November 12, 2018. https://gruene-fraktion.berlin/kampagne/hsp/.

Gujer, Eric. "'Der andere Blick': Warum die AfD keine bürgerliche Partei ist." *Neue Zürcher Zeitung*, September 13, 2019. https://www.nzz.ch/meinung /der-andere-blick/die-afd-ist-keine- buergerliche-partei-aber-auch-cdu -und-spd-machen-propaganda-ld.1508195.

Guyton, Patrick. "Der lange Marsch der Flüchtlinge." *Süddeutsche Zeitung*, September 24, 2012. https://www.tagesspiegel.de/politik/asylpolitik-der -lange-marsch-der-fluechtlinge/7173520.html.

–. "Hungerstreikgebiet, bitte nicht betreten." *Der Tagesspiegel*, June 28, 2013. https://www.tagesspiegel.de/politik/asylbewerber-protestieren-in -muenchen-hungerstreikgebietbitte-nicht-betreten/8421734.html.

–. "Vom großen Gefängnis ins kleine." *Der Tagesspiegel*, July 11, 2013. https:// www.tagesspiegel.de/politik/asylbewerber-vom-grossen-gefaengnis-ins -kleine/6862636.html.

Hà, Kiên Nghị, Nicola Lauré al-Samarai, and Sheila Mysorekar, eds. *re/ Visionen: Postkoloniale Perspektiven von People of Color auf Rassismus, Kulturpolitik und Widerstand in Deutschland*. Münster: Unrast Verlag, 2007.

Haak, Julia. "Vor der Europa-Wahl: Flüchtlinge wollen zu Fuß nach Brüssel." *Berliner Zeitung*, May 16, 2014. https://www.berliner-zeitung.de/mensch -metropole/vor-der-europa-wahl-fluechtlinge-wollen- zu-fuss-nach-bruessel -li.66636.

Halser, Marlene. "Kommentar Hungerstreik: Bis einer stirbt!" *Die Tageszeitung*, June 27, 2013. https://taz.de/!5064415/.

Hamberger, Katharina. "Reaktionen auf Petry-Äußerungen – 'Kein deutscher Polizist würde auf Flüchtlinge schießen.'" *Deutschlandfunk*, January 30, 2016. https://www.deutschlandfunk.de/reaktionen-auf-petry-aeusserungen -kein-deutscher-polizist-100.html.

Hampel, Lea. "Iranische Flüchtlinge protestieren: Hungern für die Normalität." *Die Tageszeitung*, April 4, 2012. https://taz.de/!5096782/.

Hans, Silke. "Theorien der Integration von Migranten – Stand und Entwicklung." In *Einwanderungsgesellschaft Deutschland*, edited by H. Brinkman. and M. Sauer, 23–50. Wiesbaden: Springer VS, 2016. https://doi .org/10.1007/978-3-658-05746-6_2.

Harbach, Heinz. "Konzepte der Ausländerpolitik in der Bundesrepublik Deutschland 1955–1982." *Institut für höhere Studien* 6 (1982): 235–45.

Hark, Sabine. *Gemeinschaft der Ungewählten: Umrisse eines politischen Ethos der Kohabitation*. Berlin: Suhrkamp Verlag, 2021.

Harvey, David. *A Brief History of Neoliberalism*. Oxford: Oxford University Press, 2007.

Haselberger, Stephan, and Antje Sirleschtov. "Gauck attestiert Sarrazin 'Mut.'" *Der Tagesspiegel*, December 30, 2010. https://www.tagesspiegel.de/politik /integration-gauck-attestiert-sarrazin-mut/3685052.html.

heb. "Dresden OB-Wahl: NPD Unterstützt Pegida-Frau Festerling." *Der Spiegel*, April 21, 2015. https://www.spiegel.de/politik/deutschland/ dresden-ob-wahl-npd-unterstuetzt-pegida-frau-festerling-a-1029656.html.

Hein, Jürgen. "Afghanistan: Verband afghanischer Frauen befürchtet neue Unterdrückung." *Frankfurter Allgemeine Zeitung*, November 25, 2001. http://www.faz.net/1.37404.

Heise, L., M. Ellsberg, and M. Gottmoeller. "A Global Overview of Gender-Based Violence." *International Journal of Gynecology & Obstetrics* 78 (2002): S5–14. https://doi.org/10.1016/S0020-7292(02)00038-3.

Heisig, Kirsten. *Das Ende der Geduld: Konsequent gegen jugendliche Gewalttäter.* Freiburg: Herder Verlag, 2010.

Heitmeyer, Wilhelm. "Für türkische Jugendliche in Deutschland spielt der Islam eine wichtige Rolle." *Die Zeit*, August 23, 1996. https://www.zeit .de/1996/35/heitmey.txt.19960823.xml/komplettansicht.

Heitmeyer, Wilhelm, Joachim Müller, and Helmut Schröder. *Verlockender Fundamentalismus.* Frankfurt am Main: Suhrkamp Verlag, 1997.

Heng, Geraldine. *The Invention of Race in the European Middle Ages.* Cambridge: Cambridge University Press, 2018.

Hense, Kerstin. "Gedenkfeier mit den Heroes: Blumen am Grab Hatun Sürücüs." *Der Tagesspiegel*, February 7, 2013. https://www.tagesspiegel .de/berlin/gedenkfeier-mit-den-heroes-blumen-am-grab-hatun-sueruecues /7753018.html.

–. "Integrationsprojekt erinnert an getötete Hatun Sürücü." *Der Tagesspiegel*, February 7, 2013. https://www.tagesspiegel.de/berlin/gedenkfeier -fuer-deutsch-kurdin-integrationsprojekt-erinnert-an-getoetete-hatun -sueruecue/7746166.html.

Herbert, Ulrich. *A History of Foreign Labor in Germany, 1880–1980: Seasonal Workers, Forced Laborers, Guest Workers.* Ann Arbor: University of Michigan Press, 1990.

–. "'Asylpolitik im Rauch der Brandsätze' – der zeitgeschichtliche Kontext." In *20 Jahre Asylkompromiss*, edited by Stefan Luft and Peter Schimany, 87–104. Bielefeld: transcript Verlag, 2014.

Herbert, Ulrich, and Karin Hunn. "Guest Workers and Policy on Guest Workers in the Federal Republic: From the Beginning of Recruitment in 1955 until Its Halt in 1973." In *The Miracle Years: A Cultural History of West Germany, 1949–1968*, edited by Hanna Schissler, 187–218. Princeton: Princeton University Press, 2001.

Heroes-Duisburg. "Mein Testgelände: Das Gender Magazin." Accessed March 10, 2024. https://www.meintestgelaende.de/author/heroes_neu/.

HEROES. "HEROES – gegen Unterdrückung in Namen der Ehre. Ein Projekt für Gleichberechtigung von Strohalm e.V." Accessed September 24, 2021. https://www.heroes-net.de.

Hessischer Rundfunk. "AfD: Was bedeutet "bürgerlich"?" *hr-Info: Aktuell.* Hessen, Germany, 2019. https://www.hr-inforadio.de/podcast/aktuell /afd-was-bedeutet-buergerlich,podcast-episode- 56760.html.

Hildebrandt, Antje. "So gesund ist Sarrazins Hartz-IV-Diät," *Berliner Morgenpost*, November 20, 2008. https://www.morgenpost.de/vermischtes /article103236011/So-gesund-ist-Sarrazins-Hartz-IV-Diaet.html.

Hoffmann-Nowotny, Hans-Joachim. *Soziologie des Fremdarbeiterproblems: Eine theoretische und empirische Analyse am Beispiel der Schweiz.* Stuttgart: Ferdinand Enke Verlag, 1973.

Holzner, Burkart. "The Concept 'Integration' in Sociological Theory." *The Sociological Quarterly* 8, no. 1 (1967): 51–62. https://doi.org/10.1111/j.1533-8525.1967.tb02273.x.

Hömke, Andrea, and Michael Pagel. "Schüler der Thomas-Morus-Oberschule freuten sich über Ermordung der schönen Hatin [sic] und beleidigten Mädchen ohne Kopftuch." *BZ*, February 18, 2005. https://www.bz-berlin.de/artikel-archiv/schueler-der-thomas-morus-oberschule-freuten-sich-ueber-ermordung-der-schoenen-hatin-und-beleidigten-maedchen-ohne-kopftuch.

Honnigfort, Bernhard. "Lutz Bachmann nutzt Spendenkasse." *Frankfurter Rundschau*, October 25, 2016. https://www.fr.de/politik/lutz-bachmann-nutzt-spendenkasse-11050550.html.

–. "Unterstützung von den Hetzern." *Frankfurter Rundschau*, June 9, 2015. https://www.fr.de/politik/unterstuetzung-hetzern-11178651.html.

Hooper, John. "Anti-Islamic Italian Author in New Legal Fight." *The Guardian*, July 12, 2005. https://www.theguardian.com/world/2005/jul/13/books.italy.

Horvath, Miranda A.H., and Jessica Woodhams. *Handbook on the Study of Multiple Perpetrator Rape: A Multidisciplinary Response to an International Problem*. London: Taylor & Francis Group, 2013.

Hüetlin, Thomas. "Blut, Schweiß, Weißwein." *Der Spiegel*, no. 51 (2009). https://www.spiegel.de/panorama/blut-schweiss-weisswein-a-c23b72e9-0002-0001-0000-000068167770.

Hughey, Matthew W. "The (Dis)Similarities of White Racial Identities: The Conceptual Framework of 'Hegemonic Whiteness.'" *Ethnic and Racial Studies* 33, no. 8 (2010): 1289–1309. https://doi.org/10.1080/01419870903125069.

Hunn, Karin. *"Nächstes Jahr kehren wir zurück--": die Geschichte der türkischen "Gastarbeiter" in der Bundesrepublik*. Göttingen: Wallstein Verlag, 2005.

Hür, Kemal. "Zehn Jahre nach Mord an Hatun Sürücü – Nichts ist vergessen." *Deutschlandfunk Kultur*, February 7, 2015. https://www.deutschlandfunkkultur.de/zehn-jahre-nach-mord-an-hatun-sueruecue-nichts-ist-vergessen-100.html.

hut/ddp/dpa. "Umstrittene Thesen zu Migration: Merkel entrüstet über Sarrazin." *Spiegel Online*, August 25, 2010. https://www.spiegel.de/politik/deutschland/umstrittene-thesen-zu-migration-merkel-entruestet-ueber-sarrazin-a-713752.html.

hut/dpa/dapd. "Spendenbetrug: Fast fünf Jahre Haft für Gründer von Hatun & Can." *Der Spiegel*, September 21, 2011. https://www.spiegel.de/panorama/justiz/spendenbetrug-fast-fuenf-jahre-haft-fuer-gruender-von-hatun-can-a-787680.html.

Imbusch, Peter, and Dieter Rucht. "Integration und Desentegration in modernen Gesellschaften." In *Integrationspotenziale einer modernen Gesellschaft*, edited by Wilhelm Heitmeyer and Peter Imbusch, 13–74. Wiesbaden: VS Verlag für Sozialwissenschaften, 2005.

"Integrationsdebatte: Joachim Gauck – Politiker können von Sarrazin Lernen."
   Die Welt, December 30, 2010. https://www.welt.de/politik/deutschland
   /article11902962/Joachim-Gauck-Politiker-koennen-von-Sarrazin-lernen.html
"Integrationsgipfel: 'Zuwanderung gezielt nutzen'." *Frankfurter Allgemeine
   Zeitung*, July 12, 2006. https://www.faz.net/aktuell/politik/inland
   /integrationsgipfel-zuwanderung-gezielt-nutzen-1353214.html.
Irrgang, Ulrike. "Beyond Sarrazin? Zur Darstellung von Migration in
   deutschen Medien am Beispiel der Berichterstattung in SPIEGEL und
   BILD." *Global Media Journal: German Edition* 1, no. 2 (2011). https://www
   .globalmediajournal.de/index.php/gmj/article/view/127.
Jähn, Christine. "Integration: Kein Muslimtest mehr." *Die Zeit*, April 1, 2009.
   http://www.zeit.de/online/2006/04/bundestag_fragebogen.
Jahn, Egbert. "The Offences and Repudiation of Thilo Sarrazin. Are There
   Limits to Freedom of Political Opinion in Germany?" In *German Domestic
   and Foreign Policy: Political Issues Under Debate*, edited by Egbert Jahn, 17–42.
   Heidelberg: Springer, 2015. https://doi.org/10.1007/978-3-662-47929-2_2.
Jakob, Christian. "Kommentar Flüchtlingscamps: Rückfall in trennende
   Konzepte." *Die Tageszeitung*, August 8, 2013. https://taz.de/!5061706/.
Jansen, Jonas. "Rassistische Kommentare: 'Die kannst du nur erschlagen'."
   Frankfurter Allgemeine Zeitung, August 7, 2015. https://www.faz.net/aktuell
   /gesellschaft/kriminalitaet/perlen-aus-freital-tumblr-sammelt-rassistische
   -kommentare-13691724.html.
Jarausch, Konrad. *The Rush to German Unity*. Oxford: Oxford University Press,
   1994.
Jervis, Robert. "Understanding the Bush Doctrine." *Political Science Quarterly*
   118, no. 3 (2003): 365–88.
jof/dpa/ddp/mim/hed. "Sarrazin empfiehlt zum Energiesparen warme Pullis."
   Berliner Morgenpost, July 29, 2008. https://www.morgenpost.de/berlin
   /article102243278/Sarrazin-empfiehlt-zum-Energiesparen-warme-Pullis.html.
jof/sh. "Sarrazin ist für mich ein verbaler Triebtäter." *Berliner Morgenpost*,
   March 21, 2010. https://www.morgenpost.de/berlin-aktuell/article
   104049999/Sarrazin-ist-fuer-mich-ein-verbaler-Triebtaeter.html.
John, Barbara. "Ausländerpolitik für Inländer – zur konzeptionellen
   Weiterentwicklung der Integrationspolitik." *Zeitschrift für Ausländerrecht und
   Ausländerpolitik: Abhandlungen* 1 (1985): 3–7.
Jüdische Gemeinde zu Berlin. "Rabbiner Alter widmet seinen Integrations-
   Bambi dem Projekt Heroes," December 9, 2012. http://www.jg-berlin.org
   /beitraege/details/rabbiner-alter-widmet-seinen-integrations-bambi-dem
   -projekt-heroes-i613d-2012-12-09.html.
Kaddor, Lamya. "Nicht nur Flüchtlinge brauchen Demokratieunterricht."
   T-Online, May 11, 2018. https://www.t-online.de/nachrichten/deutschland
   /id_83755144/nicht-nur-fluechtlinge-brauchen-demokratieunterricht.html.

"Kalt duschen ist viel gesünder." *Süddeutsche Zeitung*. March 10, 2010. https://
www.sueddeutsche.de/politik/thilo-sarrazin-ein-mann-und-seine-sprueche
-1.592750-4.

Kaplan, Marion. "Redefining Judaism in Imperial Germany: Practices,
Mentalities, and Community." *Jewish Social Studies* 9, no. 1 (2002): 1–33.

Karakaşoğlu, Yasemin and Mark Terkessidis. "Integration: Gerechtigkeit für
die Muslime!" *Die Zeit*, February 2, 2006. http://www.zeit.de/2006/06
/islam_integration/komplettansicht.

Karakayli, Serhat. Heimatkunde – migrationspolitisches Portal. "Ambivalente
Integration." Accessed June 15, 2018. https://heimatkunde.boell.de/2007
/11/18/ambivalente-integration.

Karapin, Roger. "Antiminority Riots in Unified Germany: Cultural Conflicts
and Mischanneled Political Participation." *Comparative Politics* 34, no. 2
(2002): 147–67. https://doi.org/10.2307/4146935.

Keilani, Fatina, and Annette Kögel. "Sarrazin ist nah dran und doch
daneben." *Der Tagesspiegel*, October 8, 2009. https://www.tagesspiegel
.de/berlin/umstrittene-aeusserungen-sarrazin-ist-nah-dran-und-doch
-daneben/1611714.html.

Kelek, Necla. "Der Individuationsprozess der muslimischen Frau in
der Moderne." In *Fachtagung Integration und Islam*, 102–19. Nürnberg:
Bundesministerium für Migration und Flüchtlinge, 2006.

–. "Die Braut als Schnäppchen." *Die Zeit*, January 27, 2005.

–. *Die fremde Braut: Ein Bericht aus dem Inneren des türkischen Lebens in
Deutschland*. Cologne: Kiepenheuer & Witsch, 2005.

–. *Die verlorenen Söhne: Plädoyer für die Befreiung des türkisch-muslimischen
Mannes*. Kiepenheuer & Witsch, 2006.

–. "Integration: Entgegnung." *Die Zeit*, February 8, 2006. http://www.zeit.de
/online/2006/06/kelek_replik.

–. *Islam im Alltag: Islamische Religiosität und ihre Bedeutung in der Lebenswelt von
Schülerinnen und Schülern türkischer Herkunft*. Münster: Waxmann, 2002.

Keller, Claudia. "Familien-Union: Die Clanchefs bitten zum Tee." *Der
Tagespiegel*, February 26, 2011. https://www.tagesspiegel.de/berlin
/familien-union-die-clanchefs-bitten-zum-tee/3887376.html.

Kelly, Natasha. Digitales Deutsches Frauenarchiv. "May Ayim." 2018.
Accessed March 10, 2024. https://www.digitales-deutsches-frauenarchiv
.de/akteurinnen/may-ayim.

Kiepenheuer und Witsch. "Necla Kelek." Accessed September 18, 2017.
http://www.kiwi-verlag.de/autor/necla-kelek/1058/.

Kilb, Andreas. "Sarrazins Buchvorstellung: Erst mal lesen, dann gratulieren."
Frankfurter Allgemeine Zeitung, August 31, 2010. https://www.faz.net/aktuell
/feuilleton/sarrazin/das-buch/sarrazins-buchvorstellung-erst-mal-lesen
-dann-gratulieren-11024362.html.

"Das Kinderelend der Ausgewiesenen." *Süddeutsche Zeitung*. March 1, 1946.

Kirschey, Peter. "Mord ist keine Ehre – ein Verbrechen." *neues deutschland,*
February 23, 2005. https://www.neues-deutschland.de/artikel/67911
.mord-ist-keine-ehre-ein-verbrechen.html.

Kitschelt, Herbert. *The Radical Right in Western Europe*. Ann Arbor: University
of Michigan Press, 1995.

Klovert, Heike. "Begrüßung im Job: es geht auch ohne Handschlag." *Spiegel
Online*, August 3, 2016. http://www.spiegel.de/karriere/handschlag-im
-beruf-es-geht-auch-ohne-a-1105141.html.

–. "Kritik an Unionsplänen: Brauchen geflüchtete Kinder einen eigenen
Werteunterricht?" *Spiegel Online*, May 8, 2018. http://www.spiegel.de
/lebenundlernen/schule/wertekunde-fuer-fluechtlingskinder-macht-das
-sinn-a-1206763.html.

Knight, Ben. "Pegida Head Lutz Bachmann Reinstated after Furore over Hitler
Moustache Photo." *The Guardian*, February 23, 2015. http://www.theguardian
.com/world/2015/feb/23/pegida-head-lutz-bachmann-reinstated-hitler
-moustache-photo.

Knight, Mary L. "(L)Earned Monsters: Psychopathic Masculinities in
Contemporary German Film and Fiction." *Colloquia Germanica* 46, no. 1
(2013): 4–20.

Kober, Henning. "Ehre vor Gericht." *Die Welt*, April 1, 2006. https://www
.welt.de/print-wams/article140501/Ehre-vor-Gericht.html.

Koehler, Daniel. "Violent Extremism, Mental Health and Substance Abuse
among Adolescents: Towards a Trauma Psychological Perspective on
Violent Radicalization and Deradicalization." *Journal of Forensic Psychiatry &
Psychology*, no. 3 (2020): 455–72. https://doi.org/10.1080/14789949.2020.17
58752.

–. *Right-Wing Terrorism in the 21st Century: The 'National Socialist Underground' and
the History of Terror from the Far-Right in Germany*. London: Routledge, 2017.

Kögel, Annette. "Mut zur Öffentlichkeit." *Der Tagesspiegel*, February 19, 2005.
https://www.tagesspiegel.de/berlin/mut-zur-oeffentlichkeit/586364.html.

Kohl, Helmut. "Coalition of the Center: 'For a Politics of Renewal.'" In
Germany in Transit: Nation and Migration 1955–2005, edited by Deniz
Göktürk, Anton Kaes, and David Gramling. Translated by David Gramling,
45–6. Oakland: University of California Press, 2007.

Köhler, Michael. "Integrationsforscherin Edele – 'Es könnte eine
Zweiklassengesellschaft unter Geflüchteten geben.'" *Deutschlandfunk*, March
26, 2022. https://www.deutschlandfunk.de/vieles-ist-diesmal-einfacher
-integrationsforscherin-aileen-edele-dlf-eefcc300-100.html.

Köhler, Regina. "Schule hat viel zu wenig Einfluß." *Die Welt*, February 18,
2005. https://www.welt.de/print-welt/article471295/Schule-hat-viel-zu
-wenig-Einfluss.html.

Komska, Yuliya. *The Icon Curtain: The Cold War's Quiet Border*. Chicago: University of Chicago Press, 2015.

Konrad Adenauer Stiftung. "Regierungserklärung von Bundeskanzler Kohl in der 121. Sitzung des Deutschen Bundestages." October 13, 1982. No longer available. https://www.helmut-kohl-kas.de/index.php?menu_sel=17&menu_sel2=&menu_sel3=&menu_sel4=&msg=1934

Köpping, Petra. *"Integriert doch erst mal uns!" – Eine Streitschrift für den Osten*. Berlin: Ch. Links Verlag, 2018.

Krämer-Badoni, Thomas. "Assimilierte Differenz oder differenzierte Assimilation? Riskante Integrationsmuster in eine desintegrierte Welt." In *Was heißt hier Parallelgesellschaft?: Zum Umgang mit Differenzen*, edited by Bukow, Wolf-Dietrich, Claudia Nikodem, Erika Schulze, and Erol Yildiz, 53–64. Wiesbaden: VS Verlag für Sozialwissenschaften, 2007.

"Kurds Stage Major Kobani Protest in Düsseldorf." *Deutsche Welle*, October 11, 2014. https://p.dw.com/p/1DTY1.

Kurthen, Hermann, and Michael Minkenberg. "Germany in Transition: Immigration, Racism and the Extreme Right." *Nations and Nationalism* 1, no. 2 (1995): 175–96. https://doi.org/10.1111/j.1354-5078.1995.00175.x.

Kurylo, Friedrich K. "The Turks Rehearsed the Uprising." In *Germany in Transit: Nation and Migration 1955–2005*, edited by Deniz Göktürk, Anton Kaes, and David Gramling. Translated by David Gramling, 42–4. Oakland: University of California Press, 2007.

Die Landesregierung Nordrhein-Westfalen. Gesetz zur Förderung der gesellschaftlichen Teilhabe und Integration in Nordrhein-Westfalen (Teilhabe- und Integrationsgesetz). Pub. L. No. GV. NRW. S. 97. Düsseldorf: Landesregierung Nordrhein-Westfalen, 2012. Accessed June 20, 2021. https://recht.nrw.de/lmi/owa/br_text_anzeigen?v_id=10000000000000000486.

"Lange Haft wegen Spendenbetrugs." *BZ*, September 21, 2011. https://www.bz-berlin.de/artikel-archiv/lange-haft-wegen-spendenbetrugs.

Laninger, Tanja, and Dirk Banse, "Mord an einer Türkin–Ermordet, weil sie frei sein wollten," *Berliner Morgenpost*, Feb. 16, 2005: 20.

Lau, Jörg. "Kulturbedingte 'Ehrenmorde.'" *Die Zeit*, March 3, 2005. https://www.zeit.de/2005/10/Ehrenmorde/komplettansicht.

–. "Sarrazin-Debatte: unter Deutschen." *Die Zeit*, October 8, 2009. https://www.zeit.de/2009/42/01-Sarrazin-Integration.

–. "Wie eine Deutsche." *Die Zeit*, February 24, 2005. https://www.zeit.de/2005/09/Hatin_S_9fr_9fc_9f_09/komplettansicht.

Ledebur, Mareen. "Münchner Asylbewerber im Trinkstreik: 'Wir gehen bis zum Ende'." *Die Tageszeitung*, June 26, 2013. https://taz.de/!5064541/.

Lehming, Malte. "Wenn ein Schimpfwort zum Ehrbegriff wird." *Der Tagesspiegel*, September 3, 2019. https://www.tagesspiegel.de/politik/ist-die-afd-buergerlich-wenn-ein-schimpfwort-zum-ehrbegriff-wird/24975010.html.

ler/apn. "Hartz-IV-Debatte: Sarrazin attestiert Westerwelle geistige Armut."
    Spiegel Online, March 1, 2010. https://www.spiegel.de/politik/deutschland
    /hartz-iv-debatte-sarrazin-attestiert-westerwelle-geistige-armut-a-680976.html.

Lichtenberg, Arne. "9/11 – Die Hamburger Zelle." *DW.COM*, May 2, 2011.
    http://www.dw.com/de/9-11-die-hamburger-zelle/a-15349371.

"Lieber sterben als nach Sachsen." *Der Spiegel*, September 29, 1991. 30–8.

Lindner, Jenny. "Jeder Zweite in Deutschland mit Migrationshintergrund?"
    Mediendienst Integration, January 7, 2015, https://mediendienst-integration
    .de/artikel/kermani-rede-jeder-zweite-hat-migrationshintergrund.html.

Litschko, Konrad. "Flüchtlingsprotest in Berlin: Wieder im Hungerstreik." *Die
    Tageszeitung*, November 16, 2012. https://taz.de/!5079274/.

Litten, Margot. "Vertriebene – Ablehnung und Verachtung für Landsleute
    aus dem Osten." *Deutschlandfunk Kultur*, August 24, 2016. https://www
    .deutschlandfunkkultur.de/vertriebene-ablehnung-und-verachtung-fuer
    -landsleute-aus-100.html.

Lohre, Matthias. "'Wenn ich komisch bin, dann meist unfreiwillig'." *Die
    Tageszeitung*, March 4, 2006.

Lokshin, Pavel. "AfD und die Medien: 'Ein symbiotisches Verhältnis.'"
    Mediendienst Integration, September 22, 2016. https://mediendienst-integration
    .de/artikel/ein-symbiotisches-verhaeltnis.html.

Löwenstein, Stephan. "Integrationsgipfel: Merkel: 'Fast ein historisches
    Ereignis'." *Frankfurter Allgemeine Zeitung*, July 14, 2006. https://www.faz
    .net/aktuell/politik/inland/integrationsgipfel-merkel-fast-ein-historisches
    -ereignis-1357015.html.

Lucassen, Leo, and Charlotte Laarman. "Immigration, Intermarriage and the
    Changing Face of Europe in the Post War Period." *The History of the Family*
    14, no. 1 (2009): 52–68. https://doi.org/10.1016/j.hisfam.2008.12.001.

Ludwig, Kristiana. "Flüchtlinge protestieren: Ein Camp auf der
    Verkehrsinsel." *Die Tageszeitung*, May 21, 2013. https://taz.de/!5066959/.

Luft, Stefan and Peter Schimany. "Asylpolitik im Wandel: Einführung in die
    Thematik des Bandes." In *20 Jahre Asylkompromiss*, edited by Stefan Luft and
    Peter Schimany, 11–29. Bielefeld: transcript Verlag, 2014.

Lummer, Heinrich. "Victims of Freeloaders?" In *Germany in Transit: Nation
    and Migration 1955–2005*, edited by Deniz Göktürk, Anton Kaes, and David
    Gramling. Translated by Tess Howell, 113–14. Oakland: University of
    California Press, 2007.

Lüttinger, Paul. "Der Mythos der schnellen Integration: Eine empirische
    Untersuchung zur Integration der Vertriebenen und Flüchtlinge in der
    Bundesrepublik Deutschland bis 1971." *Zeitschrift für Soziologie* 15, no. 1
    (1986): 20–36. https://doi.org/doi:10.1515/zfsoz-1986-0102.

Lüttinger, Paul, and Rita Rossman. *Integration der Vertriebenen: Eine empirische
    Analyse*. Frankfurt am Main: Campus Verlag, 1989.

"Lutz Bachmann: Pegida-Gründer spielt Hitler." *Frankfurter Allgemeine Zeitung*, January 21, 2015. https://www.faz.net/aktuell/politik/inland/lutz-bachmann-pegida-gruender-spielt-hitler-13382531.html.

Madloch, Norbert. "Rechtsextremistische Tendenzen und Entwicklungen in der DDR, speziell in Sachsen, bis Oktober 1990." In *Rechtsextremismus und Antifaschismus: historische und aktuelle Dimensionen*, edited by Klaus Kinner and Rolf Richter, 63–145. Berlin: Dietz, 2000.

Mahmood, Saba. "Feminism, Democracy, and Empire: Islam and the War of Terror." In *Women's Studies on the Edge*, edited by Joan Wallach Scott, 81–114. Durham: Duke University Press, 2008.

Mangold, Ijoma. "'Manifest der Vielen': Seht ihr uns?" *Die Zeit*, March 3, 2011. https://www.zeit.de/2011/10/Manifest-gegen-Sarrazin.

–. "#MeTwo: Was ist Rassismus? Und was ist keiner?" *Zeit Online*, August 1, 2018. https://www.zeit.de/2018/32/metwo-rassismus-alltag-twitter-diskussion.

Manji, Irshad. *The Trouble with Islam: A Muslim's Call for Reform in Her Faith*. New York: St. Martin's Press, 2004.

Mansour, Ahmad. "Essay Linke und Muslime: Wir sind nicht eure Kuscheltiere." *Die Tageszeitung*, July 9, 2016. https://taz.de/!5317219/.

Marin, Angelica. "This Liberian Italian Beatmaker Uses Music to Tackle Racism in Italy." *The World from PRX*, June 29, 2020, https://www.pri.org/stories/2020-06-29/liberian-italian-beatmaker-uses-music-tackle-racism-italy.

Martens, Daniela. "Nach Besetzung der nigerianischen Botschaft – Flüchtlinge klagen Berliner Polizei an." *Der Tagesspiegel*, November 10, 2012. https://www.tagesspiegel.de/berlin/nach-besetzung-der-nigerianischen-botschaft-fluechtlinge-klagen-berliner-polizei-an/7372032.html.

Maschner, W. "Die Vorhut einer Million." *Süddeutsche Zeitung*. December 21, 1945.

Matussek, Matthias. "Jagdzeit in Sachsen." *Der Spiegel* 40, September 29, 1991.

Mayblin, Lucy. "Colonialism, Decolonisation, and the Right to Be Human: Britain and the 1951 Geneva Convention on the Status of Refugees." *Journal of Historical Sociology* 27, no. 3 (2014): 423–41. https://doi.org/10.1111/johs.12053.

mbe. "Alleinerziehende mit Mindestlohn verdienen weniger als Hartz-IV-Empfänger." *FOCUS Online*, December 12, 2018. https://www.focus.de/finanzen/news/bundesregierung-ermittelt-selbst-in-vollzeit-alleinerziehende-mit-mindestlohn-verdienen-weniger-als-hartz-iv-empfaenger_id_10031493.html.

McClintock, Anne. *Imperial Leather: Race, Gender, and Sexuality in the Colonial Contest*. New York: Routledge, 1995.

McKee, Kim. "Post-Foucauldian Governmentality: What Does It Offer Critical Social Policy Analysis?" *Critical Social Policy* 29, no. 3 (2009): 465–86. https://doi.org/10.1177/0261018309105180.

MDR Exactly / mpö. "Afghanistan oder Ukraine: Deutschland behandelt nicht alle Geflüchtete gleich." *Mitteldeutscher Rundfunk*. Last modified May

14, 2022. https://www.mdr.de/nachrichten/deutschland/gesellschaft
/ukraine-syrien-fluechtlinge-deutschland-unterschied-100.html.

MDR. "Hoyerswerda 1991: Nach drei Jahrzehnten aufeinander zugehen."
Mitteldeutscher Rundfunk. May 15, 2021. https://www.mdr.de/nachrichten
/sachsen/bautzen/bautzen-hoyerswerda-kamenz/angriffe-jahrestag
-fremdenfeindlichkeit-erinnerung-100.html.

MDR Sachsen. "Landesverfassungsschutz stuft Pegida als extremistisch ein."
Mitteldeutscher Rundfunk. May 7, 2021. https://www.mdr.de/nachrichten
/sachsen/verfassungsschutz-stuft-pegida-als-exteremistisch-ein-100.html.

Mecheril, Paul. "Wirklichkeit schaffen: Integration als Dispositiv." *Aus
Politik und Zeitgeschichte: 50 Jahre Anwerbabkommen mit der Türkei* 61, no. 43
(October 24, 2011): 49–54.

Meisner, Matthias. "Pegida, Freital, Meißen… : … und die CDU. In Sachsen ist
was faul." *Der Tagesspiegel*, June 29, 2015. https://www.tagesspiegel
.de/politik/pegida-freital-meissen-und-die-cdu-in-sachsen-ist-was-faul
/11982850.html.

–. "'Besorgte Bürger' brüllen Asyl-Aktivisten nieder." *Der Tagesspiegel*, July 7,
2015. https://www.tagesspiegel.de/politik/freital-besorgte-buerger
-bruellen-asyl-aktivisten- nieder/12020774.html.

Meisner, Matthias, and Lars Radau. "Vergleiche mit Hoyerswerda sind
angebracht." *Der Tagesspiegel*, June 23, 2015. https://www.tagesspiegel.de
/politik/anti-asyl-proteste-in-freital-vergleiche-mit-hoyerswerda-sind
-angebracht/11955918.html.

Memarnia, Susanne. "Nachfolger der 'Werkstatt der Kulturen': Der misslungene
Neustart." *Die Tageszeitung*, March 13, 2020. https://taz.de/!5667538/.

Meng, Michael. "Silences about Sarrazin's Racism in Contemporary
Germany." *The Journal of Modern History* 87, no. 1 (2015): 102–35. https://
doi.org/10.1086/680259.

Menschen in Dresden. "Positionspaper der PEGIDA," December 10, 2014.
https://www.menschen-in-dresden.de/wp-content/uploads/2014/12
/pegida-positionspapier.pdf.

Mensing, Hans Peter. *Konrad Adenauer im Briefwechsel mit Flüchtlingen und
Vertriebenen*. Bonn: Kulturstiftung der Deutschen Vertribenen, 1999.

Mertins, Silke. "Was sollen die letzten Worte sein." *Die Tageszeitung*, December
23, 1997.

Messerschmidt, Rolf. "Vertriebene und Flüchtlinge in der unmittelbaren
Nachkriegszeit: Erkenntnisse der jüngeren Zeitgeschichtsforschung." In *Die
Bundesrepublik Deutschland und die Vertriebenen: Fünfzig Jahre Eingliederung,
Aufbau und Verständigung mit den Staaten des östlichen Europa*, edited by
Christof Dahm and Hans-Jakob Tebarth, 9–36. Bonn: Kulturstiftung der
deutschen Vertriebenen, 2000.

"Mesut Özil tritt aus Nationalmannschaft zurück." *tagesschau.de*, July 23, 2018. https://www.tagesschau.de/sport/oezil-ruecktritt-101.html.

Mielke, Michael. "Warum Hatun Sürücü sterben musste." *Berliner Morgenpost*, February 7, 2010. https://www.morgenpost.de/berlin/article103961528/Warum-Hatun-Sueruecue-sterben-musste.html.

Miller, Jennifer A. *Turkish Guest Workers in Germany: Hidden Lives and Contested Borders, 1960s to 1980s*. Toronto: University of Toronto Press, 2018.

Miller-Idriss, Cynthia. *The Extreme Gone Mainstream: Commercialization and Far Right Youth Culture in Germany*. Princeton: Princeton University Press, 2018.

–. "The Rise of Fascist Fashion: Clothing Helps the Far Right Sell Their Violent Message." *Salon*, April 21, 2018. https://www.salon.com/2018/04/21/the-rise-of-fascist-fashion-clothing-helps-the-far-right-sell-their-violent-message/.

Minkmar, Nils. "AfD nennt sich 'bürgerlich': Das ist Bürgerbeleidigung." *Spiegel Online*, September 3, 2019. https://www.spiegel.de/kultur/gesellschaft/afd-nennt-sich-buergerlich-das-ist-buergerbeleidigung-debattenbeitrag-a-1285112.html.

Mitchell, Koritha. "Identifying White Mediocrity and Know-Your-Place Aggression: A Form of Self-Care." *African American Review* 51, no. 4 (2018): 253–62. https://doi.org/10.1353/afa.2018.0045.

Mohanty, Chandra Talpade. "Under Western Eyes: Feminist Scholarship and Colonial Discourses." *Boundary* 2, no. 12/13 (1984): 333–58. https://doi.org/10.2307/302821.

Mojab, Shahrzad. "Tracing Dollars, Mapping Colonial Feminism: America Funds Women's 'Democracy' Training in Iraq." In *Arab Feminisms: Gender and Equality in the Middle East*, edited by Jean Said Makdisi, Noha Bayoumi and Rafif Rida Sidawi, 379-88. London: I.B. Tauris Publishers, 2014.

Molloy, Peter, director. *The Savage Peace*. London: BBC Two. Netflix. 2015.

Mudde, Cas. *Populist Radical Right Parties in Europe*. Cambridge: Cambridge University Press, 2007.

–. *The Ideology of the Extreme Right*. Manchester: Manchester University Press, 2013.

–. "The Populist Radical Right: A Pathological Normalcy." *West European Politics* 33, no. 6 (2010): 1167–86. https://doi.org/10.1080/01402382.2010.508901.

Müller, Jan. "Ehrenmord-Prozess: Verdächtige SMS – Bundesrichter kippen Sürücü-Urteil." *Spiegel Online*, August 28, 2007. http://www.spiegel.de/politik/deutschland/ehrenmord-prozess-verdaechtige-sms-bundesrichter-kippen-sueruecue-urteil-a-502533.html.

Müller, Ursula, Monika Schröttle, Sandra Glammeier, and Christa Oppenheimer. "Lebenssituation, Sicherheit und Gesundheit von Frauen in Deutschland: Eine repräsentative Untersuchung zu Gewalt gegen Frauen in Deutschland. Zusammenfassung zentraler Studienergebnisse." Rostock: Bundesministerium für Familie, Senioren, Frauen und Jugend, 2004. https://www.bmfsfj.de/blob/84316/10574a0dff2039e15a9d3dd6f9eb2dff /kurzfassung-gewalt-frauen-data.pdf.

Münch, Ursula. "Asylpolitik in Deutschland – Akteure, Interessen, Strategien." In *20 Jahre Asylkompromiss*, edited by Stefan Luft and Peter Schimany, 69–86. Bielefeld: transcript Verlag, 2014.

"München und die Flüchtlinge 2015: 'Ich kämpfte kurz mit den Tränen.'" *tagesschau.de*, September 5, 2020. https://www.tagesschau.de/fluechtlingshelfer -muenchen-2015-101.html.

Musch, Elisabeth. "Consultation Structures in German Immigrant Integration Politics: The National Integration Summit and the German Islam Conference." *German Politics* 21, no. 1 (2012): 73–90. https://doi.org/10.1080 /09644008.2011.653342.

Musharbash, Yassin. "#MeTwo: Einfach mal zuhören!" *Die Zeit*, July 27, 2018. https://www.zeit.de/gesellschaft/zeitgeschehen/2018-07/metwo -deutschland-migrationshintergrund-erfahrungen-rassismus-alltag -grosszuegigkeit.

Nagle, John David. *The National Democratic Party: Right Radicalism in the Federal Republic of Germany*. Oakland: University of California Press, 1970.

National Congress of American Indians. "Demographics." June 1, 2020. https://www.ncai.org/about-tribes/demographics.

NDR. "Flüchtlinge aus der Ukraine: Kritik an unterschiedlicher Behandlung." *NDR.DE*, April 1, 2022. https://www.ndr.de/nachrichten/hamburg /Fluechtlinge-aus-der-Ukraine-Kritik-an-unterschiedlicher-Behandlung, ukraine2524.html.

NDR. "'Lausbuben': Wie man in Freital Terroristen verharmlost." *Panorama*, ARD, December 14, 2017. https://daserste.ndr.de/panorama/archiv/2017 /Lausbuben-Wie-man-in-Freital-Terroristen-verharmlost,freital112.html.

"Necla Kelek, 49, Best-Selling Author." *The New York Times*, December 1, 2005. https://www.nytimes.com/2005/12/01/news/necla-kelek-49-bestselling -author.html.

Neubach, Helmut. "Heimatvertriebene in den politischen Parteien." In *Die Bundesrepublik Deutschland und die Vertriebenen: Fünfzig Jahre Eingliederung, Aufbau und Verständigung mit den Staaten des östlichen Europa*, edited by Christof Dahm and Hans-Jakob Tebarth, 37–66. Bonn: Kulturstiftung der deutschen Vertriebenene, 2000.

Nghị Hà, Kiên. "Deutsch Integrationspolitik als koloniale Praxis." In *re/ visionen: Postkoloniale Perspektiven von People of Colour auf Rassismus, Kulturpolitik und Widerstand in Deutschland*, edited by Kiên Nghị Hà, Sheila Mysorekar, and Nicola Lauré al-Samarai, 113–28. Münster: Unrast Verlag, 2007.

Nimz, Ulrike, and Cornelius Pollmer. "Freital: Wo der Hass regiert." *Süddeutsche Zeitung*, June 25, 2015. https://www.sueddeutsche.de/politik /proteste-gegen-fluechtlinge-in-freital-wo-der-mob-skandiert-1.2537601.

nto./Reuters. "Beatrix von Storch: AfD-Vizechefin will Polizei sogar auf Kinder schießen lassen." *Frankfurter Allgemeine Zeitung*, January 31, 2016. https://www.faz.net/aktuell/politik/fluechtlingskrise/beatrix-von-storch -afd-vizechefin-will-polizei-sogar-auf-kinder-schiessen-lassen-14044186.html.

"Oberstes SPD-Gericht bestätigt Parteiausschluss Sarrazins." *tagesschau.de*, July 31, 2020. https://www.tagesschau.de/inland/spd-sarrazin-ausschluss-105.html.

Oberwittler, Dietrich, and Julia Kasselt. *Ehrenmorde in Deutschland 1996–2005*. Bundeskriminalamt, Kriminalistisches Institut. Cologne: Luchterhand, 2011.

Olsen, Erik, and Melissa Eddy. "Video Feature: Pegida Movement Divides Germany." *The New York Times*, February 11, 2015. https://www.nytimes .com/2015/02/12/world/europe/pegida-movement-divides-germany.html.

Ong, Aihwa. *Buddha Is Hiding: Refugees, Citizenship, the New America*. Oakland: University of California Press, 2003.

Onken, Henning. "Sarrazin: So sollten Arbeitslose einkaufen." *Der Tagesspiegel*, February 11, 2008. https://www.tagesspiegel.de/berlin/landespolitik /hartz-iv-menue-sarrazin-so-sollten-arbeitslose-einkaufen/1164148.html.

Osterloh, Katrin, and Nele Westerholt. "Kultur." In *Wie Rassismus aus Wörtern spricht: (K)Erben des Kolonialismus im Wissensarchiv deutscher Sprache: ein kritisches Nachschlagewerk*, edited by Susan Arndt and Nadja Ofuatey-Alazard, 412–16. Münster: Unrast-Verlag, 2011.

O'Sullivan, Rachel. "Integration and Division: Nazi Germany and the 'Colonial Other' in Annexed Poland." *Journal of Genocide Research* 22, no. 4 (2020): 1–22. https://doi.org/10.1080/14623528.2020.1757904.

"Otto-Wels-Preis geht nach Neukölln: Die Neuköllner Heroes gewinnen den 1. Platz – Dr. Fritz Felgentreu, MdB." Accessed September 10, 2021. https:// fritz-felgentreu.de/2018/03/20/otto-wels-preis-geht-nach-neukoelln-die -neukoellner-heroes-gewinnen-den-1-platz/.

Overseas Security Advisory Council. "Security Message for US Citizens: Berlin (Germany), Demonstration Notice." US Department of State, January 26, 2015.

Özkan, Yilmaz. "Stabilisierungsfaktor oder Revolutionäres Potential? Politische Sozialisation der Gastarbeiter." PhD diss., Free University of Berlin, 1975.

Painter, Nell Irvin. *The History of White People*. New York: W. W. Norton & Company, 2010.

Panayi, Panikos. "Racial Violence in the New Germany 1990–93." *Contemporary European History* 3, no. 3 (1994): 265–87.

"Partizipations- und Integrationsgesetz des Landes Berlin," Pub. L. No. GVBl S. 842, 850–2 PartIntG (2010). https://gesetze.berlin.de/bsbe/document /jlr-PartIntergrGBERahmen.

Partridge, Damani J. "Articulating a Noncitizen Politics: Nation-State Pity vs. Democratic Inclusion." In *Refugees Welcome?: Difference and Diversity in a Changing Germany*, edited by Jan-Jonathan Bock and Sharon Macdonald. New York City: Berghahn Books, 2019.

Payandeh, Mehrdad. "Die Entscheidung des UN-Ausschusses gegen Rassendiskriminierung im Fall Sarrazin: Chancen und Grenzen des menschenrechtlichen Individualbeschwerdeverfahrens aus der Perspektive der deutschen Rechtsordnung." *Juristen Zeitung* 68, no. 20 (2013): 980–90.

"Pegida-Gründer Lutz Bachmann verurteilt." *Frankfurter Allgemeine Zeitung*, May 3, 2016. https://www.faz.net/aktuell/politik/inland/wegen -volksverhetzung-pegida-gruender-lutz-bachmann-verurteilt-14214054.html.

"Pegida-Gründer macht gegen Asylantenheim mobil." *NWZOnline.de*, June 25, 2015. https://www.nwzonline.de/panorama/pegida-gruender-macht -gegen-asylantenheim-mobil_a_29,0,2401981158.html.

Peil, Florian. "Mahnwache für ermordete Türkin: 'Alles Liebe in einer anderen Welt'." *Spiegel Online*, February 22, 2005. https://www.spiegel .de/panorama/mahnwache-fuer-ermordete-tuerkin-alles-liebe-in-einer -anderen-welt-a-343155.html.

Peşmen, Azadê. "Nicht-weißer Blick auf die Wende – Das neue 'Wir' ohne uns." *Deutschlandfunk Kultur*, November 6, 2019. https://www .deutschlandfunkkultur.de/nicht-weisser-blick-auf-die-wende-das-neue -wir-ohne-uns.976.de.html?dram:article_id=462792.

Peters, Freia. "Integration: Araber in Berlin haben ihren eigenen Richter." *Die Welt*, January 15, 2011. https://www.deutschlandfunkkultur.de/nicht -weisser-blick-auf-die-wende-das-neue-wir-ohne-uns-100.html.

–. "Mord Ohne Reue." *Die Welt*, July 27, 2011. https://www.welt.de/print /die_welt/politik/article13509815/Mord-ohne-Reue.html.

Pfeifer, Hans. "Right-Wing Terror Trial Stirs up Violent Memories in Germany's Freital." *DW.COM*, July 9, 2020. https://www.dw.com/en /germany-freital/a-54818274.

Pfreundschuh, Wolfram. "Kulturalisierung." *Kulturkritik*, accessed March 10, 2024. https://kulturkritik.net/begriffe/begr_txt.php?lex=kulturalisierung.

Phalnikar, Sonia. "Die Freiheit war ihr Todesurteil." *DW.COM*, February 25, 2005. https://www.dw.com/de/die-freiheit-war-ihr-todesurteil/a-1499642.

Phillips, David. "The Legacy of Unification." In *Education in Germany since Unification*, edited by David Phillips, 7–12. Cambridge: Symposium Books, 2000.

Phillips, Whitney. "The Oxygen of Amplification." *Data and Society*, May 22, 2018. https://datasociety.net/library/oxygen-of-amplification/.

phoenix. *Integrationsgesetz: Thomas de Maizière und Andrea Nahles geben Pressekonferenz am 25.05.16*, Streamed May 25, 2016, YouTube, 40:04, https:// www.youtube.com/watch?v=Lt_3SrCXTH8.

phw/AP/dpa. "Debatte um Ausländerschelte: Ökonom fordert Integrationsministerium." *Spiegel Online*, October 11, 2009. https://www.spiegel.de/politik/deutschland/debatte-um-auslaenderschelte-oekonom-fordert-integrationsministerium-a-654465.html.

phw/dpa/AFP. "Integrationsgipfel: 'Ein fast historisches Ereignis.'" *Der Spiegel*, July 14, 2006. https://www.spiegel.de/politik/deutschland/integrationsgipfel-ein-fast-historisches-ereignis-a-426823.html.

phw/dpa/AP/ddp. "Soziale Kälte: Empörung über Sarrazins Pulli-Provokation." *Spiegel Online*, July 29, 2008. https://www.spiegel.de/politik/deutschland/soziale-kaelte-empoerung-ueber-sarrazins-pulli-provokation-a-568833.html.

Piesche, Peggy. "Der 'Fortschritt' der Aufklärung – Kants 'Race' und die Zentrierung des Weißen Subjekts." In *Mythen, Masken und Subjekte: kritische Weissseinsforschung in Deutschland*, edited by Maureen Maischa Eggers, Grada Kilomba, Peggy Piesche, and Susan Arndt, 30–9. Münster: Unrast, 2005.

–, ed. *Labor89: intersektionale Bewegungsgeschichte*n aus West und Ost*. Berlin: Verlag Yilmaz-Günay, 2019.

Piorkowski, Christoph David. "'Nur tagsüber sind Universitäten weiße Institutionen'." *Der Tagesspiegel*, December 18, 2020. https://www.tagesspiegel.de/wissen/struktureller-rassismus-an-deutschen-hochschulen-nur-tagsueber-sind-universitaeten-weisse-institutionen/26730214.html.

Pollmer, Cornelius. "Auftritt der pöbelnden Schaummünder." *Süddeutsche Zeitung*, July 7, 2015. https://www.sueddeutsche.de/politik/freital-ausdauernd-aufgeheizt-1.2554805.

Popp, Maximillian, and Andreas Wassermann. "Where Did Germany's Islamophobes Come From?" *Spiegel Online*, January 12, 2015. https://www.spiegel.de/international/germany/origins-of-german-anti-muslim-group-pegida-a-1012522.html.

Poutrus, Patrice. "Asylum in Postwar Germany: Refugee Admission Policies and Their Practical Implementation in the Federal Republic and the GDR Between the Late 1940s and the Mid-1970s." *Journal of Contemporary History* 49, no. 1 (2014): 115–33. https://doi.org/10.1177/0022009413505667.

–. *Umkämpftes Asyl: Vom Nachkriegsdeutschland bis in die Gegenwart*. Berlin: Ch. Links Verlag, 2019.

pr/adi. "Prozess gegen Pegida-Gründer – Bachmann wegen Volksverhetzung verurteilt." *Deutschlandfunk Kultur*, May 3, 2016. https://www.deutschlandfunkkultur.de/prozess-gegen-pegida-gruender-bachmann-wegen.1895.de.html?dram:article_id=353211.

Projekt Heroes. "Concept – English Translation." Access date from text. https://heroesnetzwerk.de/wpcontent/uploads/2021/09/HEROES_Concept_EnglishTranslation.pdf.

"Pro-kurdische Proteste: Mehr als ein Dutzend Tote." *Kurier*, October 8, 2014. https://kurier.at/politik/ausland/europas-kurden-fordern-hilfe-mehr-als -ein-dutzend-bei-pro-kurdischen-protesten/89.766.076.

"Protestmarsch von Asylbewerbern – Würzburger Flüchtlinge erreichen Berlin." *Süddeutsche Zeitung*, October 5, 2012. https://www.sueddeutsche .de/bayern/protestmarsch-von-asylbewerbern-wuerzburger-fluechtlinge -erreichen-berlin-1.1488037.

Przybilla, Olaf. "Zirndorf – Menschenwürdig ist das nicht." *Süddeutsche Zeitung*, August 28, 2014. https://www.sueddeutsche.de/bayern /fluechtlinge-in-zirndorf-menschenwuerdig-ist-das-nicht-1.2108279.

Pugach, Sara. "African Students and the Politics of Race and Gender in the German Democratic Republic." In *Comrades of Color: East Germany in the Cold War World*, edited by Quinn Slobodian, 131–56. New York: Berghahn Books, 2015.

Rasche, Ute. "Smear Campaign against German-Turkish Female Activists." *Qantara.de – Dialog mit der islamischen Welt*, April 26, 2005. https:// en.qantara.de/content/german-edition-of-hurriyet-newspaper-smear -campaign-against-german-turkish-female-activists.

Rassismustötet. *Pogrom Hoyerswerda:"Ausländerjagd – Rassismus im neuen Deutschland?" ARD Im Brennpunkt*. Hoyerswerda: ARD 1991. https://www .youtube.com/watch?v=0gjFyPnCQnU&t=544s.

"Record Pegida Rally in Dresden Sparks Mass Rival Protests." *BBC News*, January 12, 2015. https://www.bbc.com/news/world-europe-30777841.

Reimann, Anna. "Ehrenmord: Sorgerechts-Gezerre um Hatun Sürücüs Sohn." *Spiegel Online*, February 5, 2007. http://www.spiegel.de/panorama/justiz/ ehrenmord-sorgerechts-gezerre-um-hatun-sueruecues-sohn-a-464439.html.

–. "Integrationskurse: Sparwut der Regierung bremst Einwanderer aus." *Spiegel Online*, September 22, 2010. http://www.spiegel.de/politik/deutschland /integrationskurse-sparwut-der-regierung-bremst-einwanderer-aus-a-718855 .html.

Reinhard, Doreen. "Freital: Lust auf Lynchen." *Die Zeit*, July 7, 2015. https:// www.zeit.de/politik/deutschland/2015-07/freital-fluechtlinge -buergerversammlung

–."Freital: Rassismus als Happening." *Zeit Online*, June 25, 2015. https:// www.zeit.de/politik/deutschland/2015-06/freital-fluechtlingsheim -proteste-stellungskrieg.

"Rektor: 'Kollegen haben mir den Rücken gestärkt.'" *Berliner Morgenpost*, February 18, 2005. https://www.morgenpost.de/printarchiv/berlin /article104159781/Rektor-Kollegen-haben-mir-den-Ruecken-gestaerkt.html.

Retterath, Hans-Werner. "Vom Barackenlager zum Übergangswohnheim. Volkskundliche Anmerkungen zur Aufnahme von Vertriebenen im Freiburger Stattteil Bischofslinde." In *Flucht und Vertreibung: 50 Jahre Danach*, edited by Gottfried Habenicht, 76–88. Freiburg: Johannes-Künzig-Institut für ostdeutsche Volkskunde, 1996.

Richards, Fred H. *Die NPD: Alternative oder Weiderkehr?* Munich: Olzog, 1967.

Riedel, Katja, Lena Kampf, and Sebastian Pittelkow. "Chemnitz: Rechtsextreme wollten Migranten jagen." *tagesschau.de*, August 26, 2019. https://www.tagesschau.de/investigativ/ndr-wdr/chemnitz-rechtsextreme-ausschreitungen-101.html.

Rights, Equality and Citizenship Programme. "ENGAGE: Roadmap for Frontline Professionals Interacting with Male Perpetrators of Domestic Violence and Abuse." European Union, 2019. https://www.work-with-perpetrators.eu/fileadmin/WWP_Network/redakteure/Projects/ENGAGE/Final_roadmaps/engage_EN_191127_web.pdf.

Ringelstein, Ronja. "So begründet die SPD den Parteiausschluss von Thilo Sarrazin." *Der Tagesspiegel*, January 24, 2020. https://www.tagesspiegel.de/berlin/rassistisch-herabwuerdigend-diskriminierend-so-begruendet-die-spd-den-parteiausschluss-von-thilo-sarrazin/25469256.html.

Rist, Ray C. *Guestworkers in Germany: The Prospects for Pluralism*. New York: Praeger, 1978.

–. "Migration and Marginality: Guestworkers in Germany and France." *Daedalus* 108, no. 2 (1979): 95–108.

Prof. Dr. Rolf Rosenbrock, Prof. Dr. Werner Schiffauer, Andreas Lipsch, and Maria Loheide, ProAsyl, "Referentenentwurf zu einem Integrationsgesetz vom 29.04.2016." Last modified May 19, 2016, accessed June 20, 2023. https://www.proasyl.de/wp-content/uploads/2015/12/2016-05-19-Brandbrief-an-Bundesregierung-zum-Integrationsgesetz.pdf.

Rommelspacher, Birgit. "Kulturelle Grenzziehungen in der Sozialarbeit: Doing and undoing differences." In *Diversität und soziale Ungleichheit: Analytische Zugänge und professionelles Handeln in der sozialen Arbeit*, edited by Herbert Effinger, Stefan Borrmann, Silke Birgitta Gahleitner, Michaela Koettig, Björn Kraus, and Sabine Stövesand, 43–55. Leverkusen: Verlag Barbara Budrich, 2012.

–. "Ungebrochene Selbstidealisierung." *Die Tageszeitung*, January 18, 2010.

Rosch, Benjamin, and Jonas Hoskyn. "Denn sie weiss, was sie tut: Islamgegnerin neu im Basler Kirchenrat." *Aargauer Zeitung*, September 7, 2019. https://www.aargauerzeitung.ch/schweiz/denn-sie-weiss-was-sie-tut-islamgegnerin-neu-im-basler-kirchenrat-135581135.

Rubin, Gayle. "The Traffic in Women." In *Literary Theory: An Anthology*, edited by Julie Rivkin and Michael Ryan, 770–94. Malden, MA: Blackwell Publishing, 2004.

Ruddick, Susan. "Constructing Difference in Public Spaces: Race, Class, and Gender as Interlocking Systems." *Urban Geography* 17, no. 2 (1996): 132–51. https://doi.org/10.2747/0272-3638.17.2.132.

Ruttig, Thomas. "Afghan Exodus: Afghan Asylum Seekers in Europe (3) – Case Study Germany." *Afghanistan Analysts Network*, February 17, 2017. https://www.afghanistan-analysts.org/wp-admin/post.php.

Sachverständigenrat deutscher Stiftungen für Integration und Migration (SVR). *Einwanderungsgesellschaft 2010: Jahresgutachten 2010 mit Integrationsbarometer.* Berlin: SVR, 2010.

Said, Edward W. "Orientalism," *The Georgia Review* 31, no. 1 (1977): 162–206, www.jstor.org/stable/41397448.

Sammann, Luise. "Eine EU-Richtlinie und ihre Auswirkungen – Unmut über ungleiche Behandlung von Kriegsflüchtlingen," *Deutschlandfunk*, last modified May 6, 2022, https://www.deutschlandfunk.de/zwei-klassen -gefluechtete-100.html.

Sarrazin, Thilo. *Deutschland schafft sich ab: Wie wir unser Land aufs Spiel setzen.* 18th printing, 2011. Munich: Deutsche Verlags-Anstalt, 2010.

–. "Thilo Sarrazin im Gespräch mit 'Lettre International'." *Bild.de*, October 8, 2009. https://eppinger.files.wordpress.com/2009/10/klasse-statt-masse.pdf.

"Sarrazins Schelte." *Spiegel Chronik*, December 9, 2009. https://www.spiegel .de/spiegel/dokument/d-68105096.html.

Säuberlich, Jörg. "Merkel 'außerordentlich zufrieden.'" *Der Tagesspiegel*, July 14, 2006. https://www.tagesspiegel.de/politik/integrationsgipfel-merkel -ausserordentlich-zufrieden/731042.html.

"Schießen auf Flüchtlinge: Frauen ja, Kinder nein." *tagesschau.de*, January 31, 2016. https://www.tagesschau.de/inland/afd-schusswaffen-103.html.

Schiffauer, Werner. "Der unheimliche Muslim: Staatsbürgerschaft und zivilgesellschaftliche Ängste." In *Konfliktfeld Islam in Europa*, edited by Monika Wohlrab-Sahr and Levent Tezcan, 111–33. Baden-Baden: Nomos, 2007.

–. *Die Gewalt der Ehre: Erklärungen zu einem deutsch-türkischen Sexualkonflikt.* Frankfurt am Main: Suhrkamp, 1983.

–. *Die Migranten aus Subay: Türken in Deutschland, Eine Ethnographie.* Stuttgart: Klett-Cotta, 1991.

–. *Parallelgesellschaften: Wie viel Wertekonsens braucht unsere Gesellschaft. Für eine kluge Politik der Differenz.* Bielefeld: transcript verlag, 2008.

Schillinger, Reinhold. "Der Lastenausgleich." In *Die Vertreibung der Deutschen aus den Osten*, edited by Wolfgang Benz, 183–92. Frankfurt am Main: Fischer Verlag, 1985.

Schily, Otto. "Integration: 'Alarmierender Einblick.'" *Der Spiegel* 4, 2005.

Schimany, Peter. "Asylmigration nach Deutschland." In *20 Jahre Asylkompromiss*, edited by Stefan Luft and Peter Schimany, 33–68. Bielefeld: transcript verlag, 2014.

Schlicht, Raphaela. *Determinanten der Bildungsungleichheit.* Wiesbaden: VS Verlag für Sozialwissenschaften, 2011. https://doi.org/10.1007 /978-3-531-92626-1.

Schmale, Holger. "Der Tag des Provokateurs." *Frankfurter Rundschau*, August 31, 2010. https://www.fr.de/panorama/provokateurs-11461356.html.

Schmidt, Ute. "Vom Flüchtling zum 'Neubürger': Die Vertriebenen in der SBZ und in der DDR vor dem Hintergrund 'verordneter' Verständigung mit dem Osten." In *Die Bundesrepublik Deutschland und die Vertriebenen: Fünfzig Jahre Eingliederung, Aufbau und Verständigung mit den Staaten des östlichen Europa*, edited by Christof Dahm and Hans-Jakob Tebarth, 76–7. Bonn: die Kulturstiftung der deutschen Vertriebenen, 2000.

Schmidtke, Oliver. "Reinventing the Nation: Germany's Post-Unification Drive Towards Becoming a 'Country of Immigration.'" *German Politics* 26, no. 4 (2017): 498–515. https://doi.org/10.1080/09644008.2017.1365137.

Schmoll, Heike. "Bildung in Berlin: Sarrazin gab den Sparkommissar." *Frankfurter Allgemeine Zeitung*, September 13, 2010. https://www.faz.net/1.1040135.

Schneider, Jan. Bundeszentrale für politische Bildung. "Rückblick: Zuwanderungsgesetz 2005." May 15, 2007. http://www.bpb.de/gesellschaft /migration/dossier-migration/56351/zuwanderungsgesetz-2005?p=all.

Schneider, Peter. "The New Berlin Wall." *The New York Times Magazine*, December 4, 2005. https://www.nytimes.com/2005/12/04/magazine/the -new-berlin-wall.html.

Schomaker, Gilbert. "Essen für 4,25 Euro: Sarrazin entwickelt Hartz-IV-Speiseplan." *Die Welt*, February 8, 2008. https://www.welt.de/politik /article1649762/Sarrazin-entwickelt-Hartz-IV-Speiseplan.html.

Schönwälder, Karen. *Einwanderung und ethnische Pluralität: politische Entscheidungen und öffentliche Debatten in Grossbritannien und der Bundesrepublik von den 1950er bis zu den 1970er Jahren*. Essen: Klartext, 2001.

–. "The Difficult Task of Managing Migration: The 1973 Recruitment Stop." In *German History from the Margins*, edited by Neil Gregor, Nils Roemer, and Mark Roseman, 252–67. Bloomington: Indiana University Press, 2006.

–. "Why Germany's Guestworkers Were Largely Europeans: The Selective Principles of Post-War Labour Recruitment Policy." *Ethnic and Racial Studies* 27, no. 2 (2004): 248–65. https://doi.org/10.1080/0141987042000177324.

Schönwälder, Karen, and Triadafilos Triadafilopoulos. "A Bridge of Barrier to Incorporation? Germany's 1999 Citizenship Reform in Critical Perspective." *German Politics and Society* 30, no. 1 (2012): 52–70.

Schreiter, N. "Demo für mehr Flüchtlingsrechte: 'Das war Berlin, jetzt kommt Europa'." *Die Tageszeitung*, October 14, 2012. https://taz.de/!5081849/.

Schröttle, Monika, and Nadia Khelaifat. "Gesundheit – Gewalt – Migration." Kurzfassung. Rostock: Bundesministerium für Familie, Senioren, Frauen und Jugend, 2009. https://www.bmfsfj.de/bmfsfj/service/publikationen /gesundheit-gewalt-migration/80598.

Schuler, Katharina. "Nun aber mal konkret." *Zeit Online*, July 14, 2006. https://www.zeit.de/online/2006/29/Integrationsgipfel.

Schulte von Drach, Markus C. "Pro: Der Handschlag ist eine für Muslime zumutbare Geste." *Süddeutsche Zeitung*, April 7, 2016. http://www .sueddeutsche.de/politik/pro-haendeschuetteln-der-handschlag-ist-fuer -muslime-eine-zumutbare-geste-1.2675574-2.

Schulz, Wolfgang. "Deutsche Künstlerinnen und Künstler aus dem Osten: Bewahrung der kulturellen Traditionen in der Bundesrepublik Deutschland als Elemente einer frühen Verständigung mit den Nachbarn." In *Die Bundesrepublik Deutschland und die Vertriebenen: Fünfzig Jahre Eingliederung, Aufbau und Verständigung mit den Staaten des östlichen Europa*, edited by Christof Dahm and Hans-Jakob Tebarth, 67–74. Bonn: die Kulturstiftung der deutschen Vertriebenen, 2000.

Schuster-Craig, Johanna. "Integration Politics as an Apparatus." *German Studies Review* 40, no. 3 (2017): 607–27. https://doi.org/10.1353/gsr.2017.0096.

–. "Mass-Market Paperbacks and Integration Politics." *German Politics and Society* 39, no. 2 (2021): 22–46. https://doi.org/10.3167/gps.2021 .390202.

–. "Resisting Integration: Neukölln Artist Reponses to Integration Politics." In *Cultural Topographies of the New Berlin*, edited by Karin Bauer and Jennifer Ruth Hosek, 228–52. New York: Berghahn Books, 2018.

–. "'Well-Integrated Muslims' and Adolescent Anti-Violence Activism in Berlin." *German Life & Letters* 68, no. 1 (2015): 125–44. https://doi.org /10.1111/glal.12072.

Schwartz, Michael. "Vertriebene im doppelten Deutschland. Integrations- und Erinnerungspolitik in der DDR und in der Bundesrepublik." *Vierteljahrshefte für Zeitgeschichte* 1 (2008): 101–51.

Schwarzer, Alice. "Hatun & Can: Die bittere Wahrheit." *Emma*, July 1, 2010. https://www.emma.de/artikel/hatun-can-die-bittere-wahrheit-265142.

Schweitzer, Helmuth. "Durch periodisches Wiegen wird die Sau nicht fetter." *Sozial Extra* 36, no. 7 (2012): 27–30. https://doi.org/10.1007 /s12054-012-0081-z.

Scott, Joan Wallach. *The Politics of the Veil*. Princeton: Princeton University Press, 2010.

Seibert, Thomas. "Blutsverwandte – der Fall Sürücü." *Der Tagesspiegel*, February 2, 2016. https://www.tagesspiegel.de/themen/reportage/neuer-ehrenmord -prozess-blutsverwandte-der-fall-sueruecue/12877474.html.

Seipp, Adam R. *Strangers in the Wild Place: Refugees, Americans, and a German Town, 1945–1952*. Bloomington: Indiana University Press, 2013.

Sen, Purna. "'Crimes of Honour,' Value and Meaning." In *"Honour": Crimes, Paradigms, and Violence against Women*, edited by Lynn Welchman and Sara Hossain, 42–63. London: Zed Books, 2005.

Serif, Walter, and Steffen Mack. "Sie können es nicht lassen!" *Mannheimer Morgen*, January 29, 2016. https://www.mannheimer-morgen.de/politik_ artikel,-politik-sie-koennen-es-nicht-lassen-_arid,751556.html.

Sezgin, Hilal. *Manifest der Vielen: Deutschland erfindet sich neu.* Berlin: Blumenbar, 2011.

Shiva, Vandana. *Stolen Harvest: The Hijacking of the Global Food Supply.* Lexington: University Press of Kentucky, 2016.

Simon, Anne-Catherine. "Necla Kelek: 'Sarrazins Gegner haben ihr Ziel erreicht.'" *Die Presse,* January 20, 2013. https://www.diepresse.com /1334649/necla-kelek-sarrazins-gegner-haben-ihr-ziel-erreicht.

Slobodian, Quinn. "Introduction." In *Comrades of Color: East Germany in the Cold War World,* edited by Quinn Slobodian, 1–19. New York: Berghahn Books, 2015.

–. "Socialist Chromatism: Race, Racism, and the Racial Rainbow in East Germany." In *Comrades of Color: East Germany in the Cold War World,* edited by Quinn Slobodian, 23–42. New York: Berghahn Books, 2015.

Smale, Alison. "German Anti-Immigrant Leaders Resign." *The New York Times,* January 28, 2015. https://www.nytimes.com/2015/01/29/world/europe /pegida-german-protest-group-announce-resignatons.html.

Smoydzin, Werner. *NPD: Die Geschichte und Umwelt einer Partei.* Pfaffenhofen: Ilmgau Verlag, 1967.

Sneyder, Bon. *Necla Kelek stellt Sarrazins Buch vor 1/2.* August 30, 2010, YouTube, 7:55, https://www.youtube.com/watch?v=nQnSfxlsUsw&t=21s.

–. "Necla Kelek stellt Sarrazins Buch vor 2/2," August 31, 2010, YouTube, 10:01, https://www.youtube.com/watch?v=6ypBu9k4oGw&t=12s.

Speckner, Kerstin. "Mach den Muslim-Test!" *Die Tageszeitung,* January 6, 2006.

Spicka, Mark E. "Cultural Centres and Guest Worker Integration in Stuttgart, Germany, 1960–1976." *Immigrants & Minorities* 33, no. 2 (2015): 117–40. https://doi.org/10.1080/02619288.2014.904639.

Spiegel Online. "Six Decades of Quality Journalism: The History of *Der Spiegel,*" October 5, 2011. http://www.spiegel.de/international/six-decades -of-quality-journalism-the-history-of-der-spiegel-a-789853.html.

Spivak, Gayatri. "Can the Subaltern Speak?" In *Marxism and the Interpretation of Culture,* edited by Cary Nelson and Lawrence Grossberg, 271–313. Urbana and Chicago: University of Illinois, 1988.

Statista. "Population of East and West Germany 1950–2016." Accessed May 21, 2021. https://www.statista.com/statistics/1054199/population-of-east -and-west-germany/.

Statistische Berichte Baden-Württemberg. *Endgültige Ergebnisse der Wahl zum 15. Landtag von Baden-Württemberg am 27. März 2011.* Artikel-Nr. 4232 11001. Stuttgart: Statistisches Landesamt Baden-Württemberg, 2011. PDF, https:// www.statistik-bw.de/Service/Veroeff/Statistische_Berichte/423211001.pdf. Accessed February 23, 2024.

stb. "Kathrin Oertel macht jetzt was Eigenes." *Stern,* January 29, 2015. https:// www.stern.de/politik/deutschland/kathrin-oertel-will-nach-pegida-neues -buendnis-gruenden-3462168.html.

Steffen, Tilman. "Pegida: Bachmann wird weiter hetzen." *Die Zeit*, May 3, 2016. https://www.zeit.de/gesellschaft/zeitgeschehen/2016-05/pegida -gruender-lutz-bachmann-volksverhetzung-geldstrafe.

Steffens, Volker. "Der offene Brief des Schulleiters nach dem Mord und das Dankschreiben von Bundespräsident Köhler." *Spiegel Online*, August 18, 2005. https://www.spiegel.de/lebenundlernen/schule/ehrenmord -an-hatin-sueruecue-bundespraesident-koehler-dankt-couragiertem -schulleiter-a-369481-2.html.

Stehle, Maria. "Narrating the Ghetto, Narrating Europe: From Berlin, Kreuzberg to the Banlieues of Paris." *Westminster Papers in Communication and Culture* 3, no. 3 (2006): 48–70. https://doi.org/10.16997/wpcc.59.

–. "White Ghettos: The 'Crisis of Multiculturalism' in Post-Unification Germany." *European Journal of Cultural Studies* 15, no. 2 (2012): 167–81. https://doi.org/10.1177/1367549411432025.

Stein, Christina. *Die Sprache der Sarrazin-Debatte: Eine diskurslinguistische Analyse*. Marburg: Tectum Wissenschaftsverlag, 2012.

Steiner, Viktor, and Johannes Velling. "Re-Migration Behavior and Expected Duration of Stay of Guest Workers in Germany." In *The Economic Consequences of Immigration to Germany*, 101–19. Heidelberg: Physica, 1994. https://doi.org/10.1007/978-3-642-51177-6_6.

Steinert, Jörg. "Mahnwache für Hatin [sic] Sürücü." Press Release. *LSVD- Landesverband Berlin-Brandenburg*, February 18, 2005. https://www.lsvd.de /bund/presse/0502180.html.

Steinweis, Alan E. "Ideology and Infrastructure: German Area Science and Planning for the Germanization of Eastern Europe, 1939–1944." *East European Quarterly* 28, no. 3 (1994): 335–47.

Stern, Alexandra Minna. *Proud Boys and the White Ethnostate: How the Alt-Right Is Warping the American Imagination*. Boston: Beacon Press, 2019.

Stokes, Lauren. "The Permanent Refugee Crisis in the Federal Republic of Germany, 1949–." *Central European History* 52 (2019): 19–44. https://doi.org /10.1017/S0008938919000025.

–. "'Fear of the Family': Migration and Integration in West Germany, 1955–2000." PhD diss., University of Chicago, 2016.

–. *Fear of the Family*. New York: Oxford University Press, 2022.

Stoldt, Till. "Die war halt zu deutsch." *Welt am Sonntag*, February 20, 2005. https: //www.welt.de/print-wams/article123850/Die-war-halt-zu-deutsch.html.

Storch, Beatrix von. "AfD-Vizechefin will Polizei auf Kinder schießen lassen – Bild 2 von 3." *Frankfurter Allgemeine Zeitung*, January 31, 2016. https:// www.faz.net/aktuell/politik/fluechtlingskrise/beatrix-von-storch-afd -vizechefin-will-polizei-sogar-auf-kinder-schiessen-lassen-14044186.html.

Stuckrad-Barre, B. von. "Ortstermin: Thilo Sarrazin kritisiert türkischstämmige Fußballfans." *Die Welt*, October 9, 2010. https://www

.welt.de/politik/deutschland/article10179969/Thilo-Sarrazin-kritisiert
-tuerkischstaemmige-Fussballfans.html.

Süddeutsche Zeitung/AFP/dpa/sks/anri. "Pegida-Hochburg – Proteste
gegen Flüchtlingsheim in Freital bei Dresden." *Süddeutsche Zeitung*, June 24,
2015. https://www.sueddeutsche.de/politik/wohnort-von-pegida
-gruender-lutz-bachmann-proteste-gegen-fluechtlingsheim-in-freital-bei
-dresden-1.2535171?print=true.

"'Suicides' Really Honor Killings?" *Sveriges Radio*, October 18, 2011. https://
sverigesradio.se/artikel/4771356.

"Sürücü-Mörder in die Türkei abgeschoben." *rbb24*, July 4, 2014. https://
www.rbb24.de/politik/beitrag/2014/07/hatun-sueruecue-bruder-ayhan
-in-die-tuerkei-abgeschoben.html.

Syd/dpa. "AfD: Beatrix von Storch nimmt Äußerung über Schüsse auf
Flüchtlinge zurück." *Der Spiegel*, February 10, 2016. https://www.spiegel
.de/politik/deutschland/afd-beatrix-von-storch-nimmt- aeusserung-ueber
-schuesse-auf-fluechtlinge-zurueck-a-1076757.html.

SZ.de/dpa/dayk. "Lutz Bachmann: Geldstrafe wegen Volksverhetzung."
Süddeutsche Zeitung, May 3, 2016. https://www.sueddeutsche.de/politik
/pegida-gruender-bachmann-geldstrafe-wegen-volksverhetzung-1.2979363.

–. "Pegida-Gründer Bachmann erhält Geldstrafe wegen Volksverhetzung."
Süddeutsche Zeitung, May 3, 2016. https://www.sueddeutsche.de/politik
/pegida-gruender-bachmann-geldstrafe-wegen-volksverhetzung-1.2979363.

SZ.de/dpa/jobr. "Sarrazin wird aus der SPD ausgeschlossen." *Süddeutsche
Zeitung*, July 31, 2020. https://www.sueddeutsche.de/politik/sarrazin
-ausschluss-spd-1.4985099.

SZ.de/dpa/Reuters/gal/dit. "Unionsfraktionschefs fordern Wertekunde
-Unterricht für Flüchtlingskinder." *Süddeutsche Zeitung*, May 7, 2018.
http://www.sueddeutsche.de/politik/union-wertekunde-unterricht
-fluechtlingskinder-1.3970311.

SZ/lex. "Ereignisprotokoll: Der erste Tag im Bachmann-Prozess." *Sächsische
Zeitung*, April 19, 2016. https://www.saechsische.de/ereignisprotokoll-der
-erste-tag-im-bachmann-prozess-3375694.html.

SZ/wei. "Asylforum in Freital abgesagt." *Sächsische Zeitung*, March 12, 2015.
https://www.saechsische.de/asylforum-in-freital-abgesagt-3056177.html.

Taft, Casey T., Christopher M. Murphy, Daniel W. King, Peter H. Musser,
and Judith M. DeDeyn, "Process and Treatment Adherence Factors in
Group Cognitive–Behavioral Therapy for Partner Violent Men," *Journal of
Consulting and Clinical Psychology* 71, no. 4, 812–20. https://doi.org
/10.1037/0022-006X.71.4.812.

Der Tagesspiegel. "10 Jahre Gedenken an Hatun Sürücü in Berlin." No longer
available. February 8, 2015, YouTube, 3:58, https://www.youtube.com
/watch?v=qzyouxBpn5c.

Der Tagesspiegel/AFP. "Spitzentreffen: Gehen dem Integrationsgipfel die Migranten aus?" *Der Tagesspiegel*, July 5, 2007. https://www.tagesspiegel.de/politik/spitzentreffen-gehen-dem-integrationsgipfel-die-migranten-aus/978700.html.

Tang, Eric. *Unsettled: Cambodian Refugees in the New York City Hyperghetto.* Philadelphia: Temple University Press, 2015.

Tayeb, Fatima El. "'Blood Is a Very Special Juice'*: Racialized Bodies and Citizenship in Twentieth-Century Germany." *International Review of Social History* 44, no. S7 (1999): 149–69. https://doi.org/10.1017/S0020859000115238.

Ter Haseborg, Volker. "Wo Thilo Sarrazin recht hat." *Hamburger Abendblatt*, September 17, 2010. https://www.abendblatt.de/hamburg/article107854160/Wo-Thilo-Sarrazin-recht hat.html.

Theil, Stefan, and Sarah Sennott. "The Barbarians Within: A Rash of Honor Killings Sends Shock Waves through Europe." *Newsweek*, March 28, 2005. https://www.newsweek.com/barbarians-within-114953

Theweleit, Klaus. *Male Fantasies: Volume 1.* Translated by Stephen Conway, Erika Carter, and Chris Turner. Minneapolis: University of Minnesota Press, 1987.

Thränhardt, Dietrich. "Germany: An Undeclared Immigration Country." *Journal of Ethnic and Migration Studies* 21, no. 1 (1995): 19–35. https://doi.org/10.1080/1369183X.1995.9976470.

–. "The Political Uses of Xenophobia in England, France and Germany." *Party Politics* 1, no. 3 (1995): 323–45. https://doi.org/10.1177/1354068895001003002.

"Tod umsonst." *Spiegel Online*, August 30, 1987. https://www.spiegel.de/politik/tod-umsonst-a-e9e0faa0-0002-0001-0000-000013526485.

Triadafilopoulos, Triadafilos. *Becoming Multicultural: Immigration and the Politics of Membership in Canada and Germany.* Vancouver: UBC Press, 2012.

Triadafilopoulos, Triadafilos, and Karen Schönwälder. "How the Federal Republic Became an Immigration Country: Norms, Politics and the Failure of West Germany's Guest Worker System." *German Politics & Society* 24, no. 3 (2006): 1–19.

Tribune Newspapers. "Emerging from Darkness, Shrouded in Doubt." *Chicago Tribune*, January 30, 2002. https://www.chicagotribune.com/2002/01/30/emerging-from-darkness-shrouded-in-doubt/.

tsp/AFP. "Lutz Bachmann ist wieder Pegida-Chef." *Der Tagesspiegel*, February 23, 2015. https://www.tagesspiegel.de/politik/anti-islam-bewegung-lutz-bachmann-ist-wieder-pegida-chef/11408898.html.

tsp/ddp. "Gedenktafel für ermordete Hatun Sürücü." *Der Tagespiegel*, June 11, 2008. https://www.tagesspiegel.de/berlin/ehrenmord-gedenktafel-fuer-ermordete-hatun-sueruecue/1253802.html.

"Die Türken erobern Deutschland." *Berliner Morgenpost*, October 2, 2009. https://www.morgenpost.de/printarchiv/berlin/article104594137/Die-Tuerken-erobern-Deutschland.html.

uh mit Stadt Schwandorf/Pressemitteilung. "Schwandorf gedenkt Opfer des Brandanschlages von 1988 – 'kein Platz für Gewalt und Extremismus'." *Wochenblatt*, December 15, 2018. https://www.wochenblatt.de/archiv /schwandorf-gedenkt-opfer-des-brandanschlages-von-1988-kein-platz-fuer -gewalt-und-extremismus-268777.

Ulrich, Bernd. "Flüchtlinge: Naivität des Bösen." *Die Zeit*, October 8, 2015. https://www.zeit.de/2015/41/fluechtlinge-krise-deutschland-zaun-angela -merkel.

United States Holocaust Museum Memorial. *Holocaust Encyclopedia*. "Germany: Jewish Population in 1933." Accessed May 21, 2021. https://encyclopedia .ushmm.org/content/en/article/germany-jewish-population-in-1933.

Universität Duisburg-Essen. "Mercatorprofessur 2006." Accessed January 25, 2018. https://www.uni-due.de/de/mercatorprofessur/2006.shtml.

UN Security Council. "ISIL/Da'esh Committed Genocide of Yazidi, War Crimes against Unarmed Cadets, Military Personnel in Iraq, Investigative Team Head Tells Security Council." May 10, 2021. https://www.un.org/ press/en/2021/sc14514.doc.htm.

Upchurch, Martin. "Institutional Transference and Changing Workplace Relations in Post Unification East Germany: A Case Study of Secondary Education Teachers." *Work, Employment and Society* 12, no. 2 (1998): 195–218. https://doi.org/10.1177/0950017098122001.

USA for UNHCR: The UN Refugee Agency. "Refugee Crisis in Europe: Aid, Statistics, and Relief Efforts." 2018. https://www.unrefugees.org /emergencies/refugee-crisis-in-europe/.

Virchow, Fabian. "The Groupuscularization of Neo-Nazism in Germany: The Case of the Aktionsbüro Norddeutschland." *Patterns of Prejudice* 38, no. 1 (2004): 56–70. https://doi.org/10.1080/0031322032000185587.

Voelker, Gottfried E. "More Foreign Workers – Germany's Labour Problem No. 1?" In *Turkish Workers in Europe 1960–1975:A Socio-Economic Reappraisal*, edited by Nermin Abadan-Unat, 331–45. Leiden: Brill, 1976.

Vogel, Kerstin. "Protestmarsch von Asylsuchenden – Polizei stoppt Flüchtlinge." *Süddeutsche Zeitung*, September 1, 2013. https://www.sueddeutsche.de /muenchen/freising/einkesselte-fluechtlinge-schimpfende-demonstranten -unmittelbarer-zwang-1.1760048.

Volpp, Leti. "Framing Cultural Difference: Immigrant Women and Discourses of Tradition." *Differences* 22, no. 1 (2011): 90–110. https://doi .org/10.1215/10407391-1218256.

von Altenbockum, Jasper. "AfD: Unheimlich bürgerlich." *Frankfurter Allgemeine Zeitung*, September 12, 2019. https://www.faz.net/1.6379477.

von Drach, Markus C. Schulte. "Existieren Parallelgesellschaften in Deutschland?" *Süddeutsche Zeitung*, August 10, 2016. https://www.sueddeutsche.de

/politik/muslime-und-migranten-gibt-es-parallelgesellschaften-in
-deutschland-1.3012266.

von Münch, Ingo. *Die deutsche Staatsangehörigkeit: Vergangenheit – Gegenwart – Zukunft*. Berlin: Walter de Gruyter, 2007.

"Vor 30 Jahren: Ausreise aus der Prager Botschaft." *Bundeszentrale der politischen Bildung*, September 27, 2019. https://www.bpb.de/politik /hintergrund-aktuell/297704/prager-botschaft.

Vorländer, Hans, Maik Herold, and Steven Schäller. *PEGIDA and New Right-Wing Populism in Germany*. Cham, Switzerland: Palgrave Macmillan, 2018. https://doi.org/10.1007/978-3-319-67495-7.

Wagner, Peter M. *NPD-Hochburgen in Baden-Württemberg: Erklärungsfaktoren für die Wahlerfolge einer rechtsextremistischen Partei in ländlichen Regionen 1972–1994*. Berlin: Duncker & Humblot, 1997.

Wahlrecht.de. "Wahlergebnisse – Bundestag (Bundestagswahl)." Accessed October 14, 2019. http://www.wahlrecht.de/ergebnisse/bundestag.htm.

Wallet, Norbert. "Bosbach: Thilo Sarrazin hat recht." *Stuttgarter Nachrichten*, September 2, 2010. https://www.stuttgarter-nachrichten.de/inhalt.bosbach -thilo-sarrazin-hat-recht.b40a6051-90b1-4357-ad95-9250f395439e.html.

Warda, Katharina. "Dunkeldeutschland." *Journal der Künste* 12 (2020): 24–26.

Warsaw Press Agency. *Transfer of the German Population from Poland: Legend and Reality*. Warsaw: Western Press Agency, 1966.

Weber, Beverly. "'We Must Talk about Cologne': Race, Gender, and Reconfigurations of 'Europe.'" *German Politics and Society* 34, no. 4 (2016): 68–86. https://doi.org/10.3167/gps.2016.340405.

–. *Violence and Gender in the "New" Europe: Islam in German Culture*. New York: Palgrave MacMillan, 2013.

Weiss, Hermann. "Die Organisationen der Vertriebenen und ihre Presse." In *Die Vertreibung der Deutschen aus dem Osten*, edited by Wolfgang Benz, 193–208. Frankfurt am Main: Fischer Verlag, 1985.

Wendt, Johannes. "Protest gegen Anhörungen: Flüchtlinge besetzen Botschaft." *Die Tageszeitung*, October 15, 2012. https://taz.de/!5081767/.

Werkstatt der Kulturen. "8. Spieglein, Spieglein an der Wand, wer ist der Integrierteste im ganzen Land?," January 25, 2012, YouTube, 14:43. https:// www.youtube.com/watch?v=RtL4xpoW4Zc&t=4s.

Wiesemann, Falk. "Flüchtlingspolitik in Nordrhein-Westfalen." In *Die Vertreibung der Deutschen aus den Osten: Ursachen, Ereignisse, Folgen*, edited by Wolfgang Benz, 173–82. Frankfurt am Main: Fischer Verlag, 1985.

Wiessala, Georg. "Problems of Nationalism, Neo-fascism and National Identity in Post-unification Germany." *Journal of Area Studies* 5, no. 10 (1997): 66–86. https://doi.org/10.1080/02613539708455797.

Wilde, Stephanie. "A Study of Teacher's Perceptions in Brandenburg Gesamtschulen." In *Education in Germany since Unification*, edited by David Phillips, 37–56. Cambridge: Symposium Books, 2000.

Wilson, Reid. "Census: More Americans Have College Degrees Than Ever Before." *The Hill*, April 3, 2017. https://thehill.com/homenews/state-watch/326995-census-more-americans-have-college-degrees-than-ever-before.

Woesthoff, Julia. "Ambiguities of Antiracism: Representations of Foreign Labourers and the West German Media, 1955–1990." PhD diss., Michigan State University, 2004.

–. "'Foreigners and Women Have the Same Problems': Binational Marriages, Women's Grassroots Organizing, and the Quest for Legal Equality in Post-1968 Germany." *Journal of Family History* 38, no. 4 (2013): 422–42. https://doi.org/10.1177/0363199013504386.

–. "'When I Marry a Mohammedan': Migration and the Challenges of Interethnic Marriages in Post-War Germany." *Contemporary European History* 22, no. 2 (2013): 199–231. https://doi.org/10.1017/S0960777313000052.

Wyatt, Ronald. "Pain and Ethnicity." *AMA Journal of Ethics* 15, no. 5 (2013): 449–54. https://doi.org/10.1001/virtualmentor.2013.15.5.pfor1-1305.

Yaghoobifarah, Hengameh. "Blicke." In *Eure Heimat ist unser Albtraum*, edited by Fatma Aydemir and Hengameh Yaghoobifarah, 69–81. Berlin: Ullstein, 2019.

Yildiz, Yasemin. "Turkish Girls, Allah's Daughters, and the Contemporary German Subject: Itinerary of a Figure." *German Life and Letters* 62, no. 4 (2009): 465–81. https://doi.org/10.1111/j.1468-0483.2009.01475.x.

–. "Governing European Subjects: Tolerance and Guilt in the Discourse of 'Muslim Women.'" *Cultural Critique* 77, no. 1 (2011): 70–101. https://doi.org/10.1353/cul.2011.0002.

–. "Reading Racialization: Yadé Kara's Selam Berlin." *German Studies Review* 46, no. 1 (2023): 97–115.

Yoder, Jennifer A. *From East Germans to Germans?: The New Postcommunist Elites*. Durham: Duke University Press, 1999.

YouTube. "WERKSTATT DER KULTUREN – Diskussion," 2010. Accessed March 11, 2024. https://www.youtube.com/channel/UC2GFAmAfvDnnXX-GldoGBAw.

Yurdakul, Gökçe. *From Guest Workers into Muslims: The Transformation of Turkish Immigrant Associations in Germany*. Newcastle upon Tyne: Cambridge Scholars Publishing, 2009.

Zahra, Tara. "Looking East: East Central European 'Borderlands' in German History and Historiography." *History Compass* 3, no. 1 (2005). https://doi.org/10.1111/j.1478-0542.2005.00175.x.

Zawatka-Gerlach, Ulrich, Sandra Dasslef, and Mariz Hubschmid. "Sarrazin stellt seine Weltsicht vor." *Der Tagesspiegel*, August 31, 2010. https://www.tagesspiegel.de/berlin/pressekonferenz-sarrazin-stellt-seine-weltsicht-vor/1914788.html.

Zayas, Alfred M. de. *Nemesis at Potsdam: The Anglo-Americans and the Expulsion of the Germans: Background, Execution, Consequences*. London: Routledge, 1977.

Zeit Online/afp/ces. "Frauke Petry: AfD will Flüchtlinge notfalls mit Waffengewalt stoppen." *Die Zeit*, January 30, 2016. https://www.zeit .de/politik/deutschland/2016-01/frauke-petry-afd-grenzschutz -auf-fluechtlinge-schiessen.

Zeit Online/dpa/mp. "Tumulte bei Bürgerversammlung in Freital," *Die Zeit*, July 7, 2015. https://www.zeit.de/politik/deutschland/2015-07 /freital-buergerversammlung-tumulte.

Zeit Online/dpa/sk. "Pegida: Lutz Bachmann wieder im Vorstand von Pegida." *Die Zeit*, February 23, 2015. http://www.zeit.de/gesellschaft /zeitgeschehen/2015-02/pegida-lutz-bachmann-zurueck-im-vorstand.

–. "Freital: Polizei nimmt Rechtsextremisten in Sachsen fest." *Die Zeit*, November 5, 2015. https://www.zeit.de/gesellschaft/zeitgeschehen/2015-11/freital -razzia-buegerwehr- mitglieder?utm_referrer=https%3A%2F%2Fwww .google.com%2F.

Index

GERMAN AND EUROPEAN STUDIES

General Editor: James Retallack

www.ingramcontent.com/pod-product-compliance
Lightning Source LLC
Chambersburg PA
CBHW031137020426
42333CB00013B/415